CLARENDON LAW SERIES

Edited by
Paul Craig

Works of John Finnis available from
Oxford University Press

Reason in Action
Collected Essays: Volume I

Intention and Identity
Collected Essays: Volume II

Human Rights and Common Good
Collected Essays: Volume III

Philosophy of Law
Collected Essays: Volume IV

Religion and Public Reasons
Collected Essays: Volume V

Natural Law and Natural Rights
Second Edition

Aquinas
Moral, Political, and Legal Theory

Nuclear Deterrence, Morality and Realism
with Joseph Boyle and Germain Grisez

NATURAL LAW AND NATURAL RIGHTS

Second Edition

JOHN FINNIS

OXFORD
UNIVERSITY PRESS

OXFORD
UNIVERSITY PRESS

Great Clarendon Street, Oxford ox2 6DP

Oxford University Press is a department of the University of Oxford.
It furthers the University's objective of excellence in research, scholarship,
and education by publishing worldwide in

Oxford New York

Auckland Cape Town Dar es Salaam Hong Kong Karachi
Kuala Lumpur Madrid Melbourne Mexico City Nairobi
New Delhi Shanghai Taipei Toronto

With offices in

Argentina Austria Brazil Chile Czech Republic France Greece
Guatemala Hungary Italy Japan Poland Portugal Singapore
South Korea Switzerland Thailand Turkey Ukraine Vietnam

Oxford is a registered trade mark of Oxford University Press
in the UK and in certain other countries

Published in the United States
by Oxford University Press Inc., New York

First published 2011 (first edition 1980)

British Library Cataloguing in Publication Data

Data available

Library of Congress Cataloging in Publication Data

Data available

Typeset by SPI Publisher Services, Pondicherry, India

ISBN: 978–0–19–959913–4
ISBN: 978–0–19–959914–1 (Pbk.)

3 7 9 10 8 4 2

PREFACE

THE core of this book is its second Part. In one long movement of thought, these chapters (III–XII) sketch what the textbook taxonomists would label an 'ethics', a 'political philosophy', and a 'philosophy of law' or 'jurisprudence'. We may accept the labels, as a scholarly convenience, but not the implication that the 'disciplines' they identify are really distinct and can safely be pursued apart. Parts One and Three are, in a sense, outriders. Anyone interested in natural law simply as an ethics may omit Chapter I; anyone whose concerns are limited to jurisprudence may omit Chapter XIII. And those who want to see, in advance, how the whole study yields an understanding very different from the accounts of 'natural law' in their textbooks of jurisprudence and philosophy might turn first to Chapter XII, and then perhaps to Chapter II.

The book is no more than introductory. Countless relevant matters are merely touched upon or are passed over altogether. Innumerable objections receive no more than the silent tribute of an effort to draft statements that would prove defensible if a defence against objections were explicitly undertaken. No effort is made to give an ordered account of the long history of theorizing about natural law and natural rights. For experience suggests that such accounts lull rather than stimulate an interest in their subject-matter. And indeed, the history of these theories can only be properly understood by one who appreciates the intrinsic problems of human good and practical reasonableness with which the theorists were grappling. So my prior concern is to give my own response to those problems, mentioning other theories only where I think they can both illuminate and be illuminated by the theory presented in this book. My hope is that a re-presentation and development of main elements of the 'classical' or 'mainstream' theories of natural law, by way of an argument on the merits (as lawyers say), will be found useful by those who want to understand the history of ideas as well as by those interested in forming or reforming their own view of the merits.

Every author has his milieu; this book has roots in a modern tradition that can be labelled 'analytical jurisprudence', and my own interest in that tradition antedates the time when I first began to suspect that there might be more to theories of natural law than superstition and darkness. Someone who shared my theory of natural law, but whose focus of interest and competence was, say, sociological jurisprudence or political theory or moral theology, would have written a different book.

In 1953 Leo Strauss prefaced his study of natural law with the warning that 'the issue of natural right presents itself today as a matter of party allegiance. Looking around us, we see two hostile camps, heavily fortified and guarded. One is occupied by the liberals of various descriptions, the other by the Catholic and non-Catholic disciples of Thomas Aquinas'.[1] Things have changed during the last 25 years, and the debate need no longer be regarded as so polarized. Still, the issues tackled in this book go to the root of every human effort, commitment, and allegiance, and at the same time are overlaid with a long and continuing history of fierce partisanship. So it may be as well to point out that in this book nothing is asserted or defended by appeal to the authority of any person or body. I do quite frequently refer to Thomas Aquinas, because on any view he occupies a uniquely strategic place in the history of natural law theorizing. Likewise, I refer occasionally to the Roman Catholic Church's pronouncements on natural law, because that body is perhaps unique in the modern world in claiming to be an authoritative exponent of natural law. But, while there is place for appeal to, and deference to, authority, that place is not in philosophical argument about the merits of theories or the right response to practical problems, and so is not in this book.

My arguments, then, stand or fall by their own reasonableness or otherwise. But that is not to say that there is much that is original in them. My debts to Plato, Aristotle, Aquinas, and other authors in that 'classical' tradition are recorded in the

---

[1] Strauss, *Natural Right and History* (Chicago: 1953), 7.

footnotes and in the more discursive notes following each chapter. My debt to Germain Grisez is similarly acknowledged, but calls for explicit mention here. The ethical theory advanced in Chapters III–V and the theoretical arguments in sections VI.2 and XIII.2 are squarely based on my understanding of his vigorous re-presentation and very substantial development of the classical arguments on these matters.

I have, of course, many other debts, particularly to David Alston, David Braine, Michael Detmold, Germain Grisez, H. L. A. Hart, Neil MacCormick, J. L. Mackie, Carlos Nino, and Joseph Raz, who from their diverse standpoints offered comments on the whole or substantial parts of a draft.

The book was conceived, begun, and finished in the University of Oxford, whose motto could be placed at the end of Part Three. But the book was mainly written in Africa, in Chancellor College at the University of Malawi, in an environment at once congenial and conducive to contemplation of the problems of justice, law, authority, and rights.

March 1979

PREFACE TO THE SECOND EDITION

THE text of the first edition, including its footnotes and the endnotes to each chapter, is almost unchanged. Typographical and other formal errors have been corrected, and two or three kinds of locution whose connotations have altered significantly since 1979 have been adjusted. Although everything has been reset, the pagination is the same, within one line per page, up to the point where the Postscript begins, after which there is also an enlarged Index to both the original book and the Postscript.

The aim of the Postscript is not to say everything that might well be said if these matters were to be treated afresh. Rather it is to indicate where the original needs, I think, amendment or supplementation. The Postscript begins with some general observations, by way of introductory Overview, and then comments on each chapter section by section, in sequence. In the Index, references to pages numbered above 413 are to new material.

This new edition was prepared in conjunction with the five volumes of my *Collected Essays* (hereafter *CEJF*). References in the Postscript to items republished in those volumes use the form essay II.13 and so forth. Where the original edition cited something republished in *CEJF*, a supplementary reference in that form has also been inserted. Each of those five volumes contains a substantially complete Bibliography of my publications both before and after *Natural Law and Natural Rights*. The short Bibliography of Cited Essays, after the Postscript, locates each of the works of mine cited in the Postscript, whether or not republished in *CEJF*.

The editor of the Clarendon Law Series kindly allowed me to use a cover picture in the style of the *Collected Essays*. Like the picture for *CEJF* I, but not the other volumes, this is an oil painting. Done in 1898 by John White, it is called *Land of the salt bush*, and depicts results of human purpose and action, to 'subdue the earth', in vast areas of marginal land in South Australia that are neither as near-desert as Lake Torrens (*CEJF* V) nor as hospitable and fertile as Adelaide (*CEJF* III and IV) or the Barossa Valley (*CEJF* II).

February 2011

POSTSCRIPT ABBREVIATIONS

Aquinas	John Finnis, *Aquinas: Moral, Political and Legal Theory* (OUP: 1998)
CL²	H.L.A. Hart, *The Concept of Law* (2nd edn) (OUP: 1994)
FoE	John Finnis, *Fundamentals of Ethics* (OUP; Georgetown University Press: 1983)
LCL	Germain Grisez, *Living a Christian Life* (Franciscan Press: 1993)
LE	Ronald Dworkin, *Law's Empire* (Harvard University Press; Fontana: 1986)
NDMR	John Finnis, Joseph Boyle and Germain Grisez, *Nuclear Deterrence, Morality and Realism* (OUP: 1987)
NLNR	John Finnis, *Natural Law and Natural Rights* (OUP: 1980; 2nd edn 2011)

CONTENTS

ABBREVIATIONS

Adel L. R.	*Adelaide Law Review.*
Am. J. Int. L.	*American Journal of International Law.*
Am. J. Juris.	*American Journal of Jurisprudence* (formerly *Nat. L.F.*).
Arch.Phil.Dr.	*Archives de Philosophic du Droit.*
Arch.R.S.P.	*Archiv fur Rechts- und Sozialphilosophie.*
British Moralists	D. D. Raphael (ed.), *British Moralists 1650–1800* (Oxford: 1969).
Camb. L.J.	*Cambridge Law Journal.*
Comm.	William Blackstone, *Commentaries on the Laws of England* ((Oxford: 1765–9) cited to 9th edn, 1783, the last revised by Blackstone).
Concept of Law	H. L. A. Hart, *The Concept of Law* (Oxford: 1961) [page numbers in the 2nd edn, 1994 have been added in brackets where the pagination of editions diverges].
De Legibus	Francisco Suarez, SJ, *De Legibus ac Deo Legislatore* (Coimbra: 1612).
Doctor and Student	Christopher St. German, *Doctor and Student* [1523 (First Dialogue, Latin), 1530 (Second Dialogue, English), 1531 (First Dialogue, Eng.)], eds Plucknett and Barton (London: 1975).
Essays	P. M. S. Hacker and J. Raz, *Law, Morality and Society: Essays in honour of H. L. A. Hart* (Oxford: 1977).
Eud. Eth.	Aristotle, *Eudemian Ethics.*
Gauthier-Jolif	R. A. Gauthier and J. Y. Jolif, *L'Ethique à Nicomaque* (revised edn, Paris: 1970).
General Theory	Hans Kelsen, *General Theory of Law and State* (Cambridge, Mass.: 1945).
Harv. L. Rev.	*Harvard Law Review.*
I. C. J. Rep.	*Reports of the International Court of Justice.*
in Eth.	Thomas Aquinas, *In Decem Libros Ethicorum Aristotelis ad Nicomachum Expositio*, ed. R. M. Spiazzi (Turin and Rome: 1949).

in Pol.	Thomas Aquinas, *In Octo Libros Politicorum Aristotelis Expositio,* ed. R. M. Spiazzi (Turin and Rome: 1951).
in Primam Secundae	Gabriel Vazquez, SJ, *Commentariorum ac Disputationum in Primam Secundae Sancti Thomae...* (1605).
Int. J. Ethics	*International Journal of Ethics.*
Legal System	J. Raz, *The Concept of a Legal System* (Oxford: 1970).
L.Q.R.	*Law Quarterly Review.*
Meta.	Aristotle, *Metaphysics.*
Methodology	E. A. Shils and H. A. Finch (eds.), *Max Weber on the Methodology of the Social Sciences* (Glencoe, Ill.: 1949).
Morality of Law	Lon L. Fuller, *The Morality of Law* (revised edn, 1969, New Haven and London).
Nat. L.F.	*Natural Law Forum* (now *Am. J. Juris.*).
Nic. Eth.	Aristotle, *Nicomachean Ethics.*
Of Laws	Jeremy Bentham, *Of Laws in General* (ed. H. L. A. Hart, London: 1970).
On Law	Max Rheinstein (ed.), *Max Weber on Law in Economy and Society* (Cambridge, Mass.: 1954).
Oxford Essays II	A. W. B. Simpson (ed.), *Oxford Essays in Jurisprudence: Second Series* (Oxford: 1971).
Phil. Pub. Aff.	*Philosophy and Public Affairs.*
Phil. Rev.	*Philosophical Review.*
Pol.	Aristotle, *Politics.*
Post. Anal.	Aristotle, *Posterior Analytics.*
Practical Reason	J. Raz, *Practical Reason and Norms* (London: 1975).
Proc. Aris. Soc.	*Proceedings of the Aristotelian Society.*
Province	John Austin, *The Province of Jurisprudence Determined* (1832; ed. H. L. A. Hart, London: 1954).
Rev. Thom.	*Revue Thomiste.*
S.T.	Thomas Aquinas, *Summa Theologiae,* cited by Part (I, I–II, II–II, III), Question (q. 94), and Article (a. 2); (a. 2c = body of the reply, in a. 2; ad 4 = reply to fourth objection in relevant Article).
Theory of Justice	John Rawls, *A Theory of Justice* (Cambridge, Mass.: 1971, Oxford: 1972).
U. Pa. L. Rev.	*University of Pennsylvania Law Review.*

Part One

I

EVALUATION AND THE DESCRIPTION
OF LAW

I.1 THE FORMATION OF CONCEPTS FOR
DESCRIPTIVE SOCIAL SCIENCE

THERE are human goods that can be secured only through the institutions of human law, and requirements of practical reasonableness that only those institutions can satisfy. It is the object of this book to identify those goods, and those requirements of practical reasonableness, and thus to show how and on what conditions such institutions are justified and the ways in which they can be (and often are) defective.

It is often supposed that an evaluation of law as a type of social institution, if it is to be undertaken at all, must be preceded by a value-free description and analysis of that institution as it exists in fact. But the development of modern jurisprudence suggests, and reflection on the methodology of any social science confirms, that no theorist can give a theoretical description and analysis of social facts without also participating in the work of evaluation, of understanding what is really good for human persons, and what is really required by practical reasonableness.

A social science, such as analytical or sociological jurisprudence, seeks to describe, analyse, and explain some object or subject-matter. This object is constituted by human actions, practices, habits, dispositions, and by human discourse. The actions, practices, etc., are certainly influenced by the 'natural' causes properly investigated by the methods of the natural sciences, including a part of the science of psychology. But the actions, practices, etc., can be fully understood only by understanding their point, that is to say their objective, their value, their significance or importance, as conceived by the people who performed them, engaged in them, etc. And these conceptions of point, value, significance, and importance will be reflected in the discourse of those same people, in the con-

ceptual distinctions they draw and fail or refuse to draw. Moreover, these actions, practices, etc., and correspondingly these
concepts, vary greatly from person to person, from one society
to another, from one time and place to other times and
places. *How, then, is there to be a general descriptive theory of these
varying particulars?*

A theorist wishes to describe, say, law as a social institution.
But the conceptions of law (and of *jus, lex, droit, nomos,...*)
which people have entertained, and have used to shape their
own conduct, are quite varied. The subject-matter of the
theorist's description does not come neatly demarcated from
other features of social life and practice. Moreover, this social
life and practice bears labels in many languages. The languages
can be learned by speakers of other languages, but the principles
on which labels are adopted and applied—i.e. the practical
concerns and the self-interpretations of the people whose conduct
and dispositions go to make up the theorist's subject-
matter—are not uniform. Can the theorist do more, then, than
list these varying conceptions and practices and their corresponding labels? Even a list requires some principle of selection of
items for inclusion in the list. And jurisprudence, like other
social sciences, aspires to be more than a conjunction of lexicography with local history, or even than a juxtaposition of all
lexicographies conjoined with all local histories.

How does the theorist decide what is to count as law for the
purposes of his description? The early analytical jurists do not
show much awareness of the problem. Neither Bentham nor
Austin advances any reason or justification for the definitions
of law and jurisprudence which he favours. Each tries to show
how the data of legal experience can be explained in terms
of those definitions. But the definitions are simply posited at the
outset and thereafter taken for granted. Bentham's notion of the
'real elements' of ideas encourages us to speculate that he was
attracted to his definition of a law ('an assemblage of signs de-
clarative of a volition conceived or adopted by the sovereign in
a state...'[1]) by the fact that assemblages of signs (and the
commands and prohibitions of a definite individual or set of
individuals) are 'real entities' that make an empirical impres-

---

[1] Bentham, *Of Laws*, 1; on 'real elements' and 'real entities', see *ibid.*, 2–3, 251–2, 278, 294, and *A Fragment on Government* (1776), ch. V, para, vi, note 1(6).

sion on the mind. Austin's *obiter dicta* on methodology suggest that for him the attraction of the notions of command, political superior, and habit of obedience was precisely their simplicity and definiteness. He seems to have wanted the 'leading terms' of his explanatory system to have the 'simplicity and definiteness' found in the 'method so successfully pursued by geometers'.[2] So he did not mind either the complexity of some of the conclusions (e.g. as to sovereignty in federations) necessitated by his definitional premises, or the novelty and artificiality of others among those conclusions (e.g. as to the extralegal character of constitutional law, or the non-existence of legal rights of the sovereign). He prized the 'fewness' of his leading terms;[3] every reader of Austin becomes aware of the consequent flattening or thinning-out of the account of legal experience.

In Kelsen's 'general theory of law' we find no critical attention to the methodological problem of selecting concepts for the purposes of a value-free or descriptive general theory. We do find an awareness, not apparent in Bentham and Austin, that point or function is intrinsic to the constitution, and hence to the descriptive understanding, of the subject-matter. So Kelsen defines law as a specific social technique: 'the social technique which consists in bringing about the desired social conduct of men through the threat of a measure of coercion which is to be applied in case of contrary conduct'.[4] From this he derives his characterization of the individual legal norm as a norm for the application of a sanction, and from this in turn follow the other features of his 'nomostatics' and several features of his 'nomodynamics'. But how does Kelsen propose to justify the definition itself? Simply as follows:

What could the social order of a negro tribe under the leadership of a despotic chieftain—an order likewise called 'law'—have in common with the constitution of the Swiss republic?

---

[2] Austin, *Province*, 77–8.
[3] *Ibid.*, 78.
[4] Kelsen, *General Theory*, 19. So law is a specific means to a specific end: 'The law is ... an ordering for the promotion of peace' (*ibid.*, 21); hence 'Law is an order according to which the use of force is generally forbidden but exceptionally, under certain circumstances and for certain individuals, permitted as a sanction' (*ibid.*, 22); see also *ibid.*, 392, 399.

[Let us interject to ask: Who is doing this calling, this naming? Whose willingness so to refer to the tribe's social order (in language expressing distinctions which the despotic chieftain and his subjects do not care to make) is thus being made decisive?]

Yet there is a common element that fully justifies this terminology... for the word refers to that specific social technique which, despite the vast differences... is yet essentially the same for all these peoples differing so much in time, in place, and in culture...

What could be simpler? One takes the word 'law'. Ignoring a wide range of meanings and reference (as in 'law of nature', 'moral law', 'sociological law', 'international law', 'ecclesiastical law', 'law of grammar'), and further ignoring alternative ways of referring to, e.g., the 'negro tribe's' social order, one looks at the range of subject-matter signified by the word in the usage which one has (without explanation) selected. One looks for 'a common element'. This *one thing common* is the criterion of the 'essence' of law, and thus *the one feature* used to characterize and to explain descriptively the whole subject-matter. There is thus one concept, which can be predicated equally and *in the same sense* (i.e. univocally) of everything which, in a pre-theoretical usage (which the theorist allows to determine his theoretical usage), somebody was willing to call 'law'.

The noticeably greater explanatory power of later descriptive analyses of law, such as those of H. L. A. Hart and Joseph Raz, is to be attributed to their fairly decisive break with the rather naive methodologies of Bentham, Austin, and Kelsen. This sophistication of method has three principal features, discussed in the following three sections.

1.2   ATTENTION TO PRACTICAL POINT

Hart's critique of Austin and Kelsen retains their fundamentally descriptive theoretical purpose: for his objection is that their theory 'failed to fit the facts'.[5] But the facts which their theory failed to fit, according to Hart, were facts about function. If Kelsen identifies law as a 'specific social technique', Hart replies that Kelsen's description in fact obscures 'the specific character of law as a means of social control' by 'distorting the different social functions which different types of legal rule

---

[5] Hart, *Concept of Law*, 78 [80].

perform'.[6] Hart's description ('concept') of law is built up by appealing, again and again, to the practical point of the components of the concept. Law is to be described in terms of rules *for* the guidance of officials and citizens alike, not merely as a set of predictions of what officials will do. A legal system is a system in which 'secondary' rules have emerged *in order to* remedy the *defects* of a pre-legal regime comprising only 'primary rules'. Law must[7] have a minimum content of primary rules and sanctions *in order to* ensure the survival of the society or its members and to give them *practical reason for* compliance with it.

Raz refines these elements by a description of law which moves still further away from the 'despotic chieftain's' monopolization of force by threats of force. For Raz, as for Hart, the law is not *any* set of norms; it is a system of norms which provides a method (i.e. technique) of settling disputes authoritatively, by means of norms which both (a) provide binding guidance for 'primary institutions' (which settle the disputes by 'binding applicative determinations') and (b) also ('the very same norms') guide the individuals whose behaviour may fall to be evaluated and judged by those institutions.[8] Because of this dual function of its norms, a legal system differs fundamentally from any social order in which an authority may determine matters by deciding each problem as it thinks best, in its unfettered discretion.[9] Moreover, law does not seek merely to monopolize the use of force and thus to secure peace; it characteristically claims authority to regulate any form of behaviour, and to regulate all normative institutions to which the members of its subject-community belong;[10] finally, it contains norms 'the purpose of which is to give binding force within the system to norms which do not belong to it'.[11] 'By making these claims the law claims to provide the general framework for the

---

[6] *Ibid.*, 38, 39. For a brief account of these differing 'social functions', see *ibid.*, 27–8.

[7] See *ibid.*, 189–90 [193–4], 193 [198–9], 194–5 [199–200]; also Hart, 'Positivism and the Separation of Law and Morals' (1958) 71 *Harv. L. Rev.* 593, in Dworkin (ed.), *The Philosophy of Law* (Oxford: 1977), 17 at 35.

[8] Raz, *Practical Reason*, 136, 137, 139.

[9] *Ibid.*, 138, 141.

[10] *Ibid.*, 151.

[11] *Ibid.*, 153.

conduct of all aspects of social life and sets itself as the supreme guardian of society'.[12] It follows, of course, that sanctions and their enforcement by force, so far from being the specific identifying criterion of law as a social order, are 'not a feature which forms part of our concept of law'.[13] Human nature being what it is, resort to sanctions is universal and the operation of law without such resort, though 'logically possible', is 'humanly impossible'.[14] But the co-ordinating, dispute-resolving, and damage-remedying functions of law would require a *fully* legal social order even in 'a society of angels' which would have no use for sanctions.[15]

Raz builds up his account of law with a full awareness (not apparent in the earlier theorists of law) that there are social scientists who find no use for the concept of law or legal system in their description of human social, even political order.[16] He is aware that their theoretical decision to replace it with other concepts can be contested (as he wishes to contest it) only by showing that they have overlooked (i) important functions (or objectives and techniques) of social order, and (ii) the way in which those functions can be interrelated in a multi-faceted institution worth maintaining as a distinct unit of, or component in, social order.

By emphasizing (in his recent work) the distinction between law and social systems of absolute discretion, inasmuch as legal norms for guiding the citizen are also *binding* upon the courts (the legal 'primary organs'), Raz goes far towards Lon Fuller's analysis of the social function of law. Where Hart had retained Kelsen's notion that law is a method of social control but rejected as insufficiently differentiated Kelsen's account of the method, Fuller rejects, as an insufficiently differentiated and inappropriate general category, the notion of a 'means of social control'. For Fuller, law is indeed a social order in which there are rulers and subjects, but it is to be distinguished from any social order in which the rulers are exercising a 'managerial

---

[12] *Ibid.*, 154.

[13] *Ibid.*, 159.

[14] Raz, *Practical Reason*, 158.

[15] *Ibid.*, 159.

[16] See Raz, 'On the Functions of the Law', in *Oxford Essays II*, 278–304 at 300–3, analysing G. A. Almond and G. B. Powell, *Comparative Politics* (Boston: 1966).

direction' over their subjects. Law is distinguished from such managerial direction partly by the generality of its major rules, and above all by the fact that its officials are bound to apply the rules which they have previously announced to their subjects. There is thus an essential component of collaboration and reciprocity in the enterprise of subjecting human conduct to the governance of legal as distinct from merely managerial norms.[17]

All these accounts of law, even that part of Fuller's which I have just mentioned, are intended as descriptive. They seek to 'identify law on the basis of non-evaluative characteristics only'.[18] As Raz says, such 'non-evaluative identifying criteria ...should single out those phenomena which form a special sort of social institution, an institution to be found as an important component of many social systems and which differs significantly from other social institutions'.[19] It is obvious, then, that the differences in description derive from differences of opinion, amongst the descriptive theorists, about what is *important* and *significant* in the field of data and experience with which they are all equally and thoroughly familiar.

I.3   SELECTION OF CENTRAL CASE AND FOCAL MEANING

The obvious question provoked by the course of theorizing sketched in the preceding section is: From what viewpoint, and relative to what concerns, are *importance* and *significance* to be assessed? Before we consider that question, however, it will be as well to identify the philosophical device which enables an increasingly *differentiated* description of law to be offered as still a *general* theory of law.

Aristotle introduced, discussed, and regularly employed the device, not least in his philosophy of human affairs. He called it the identification of *focal meaning (pros hen* or *aph'henos* homonymy). The device is or corresponds to a main component in Max Weber's not too clearly explained methodological device, the *ideal-type*. It involves a conscious departure from the assumption upon which, as we saw, Kelsen proceeded: that

---

[17] Fuller, *Morality of Law*, 210, 214, 216; 39–40, 61, 155; 20.
[18] Raz, *Practical Reason*, 165.
[19] *Ibid.*, 165.

descriptive or explanatory terms must be employed by the theorist in such a way that they extend, straightforwardly and in the same sense, to *all* the states of affairs which could reasonably, in non-theoretical discourse, be 'called "law"', however undeveloped those states of affairs may be, and however little those states of affairs may manifest any concern of their authors (e.g. the 'despotic chieftains') to differentiate between law and force, law and morality, law and custom, law and politics, law and absolute discretion, or law and anything else. Such insistence on a flatly univocal meaning of theoretical terms, leading to the search for a lowest common denominator or highest *common* factor or for the 'one thing common', was directly attacked by Aristotle,[20] and is consciously abandoned by Hart and Raz. Thus Hart rejects the view that 'the several instances of a general term must have the same characteristics'. Instead, he proceeds on the assumption that 'the extension of the general terms of any serious discipline is never without its principle or rationale'.[21] What Aristotle says in relation to 'friend[ship]', 'constitution[ality]', and 'citizen-[ship]'[22] is well said by Raz in relation to 'legal system':

The general traits which mark a system as a legal one are several and each of them admits, in principle, of various degrees. In typical instances of legal systems all these traits are manifested to a very high degree. But it is possible to find systems in which all or some are present only to a lesser degree or in which one or two are absent altogether... When faced with borderline cases it is best to admit their problematic credentials, to enumerate their similarities and dissimilarities to the typical cases, and leave it at that.[23]

Because the word 'typical' may suggest that the relevant criterion is statistical frequency (whether in human history, or today), I prefer to call the states of affairs referred to by a theoretical concept in its focal meaning the *central case(s)*.

By exploiting the systematic multi-significance of one's theoretical terms (without losing sight of the 'principle or rationale' of this multi-significance), one can differentiate the mature from the undeveloped in human affairs, the sophis-

---

[20] *Eud. Eth.* VII.2: 1236a16–30.
[21] Hart, *Concept of Law*, 15, 210 [215]; see also 234 [279–80].
[22] *Nic. Eth.* VIII.4: 1157a30–3: *Pol.* III.1: 1275a33–1276b4.
[23] Raz, *Practical Reason*, 150.

ticated from the primitive, the flourishing from the corrupt, the fine specimen from the deviant case, the 'straightforwardly', 'simply speaking' (*simpliciter*), and 'without qualification' from the 'in a sense', 'in a manner of speaking', and 'in a way' (*secundum quid*)—but all without ignoring or banishing to another discipline the undeveloped, primitive, corrupt, deviant, or other 'qualified sense' or 'extended sense' instances of the subject-matter: see XII.4.

So there are central cases, as Aristotle insisted, of friendship, and there are more or less peripheral cases (business friendship, friendship of convenience, cupboard love, casual and play relations, and so on: see VI.4). There are central cases of constitutional government, and there are peripheral cases (such as Hitler's Germany, Stalin's Russia, or even Amin's Uganda). On the one hand, there is no point in denying that the peripheral cases *are* instances (of friendship, constitutionality...). Indeed, the study of them is illuminated by thinking of them as watered-down versions of the central cases, or sometimes as exploitations of human attitudes shaped by reference to the central case. And, on the other hand, there is no point in restricting one's explanation of the central cases to those features which are present not only in the central but also in each of the peripheral cases. Rather, one's descriptive explanation of the central cases should be as conceptually rich and complex as is required to answer all appropriate questions about those central cases. And then one's account of the other instances can trace the network of similarities and differences, the analogies and disanalogies, for example, of form, function, or content, between them and the central cases. In this way, one uncovers the 'principle or rationale' on which the general term ('constitution', 'friend', 'law'...) is extended from the central to the more or less borderline cases, from its focal to its secondary meanings.

I.4 SELECTION OF VIEWPOINT

But by what criteria is one meaning to be accounted focal and another secondary, one state of affairs central and another borderline? This is simply a reformulation of the question left over from I.2: From what viewpoint, and relative to what concerns, are *importance* and *significance* to be assessed?

Hart and Raz are clear that a descriptive theorist, in 'deciding to attribute a central role'[24] to some particular feature or features in his description of a field of human affairs, must 'be concerned with',[25] 'refer to',[26] or 'reproduce'[27] one particular *practical* point of view (or set of similar viewpoints). By 'practical', here as throughout this book, I do not mean 'workable' as opposed to unworkable, efficient as opposed to inefficient; I mean 'with a view to decision and action'. Practical thought is thinking about what (one ought) to do. Practical reasonableness is reasonableness in deciding, in adopting commitments, in choosing and executing projects, and in general in acting. Practical philosophy is a disciplined and critical reflection on the goods that can be realized in human action and the requirements of practical reasonableness. So when we say that descriptive theorists (whose purposes are not practical) must proceed, in their indispensable selection and formation of concepts, by adopting a practical point of view, we mean that they must assess importance or significance in similarities and differences within their subject-matter by asking what would be considered important or significant in that field by those whose concerns, decisions, and activities create or constitute the subject-matter.

Thus Hart gives descriptive explanatory priority to the concerns and evaluations (and consequently to the language) of people with an 'internal point of view', viz. those who do not 'merely record and predict behaviour conforming to rules', or attend to rules 'only from the external point of view as a sign of possible punishment', but rather '*use* the rules as standards for the appraisal of their own and others' behaviour'.[28] Raz, in his earlier work, adopts 'the ordinary man's point of view',[29] but in his more recent work shifts to 'the legal point of view', which is the point of view of people who 'believe in the

[24] See Raz, *Legal System*, 201.
[25] *Ibid.*, 200 n. 2.
[26] Hart, *Concept of Law*, 96 [98].
[27] *Ibid.*, 88 [90].
[28] *Ibid.*, 95–6 [98]; also 86–8 [88–90], 59–60 [60–1], 113 [116–17], 197 [201–2], 226 [231–2].
[29] Raz, *Legal System*, 200 n. 2.

validity of the norms and follow them' (paradigmatically, the viewpoint of the judge *qua* judge).[30]

Rather obviously, this position of Hart and Raz is unstable and unsatisfactory. As against Austin and Kelsen they have sharply differentiated the 'internal' or 'legal' point of view from the point of view of those who merely acquiesce in the law and who do so only because, when, and to the extent that they fear the punishments that will follow non-acquiescence. But both theorists firmly refuse to differentiate further. They recognize that the 'internal' or 'legal' viewpoint, as they describe it, is an amalgam of very different viewpoints. '[A]llegiance to the system may be based on many different considerations: calculations of long-term interest; disinterested interest in others; an unreflecting inherited or traditional attitude; or the mere wish to do as others do'.[31] Raz is willing to extend his conception of 'the legal point of view' to encompass the viewpoint of 'an anarchist' who becomes a judge 'on the ground that if he follows the law most of the time he will be able to disobey it on the few but important occasions when to do so will most undermine it'.[32] But all this is unstable and unsatisfactory because it involves a refusal to attribute significance to differences that any actor in the field (whether the subversive anarchist or his opponent the 'ideal law-abiding citizen'[33]) would count as practically significant. And, given the technique of analysis by central case and focal meaning, which elsewhere Hart and Raz use with such fruitful resolution, there seems to be no good reason for this refusal to differentiate the central from the peripheral cases *of the internal or legal point of view itself.*

For it is not difficult to discern that the viewpoint of Raz's anarchistic judge, who covertly picks and chooses amongst the laws he will enforce, with the intention of overthrowing the whole system, is not a paradigm of either the judicial or the legal point of view. Neither the anarchist nor his fellows would consider it as such. Why then should the descriptive theorist? Similarly with Hart's 'unreflecting inherited

---

[30] Raz, *Practical Reason*, 177, 171.
[31] Hart, *Concept of Law*, 198 [203]; also 111 [114], 226 [231–2].
[32] Raz, *Practical Reason*, 148.
[33] *Ibid.*, 171.

or traditional attitude…or mere wish to do as others do'. These are attitudes which will, up to a point, tend to maintain in existence a legal system (as distinct from, say, a system of despotic discretion) if one already exists. But they will not bring about the transition from the pre-legal (or post-legal!) social order of custom or discretion to a legal order, for they do not share the concern, which Hart himself recognizes as the explanatory source of legal order, to remedy the defects of pre-legal social orders. Similarly, Hart's persons who are moved by 'calculations of long-term interest' (sc. self-interest) water down any concern they may have for the function of law as an answer to real social problems; like Raz's anarchistic judge, they dilute their allegiance to law and their pursuit of legal methods of thought with doses of that very self-interest which it is an elementary function of law (on everybody's view) to subordinate to social needs. All these considerations and attitudes, then, are manifestly deviant, diluted, or watered-down instances of the practical viewpoint that brings law into being as a significantly differentiated type of social order and maintains it as such. Indeed, they are parasitic upon that viewpoint.

From the list of types of internal or legal viewpoint offered by Hart and Raz, we are now left only with 'disinterested interest in others', and the view of those who consider the rules, or at least the rules of recognition, to be 'morally justified'.[34] If disinterested concern for others is detached from moral concern, as it is by Hart,[35] then what it involves is quite unclear, and, in the absence of clarification, it must be considered to have a relationship to law and legal concerns as uncertain and floating as its relationship (on this view) to moral concern.

The conclusion we should draw is clear. If there is a point of view in which legal obligation is treated as at least presumptively a moral obligation (and thus as of 'great importance', to be maintained 'against the drive of strong passions' and 'at the cost of sacrificing considerable personal interest'),[36] a viewpoint in which the establishment and maintenance of legal as distinct from discretionary or statically customary order is regarded as a moral ideal if not a compelling demand of justice, then such a

---

[34] See Raz, *Practical Reason*, 147–8.
[35] Hart, *Concept of Law*, 226 [231–2].
[36] *Ibid.*, 169 [173–4].

viewpoint will constitute the central case of the legal view-point. For only in such a viewpoint is it a matter of over-riding importance that law as distinct from other forms of social order should come into being, and thus become an object of the theorist's description. But the term 'moral' is of somewhat un-certain connotation. So it is preferable to frame our conclusion in terms of practical reasonableness (see V.1, V.10, VI.1, XI.1, XI.4). If there is a viewpoint in which the institution of the Rule of Law (see X.4), and compliance with rules and principles of law according to their tenor, are regarded as at least presumptive requirements of practical reasonableness itself, such a viewpoint is the viewpoint which should be used as the standard of reference by the theorist describing the features of legal order.

One further differentiation remains possible. Among those who, from a practical viewpoint, treat law as an aspect of practical reasonableness, there will be some whose views about what practical reasonableness actually requires in this domain are, in detail, more reasonable than others. Thus, the central case viewpoint itself is the viewpoint of those who not only appeal to practical reasonableness but also *are* practically reasonable, that is to say: consistent; attentive to all aspects of human opportunity and flourishing, and aware of their limited commensurability; concerned to remedy deficiencies and break-downs, and aware of their roots in the various aspects of human personality and in the economic and other material conditions of social interaction.[37] What reason could one as a descriptive theorist have for rejecting the conceptual choices and discriminations of these persons, when one is selecting the concepts with which one will construct one's description of the central case and then of all the other instances of law as a specific social institution?

As a descriptive theorist, one is indeed not bound to adopt into one's theory all the concepts which the societies one is studying have

---

[37] Behind Aristotle's cardinal principle of method in the study of human affairs—viz. that concepts are to be selected and employed substantially as they are used in practice by the *spoudaios* (the mature person of practical reasonableness): see XII. 4, below—lies Plato's argument (*Rep.* IX: 582a–e) that the lover of wisdom can understand the concerns of people of other character, while the converse does not hold; in other words, the concerns and understanding of the mature and reasonable person provide a better *empirical* basis for the reflective account of human affairs: see also *Rep.* III: 408d–409c.

used in their own self-interpretation of their own practices. Many such concepts betray a weak sensitivity to certain aspects of human well-being; others betray the influence of ideological myth, for example, that 'the people' rules 'itself' (cf. IX.4), or that 'the revolution' is replacing the rule of law with 'the administration of things'. But it is precisely a disciplined and informed *practical* thought (whether 'theoretical', i.e. reflective, in intent, or more immediately directed to action) that can provide a critique of these concepts, in order to overcome the obstacles they place in the way of clear thinking about what ought to be done. Descriptive social theory does not share this concern about what ought to be done. But it cannot in its descriptions do without the concepts found appropriate by persons of *practical* reasonableness to *describe to themselves* what they think worth doing and achieving in the face of all the contingencies, misunderstandings, and myths confronting them in their practice.

Thus, by a long march through the working or implicit methodology of contemporary analytical jurisprudence, we arrive at the conclusion reached more rapidly (though on the basis of a much wider social science) by Max Weber: namely, that the evaluations of the theorist himself are an indispensable and decisive component in the selection or formation of any concepts for use in description of such aspects of human affairs as law or legal order. For theorists cannot identify the central case of that practical viewpoint which they use to identify the central case of their subject-matter, unless they decide what the requirements of practical reasonableness really are, in relation to this whole aspect of human affairs and concerns. In relation to law, the most important things for the theorist to know and describe are the things which, in the judgment of the theorist, make it important from a *practical* viewpoint to have law—the things which it is, therefore, important in practice to 'see to' when ordering human affairs. And when these 'important things' are (in some or even in many societies) in fact missing, or debased, or exploited or otherwise deficient, then the most important things for the theorist to describe are those aspects of the situation that manifest this absence, debasement, exploitation, or deficiency.

Does this mean that descriptive jurisprudence (and social science as a whole) is inevitably subject to every theorist's conceptions and prejudices about what is good and practically reasonable? Yes and no. 'Yes', in so far as there is no escaping the theoretical requirement that a judgment of *significance* and *importance* must be made if theory is to be more than a vast rubbish heap of miscellaneous facts described in a multitude of incommensurable terminologies. 'No', in so far as the disciplined acquisition of accurate knowledge about human affairs—and thus about what other persons have considered practically important, and about the actual results of their concern—is an important help to reflective and critical theorists in their effort to convert their own (and their culture's) practical 'prejudices' into truly reasonable judgments about what is good and practically reasonable. Descriptive knowledge thus can occasion a modification of the judgments of importance and significance with which one first approached the data as a theorist, and can suggest a reconceptualization. But the knowledge will not have been attained without a preliminary conceptualization and thus a preliminary set of principles of selection and relevance drawn from some practical viewpoint.

There is thus a movement to and fro between, on the one hand, assessments of human good and of its practical re-quirements, and on the other hand, explanatory descriptions (using all appropriate historical, experimental, and statistical techniques to trace all relevant causal interrelationships) of the human context in which human well-being is variously realized and variously ruined. Just as (as we shall see: II.4) there is no question of deriving one's basic judgments about human values and the requirements of practical reasonableness by some inference from the facts of the human situation, so there is no question of reducing descriptive social science to an apologia for one's ethical or political judgments, or to a project for apportioning praise or blame among the actors on the human scene: in this sense, descriptive social science is 'value-free'. But when all due emphasis has been given to the differences of objective and method between practical philosophy and descriptive social science, the methodological problems of concept-formation as we have traced it in this chapter compel us to recognize that the point of reflective equilibrium in descriptive social science is attainable only by one in whom wide knowledge of the data, and penetrating understanding of other persons' practical viewpoints and concerns, are allied to a sound judgment about all aspects of genuine human flourishing and authentic practical reasonableness.

I.5   THE THEORY OF NATURAL LAW

Bentham, Austin, Kelsen, Weber, Hart, and Raz all published stern repudiations of what they understood to be the theory of natural law; and Fuller carefully dissociated himself from that theory in its classical forms. But the theoretical work of each of these writers was controlled by the adoption, on grounds left inexplicit and inadequately justified, of some practical viewpoint as the standard of relevance and significance in the construction of his descriptive analysis. A sound theory of natural law is one that explicitly, with full awareness of the methodological situation just described, undertakes a critique of practical viewpoints, in order to distinguish the practically unreasonable from the practically reasonable, and thus to diff- erentiate the really important from that which is unimportant or is important only by its opposition to or unreasonable exploitation of the really important. A theory of natural law claims to be able to identify conditions and principles of practical right-mindedness, of good and proper order among persons, and in individual conduct. Unless some such claim is justified, analytical jurisprudence in particular and (at least the major part of) all the social sciences in general can have no critically justified criteria for the formation of general concepts, and must be content to be no more than manifesta- tions of the various concepts peculiar to particular peoples and/or to the particular theorists who concern themselves with those people.

A theory of natural law need not be undertaken primarily for the purpose of thus providing a justified conceptual frame- work for descriptive social science. It may be undertaken, as this book is, primarily to assist the practical reflections of those concerned to act, whether as judges, or as statesmen, or as citizens. But in either case, the undertaking cannot proceed securely without a knowledge of the whole range of human possibilities and opportunities, inclinations and capacities—a knowledge that requires the assistance of descriptive and analytical social science. There is thus a mutual though not quite symmetrical interdependence between the project of describing human affairs by way of theory and the project of evaluating human options with a view, at least remotely, to acting reasonably and well. The evaluations are in no way deduced from the descriptions (see II.4); but one whose knowledge of the facts of the human situation is very limited is unlikely to judge well in discerning the practical implications of the basic values. Equally, the descriptions are not deduced from the evaluations; but without the evaluations one cannot determine what descriptions are really illuminating and significant.

NOTES

I.1

Description of human institutions and practices requires identification of their point... See Max Weber, *Theory of Social and Economic Organization* (ed. T. Parsons, New York and London: 1947), 88–126; *On Law*, 1–10; Alfred Schütz, 'Concept and Theory Formation in the Social Sciences' (1954) 5 *J. of Philosophy*, reprinted in his *Collected Papers*, vol. I (ed. M. Natanson, The Hague: 1967), 48 at 58–9; Eric Voegelin, *The New Science of Politics* (Chicago and London: 1952), 27–9.

Bentham on definition of law... See also Bentham, *Collected Works* (ed. J. Bowring, Edinburgh: 1863), vol. IV, 483; and excursus to XI.8 (notes).

Kelsen's technique of definition... See also Hans Kelsen, *Pure Theory of Law* (Berkeley and Los Angeles: 1967), 30–1.

I.2

Description of social institutions, such as law, requires identification of their point or function(s)... See also J. Raz, 'On the Functions of the Law', in *Oxford Essays II*, 278–304 at 278; *Legal System*, 145.

Raz on the criterion of law... Raz is clear that any theorist seeking to describe law must decide between different theoretical concepts, and that 'the explicit formulation of meta-theoretical criteria is a condition for a rational and reasoned comparison of theories': Raz, *Legal System*, 146. Central to his own account of meta-theoretical criteria is his decision that legal theory should explicate 'common sense and professional opinion' (201). In *Legal System*, he offers a 'jurisprudential criterion' (200): viz. that 'a momentary legal system contains all, and only all, the laws recognized by a primary law-applying organ which it institutes' (192). He underlines that this criterion 'is concerned with the actual behaviour of primary organs, not with what they ought to do...' (198). But in *Practical Reason* he criticizes those legal theorists 'who concluded that the law consists of all the standards which the courts do apply. This...confuses institutionalized systems with systems of absolute discretion' (142). So his new criterion is: a legal system contains 'only those norms which its primary organs are bound to obey' (142; also 148). This shift in Raz's jurisprudential criterion for membership of a legal system is to be traced to his shift from a concern to reproduce the rather undifferentiated 'ordinary man's' point of view to a concern to reproduce the 'legal point of view', the view of one (paradigmatically a judge, or an 'ideal law-abiding citizen') who believes that people are in some way *justified* in following the rules of the system (139, 143, 171).

I.3

Aristotle on focal meaning and analysis of central cases...See W. F. R. Hardie, *Aristotle's Ethical Theory* (Oxford: 1968), 59–60, 63–5; *Gauthier-Jolif* II/1, 45–6; II/2, 686ff.; cf. W. W. Fortenbaugh, 'Aristotle's Analysis of Friendship: Function and Analogy, Resemblance and Focal Meaning' (1975) 20 *Phronesis* 51–62; and XII.4. Hart's discussion in *Concept of Law*, 15–16, 234 [279] does not clearly distinguish what Aristotle called analogy (and the medievals called 'analogy of proportionality') from what he called *pros hen* homonymy or focal meaning (called by the medievals 'analogy of attribution or proportion'). Hart's account (at 15–16) seems to concentrate on the former, but the latter is the more important device in the theory of human affairs. Having noted this distinction, however, I find it convenient to use the broad concept of 'analogy' and 'analogical', introduced by the medievals and more or less retained in philosophical usage thereafter. In this broad sense, a term is analogical when its meaning shifts systematically (i.e. according to some principle or rationale) as one shifts from one context or use to another. On the search for the principle or rationale in such cases, see also Hart, 'Definition and Theory in Jurisprudence' (1954) 70 *L.Q.R.* 37 at 38, 44n, 56–9.

Max Weber on the construction of ideal-type concepts for general sociology...See Weber, *Methodology*, 89–93. See also Alfred Schütz, 'The Problem of Rationality in the Social World', in his *Collected Papers*, vol. II (The Hague: 1964), 64 at 81–8.

Differentiation of 'mature' from 'impoverished' specimens of law and legal system...Austin recognized that jurisprudence should study primarily the 'ampler and maturer' legal systems: see Austin, *Province*, 367. See also Raz, *Legal System*, 140; *Practical Reason*, 150.

Frequency of occurrence or instantiation is not a decisive criterion of relevance or centrality...See Weber, *Methodology*, 72–80; Eric Voegelin, 'The Theory of Legal Science: a Review' (1942) 4 *Louisiana Law Rev.* 554 at 558–64.

I.4

Practical thought, reasonableness, philosophy, etc..... For my use of 'practical', throughout the book, see Aristotle, *Nic. Eth.* VI.2: 1139a26–31; *De Anima* III.9: 432b27; Aquinas, *S.T.* I q. 79 a. 11; Raz, *Practical Reason*, 10–13. In Aristotle, 'practical' is distinguished from *theoretikē*, translated by the medievals as *speculativa*: see Aristotle, loc. cit. and *Meta.* VI.1: 1025b19–29. Neither 'theoretical' nor 'speculative' is very suitable for drawing the necessary distinctions in English; in this chapter 'descriptive' and 'descriptive explanation' have been used for the purpose. The Aristotelian/Thomist distinction has intrinsic difficulties, since practical philosophy is 'directed to action' only somewhat remotely, i.e. in a 'theoretical way'. Despite the difficulties, the distinction should be retained; it witnesses to the ancient awareness of the basic distinction between 'is' and 'ought' (a distinction which itself is not altogether simple in its applications).

Weber on the necessity of the theorist using his own evaluations in order to assess significance for descriptive theory... See, above all, *Methodology,* 58, 76–82, 24; also Julien Freund, *The Sociology of Max Weber* (London: 1968), 51–61. Of course, Weber regarded these evaluations by the theorist as non-scientific, i.e. as lacking the dignity of objectivity: see II.3 (notes). Hence, he would not accept that the task of theorists, in this part of their work, is to decide what the basic forms of human good and the requirements of practical reasonableness 'really are'. I may add that in referring to Weber's contention that evaluation is necessary for any social science, I am not subscribing to every aspect of his argument for this contention, an argument not free from the neo-Kantian notion that all concepts have to be imposed by the human mind on the flux of phenomena—a flux that has no intelligible structure of its own to be discovered.

Descriptive social theory is not about what ought to be done... Thus, the objective and methods of a general descriptive and analytical jurisprudence such as Hart's or Raz's are to be clearly distinguished from the objective and methods of a 'legal theory' as conceived by R. M. Dworkin. For Dworkin, a main function of a 'theory of law' is 'to provide a basis for judicial duty'; 'the principles it sets out must try to *justify* the settled rules [of a given community] by identifying the political or moral concerns and traditions which, in the opinion of the lawyer whose theory it is, do in fact support the rules': Dworkin, *Taking Rights Seriously* (London: 1977), 67. (The phrase 'in fact' here means 'really' (as assessed normatively), not 'as a matter of cause-and-effect'; see also 51, lines 6, 11.) See also 117; Dworkin, 'No Right Answer?', in *Essays* at 82. Of course, a theory so relative to the moral opinions and practices of a given community is not a general theory such as theories of natural law aspire to be. But Dworkin contemplates a 'general theory of law' which in its (quite ambitious) 'normative part' would set out, *inter alia,* 'standards that judges should use to decide hard cases at law' and would explain 'why and when judges, rather than other groups or institutions, should make the decisions required by the theory...' (*Taking Rights Seriously,* vii–viii). For reasons that are unclear, he contemplates a distinct though related 'conceptual part' that would determine (how is not explained) such questions as 'Can the most fundamental principles of the constitution... themselves be considered as part of the law?'. In any event, his debate with 'positivists' such as Hart and Raz miscarries, because he fails to acknowledge that their theoretical interest is not, like his, to identify a fundamental 'test for law' in order to identify (even in the most disputed 'hard' cases) where a judge's legal (moral and political) duty really lies, in a given community at a given time. Rather, their interest is in describing what is treated (i.e. accepted and effective) as law in a given community at a given time, and in generating concepts that will allow such descriptions to be clear and explanatory, but without intent to offer solutions (whether 'right answers' or standards that would if properly applied yield right answers) to questions disputed among competent lawyers. The 'embarrassing questions' listed by Dworkin, *Taking Rights Seriously,* 14, 15, 44, are not questions that either Hart or Raz offers to answer. So Dworkin's is, fundamentally (though with many illuminating moments of description), a normative theory of law, offering guidance to the judge as to his judicial duty; theirs is a descriptive theory, offered to historians to enable a discriminating history of legal systems to be written. The fact that, as I have argued in this chapter, the descriptive theorist needs the assistance of a general normative theory in developing sufficiently differentiated concepts and reasonable standards of relevance does not eliminate the different uses to which the more or less common stock of theoretical concepts will be put by the normative and the descriptive (historical) theorists, respectively.

Reflective equilibrium in descriptive social science... The theorist who could attain this point would be one whose viewpoint systematically approximated the 'universal viewpoint' postulated by B. J. F. Lonergan, *Insight: A Study of Human Understanding* (London: 1957), 554–68. As Lonergan remarks (566), such a viewpoint 'is universal not by abstractness but by potential completeness. It attains its inclusiveness, not by stripping objects of their peculiarities' (cf. Kelsen, Austin...) 'but by envisaging subjects' (i.e. persons) 'in their necessities'.

II

IMAGES AND OBJECTIONS

II.1 NATURAL LAW AND THEORIES OF NATURAL LAW

WHAT are *principles of natural law*? The sense that the phrase 'natural law' has in this book can be indicated in the following rather bald assertions, formulations which will seem perhaps empty or question-begging until explicated in Part Two. There is (i) a set of basic practical principles which indicate the basic forms of human flourishing as goods to be pursued and realized, and which are in one way or another used by everyone who considers what to do, however unsound his conclusions; and (ii) a set of basic methodological requirements of practical reasonableness (itself one of the basic forms of human flourishing) which distinguish sound from unsound practical thinking and which, when all brought to bear, provide the criteria for distinguishing between acts that (always or in particular circumstances) are reasonable-all-things-considered (and not merely relative-to-a-particular purpose) and acts that are unreasonable-all-things-considered, i.e. between ways of acting that are morally right or morally wrong—thus enabling one to formulate (iii) a set of general moral standards.

To avoid misunderstandings about the scope of our subject-matter in this book, I should add here that the principles of natural law, thus understood, are traced out not only in moral philosophy or ethics and 'individual' conduct, but also in political philosophy and jurisprudence, in political action, adjudication, and the life of the citizen. For those principles justify the exercise of authority in community. They require, too, that that authority be exercised, in most circumstances, according to the manner conveniently labelled the Rule of Law, and with due respect for the human rights which embody the requirements of justice, and for the purpose of promoting a common good in which such respect for rights is a component. More particularly, the principles of natural law explain the obligatory force (in the fullest sense of 'obligation') of positive laws, even when those laws cannot be deduced from those principles. And attention to the principles, in the context of these explanations of law and legal obligation, justifies regarding certain positive laws as radically defective, *precisely as laws*, for want of conformity to those principles.

My present purpose, however, is not to anticipate later chapters, but to make some preliminary clarifications. A first essential distinction is that between a theory, doctrine, or account and the subject-matter of that theory, doctrine, or account. There can be a history of theories, doctrines, and accounts of matters that have no history. And principles of natural law, in the sense formulated in the two preceding paragraphs, have no history.

Since I have yet to show that there are indeed any principles of natural law, let me put the point conditionally. Principles of this sort would hold good, as principles, however extensively they were overlooked, misapplied, or defied in practical thinking, and however little they were recognized by those who reflectively theorize about human thinking. That is to say, they would 'hold good' just as the mathematical principles of accounting 'hold good' even when, as in the medieval banking community, they are unknown or misunderstood. So there could be a history of the varying extent to which they have been used by people, explicitly or implicitly, to regulate their personal activities. There could also be a history of the varying extent to which reflective theorists have acknowledged the sets of principles as valid or 'holding good'. And there could be a history of the popularity of the various theories offered to explain the place of those principles in the whole scheme of things. But of natural law itself there could, strictly speaking, be no history.

Natural law could not rise, decline, be revived, or stage 'eternal returns'. It could not have historical achievements to its credit. It could not be held responsible for disasters of the human spirit or atrocities of human practice.

But there is a history of the opinions or set of opinions, theories, and doctrines which assert that there are principles of natural law, a history of origins, rises, declines and falls, revivals and achievements, and of historical responsibilities. Anyone who thinks that there really are no such principles will consider that a book about natural law must be a book about mere opinions, and that the principal interest of those opinions is their historical causes and effects. But anyone who considers that there are principles of natural law, in the sense already outlined, ought to see the importance of maintaining a distinction between discourse about natural law and discourse about a doctrine or doctrines of natural law. Unhappily, people often fail to maintain the distinction.[1]

This is a book about natural law. It expounds or sets out a theory of natural law, but is not *about* that theory. Nor is it about other theories. It refers to other theories only to illuminate the theory expounded here, or to explain why some truths about natural law have at various times and in various ways been overlooked or obscured. The book does not enter into discussions about whether natural law doctrines have exerted a conservative or radical influence on Western politics, or about the supposed psychological (infantile)[2] origins of such doctrines, or about the claim that some or all specific natural law doctrines are asserted hypocritically,[3] arrogantly,[4] or as a disguise or vehicle for expressions of ecclesiastical faith. For none of these discussions has any real bearing on the question whether there is a natural law and, if so, what its content is. Equally irrelevant to that question is the claim that disbelief in natural law yields bitter fruit. Nothing in this book is to be interpreted as either advancing or denying such claims; the book simply prescinds from all such matters.

II.2   LEGAL VALIDITY AND MORALITY

The preceding section treated theories of natural law as theories of the rational foundations for moral judgment, and this

---

[1] Notable examples of this failure include A. P. D'Entrèves, *Natural Law* (London: 1951, rev. edn 1970), 13, 18, 22, etc.; Julius Stone, *Human Law and Human Justice* (London: 1965), chs 2 and 7.

[2] See Alf Ross, *On Law and Justice* (London: 1958), 258, 262–3.

[3] See Wolfgang Friedmann, letter (1953) 31 *Canadian Bar Rev.* 1074 at 1075.

[4] See Wolfgang Friedmann, review (1958) 3 *Nat. L.F.* 208 at 210; also Hans Kelsen, *Allgemeine Staatslehre* (Berlin: 1925), 335, on 'natural law naivety or arrogance' (in the passage, omitted from the 1945 English translation *(General Theory*, cf. 300), about the fully legal character of despotism).

will be the primary focus of subsequent sections of this chapter. But in the present section I consider the more restricted and juristic understanding of 'natural law' and 'natural law doctrine(s)'.

Here we have to deal with the image of natural law entertained by jurists such as Kelsen, Hart, and Raz. This image should be reproduced in their own words, since they themselves scarcely identify, let alone quote from, any particular theorist as defending the view that they describe as the view of natural law doctrine. Joseph Raz usefully summarizes and adopts Kelsen's version of this image:

Kelsen correctly points out that according to natural law theories there is no specific notion of legal validity. The only concept of validity is validity according to natural law, i.e., moral validity. Natural lawyers can only judge a law as morally valid, that is, just or morally invalid, i.e., wrong. They cannot say of a law that it is legally valid but morally wrong. If it is wrong and unjust, it is also invalid in the only sense of validity they recognise.[5]

In his own terms, Raz later defines 'Natural Law theorists' as 'those philosophers who think it a criterion of adequacy for theories of law that they show... that it is a necessary truth that every law has moral worth'.[6]

For my part, I know of no philosopher who fits, or fitted, such a description, or who would be committed to trying to defend that sort of theoretical or meta-theoretical proposal. Sections IX.2, X.2, X.5, X.6, XI.4, XII.3, and XII.4 are devoted to correcting this image. Suffice it here to say that the root of the misunderstanding seems to be the failure of the modern critics to interpret the texts of natural law theorists in accordance with the principles of definition which those theorists have, for the most part, consistently and self-consciously used. I have already given a sketch of those

[5] Raz, 'Kelsen's Theory of the Basic Norm' (1974) 19 *Am. J. Juris.* 94 at 100.

[6] Raz, *Practical Reason*, 162. This formulation corresponds to the contradictory of the characterization of 'Legal Positivism' constructed by Hart in order to define 'the issue between Natural Law and Legal Positivism': *Concept of Law*, 181 [185]. See also *Practical Reason*, 155, 162; all these formulations seem to be intended by Raz to apply equally to 'definitional' and 'derivative approach' theories of natural law. (Since no one uses the 'definitional' approach, there is no need to inquire into the value of the supposed distribution between 'definitional' and 'derivative' approaches.)

principles in I.3, under the rubric 'central cases and focal meanings'.

The image of natural law theory which we have just been dealing with is closely related, in the mind of Kelsen, with another image. For Kelsen says it is a 'cardinal point of the historical doctrine of natural law...over two thousand years' that it attempts 'to found positive law upon a natural law delegation'.[7] So far, so good (though the formulation is not classical). But Kelsen regards the attempt as 'logically impossible', on the ground that such a delegation would entail ascribing legal validity to norms not because of their justice but because of their origination by the delegate; and this in turn would entail, he says, that the delegate could override and 're-place' the natural law, 'in view of the fact that positive law is not, on principle, subject to limitations of...its...material validity'.[8] The *non sequitur* is Kelsen's, I am afraid, and is not in his sources; the 'principle' to which he appeals is a mere *petitio principii*. If we may translate the relevant portion of, for example, Thomas Aquinas's theory into Kelsenian terminology (as far as possible), it runs as follows: The legal validity (in the focal, moral sense of 'legal validity') of positive law is derived from its rational connection with (i.e. derivation from) natural law, and this connection holds good, normally, if and only if (i) the law originates in a way which is legally valid (in the specially restricted, purely legal sense of 'legal validity') and (ii) the law is not materially unjust either in its content or in relevant circumstances of its positing.[9] Aquinas's discussion of these points is under-elaborated, in relation to the modern jurisprudential debate: see XII.4. But it avoids the self-contradiction and/or vacuity of which Kelsen accuses it. To delegate is not to delegate unconditionally.

---

[7] Kelsen, *General Theory*, 412.

[8] *Ibid.*, 412–13. See also 411: 'Any attempt to establish a relationship between the two systems of norms in terms of simultaneously valid orders ultimately leads to their merging in terms of sub- and super-ordination, that is [*non sequitur*] to the recognition of positive as natural law or of natural as positive law'.

[9] See *S.T.* I–II q. 96 a. 4c; the Thomist equivalent of Kelsen's principal sense of legal validity is the notion of an act of purported law-creation being *infra potestatem commissam*. See X.7 and XII.2.

In view of the foregoing, it is not surprising to find Kelsen propagating another misleading, and not uncommon, image of natural law juristic theory:

The natural-law teachers contend, in a version which has remained a stereotype from the church fathers down to Kant, that positive law derives its entire validity from natural law; it is essentially a mere emanation of natural law; the making of statutes or of decisions does not freely create, it merely reproduces the true law which is already somehow in existence...[10]

Positive law, he says, is thus treated as a mere 'copy' of natural law. But all this is travesty. We may refer again to Thomas Aquinas—as always, not because there is any presumption that whatever he asserts is true, but simply because he is un-questionably a paradigm 'natural law theorist' and dominates the period 'from the church fathers down to Kant', by synthe-sizing his patristic and early medieval predecessors and by fixing the vocabulary and to some extent the doctrine of later scholastic and, therefore, early modern thought. Now Aquinas indeed asserts that positive law derives its validity from natural law; but in the very same breath he shows how it is *not* a mere emanation from or copy of natural law, and how the legislator enjoys all the creative freedom of an architect: the analogy is Aquinas's.[11] Aquinas thinks that positive law is needed for two reasons, of which one is that the natural law 'already somehow in existence' does *not* itself provide all or even most of the solutions to the co-ordination problems of communal life. On any reasonable view, Aquinas's clear elaborations of these points (based on a hint from Aristotle)[12] must be considered one of the more successful parts of his not always successful work on natural law. My own discussion of the relations between natural law and the content of positive law is principally in X.7.

Finally we may note that the other of the two justifications for constructing a system of positive law to supplement the 'natural' requirements of morality, according to Aquinas (who

---

[10] *General Theory*, 416.
[11] See *S.T.* I–II q. 95 a. 2 (q. 91 a. 3 and q. 95 a. 1 must be read in the light of this very precise article, and of q. 99 a. 3 ad 2; q. 99 a. 5c; q. 100 a. 11c). The analogy is explained at X.7.
[12] See *Nic. Eth.* V. 7: 1134b20–24 (reproduced in notes to X.7); Aquinas, *in Eth.* V, lect. 12, no. 1023; cf. Aristotle, *Rhetoric* I.13: 1373b.

gives this justification a perhaps excessive prominence), is the need for compulsion, to force selfish people to act reasonably.[13] How strange, then, to read Kelsen finding yet another 'necessary contradiction between positive and natural law', this time 'because the one is a coercive order, while the other, ideally, is not only non-coercive, but actually has to forbid any coercion among men'.[14] This, alas, is yet another distorted image; a sound theory of natural law is an attempt to express reflectively the requirements and ideals of practical reasonableness, not of idealism: see X.1.

II.3   THE VARIETY OF HUMAN
OPINIONS AND PRACTICES

H. L. A. Hart has said that 'natural law theory in all its protean guises attempts to assert that human beings are equally devoted to and united in their conception of aims (the pursuit of knowledge, justice to their fellow men) other than that of survival'.[15] For my part, I know of no one who has ever asserted this. Certainly the classical theorists of natural law all took for granted, and often enough bluntly asserted, that human beings are not all equally devoted to the pursuit of knowledge or justice, and are far from united in their conception of what constitutes worthwhile knowledge or a demand of justice. There is much to be said for Leo Strauss's judgment that 'knowledge of the indefinitely large variety of notions of right and wrong is so far from being incompatible with the idea of natural right that it is the essential condition for the emergence of that idea: realization of the variety of notions of right is *the* incentive for the quest for natural right'.[16]

Thomas Aquinas frequently tackled the question of the extent of human recognition of the natural law.[17] When his re-

---

[13] *S.T.* I–II q. 90 a. 3 ad 2; q. 95 a. 1c and ad 1; q. 96 a. 5c; see also Plato, *Rep.* 519e; Aristotle, *Nic. Eth.* X. 9: 1180a22.

[14] *General Theory*, 411.

[15] Hart, 'Positivism and the Separation of Law and Morals' (1958) 71 *Harv. L. Rev.* 593, reprinted in Dworkin (ed.), *Philosophy of Law* (Oxford: 1977), 17 at 36.

[16] Strauss, *Natural Right and History* (Chicago: 1953), 10. Likewise H. Rommen, *The Natural Law* (St. Louis and London: 1947), 4. For the ancients awareness of the variety of moral notions see Aristotle, *Nic. Eth.* V.7: 1134b27–35; I.3: 1094b14–16; and for sceptical appeals to this variety, see Sextus Empiricus, *Pyrrhonean Hypotyposes* III, xxiv, 198–238.

[17] *S.T.* I–II q. 93 a. 2c; q. 94 a. 2c, a. 4, a. 5 ad 1, a. 6c; q. 99 a. 2 ad 2; q. 100 a. 1c, a. 3c, a. 6c, a. 11c.

marks are taken together, it can be seen that he is working with a threefold categorization of the principles or precepts of natural law. *First* there are the most general (*communissima*) principles, which are not so much precepts as, 'so to speak, the ends [or point] of the precepts';[17b] they state the basic forms of human good; at least to the extent that they concern his own good, they are recognized by anyone who reaches the age of reason and who has enough experience to know what they refer to, and in this sense they 'cannot, as general principles [*in universali*], be eliminated from the human heart'.[18] This is the nearest Aquinas gets to making the assertion which Hart suggests is the core of natural law theorizing. It amounts to no more than saying that any sane person is capable of seeing that life, knowledge, fellowship, offspring, and a few other such basic aspects of human existence are, as such, good, i.e. worth having, leaving to one side all particular predicaments and implications, all assessments of relative importance, all moral demands, and in short, all questions of whether and how one is to devote oneself to these goods.

For, *secondly*, even the most elementary and easily recognizable moral implications of those first principles are capable of being obscured or distorted for particular people and, indeed, for whole cultures, by prejudice, oversight, convention, the sway of desire for particular gratifications, etc.;[19] for example, many people (in Aquinas's day, as now) think that morality touches only interpersonal relations and that 'everyone is free to do what he will in those matters that concern only himself', while others cannot see that they have any obligations to other people.[20] And, *thirdly*, there are many moral questions which can only be rightly answered by someone who is wise, and who considers them searchingly.[21]

So when Hart objects that the conception of 'the human end or good for man' which was entertained by 'the classical exponents' of natural law was 'complex', 'debatable', and

---

[17b] *S.T.* I–II q. 100 a. 11c; see also q. 90 a. 2 ad 1.

[18] *S. T.* I–II q. 94 a. 6c; also a. 2c; q. 99 a. 2 ad 2; q. 100 aa. 5 ad 1, 11c; q. 58 a. 5c; q. 77 a. 2c; *De Veritate*, q. 16 a. 3c.

[19] *S. T.* I–II q. 100 a. 1c (anyone's natural reason can immediately grasp that theft is not to be committed); q. 94 a. 4c, 6c (but whole peoples have failed to see the wrongfulness of theft or brigandage).

[20] *S.T.* I–II q. 100 a. 5 ad 1; II–II q. 122, a. 1c.

[21] *S.T.* I–II q. 100 a. 1c, a. 3c, a. 11c.

'disputable',[22] the classical exponents would have replied that indeed it was complex, debated, and disputed, and that they had made rather extensive contributions to the debate.[23] For the real problem of morality, and of the point or meaning of human existence, is not in discerning the basic aspects of human well-being, but in integrating those various aspects into the intelligent and reasonable commitments, projects, and actions that go to make up one or other of the many admirable forms of human life. And by no means everybody can see these things steadily and whole, let alone put them into practice. The fact that there is controversy is not an argument against one side in that controversy. A genuine requirement of practical reasonableness is not the less a part of natural law (to use the classical phrase) just because it is not universally recognized or is actively disputed.

Julius Stone discerned three 'decisive issues between positivists and natural lawyers', and one of the them was: 'Are [natural lawyers] entitled to claim that what they assert as self-evident must be recognized as self-evident by all?'[24] The formulation of the issue is confused: the pertinent claim would be 'that what they assert to be self-evident is [or should be?] recognized as *true* by all'. For the important thing about a self-evident proposition is that people (with the relevant experience, and understanding of terms) *assent* to it without needing the proof of argument; it matters not at all whether they further recognize it as belonging to the relatively sophisticated philosophical category, 'self-evident'. But even if we correct Stone's formulation accordingly, it remains a non-issue, another imaginary image of natural law theory.

Near the very beginning of the tradition of theorizing about natural right, we find Aristotle quite explicit that ethics can only be usefully discussed with experienced and mature people, and that age is a necessary but not a sufficient

[22] *Concept of Law*, 187 [191].
[23] See, e.g., *Nic. Eth.* I.5: 1095b14–1096a10; *Eud. Eth.* I.5: 1215b 5–1216a10; and *S.T.* I–II q. 2 aa. 1–6, on the claims of wealth, honour, reputation, power, bodily well-being, and pleasure, respectively, to be the integrating goods of human existence. The existence of 'dispute' and 'debate' about the ultimate ends of human existence is a topic of *S.T.* I–II q. 1 a. 7; also I q. 2 a. 1 ad 1.
[24] Stone, *Human Law and Human Justice*, 212.

condition for the required maturity.[25] He does not explicitly ascribe self-evidence or indemonstrability or axiomatic status to any ethical or practical principles, though he treats certain things as beyond question: for example, that no one would wish to attain 'happiness' at the cost of losing his identity.[26] Aquinas, on the other hand, has a discussion of self-evidence, if we translate *propositio per se nota* as 'self-evident proposition'. But, *pace* Stone, Aquinas's discussion begins by pointing out that while some propositions are self-evident to 'everyone', since everyone understands their terms, other propositions are self-evident only to 'the wise', since only the relatively wise (or learned) understand what they mean.[27] He gives two examples of the latter sort of self-evident propositions, from the field of speculative philosophy; one is that 'a human being is a rational being', and the other is that 'a disembodied spirit does not occupy space'. He then proceeds to speak about the self-evident pre-moral principles that he later calls *communissima*, without, unfortunately, indicating which if any of them he thinks self-evident only to the relatively wise. An example is, perhaps, the principle 'to know about God is a good'.[28] For Aquinas denied that the existence of God is self-evident, even to the relatively wise, in this life.[29]

It does seem to be the case that a good many of the principles of logic and mathematics employed in natural science and technology, and in historical and archaeological science, are such that it would be absurd to say that they either have been proved or are in need of proof. But what is certain is that the natural sciences and in general all theoretical disciplines rest implicitly on epistemic principles, or norms of theoretical rationality, which are undemonstrated, indemonstrable, but self-evident in a manner strongly analogous to the self-evidence ascribed by Aquinas to the basic principles of practical reasonableness: for an identification of some of these

---

[25] *Nic. Eth.* I.3: 1094b28–a12; 4: 1095a31–b13.

[26] *Nic. Eth.* IX.4: 1166a20–23; VIII.7: 1159a9–12.

[27] *S.T.* I–II q. 94 a. 2c; q. 66 a. 5 ad 4. Note that, like Aristotle *(Post. Anal.* B, 19), Aquinas vigorously denies that there are any innate ideas; no proposition, however self-evident, is either formed or assented to by a human mind without an act of understanding of data of experience: *S.T.* I q. 79 a. 2c; *De Veritate* q. 16 a. 1c.

[28] *S.T.* I–II q. 94 a. 2c.

[29] *S.T.* I q. 2 a. 1.

epistemic principles, see III.4; for a use of one of them, see XIII.2.

II.4   THE ILLICIT INFERENCE FROM FACTS TO NORMS

Another of the three 'decisive issues' formulated by Stone was this: 'Have the natural lawyers shown that they can derive ethical norms from facts?'[30] And the answer can be brisk: They have not, nor do they need to, nor did the classical exponents of the theory dream of attempting any such derivation.

This answer will doubtless give widespread dissatisfaction. For if it is correct, the most popular image of natural law has to be abandoned. The corresponding and most popular objection to all theories of natural law has to be abandoned, too, and the whole question of natural law thought through afresh by many.

Thus it is simply not true that 'any form of a natural-law theory of morals entails the belief that propositions about man's duties and obligations can be inferred from propositions about his nature'.[31] Nor is it true that for Aquinas 'good and evil are concepts analysed and fixed in metaphysics before they are applied in morals'.[32] On the contrary, Aquinas asserts as plainly as possible that the first principles of natural law, which specify the basic forms of good and evil and which can be adequately grasped by anyone of the age of reason (and not just by metaphysicians), are *per se nota* (self-evident) and indemonstrable.[33] They are not inferred from speculative principles. They are not inferred from facts. They are not inferred from metaphysical propositions about human nature, or about the nature of good and evil, or about 'the function of a human being';[34] nor are they inferred from a

---

[30] Stone, *Human Law and Human Justice*, 212.

[31] D. J. O'Connor, *Aquinas and Natural Law* (London: 1967), 68; similarly, amongst countless others, Norberto Bobbio, 'Quelques arguments contre le droit naturel' (1959) 3 *Annales de philosophie politique* 180; *Locke e il Diritto Naturale* (Turin: 1963), 70–1.

[32] O'Connor, *Aquinas and Natural Law*, 19.

[33] Aquinas, *in Eth.* V, lect. 12, para. 1018; *S.T.* I–II q. 94 a. 2; q. 91 a. 3c; q. 58 aa. 4c, 5c.

[34] Cf. the objections of Margaret MacDonald, 'Natural Rights', in P. Laslett (ed.), *Philosophy, Politics and Society* (Oxford: 1956), 35 at 44; Kai Nielsen, 'The Myth of Natural Law', in S. Hook (ed.), *Law and Philosophy* (New York: 1964), 122 at 132.

teleological conception of nature[35] or any other conception of nature. They are not inferred or derived from anything. They are underived (though not innate). Principles of right and wrong, too, are derived from these first, pre-moral principles of practical reasonableness, and not from any facts, whether metaphysical or otherwise. When discerning what is good, to be pursued (*prosequendum*), intelligence is operating in a different way, yielding a different logic, from when it is discerning what is the case (historically, scientifically, or metaphysically); but there is no good reason for asserting that the latter operations of intelligence are more rational than the former.

Of course, Aquinas would agree that 'were man's nature different, so would be his duties'.[36] The basic forms of good grasped by practical understanding are what is good for human beings with the nature they have. Aquinas considers that practical reasoning begins not by understanding this nature from the outside, as it were, by way of psychological, anthropological, or metaphysical observations and judgments defining human nature,[37] but by experiencing one's nature, so to speak, from the inside, in the form of one's inclinations. But again, there is no process of inference. One does not judge that 'I have [or everybody has] an inclination to find out about things' and then infer that therefore 'knowledge is a good to be pursued'. Rather, by a simple act of non-inferential understanding one grasps that the object of the inclination which one experiences is an instance of a general form of good, for oneself (and others like one).

There are important objections to be made to Aquinas's theory of natural law. O'Connor rightly identifies the main one: Aquinas fails to explain 'just how the specific moral rules which we need to guide our conduct can be shown to be connected with allegedly self-evident principles'.[38] But the objection that Aquinas's account of natural law proposes an illicit inference from 'is' to 'ought' is quite unjustified.

[35] *Pace* Strauss, *Natural Right and History*, 7–8; and Hart, *Concept of Law*, 182–7 [186–92].

[36] O'Connor, *Aquinas and Natural Law*, 18.

[37] *Pace* O'Connor who says, *ibid.*, 15, that 'the theory of natural law...turns on the idea that human nature is constituted by a unique set of properties which can be understood and summed up in a definition'.

[38] *Ibid.*, 73. For my own attempt to explain this, see Chapter V.

How can this objection have become so popular? There are a number of probable reasons, of which I may mention three. The first is that the very phrase 'natural law' can lead one to suppose that the norms referred to, in any theory of natural law, are based upon judgments about nature (human and/or otherwise).[39] The second reason is that this supposition is in fact substantially correct in relation to the Stoic theory of natural law (see XIII.1) and, as we shall shortly see, in relation to some Renaissance theories, including some that claimed the patronage of Thomas Aquinas and have been influential almost to the present day (see II.6).

Thirdly, Aquinas himself was a writer not on ethics alone but on the whole of theology. He was keen to show the relationship between his ethics of natural law and his general theory of metaphysics and the world-order. He wished to point out the analogies running through the whole order of being. Thus human virtue is analogous to the 'virtue' that can be predicated of anything which is a fine specimen of things of its nature, in good shape, *bene disposita secundum convenientiam suae naturae*.[40] So he is happy to say that human virtue, too, is in accordance with the nature of human beings, and human vice is *contra naturam*. If we stopped here, the charge against him would seem to be proved, or at least plausible (and certain later philosophical theologians would seem to have been justified in claiming his patronage). But in fact Aquinas takes good care to make his meaning, his order of explanatory priorities, quite clear. The criterion of conformity with or contrariety to human nature is reasonableness.

And so whatever is contrary to the order of reason is contrary to the nature of human beings as such; and what is reasonable is in accordance

---

[39] This sort of a *priori* reasoning from words, without inquiry into their use by particular theorists, is indulged in by those who generalize J. S. Mill's exposé of the confusions of Montesquieu and Combe (between 'is' laws and 'ought' laws: see 'Nature', in Mill, *Three Essays on Religion* (London and New York: 1874), 8–15) into a general condemnation of natural law theories. Of the classic theories, the Stoic variety is perhaps exposed to Mill's objection (cf. XIII.1); Plato's is not (as Mill himself points out: *ibid.*, 4); and the Aristotelian variety is not (as ought to be clear from the Aristotelian distinction between theoretical and practical reason, from Aristotle's sharp differentiation between the senses of 'necessary' (*Meta.* V, 5: 1015a20), and from Aquinas's willingness to draw, when appropriate, a sharp distinction between the 'natural' and the 'reasonable' (e.g. *S.T.* I–II q. 1 a. 2c)).

[40] *S.T.* I–II q. 71 a. 2c.

with human nature as such. *The good of the human being is being in accord with reason, and human evil is being outside the order of reasonableness...* So human virtue, which makes good both the human person and his works, is in accordance with human nature *just* in *so* far as [*tantum...inquantum*] it is in accordance with reason; and vice is contrary to human nature just in so far as it is contrary to the order of reasonableness.[41]

In other words, for Aquinas, the way to discover what is morally right (virtue) and wrong (vice) is to ask, not what is in accordance with human nature, but what is reasonable. And this quest will eventually bring one back to the *underived* first principles of practical reasonableness—principles which make no reference at all to human nature, but only to human good. From end to end of his ethical discourses, the primary categories for Aquinas are the 'good' and the 'reasonable'; the 'natural' is, from the point of view of his ethics, a speculative appendage added by way of metaphysical reflection, *not* a counter with which to advance either to or from the practical *prima principia per se nota*.

Since Aquinas's Aristotelian distinction between 'speculative' and practical reason corresponds so neatly with the modern (but not only modern!) distinction which we (roughly!) indicate by contrasting 'fact' and 'norm' or 'is' and 'ought', it will be helpful to examine in greater depth the historical process by which the theory of natural law has come to be associated with a fundamental disregard of this distinction. To this examination the next two sections are devoted; they are, however, no more than an introduction to a much-needed investigation, still to be made.

II.5   HUME AND CLARKE ON 'IS' AND 'OUGHT'

In every system of morality, which I have hitherto met with, I have always remarked, that the author proceeds for some time in the ordinary way of reasoning, and establishes the being of a God, or makes observations concerning human affairs; when of a sudden I am surprised to find, that instead of the usual copulations of propositions,

---

[41] *Ibid.* (emphasis added). For similar formulations, see *S.T.* I–II q. 94 a. 3 ad 2; q. 18 a. 5. The same order of explanatory priorities can be observed in Plato's remarks about acting according to reason and thus according to nature: *Rep.* IV: 444d; IX: 585–6.

is, and *is not*, I meet with no proposition that is not connected with an *ought*, or an *ought not*. This change is imperceptible; but is, however, of the last consequence. For as this *ought*, or *ought not*, expresses some new relation or affirmation, it is necessary that it should be observed and explained; and at the same time that a reason should be given, for what seems altogether inconceivable, how this new relation can be a deduction from others, which are entirely different from it.... this small attention would...let us see, that the distinction of vice and virtue is not founded merely on the relations of objects, nor is perceived by reason.[42]

There have been many interpretations of this passage, but it will be safe to attend here only to the two most plausible. The first and standard interpretation treats Hume as announcing the logical truth, widely emphasized since the later part of the nineteenth century, that no set of non-moral (or, more generally, non-evaluative) premisses can entail a moral (or evaluative) conclusion. The second interpretation places the passage in its historical and literary context, and sees it as the tailpiece to Hume's attack on the eighteenth-century rationalists (notably Samuel Clarke), an attack whose centrepiece is the contention that rational perception of the moral qualities of actions could not of itself provide a motivating guide to action. While the second interpretation has more to commend it as an interpretation, there is no harm in accepting the first, since if Hume is not to be credited with announcing the logical principle in question, somebody else is to be; and the important thing is that the principle is true and significant. To the discussion in the preceding section I may here simply add that this principle itself in no way entails or authorizes Hume's conclusion that distinctions between 'vice and virtue' are not 'perceived by reason'.[43] That said, we may consider the second interpretation.

[42] David Hume, *A Treatise of Human Nature* (1740), Book III, Part i, sec. 1 (Raphael, *British Moralists*, para. 504: here as elsewhere I follow Raphael's revision of spelling).

[43] But for the fact that Hume offers, as his own, four or five inconsistent views about the nature and basis of moral propositions (see the careful analysis in Jonathan Harrison, *Hume's Moral Epistemology* (Oxford: 1976), 110–25), I should have to add that Hume himself conspicuously offends against the principle that 'ought' cannot be derived from 'is'. To the extent that his 'predominant' view (*ibid.*, 124) is that moral judgments are judgments about what characteristics and actions arouse approval or disapproval (so that, as Hume puts it, systems of ethics should be 'founded on fact and observations': *An Enquiry concerning the Principles*

Hume's aim, in the section which concludes with the *is-ought* paragraph, is to 'consider, whether it be possible, from reason alone, to distinguish betwixt moral good and evil, or whether there must concur some other principles to enable us to make that distinction'.[44] His arguments are expressly directed against 'those who affirm that virtue is nothing but a conformity to reason; that there are eternal fitnesses and unfitnesses of things, which are the same to every rational being that considers them; that the immutable measures of right and wrong impose an obligation, not only on human creatures, but also on the Deity himself...'.[45]

Who are 'those who affirm' these propositions? It is possible to point to passages in Joseph Butler's *Fifteen Sermons* (1726) and Ralph Cudworth's *A Treatise concerning Eternal and Immutable Morality* (c. 1685, first printed 1731). But the obvious source, identified twice in this connection by Hume himself,[46] is Samuel Clarke's *A Discourse concerning the Unchangeable Obligations of Natural Religion...*(1706, 8th edn, 1732). Clarke's *Discourse*, popular and influential in its day, is loose, prolix, and repetitive; but towards the end of his life, Clarke offered a summary: 'Thus have I endeavoured to deduce the *original*

---

of Morals (1751), sec. 1 (Raphael, *British Moralists*, para. 563)), Hume plainly attempts the logically illegitimate derivation. This is certainly some evidence against the first interpretation of the *is-ought* paragraph of his *Treatise*, *qua* interpretation: for an interpreter ought not to postulate inconsistencies beyond necessity. But it is more interesting to observe that many modern epigones of Hume, who regard him as having laid the basis for a sound ethical theory by discovering the principle 'no *ought* from an *is*', themselves fall into the same inconsistency as their master: the *fact* that one has opted for, adopted, chosen, or decided upon some practical principle is no more a logically legitimate ground for asserting that ϕ ought to be done than is the fact (which Hume fixed upon) that ϕ arouses sentiments of approval or disapproval in oneself or in people in general.

[44] *Treatise*, III, i, 1 (*British Moralists*, para. 488). By 'principle' Hume here means mental factors, such as conscience, moral sense, sentiment, and other passions: see *British Moralists*, paras 489, 490, 505, etc.

[45] *Ibid.*; *British Moralists*, para. 488. For further references to the 'natural fitness and unfitness of things', see paras 497 and 500. For the importance to Hume of the problem whether God could be known to be bound by them, see paras 500 and 634 (the latter is Hume's letter of 16 March 1740 to Francis Hutcheson).

[46] See Hume, *A Letter from a Gentleman* (1745), quoted by Raphael in W. B. Todd (ed.), *Hume and the Enlightenment* (Edinburgh and Austin: 1974), 27; and Hume, *An Enquiry concerning the Principles of Morals* (1751), sec. III, part ii, para. 158 n., mentioning also Cudworth, Malebranche, and Montesquieu's *L'esprit des lois* (which appeared, however, eight years after Hume's *Treatise*).

obligations of *morality*, from the *necessary and eternal reason* and *proportions of things*.[47] More precisely, we may say that Clarke has offered to prove that:

[i] the same necessary and eternal *different relations*, that different things bear one to another; with regard to which [ii] the will of God always and necessarily does determine itself, to choose to act only what is agreeable to [the eternal rules of] justice, equity, goodness and truth, in order to the welfare of the whole universe; [iii] *ought* likewise constantly to determine the wills of all subordinate rational beings, to govern all their actions by the same rules, for the good of the public, in their respective stations. That is: [i] these eternal and necessary differences of things make it *fit and reasonable* for creatures so to act; they [ii] cause it to be their *duty*, or lay an *obligation* upon them, so to do; even separate from the consideration of these rules being the *positive will or command of God*...[48]

My present interest is in stage (iii) of this argument, the proof that actions which are fit and reasonable are thereby *obligatory*. But I may first reproduce one of the examples which Clarke offers in order to illustrate what he means by an eternal, unalterable, or absolute proportion or fitness of things: '...in men's dealing and conversing one with another; it is undeniably more fit, absolutely and in the nature of the thing itself, that all men should endeavour to promote the universal good and welfare of all; than that all men should be continually contriving the ruin and destruction of all'.[49] Clarke regards such propositions as 'plain and self-evident',[50] and in need of no proof. What he wants to *prove* is that the 'eternal reason of

---

[47] Clarke, *A Discourse concerning the Unchangeable Obligations of Natural Religion*, 225, reproduced in Raphael, *British Moralists*, para. 251 (Clarke's emphases); the passage was added after the 5th edn (1719). Earlier (Raphael, para. 244), speaking of the duty of universal benevolence, Clarke says: 'the obligation to this great duty, may also otherwise be deduced from the *nature of man*...' (his emphasis).

[48] *Ibid.*, para. 225 (Clarke's emphases). The numerals in square brackets, which I have inserted here and in later quotations from Clarke, correspond to the first three of the seven numbered stages of Clarke's subsequent argument; stages four to seven overlap with each other and with the first three. The words in square brackets are taken from the equivalent passage in para. 231; I have inserted them here to make the passage more readily comprehensible.

[49] *Ibid.*, para. 226. Cf. Hume, *Treatise* II, iii, 3 (*British Moralists*, para. 483): 'it is not contrary to reason to prefer the destruction of the whole world to the scratching of my finger'.

[50] Clarke, *A Discourse concerning the Unchangeable Obligations of Natural Religion*, *British Moralists*, para. 227.

things',[51] [i] known and expressed in such propositions, [iii] 'ought...indispensably to govern men's actions', i.e. that it creates (or is) an *obligation*, indeed 'the truest and formallest obligation', 'the original obligation of all'.[52]

Clarke's proof of obligation, so far as it can be disentangled from his constant reassertions of the conclusion to be proved, appears to be this: Just as 'it would be absurd and ridiculous for a man in arithmetical matters, [i] ignorantly to believe that twice two is not equal to four; or [iii] wilfully and obstinately to contend, against his own clear knowledge, that the whole is not equal to all its parts', so it is 'absurd and blameworthy, [i] to mistake negligently plain right and wrong, that is, to understand the proportions of things in morality to be what they are not; or [iii] wilfully to act contrary to known justice and equity, that is, to will things to be what they are not and cannot be'.[53] He repeats this argument: the rules of right oblige because those who contravene them 'endeavour (as much as in them is) to make things be what they are not, and cannot be', which is presumptuous, insolent, contrary to understanding, reason, and judgment, an attempt to destroy the order by which the universe subsists, and above all, as *absurd* as 'to pretend to alter the certain proportions of numbers' or to call light darkness.[54]

This argument is a failure. To try to alter the proportions of numbers, or to shut one's eyes to the difference between light and dark, is (where it is not logically impossible) *pointless*, profitless, devoid of potential advantage to oneself or others. But to act contrary to justice is frequently advantageous to oneself and one's friends. (And for that reason alone, such action need not be interpreted as endeavouring to 'make things be what they are not and cannot be'.) The demand for a proof of obligation is a demand to be shown the *point* of acting in ways that will certainly sometimes run counter to one's desires and (at least certain of) one's interests. Clarke's argument fails to make the transition from *is* (in this case, 'is reasonable', 'is just', etc.) to

---

[51] Also called by him 'right reason' and 'the law of nature': para. 246.

[52] *Ibid.*, para. 233.

[53] *Ibid.*, para. 232. For my use of bracket numerals, see n. 48 above.

[54] *Ibid.* See also para. 230, med. In a later reference to this kind of 'absurdity', Clarke, *A Discourse concerning the Unchangeable Obligations of Natural Religion*, 232 cites Cicero, *De Legibus* I, 44.

ought because it fails to advert to any desire or interest of the agent's that might be satisfied by acting rightly. His argument does (rather sketchily) attend to human desires, interests, and well-being, but only in order to arrive at the judgment that certain actions are fitting and reasonable. It fails to consider whether acting fittingly and reasonably is an aspect of (or way of realizing) the agent's well-being or is in any other way worth while or desirable.

Now this objection to Clarke is not Hume's, for it treats the problem of obligation as the problem of finding justifying reasons, i.e. adequate point, for acting in certain ways, whereas Hume lacks any clear conception of, or systematic interest in the concept of, justifying reasons. For him, the problem of obligation seems to come down to the problem of finding a motive that *will* move someone to act in certain ways. So the central objection he raises against Clarke's type of argument is this:

It is one thing to know virtue, and another to conform the will to it. In order, therefore, to prove that the measures of right and wrong are eternal laws, *obligatory* on every rational mind, it is not sufficient to show the relations upon which they are founded: we must also point out the connection betwixt the relation and the will; and must prove that this connection is so necessary, that in every well-disposed mind, it must take place and have its influence ...Now...in human nature no relation can ever alone produce any action...[W]e cannot prove *a priori*, that these relations [of right and wrong], if they really existed and were perceived, would be universally forcible and obligatory.[55]

Supporters of the 'first', standard interpretation of the *is-ought* paragraph (which follows four paragraphs after that just quoted) should be disconcerted by this manifestation of Hume's indifference to the distinction between the 'forcible' and the 'obligatory', between what ought to move the will and what 'must' (i.e. necessarily does) move it.

Supporters of the second interpretation of the *is-ought* paragraph have no such difficulty. In their view, Hume's concern in the *is-ought* paragraph is essentially the same as his concern in the passage just quoted, where it is clear that the gap which

---

[55] *Treatise*, III, i, 1 (*British Moralists*, para. 500) (Hume's emphasis).

Hume says cannot be bridged is *not* the gap between the factual and the normative, but the gap between *any truth* (even a 'normative truth', a true proposition about what is good or bad, right or wrong) and motivating conclusions about what ought to be done. This interpretation of the *is-ought* paragraph seems to me to be very plausible; it integrates that paragraph with the main thread of thought running right through that section of the *Treatise* which it concludes (viz. the view that morals move one to action but reason does not), and it explains Hume's pervasive indifference to the logical difference between obligation and influence. (This interpretation does not, of course, *defend* Hume against the charge of ignoring that difference; the principle that *ought* is not inferable from *is* retains its validity even if Hume neither announced it nor conformed his arguments to its requirements.)

The problem Clarke set himself was to show that moral truths provide a (conclusive) reason for action. He failed to solve the problem because he ignored the logic of practical reasoning, in which the fundamental category is the good (not necessarily moral) that is to be[56] pursued and realized. Instead he looked exclusively to the logic of speculative or theoretical reasoning, in which the fundamental category is 'what is the case' and the fundamental principle is that contradictions are excluded. Hume saw that Clarke's problem was a real one, and that Clarke was looking in the wrong direction for its solution. Hume himself lacked a viable conception of practical reason and practical principles. So he was able to offer no more than a scatter of notoriously inconsistent and puzzling responses to the problem, some purporting to solve it, others to dissolve it. But his historical importance is that the vigour of his attack brought to an end a line of argument that by then had dominated the main-line theories of natural law for 150 years or more.

II.6   CLARKE'S ANTECEDENTS

The conceptual framework of Clarke's confused and rhetorical discourse is to be found, tersely expressed, in Hugo Grotius,

---

[56] I use the phrase 'is to be' as a gerundive, i.e. in the sense it has when we ask 'What is to be done?' ('Quid est *faciendum*?'). Thus, it can be understood as equivalent to 'ought to be...', across a wide range of meanings of 'ought': see II.6, III.2, 3, 5.

De Jure Belli ac Pacis (1625) and in Grotius's sources, which certainly included Suarez, *De Legibus* (1612) and probably also Gabriel Vazquez's *Commentary* on Aquinas (1605). Clarke, like all educated persons of his time, would have been familiar with Grotius's incomparably influential treatise, and may well have been familiar with the relevant passages of Suarez and Vazquez, either at first hand or through English commentators on their argument such as the Cambridge Platonist, Nathaniel Culverwel.

Grotius is standardly said to have inaugurated a new, modern, and secular era in natural law theorizing by his *'etiamsi daremus...'*:

> ...what we have been saying would have a degree of validity [*locum aliquem*] even if we were to grant [*etiamsi daremus*] that which cannot be conceded without the utmost wickedness, that there is no God, or that the affairs of men are of no concern to him.[57]

But this standard reading of Grotius is a mere misunderstanding. Grotius must be assumed to have known (if only from his reading of Suarez) that, for the purpose of discussing the roots of obligation, the hypothesis of God's non-existence (or indifference) had been a commonplace of theological debate since, at latest, the mid-fourteenth century. And very many of the scholastics used the hypothesis to just the same effect as Grotius. For what had Grotius just 'been saying'? In the preceding sentence but one, he had remarked:

> Since...man has...judgment, which enables him to determine what things are agreeable or harmful...and what can lead to either alternative: in such things it is understood, within the limitations of human understanding, to be fitting to human nature [*conveniens humanae naturae*] to follow a well-ordered judgment...Whatever is clearly repugnant to such judgment is likewise understood to be against the law of nature, that is, of human nature [*contra jus naturae, humanae scilicet*].

And the 'degree of validity' which Grotius would accord the law of nature in the absence of divine command is indicated in the first chapter of the treatise, in a formulation which preserves all the ambiguity of the phrase 'a degree of validity':

---

[57] *De Jure Belli ac Pacis*, Prolegomena, para. 11 (trans. Kelsey, Oxford: 1925; adjusted).

The law of nature is a dictate of right reason, pointing out [*indicans*] that an act, according as it is fitting or unfitting [*ex ejus convenientia aut disconvenientia*] to rational nature, has in it a quality of moral turpitude or moral necessity; and that, in consequence, such an act is either forbidden or enjoined by the author of nature, God. The acts in regard to which a dictate exists are in themselves either *debiti* or *illiciti*, and so are understood to be necessarily enjoined or forbidden by God.[58]

Translators of the last sentence often render '*debiti*' as 'obligatory'. But this fails to preserve the delicate ambiguity in the thought of Grotius and his sources. The problem that they were uneasily indicating by way of the hypothesis *etiamsi daremus* is essentially the problem so directly confronted later by Clarke and, polemically, by Hume: Granted that we can discern right and wrong, due and undue, by reasoning, what makes it *obligatory* to choose the right and the due and to avoid the wrong and the undue? Grotius himself, of course, had no need to elaborate on this problem in what, after all, is simply the introduction to a law book. But his approach hints at the answer which, by the beginning of the seventeenth century, had become standard among the philosophical theologians: What is right and wrong depends on the nature of things (and what is *conveniens* to such nature), and not on a decree of God; but the normative or motivating significance of moral rightness and wrongness, in particular the obligatoriness of the norm of right and wrong, depends fundamentally upon there being a decree expressing God's will that the right be done (as a matter of obligation) and that the wrong be avoided (likewise). As Grotius put it, 'due and undue acts are therefore understood to be necessarily enjoined or forbidden by God', though they would remain due or undue, even if (*etiamsi daremus*) there were no such divine decrees.

Clarke's difficulties arose from the fact that, while rejecting one part of this twofold thesis, he accepted the other part. Not unreasonably, he rejected the assumption that obligation is

---

[58] *De Jure Belli ac Pacis*, I, c. i, sec. 10, paras 1, 2. Grotius, like Clarke, regards the 'fundamental conceptions' in the law of nature as so 'manifest and clear, almost as self-evident as are those things which we perceive by the external senses', that 'no one can deny them without doing violence to himself' (*ibid.*, Prolegomena: in the Kelsey trans., para. 39). He also uses the comparison with 2 x 2 = 4: *ibid.*, I, c. i, sec. 10, para. 5.

essentially the effect of a superior's act of will. But he remained so firmly within the grip of the thesis that practical reasoning is a matter of discerning relations of fittingness to or consistency with nature that he tried to treat obligation as just one more of the set of relations of consistency.

The ethical theory espoused by Vazquez and Suarez was constructed from terms quarried from the works of Aristotle and, above all, Aquinas. But it differed radically from the ethical theories actually maintained by Aristotle and Aquinas. Vazquez and Suarez maintained, *first*, that in discerning the content of the natural law, reason's decisive act consists in discerning precepts of the form 'ϕ is unfitting to human, i.e. rational, nature and thus has the quality of moral wrongfulness' or 'ϕ befits human, i.e. rational nature and thus has the quality of moral rectitude and, if ϕ is the only such act possible in a given context, the additional quality of moral necessity or dueness'.[59] (We can call this thesis 'rationalist'.) For Aquinas, on the other hand, what is decisive, in discerning the content of the natural law, is one's understanding of the basic forms of (not-yet-moral) human well-being as desirable and potentially realizable ends or opportunities and thus as to-be-pursued and realized in one's action—action to which one is already beginning to direct oneself in this very act of practical understanding.[60] *Secondly*, Suarez and (it seems) Vazquez maintained that obligation is essentially the effect of an act of will by a superior, directed to moving the will of an inferior:[61] see also XI.8, XI.9. (We can call this thesis 'voluntarist'.) Aquinas, on the other hand, treats obligation as the rational

[59] See Vazquez, *in Primam Secundae*, disp. 90, c. 3; disp. 97, c. 3; Suarez, *De Legibus*, Book II, c. 7, paras 4–7; c. 5, paras 4–5; c. 6, para. 17.

[60] *S.T.* I–II q. 94 a. 2. Aquinas would not reject the Vazquez-Suarez formulae, but would give them a subordinate and derivative place in the methodology of ethics.

[61] See Vazquez, *in Primam Secundae*, disp. 49, c. 3; Suarez, *De Legibus*, Book I, c. 5, paras 12, 15, 16, 24; Book II, c. 6, paras 6–7, 8, 12, 13, 22. Nothing is more striking than the unquestioned, almost undiscussed assumption of this view amidst the luxuriant subtleties of late scholasticism. Even a writer like Vitoria, who is credited with leading the 'Thomist' revival in the early sixteenth century, says 'it is unintelligible to me how anyone can sin unless he is under some obligation, *and I don't see how anyone can be obligated unless he has a superior*': *De eo ad quod tenetur homo cum primum venit ad usum rationis* (1535; Lyons: 1586), Part II, para. 9; and see notes to XI.9.

necessity of some means to (or way of realizing) an end or objective (i.e. a good) of a particular sort. What sort? Primarily (i.e. apart from special forms of obligation) the good of a form of life which, by its full and reasonably integrated realization of the basic forms of human well-being, renders one a fitting subject for the friendship of the being whose friendship is a basic good that in its full realization embraces all aspects of human well-being, a friendship indispensable for every person.[62] Aquinas's treatment of all these issues is saturated with the interrelated notions, 'end' and 'good'; the terms 'obligation', 'superior', and 'inferior' scarcely appear, and the notion of conformity to nature is virtually absent. In Suarez and Vazquez the terms 'end' and 'good' are almost entirely gone, replaced by 'right' and 'wrong' and cognate notions.

The reader will ask how Aquinas explained the difference between moral thinking and merely prudential reasoning (in the modern sense of 'prudential'), and how he accounted for the peculiarly conclusory sense of the moral 'ought'. The answer must be that Aquinas's account of these matters is, at best, highly elliptical, scattered, and difficult to grasp, and at worst, seriously underdeveloped; and that these deficiencies occasioned the unsatisfactory responses of those who professed to follow him in the later history of philosophical theology. But to this I must add that the materials for a satisfactory development of the sort of position espoused by Aquinas are available, and that the attempt to put these materials to use is encouraged by the impasse in which the sixteenth- and seventeenth-century theories of natural law manifestly found themselves. The subsequent chapters of this book incorporate such an attempt.

It is not respect for Aquinas that inspires this attempt; after all, the Jesuit theologians of early seventeenth-century Spain did not lack respect for Aquinas, yet felt themselves intellectually compelled to oppose, explicitly, certain strategic theses in his philosophy (see, e.g., XI.8, on *imperium*). No; the reason for making the attempt is that a theory of practical reasonableness, of forms of human good, and of practical

---

[62] See *S.T.* I–II q. 1 a. 6; q. 4 a. 8c and ad 3; q. 5 a. 7c; q. 90 a. 1c; q. 99 aa. 1c, 2c; II–II q. 44 a. 1c; q. 47 a. 2 ad 1.

principles, such as the theory Aquinas adumbrated but left insufficiently elaborated, is untouched by the objections which Hume (and after him the whole Enlightenment and post-Enlightenment current of ethics) was able to raise against the tradition of rationalism eked out by voluntarism. That tradition presented itself as the classical or central tradition of natural law theorizing, but in truth it was peculiar to late scholasticism. It was attractive to non-Catholics (like Grotius, Culverwel, and Clarke) who adopted its major concepts not least because of its strong verbal and conceptual resemblances to the Stoicism (see XIII.1) so much admired in European culture from the Renaissance to the end of the eighteenth century The substantive differences between the theory of natural law espoused by Vazquez and Suarez (and most Catholic manuals until the 1960s) and the theory espoused by Aquinas are scarcely less significant and extensive than the better-known differences between Aristotelian and Stoic ethics. But ecclesiastical deference to a misread Aquinas obscured the former differences until well into this century.

We can put Hume's attack on the ethics of his predecessors into perspective by the following summary remarks: (i) Aristotle and Aquinas would readily grant that *ought* cannot be deduced from *is* (whether or not Hume really formulated and adhered to that principle); (ii) Both would go along with Hume's view that the speculative discernment of 'eternal relations', even relations of 'fitness to human nature', leaves open the question what motive anybody has for regulating his actions accordingly; (iii) Aquinas would deplore both the confusion (shared by Hume and Suarez![63]) of obligation with impulse or influence, and Hume's failure to see that reason is an 'active principle' because one is motivated according to one's *understanding* of the goodness and desirability of human opportunities, including the opportunity of extending intelligence and reasonableness into one's choices and actions; (iv) Aquinas would reject the assumption of Clarke, Grotius, Suarez, and Vazquez that the primary and self-evident principles of natural law are moral principles (in

[63] Suarez, *De Legibus*, Book II, c. 6, para. 22: 'obligation is a certain moral impulse [*motio*] to action'; Hume, *Treatise* III, ii, 5 (*British Moralists*, para. 541): 'promises...create [a] new motive or obligation.... [A] sense of interest...is the first obligation to the performance of promises'.

the modern sense of 'moral'), or that they are initially grasped as principles concerned with self-evident relations of conformity or disconformity to human nature; (v) Aquinas, like Clarke and Hume, would reject the view that the will or imperative of a superior accounts for obligation; like Hume he would reject Clarke's view that obligation is essentially a matter of avoiding intellectual inconsistencies; and finally he would reject both Hume's view that it is a matter of, or intrinsically related to, a peculiar sentiment, and equally the recent neo-Humean view that statements of obligation are merely prescriptions expressing a certain sort of commitment or decision.

II.7   THE 'PERVERTED FACULTY' ARGUMENT

A late but traceable descendant of the Vazquez-Suarez conception of natural law is the argument, which looms large among the modern images of natural law theory, that natural functions are never to be frustrated or that human faculties are never to be diverted ('perverted') from their natural ends. But, as a general premiss, in any form strong enough to yield the moral conclusions it has been used to defend, this argument is ridiculous.

II.8   NATURAL LAW AND THE EXISTENCE
AND WILL OF GOD

'[T]raditional concepts of natural law are completely dependent for their viability on the soundness of such claims [as that natural theology is intelligible, let alone true, and that God exists]'.[64] It is tempting to dismiss this as yet another phantom. Aquinas, for example, considers that the first principles of natural law are self-evident, but that (i) the existence of God is *not* self-evident to the human mind, (ii) a knowledge that friendship with God is our last end is *not* available by 'natural' reasoning but only by revelation, (iii) attainment of that end is not possible by natural means but only by supernatural grace, and (iv) the will of God, so far as it

---

[64] Kai Nielsen, 'The Myth of Natural Law', in Hook (ed.), *Law and Philosophy*, 130.

concerns creatures (such as mankind), cannot be discovered by reasoning. A neo-Suarezian supposes that the first principle of natural law is 'Follow nature' and that this principle has normative significance by being the content of an act of divine will.[65] But neo-Suarezian theory, however widespread it became in Catholic seminaries until the 1960s, is by no means the most important of the 'traditional concepts of natural law'. And Part II of this book offers a rather elaborate sketch of a theory of natural law without needing to advert to the question of God's existence or nature or will.

That perhaps suffices to dispose of the claim which Nielsen actually made. But just as the fact that a good explanation of molecular motion can be provided, without adverting to the existence of an uncreated creator of the whole state of affairs in which molecules and the laws of their motion obtain, does not of itself entail either (i) that no further explanation of that state of affairs is required or (ii) that no such further explanation is available, or (iii) that the existence of an uncreated creator is not that explanation, so too the fact that natural law can be understood, assented to, applied, and reflectively analysed without adverting to the question of the existence of God does not of itself entail either (i) that no further explanation is required for the fact that there are objective standards of good and bad and principles of reasonableness (right and wrong), or (ii) that no such further explanation is available, or (iii) that the existence and nature of God is not that explanation. For this reason, and for others that will appear in the course of our study, Part III of this book undertakes a brief examination of such questions. They are in themselves not practical but theoretical or metaphysical questions. But their exploration, and the answers yielded by it, and the further questions suggested by those answers, all add significance to the integrating good (in itself self-evident) of practical reasonableness and thus to the moral principles involved in the pursuit of that good.

---

[65] See, among countless examples, Rommen, *The Natural Law*, 49, 63–4. For Suarez himself, see XI.9.

NOTES

II.1

History of theories of natural law, and of their influence... An informative study (rather wider than its subtitle) is C. G. Haines, *The Revival of Natural Law: A study of the establishment and of the interpretation of limits on legislatures with special reference to the development of certain phases of American constitutional law* (Cambridge, Mass.: 1930).

Natural law has no history... 'But what about changes in human nature?' 'What about the fact that man is a historical being?' 'Does this thesis derive from a theory of eternal or ahistorical essences?' Well, the thesis in the text concerns the basic forms of human flourishing, and the basic requirements of practical reasonableness. So if a critic wishes to propose that what, in Chapters III–IV, I identify as basic forms of human flourishing would not have been flourishing for human beings of some epoch, or that what, in Chapters V–VI, I identify as basic requirements of practical reasonableness would not have been applicable to such other human beings (because of some difference between their condition and ours), the onus is on this critic to show us these beings and those differences. I have read countless proclamations of the historicity, etc., of man, but no serious attempt to meet this challenge. Abstract discussions of the mutability or immutability of human nature are beside the point: the argument of this book does not rely, even implicitly, on the term 'human nature'.

II.2

Natural law theory and legal validity... Kelsen, Hart, and Raz, to validate their image of natural law theory, could point to Blackstone, I *Comm.* 41: '...no human laws are of any validity, if contrary to this [sc. natural law]'. But Blackstone simply does not mean what he there says; on the very next page, he is saying '...no human laws should be suffered to contradict these [sc. the law of nature and the law of revelation]...Nay, if any human law should allow or injoin us to commit it [sc. murder, demonstrably forbidden by the natural law], we are bound to transgress *that human law...*' (emphasis added). The truth is that, though they are not negligible for an understanding of the *Commentaries* (see Finnis, 'Blackstone's Theoretical Intentions' (1967) 12 *Nat. L.F.* 163 [*CEJF* IV.8]), Blackstone's remarks in this Introduction to his work cannot be dignified with the title 'a theory'.

'Natural law' and the notion that statutes are merely declaratory... The mistaken idea that mainstream natural law theories taught that just enactments must be merely declaratory of natural law (or: cannot be identified as enactments without some moral reasoning about their content) has engendered very serious misunderstandings of the history of Western (not least English) law and legal thought. Morris Arnold, 'Statutes as Judgments: the Natural Law Theory of Parliamentary Activity in Medieval England' (1977) 126 *U. Pa. L. Rev.* 329, identifies and refutes the bad history, but not the bad jurisprudence underlying it.

II.3

Variety and conflict in moral opinions... Weber rightly refused to base his claim that social science is ethically neutral upon the view that the variety of ethical evaluations proves them to be merely subjective: *Methodology*, 12, 55. Why then does Weber maintain that competing values or ideals are all of equal rank in the eye of science? He seems to have three lines of thought. (i) The gap between 'ought' and 'is' proves that value-judgments are inevitably subjective. (This is a *non sequitur*: see

II.4.) (ii) He slides from saying that *empirical science* cannot adjudicate between values to saying that such adjudication is beyond reason and objectivity altogether, and is a matter of faith, demonic decision, radical subjectivity. (But this is just a slide.) (iii) Like Sartre after him, Weber relies mainly upon certain ethical dilemmas, in which it is, he thinks, impossible to show that one of two competing ideals or morally motivated courses of action is superior to the other: for a discussion of Weber's examples, see Strauss, *Natural Right and History*, 67–74; for a discussion of Sartre's main example, see VII.4 at p. 176. But all these dilemmas arise from the *complexity* of ethical considerations; they do not show that all value-judgments, or even all ethical value-judgments, are likewise perplexed and beyond rational discrimination (and see III.5).

The 'universally acknowledged' first practical principles are not moral principles... A very frequent misreading of Aquinas, fostered by the main currents of post-Renaissance scholasticism, treats the deliverances of *synderesis* (i.e. the first principles of practical reasonableness: *S.T.* I q. 79 a. 12; I–II q. 94 a. 1 ad 2) as already crystallized moral principles (in the form of e.g. the last six of the Ten Commandments). This interpretation finds some support in the wording of occasional passages (e.g. *S.T.* II–II q. 122 a. 1c). But it makes nonsense of Aquinas's notion of *prudentia*, reducing it to a mere ability to judge when such a crystallized moral rule is applicable, working with such banal 'arguments' as 'murder is wrong; this is an act of murder; therefore this act is wrong and must not be done'. The capacity to make such arguments could never earn the paramount dignity of status accorded to *prudentia* by Aquinas: *S.T.* II–II q. 47 a. 6 ad 3; I–II q. 61 a. 2c; q. 66 a. 3 ad 3. Above all, this neo-scholastic theory discards Aquinas's repeated teaching that the first principles of human action are ends (*fines*), so that one cannot reason rightly in matters of practice, i.e. cannot have *prudentia*, unless one is well-disposed towards those ultimate ends: *S.T.* I–II q. 57 a. 4c; q. 58 a. 5c; II–II q. 47 a. 6.

Aquinas on self-evidence... Aquinas is regrettably obscure on the question of which practical principles or precepts are self-evident (whether *per se*, *quoad omnes*, or *quoad sapientes*) and which are deduced conclusions. This is one aspect of his very important failure to discuss the principles which *prudentia* uses to transform the first principles of natural law (which even the most evil employ in their practical reasoning: *S.T.* Supp., q. 98 a. 1) into truly moral principles, norms, and judgments. For an effort to fill this gap, see Chapter V.

'Intersubjectively transmissible knowledge'... Arnold Brecht's distinction, in his *Political Theory: the Foundations of Twentieth Century Political Thought* (Princeton: 1959, paperback edn, 1967), between (i) intersubjectively transmissible scientific knowledge, (ii) non-transmissible but genuine knowledge, and (iii) speculation, leans heavily (as he recognizes, 181) on neo-positivism or logical positivism, and suffers from the irremediable weakness that it allows no place for, e.g., the philosophical knowledge embodied (purportedly) in the distinction itself. In view of the vagueness and inconsistencies in his set-piece account (113–16) (a) of what is intersubjectively transmissible, and (b) of the senses in which 'Scientific Method' is 'exclusive', it is not really surprising to find Brecht advancing (573), as an example of *scientia transmissibilis* the 'scientific postulate of adequate proportions' which enables 'science' to 'point to such faults in religious arguing as a gross lack of proportion between ideas of God's greatness, wisdom, and power on one side, and trivial acts, such as table-rapping... on the other'. No one who argues that certain basic values are self-evident, and that there are objective basic principles of practical reasonableness, need be concerned about exclusion from a 'science' so elastically and arbitrarily conceived. But one should reject the exclusive equation which Brecht (despite all his protestations

to the contrary) makes between 'according to the method of the natural sciences' and 'rational' (see e.g. *ibid.*, 430, quoting and commenting upon Einstein): such an equation is self-refuting. (On self-refutation, see III.6.) The basic principles and requirements of practical reasonableness are intersubjectively transmissible; their transmissibility can be appreciated by anyone who steadily attends to the matter (i.e. to the basic forms of human good) and who is not deflected by the irrelevant objections that not everyone happens to agree in pronouncements on these or related matters, and that the subject-matter and procedures of other disciplines differ from those of practical reasonableness.

For Aquinas, the existence of God is not self-evident . . . Still, he thinks that, since the existence and something of the nature of God can be known by demonstration and/or revelation, the principle that God is to be loved is a basic principle of natural law: *S.T.* I–II q. 100 aa. 3 ad 1, 4 ad 1; cf. q. 100 a. 11c; *De Veritate* q. 16 a. 1 ad 9. Cf. XIII.5.

II.4

Stone on 'the three decisive issues' . . . I discussed one of these issues in II.3; the remaining one of the three was: 'Have [the natural lawyers] explained how positive law ceases to be law simply by virtue of its violation of natural law?': Stone, *Human Law and Human Justice*, 212. This presupposes the over-simplified image discussed in II.2.

Natural law, or morality, can be understood, assented to and applied without knowledge of metaphysics or anthropology . . . Aquinas, *S.T.* I–II q. 58 a. 4c, is very clear: no one can be morally upright without (a) an understanding of the first principles of practical reasoning and (b) the practical reasonableness (*prudentia*) which brings those principles to bear, reasonably, on particular commitments, projects, actions; but one can indeed be morally upright without speculative (i.e. theoretical, 'is'-knowledge) wisdom, without the practical knowledge of a craftsman (art), and without speculative knowledge (*scientia*). As I mentioned in the notes to II.3, Aquinas considered that *prudentia* can exist only in one who is well-disposed (*bene dispositus*) towards the basic ends of human existence; but he would have rejected as absurd the view imputed to him by O'Connor, *Aquinas and Natural Law*, 29, that 'having "well-disposed affections" (*affectum bene dispositum*) [*sic*] will be a consequence of having a correct insight into the nature of man'.

Natural law and ideological conceptions of nature . . . So far as I can see, Strauss, in his exposition of 'classic natural right' (*Natural Right and History*, ch. 4), makes no attempt to justify his prominent but vague assertion (*ibid.*, 7) that 'natural right in its classic form is connected with a teleological view of the universe'. Hart too gives much prominence to this claim (*Concept of Law*, 182–7 [186–92]), but actually refers only to such minor figures (for the history of natural law theory) as Montesquieu and Blackstone. It is true that the natural law theory of, say, Aristotle and Aquinas goes along with a teleological conception of nature and, in the case of Aquinas, with a theory of divine providence and eternal law. But what needs to be shown is that the conception of human good entertained by these theorists is *dependent* upon this wider framework. There is much to be said for the view that the order of dependence was precisely the opposite—that the teleological conception of nature was made plausible, indeed conceivable, by analogy with the introspectively luminous, self-evident structure of human well-being, practical reasoning, and human purposive action: read Aristotle, *Physics* II.8: 199a9–19. Despite the irrelevance of general teleology to my own argument, two further remarks seem in place: (i) Hart's account of 'the teleological view of nature' is a little extravagant—of what serious writer was it ever true that 'the questions whether [events] *do* occur regularly and whether they *should* occur or whether it is *good* that they occur [were] not regarded as separate questions' (*Concept of Law*, 185)? In Aristotelian thought 'good' is never used at large, in this fashion, and what is good for the spider is recognized as not good for the fly, while neither spider nor fly is conceived as good for us. (ii) The question of teleology is not philosophically closed, whatever may be the case in the methodology of the natural sciences: see, e.g., Peter Geach, *The Virtues* (Cambridge: 1977), 9–12.

Aquinas on first principles of natural law...Fundamental for the understanding of Aquinas's widely misunderstood account is G. Grisez, 'The First Principle of Practical Reason: A Commentary on the *Summa Theologiae*, 1–2, Question 94, Article 2' (1965) 10 *Nat. L. F.* 168–96, reprinted in A. Kenny (ed.), *Aquinas: A Collection of Critical Essays* (London: 1970), 340–82 (slightly abbreviated).

'Fact' and 'norm'...'Since the term "fact" is properly used as a synonym for "truth" even in its most generic sense,...we can speak of mathematical and even ethical facts...': Wilfrid Sellars, *Science and Metaphysics* (London and New York: 1968), 116. But, since I am accepting that there is *a* distinction to be drawn, relevant to the *justification* of practical (including ethical) judgments, I need not here try to refine the terms in which the distinction *of fact* from *norm* is drawn.

II.5

The gap between 'is' and 'ought'...A useful history of the growth of explicit attention to this, and of a relativistic conception of ethics as the supposed implication of it, is Arnold Brecht, *Political Theory: the Foundations of Twentieth Century Political Thought* (Princeton: 1959), ch. VI. For explorations of the rational relationship between some sorts of 'facts' and conclusions about what ought to be done, see Jonathan Harrison, *Hume's Moral Epistemology* (Oxford: 1976), 74–82.

Hume's is-ought argument(s)...The structure and arguments of this section of the *Treatise* are carefully disentangled in D. D. Raphael, 'Hume's critique of ethical rationalism' in W. B. Todd (ed.), *Hume and the Enlightenment* (Edinburgh, 1974), 14 at 20–9; Harrison, *Hume's Moral Epistemology*; and R. David Broiles, *The Moral Philosophy of David Hume* (The Hague: 2nd edn, 1969).

The second interpretation of Hume's is-ought paragraph...is defended by Broiles, *The Moral Philosophy of David Hume*, ch. 6.

Butler and Cudworth on fitnesses and conformity to human nature...See Joseph Butler, 'Dissertation of the Nature of Virtue', appendix II to *The Analogy of Religion* (1736, 3rd edn, 1740), in Raphael, *British Moralists*, para. 432; *Fifteen Sermons* (1726, 4th edn, 1749), in *British Moralists*, paras 374, 377, 384, 391 (reference to 'speculative absurdity'), 395, 400, 402, 404, 409 (summary), 423. For Cudworth, see *A Treatise concerning Eternal and Immutable Morality* (c. 1685; 1st edn, 1731), Book I, c. ii, paras 3, 4; Book IV; c. vi, para. 4; in *British Moralists*, paras 122–4, 135.

Confusion in Hume between obligation and motivating or necessitating causes...This accounts for, and is evidenced by, such otherwise surprising remarks in the *Treatise* as: 'the moral obligation, or the sentiment of right and wrong...' (*British Moralists*, para. 533); 'when the neglect or non-performance of [an action] displeases us after a [certain] manner, we say that we lie under an obligation to perform it. A change of the obligation supposes a change of the sentiment; and a creation of a new obligation supposes some new sentiment to arise' (para. 537); 'No action can be required of us as our duty, unless there be implanted in human nature some actuating passion or motive, capable of producing the action' (para. 538); 'were there no more than a resolution..., promises would only declare our former motives, and would not create any new *motive or obligation*' (para. 541, emphasis added); 'interest is the first obligation to performance of promises' (para. 542); 'afterwards a sentiment of morals concurs with interest, and becomes a new obligation upon mankind' (para. 543). Interpretation of some of these passages is complicated by Hume's assumption that the subject-matter of moral assessments is always motives, not actions (except in so far as these reflect motives). A confusion analogous to Hume's is found in Adam Smith (an early Humean moralist), *The Theory of Moral Sentiments* (1776), I, ii, 4, 1; see T. D. Campbell, in A. S. Skinner and T. B. Wilson (eds.), *Essays on Adam Smith* (Oxford: 1975), 78.

II.6

Clarke and Grotius... The connection cannot, I think, and need not be established directly. Available to an English scholar in 1704 were at least 14 editions, at least two English translations, and at least four additional commentaries on or digests of the *De Jure Belli ac Pacis*. Note that the 'modern' author most cited by Clarke (and very frequently and copiously on the law of nature) is Richard Cumberland, *De Legibus Naturae* (1672), and that Cumberland goes out of his way to say on the first page of his Prolegomena that the *De Jure Belli ac Pacis* deserves especially well of mankind, being the first of its kind, truly worthy of its great author and of immortality.

'Etiamsi daremus...'... See J. St. Leger, *The 'Etiamsi Daremus' of Hugo Grotius* (Rome: 1962). For the debate in classical thought, see Plato, *Rep.* II: 365d-e; *Laws* X: 885b: 907b. For the scholastic formulations of the 'etiamsi daremus', see, e.g., Gregory of Rimini, *In Librum Secundum Sententiarum* [c. 1350; Venice: 1503], dist. 34. q. 1. a. 2 (quoted in Pereña's edition of Suarez, *De Legibus*, vol. III (Madrid: 1974), 80 n.); Vitoria, *De eo ad quod tenetur homo*, n. 61 above; Suarez, *De actibus humanis*...(1581; first published, in part, by Pereña and Abril, op. cit., 210), q. 9 (*ibid.*, 211): Vazquez, *In Primam Secundae*, disp. 97, c. 1. Suarez reports the first of these, and some other scholastic sources where, he says, the hypothesis is raised: *De Legibus*, Book II, c. 6, para. 3. For Culverwel's citations of Vazquez and Suarez, especially on the *etiamsi daremus*, see his *An Elegant and Learned Discourse of the Light of Nature* ([1652, 4th edn, 1669], ed. Brown, 1857), 45, 55, 74–7.

The ethical theory of Vazquez and Suarez... It is commonly said that Vazquez and Suarez differ as extreme rationalism differs from moderate voluntarism in ethics: see e.g. A.-H. Chroust, 'Hugo Grotius and the Scholastic Natural Law Tradition' (1943) 17 *New Scholasticism* 101 at 114, 117; Rommen, *The Natural Law*, 64, 71, 196; and Suarez himself, *De Legibus*, Book II, c. 5, paras 2, 5–8. But, *pace* Chroust and Rommen, Vazquez rejected as 'empty' the distinction which they ascribe to him, between *lex praecipens* and *lex indicans*: see Vazquez, *in Primam Secundae*, disp. 97, c. 1, no. 1. *Pace* Chroust, 'Hugo Grotius and the Scholastic Natural Law Tradition', 114, he does not say that the natural law is '*compelling* without being expressly commanded'. His theory of obligation is undeveloped, but seems to be the same as Suarez's: obligation is the effect of the *imperium* of a superior. Like Suarez, he rejects out of hand Aquinas's theory of *imperium* in the individual human act (see XI.8). Vazquez regards law as an act of intellect, rather than of will; but those who seize on this to liken him to Aquinas and oppose him to Suarez altogether overlook that for Vazquez the relevant 'act of intellect' is no more than an *intimatio* to an inferior of the will of his superior: Vazquez, *in Primam Secundae*, disp. 150, c. 3, no. 19; disp. 49, c. 2, no. 6 (and this is essentially the view of Suarez, *De Legibus*, Book I, c. 4, para. 14; c. 5, paras 21–5). Compare this with Aquinas's reason for saying that law is an act of intellect; this reason has nothing to do with the will of a superior needing to be made known, but only with the fact that it is intelligence that grasps ends, and arranges means to ends, and grasps the necessity of those arranged means; and this is the source of obligation: *S.T.* I–II q. 90 a. lc.

Aquinas on 'convenientia'... For his use of this term and its cognates, in a moral context (but not so as to amount to the Vazquez-Suarez-Grotius *convenientia* to 'rational nature' as such), see particularly *S.T.* I–II q. 18 aa. 2c, 5c ad 2, 8c ad 2, 9c, 10c ad 3; q. 10 a. 1c; q. 71 a. 2; q. 94 a. 3 ad 3. Vazquez is sometimes said to have originated the later use of the notion, but it is found in a manuscript of Suarez dated 1592, well before the publication of Vazquez's commentary: see vol. Ill of the Pereña edition of *De Legibus*, 220. For the Stoic use of '*convenientia*', see XIII.1.

Stoic influence on post-Renaissance ethical theory... In considering this influence, note that Cicero's moral works are the most frequently cited of all the works cited or quoted with approval by Clarke, and that all the Ciceronian texts on natural law are translated in the text of Clarke's lectures, as well as referred to and reproduced in his marginal notes: see Clarke, *A Discourse concerning the Unchangeable Obligations of Natural Religion*, 213–17, 221–2. Though Clarke, *ibid.*, 210, denounces the 'ranting discourses' of the Stoics on suicide, he praises Cicero, 'that great master', for his 'knowledge and understanding of the true state of things, and of the original obligations of human nature...': *ibid.*, 209 (*British Moralists*, para. 244).

'Is' and 'ought' in Aristotle and Aquinas... Quite unfounded is the notion that 'in its classical formulations, natural law...asserted...that there is a connection between morality and the natural order, such that true statements about morality are realized in the actual course of events. What ought to be and what is were believed to be united in a way that contradicts the logical separation that we now maintain between normative and descriptive discourse': Lloyd L. Weinreb, 'Law as Order' (1978) 91 *Harv. L. Rev.* 909 at 911; similarly misleading is R. M. Unger, *Law in Modern Society* (New York and London: 1976), 79. For Aristotle's account of obligation, see *Nic. Eth.* IX.8: 1168b29–30, 1169a11–22, an account which needs a supplementation such as is offered at XIII.5; see also XI.1.

II.7

The 'perverted faculty' argument... A careful exposition and critique of this argument, adverting to its roots in Suarezian conceptions of natural law, is Germain Grisez, *Contraception and the Natural Law* (Milwaukee: 1964), 19–31. Grisez shows that the argument was tailor-made to meet the demand for a major premiss for arguments against contraception and other sexual vices; he definitively criticizes the inadequate arguments thus yielded (and replaces them). There is room for a deeper historical study of the perverted faculty argument, and for a close study of an argument employed by Aquinas against lying (*S.T.* II–II q. 110 a. 3c), which can, but need not (and, I think, should not), be read as employing the perverted faculty argument as its general premiss, and was (I imagine) historically important in suggesting the perverted faculty argument to theologians in a hurry.

Part Two

III

A BASIC FORM OF GOOD: KNOWLEDGE

III.1   AN EXAMPLE

NEITHER this chapter nor the next makes or presupposes any moral judgments. Rather, the two chapters concern the evaluative substratum of all moral judgments. That is to say, they concern the acts of practical understanding in which we grasp the basic values of human existence and thus, too, the basic principles of all practical reasoning.

The purpose of this chapter, in particular, is to illustrate (i) what I mean by 'basic value' and 'basic practical principle', (ii) how such values and principles enter into any consideration of good reasons for action and any full description of human conduct, and (iii) the sense in which such basic values are obvious ('self-evident') and even unquestionable. For this purpose, I discuss only one basic value, leaving to the next chapter the identification of the other forms of human good that, so far as I can see, are likewise irreducibly basic.

The example of a basic value to be examined now is: knowledge. Perhaps it would be more accurate to call it 'speculative knowledge', using the term 'speculative' here, not to make the Aristotelian distinction between the *theoretikē* and the *praktikē*, but to distinguish knowledge as sought for its own sake from knowledge as sought only instrumentally, i.e. as useful in the pursuit of some other objective, such as survival, power, popularity, or a money-saving cup of coffee. Now 'knowledge', unlike 'belief', is an achievement-word; there are true beliefs and false beliefs, but knowledge is of truth. So one could speak of truth as the basic good with which we are here concerned, for one can just as easily speak of 'truth for its own sake' as of 'knowledge for its own sake'. In any event, truth is not a mysterious abstract entity; we want the truth when we want the judgments in which we affirm or deny propositions to be true judgments, or (what comes to the same) want the propositions affirmed or denied, or to be affirmed or denied, to be true propositions. So, to complete the explanation of what is meant by the knowledge under discussion here, as distinct from instrumental knowledge, I can add that the distinction I am drawing is not between one set of propositions and another. It is not a distinction between fields of knowledge. Any proposition, whatever its subject-matter, can be inquired into (with a view to affirming or denying it) in either of the two distinct ways, (i) instrumentally or (ii) out of curiosity, the pure desire to know, to find out the truth about it simply out of an interest in or concern for truth and a desire to avoid ignorance or error as such.

This chapter, then, is an invitation to reflect on one form of human activity, the activity of trying to find out, to understand, and to judge matters correctly. This is not, perhaps, the easiest activity to understand; but it has the advantage of being the activity in which the reader himself is actually engaged. But if it seems too abstruse and tricky to try to understand this form of activity reflexively (i.e. by reflecting on one's attempt to understand and assess the truth of this chapter itself), one can reflect on any other exercise of curiosity. One could consider, for example, the wide-ranging effort of historical inquiry involved in discovering the actual intentions of the principal authors of the Statute of Uses (1536) or of the Fourteenth Amendment of the US Constitution (1866). Or something more humble (like weighing the truth of some gossipy rumour), or more 'scientific'—it makes no difference, for present purposes.

III.2   FROM INCLINATION TO GRASP OF VALUE

Curiosity is a name for the desire or inclination or felt want that we have when, just for the sake of knowing, we want to find out about something. One wants to know the answer to a particular question. Quite apart from my brief or assignment, from the fee or the examination, what does this statutory provision mean? What did the authors of the Fourteenth Amendment care for economic equality? What happened on the night of the murder? Are 'desire', 'inclination', and 'want' as synonymous as the first sentence of this paragraph supposes? Does $e = mc^2$? How does this clock work? *It would be good to find out.* Quite often, of course, the raising of questions is not accompanied by any particular state of feelings. Quite often the inclination is to be described, more colourlessly (and ambiguously), as 'having an interest'.

Commonly one's interest in knowledge, in getting to the truth of the matter, is not bounded by the particular questions that first aroused one's desire to find out. So readily that one notices the transition only by an effort of reflection, it becomes clear that knowledge is a good thing to have (and not merely for its utility), without restriction to the subject-matters that up to now have aroused one's curiosity. In explaining, to oneself and others, what one is up to, one finds oneself able and ready to refer to *finding out, knowledge, truth* as sufficient explanations of the point of one's activity, project, or commitment. One finds oneself reflecting that ignorance and muddle are to be avoided, simply as such and not merely in relation to a closed list of questions that one has raised. One begins to consider the well-informed and clear-headed person as, to that extent, well-off (and not only for the profitable use he can make of his knowledge). 'It's good to find out...' now seems to be applicable not merely in relation to oneself and the question that currently holds one's attention, but at large—in relation to an inexhaustible range of questions and subject-matters, and for anyone.

To mark this distinction between 'good', referring to some particular objective or goal that one is considering as desirable, and 'good', referring to a general form of good that can be participated in or realized in indefinitely many ways on indefinitely many occasions, it will be useful to reserve the word 'value' so that (for the purposes of this book) it signifies only the latter sense of 'good'. But, to avoid an artificially constricted vocabulary, I will still use the term 'good' to signify both the particular object of a particular person's desire, choice, or action, and the general form, of which that particular object is (or is supposed to be) an instance. For there is typically some general description that makes manifest the aspect under which a particular objective has its interest, attracts desire, choice, and efforts and thus is (or is considered to be) a good thing.

It is important not to allow one's reflection on the value of knowledge to become muddled here. A number of common misunderstandings threaten to short-circuit our understanding of practical reason and its relationship to morality, just at this point. So we should bracket out these misunderstandings one by one: the reasons for doing so will appear more fully in the next chapter. (i) To think of knowledge as a value is not to think that every true proposition is equally worth knowing, that every form of learning is equally valuable, that every subject-matter is equally worth investigating. Except for some exceptional purpose, it is more worthwhile to know whether the contentions in this book are true or false than to know how many milligrams of printer's ink are used in a copy of it. (ii) To think of knowledge as a basic form of good is not to think that knowledge, for example, of the truth about these contentions, would be equally valuable for every person. (iii) Nor is it to think that such knowledge, or indeed any particular item of knowledge, has any priority of value even for the reader or writer at this moment; perhaps one would be better off busying oneself with something else, even for the rest of one's life . . . (iv) Just as 'knowledge is good' does not mean that knowledge is to be pursued by everybody, at all times, in all circumstances, so too it does not mean that knowledge is the only general form of good, or the supreme form of good. (v) To think of knowledge as a value is not, as such, to think of it as a 'moral' value; 'truth is a good' is not, here, to be understood as a moral proposition, and 'knowledge is to be pursued' is not to be understood, here, as stating a moral obligation, requirement, prescription, or recommendation. In our reflective analysis of practical reasonableness, morality comes later. (vi) At the same time, finally, it is to be recalled that the knowledge we here have in mind as a value is the knowledge that one can call an *intrinsic* good, i.e. that is considered to be desirable for its own sake and not merely as something sought after under some such description as 'what will enable me to impress my audience' or 'what will confirm my instinctive beliefs' or 'what will contribute to my survival'. In sum, (vii) to say that such knowledge is a value is simply to say that reference to the pursuit of knowledge makes intelligible (though not necessarily reasonable-all-things-considered) any particular instance of the human activity and commitment involved in such pursuit.

III.3   PRACTICAL PRINCIPLE AND PARTICIPATION
IN VALUE

'Knowledge is something good to have'. 'Being well-informed and clear-headed is a good way to be'. 'Muddle and ignorance are to be avoided'. These are formulations of a practical principle. Any such expression of our understanding of a value can provide the starting-point (in Latin, *principium*) for reasoning about what to do, and thus is a principle of practical reasonableness.

For example: '(i) It would be good to find out the truth about the alleged principles of natural law; (ii) reading this book critically seems likely to help me find out what I want to find out about these matters; (iii) so, despite its tedium, I'll read it right through and think its main arguments out'. The first premiss is expressed as a practical principle; it formulates a want but makes the want more than a blind urge by referring its object (one's finding-out about natural law) to the intelligible and general form of good which that object is one possible way of participating in or instantiating. When combined with the second premiss, which is a straightforward factual judgment about the relevance, coherence, etc., of a particular book, the first premiss or practical principle expresses a reason for acting in the manner signified in the conclusion, the third step in the train of reasoning. The force of this reason varies, of course, depending on how much one values these matters in particular (and in one's particular circumstances), and on the certainty or uncertainty of one's factual estimate of the appropriateness of the proposed means for realizing that value in this particular case.

Basic practical principles, such as that knowledge is a good to be pursued and ignorance is to be avoided, do not play the same role as rules do, in practical reasoning or the explanation and description of intelligent action. A basic practical principle serves to orient one's practical reasoning, and can be instantiated (rather than 'applied') in indefinitely many, more specific, practical principles and premisses. Rather than restrict, it suggests new horizons for human activity.

The basic practical principle that knowledge is good need hardly ever be formulated as the premiss for anyone's actual practical reasoning. Particular practical premisses (such as that knowledge about natural law would be good to have) are not usually adopted as the conclusions of an inferential train of reasoning from the more general and basic principle. In this respect, practical reasoning is like 'theoretical' reasoning, which has its own basic and usually tacit presuppositions and principles. We often say 'Too late!'; but how often do we formulate the presupposition on which our conclusion rests—the guiding presupposition that time cannot be reversed?

Yet such presuppositions and principles can be disengaged and identified, by reflection not only on our own thinking but also on the words and deeds of others. In trying to make sense of someone's commitments, projects, and actions over a period, we may say that he acted 'on the basis that' knowledge is a good worthy of a life-shaping devotion. The good of knowledge was not for him an 'end' external to the 'means' by which he 'pursued' it or sought to 'attain' it. Rather, it was a good in which, we may say, he *participated*, through or in those of his commitments, projects, and actions which are explicable by reference to that basic practical principle, that basic form of good. A particular action (say, reading a book) and a particular project (such as understanding a certain body of theory) can be more or less completely attained, completed, finished off. But it may be helpful to reserve the word 'commitment' for that sort of participation-in-a-value which is never finished and done with (except by abandonment of the commitment) and which takes shape in a potentially inexhaustible variety of particular projects and actions, each with its particularized first premiss of practical reasoning.

III.4   THE SELF-EVIDENCE OF THE GOOD
OF KNOWLEDGE

Is it not the case that knowledge is really a good, an aspect of authentic human flourishing, and that the principle which expresses its value formulates a real (intelligent) reason for action? It seems clear that such indeed is the case, and that there are no sufficient reasons for doubting it to be so. The

good of knowledge is self-evident, obvious. It cannot be demonstrated, but equally it needs no demonstration.

This is not to say that everyone actually does recognize the value
of knowledge, or that there are no preconditions for recognizing
that value. The principle that truth (and knowledge) is worth
pursuing is not somehow innate, inscribed on the mind at birth.
On the contrary, the value of truth becomes obvious only to one
who has experienced the urge to question, who has grasped the
connection between question and answer, who understands that
knowledge is constituted by correct answers to particular questions, and who is aware of the possibility of further questions and
of other questioners who likewise could enjoy the advantage of
attaining correct answers. A new-born child, for example, has
presumably not had any such set of felt inclinations, memories,
understandings, and (in short) experiences.

In asking oneself whether knowledge is indeed a value (for its
own sake: thus, a basic value), one should not be deflected by the
fact that one's inclination to seek truth has psychological roots.
It may well be that at an early stage in the life of the mind the
urge to know is scarcely differentiated from other urges, such as
the sexual drive. This early lack of differentiation may never be
wholly surmounted, so that the one urge remains capable not
only of deflecting but also of reinforcing the other. Such facts,
interesting and important as they may be in some contexts,
are not relevant to the question 'Is knowledge indeed a good,
objectively worth pursuing?'. In considering the question 'Is
the opinion of these psychologists that curiosity is a form of
sexuality a true or at least a warranted opinion?', it is relevant
to attend to the coherence of these psychologists' hypothesis, to
the pertinence of their evidence, to the soundness of their inferences. But it is *not* relevant to ask whether the psychologists'
opinion emerged in their psyches at the call of their sexuality
or as a reflection of their organic constitution or under the
influence of any other such sub-rational cause. The soundness
of an answer to a particular question is never established or
disconfirmed by the answer to the *entirely different* question of
what are the physical, biological, and psychological preconditions
and concomitants of the raising of that question (or any question) and of the proposing of that answer (or any answer).

And all this holds true of the answer 'Yes, obviously' to the question 'Is knowledge worth having?'.

Just as we should not appeal to causes, preconditions, and concomitants in order to raise an illegitimate doubt about the self-evidence of the value of knowledge, so we should not seek a deduction or inference of that value from facts. If one is to go beyond the felt urge of curiosity to an understanding grasp of the value of knowledge, one certainly must know at least the fact that some questions can be answered. Moreover, one certainly will be assisted if one also knows such facts as that answers tend to hang together in systems that tend to be illuminating over as wide a range as the data which stimulate one's questions. But one who, thus knowing the possibility of attaining truth, is enabled thereby to grasp the value of that possible object and attainment is not inferring the value from the possibility. No such inference is possible. No value can be deduced or otherwise inferred from a fact or set of facts.

Nor can one validly infer the value of knowledge from the fact (if fact it be) that 'all human persons desire to know'. The *universality* of a desire is not a sufficient basis for inferring that the object of that desire is really desirable, objectively good. Nor is such a basis afforded by the fact that the desire or inclination manifests, or is part of, a *deep* structure shaping the human mind, or by the fact that the desire, or the structure, is *ineradicable*, or by the fact that in whole or part the desire is (or is not) *common* to all animals, or by the fact that it is (or is not) *peculiar* to human beings.

Nor would it be logically decisive to establish that all human persons not only desire to know (have the urge of curiosity) but also affirm the value of knowledge and respect and pursue it in their lives. (Conversely, the fact that not everyone pursues or admits to pursuing or even give lip-service to the value of knowledge does not give sufficient ground for denying or rejecting that value.) To know that and how other persons have valued knowledge is *relevant*, for it serves as a disclosure or intimation or reminder of the range of opportunities open to one. The life and death of a Socrates, and the disciplined, exact, profound, and illuminating investigations of a Plato (or a Galileo or a Maitland), reveal an aspect of human possibility only vaguely prefigured by one's own relatively feeble or fickle curiosity (see IV.1). But to say that knowledge *must* be a real value, because intelligent people, or great or mature persons have regarded it as a value and as an aspect of their own flourishing, is not to make what could be called an inference. For one's assessment of a person as flourishing, mature, great, or, in the relevant respect, intelligent is made possible only by one's own underived understanding that what that person is and does is really good (in the relevant respects). The 'premiss' of the apparent inference thus rests on its 'conclusion'.

But is there not something fishy about appeal to self-evidence? Do modern sciences and other theoretical disciplines rest on self-evident concepts or principles? Or is it not rather the case that appeal to allegedly self-evident principles is a relic of the discredited Aristotelian conception of axiomatized sciences of nature?

A proper discussion of self-evidence would have to be embarrassingly complex, not only because almost every controverted question in epistemology is here brought to a focus, but also because the modern conception of an axiom is not the conception taken for granted by Aristotle and Aquinas. For the axioms of, say, modern geometries are not selected, as those of Euclid apparently were, for their purported self-evidence, but rather for their capacity to generate a system of theorems, proofs, etc., which is consistent and complete. We may observe in passing that appeal to self-evidence does seem to be made (though without much advertisement) in a modern geometry: (i) in establishing the meaning of at least some of the 'primitive' terms employed to formulate the axioms and theorems (e.g. in Hilbert's or Veblen's postulates for Euclidean geometry, the term 'between', as in 'C is between A and B'); (ii) in generating the theorems and proofs, by employing as inference rules a logic which (as geometers rather freely admit) is imported into geometry without too much scrutiny; (iii) at some point in the assessment of consistency; and (iv) at some point in the assessment of completeness. Still, someone may ask whether a modern pure geometry is intended to state truths or to amount to knowledge at all. So, leaving that question to one side, it may be more pertinent to observe that the natural sciences (not to mention the historical sciences, and the disciplined common sense of forensic assessment of evidence) certainly rest, implicitly but thoroughly, on the principles of elementary formal logic (though those principles are far from exhausting the rational principles on which the elaboration of such sciences and disciplines proceeds).

It may be still more helpful, for the purposes of this brief reflection on self-evidence, to consider some of the principles or norms of sound judgment in every empirical discipline. These principles might be described as methodological; in this respect they resemble the basic requirements of practical reasonableness to be discussed in Chapter V, rather than the principles of practical reasonableness considered in this chapter and the next—principles identifying substantive forms of human good. But reflection on what it means to say that the principles or norms of sound empirical judgment are self-evident will help to eliminate some misunderstandings of what it means to say that the substantive principles of practical reasonableness are self-evident. In particular, it will help to show that the self-evidence of a principle entails neither (a) that it is formulated reflectively or at all explicitly by those who are guided by it, nor (b) that when one so formulates it, one's formulation will invariably be found to be accurate or acceptably refined and sufficiently qualified, nor (c) that it is arrived at, even only implicitly, without experience of the field to which it relates.

There are indeed many principles of sound empirical judgment or, more generally, of rationality in theoretical inquiries. One such principle is that the principles of logic, for example the forms of deductive inference, are to be used and adhered to in all one's thinking, even though no non-circular proof of their validity is possible (since any proof would employ them). Another is that an adequate reason why anything is so rather than otherwise is to be expected, unless one has a reason not to expect such a reason: cf. XIII.2. A third is that self-defeating theses are to be abandoned: see III.6. A fourth is that phenomena are to be regarded as real unless there is some reason to distinguish between appearance and reality. A fifth is that a full description of data is to be preferred to partial descriptions, and that an account or explanation of phenomena is not to be accepted if it requires or postulates something inconsistent with the data for which it is supposed to account. A sixth is that a method of interpretation which is successful is to be relied upon in further similar cases until contrary reason appears. A seventh is that theoretical accounts which are simple, predictively successful, and explanatorily powerful are to be accepted in preference to other accounts. And there are many others: see XIII.2.

Such principles of theoretical rationality are not demonstrable, for they are presupposed or deployed in anything that we would count as a demonstration. They do not describe the world. But although they cannot be verified by opening one's eyes and taking a look, they are obvious—obviously valid—to anyone who has experience of inquiry into matters of fact or of theoretical (including historical and philosophical) judgment; they do not stand in need of demonstration. They are objective; their validity is not a matter of convention, nor is it relative to anybody's individual purposes. They can be meaningfully denied, for they are not principles of logic, conformity to which is essential if one is to *mean* anything. But to defy them is to disqualify oneself from the pursuit of knowledge, and to deny them is as straightforwardly unreasonable as anything can be. In all these respects, the principles of *theoretical* rationality are self-evident. And it is in these respects that we are asserting that the basic *practical* principle that knowledge is a good to be pursued is self-evident.

Nowadays, any claim that something is self-evident is commonly misunderstood by philosophers. They think that any such claim either asserts or presupposes that the criterion of the truth of the allegedly self-evident principle, proposition, or fact is one's *feeling of certitude* about it. This is indeed a misunderstanding. Self-evident principles such as those I have been discussing are not validated by feelings. On the contrary, they are themselves the criteria whereby we discriminate between feelings, and discount some of our feelings (including feelings of certitude), however intense, as irrational or unwarranted, misleading or delusive.

III.5 'OBJECT OF DESIRE' AND OBJECTIVITY

The principle that truth is worth pursuing, knowledge is worth having, is thus an underived principle. Neither its intelligibility nor its force rests on any further principle.

This may tempt us to say that knowledge is a good *because* we desire it, are interested in it, value it, pursue it. But the temptation has plausibility only if we abandon the effort to understand the value of knowledge. And we are tempted to abandon that effort only when, for bad philosophical reasons, we confuse a principle's lack of derivation with a lack of justification or lack of objectivity. Non-derivability in some cases amounts to lack of justification and of objectivity. But in other cases it betokens self-evidence; and these cases are to be found in every field of inquiry. For in every field there is and must be, at some point or points, an end to derivation and inference. At that point or points we find ourselves in face of the self-evident, which makes possible all subsequent inferences in that field.

In the next section I look to see what can be said in defence of the underived and underivable principle that knowledge is an intrinsic value. For the moment let us reflect on the fact that, for all who consider something like knowledge to be a good, the true expression of their opinion and attitude is *not* 'it is good because or in so far as I desire it', *but* 'I desire it because and in so far as it is good'.

It is easy to be confused by the Aristotelian tag that 'the good is what all things desire'—as if the goodness were consequential on the desires. But, as it applies to human good and human desire, this tag was intended to affirm simply that (i) our primary use of the term 'good' (and related terms) is to express our practical thinking, i.e. our thinking, in terms of reasons for action, towards decision and action; and that (ii) we would not bother with such thinking, or such action, unless we were in fact interested in (*desirous* of . . .) whatever it is we are calling good. Those who used the tag were equally insistent that one's human desire is a pursuit of something in so far as it seems desirable, and that things seem desirable to one in so far as they (appear to) promise to make one better-off (not necessarily 'materially', or instrumentally).

Other people, sceptical about the objectivity of value judgments, do grant that, from one's 'internal' or 'practical' viewpoint as someone who is judging something to be good and desirable, one's desire and decision to pursue the object are consequential on one's judgments (i) that the object *is* good and (ii) that one will *really* be better-off for getting or doing or effecting it. But, in their philosophizing, these sceptics argue that the internal viewpoint or practical mode of thinking is systematically delusory, precisely in this respect. Our practical judgments of value, they say, are ultimately no more than expressions of our feelings and desires; we *project* our desires on to objects, and *objectify* our feelings about objects by mistakenly ascribing to those objects such 'qualities' as goodness, value, desirability, perfection, etc. If one says 'knowledge is good and ignorance is bad', one may think one is affirming something objective, something that is correct and would be so even if one were not aware of the value of knowledge and were content with ignorance. Indeed (the sceptics grant), some such beliefs are built into our ordinary thought and language. But if one thinks this about what one is affirming, one is, they say, in error. Really one's affirmations express only a subjective concern. One can affirm, correctly or truly, no more than that one regards knowledge as something satisfying an aim or desire which one happens to have (and which one has, probably, because it is an aim widely shared or commended in one's community).

It is important to see both how much such sceptics are claiming, and how precise must be their grounds for claiming it. They are claiming much, because their claim, if true, would render mysterious the rational characteristics of the principle that knowledge is a good worth pursuing. These rational characteristics can be summed up as self-evidence or obviousness, and peremptoriness. As to self-evidence I have said enough already: to those who fix their attention on the possibilities of attaining knowledge, and on the character of the open-minded, wise, and clear-headed person, the value of knowledge is obvious. Indeed, sceptics do not really deny this. How could they? What they do instead is invite us to shift our attention, away from the relevant subject-matter, to other features of the world and of human understanding.

Now understanding the value of truth, grasping a practical principle, is not just like understanding a principle of logic, or mathematics, or physical science. It is not just like opening one's eyes and perceiving the black marks on this page, or even like 'seeing' those marks as words with meanings. Judging that certain people are well-off because they are wise is not like judging that they are bearers of infection because they have tuberculosis. By referring us to these differences between evaluation and other forms of human understanding, the sceptics hope to raise a philosophical doubt about what seems beyond doubt when one is considering the relevant subject-matter itself. They argue that our belief in the objectivity of values amounts to a belief in very queer 'things', perceived by a very queer faculty of 'intuition': all very fishy.

But we should not be deflected. It is obvious that those who are well-informed, etc., simply *are* better-off (other things being equal) than someone who is muddled, deluded, and ignorant, that the state of the former is better than the state of the latter, not just in this particular case or that, but in all cases, as such, universally, and *whether I like it or not*. Knowledge is better than ignorance. Am I not compelled to admit it, willy-nilly? It matters not that I may be feeling incurious myself. For the understanding affirmation of the practical principle is neither a reference to nor an expression of any desire or urge or inclination of mine. Nor is it merely a reference to (or implied presupposition of) any desires that my fellows happen to have. It goes beyond the desires and inclinations which may first have aroused my interest in the possibility of knowledge and which may remain a necessary substratum of any interest in truth sufficient to *move* me to pursue it *for myself.* It is a rational judgment about a general form of human well-being, about the fulfilment of a human potentiality. As such, it has (in its own way) the peremptoriness of all other rational judgments. It constitutes a critique of my passing likes and dislikes. The practical principle is hard to play fast and loose with; I may ignore it or reject it, but again and again it will come to mind, and be implicit in my deliberations and my discourse, catching me out in inconsistency. To avoid it, I have to be arbitrary.

To gainsay the rational force or objectivity of this practical principle, it is not enough for the sceptic to point to the diversity of moral opinions. For the principle that truth is worth knowing and that ignorance is to be avoided is not itself a moral principle. In due course we shall see that it is a principle relevant to the making of moral judgments, in the sense that it is a necessary condition of the truth or validity of certain moral norms: see V.3, V.7, V.10. But at the moment we are assuming or asserting nothing about 'morality' or 'ethics', and are ascribing no 'moral' force to the value judgment under consideration. Problems about morality and moralities are therefore beside the point.

It is equally irrelevant for the sceptic to argue that values cannot be derived from facts. For my contention is that, while awareness of certain 'factual' possibilities is a necessary condition for the reasonable judgment that truth is a value, still that judgment itself is derived from no other judgment whatsoever.

Moreover, it is insufficient for the sceptic to point out that not everyone who might be asked would affirm that truth is a value worth pursuing. For I am saying nothing about whether the principle happens to be universally affirmed, or will be in the future. I am contending only (i) that if one attends carefully and honestly to the relevant human possibilities one can understand, without reasoning from any other judgment, that the realization of those possibilities is, as such, good and desirable for the human person; and (ii) that one's understanding needs no further justification. To refer, at this point, to the opinions of other people is simply to change the subject.

Thus, the usual general arguments of sceptics in ethics give no support to the sceptics' denial of the objectivity of the value of knowledge. Much more precise grounds for this claim can rightly be demanded of the sceptics. Can they be forthcoming?

III.6   SCEPTICISM ABOUT THIS BASIC VALUE
IS INDEFENSIBLE

In the case of the basic values and practical principles to be identified in the next chapter, the discussion of their self-evidence and objectivity would have to rest at this point. But in the case of the basic value of knowledge we can go one step further. We can show that *any* argument raised by the sceptic is going to be self-defeating. To show this is not to show that the basic value of knowledge is self-evident or objective; it is only to show that counter-arguments are invalid. But to make even this limited defensive point, in relation to only one basic value, may help to undermine sceptical doubts about all and any of the basic principles of practical reasoning.

Some propositions refute themselves either because they are directly self-contradictory or because they logically entail their contradictory: for example, 'I know that I know nothing'; 'It can be proved that nothing can be proved'; 'All propositions are false'.

Then again, there are some statements whose occurrence *happens* to refute their content. An example of this pragmatic self-refutation is afforded by someone singing 'I am not singing'. Here there is what we may call performative inconsistency, that is, inconsistency between what is asserted by a statement and facts that are given in and by the making of the statement.

Thirdly, there are propositions which cannot be coherently asserted, because they are *inevitably* falsified by any assertion of them. The proposition 'I am not singing' is not such a proposition, for it can be asserted in writing. But the proposition 'I do not exist' is inevitably falsified by an assertion of it. Another example of this operational self-refutation is 'No one can put words (or other symbols) together to form a sentence'. Operationally self-refuting propositions are not logically incoherent. Nor are they meaningless or empty or semantically paradoxical, as are 'This sentence is false' or 'This provision shall come into effect on 1 January' (where 'this sentence' or 'this provision' in each case is not a colloquial reference to some other sentence or norm but is self-referential and fails to establish any definite reference). Operationally self-refuting propositions have a quite definite reference and so can be (and inevitably are) false. They have a type of performative inconsistency; that is, they are inconsistent with the facts that are given in and by *any* assertion of them. An operationally self-refuting proposition cannot be coherently asserted, for it contradicts either the proposition that someone is asserting it or some proposition entailed by the proposition that someone is asserting it.

The sceptical assertion that knowledge is not a good is operationally self-refuting. For if one makes such an assertion, intending it as a serious contribution to rational discussion, one is implicitly committed to the proposition that one believes that one's assertion is worth making, and worth making *qua* true; one thus is committed to the proposition that one believes that truth is a good worth pursuing or knowing. But the sense of one's original assertion was precisely that truth is not a good worth pursuing or knowing. Thus, one is implicitly committed to formally contradictory beliefs.

One can certainly toy with the notion that knowledge is not a good worth pursuing. But the fact that to *assert* this (whether to an audience, or as the judgment concluding one's own inner cogitations) would be operationally self-refuting should persuade the sceptic to cut short idle doubting. Self-defeating positions should be abandoned. The sceptic, on this as on other matters, can maintain coherence by *asserting* nothing; but coherence is not the only requirement of rationality.

A judgment or belief is objective if it is correct. A proposition is objective if one is warranted in asserting it, whether because there is sufficient evidence for it, or compelling grounds, or because (to one who has the experience and intelligence to understand the terms in which it is expressed) it is obvious or self-evidently correct. And if a proposition *seems* to be correct *and* could never be coherently denied, we are certainly justified in affirming it and in considering that what we are affirming is indeed objectively the case (in the relevant sense of 'what is the case'). But all this is true of the proposition we have been considering, viz. that knowledge is a good to be pursued. We do not thereby directly demonstrate that knowledge is a good to be pursued; that principle remains indemonstrable, self-evident. What we demonstrate is simply that it is presupposed in all demonstrations, indeed in all serious assertions, whatsoever, and has as much title to be called 'objective' as any other proposition whose contradictory is inevitably falsified by the act of asserting it.

NOTES

III.2

'Value' as a general form of good, the aspect or description under which particular objects are (or are regarded as) good...Aquinas's exposition of his ethics particularly suffers for want of a term reserved for signifying this. He has to make do with *bonum commune* (which has other quite different meanings in his work) or *bonum generale* or *bonum universale* or plain *bonum*. Endless confusion has resulted, notwithstanding that Aquinas himself was quite clear that, while the object of intelligent desire is always a particular (thing, action, state of affairs), nevertheless that particular is always so desired *secundum aliquam rationem universalem* or *sub communi ratione boni*: see *S.T.* I q. 80 a. 2 ad 2;

II–II q. 24 a. 1c. For the notion of value (as contrasted with particular objective) used here, see G. Grisez and R. Shaw, *Beyond the New Morality* (Notre Dame and London: 1974), chs 2 and 7.

The shift of interest from urge or inclination to concern for value...Hence, at this second level, 'something's being good is its having the properties that it is *rational* to want in things of its kind...the criteria of evaluation differ from one kind of thing to another. Since we want things for different purposes, it is obviously rational to assess them by different features': Rawls, *Theory of Justice*, 405–6 (emphasis added). But intelligence or reason also evaluates the various 'different purposes', by reference to *basic* values ('things' which it is 'rational to want' simply for one's 'well-being'), such as truth (and knowledge of it).

Knowledge is an intrinsic and basic form of good...Thus, knowledge is a *bonum honestum*, in the classical distinction between *bonum honestum*, *bonum utile*, and *bonum delectabile*: see Aquinas, *S.T.* I–II q. 94 a. 2; q. 100 a. 5 ad 5. For *honestum* does not necessarily mean *morally* worthy, as many English translations suggest. A *bonum honestum* is simply a good that is worth while having or doing or effecting for its own sake, and not just for the sake of any utility it may have as a means to some other good, nor just for the pleasure it may afford. Moral good is thus just one sort of *bonum honestum*. For the threefold distinction, see Aquinas, *in Eth.*, para. 58 (on 1095b17–18); *S.T.* I q. 5 a. 6; I–II q. 34 a. 2 ad 1; II–II q. 145 a. 3; following Ambrose, *De Officiis*, I, c. 9, following Cicero, *De Officiis*, II, c. 3. See also Aristotle, *Nic. Eth.* VIII.2: 1155b18–20; II.2: 1104b31–32 with *Gauthier-Jolif*, which points out that Aristotle is simply adopting a commonplace and is not ascribing great importance to it; also *Topics* I.13: 105a28; III.3: 118b28. See notes to VI.3–4 on the three types of *philia* (friendship).

Knowledge is good but can be inappropriately pursued...See Aquinas, *S.T.* II–II q. 167 a. 1c on the vice of *curiositas*.

III.3

'*Knowledge is a good to be pursued*...'...This is the mode of formulation of each of the first principles of natural law (of which this principle about truth and knowledge is one), according to Aquinas, *S.T.* I–II q. 94 a. 2. For the sense of the formula, and sound exegesis of the whole article, see G. Grisez, 'The First Principle of Practical Reason: A Commentary on the *Summa Theologiae*, 1–2, Question 94, Article 2' (1965) 10 *Nat. L. F.* 168, also (abbreviated) in A. Kenny (ed.), *Aquinas: A Collection of Critical Essays* (London: 1970), 340–82.

One's objective constitutes a principle in one's practical reasoning...See Aristotle, *Nic. Eth.* VI.5: 1140b17; VI.12: 1144a31–33; VII.8: 1151a15–20, with Aquinas, *in Eth.* on the same passages (i.e. paras 1170, 1273, 1431) and para. 286.

Trains of practical reasoning (the 'practical syllogism')...See Aristotle, *Nic. Eth.* VI.9, 12: 1142b22–26, 1144a31–36; VII.3: 1146b34–1147a36; *de Anima* III.11: 434a16–21; *de Motu Animalium*, 7: 701a7–33; W. F. R. Hardie, *Aristotle's Ethical Theory* (Oxford: 1968), ch. XII; J. Donald Monan, *Moral Knowledge and its Methodology in Aristotle* (Oxford: 1968), 61–3, 68–72; *Gauthier-Jolif* II/1, 209–12; II/2, 605–14; David Shwayder, *The Stratification of Behaviour* (London: 1965), 92–104; G. E. M. Anscombe, *Intention* (Oxford: 1957), 57–79.

'*"Principles" and "rules"*...'*' "*Principles" and "rules" are often used interchangeably, though the word "principle" usually carries an implication of greater generality and greater importance than the word "rules". Many of the features which mark the distinction between rules and principles in common discourse are devoid of philosophical importance... It should be mentioned, however, that the word "principle" is sometimes used to assert an ultimate value or to assert that a value is a reason for action...': Raz, *Practical Reason*, 49. It is the latter use of 'principle', not the 'rule'-like use, that concerns us here. For the more 'rule'-like use of 'principle', see e.g. X.7.

Ends and Means... It is hazardous to use the terms 'ends' and 'means'; readers must take care lest their thought about ends and means be dominated by any one instance of the relationship. A useful introduction to the different sorts of ends and means is Shwayder, *The Stratification of Behaviour*, 144–8. All the discussions of practical reasoning cited in the last note but one underline the necessity, as a minimum, of distinguishing between (i) actions which are means materially (spatially or temporally...) *external* to that-to-which-they-are-means (as drawing money from the bank is external to buying this book, and buying this book is external to reading it...), and (ii) actions which are means *constitutive* of, or *components* or *ingredients* in, or *materially identified* with that-to-which-they-are-means (as reading this book is a way of thinking about certain important matters, which in turn is a way of realizing, actualizing, or instantiating the value of knowledge). To the above citations add, likewise, J. L. Ackrill, 'Aristotle on *Eudaimonia*' (1974) 60 *Proc. Brit. Acad.* 339 at 342–4.

'Participation in value' and 'commitment'... These notions, as I use them, are rather similar to the existentialist concept *of project*, as explained by George Kateb, 'Freedom and Worldliness in the Thought of Hannah Arendt' (1977) 5 *Political Theory* 141 at 153: 'The project is a task without boundaries; one can never say that it is done, yet the whole meaning of it is found in every action done for its sake. ("For the sake of" does not mean "in order to" [Arendt, *The Human Condition* (Chicago and London: 1958), 154, 156–7]). It is never realized. The fact that I adopt a principle prevents no one else from adopting it; it is inexhaustible... A principle is not a consideration external to the act and reachable by a neutral method'. Of course, as a matter *of words*, this is precisely *not* my concept of project.

III.4

Self-evidence and having no reason to doubt what seems to be the case... See Roy Edgley, *Reason in Theory and Practice* (London: 1969), 156.

First principles are indemonstrable and self-evident but not innate... See Aristotle, *Post. Anal.* II.15: 100a; *Meta.* I.1: 980b–981a (these texts relate to speculative or theoretical indemonstrable principles, and Aristotle seems to lack any explicit concept of indemonstrable *practical* first principles). Aquinas followed Aristotle's theory of the 'induction' of indemonstrable first principles by insight working on observation, memory, and experience, but extended the account to a parallel 'induction' of indemonstrable first principles of practical reason (i.e. of natural law) by insight working on felt inclinations and a knowledge of possibilities: *S.T.* I–II q. 94 a. 2 (first principles, naturally known, of natural law); I q. 79 a. 12 (our natural disposition to know these first practical principles: *synderesis*); I–II q. 94 a. 1 ad 2 (*synderesis* is the habit of mind which holds the precepts of natural law, which are the first principles of human actions); I–II q. 10 a. 1c; II–II q. 47 a. 6c; II–II q. 79 a. 2 ad 2; *In 2 Sent.* d. 24, q. 2 a. 3 (for any definite knowledge of first principles we need both sense-experience and memory); d. 39 q. 3 a. 1; *de Veritate* q. 16 a. 1; *in Eth.* VI, lect. 12 (para. 1249).

Sexuality and curiosity...Charles Fried, *An Anatomy of Values* (Cambridge, Mass.: 1970), 88–9, sug-gests reasons for setting aside the psychologists' hypotheses when considering the *value* of truth.

Self-evident principles of theoretical rationality...See Michael Slote, *Reason and Scepticism* (London and New York: 1970), 220 ('Index of Principles'); G. Grisez, *Beyond the New Theism* (Notre Dame and London: 1975), 76–81, 114, 134–5, 168–72, 392; J. Boyle, G. Grisez, and O. Tollefsen, *Free Choice: A Self-Referential Argument* (Notre Dame and London: 1976), 144–52, 168–77.

Principles of formal logic in scientific reasoning...See, e.g., R. Harré, *The Principles of Scientific Thinking* (London: 1970), 140–1; W. Sellars, *Science, Perception and Reality* (London and New York: 1963), 295; and generally Henry E. Kyburg, *Philosophy of Science: A Formal Approach* (New York and London: 1968).

III.5

'*The good is what all things desire*'...See Aristotle, *Topics* III.1: 116a19–20; *Rhet.* I.6: 1362a23; *Nic. Eth.* I.1: 1094a3. As Aquinas points out in his commentary on this last-mentioned passage, Aristotle is not asserting that there is some one good thing which everything is tending towards; rather he is indicating the general conception of good (*bonum communiter sumptum*). As Aquinas also points out, 'desire' here really means 'tend towards', such 'tending' being unconscious, instinctive, conscious, or truly volitional depending on the nature of the subject of the tendency. It is only by an extended analogy that our notions of desire or *appetitus*, and even of good, are applied to beings which act without awareness of objectives and without freedom to choose to pursue or reject them: see Aquinas, *in Meta.* paras 999–1000 (on *Meta.* V.14: 1020b24). True, as metaphysicians both Aristotle and Aquinas hold a 'teleological view of the world' something like that described by Hart, *Concept of Law*, 182–7 [186–92] (but see third note to II.4). But both would have regarded as a false contrast the view, ascribed to them by Hart (*ibid.*, 186 [190]), that man's 'optimum state is not man's good or end because he desires it; rather he desires it because it is already his natural end'. Metaphysically, in their view, desire is explained by end *in one explanatory perspective* (see the next note, below), while end is explained by desire *in another explanatory perspective* (see, e.g., *S.T.* I–II q. 94 a. 2c); and in a third explanatory perspective (equally legitimate, in their view), both desire and end are accounted for by the essence or nature of the being (here, man) (see, e.g., *S.T.* I q. 77 a. 6; and see XIII.4). But both Aristotle and Aquinas consider that 'practical philosophy' (including ethics) is a rational inquiry distinct from metaphysics; both are clear that in ethics one looks not for explanations of the form 'A desires X because it is his natural end'; rather, one is looking for reasons for action that are good as reasons. And Aquinas, at least, is quite explicit that the search for good reasons for desiring and choosing and acting comes to an end not in the speculative (i.e. theoretical) propositions of meta-physics but in indemonstrable *practical* principles which are self-evident (*per se nota*) and in need of no further justificatory explanation: such as '*truth* is a good to be pursued...': see *S.T.* I–II q. 94 a. 2; see also second note to III.4.

Objects are desired as desirable, and considered desirable as making one better-off...This is implicit throughout Aristotle's ethics and is made explicit in sympathetic commentaries such as Aquinas, *in Eth.*, paras 1552 (on 1155b20) and 257 (on 1103b31–33). The tersest formulations are in Aquinas, *S.T.* I q. 5 a. 1c ad 1: 'The goodness of something consists in its being desirable [*appetibile*]; hence Aristotle's *dictum* that *good is what all things desire*. Now desirability is consequent upon completion (or fulfilment) for things always desire their completion…The term "good" expresses the idea of desirable completion [*bonum dicit rationem perfecti quod est appetibile*]'; see also I q. 5 a. 3c; q. 48 a. 1c; q. 6 a. 3c: '…a thing is called "good" in so far as it is [considered by the speaker to be] complete…' In the present instance, one's being well-informed etc. is the relevant 'completion', and knowledge and the means involved in acquiring and retaining it are good and desirable as 'completing' ('perfecting'). Thus, Aquinas himself remarks, commenting on Aristotle: 'All knowledge is obviously good, because the good of anything is that which belongs to the fullness of being which all things seek after and desire; and man as man reaches fullness of being through knowledge'; *in De Anima*, intro., s. 3; cf., as to 'good' and 'fullness of being', *S.T.* I–II q. 18 a. 1c. Or again: 'by the fact that they [persons] know something, they are completed by the true': *De Veritate* q. 21 a. 3c. On the relation between the desired, the desirable, and the perfective in Aquinas's notion of good, see Ronald Duska, 'Aquinas's Definition of Good: Ethical-Theoretical Notes on *De Veritate*, Q. 21' (1974) 58 *The Monist* 151 at 152–8 (only).

'*Value judgments seem to those who make them to be objective but really succeed in saying nothing more about the world than that the speakers have certain desires*'… J.L. Mackie, *Ethics: Inventing Right and Wrong* (Harmondsworth: 1977), ch. 1, lucidly argues for a sceptical thesis like this; he mentions 'objectification', in order to explain why people are under the delusion (as he deems it) that their practical principles are fundamentally objective and rational; similar, in both respects, is E. Westermarck, *Ethical Relativity* (London: 1932), 143 and *passim*. Both Mackie's main arguments (the one from 'queerness', the other from the diversity of human opinions about value) are briefly attended to in the text, above. Fundamental to such positions as Mackie's (and explicit on pp. 39–40 of his book) is a metaphysics and epistemology of a philosophical doctrine (which can be more or less subtle) of empiricism. For a fundamental critique of empiricism and of its conception of objectivity, see B. J. Lonergan, *Insight: A Study of Human Understanding* (London: 1957), chs I–V, VIII–XIV, esp. 411–16. In assessing Mackie's difficulties with the notion of 'objective prescriptivity' (*Ethics: Inventing Right and Wrong*, 47) (e.g. with the notion that knowledge really is a good and really is to be pursued), observe that he considers that, while the prescriptivity (to-be-pursuedness) of a way of being is *not* self-evident even for one who understands correctly that that way of being is thoroughly appropriate for human beings (because it fully develops their capacities and gives deepest satisfaction), nevertheless the *objective* prescriptivity of a way of being *would* be established by the fact that God (if there were a God) had issued a command requiring men to live in that way: *ibid.*, 230–2. For a critique of this and other 'will' theories of prescriptivity, normativity, and obligation, see XI.8 (excursus to notes), XI.9; and cf. XIII.5.

The significance of the variety of ethical opinions…See notes to II.3; see also V.10. Bear in mind the remark of Wilfrid Sellars, *Science and Metaphysics* (London and New York: 1968), 223: '…reasoning from the moral point of view proceeds in a context of ignorance and diversity of opinion. But, then, the same is true of consensus on matters of fact, scientific laws and theoretical principles'. To like effect, see Alan Gewirth, 'Positive "Ethics" and Normative "Science"' (1960) 69 *Philosophical Review* 311–330, reprinted in Thomson and Dworkin (eds), *Ethics* (New York: 1968), 27–47, at 32; and P. T. Geach, *The Virtues* (Cambridge: 1977), 14–15.

III.6

Self-refutation…For a much fuller statement of the argument of this section, including explanation of my use of terms such as 'proposition', 'statement', 'sentence', etc., see J. Finnis, 'Scepticism, Self-Refutation and the Good of Truth', in *Essays*, 247 at 250–4, 258–66 [*CEJF* I.3 at 65–8, 72–80]. To the references to the literature given there, add (more recent), Boyle, Grisez, and Tollefsen, *Free Choice: A Self Referential Argument*, 122–38.

IV
THE OTHER BASIC VALUES

IV.1   THEORETICAL STUDIES OF 'UNIVERSAL' VALUES

CURIOSITY is not the only basic urge, inclination, or interest. Knowledge is not the only basic aspect of human well-being. The last chapter was devoted to a reflection on the value of knowledge, not because that value is more important or basic than all other values, but simply because the materials for an analysis were so readily available, in a form substantially common to each reader, in the shape of each's own commitment to understanding (including understanding that chapter itself). So we may now widen our reflections on our interests and commitments, and ask whether there are other basic values besides knowledge, other indemonstrable but self-evident principles shaping our practical reasoning.

Such a course of reflection is, in a way, an attempt to understand one's own character, or nature. The attempt thus parallels attempts made, in quite another way, by those anthropologists and psychologists who ask (in effect) whether there is a human nature and what are its characteristics. The anthropological and psychological studies ought to be regarded as an aid in answering our own present question— not, indeed, by way of any 'inference' from universality or 'human nature' to values (an inference that would be merely fallacious), but by way of an assemblage of reminders of the range of possibly worthwhile activities and orientations open to one.

To anyone who surveys the literature, whether on ethics (or other practical modes of thinking about values) or on anthropology (or other 'theoretical' modes of investigating what humans value) it is obvious that investigation of the basic aspects of human well-being (real or supposed) is not easy. The difficulty manifests itself: (a) in arbitrary and implausible reductions of the many basic values to one (or two, or three) values, or of the many basic inclinations or interests to one (or two, or three) basic inclinations or interests; (b) in lists of basic tendencies (or values, or features of human nature) which as lists are incoherent because drawn up on shifting criteria; and (c) in short-winded analyses which mention a few tendencies, values, or features, and then tail off into 'etc.' or 'and other basic values' . . . etc. (not for convenience, as in this sentence, but for want of sustained attention to the problem).

Reductionism, cross-categorization, and the daunting variety of the lists offered by investigators, can be overcome by steady attention to distinctions drawn and emphasized in the preceding chapter. Recall, first of all, the distinction between the brute fact of an urge (or drive or inclination or tendency) and the forms of good which one who has such urges can think it worthwhile to pursue and realize, on the ground not that he has the urges but that he can see the good of such pursuit and realization. Secondly, and *a fortiori*, recall the distinction between the material conditions for, or affecting, the pursuit of a value and the value itself. A sound brain and intelligence are necessary conditions for the understanding, pursuit, and realization of truth, but neither brainpower nor intelligence should appear in a list of basic values: knowledge is the relevant value. Or again, H. L. A. Hart's 'natural facts and aims',[1] or 'truisms' about human beings, concern the material and psychological conditions ('the setting') under which persons seek their various ends (and his list of universally recognized or 'indisputable' ends contains only one entry: survival). Thirdly, in listing the basic values in which human beings may participate, recall the distinctions between general value and particular goal, and between ends and the means for attaining, realizing, or participating in those ends. Amongst these means are to be included the many intermediate and subordinate ends involved in such wide-ranging, long-lasting, and fecund means as languages, institutions like laws or property, or an economy. Thus, for example, John Rawls's 'primary goods' (liberty, opportunity, wealth, and self-respect) are primary, in his view, not because they are the basic *ends* of human life but because 'it is rational to want these goods whatever else is wanted, *since* they are in general *necessary for* the

---

[1] *Concept of Law*, 190 [194], 191 [196], 195 [199].

framing and the execution of a rational plan of life';[2] see V.3, VIII.5.

Students of ethics and of human cultures very commonly assume that cultures manifest preferences, motivations, and evaluations so wide and chaotic in their variety that no values or practical principles can be said to be self-evident to human beings, since no value or practical principle is recognized in all times and all places: cf. II.3. But those philosophers who have recently sought to test this assumption, by surveying the anthropological literature (including the similar general surveys made by professional anthropologists), have found with striking unanimity that this assumption is unwarranted.

These surveys entitle us, indeed, to make some rather confident assertions. All human societies show a concern for the value of human life; in all, self-preservation is generally accepted as a proper motive for action, and in none is the killing of other human beings permitted without some fairly definite justification. All human societies regard the procreation of a new human life as in itself a good thing unless there are special circumstances. No human society fails to restrict sexual activity; in all societies there is some prohibition of incest, some opposition to boundless promiscuity and to rape, some favour for stability and permanence in sexual relations. All human societies display a concern for truth, through education of the young in matters not only practical (e.g. avoidance of dangers) but also speculative or theoretical (e.g. religion). Human beings, who can survive infancy only by nurture, live in or on the margins of some society which invariably extends beyond the nuclear family, and all societies display a favour for the values of co-operation, of common over individual good, of obligation between individuals, and of justice within groups. All know friendship. All have some conception of *meum* and *tuum*, title or property, and of reciprocity. All value play, serious and formalized, or relaxed and recreational. All treat the bodies of dead members of the group in some traditional and ritual fashion different from their procedures for rubbish disposal. All display a concern for powers or principles which

---

[2] *Theory of Justice*, 433 (emphasis added).

are to be respected as suprahuman; in one form or another, religion is universal.

Certainly, there seems to be no practical principle which has the specificity we expect of a 'moral rule' and which is accepted, even 'in principle' or 'in theory', amongst all human beings. But my present concern is not at all with 'morals' or 'ethics'. The emergence of ethical judgment as a mode of practical judgment is treated in the next chapter. My present concern is the universality of those basic value judgments that are manifested not only in various moral requirements and restrictions but also in the many forms of human culture, institutions, and initiative. For in so far as we can 'see the point' of a human institution, art, or endeavour, even one very remote from us and open to our criticism or distaste, there is put before us a revelation or reminder of the range of opportunities open to us in shaping our own life through the free and selective pursuit of the basic values: see III.4. The universality of a few basic values in a vast diversity of realizations emphasizes *both* the connection between a basic human urge/drive/inclination/tendency and the corresponding basic form of human good, *and* at the same time the great difference between following an urge and intelligently pursuing a particular realization of a form of human good that is never completely realized and exhausted by any one action, or lifetime, or institution, or culture (nor by any finite number of them): see III.3.

This plasticity of human inclinations, which correlates with the generality or universality of the corresponding values understood by one's practical intelligence, is important for an accurate grasp not only of human anthropology and history but also of the human virtues and vices, conscience, and ethics (the subjects of the next chapter). So it is worth dwelling upon.

Consider again the drive of curiosity. It finds its response and satisfaction in the intellectual cathedrals of science, mathematics, and philosophy, whose ramifications and sophistications are beyond the grasp of even the most dedicated individual. But equally it finds a response and satisfaction in detective stories, daily newspapers, and gossip. Universally the practical principle that truth is a good worth attaining (and that mistake, muddle, and misinformation are to be avoided) is applied by human beings to whatever form of knowledge-gathering they choose to interest themselves in or commit themselves to. The unity of practical principle is as important as the immense diversity of method.

Besides limitless diversity in such forms of pursuit, there is diversity in the depth, intensity, and duration of commitment, in the extent to which the pursuit of a given value is given priority in the shaping of one's life and character. Some people's recognition of the value of truth may elicit from them the response of a lifetime of austere self-discipline and intellectual grind; others' may evoke a commitment sufficient only to enjoy the intellectual play of a good argument; others' may carry them no further than a disposition to grumble at the lying propaganda on the television...This diversity results not only from the fact that truth is not the only basic value, but also from the fact that human beings (and thus whole cultures) differ in their determination, enthusiasm, sobriety, farsighted-ness, sensitivity, steadfastness, and all the other modalities of response to *any* value.

IV.2   THE BASIC FORMS OF HUMAN GOOD:
A PRACTICAL REFLECTION

It is now time to revert, from the descriptive or 'speculative' findings of anthropology and psychology, to the critical and essentially practical discipline in which readers all must ask themselves: What *are* the basic aspects of my well-being? Here each one of us, however extensive one's knowledge of the interests of other people and other cultures, is alone with one's own intelligent grasp of the indemon-strable (because self-evident) first principles of one's own practical reasoning. From one's capacity to grasp intelligently the basic forms of good as 'to-be-pursued' one gets one's ability, in the descriptive disciplines of history and anthropology, to sympathetically (though not uncritically) see the point of actions, lifestyles, characters, and cultures that one would not choose for oneself. And one's speculative knowledge of other people's interests and achievements does not leave unaffected one's practical understanding of the forms of good that lie open to one's choice. But there is no inference from fact to value. At this point in our discourse (or private meditation), inference and proof are left behind (or left until later), and the proper form of discourse is: '...is a good, in itself, don't you think?'.

Remember: by 'good', 'basic good', 'value', 'well-being', etc. I do *not* yet mean 'moral good', etc.

What, then, are the basic forms of good for us?

A. Life

A first basic value, corresponding to the drive for self-preservation, is the value of life. The term 'life' here signifies every aspect of the vitality (*vita*, life) which puts a human being in good shape for self-determination. Hence, life here includes bodily (including cerebral) health, and freedom from the pain that betokens organic malfunctioning or injury. And the recognition, pursuit, and realization of this basic human purpose (or internally related group of purposes) are as various as the crafty struggle and prayer of someone fallen overboard seeking to stay afloat until the ship turns round; the teamwork of surgeons and the whole network of supporting staff, ancillary services, medical schools, etc.; road safety laws and programmes; famine relief expeditions; farming and rearing and fishing; food marketing; the resuscitation of suicides; watching out as one steps off the kerb...

Perhaps we should include in this category the transmission of life by procreation of children. Certainly it is tempting to treat procreation as a distinct, irreducibly basic value, corresponding to the inclination to mate/reproduce/rear. But while there are good reasons for distinguishing the urge to copulate from both the urge to self-preservation and the maternal or paternal instincts, the analytical situation is different when we shift from the level of urges/instincts/drives to the level of intelligently grasped forms of good. There may be said to be one drive (say, to copulate) and one physical release for that drive (or a range of such physical forms); but as a human action, pursuit, and realization of value, sexual intercourse may be play, and/or an expression of love or friendship, and/or an effort to procreate. So, likewise, we need not be analytically content with an anthropological convention which treats sexuality, mating, and family life as a single category or unit of investigation; nor with an ethical judgment that treats the family, and the procreation and education of children, as an indistinguishable cluster of moral responsibilities. We can distinguish the desire and decision to have a child, simply for the sake of bearing a child, from the desire and decision to cherish and to educate the child. The former desire and decision is a pursuit of the good of life, in this case life-in-its-transmission; the latter desires and decisions are aspects of the pursuit of the distinct basic values of sociability (or friendship) and truth (truth-in-its-communication), running alongside the continued pursuit of the value of life that is involved in simply keeping the child alive and well until it can fend for itself.

B. Knowledge

The second basic value I have already discussed: it is knowledge, considered as desirable for its own sake, not merely instrumentally.

C. Play

The third basic aspect of human well-being is play. A certain sort of moralist analysing human goods may overlook this basic value, but an anthropologist will not fail to observe this large and irreducible element in human culture. More importantly, each one of us can see the point of engaging in performances which have no point beyond the performance itself, enjoyed for its own sake. The performance may be solitary or social, intellectual or physical, strenuous or relaxed, highly structured or relatively informal, conventional or *ad hoc* in its pattern ... An element of play can enter into any human activity, even the drafting of enactments, but is always analytically distinguishable from its 'serious' context; and some activities, enterprises, and institutions are entirely or primarily pure play. Play, then, has and is its own value.

D. Aesthetic experience

The fourth basic component in our flourishing is aesthetic experience. Many forms of play, such as dance or song or football, are the matrix or occasion of aesthetic experience. But beauty is not an indispensable element of play. Moreover, beautiful form can be found and enjoyed in nature. Aesthetic experience, unlike play, need not involve an action of one's own;

what is sought after and valued for its own sake may simply be the beautiful form 'outside' one, and the 'inner' experience of appreciation of its beauty. But often enough the valued experience is found in the creation and/or active appreciation of some *work* of significant and satisfying form.

E. Sociability (friendship)

Fifthly, there is the value of that sociability which in its weakest form is realized by a minimum of peace and harmony amongst persons, and which ranges through the forms of human community to its strongest form in the flowering of full friendship. Some of the collaboration between one person and another is no more than instrumental to the realization by each of his or her own individual purposes. But friendship involves acting for the sake of one's friend's purposes, one's friend's well-being. To be in a relationship of friendship with at least one other person is a fundamental form of good, is it not?

Friendship and, to a lesser degree, the other forms of sociability are of special significance for the theme of this book, and so are more amply discussed later: see VI.2–4.

F. Practical reasonableness

Sixthly, there is the basic good of being able to bring one's own intelligence to bear effectively (in practical reasoning that issues in action) on the problems of choosing one's actions and lifestyle and shaping one's own character. Negatively, this involves that one has a measure of effective freedom; positively, it involves that one seeks to bring an intelligent and reasonable order into one's own actions and habits and practical attitudes. This order in turn has (i) an internal aspect, as when one strives to bring one's emotions and dispositions into the harmony of an inner peace of mind that is not merely the product of drugs or indoctrination nor merely passive in its orientation; and (ii) an external aspect, as when one strives to make one's actions (which are external in that they change states of affairs in the world and often enough affect the relations between persons) authentic, that is to say, genuine realizations of one's own freely ordered evaluations, preferences, hopes, and self-determination. This value is thus complex, involving freedom and reason, integrity and authenticity. But it has a sufficient unity to be treated as one; and for a label I choose 'practical reason-ableness'. This value is the theme of Chapter V.

G. 'Religion'

Seventhly, and finally in this list, there is the value of what, since Cicero, we summarily and lamely call 'religion'. For, as there is the order of means to ends, and the pursuit of life, truth, play, and aesthetic experience in some individually selected order of priorities and pattern of specialization, and the order that can be brought into human relations through collaboration, community, and friendship, and the order that is to be brought into one's character and activity through inner integrity and outer authenticity, so, finally, there arise such questions as: (a) How are all these orders, which have their immediate origin in human initiative and pass away in death, related to the lasting order of the whole cosmos and to the origin, if any, of that order? (b) Is it not perhaps the case that human freedom, in which one rises above the determinism of instinct and impulse to an intelligent grasp of worthwhile forms of good, and through which one shapes and masters one's environment but also one's own character, is itself somehow subordinate to something which makes that human freedom, human intelligence, and human mastery possible (not just 'originally' but from moment to moment) and which is free, intelligent, and sovereign in a way (and over a range) no human being can be?

Misgivings may be aroused by the notion that one of the basic human values is the establishment and maintenance of proper relationships between oneself (and the orders one can create and maintain) and the divine. For there are, always, those who doubt or deny that the universal order-of-things has any origin beyond the 'origins' known to the natural sciences, and who answer question (b) negatively. But is it reasonable to deny that it is, at any rate, peculiarly important to have thought reasonably and (where possible) correctly about these questions of the origins of cosmic order and of human freedom and reason—whatever the answer to those questions turns out to be, and even if the answers have to be agnostic or negative? And does not that importance in large part consist in this: that if there is a transcendent origin of the universal order-of-things and of human freedom and reason, then one's life and actions are in fundamental disorder if they are not brought, as best one can, into some sort of harmony with whatever can be known or surmised about that transcendent other and its lasting order? More important for us than the ubiquity of expressions of religious concerns, in all human cultures, is the question: Does not one's own sense of 'responsibility', in choosing what one is to be and do, amount to a concern that is not reducible to the concern to live, play, procreate, relate to others, and be intelligent? Does not even a Sartre, taking as his *point de départ* that God does not exist (and that therefore 'everything is permitted'), none the less appreciate that he is 'responsible'—obliged to act with freedom and authenticity, and to will the liberty of other persons equally with his own—in choosing what he is to be; and all this, because, *prior to* any choice of his, 'man' is and is-to-be free?[3] And is this not a recognition (however residual) of, and concern about, an order of things 'beyond' each and every one of us? And so, without wishing to beg any question, may we not for convenience call that concern, which is concern for a good consisting in an irreducibly distinct form of order, 'religious'? The present remarks are no more than place-holders; I discuss the issue on its merits in XIII.5.

IV.3   AN EXHAUSTIVE LIST?

Now besides life, knowledge, play, aesthetic experience, friendship, practical reasonableness, and religion, there are countless objectives and forms of good. But I suggest that these other objectives and forms of good will be found, on analysis, to be ways or combinations of ways of pursuing (not always sensibly) and realizing (not always successfully) one of the seven basic forms of good, or some combination of them.

Moreover, there are countless aspects of human self-determination and self-realization besides the seven basic aspects which I have listed. But these other aspects, such as courage, generosity, moderation, gentleness, and so on, are not themselves basic values; rather, they are ways (not means, but

---

[3] J.-P. Sartre, *L'Existentialisme est un humanisme* (Paris: 1946), 36, 83–4.

modes) of pursuing the basic values, and fit (or are deemed by some individual, or group, or culture, to fit) a person for their pursuit.

In this way we can analytically unravel even very 'peculiar' conventions, norms, institutions, and orders of preference, such as the aristocratic code of honour that demanded direct attacks on life in duelling.

Again, though the pursuit of the basic values is made psychologically possible by the corresponding inclinations and urges of one's nature, still there are many inclinations and urges that do not correspond to or support any basic value: for example, the inclination to take more than one's share, or the urge to gratuitous cruelty. There is no need to consider whether these urges are more, or less, 'natural' (in terms of frequency, universality, intensity, etc.) than those urges which correspond to the basic values. For I am not trying to justify our recognition and pursuit of basic values by deducing from, or even by pointing to, any set of inclinations. The point, rather, is that selfishness, cruelty, and the like, simply do not stand to something self-evidently good as the urge to self-preservation stands to the self-evident good of human life. Selfishness, cruelty, etc., stand in need of some explanation, in a way that curiosity, friendliness, etc., do not. (This is not to say that physiologists and psychologists should not investigate the physical and psychosomatic substructure of curiosity, friendliness, etc.) Often enough the explanation will be that the pursuit of a value (say, truth), or of a standard material means to sustaining a value (say, food), becomes locked into a pattern of exclusiveness or inversion—producing selfish indifference to the inclusive realization of that same value in the lives of others, and to the intrinsic value of sharing goods in friendship. Or again, cruelty may be found to be an inverted form of pursuit of the value of freedom and self-determination and authenticity: some people may make themselves 'feel real' to themselves by subjecting others to their utter mastery. In the absence of such explanations, and of psychosomatic disease, we find these urges as baffling as persistent illogicality, as opaque and pointless as, say, a demand for a plate of mud for no reason at all.

But are there just seven basic values, no more and no less? And what is meant by calling them basic?

There is no magic in the number seven, and others who have reflected on these matters have produced slightly different lists, usually slightly longer. There is no need for the reader to accept the present list, just as it stands, still less its nomenclature (which simply gestures towards categories of human purpose that are each, though unified, nevertheless multi-faceted). My brief discussion of the problem of whether procreation should be treated as an analytically distinct category of human good illustrates the scope that exists for modification of the details of the list. Still, it seems to me that those seven purposes are all of the basic purposes of human action, and that any other purpose which you or I might recognize and pursue will turn out to represent, or be constituted of, some aspect(s) of some or all of them.

IV.4   ALL EQUALLY FUNDAMENTAL

More important than the precise number and description of these values is the sense in which each is basic. First, each is equally self-evidently a form of good. Secondly, none can be analytically reduced to being merely an aspect of any of the others, or to being merely instrumental in the pursuit of any of the others. Thirdly, each one, when we focus on it, can reasonably be regarded as the most important. Hence, there is no objective hierarchy amongst them. Let me amplify this third point, which includes the other two.

If one focuses on the value of speculative truth, it can reasonably be regarded as more important than anything; knowledge can be regarded as the most important thing to acquire; life can be regarded as merely a precondition, of lesser or no intrinsic value; play can be regarded as frivolous; one's concern about 'religious' questions can seem just an aspect of the struggle against error, superstition, and ignorance; friendship can seem worth forgoing, or be found exclusively in sharing and enhancing knowledge; and so on. But one can shift one's focus. If one is drowning, or, again, if one is thinking about one's child who died soon after birth, one is inclined to shift one's focus to the value of life simply as such. The life will not be regarded as a mere precondition of anything else; rather, play and knowledge and religion will seem secondary, even rather optional extras. But one can shift one's focus, in this way, one-by-one right round the circle of basic values that constitute the horizon of our opportunities. We can focus on play, and reflect that we spend most of our time working simply in order to afford leisure; play is performances enjoyed for their own sake as performances and thus can seem to be the point of everything; knowledge and religion and friendship can seem pointless unless they issue in the playful mastery of wisdom, or participation in the play of the divine puppet master (as Plato said),[4] or in the playful intercourse of mind or body that friends can most enjoy.

Thus, I have illustrated this point in relation to life, truth, and play; the reader can easily test and confirm it in relation to each of the other basic values. Each is fundamental. None is more fundamental than any of the others, for each can reasonably be focused upon, and each, when focused upon, claims a priority of value. Hence there is no objective priority of value amongst them.

Of course, each one of us can reasonably *choose* to treat one or some of the values as of more importance in *one's own* life. As (say) a scholar, one chooses to dedicate oneself to the pursuit of know-ledge, and thus gives its demands priority, to a greater or lesser degree (and perhaps for a whole lifetime), over the friendships, the worship, the games, the art and beauty that one might otherwise enjoy. One might have been out saving lives through medicine or famine relief, but one chooses not to. But one may change one's priorities; one may risk one's life to save someone drowning, or give up one's career to nurse a sick spouse or to fight for one's community. The change is not in the relation between the basic values as that relation might reasonably have seemed to one before one chose one's life-plan (and as it should always seem to one when one is considering human opportunity and flourishing in general); rather, the change is in one's chosen life-plan. That chosen plan *made* truth more important and fundamental for one. One's new choice changes the status of that value *for oneself*; the change is in oneself. Each of us has a subjective order of priority amongst the basic values; this ranking is no doubt partly shifting and partly stable, but is in any case essential if we are to

----

[4] *Laws*, VII: 685, 803–4; see XIII.5, at 408–9 below.

act at all to some purpose. But one's reasons for choosing the particular ranking that one does choose are reasons that properly relate to one's temperament, upbringing, capacities, and opportunities, not to differences of rank of intrinsic value between the basic values.

Thomas Aquinas, in his formal discussion of the basic forms of good and self-evident primary principles of practical reasoning—which he calls the first principles and most general precepts of natural law[5]—sets a questionable example. For he arranges the precepts in a threefold order: (i) human life is a good to be sustained, and what threatens it is to be prevented; (ii) the coupling of man and woman, and the education of their young, etc., is to be favoured, and what opposes it is to be avoided; (iii) knowledge (especially of the truth about God), sociable life, and practical reasonableness are goods, and ignorance, offence to others, and practical unreasonableness are to be avoided. And his rationale for this threefold ordering (which all too easily is interpreted as a ranking) is that the self-preservative inclinations corresponding to the first category are common not just to all men but to all things which have a definite nature; that the sexual-reproductive inclinations corresponding to the second category of goods are shared by human beings with all other animate life; and that the inclinations corresponding to the third category are peculiar to mankind. Now all this is no doubt true, and quite pertinent in a metaphysical meditation on the continuity of human order with the universal order-of-things (of which human nature is a microcosmos, incorporating all levels of being: inorganic, organic,... mental...). But is it relevant to a meditation on the *value* of the various basic aspects of human well-being? Are not speculative considerations intruding into a reconstruction of principles that are practical and that, being primary, indemonstrable, and self-evident, are not derivable (nor sought by Aquinas to be derived) from any speculative considerations? As it happens, Aquinas's threefold ordering quite properly plays no part in his practical (ethical) elaboration of the significance and consequences of the primary precepts of natural law: for example, the 'first-order' good of life may not, in his view, be deliberately attacked

---

[5] *S.T.* I–II q. 94 a. 2c.

even in order to preserve the 'third-order' good of friendship with God.[6] In ethical reflection the threefold order should be set aside as an irrelevant schematization.

IV.5   IS PLEASURE THE POINT OF IT ALL?

At the opposite extreme, so to speak, from Thomas Aquinas's injection of metaphysical considerations into the reconstruction of practical discourse, is the characteristically modern mistake of trying to find a form of human well-being yet more basic and important to man than any of the seven basic values—namely some form of experience (such as 'pleasure', or 'peace of mind', or 'freedom' considered as an experience of 'floating', etc.) or set of experiences (such as 'happiness', in the common, casual sense of that word, or 'bliss'). But this notion that pleasure, or any other real or imagined internal feeling, is the point of everything is mistaken. It makes nonsense of human history and anthropology. More importantly, it simply mis-locates what is really worthwhile.

Carry out the thought-experiment skillfully proposed by Robert Nozick.[7] Suppose you could be plugged into an 'experience machine' which, by stimulating your brain while you lay floating in a tank, would afford you all the experiences you choose, with all the variety (if any) you could want: but you must plug in for a lifetime or not at all. On reflection, is it not clear, first, that you would not choose a lifetime of 'thrills' or 'pleasurable tingles' or other experiences of that type? But, secondly, is it not clear that one would not choose the *experiences* of discovering an important theorem, or of winning an exciting game, or of sharing a satisfying friendship, or of reading or writing a great novel, or even of seeing God ... or any combination of such experiences? The fact is, is it not, that if one were sensible one would not choose to plug into the experience machine *at all*. For, as Nozick rightly concludes, one wants to *do* certain things (not just have the experience of doing them); one wants to *be* a certain sort of person, through one's own authentic, free self-determination and self-realization; one

---

[6] *S.T.* II–II q. 64 a. 5 ad 3; q. 64 a. 6 ad 2; III q. 68 a. 11 ad 3.
[7] *Anarchy, State and Utopia* (Oxford: 1974), 42–5. See also Aristotle, *Eud. Eth.* I.5: 1216a.

wants to *live* (in the active sense) oneself, making a real world through that real pursuit of values that inevitably involves making one's personality in and through one's free commitment to those values.

The pursuit and realization of any of the basic values is effected partly through physical routines (many of which, when successfully consummated, give more-or-less physical pleasure); and partly through programmes, schemes, and courses of action (each of which includes physical routines, has a more-or-less specific goal, and gives satisfaction when successfully completed). But one's self-determination and self-realization is never consummated, never successfully and finally completed. And none of the basic aspects of one's well-being is ever fully realized or finally completed. Nor does a basic value lie at the end of one's choice, activity, and life in the way that the culmination of a physical performance and the goal of a definite course of action typically lie at the end of the performance or course of action. So 'pursuit' and 'realization' are rather misleading in their connotations here, and it is convenient to say that one *participates* in the basic values: see III.3. By participating in them in the way one chooses to, one hopes not only for the pleasure of successfully consummated physical performance and the satisfaction of successfully completed projects, but also for 'happiness' in the deeper, less usual sense of that word in which it signifies, roughly, a fullness of life, a certain development as a person, a meaningfulness of one's existence.

The experiences of discovery ('Eureka!') or creative play or living through danger are pleasurable, satisfying, and valuable; but it is because we want to make the discovery or to create or to 'survive' that we want the experiences. What matters to us, in the final analysis, is knowledge, significantly patterned or testing performances (and performing them), beautiful form (and appreciating it), friendship (and being a friend), freedom, self-direction, integrity, and authenticity, and (if such there be) the transcendent origin, ground, and end of all things (and *being* in accord with it). If these give pleasure, this experience is one aspect of their reality as human goods, which are not participated in fully unless their goodness is experienced as such. But a participation in basic goods which is emotionally dry, subjectively unsatisfying, nevertheless is good and meaningful as far as it goes.

So it is that the practical principles which enjoin one to participate in those basic forms of good, through the practically intelligent decisions and free actions that constitute the person one is and is to be, have been called in the Western philosophical tradition the first principles of natural law, because they lay down for us the outlines of everything one could reasonably want to do, to have, and to be.

NOTES

IV. 1

Lists of basic tendencies, or values, or features of human nature... Thomas E. Davitt, 'The Basic Values in Law: A Study of the Ethicolegal Implications of Psychology and Anthropology' (1968) 58 *Trans. Amer. Phil. Soc.* (NS), Part 5, surveys the anthropological, psychological, and philosophical literature and reports: 'Some have said there is only one basic drive be it regarding sex, economics, will-to-power, or inquiry. Some have claimed that there are two drives, feeding and breeding. Some have said there are three drives, self-preservation, reproduction, and gregariousness; or feeding, breeding and inquiring. Others have said there are four fundamental drives, hunger, thirst, sex and seeking physical wellbeing; or self-maintenance, self-perpetuation, self-gratification and religion; or self-preservation, procreation, organized co-operation, and religion; or the visceral, the active, the esthetic, the emotional; or the avoidance of injury, maintenance, reproduction, and creativity; or self-preservation, nutrition, sex and gregariousness. Still others have maintained that there are five basic drives which stand in hierarchical relation to each other, namely, the physical, safety, love, esteem and self-actualization... Still others, relating drives to values, list as many as twelve drives and fourteen values' (13–14, where Davitt provides bibliographical references, criticisms, and a list of his own).

Universally recognized values... Surveys, by philosophers, of the anthropological evidence and the testimony of general anthropologists include the following (each of which affirms the universality or virtual universality of the values and norms mentioned in this section): E. Westermarck, *Ethical Relativity* (London: 1932), ch. VII (Westermarck was defending ethical relativism but found that all the important 'differences of moral opinion' between 'savage peoples' and 'civilized nations' 'depend on knowledge or ignorance of facts, on specific religious or superstitious beliefs, on different degrees of reflection, or on different conditions of life or other external circumstances': 196) with the exception of differences of opinion concerning the range of persons to whom moral duties might be owed); Alexander MacBeath, *Experiments in Living: A Study of the Nature and Foundations of Ethics or Morals in the Light of Recent Work in Social Anthropology* (London: 1952); Morris Ginsberg, *On the Diversity of Morals* (London: 1956), chs VII and VIII; M. Edel and A. Edel, *Anthropology and Ethics* (Springfield: 1959). For the most detailed bibliography, see Richard H. Beis, 'Some Contributions of Anthropology to Ethics' (1964) 28 *Thomist* 174; and Davitt, 'The Basic Values in Law'.

IV.2

The basic forms of good for us... My account is substantially similar to G. Grisez and R. Shaw, *Beyond the New Morality: The Responsibilities of Freedom* (Notre Dame and London: 1974), ch. 7. See also (i) the list assembled from philosophical accounts of the 'sorts of things it is rational to desire for their own sakes', in W. K. Frankena, *Ethics* (New Jersey, 2nd edn: 1973), 87–8; (ii) A. H. Maslow's psychological account of basic human needs, in *Motivation and Personality* (New York: 1954), 80–106; (iii) the chapter headings in Robert H. Lowrie, *An Introduction to Cultural Anthropology* (London: 1934). Morris Ginsberg, 'Basic Needs and Moral Ideals' in *The Diversity of Morals*, ch. VII, gives a shorter list, but analyses the relation between self-evident values ('ideals') and corresponding inclinations ('needs') in a manner similar to mine. Cf. Aquinas's rather similar, short but explicitly open-ended lists: *ST* I–II q. 10 a. 1c; q. 94 a. 2c.

Play as a basic aspect of human well-being... See Johan Huizinga, *Homo Ludens: A Study of the Play-Element in Culture* ([1938] London: 1949; paperback 1970); Josef Pieper, *Leisure, the Basis of Culture* (London: 1952); Hugo Rahner, *Man at Play* ([1949] London: 1965). Huizinga, *Homo Ludens* (1970 edn), 32 says: 'Summing up the formal characteristics of play, we might call it a free activity standing quite consciously outside "ordinary" life as being "not serious", but at the same time absorbing the player intensely and utterly. It is an activity connected with no material interest, and no profit can be gained by it. It proceeds within its own proper boundaries of time and space according to fixed rules and in an orderly manner...'. For a reminder that not every element in such a definition is to be found literally obtaining in every instance of what we call games, see L. Wittgenstein, *Philosophical Investigations* (London: 1953), 66–71, 75, 83–4.

Play in drafting enactments... See the beautiful examples from Old Frisian and Old Icelandic law, quoted in Huizinga, *Homo Ludens* (1970 edn), 149–51.

Aesthetic experience... See further the discussion and citations in Finnis, 'Reason and Passion: The Constitutional Dialectic of Free Speech and Obscenity' (1967) 116 *U. Pa. L. Rev.* 222 at 232–7 [*CEJF* I.17 at 286–91].

Practical intelligence is a basic form of good to be cultivated... See Aquinas, *S.T.* I–II q. 94 a. 3c; *De Veritate* q. 16 a. 1 ad 9. Grisez and Shaw, *Beyond the New Morality*, 67–8, prefer to speak here of two basic human purposes, which they label 'integrity' and 'authenticity'.

'Religion' as a basic form of human good... I follow Grisez in using this label, but am aware that '*religion* is not an analytical concept of anything, but a topical response to certain problems in the Roman subsection of an ecumenic-imperial society': Eric Voegelin, *Order and History*, vol. 4, *The Ecumenic Age* (Baton Rouge: 1974), 45; cf. also *ibid.*, vol. I, *Israel and Revelation* (1956), 288 n. 47 and 376. See Cicero, *De Natura Deorum* I, 2–4, II, 70–2, analysed by Voegelin, *Order and History*, vol. 4, 44–5. On the universality of (i) the search for ultimate explanations of the universal order-of-things and of human life and destiny, and (ii) the attempt to bring human affairs into harmony, actual or ritualistic, with the source of such explanations, see e.g. Davitt, 'The Basic Values in Law', 70–4, citing many anthropologists' affirmations of this universality, e.g. Ruth Benedict, 'Religion' in F. Boas (ed.), *General Anthropology* (Boston: 1938), 628.

IV.3

Reputation, though not a mere 'means', is not a basic end or value... A good short exposition of the classical analysis of the worth of reputation is Henry B. Veatch, *Rational Man*

(Bloomington, Ind.: 1962), 60–1, showing that reputation is valuable only as a reassuring sign or mark of one's own real achievements and perfections (as measured by the basic values). An intelligent concern for one's reputation is in fact a very complex and close weave of aspects of one's concern for truth, one's concern to be in harmony with other persons, and one's concern for practical reasonableness (an authentic realization of one's basic concerns).

V
THE BASIC REQUIREMENTS OF
PRACTICAL REASONABLENESS

V.1 THE GOOD OF PRACTICAL
REASONABLENESS STRUCTURES OUR
PURSUIT OF GOODS

THERE is no reason to doubt that each of the basic aspects of human well-being is worth seeking to realize. But there are many such basic forms of human good; I identified seven. And each of them can be participated in, and promoted, in an inexhaustible variety of ways and with an inexhaustible variety of combinations of emphasis, concentration, and specialization. To participate thoroughly in any basic value calls for skill, or at least a thoroughgoing commitment. But our life is short.

By disclosing a horizon of attractive possibilities for us, our grasp of the basic values thus creates, not answers, the problem for intelligent decision: What is to be done? What may be left undone? What is not to be done? We have, in the abstract, no reason to leave any of the basic goods out of account. But we do have good reason to choose commitments, projects, and actions, knowing that choice effectively rules out many alternative reasonable or possible commitments, projects, and actions.

To have this choice between commitment to concentration upon one value (say, speculative truth) and commitment to others, and between one intelligent and reasonable project (say, understanding this book) and other eligible projects for giving definite shape to one's participation in one's selected value, and between one way of carrying out that project and other appropriate ways, is the primary respect in which we can call ourselves both free and responsible.

For amongst the basic forms of good that we have no good reason to leave out of account is the good of practical reasonableness, which is participated in precisely by shaping one's participation in the other basic goods, by guiding one's commitments, one's selection of projects, and what one does in carrying them out.

The principles that express the general ends of human life do not acquire what would nowadays be called a 'moral' force until they are brought to bear upon definite ranges of project, disposition, or action, or upon particular projects, dispositions, or actions. How they are thus to be brought to bear *is* the problem for practical reasonableness. 'Ethics', as classically conceived, is simply a recollectively and/or prospectively reflective expression of this problem and of the general lines of solutions which have been thought reasonable.

How does one tell that a decision is practically reasonable? This question is the subject-matter of the present chapter. The classical exponents of ethics (and of theories of natural law) were well aware of this problem of criteria and standards of judgment. They emphasize that an adequate response to that problem can be made only by one who has experience (both of human wants and passions and of the conditions of human life) and intelligence and a desire for reasonableness stronger than the desires that might overwhelm it. Even when, later, Thomas Aquinas clearly distinguished a class of practical principles which he considered self-evident to anyone with enough experience and intelligence to understand the words by which they are formulated, he emphasized that moral principles such as those in the Ten Commandments are *conclusions from* the primary self-evident principles, that reasoning to such conclusions requires good judgment, and that there are many other more complex and particular moral norms to be followed and moral judgments and decisions to be made, all requiring a degree of practical wisdom which (he says) few men in fact possess: see II.3.

Now, you may say, it is all very well for Aristotle to assert that ethics can be satisfactorily expounded only by and to those who are experienced and wise and indeed of good habits,[1] and that these characteristics are only likely to be found in societies that already have sufficiently sound standards of conduct,[2] and that the popular morality of such societies (as crystallized and detectable in their language of praise and blame, and their lore) is a generally sound pointer in the

---

[1] *Nic. Eth.* I.3: 1095a7–11; 4: 1095b5–13; X.9: 1179b27–30.
[2] *Nic. Eth.* X.9: 1179b27–1180a5.

elaboration of ethics.[3] He may assert that what is right and morally good is simply *seen* by the person (the *phronimos*, or again the *spoudaios*) who is right-minded and morally good,[4] and that what such a person thinks and does *is* the criterion of sound terminology and correct conclusions in ethics (and politics).[5] Such assertions can scarcely be denied. But they are scarcely helpful to those who are wondering whether their own view of what is to be done is a reasonable view *or not*. The notion of 'the mean', for which Aristotle is perhaps too well-known, seems likewise to be accurate but not very helpful (though its classification of value-words doubtless serves as a reminder of the dimensions of the moral problem). For what is 'the mean and best, that is characteristic of virtue'? It is 'to feel [anger, pity, appetite, etc.] when one ought to, and in relation to the objects and persons that one ought to, and with the motives and in the manner that one ought to...'.[6] Have we no more determinate guide than this?

In the two millennia since Plato and Aristotle initiated formal inquiry into the content of practical reasonableness, philosophical reflection has identified a considerable number of requirements of *method* in practical reasoning. Each of these requirements has, indeed, been treated by some philosophers with exaggerated respect, as if it were the exclusive controlling and shaping requirement. For, as with each of the basic forms of good, each of these requirements is fundamental, underived, irreducible, and hence is capable when focused upon of seeming the most important.

Each of these requirements concerns what one *must* do, or think, or be if one is to participate in the basic value of practical reasonableness. Someone who lives up to these requirements is thus Aristotle's *phronimos* and has Aquinas's *prudentia*; they are requirements of reasonableness or practical wisdom, and to fail to live up to them is irrational. But, secondly, reasonableness both *is* a basic aspect of human well-being and

---

[3]   See *Nic. Eth.* VI.5: 1140a24–25; II.5: 1105b30–31; III.6: 1115a20; III.10: 1117b32; cf. X.2: 1173a1.
[4]   *Nic. Eth.* VI.11: 1143a35–1143b17.
[5]   *Nic. Eth.* X.10: 1176a17–18; cf. III.6: 1113a33; IX.4: 1166a12–13: see also I.4 above.
[6]   *Nic. Eth.* II.6: 1106b21–24.

concerns one's participation in all the (other) basic aspects of human well-being. Hence its requirements concern fullness of well-being (in the measure in which any one person can enjoy such fullness of well-being in the circumstances of his lifetime). So someone who lives up to these requirements is also Aristotle's *spoudaios* (mature person); such a person's life is *eu zen* (well-living) and, unless circumstances are quite adverse, has (we can say) Aristotle's *eudaimonia* (the inclusive all-round flourishing or well-being—not safely translated as 'happiness'). But, thirdly, the basic forms of good are opportunities of *being*; the more fully one participates in them the more one is what one can be. And for this state of being fully what one can be, Aristotle appropriated the word *physis*, which was translated into Latin as *natura* (cf. XIII.1). So Aquinas will say that these requirements are requirements not only of reason, and of goodness, but also (by entailment) of (human) nature: see II.4.

Thus, speaking very summarily, we could say that the requirements to which we now turn express the 'natural law method' of working out the (moral) 'natural law' from the first (pre-moral) 'principles of natural law'. Using only the modern terminology (itself of uncertain import) of 'morality', we can say that the following sections of this chapter concern the sorts of reasons why (and thus the ways in which) there are things that morally ought (not) to be done.

V.2   A COHERENT PLAN OF LIFE

First, then, we should recall that, though they correspond to urges and inclinations which can make themselves felt prior to any intelligent consideration of what is worth pursuing, the basic aspects of human well-being are discernible only to those who think about their opportunities, and thus are realizable only if one intelligently directs, focuses, and controls one's urges, inclinations, and impulses. In its fullest form, therefore, the first requirement of practical reasonableness is what John Rawls calls a rational plan of life.[7] Implicitly or explicitly one must have a harmonious set of purposes and orientations, not as the

---

[7] *Theory of Justice*, 408–23, adopting the terminology of W. F. R. Hardie, 'The Final Good in Aristotle's Ethics' (1965) 60 *Philosophy* 277.

'plans' or 'blueprints' of a pipe-dream, but as effective commitments. (Do not confuse the adoption of a set of basic personal or
social commitments with the process, imagined by some contemporary philosophers, of 'choosing basic values'!) It is unreasonable
to live merely from moment to moment, following immediate
cravings, or just drifting. It is also irrational to devote one's
attention exclusively to specific projects which can be carried
out completely by simply deploying defined means to defined
objectives. Commitment to the practice of medicine (for the sake
of human life), or to scholarship (for the sake of truth), or to
any profession, or to a marriage (for the sake of friendship and
children)... all require both direction and control of impulses,
and the undertaking of specific projects; but they also require
the redirection of inclinations, the reformation of habits, the
abandonment of old and adoption of new projects, as circumstances
require, and, overall, the harmonization of all one's deep commitments—for which there is no recipe or blueprint, since basic
aspects of human good are not like the definite objectives of
particular projects, but are *participated in* (see III.3).

As Rawls says, this first requirement is that we should 'see our
life as one whole, the activities of one rational subject spread out in
time. Mere temporal position, or distance from the present, is not a
reason for favouring one moment over another'.[8] But since human
life is in fact subject to all manner of unforeseeable contingencies,
this effort to 'see' our life as one whole is a rational effort only if it
remains on the level of general commitments, and the harmonizing
of them. Still, generality is not emptiness (as one can confirm for
oneself by contrasting any of the basic forms of good, which as
formulated in the 'substantive' practical principles are quite general, with their opposites). So, in every age, wise men have coun-
selled 'in whatever you do remember your last days' (Ecclesiasticus
7:36), not so much to emphasize the importance of the hour of
death in relation to a life hereafter, but rather to establish the
proper perspective for choosing how to live one's present life.
For, from the imagined and heuristically postulated standpoint of
the still unknown time of one's death, one can see that many sorts
of choices would be irrational, a waste of opportunities, meaning-

---

[8] *Theory of Justice*, 420.

less, a failure, a shame. So the Christian parable of the man who devoted all his energies to gathering riches, with a view to nothing more than drinking and eating them up, makes its 'moral' point by appealing to the intelligence by which we discern folly: 'You *fool*! This night your life shall be required of you. Then whose shall that wealth be which you have heaped together?' (Luke 12:20.)

The content and significance of this first requirement will be better understood in the light of the other requirements. For indeed, all the requirements are interrelated and capable of being regarded as aspects one of another.

V.3   NO ARBITRARY PREFERENCES AMONGST VALUES

Next, there must be no leaving out of account, or arbitrary discounting or exaggeration, of any of the basic human values. Any commitment to a coherent plan of life is going to involve some degree of concentration on one or some of the basic forms of good, at the expense, temporarily or permanently, of other forms of good: see IV.4. But the commitment will be rational only if it is on the basis of one's assessment of one's capacities, circumstances, and even of one's tastes. It will be unreasonable if it is on the basis of a devaluation of any of the basic forms of human excellence, or if it is on the basis of an overvaluation of such merely derivative and supporting or instrumental goods as wealth or 'opportunity' or of such merely secondary and conditionally valuable goods as reputation or (in a different sense of secondariness) pleasure.

Some scholars may have little taste or capacity for friendship, and may feel that life for them would have no savour if they were prevented from pursuing their commitment to knowledge. None the less, it would be unreasonable for them to deny that, objectively, human life (quite apart from truth-seeking and knowledge) and friendship are good in themselves. It is one thing to have little capacity and even no 'taste' for scholarship, or friendship, or physical heroism, or sanctity; it is quite another thing, and stupid or arbitrary, to think or speak or act as if these were not real forms of good.

So, in committing oneself to a rational plan of life, and in interacting with other people (with their own plans of life), one must not use Rawls's 'thin theory of the good'. For the sake of a 'democratic'[9] impartiality between differing conceptions of human good, Rawls insists that, in selecting principles of justice, one must treat as primary goods only liberty, opportunity, wealth, and self-respect, and that one must not attribute intrinsic value to such basic forms of good as truth, or play, or art, or friendship. Rawls gives no satisfactory reason for this radical emaciation of human good, and no satisfactory reason is available: the 'thin theory' is arbitrary. It is quite reasonable for many people to choose not to commit themselves to any real pursuit of knowledge, and it is quite unreasonable for scholar-statesmen or scholar-parents to demand that each subject or child of theirs should conform willy-nilly to the modes and standards of excellence that they choose and set for themselves. But it is even more unreasonable for one—anyone—to deny that knowledge *is* (and is to be treated as) a form of excellence, and that error, illusion, muddle, superstition, and ignorance are evils that one should not wish for, or plan for, or encourage in oneself or in others. If, as statesman (see VIII.5) or father or mother or simply as a self-directing individual, one treats truth or friendship or play or any of the other basic forms of good as of no account, and never asks oneself whether one's life-plan(s) makes reasonable allowance for participation in those intrinsic human values (and for avoidance of their opposites), then one can be properly accused both of irrationality and of stunting or mutilating oneself and those in one's care.

V.4   NO ARBITRARY PREFERENCES AMONGST PERSONS

Next, the basic goods are human goods, and can in principle be pursued, realized, and participated in by any human being. Other persons' survival, their coming to know, their creativity, their all-round flourishing, may not interest me, may not concern me, may in any event be beyond my power to affect. But have I any *reason* to deny that that survival, knowledge, creativity, and flourishing are really good, and are fit matters of interest, concern, and favour by those persons and by all who have to do with them? The questions of friendship, collaboration, mutual assistance, and justice are the subject of the next chapters. Here we need not ask just who

---

[9] Cf. *Theory of Justice*, 527.

is responsible for whose well-being: see VII.4. But we can add, to the second requirement of fundamental impartiality of recognition of each of the basic forms of good, a third requirement: of fundamental impartiality among the human subjects who are or may be partakers of those goods.

My own well-being (which, as we shall see, includes a concern for the well-being of others, my friends: see VI.4; but ignore this for the moment) is reasonably the first claim on my interest, concern, and effort. Why can I so regard it? Not because it is of more value than the well-being of others, simply because it is mine: intelligence and reasonableness can find no basis in the mere fact that A is A and is not B (that I am I and am not you) for evaluating his (our) well-being differentially. No: the only *reason* for me to prefer my well-being is that it is through *my* self-determined and self-realizing participation in the basic goods that I can do what reasonableness suggests and requires, viz. favour and realize the forms of human good indicated in the first principles of practical reason.

There is, therefore, reasonable scope for self-preference. But when all allowance is made for that, this third requirement remains a pungent critique of selfishness, special pleading, double standards, hypocrisy, indifference to the good of others whom one could easily help ('passing by on the other side'), and all the other manifold forms of egoistic and group bias. So much so that many have sought to found ethics virtually entirely on this principle of impartiality between persons. In the modern philosophical discussion, the principle regularly is expressed as a requirement that one's moral judgments and preferences be *universalizable*.

The classical non-philosophical expression of the requirement is, of course, the so-called Golden Rule formulated not only in the Christian gospel but also in the sacred books of the Jews, and not only in didactic formulae but also in the moral appeal of sacred history and parable. It needed no drawing of the moral, no special traditions of moral education, for King David (and every reader of the story of his confrontation with Nathan the prophet) to feel the rational conclusiveness of Nathan's analogy between the rich man's appropriation of the poor man's ewe and the King's appropriation of Uriah the Hittite's wife, and thus the rational necessity for the King to extend his condemnation of the rich man to himself. 'You are the man' (2 Samuel 12:7).

'Do to (or for) others what you would have them do to (or for) you'. Put yourself in your neighbour's shoes. Do not condemn others for what you are willing to do yourself. Do not (without special reason) prevent others getting for themselves what you are trying to get for yourself. These are requirements of reason, because to ignore them is to be arbitrary as between individuals.

But what are the bounds of reasonable self-preference, of reasonable discrimination in favour of myself, my family, my group(s)? In the Greek, Roman, and Christian traditions of reflection, this question was approached via the heuristic device of adopting the viewpoint, the standards, the principles of justice, of one who sees the whole arena of human affairs and who has the interests of each participant in those affairs equally at heart and equally in mind—the 'ideal observer'. Such an impartially benevolent 'spectator' would condemn some but not all forms of self-preference, and some but not all forms of competition: see VII.3–4. The heuristic device helps one to attain impartiality as between the possible subjects of human well-being (persons) and to exclude mere bias in one's practical reasoning. It permits one to be impartial, too, among inexhaustibly many of the life-plans that differing individuals may choose. But, of course, it does not suggest 'impartiality' about the basic aspects of human good. It does not authorize one to set aside the second requirement of practical reason by indifference to death and disease, by preferring trash to art, by favouring the comforts of ignorance and illusion, by repressing all play as unworthy of man, by praising the ideal of self-aggrandizement and contemning the ideal of friendship, or by treating the search for the ultimate source and destiny of things as of no account or as an instrument of statecraft or a plaything reserved for leisured folk...

Therein lies the contrast between the classical heuristic device of the benevolently divine viewpoint and the equivalent modern devices for eliminating mere bias, notably the heuristic concept of the social contract. Consider Rawls's elaboration of the social contract strategy, an elaboration which most readily discloses the purpose of that strategy as a measure and instrument of practical reason's requirement of interpersonal impartiality. Every feature of Rawls's construction is designed to guarantee that if a supposed principle of justice is one that would be unanimously agreed on, behind the 'veil of ignorance', in the 'Original Position', then it must be a principle that is fair and unbiased as between persons. Rawls's heuristic device is thus of some use to anyone who is concerned for the third requirement of practical reasonableness, and in testing its implications. Unfortunately, Rawls disregards the second requirement of practical reasonableness, viz. that each basic or intrinsic human good be treated as a basic and intrinsic good. The conditions of the Original Position are designed by Rawls to guarantee that no principle of justice will systematically favour any life-plan simply because that life-plan participates more fully in human well-being in any or all of its basic aspects (e.g. by favouring knowledge over ignorance and illusion, art over trash, etc.).

And it simply does not follow, from the fact that a principle chosen in the Original Position would be unbiased and fair as between individuals, that a principle which would *not* be chosen in the Original Position must be unfair or not a proper principle of justice in the real world. For in the real world, as Rawls himself admits, intelligence can discern intrinsic basic values and their contraries.[10] Provided we make the distinctions mentioned in the previous section, between basic practical principles and mere matters of taste, inclination, ability, etc., we are able (and are required in reason) to favour the basic forms of good and to avoid and discourage their contraries. In doing so we are showing no improper favour to individuals as such, no unreasonable 'respect of persons', no egoistic or group bias, no partiality opposed to the Golden Rule or to any other aspect of this third requirement of practical reason: see VIII.5–6.

V.5 DETACHMENT AND COMMITMENT

The fourth and fifth requirements of practical reasonableness are closely complementary both to each other and to the first requirement of adopting a coherent plan of life, order of priorities, and set of basic commitments.

---

[10] *Theory of Justice*, 328.

In order to be sufficiently open to all the basic forms of good in all the changing circumstances of a lifetime, and in all one's relations, often unforeseeable, with other persons, and in all one's opportunities of effecting their well-being or relieving hardship, one must have a certain detachment from all the specific and limited projects which one undertakes. There is no good reason to take up an attitude to any of one's particular objectives, such that if one's project failed and one's objective eluded one, one would consider one's life drained of meaning. Such an attitude irrationally devalues and treats as meaningless the basic human good of authentic and reasonable self-determination, a good in which one meaningfully participates simply by trying to do something sensible and worthwhile, whether or not that sensible and worthwhile project comes to nothing. Moreover, there are often straightforward and evil consequences of succumbing to the temptation to give one's particular project the overriding and unconditional significance which only a basic value and a general commitment can claim: they are the evil consequences that we call to mind when we think of fanaticism. So the fourth requirement of practical reasonableness can be called detachment.

The fifth requirement establishes the balance between fanaticism and dropping out, apathy, unreasonable failure, or refusal to 'get involved' with anything. It is simply the requirement that having made one's general commitments one must not abandon them lightly (for to do so would mean, in the extreme case, that one would fail ever to really participate in any of the basic values). And this requirement of fidelity has a positive aspect. One should be looking creatively for new and better ways of carrying out one's commitments, rather than restricting one's horizon and one's effort to the projects, methods, and routines with which one is familiar. Such creativity and development shows that a person, or a society, is really living on the level of practical *principle*, not merely on the level of conventional rules of conduct, rules of thumb, rules of method, etc., whose real appeal is not to reason (which would show up their inadequacies) but to the sub-rational complacency of habit, mere urge to conformity, etc.

V.6   THE (LIMITED) RELEVANCE OF
CONSEQUENCES: EFFICIENCY, WITHIN REASON

The sixth requirement has obvious connections with the fifth, but introduces a new range of problems for practical reason, problems which go to the heart of 'morality'. For this is the requirement that one bring about good in the world (in one's own life and the lives of others) by actions that are efficient for their (reasonable) purpose(s). One must not waste one's opportunities by using inefficient methods. One's actions should be judged by their effectiveness, by their fitness for their purpose, by their utility, their consequences...

There is a wide range of contexts in which it is possible and only reasonable to calculate, measure, compare, weigh, and assess the consequences of alternative decisions. Where a choice must be made it is reasonable to prefer human good to the good of animals. Where a choice must be made it is reasonable to prefer basic human goods (such as life) to merely instrumental goods (such as property). Where damage is inevitable, it is reasonable to prefer stunning to wounding, wounding to maiming, maiming to death: i.e. lesser rather than greater damage to one-and-the-same basic good in one-and-the-same instantiation. Where one way of participating in a human good includes *both* all the good aspects and effects of its alternative, *and* more, it is reasonable to prefer that way: a remedy that both relieves pain and heals is to be preferred to the one that merely relieves pain. Where a person or a society has created a personal or social hierarchy of practical norms and orientations, through reasonable choice of commitments, one can in many cases reasonably measure the benefits and disadvantages of alternatives. (Consider someone who has decided to become a scholar, or a society that has decided to go to war.) Where one is considering objects or activities in which there is reasonably a market, the market provides a common denominator (currency) and enables a comparison to be made of prices, costs, and profits. Where there are alternative techniques or facilities for achieving definite objectives, cost-benefit analysis will make possible a certain range of reasonable comparisons between techniques or facilities. Over a wide range of preferences and wants, it is reasonable for an individual or society to seek to maximize the satisfaction of those preferences or wants.

But this sixth requirement is only one requirement among a number. The first, second, and third requirements require that in seeking to maximize the satisfaction of preferences one should discount the preferences of, for example, sadists (who follow the impulses of the moment, and/or do not respect the value of life, and/or do not universalize their principles of action with impartiality). The first, third, and (as we shall see) seventh and eighth requirements require that cost-benefit analysis be contained within a framework that excludes any project involving certain intentional killings, frauds, manipulations of personality, etc. And the second requirement requires that one recognize that each of the basic aspects of human well-being is equally basic, that none is objectively more important than any of the others, and thus that none can provide a common denominator or single yardstick for assessing the utility of all projects: they are incommensurable, and any calculus of consequences that pretends to commensurate them is irrational.

As a general strategy of moral reasoning, utilitarianism or consequentialism is irrational. The utilitarian or (more generally) the consequentialist claims that (i) one should always choose the act that, so far as one can see, will yield the greatest net good on the whole and in the long run ('act-utilitarianism'), or that (ii) one should always choose according to a principle or rule the adoption of which will yield the greatest net good on the whole and in the long run ('rule-utilitarianism'). Each of these claims is not so much false as senseless (in a sense of 'senseless' that will shortly be explained). For no plausible sense can be given, here, to the notion of a 'greatest net good', or to any analogous alternative notions such as 'best consequences', 'lesser evil', 'smallest net harm', or 'greater balance of good over bad than could be expected from any available alternative action'.

Of course, modern ethical theories are most obviously distinguished from earlier theories precisely by their adoption of consequentialist method. So the claim that any such method is irrational may arouse the reader's misgivings. Now there are many features of consequentialist method which are arbitrary

or unworkable; I mention some of these briefly, later in this
section. But the fundamental problem is that the methodological
injunction to maximize good(s) is irrational. And it is important
to see that this irrationality is not merely the unreasonableness of
adopting a practically unworkable method. Consequentialist
method is indeed unworkable, and notoriously so. But more than
that, its methodological injunction to maximize good is *senseless*.
That is to say, it is senseless in the way that it is senseless to try
to sum together the size of this page, the number six, and the
mass of this book.

'Good(s)' could be measured and computed in the manner required by consequentialist ethics only if (a) human beings had some
single, well-defined goal or function (a 'dominant end'), or (b) the
differing goals which men in fact pursue had some common factor,
such as 'satisfaction of desire'. But neither of these conditions
obtains. Only an inhumane fanatic thinks that human beings are
made to flourish in only one way or for only one purpose. If a
religious person says that man is made simply for the glory of God,
or simply for eternal life in friendship with God, we must reply by
asking whether the glory of God may not be manifested in *any* of
the many aspects of human flourishing, whether these aspects are
not all equally fundamental, whether love of God may not thus
take, and be expressed in, any of the inexhaustibly many life-plans
which conform to the requirements set out in this chapter, which
are requirements of a reason-loving love of those things that can
be humanly (humanely) loved: see XIII.5. If, at the other extreme,
someone asserts that each and every human desire has the
same prima facie entitlement to satisfaction, so that the univocal
meaning of 'good' (in the consequentialist methodological
injunction) is 'satisfaction of desire', we must repeat that this has
no plausibility at all to any who steadily reflect on the basic
principles of their own practical intelligence. What reason can
you find to deny that truth (and knowledge) is a good?
What reason, then, can be found for treating the desire of
someone who wants to keep people ignorant as a desire that
even prima facie is just as much entitled to satisfaction as the
desire of someone who loves knowledge? Why should any
who desire (as consequentialists obviously do) to regulate their
conduct by practical reasonableness treat as of equal value the

desire (which they may find in themselves or in others) to live according to sheer whim, or according to a programme adopted and loved for its sheer arbitrariness? And we can ask the same question in relation to all those desires that focus on death, pain, joylessness, trash, hatred and destruction of others, incoherence, and any other form of human ruin. These evils can be embraced, as if they were intrinsic goods, by persons who once accepted them only as means to ends and whose personalities were skewed by their wrongdoing. To say that one who gives vent to these desires is 'mentally sick' (and hence not to be counted in the grand calculus of satisfactions) is, often enough, a mere form of words disguising a moral evaluation made tacitly on non-consequentialist lines.

I have already (see IV.5) discussed and rejected the view that pleasure or any other definable form of experience can provide the homogeneous and complete human good that the consequentialist needs to be able to identify before he begins computing a maximum net good. To my earlier discussion I add the following two points. First: attempts to define 'good' (for the purposes of the calculus) in terms of enjoyment, satisfaction, happiness, and desire have to assume that 'disvalues' such as pain and frustration stand to their valued opposites as cold stands to heat, viz. as just a low level of the value, on one and the same scale. But this assumption of commensurability is quite implausible. So some consequentialists have been concerned to maximize enjoyments, etc., while others have been concerned to minimize pains, etc. It is rash to assume that these two approaches can be harmonized by subtracting the disvalues from the values, to arrive at a 'net maximum (or greater) good' or 'net minimum (or lesser) evil'. Some consequentialists were so well aware of this awkward incommensurability of good and evil that they argued that *good* results were morally irrelevant: their ('negative utilitarian') methodological injunction was to choose the act (or rule) that will bring about least evil. Secondly: desires, enjoyments, and satisfactions, even when sieved to exclude those opposed to the basic forms of human good, seem to differ in kind, as well as degree. One can compare the strength and degree of one's desire to have a cup of tea now with one's desire to have a cup of coffee now, and the degree of the respective enjoyment or satisfactions. But how can either of those desires and their satisfaction be compared with one's desire to be a fine scholar, a craftsmanlike lawyer, a good father, a true friend...?

In short, no determinate meaning can be found for the term 'good' that would allow any commensurating and calculus of good to be made in order to settle those basic questions of practical reason which we call 'moral' questions. Hence, as I said, the consequentialist methodological injunction to maximize net good is senseless, in the way that it is senseless to try to sum up the quantity of the size of this page, the quantity of the number six, and the quantity of the mass of this book. Each of these quantities *is* a quantity and thus has in common with the others the feature that, of it, one can sensibly ask 'How much?' Similarly, each of the basic aspects of human good *is* a good and thus has in common with the others the feature that, of it, one can sensibly ask 'Is this something I should rather be getting/doing/being?' But the different forms of goods, like the different kinds of quantities, are objectively incommensurable. One can *adopt* a system of weights and measures that will *bring* the three kinds of quantity into a relation with each other (there might be six times as many square inches to this page as there are ounces of weight in this book, or 600 times as many square millimetres as kilograms, or...). But adopting a system of weights and measures is *nothing like* carrying out a computation in terms of the system. Similarly, one can *adopt* a set of commitments that will *bring* the basic values into a relation with each other sufficient to enable one to choose projects and, in some cases, to undertake a cost-benefit analysis (or preference-maximizing or other like analysis) with some prospect of a determinate 'best solution'. But the adoption of a set of commitments, by an individual or a society, is *nothing like* carrying out a calculus of commensurable goods, though it should be controlled by all the rational requirements which we are discussing in this chapter, and so is far from being blind, arbitrary, directionless, or indiscriminate.

Consequentialism is arbitrary in a number of other respects. And again this arbitrariness is not a matter of mere 'unworkability' that can be surmounted 'in principle', i.e. if human limitations could be surmounted.

For example, consequentialism provides no reason for preferring altruism to egoism or to exclusive concern for one's family or party or class or country or church. Jeremy Bentham oscillated and equivocated for 60 years about whether his utilitarianism was to maximize his own happiness or the happiness of 'everybody'. Particular consequentialists may *happen* to find (or think they find) their own good in maximizing the good of others or of 'all'; but their consequentialist analysis and method of practical reasoning affords them no principle by reference to which they could criticize as unreasonable or immoral any persons who set out to maximize their own happiness regardless of the welfare of others.

Again, consequentialism that goes beyond pure egoism requires a principle of distribution of goods. Supposing (what is in fact logically impossible) that human goods could be commensurated and summed, and supposing (what is for consequentialism an arbitrary importation of a principle of universalization not explicable by appeal to consequences) that 'everyone's' good is to be counted impartially, it remains that the methodological injunction to maximize good still yields no determinate result. No determinate result will follow until we further specify whether maximized good means (a) maximum amounts of good regardless of distribution ('over-all utility': a minority, or even a majority, can be enslaved, tortured, or exterminated if that will increase over-all net satisfaction/happiness/good), or (b) maximum *average* amounts of good ('average utility': any number of people can be enslaved, etc., if that will increase the average net satisfaction, etc.), or (c) maximum amounts of good for those worst-off ('maximin' or 'minimax' utility: whatever is chosen must increase the well-being of those worst-off more than any alternative choice), or (d) equal amounts of good for 'everyone' (notwithstanding that *almost* everyone might be *much* better-off in a society regulated in accordance with specifications (a), (b), or (c)). Some such specification is logically necessary: as it stands, any principle containing a term such as 'the greatest good of the greatest number' is as logically senseless as offering a prize for 'writing the most essays in the shortest time' (Who wins?—the person who turns up tomorrow with three essays, or the person who turns up in a week with 12, or...?). But there is no *consequentialist* reason for preferring any particular one of the eligible specifications. The ambition to maximize goods logically cannot be a sufficient principle of practical reasoning.

Again, consequentialist method enjoins us to make the choice that would produce greater net good than could be expected to be produced by any alternative choice. But the alternatives that are in fact 'open' or 'available' to one are innumerable. A genuine consequentialist assessment of alternative possibilities could never end, and could begin anywhere. So it should never begin at all, in reason. (To say this is not at all to say that one should ever disregard or shut one's eyes to foreseeable consequences, or look no further than one's 'good intentions'.)

Now individuals and societies do in fact 'solve' these problems for themselves, and so make the consequentialist injunctions *seem* workable. They focus on something which they have already set their hearts on (an increase in national wealth by collectivizing farming, an end to the war, the detection of those heretics or criminals, re-election as President, an end to that young woman's suffering...). 'The' good consequences of this, and 'the' bad consequences of omitting or failing to get it, are dwelt upon. Such requirements as interpersonal impartiality of focus, fidelity to commitments, etc., are brushed aside. Thus, the 'calculus' is forced through to provide a determinate solution (the quickest, cheapest way of getting what was first focused upon: hence, the forced collectivization and liquidation of the farmers, the nuclear or fire-storm bombing of the enemy's hostage civilians, the inquisitorial torture of suspects or informers, the fraudulent cover-up and obstruction of legal process, the abortion of unborn and 'exposure' of newly born children...). Of course, by focusing on some other alternatives, and on some other long-term or over-all consequences of choosing the favoured alternative, and on the life-possibilities of the proposed victims, and so on, one can in every case find reasons to condemn the favoured action 'on consequentialist grounds'. But in truth both sets of calculations, in such cases, are equally senseless. What generates the 'conclusions' is always something other than the calculus: an overpowering desire, a predetermined objective, the traditions or conventions of the group, or the requirements of practical reason discussed in this chapter.

The limits of the 'reasonable foresight' demanded by our law, and *a fortiori* the nature of the choices ('reasonable care', etc.) demanded, by our law, in view of what was 'reasonably foreseeable', are manifestly fixed almost entirely by (tacit) appeal to social commitments and moral evaluations made, not by consequentialist method, but by following out (with greater or less integrity and success) the requirements of practical reason discussed in this chapter.

The sixth requirement—of efficiency in pursuing the definite goals which we adopt for ourselves and in avoiding the definite harms which we choose to regard as unacceptable—is a real requirement, with indefinitely many applications in 'moral' (and hence in legal) thinking. But its sphere of proper application has limits, and every attempt to make it the exclusive or supreme or even the central principle of practical thinking is irrational and hence immoral. Still, we ought not to disguise from ourselves the *ultimate* (and hence inexplicable, even 'strange'[11]) character of the basic principles and requirements of reasonableness (like the basic aspects of the world...) once we go beyond the intellectual routines of calculating cost-benefit and efficiency.

V.7   RESPECT FOR EVERY BASIC VALUE
IN EVERY ACT

The seventh requirement of practical reasonableness can be formulated in several ways. A first formulation is that one should not choose to do any act which *of itself does nothing but* damage or impede a realization or participation of any one or more of the basic forms of human good. For the only 'reason' for doing such an act, other than the non-reason of some impelling desire, could be that the good *consequences* of the act *outweigh* the damage done in and through the act itself. But, outside

[11] Thus, Brian Barry rightly begins his 'Justice Between Generations', *Essays*, 269–84, by asking (quoting Wilfred Beckerman): 'Suppose that, as a result of using up all the world's resources, human life did come to an end. So what?' and concludes a thorough analysis of the issues for practical reasonableness by saying '...the continuation of human life into the future is something to be sought (or at least not sabotaged) even if it does not make for the maximum total happiness. Certainly, if I try to analyse the source of my own strong conviction that we should be wrong to take risks with the continuation of human life, I find that it does not lie in any sense of injury to the interests of people who will not get born but rather in a sense of its cosmic impertinence—that we should be grossly abusing our position by taking it upon ourselves to put a term on human life and its possibilities' (p. 284).

merely technical contexts, consequentialist 'weighing' is always and necessarily arbitrary and delusive for the reasons indicated in the preceding section.

Now an act of the sort we are considering will always be done (if it is done intelligently at all) as a means of promoting or protecting, directly or indirectly, one or more of the basic goods, in one or more of their aspects. For anyone who rises above the level of impulse and acts deliberately must be seeking to promote some form of good (even if only the good of authentically powerful self-expression and self-integration, sought through sadistic assaults or through malicious treachery or deception, with 'no ulterior motives'). Hence, if consequentialist reasoning were reasonable, acts which themselves do nothing but damage or impede a human good could often be justified as parts of, or steps on the way to carrying out, some project for the promotion or protection of some form(s) of good. For example, if consequentialist reasoning were reasonable, one might sometimes reasonably kill some innocent person to save the lives of some hostages. But consequentialist reasoning is arbitrary and senseless, not just in one respect but in many. So we are left with the fact that such a killing is an act which of itself does nothing but damage the basic value of life. The goods that are expected to be secured in and through the consequential release of the hostages (if it takes place) would be secured not in or as an aspect of the killing of the innocent man but in or as an aspect of a distinct, subsequent act, an act which would be one 'consequence' amongst the innumerable multitude of incommensurable consequences of the act of killing. Once we have excluded consequentialist reasoning, with its humanly understandable but in truth naively arbitrary limitation of focus to the purported calculus 'one life versus many', the seventh requirement is self-evident. (The following paragraphs, therefore, seek not to demonstrate, but to clarify the sense of this requirement; on self-evidence: see III.4.)

The basic values, and the practical principles expressing them, are the only guides we have. Each is objectively basic, primary, incommensurable with the others in point of objective importance. If one is to act intelligently at all one must choose to realize and participate in some basic value or values rather than others, and this inevitable concentration of effort will indirectly impoverish, inhibit, or interfere with the realization of those other values. If I commit myself to truthful scholarship, then I fail to save the lives I could save as a doctor, I inhibit the growth of the production of material goods, I limit my opportunities for serving the community through politics, entertainment, art, or preaching. And within the field of science and scholarship, my research into K means that L and M go as yet undiscovered. These unsought but unavoidable side-effects accompany every human choice, and their consequences are incalculable. But it is always reasonable to leave some of them, and often reasonable to leave all of them, out of account. Let us for brevity use the word 'damage' to signify also impoverishment, inhibition, or interference, and the word 'promote' to signify also pursuit or protection. Then we can say this: to indirectly damage any basic good (by choosing an act that directly and immediately promotes either that basic good in some other aspect or participation, or some other basic good or goods) is obviously quite different, rationally and thus morally, from directly and immediately damaging a basic good in some aspect or participation by choosing an act which in and of itself simply (or, we should now add, primarily) damages that good in some aspect or participation but which indirectly, via the mediation of expected consequences, is to promote either that good in some other aspect or participation, or some other basic good(s).

To choose an act which in itself simply (or primarily) damages a basic good is thereby to engage oneself willy-nilly (but directly) in an act of opposition to an incommensurable value (an aspect of human personality) which one treats as if it were an object of measurable worth that could be outweighed by commensurable objects of greater (or cumulatively greater) worth. To do this will often accord with our feelings, our generosity, our sympathy, and with our commitments and projects in the forms in which we undertook them. But it can never be justified in reason. We must choose rationally (and this rational judgment can often promote a shift in our perspective and consequently a realignment of initial feelings and thus of our commitments and projects). Reason requires that every basic value be at least respected in each and every action. If one could ever rightly choose a single act which *itself* damages and *itself does* not promote some basic good, then one could rightly choose whole programmes and institutions and enterprises that themselves damage and do not promote basic aspects of human well-being, for the sake of their 'net beneficial consequences'. Now we have already seen that consequences, even to the extent that they can be 'foreseen as certain', cannot be commensurably *evaluated*, which means that 'net beneficial consequences' is a literally absurd general objective or criterion. It only remains to note that if one thinks that one's rational responsibility to be always doing and pursuing good is satisfied by a commitment to act always for best consequences, one treats every aspect of human personality (and indeed, therefore, treats oneself) as a utensil. One holds oneself ready to do *anything* (and thus makes oneself a tool for all those willing to threaten sufficiently bad consequences if one does not cooperate with them).

But the objection I am making to such choices is not that programmes of mass killing, mass deception, etc. would then be morally eligible (though they would) and indeed morally required (though they would), but that no sufficient reason can be found for treating any act as immune from the only direction which we have, viz. the direction afforded by the basic practical principles. These each direct that a form of good is to be pursued and done; and each of them bears not only on all our large-scale choices of general orientations and commitments, and on all our medium-scale choices of projects (in which attainment of the objective will indeed be the good consequence of successful deployment of effective means), but also on each and every choice of an act which itself is a complete act (whether or not it is also a step in a plan or phase in a project). The incommensurable value of an aspect of personal full-being (and its corresponding primary principle) can never be rightly subordinated to any project or commitment. But such an act of subordination inescapably occurs at least whenever a distinct choice-of-act has in *itself* no meaning save that of damaging that basic value (thus violating that primary principle).

Such, in highly abstract terms, is the seventh requirement, the principle on which alone rests (as we shall later see) the strict inviolability of basic human rights: see VIII.7. There is no human right that will not be overridden if feelings (whether generous and unselfish, or mean and self-centred) are allowed to govern choice, or if cost-benefit considerations are taken outside their appropriate technical sphere and allowed to govern one's direct engagement (whether at the level of commitment, project, or individual act) with basic goods. And the perhaps unfamiliar formulation which we have been considering should not obscure the fact that this 'seventh requirement' is well-recognized, in other formulations: most loosely, as 'the end does not justify the means'; more precisely, though still ambiguously, as 'evil may not be done that good might follow therefrom'; and with a special Enlightenment flavour, as Kant's 'categorical imperative': 'Act so that you treat humanity, whether in your own person or in that of another, always as an end and never as a means only'.[12]

Obviously, the principal problem in considering the implications of this requirement is the problem of individuating and characterizing actions, to determine what is one complete act-that-itself-does-nothing-but-damage-a-basic-good. Human acts are to be individuated primarily in terms of those factors which we gesture towards with the word 'intention'. Fundamentally, a human act is a that-which-is-decided-upon (or -chosen) and its primary proper description is as what-is-chosen. A human action, to be humanly regarded, is to be characterized in the way it was characterized in the conclusion to the relevant train of practical reasoning of the man who chose to do it (cf. III.3). On the other hand, the world with its material (including our bodily selves) and its structures of physical and psycho-physical causality is not indefinitely malleable by human intention. When one is deciding what to do, one cannot reasonably shut one's eyes to the causal structure of one's project; one cannot characterize one's plans *ad lib*. One can be engaged *willy-nilly* but directly, in act, with a basic good, such as human life.

Perhaps the consequences of one's act seem likely to be very good and would themselves directly promote further basic human good. Still, these expected goods will be realized (if at all) not as aspects of one-and-the-same act, but as aspects or consequences of other acts (by another person, at another time and place, as the upshot of another free decision...). So,

---

[12] Kant, *Foundations of the Metaphysics of Morals* (1785; trans. Beck, Indianapolis: 1959), 47.

however 'certainly foreseeable' they may be, they cannot be used to characterize the act itself as, *in and of itself,* anything other than an intentional act of, say, man-killing. This is especially obvious when a blackmailer's price for sparing his hostages is 'killing that man'; the person who complies with the demand, in order to save the lives of the many, cannot deny that he is choosing an act which of itself does nothing but kill.

Sometimes, however, the 'good effects' are really aspects of one-and-the-same act, and can form part of the description of what it is in and of itself. Then we cannot characterize the act as in and of itself *nothing but* damaging to human good. But is it rationally justifiable? Not necessarily; the seventh requirement is not an isolated requirement, and such a choice may flout the second, third, fourth, and fifth requirements. The choice one makes may be a choice one would not make if one were sufficiently detached from one's impulses and one's peculiar project to avoid treating a particular act or project as if it were itself a basic aspect of human well-being; or if one were *creatively* open to all the basic goods and thus careful to adjust his projects so as to minimize their damaging 'side-effects' and to avoid substantial and irreparable harms to persons. The third requirement here provides a convenient test of respect for good: would I (the person acting) have thought the act reasonable had *I* been the person harmed? Considerations such as these are woven into the notion of *directly* choosing against a basic value. And for most practical purposes this seventh requirement can be summarized as: Do not choose directly against a basic value.

For indeed the pattern of our reflections on particular, often tragic, problem situations (*casus*) can be generalized, by lawyers and professional moralists, into 'doctrines' (such as the so-called doctrine of double effect) which press to their limit the implications of such common notions as 'direct/indirect', 'side-effect', 'intention', 'permission', etc. Such doctrines have their use as summary reminders of analogies and differences across a vast range of human affairs, many of which are hard to think straight about, both because of their complexity and because they include such factors as differential 'risks'. But the doctrines of the legal (legislative, judicial, or academic) or moral casuists are not themselves the principles of practical reasonableness— i.e. the 'substantive' principles discussed in Chapter IV and the 'methodological' requirements of reasonableness discussed in this chapter. In many problematic circumstances, the implications of the seventh requirement are clear: such-and-such an action, for all that it has such-and-such desirable expected consequences, is unreasonable. But in many *casus* the characterization of the actions calls for the 'judgment' that wisely good persons have (more or less) and other persons have not (more or less). In abstract discussions, we ought not to expect more precision than the subject-matter will bear. Still, recognition of this need for judgment is not to be confused with sliding into the morass of arbitrariness which we call consequentialism. And recognition of the tragic implications of some circumstances and decisions is not a rational ground for undertaking the heroic but absurd burden self-imposed by consequentialism—the burden of being responsible for 'over-all net good' (cf. notes to VII.4 and VIII.7).

Finally, a note about terminology. The principal bearer of an explicit theory about natural law happens, in our civilization, to have been the Roman Catholic Church. Without committing itself to any explanation of the sort attempted in this chapter and the last, that Church has stringently elaborated the implications of the seventh requirement, as those implications concern the basic values of life (including the procreative transmission of life), truth (including truth in communication), and religion. And it has formulated those implications in strict negative principles such as those declaring wrongful any killing of the innocent, any anti-procreative sexual acts, and lying and blasphemy. (The ecclesiastical formulations are more complex; but that is their gist.) Those strict negative principles have thus become popularly regarded as the distinctive content of natural law doctrine. But in fact, as the term 'natural law' is used both in this book and, it seems to me, in the pronouncements of the Roman Catholic Church, *everything* required by virtue of *any* of the requirements discussed in this chapter is required by natural law. In this use of the term, if *anything* can be said to be required by or contrary to natural law, then *everything* that is morally (i.e. reasonably) required to be done is required (either mediately or immediately: cf. X.7) by natural law, and everything that is reasonably (i.e. morally) required not to be done is contrary to natural law. The seventh requirement of practical reasonableness is no more and no less a 'natural law principle' than any of the other requirements.

V.8   THE REQUIREMENTS OF THE COMMON GOOD

Very many, perhaps even most, of our concrete moral responsibilities, obligations, and duties have their basis in the eighth requirement. We can label this the requirement of favouring and fostering the common good of one's communities. The sense and implications of this requirement are complex and manifold: see especially VI.8, VII.2–5, IX.1, XI.2, XII.2–3.

V.9   FOLLOWING ONE'S CONSCIENCE

The ninth requirement might be regarded as a particular aspect of the seventh (that no basic good may be directly attacked in any act), or even as a summary of all the requirements. But it is quite distinctive. It is the requirement that one should not do what one judges or thinks or 'feels'-all-in-all should not be done. That is to say one must act 'in accordance with one's conscience'.

This chapter has been in effect a reflection on the workings of conscience. If one were by inclination generous, open, fair, and steady in one's love of human good, or if one's milieu happened to have settled on reasonable *mores*, then one would be able, without solemnity, rigmarole, abstract reasoning, or casuistry, to make the particular practical judgments (i.e. judgments of conscience) that reason requires. If one is not so fortunate in one's inclinations or upbringing, then one's conscience will mislead one, unless one strives to be reasonable and is blessed with a pertinacious intelligence alert to the forms of human good yet undeflected by the sophistries which intelligence so readily generates to rationalize indulgence, timeserving, and self-love. (The stringency of these conditions is the permanent ground for the possibility of authority in morals, i.e. of authoritative guidance, by one who meets those conditions, acknowledged willingly by persons of conscience.)

The first theorist to formulate this ninth requirement in all its unconditional strictness seems to have been Thomas Aquinas: if one chooses to do what one judges to be in the last analysis unreasonable, or if one chooses not to do what one judges to be in the last analysis required by reason, then one's choice is unreasonable (wrongful), however erroneous one's judgments of conscience may happen to be. (A *logically* necessary feature of such a situation is, of course, that one is ignorant of one's mistake.)

This dignity of even the mistaken conscience is what is expressed in the ninth requirement. It flows from the fact that practical reasonableness is not simply a mechanism for producing correct judgments, but an aspect of personal full-being, to be respected (like all the other aspects) in every act as well as 'over-all'—whatever the consequences.

V. 10   THE PRODUCT OF THESE REQUIREMENTS: MORALITY

Now we can see why some philosophers have located the essence of 'morality' in the reduction of harm, others in the increase of well-being, some in social harmony, some in universalizability of practical judgment, some in the all-round flourishing of the individual, others in the preservation of freedom and personal authenticity. Each of these has a place in rational choice of commitments, projects, and particular actions. Each, moreover, contributes to the sense, significance, and force of terms such as 'moral', '[morally] ought', and 'right'; not every one of the nine requirements has a direct role in every moral judgment, but some moral judgments do sum up the bearing of each and all of the nine on the questions in hand, and every moral judgment sums up the bearing of one or more of the requirements.

Obligation and related notions come up for discussion later (see XI.1–2, XI.4, XIII.5). Suffice it to say here that each of the requirements can be thought of as a mode of moral obligation or responsibility. For each plays its part in reasonable deciding, by generating arguments of the form (roughly):

(1) harmony of purposes/recognition of goods/absence of arbitrariness between persons/detachment from particular realizations of good/fidelity to commitments/efficiency in the technical sphere/respect in act for every basic value/

community/authenticity in following one's reason...are (all) aspects of the real basic good of freedom and reason;

(2) that harmony of purposes, or..., can in such-and-such circumstances be achieved/done/expressed/etc. only (or best, or more fittingly) by (not) doing act ϕ; so

(3) act ϕ should (not)/must (not)/ought (not) to...be done.

Such a train of practical reasoning is not to be found on the surface of every piece of moral discourse. This chapter and the last have been explorations not of the surface but of the deep structure of practical thinking, more particularly, of moral thought. The requirements of practical reasonableness generate a moral language utilizing and appealing to moral distinctions employed more or less spontaneously. The sources of these distinctions have to be discerned by an effort of reflection which, as the history of philosophy demonstrates, is not too easy.

If, finally, we look back over the complex of basic principles and basic requirements of practical reasonableness, we can see how 'natural' is that diversity of moral opinion which the sceptic makes such play of. It is a diversity which has its source in too exclusive attention to some of the basic value(s) and/or some basic requirement(s), and inattention to others. Sometimes, no doubt, the distortion or deflection is most immediately explicable by reference to an uncritical, unintelligent spontaneity; sometimes, by reference to the bias and oversight induced by conventions of language, social structure, and social practice; and sometimes (and always, perhaps, most radically) by the bias of self-love or of other emotions and inclinations that resist the concern to be simply reasonable.

NOTES

V. 1

Freedom of choice... The notion of freedom of choice, as the matrix in which human responsibility for good is set, first becomes an explicit theme in Christian writings. It is given great prominence by Thomas Aquinas, who opens the part of his *Summa Theologiae* which deals with human action and morality by stating: 'Human beings are made in the image of God, and this implies, as St. John of Damascus said, that they are intelligent and free in judgment and self-mastery. So, having considered both the exemplar of that image, namely God, and the things that proceed by divine power and the will of God, it remains for us now to consider the image itself, i.e. human beings, precisely insofar as each is the source of his or her own actions and has freedom of judgment and power over his or her own works and deeds': *S.T.* I–II, Prologue. For a vindication of the reality of freedom of choice, see J. Boyle, G. Grisez, and O. Tollefsen, *Free Choice: A Self-Referential Argument* (Notre Dame and London: 1976).

Ethics as the reflective account of practical reasonableness. . . There is no clearly settled meaning of 'ethics' in modern philosophical discussion. But there is substantial agreement that one can usefully distinguish between (i) descriptive empirical enquiries about people's moral judgments, (ii) 'moral', 'normative', or (practically) 'critical' questions, for one's own judgment, about what is to be done, and (iii) 'analytical', 'meta-ethical', (theoretically) 'critical' questions about the language and logic used in discourse of the two preceding kinds. Still, 'meta-ethics' cannot well proceed without assuming that some 'normative' judgments are more worthy of attention than others, while normative moral judgment cannot be made with full rationality without critical reflection on itself to clarify its terms and its logic. Hence, there is no good reason to *separate* (ii) from (iii); the classical conjunction of the two, as 'ethics' or 'moral philosophy', was fully justified. For modern discussion, see, e.g., R. M. Hare, 'Ethics' in his *Essays on the Moral Concepts* (London: 1972), 39–40; William K. Frankena, *Ethics* (New Jersey: 2nd edn, 1973), 4–5 (taking 'the more traditional view' that 'ethics' should rightly include both 'meta-ethics' and 'normative ethics').

'Moral principles' are conclusions from primary practical principles. . . In Aquinas's view, most of the Ten Commandments are (a) moral principles, and (b) secondary principles of natural law, *conclusions* drawn from the primary principles by a rational elaboration which most people find easy but which can be perverted by passion and convention: *S.T*.. I–II q. 100 a. 3c ad 1; a. 6c; a. 11c ad 1; cf. also q. 94 a. 5c; a. 6c ad 3; and see note below.

Elaboration of moral principles, and particular moral decisions, both require wisdom that is far from universal. . . see, e.g., *S.T.* I–II q. 100 aa. 1, 3, 11; this wisdom is *prudentia* (*S.T.* II–II q. 47 a. 2c ad 1; aa. 6, 15; and notes to II.3 above). On the folly of the many see *S.T.* I–II q. 9 a. 5 ad 3; q. 14 a. 1 ad 3. On the corruption of practical reasonableness in various cultures and people(s), see *S.T.* I q. 113 a. 1; I–II q. 58 a. 5; q. 94 a. 4; q. 99 a. 2 ad 2; and II.3 above, and 225 n. 28 below.

'The mean'. . . Aristotle's account is circular: right action is action according to right principle (or right reason) (*Nic. Eth.* II.2: 1103b31–32); the criterion of right principle is the mean between the vices of excess and deficiency (*Nic. Eth.* II.2: 1104a12–27; II.6: 1106a25–1107a8); but the mean is itself determined by reference to the practical wisdom of the *phronimos* (as to whom see note below) and (which comes to the same thing) to the right principle (*Nic. Eth.* II.6: 1107a1; VI.1: 1133b20). The importance of this idea of the mean in Aristotle's ethics is often exaggerated.

The 'phronimos' in Aristotle. . . This is the person who has *phronēsis*, practical wisdom, full reasonableness (in the Latin writings, *prudentia*). Such a person *is* the norm of action: *Nic. Eth.* II.6: 1107a1; VI.11: 1143b15. 'Men like Pericles are considered to be *phronimoi* because they have the faculty of discerning what things are good for themselves and for mankind': *Nic. Eth.* VI.5: 1140b8–10. *Phronēsis* is 'a truth-attaining rational quality, concerned with action in relation to things that are good and bad for human beings': *Nic. Eth.* VI.5: 1140b6–8.

Aquinas's notion of 'prudentia'. . . For Aquinas, the virtue *of prudentia* is what enables one to reason well towards choice of commitments, projects, and actions, to apply the most general practical principles concretely, to choose rightly, to find the right mean, to be virtuous, to be a good person: *S.T.* II–II q. 47 aa. 1–7; notes to II.3 above.

The 'spoudaios' in Aristotle. . . The term is often translated 'good man' or 'virtuous person'. But a richer translation is 'mature person' (by contrast with the young and inexperienced who can scarcely, if at all, do ethics: *Nic. Eth.* I.3: 1095a3). It is such a person who judges practical affairs correctly, and 'who *is* the standard and measure [*kanon kai metron*, in Latin *regula et mensura*: Aquinas will take these terms into the heart of his definition of *lex*, law: *S.T.* I–II q. 90, a. 1c] of what is noble [or upright: *kalon*] and pleasant': *Nic. Eth.* III.5: 1113a32. What the *spoudaios* does is done well and properly: I.7: 1098a15. 'Those things are actually valuable and pleasant which appear so to the *spoudaios*': X.6: 1176b26. So the central case of friendship is the friendship of *spoudaioi*, who can reasonably find each other lovable simply as such: IX.9: 1170a13–15; cf. IX.4: 1166a13; and the central case of *the polis* is the *spoudaia polis*: *Pol.* VII.12: 1332a33). See I.4 above, XII.4 below.

Aristotle's notion of 'eudaimonia'... See John M. Cooper, *Reason and Human Good in Aristotle* (Cambridge, Mass., and London: 1975), and note to V.2 on 'rational plans of life'.

'*Physis*' *and* 'natura' *as fullness of being*...See Aristotle, *Meta.* XII.3: 1070a12; V.4: 1015a4–15.

Morality, for Aquinas, is fullness of reasonableness, goodness, and human nature...See especially *S.T.* I–II q. 18 a. 1c; q. 71 a. 2.

The modern notion(s) of morality... 'Morality' and cognate words have connotations and overtones that no single word (or standard set of words) has either in Plato and Aristotle's Greek or in Aquinas's Latin (though for examples of a use similar to the modern, see *S.T.* I–II q. 18; q. 99 a. 2; q. 100). A useful description of aspects of the modern concept is Hart, *Concept of Law*, 163–76 [167–80].

The basic requirements of practical reasonableness...The differentiation and analysis of these requirements is largely the work of Germain Grisez, and marks a major advance in the philosophical analysis of natural law. He calls these guidelines 'modes of obligation' ('Methods of Ethical Inquiry' (1967) 41 *Proc. Amer. Cath. Philosophical Ass.* 160) or 'modes of responsibility' (*Beyond the New Morality: The Responsibilities of Freedom* (Notre Dame and London: 1974), 108–36, 213). His list numbers eight, rather than nine, and differs in some details.

V.2

Rational plans of life...Besides Rawls, *Theory of Justice*, 408–23, see Charles Fried, *An Anatomy of Values: Problems of Personal and Social Choice* (Cambridge, Mass.: 1970), 97–101 (the 'life plan'). Like Grisez, both Rawls and Fried are drawing on Josiah Royce, *The Philosophy of Loyalty* (New York: 1908), 168, who argued that 'a person, an individual self, may be defined as a human life lived according to a plan' (a definition which makes its point by the paradox of metonymy). The term 'plan' has the serious drawback that it suggests, too much, that participation in human fullness and reasonableness is just like pursuit of a definite objective, and that commitments to basic values 'for good' (i.e. with a view to a lifetime, or 'indefinitely') are just like settling on particular concrete projects and taking efficient steps to carry them out. Nevertheless, the idea of a plan of life expresses in modern terms the rational requirement (viz. of an over-all *unity* and harmony of purpose, of an *integration* of commitments, projects, actions, habits, feelings) that the ancients preferred to express in terms of a unity *end*. This notion ('end') has much the same drawbacks as its modern counterpart, 'plan'; hence the constant temptation to treat what is really an 'inclusive end' as if it were a 'dominant end', a temptation which not only Aristotle's interpreters (often) but also Aristotle himself (occasionally) find hard to resist. See J. L. Ackrill, 'Aristotle on *Eudaimonia*' (1975) 60 *Proc. Brit. Acad.* 339, and notes to III.3; and further, notes to V.7 below, concerning 'dominant end' theories. In any event, Cooper, *Reason and Human Good in Aristotle*, 96–7, 121–5, and *passim*, has suggested that in Aristotle *eudaimonia* can be regarded as the effective possession-in-action of a rational over-all plan of life. If the matter were further investigated I think it would emerge that Aristotle's implicit conception of *eudaimonia* is of that condition in which one is (or tends to be: see note below) when one satisfies-in-action not merely this first requirement of practical reasonableness but all nine requirements traced in this chapter.

Unforeseeable contingencies in human life... The subjection of human reasonableness and fulfilment to chance and hazard is emphasized by Aristotle: see Aubenque, *La Prudence chez Aristote* (Paris: 1963), 64–91. Christian, like Stoic, reflection, introduced the notion of providence rejected by Aristotle (but not by Plato: see *Laws* X: 903–4): human affairs are subject to divine *prudentia*, which makes everything contribute to the good of the universe: Aquinas, *S.T.* I q. 22 aa. 1, 2; I–II q. 19 a. 10c; XIII.3 below. But: that 'we *do not know* what God concretely [or in particular] wills' remains a central tenet of Aquinas's theory of natural law: I–II q. 19 a. 10 ad 1; q. 91 a. 3 ad 1; XIII.5 below; so we have to cling to the general principles of reason, the general forms of good, the general structure of our nature: I–II q. 19 a. 10 ad 1 and ad 2. Moreover, on the view of Aquinas (unlike both Aristotle and the Stoics), the good of the universe includes and is in part realized by the good of creatures 'made in God's image', i.e. creatures whose good includes and is realized by their own intelligent creativity and free self-determination: I–II, prol. (quoted in notes to V.1 above). Divine providence, on this view, works itself out through, *inter alia*, human choices that are really free and self-constituting (not merely blind).

Seeing one's life from the imagined standpoint of one's death... So Plato's Socrates teaches that philosophy (which for him is always contemplatively practical) is the practice of dying: *Phaedo* 64a.

V.3

Wealth, reputation, 'opportunity' (power), and pleasure as secondary forms of good... See Aristotle, *Nic. Eth.* I.5; X.1–3; Aquinas, *S.T.* I–II q. 2 aa. 1–6; notes to IV.3 above. Cf. the notes on Rawls's 'primary goods', below.

Rawls's 'thin theory' of good... Good, in this 'thin' sense, is what it is rational for one (*any*one) to want *whatever else* one's preferences, wants, aims, etc. See *Theory of Justice*, 396–407, 433–4.

Rawls's 'primary goods'... These are the goods which 'it is rational to want... whatever else is wanted, since they are in general necessary for the framing and the execution of a rational plan of life', and are 'liberty and opportunity, income and wealth, and above all self-respect': *Theory of Justice*, 433; also 253, 260, 328. Rawls will not permit a theorist of justice to treat real primary goods (in our sense), such as truth, art, culture, religion, or friendship, as having an *intrinsic* value or as being *objective* final ends of human life (see *ibid.*, 419, 527): to do so would be out of line with his 'rejection of the principle of perfection and the acceptance of democracy in the assessment of one another's excellences': *ibid.*, 527.

Rawls on intrinsic goods, excellences, and perfections... Rawls expressly does *not* contend that 'criteria of excellence lack a rational basis from the standpoint of everyday life', and he grants that 'the freedom and well-being of individuals, when measured by the excellence of their activities and works, is vastly different in value' and that 'comparisons of intrinsic value can obviously be made': *Theory of Justice*, 328, 329. But he will not allow such differentiations (e.g. of the intrinsic value of [having] true beliefs and the intrinsic disvalue of [having] false beliefs) to enter at all into the rational determination of the basic principles of justice: see *ibid.*, 327–32.

V.4

The rationality of priority of concern for one's own good... On the proper priority of self-love—a principle that must be understood with precision—see *Nic. Eth.* IX.4: 1166a1–1166b29; *S.T.* II–II q. 26 aa. 3–5; and see VI.1, VI.4, and XIII.5 below.

'Passing by on the other side'... See Luke 10:32. On the 'Good Samaritan' principle in modern societies; see also James Ratcliffe (ed.), *The Good Samaritan and the Law* (New York: 1966).

The Golden Rule... See Tobit 4:16; Matthew 7:12; Luke 6:31. Kelsen's contention (*What is Justice?* (Berkeley: 1957), 16–18) that the Golden Rule is empty overlooks the fact that it is only one amongst (say) nine basic requirements of practical reason, which itself is only one amongst (say) seven basic practical principles. In truth, the Golden Rule is a potent solvent and determinant in moral matters.

The heuristic device of the 'ideal observer'... Plato's formulation is implicit, but central to his thought: both the Myth of the Cave (*Rep.* VII: 514a–521b) and the image of the divine puppet-master whose tug we are to follow (*Laws*, VII: 804b; see XIII.5 below) are to be understood as insisting on the need to raise one's mind's eye to this viewpoint in judging human affairs. For the modern discussion, initiated by David Hume and elaborated by Adam Smith, see e.g. D. D. Raphael, 'The Impartial Spectator' (1972) 58 *Proc. Brit. Acad.* 335.

The 'social contract' as a heuristic device for excluding bias... Rawls is particularly clear that his notion of the Original Position (which includes a requirement that the parties in it agree together, i.e. 'contract', on principles of justice) is a device for excluding bias, for guaranteeing objectivity, and for seeing the whole human situation *sub specie aeternitatis:* see especially *Theory of Justice*, 587; also 516.

V.5

The requirement of reasonable detachment... Epictetus' version of Stoicism (c. AD 100) elevates this requirement to a dominant position: see especially Arrian's *Encheiridion of Epictetus, passim.* For balance, see Josiah Royce, *The Philosophy of Loyalty* (New York: 1908), especially Lecture V, sec. 1.

The requirement of 'commitment'... See Gabriel Marcel (much influenced by Royce), e.g. *Homo Viator* (London: 1951), 125–34, 155–6.

V.6

The rational limitations of cost-benefit analysis... See E. J. Mishan, *Cost-Benefit Analysis: An Introduction* (London: 1971), 108, 307–21.

Problems of utilitarianism or consequentialism... See D. H. Hodgson, *Consequences of Utilitarianism* (Oxford: 1967), chs II–III; Dan W. Brock, 'Recent Work in Utilitarianism' (1973) 10 *Amer. Philosophical Q.* 245; Germain Grisez, 'Against Consequentialism' (1978) 23 *Am. J. Juris.* 21. Notice that what I describe as irrational is consequentialism as a general method in ethics (i.e. in open-ended practical reasoning), and *not* what Neil MacCormick, *Legal Reasoning and Legal Theory* (Oxford: 1978), 105–6 and ch. VI, calls 'consequentialist' reasoning by judges, viz. (to summarize his valuable analysis) (i) examining the *types* of decision which would 'have to be given' in other cases if a certain decision is given in the case before them, and (ii) asking about the acceptability or unacceptability of such 'consequences' of the proposed decision in that case. As MacCormick notes (*ibid.*, 105), 'there is...no reason to assume that [this mode of argument] involves evaluation in terms of a single scale...'. In fact, the evaluation will be by reference to the established commitments of a society.

Consequentialism: irrational and arbitrary, or merely 'unworkable'?... G. J. Warnock, *The Object of Morality* (London: 1971), 28–30, recites some objections to utilitarianism, not explicitly distinguishing 'practical' difficulties of unworkability from problems that go to the very sense (intelligibility) of the utilitarian method. He remarks that objections 'of this sort are not really, I think, all that impressive'. For moral problems *are* difficult. 'And as to the difficulty in comparison and computation of "happinesses", it is at any rate clear that such comparisons do somehow get made...' Warnock thus misses the point; some approximate commensuration of some goods is, of course, possible and commonplace within a 'moral' framework established by commitments, relationships, etc., which have been adopted reasonably-in-terms-of-the-nine-requirements-of-practical-reasonableness; just as some more precise commensuration of costs with benefits is possible in relation to some concrete operational goal. The trouble with utilitarianism is that it offers to replace the nine criteria of practical reasonableness with one that is in truth rationally applicable only in a subordinate, contained element of practical thinking: the recommendation could be called a sort of category mistake.

Critique of 'dominant end' theories of ethics... See Rawls, *Theory of Justice*, 548–60, esp. 554; see also Cooper, *Reason and Human Good in Aristotle*, 94–100.

'Every desire has an equal claim to satisfaction'... See William James, *The Will to Believe* (New York: 1897), 195ff.; Bertrand Russell, *Human Society in Ethics and Politics* (London: 1954), 56–9, 84. For the importation of this view into jurisprudence by Roscoe Pound, see VII.6. In a muted form this view, at least as a methodological postulate, lies at the root of Rawls's *Theory of Justice*. In a more or less straightforward way it underpins most modern versions of utilitarianism and indeed most modern ethics. John Stuart Mill rebelled against Jeremy Bentham's version of it: *Utilitarianism* (1863), ch. 1. But the utilitarian has no choice but to adopt either a strict dominant end theory or a strict equality of desires (or preferences) theory. Hence, Mill's utilitarian criterion is incoherent, as is shown e.g. by Anthony Quinton, *Utilitarian Ethics* (London: 1973), 39–47.

Maximization of good (pleasure) or minimization of evil (pain)?... See the vigorous exploration of the problem by Cicero, *De Finibus*, II. 6–25, esp. 17. For critique of the view that pain and pleasure are commensurable, see Robinson A. Grover, 'The Ranking Assumption' (1974) 4 *Theory and Decision* 277–99.

'Greatest good of the greatest number'... For the logical problems caused by the double superlative, see P. T. Geach, *The Virtues* (Cambridge: 1977), 91–4.

V.7

The seventh requirement... This is clearly and variously formulated in Germain Grisez's works, e.g. (with R. Shaw), *Beyond the New Morality*, ch. 13; *Contraception and the Natural Law* (Milwaukee: 1964), 68–71, 110–14; *Abortion: the Myths, the Realities and the Arguments* (New York: 1970), 318–19. For the classic formulation, see Romans 3:8.

'Intention' and the characterization of action... See Germain Grisez, 'Toward a Consistent Natural-Law Ethics of Killing' (1970) 15 *Am. J. Juris.* 64; J. M. Finnis, 'The Rights and Wrongs of Abortion: A Reply to Judith Thomson' (1973) 2 *Phil. Pub. Aff* 117–45 [*CEJF* III.18] (reprinted in, e.g., Dworkin, *Philosophy of Law* (Oxford: 1977)); H. L. A. Hart, *Punishment and Responsibility* (Oxford: 1968), ch. 5;

G. E. M. Anscombe, 'War and Murder' in W. Stein (ed.), *Nuclear Weapons and Christian Conscience* (London: 1961), 57–9; Charles Fried, 'Right and Wrong—Preliminary Considerations' (1976) 5 *J. Legal Studies* 165–200.

The 'doctrine' of 'double-effect'... See, e.g., J. T. Mangan, 'An Historical Account of the Principle of the Double Effect' (1949) 10 *Theological Studies* 40–61.

'Natural law' in Roman Catholic pronouncements of strict negative principles... A recent example is Vatican Council II's declaration that it is a 'principle of universal natural law' that 'every act of war which tends indiscriminately to the destruction of entire cities or extensive areas along with their population is a crime': Pastoral Constitution *Gaudium et Spes* (1965) 79, 80. As to some of the ecclesiastically recognized implications of the seventh requirement, briefly listed in the text, see J. Finnis, 'Natural Law and Unnatural Acts' (1970) 11 *Heythrop J.* 365; 'The Rights and Wrongs of Abortion: A Reply to Judith Thomson' (1973) 2 *Phil. Pub. Aff.* 117–45 [*CEJF* III.18].

V. 9

Conscience (practical reasonableness) and the obligation to follow it... See Eric D'Arcy, *Conscience and its Right to Freedom* (London: 1961), 76–125. Aquinas's discussion is clear: *S.T.* I–II q. 19 a. 5. It scarcely needs to be added that: (i) if my conscience is erroneous, what I do will be unreasonable; and (ii) if my conscience is erroneous because of my negligence and indifference in forming it, in doing what I do I will be acting culpably (notwithstanding that I am required by the ninth requirement of reasonableness to do it): see *S.T.* I–II q. 19 a. 6; and (iii) that if I am aware that I have formed my practical judgment inadequately it will be reasonable of me to bow to contrary advice or instructions or norms. Of course, it by no means follows (as D'Arcy's own argument too easily assumed) that if, because of this ninth requirement, I have an obligation to ϕ, others have no liberty to prevent me from doing ϕ, or to punish me for doing ϕ; indeed, often enough they have not only the liberty but also an obligation to do so: see X.1.

VI

COMMUNITY, COMMUNITIES, AND COMMON GOOD

VI.1 REASONABLENESS AND SELF-INTEREST

THE previous chapter, on the requirements of reasonable self-constitution, will have aroused misgivings. Certainly the discussion overlooked neither the requirement of impartiality between persons, nor the requirement that basic values be always respected not only in one's own but also in others' participation in them. But are these and all the other requirements really in the service of one's own self, one's own self-constitution, self-realization, self-fulfilment? Rather than expounding morality in terms of the 'practical reason' and 'well-being' of the moral actor, should we not be *contrasting* the requirements of morality with those of rational self-interest?

The preceding sentence plays on the terms 'rational' and 'self-interest'. The ambiguities of 'reason', 'rational', and cognate terms, are well understood. Everyone knows about the rationality, often very finely turned, of mass-murderers or drug-addicts, or of one's own egoistic little schemes; and equally, everyone knows that by shifting one's focus of attention, one can criticize these schemes as arbitrary (though not whimsical), short-sighted (though cunning), unreasonable, and indeed irrational (though not without a certain, sometimes rather overwhelming rationality). But not everyone is so much at ease with 'self-interest', which is sliding away from the dignity of 'self-constitution' towards the moral indignity of 'self-centredness' and 'selfishness'. And does not the analysis of morality as reasonableness in self-constitution overlook the fact that moral responsibilities can require one to sacrifice not merely one's selfishness, and one's self-interest, but even, on occasion, *oneself*?

This chapter undertakes a fuller analysis of the proper relationship between one's own well-being and the well-being of others. It does not complete that analysis, even in outline. The question just raised, about the reasonableness of self-sacrifice, and the related question whether the effort to be reasonable is in the end just a pursuit of self-perfection, are questions to be tackled and resolved only in Chapter XIII. Conversely, the present chapter's exploration of the network of overlapping relationships in which and for which all individual lives are to be lived is an indispensable foundation for all the subsequent explorations of justice, rights, authority, law, and obligation—explorations of practical reasonableness which finally demand the venture of speculative reason undertaken in Chapter XIII.

VI.2   TYPES OF UNIFYING RELATIONSHIP

Who has not noticed the peculiar vagueness of the term 'social'? Who has not felt slightly baffled about the 'communities', and 'societies', which are spoken of sometimes as (lots of) individuals, sometimes as if they were themselves individuals with interests, well-being, etc., and sometimes as extremely abstract 'systems' (of what?)? Little progress can be made by talking about social life, social responsibilities, social rules, etc., until what it is to be involved in community is quite particularly and concretely understood.

Two preliminary remarks may be made. First: what is here said of 'community' might equally be said of 'society'. The two words have slightly different ranges and flavours in ordinary usage; but the differences themselves differ from one European language to another, and there seems no advantage in following here the fashion, initiated by Tönnies, of appropriating the two words to signify extremes or poles in the range of forms of human community/society/friendship which we are about to study. The second preliminary point is that it is helpful to begin by thinking of community or association not as *a* community or *an* association (an 'entity' or 'substance' or 'thing' which 'exists', acts, etc.) but rather as community or association, an ongoing state of affairs, a sharing of life or of action or of interests, an associating or coming-together. Community in this sense is a matter of relationship and interaction. So, in the title of this chapter, I distinguish between community and communities; and in the development of the chapter the discussion of what it is to say that communities (groups...) *exist* is left to section VI.7.

Whatever else it is, community is a form of unifying relationship between human beings. Now such relationships in part are, and in part are not, the outcome of human intelligence, practical reasonableness, and effort. We can indeed identify four basic ways in which human understanding stands to unifying relationships, and can show that human community involves relationships in all four 'orders'. ('Order' means simply a set of unifying relationships.) My purpose in referring to these four orders is not metaphysical or epistemological; still less is it to suggest some hierarchy of value or importance. It is to give some concreteness to our discussion of human community by assembling conveniently some reminders of the complexity of human community. This complexity is often lost sight of by those who attempt to explain one order of reality using exclusively techniques of analysis suitable for another order (i.e. who try to reduce one order to another). When we are considering the connection between the basic principles of practical reasonableness and the intelligible order and existence of reality as a whole, it will be useful to recall these reminders of the ordered complexity of things (including human affairs): see XIII.2.

There is first the order which we can understand but which we do not ourselves bring about: the order which is studied by the 'natural sciences'. A simple example of this order is the unifying relationship that exists between lecturer and listeners when the listeners *hear the sounds* made by the lecturer's vocal chords; the interrelated movements of vocal chords, sound waves, air, eardrums, etc. are subjects for natural scientific study. Part of our unity in human community, then, is physical and biological. An aspect of human community is the genetic unity of the race: human beings can (and have the physical and psychological urge to) interbreed with each other and not with other animals. A family has a special physical unity of close genetic interrelationship, sexual intercourse between parents, the feeding of the unborn infant children from their mother's body, a certain degree of compatibility of blood groups and tissues, inherited similarities of physique and perhaps of feeling, temperament, intelligence...

Secondly, there is the unity or order which we can bring into our understanding itself: the order which is studied reflectively in logic, epistemology, methodology, and similar disciplines, and which is manifested more straightforwardly in the internal coherence of each body of knowledge, each field of discourse. A simple example of this order is the relationship that exists between lecturer and listeners when the listeners *hear expositions, arguments, and explanations*; the listeners bring their understanding into line with the lecturer's even if only to the degree needed to disagree with the lecturer's views. (In order to disagree with each other, we must each be thinking of the same proposition.) Part of our unity in human community, then, is unity of intelligence in its capacities, its workings, and its product, knowledge. Thus, for example, we can speak of 'what science has established', notwithstanding that no one person knows all science (or even all of 'a science'). A family can have a special unity in this order of relationships, inasmuch as its members think and learn together, acquiring a common fund of experience and insight, and even knowing how much the others know...

Thirdly, there is the unity or order which we bring into, or impose upon, whatever matter is subject to our powers. This order is studied in the arts (such as cooking, shipbuilding, sailing), in technology and all the applied sciences, but also in studies of human symbol-making (such as linguistics, and even some aspects of literary criticism). A simple example of this order is the relationship that exists between lecturer and listeners when the listeners *hear the English language* and a pedagogical technique; the listeners share with the lecturer in making and decoding the formalized symbols of a language and the less formalized symbols, signs, and expressions (e.g. gestures and smiles) which, by pedagogical or rhetorical art, can be made the bearers of meanings. Part of our unity in human community, then, is the cultural unity of shared language, common technology, common technique (as in an orchestra), a common capital stock, and so on. A family can have a special unity in this order of relationships, inasmuch as its members share not only house and property and possessions but also a range of especially subtle modes of communication with one another...

Fourthly, there is the unity or order which we bring into our own actions and dispositions by intelligently deliberating and choosing: the order which is studied in one way by psychology (in one of its branches), in another way by biography and the history of human affairs, and in another way by ethics, political philosophy, and the like. A simple example of this order is the relationship that exists between lecturer and listeners when the listeners *hear the lecturer*, as a person and a teacher; the listeners share with the lecturer in making self-constituting decisions; the lecturer's decision is to devote part of his or her life to trying to communicate knowledge to another person (perhaps for the sake of truth and a kind of friendship, perhaps only to earn a living), while the listeners' decisions are to commit part of their own lifetimes to trying to acquire knowledge from another person (perhaps for the sake of truth, perhaps only to gain a qualification which in turn will enable him to...). Part of our unity in human community, then, is the unity of common action. A family can have a special unity in this order of relationships, inasmuch as each of its members (especially the one(s) directing and shaping the common life) is devoted to finding his or her own self-fulfilment (at least in part) in helping the other members to fulfil themselves, by caring for them and helping them to grow in freedom and responsibility and other basic aspects of human flourishing.

Obviously, human community as we are concerned with it in this book's exploration of practical reasonableness is primarily a matter of community in the fourth order. Some degree of unity of the other three sorts is clearly needed if there is to be the community of joint action or of mutual commitment to the pursuit of some common good. But no degree of unity in those other three orders can substitute for such co-operation and common commitment; the most united family can just fall apart. So in the following section we consider more closely the main types of co-ordination of action. Throughout the analysis, 'collaboration', 'co-operation', and 'co-ordination' are used more or less synonymously and are to be understood without the flavour of effort or formality that they often have in ordinary usage. Where I refer to 'negative co-ordination' I mean mutual non-interference (e.g. abstaining from assault, theft, etc.); and 'co-ordination' without qualification is normally to be taken as including this negative co-ordination. Much of the analysis is in terms of two individuals; this is merely for the sake of simplicity and can be understood as 'two or more'.

VI.3   'BUSINESS' COMMUNITY AND 'PLAY' COMMUNITY

Consider first the pursuit, by each of two individuals, of some particular objective which each has in view, and which each can attain only by collaborating or at least co-ordinating with the other. For example, A wants to learn what tutor X has to say about 'natural law', and so does B. Tutor X gives tutorials only to pairs of students. So A and B must collaborate with each other to some (rather minimal) degree, co-ordinating their arrival, settling on the tutor's chairs without fighting, abstaining from incessant interruptions of each other, and so on. Each may be entirely indifferent to the other's success in pursuing the objective; indeed, their projects may to some degree conflict: they may be competing with each other for a prize or a position. But each has an interest in the maintenance of the ensemble of conditions (e.g. quiet, fresh air in the room, holding the tutor's attention to the subject, etc.) for successful pursuit of his or her own objective; and since that pursuit is required (by the tutor) to be co-ordinated, the interest of A and B in that ensemble of conditions can be said to be a common interest; and the ensemble of conditions, being a state of affairs which A and B each consider worth maintaining as a means to that personal objective, can be said to be a good common to A and B, a common good; and A's and B's pursuit (their effort and care to maintain that ensemble of conditions) can be said, notwithstanding the indifference of each to the other's objective, to be a common pursuit (common effort, care, etc.).

The relationship between A and B, here, is one of collaboration or co-ordination without contract. The relationships between A and X, and B and X are, on the other hand, contractual (in form, if not in legal effect). A wants to learn something and X wants (say) to earn a living; each, in order to attain his or her *own* objective, can agree to assist the other to attain *the other's* objective, but the condition of such assistance is that it shall be reciprocal: A will pay X if and only if X will teach, and X will teach if and only if A will pay. The performance of the contract between A and X (and, likewise, between B and X) thus becomes a common interest, a common pursuit, a common good, for A and X (and B and X), notwithstanding that A and X, apart from the contract, may have no interest in each other's objective, and notwithstanding that the reciprocity of interest between A and X is significantly different from the likeness of interest between A and B.

Aristotle classed all such relationships between A and B, A and X, and B and X, as relationships of utility. In such relationships there is some common interest, some common good and some common (co-ordinated) action—but all in the service of each attaining his or her own objective. The objective of each remains individual and private, not only in the sense that the success of other parties in attaining their objectives is a matter of indifference to each party (save to the extent, if any, that such success assists him or her to attain personal success), but also in the sense that the co-ordination of action is not valued by any party as a component or aspect of that party's objective.

This last-mentioned feature of business or 'utility' relationships serves to distinguish them from relationships in which the co-ordination of action is what the parties value, i.e. *is* the objective (or a substantial component of the objective) of each of the parties. Aristotle named this class of relationships relationships of 'pleasure', and we can see what he was getting at: we engage in these relationships 'for fun'. But a better name would be relationships *of play*. For, as we saw in IV.2, the central feature and good of play is that the activity or performance is valued by the participants for its own sake, and is itself the source of their pleasure or satisfaction. (We ought here to understand 'participant' in a broad sense: the audience at an entertainment are really 'part of the game', as is shown by the interest that both entertainers and audience have in the quality of audience reaction.)

The common good in play relationships is, thus, that there be a 'good play of the game' (in a broad sense of 'game'). Beyond that, neither of the participants need have any interest in the other participant, even when, as in *some* games or play relationships (e.g. swopping jokes), one party's evincing pleasure or satisfaction is a necessary condition of the other party's finding the game satisfying.

Thus, the community of action and interest that exists between business associates (in the broad sense that includes workmates, partners, and contracting parties), and between play-partners, is to be distinguished from the community of action and interest that exists between *friends* in the full sense. Aristotle thought that the three sorts of community of action and interest are sufficiently similar to warrant applying a common name to all these relationships, which he therefore called three sorts of *philia*. And he was willing to analyse types of constitutional order in terms of these types of *philia*. But he was, of course, insistent that what we call friendship in the full sense is the central case of *philia*.

VI.4   FRIENDSHIP

If A and B are friends, then the collaboration of each is for the sake (at least in part) *of the other*, and there is community between them not only in that there is a common interest in the conditions, and common pursuit of the means, whereby each will get what he wants for himself, but also in that what A wants for himself he wants (at least in part) under the description 'that-which-B-wants-for-himself', and vice versa. Indeed, the good that is common between friends is not simply the good of successful collaboration or co-ordination, nor is it simply the good of two successfully achieved coinciding projects or objectives; it is the common good of mutual self-constitution, self-fulfilment, self-realization.

The preceding paragraph was very summary, indeed rapid. Since our understanding of the significance of community for individual well-being and practical reasonableness will hardly be complete if only half-hearted forms of community remain in the foreground of our analysis, we need a clear and precise understanding of the most intense form of community, the friendship of true friends. This is more often treated as a matter for sentimental appreciation than for clear and precise analysis. But certainly there is no possibility of understanding the classical tradition of 'natural law' theorizing, or my own later explorations of obligation, without first appropriating the analysis of friendship in its full sense. Perhaps you or I have no real friends, in this full sense? But we can see the good of real friendships, in the lives perhaps of some of our acquaintances, and in our aspirations, or as reflected in our language, poetry, tragedy...And in real life, outside the confines of our reflections, the boundaries between business, play, and full friendship are not too clear. Many relationships initiated merely for business and private need or advantage, or for play and individual pleasure, ripen into relationships of more or less intense friendship. Conversely, friendships can readily degenerate into mutual exploitation.

In the fullest sense of 'friendship', A is the friend of B when (i) A acts (or is willing to act) for B's well-being, for the sake of B, while (ii) B acts (or is willing to act) for A's well-being, for the sake of A, (iii) each of them knows of the other's activity and willingness and of the other's knowledge, and (iv) each of them co-ordinates (at least some of) his or her activity with the activity (including acts of friendship) of the other so that there is a sharing, community, mutuality, and reciprocity not only of knowledge but also of activity (and thus, normally, of enjoyment and satisfaction). And when we say that A and B act for the sake of each other, we mean that the concern of each for the other is founded, not in devotion to some principle according to which the other (as a member of a class picked out by that principle) is entitled to concern, but in regard or affection for that individual person as such.

The core of friendship is the following dialectic:

(1) Having a friend is a basic form of good. That is to say, for one (anyone) to have a friend is a basic aspect of one's well-being. One can scarcely think of oneself as really well-off if one has no friends. The intrinsic value of having a true friend does not consist precisely in the services the friend may render one (though they may be valuable), nor precisely in the pleasure the friend may give one (though who would not welcome that?), but in the state of affairs itself that we call friendship. That state of affairs itself is the source of the deep satisfaction which normally accompanies it and which is a manifestation of the intrinsic value of the state of affairs.

(2) But if one treats one's relationship with one's friend as being for one's own sake, then the relationship will not be one of friendship and the benefits (if any) that one derives from it will not include the benefit of real friendship. For one to be one's friend's friend, one must

act (at least in substantial part) for the sake of one's friend's well-being, and must value the friend's well-being for the sake of the friend. One must treat one's friend's well-being as an aspect of one's own well-being.

(3) On the other hand, what is said in steps (1) and (2) is true equally of one's friend. That is to say: (1′) for B to be a friend of A is a constitutive element in B's well-being, and requires (2′) that B value A's well-being for the sake of A, and treat A's well-being as an aspect of B's own well-being. It follows that A must value A's own well-being for the sake of B, while B must value B's own well-being for the sake of A. And so on. The reciprocity of love does not come to rest at either pole.

Thus, self-love (the desire to participate fully, oneself, in the basic aspects of human flourishing) requires that one go beyond self-love (self-interest, self-preference, the imperfect rationality of egoism . . .). This requirement is not only in its content a component of the requirement of practical reasonableness; in its form, too, it is a parallel or analogue, for the requirement in both cases is that one's inclinations to self-preference be subject to a critique in thought and a subordination in deed. The demands of friendship thus can powerfully reinforce the other demands of practical reasonableness, not least the demands of impartiality as between persons (though it is obvious that friendship complicates those demands and can, if unmeasured, compete with and distort them).

Just as the unknown time of one's prospective death is, in thought, a vantage point from which to distinguish some reasonable alternative plans of life, so friendship establishes an analogous vantage point. In friendship one is not thinking and choosing 'from one's own point of view', nor from one's friend's point of view. Rather, one is acting from a third point of view, the unique perspective from which one's own good and one's friend's good are equally 'in view' and 'in play'. Thus, the heuristic postulate of the impartially benevolent 'ideal observer', as a device for ensuring impartiality or fairness in practical reasoning, is simply an extension of what comes naturally to friends.

Finally, to return to the analysis of community, we can say that friendship is the most communal though not the most extended or elaborated form of human community. There is community in a full sense when (i) A makes B's well-being and self-constituting participation in human goods one of A's own self-constituting commitments, and (ii) B makes A's well-being likewise one of B's own basic commitments, and (iii) A and B collaborate in pursuance of these commitments. ('Commitment' does not here refer to contracts or agreements, but to commitment in the sense that one as, say, a scholar commits oneself to scholarship; some, but by no means all, commitments to the well-being of another person or persons are expressed by bilateral agreement or unilateral promise or vow.)

VI.5 'COMMUNISM' AND 'SUBSIDIARITY'

Plato proposed a sharing of women and children, and of goods and possessions, throughout the political community (*polis*). And in every age, enthusiasm for community, for the widest sharing in friendship, has inspired the dream of a 'state of nature' (a golden age in the past, a Utopia beyond the seas, or a millennial realm of the future) in which sexual partners, and their offspring, and the whole stock of land and chattels and everything else contributing to the material matrix of human life, all would be held in common, so that no one could treat any of them as 'mine and not thine'.

So Aristotle had to begin his *Politics* with some reminders. Friendship is nothing if it is not willing the good of one's friend, committing oneself to helping in one's friend's self-constituting participation in any or all of the basic aspects of human flourishing. In the first place, then, there will be no friendship if there is no commitment, and to commit oneself is, in this finite life, to turn aside from an inexhaustible multitude of alternative commitments that one might have made. In the second place, one can give nothing to a friend unless one has something of one's own to give. One cannot even have the friend to dinner if one has no food save one's own ration. You say, let the friend come with food, it is the sharing that counts. But what am I sharing? *My* shelter, warmth, living-space. You say, have dinner together in the communal eating place. But still I have to give the friend *my* company, my attention and interest, which I thereby deny to someone else. In the third place, much that I have to give can only be given to a few and can only be fully given to a few who are specified by a relationship to me that is intrinsically permanent (e.g. genetic) or deliberately made quasi-permanent. A woman can give her maternal affection only to a child that is hers (or that she can treat as hers). Only a family or quasi-family can build up over time that common stock—of uncalculated affection, physical and psychological rapport, of shelter and means of support and material bases for new projects, of memories and experience, of symbols, signs, and gestures to bear moods and meanings, of knowledge of each other's strengths and weaknesses, loves and detestations, and of formal and informal but reliable commitment and devotion—which each member holds at the others' disposal, and which, being rich in all four orders of reality, constitutes an incomparably fine thing for a friend to give or to receive. To cut the whole matter short, we must bluntly say that Plato's proposal, made in the name of friendship, is tantamount to a drastic dilution, 'watering-down',[1] of friendship—a radical emaciation of a basic aspect of human well-being. (Notice that none of this argument goes to the justice of common or private ownership of property; this is considered in the next chapter, at VII.3.)

Still, as Aristotle also points out, if the family is thus to contribute to this growth of its members in freedom, friendship, and all-round good, it must be liberated from the requirement of unremitting toil by all its members for material necessities. Things will be better for everyone if there is a division of labour between families, specialization, technology, joint or co-operative enterprises in production and marketing, a market and a medium of exchange, in short, an economy that is more than domestic. And the same goes for the other goods participated in by the family. The resources not only of material goods and of technology, but also of language, of knowledge, of aesthetic experience, of interpersonal concern and religious aspiration, are all more ample than any family can mediate to its members by itself. Hence, the members of a family will flourish more fully if, without dissolving their family, they enter into a whole network of associations with their neighbours. Aristotle speaks of this level of associations as essentially the

---

[1] Aristotle, *Pol.* II.1: 1262b17.

community of neighbourhood. But neighbourhood, we must add, need not be merely geographical.

To Aristotle's whole analysis of this vastly ramified level of forms of community intermediate between the family and the political community, we must also add that just as the dissolution of family and property would water down human friendship, so the complete absorption by the family of its members would radically emaciate their personal freedom and authenticity, which also are basic aspects of human full-being. One who treats his or her spouse as a sheer possession, or who, when his or her children have been nurtured to the threshold of maturity, seeks to make those children's basic commitments for them, robs that spouse or those children of a basic good, just as surely as Plato's republic would rob its members of another basic good. In face of the perennial dream of a general communism in friendship, the justification for the family, for its contractual or quasi-contractual permanence and exclusiveness, for its possessiveness and its possessions, is a justification which holds good only to the extent that each member of the family is enabled to grow in self-possession (of which self-giving in friendship is one basic aspect).

To say this is to formulate, in relation to the family, a principle which in fact holds good for all other forms of human community (though only in a modified form for full friendship itself). Some recent political thinkers have given this principle the name 'subsidiarity', and this name will be convenient provided we note that it signifies not secondariness or subordination, but assistance; the Latin for help or assistance is *subsidium*. As we shall see (VII.3), the principle is one of justice. It affirms that the proper function of association is to help the participants in the association to help themselves or, more precisely, to constitute themselves through the individual initiatives of choosing commitments (including commitments to friendship and other forms of association) and of realizing these commitments through personal inventiveness and effort in projects (many of which will, of course, be co-operative in execution and even communal in purpose). And since in large organizations the process of decision-making is more remote from the initiative of most of those many members who will carry out the decision, the same principle requires that larger associations should not assume functions which can be performed efficiently by smaller associations.

What is the source of this principle? I touched on it when I discussed the 'experience machine': see IV.5. Human good requires not only that one *receive* and *experience* benefits or desirable states; it requires that one *do* certain things, that one should *act*, with integrity and authenticity; if one can obtain the desirable objects and experiences through one's own action, so much the better. Only in action (in the broad sense that includes the investigation and contemplation of truth) does one fully participate in human goods. One cannot—no one can—spend all one's time, in all one's associations, leading and taking initiatives; but anyone who is never more than a cog in big wheels turned by others is denied participation in an important aspect of human well-being.

VI.6   COMPLETE COMMUNITY

Family is a very thoroughgoing form of association, controlling or influencing every corner of the lives of its members for a considerable proportion of their lifetime. But it is incomplete and inadequate. Indeed, it cannot even properly provide for the unimpaired transmission of its own genetic basis; a family that breeds within itself is headed for physical self-destruction. And its weakness as an economic unit, capable of supporting the health and culture of its members, has already been mentioned and needs no elaboration here. Economic, cultural, and sporting associations, in turn, are more or less explicitly specialized in their concerns. And as for friendship in its full sense, if the friendship of husband and wife is an incomplete basis for ample well-being, so is any other. So there emerges the desirability of a 'complete community', an all-round association in which would be co-ordinated the initiatives and activities of individuals, of families, and of the vast network of intermediate associations. The point of this all-round association would be to secure the whole ensemble of material and other conditions, including forms of collaboration, that tend to favour, facilitate, and foster the realization by each individual of his or her personal development. (Remember: this personal development includes, as an integral element and not merely as a means or precondition, both individual self-direction and community with others in family, friendship, work, and play.)

Such an ensemble of conditions includes some co-ordination (at least the negative co-ordination of establishing restraints against interferences) of any and every individual life-plan and any and every form of association. So there is no aspect of human affairs that is outside the range of such a complete community. Aristotle, by a premature generalization from incomplete empirical data, declared that the Greek *polis* was the paradigmatic form of complete and self-sufficient community for securing the all-round good of its members. So the form of community that today claims to be complete and self-sufficient, the territorial state, retains the label 'political community' or 'body politic'; for though it does not fit Aristotle's descriptions of paradigmatic forms of *polis*, it claims the all-embracing function which Aristotle (after Plato) ascribed to the *polis*. There can be 'parish pump politics', 'College politics', and so on; but 'politics' without qualification signifies the field of action and discourse to do with the affairs of complete communities.

Nor is 'politics' the only term whose focal meaning concerns complete community. 'Law' is another such term. We can certainly speak intelligibly and usefully of the law of some lesser group, even of a gang. But, as the common understanding of the unqualified expressions 'law' and 'the law' indicates, the central case of law and legal system is the law and legal system of a complete community. That is why it is characteristic of legal systems that: (i) they claim authority to regulate all forms of human behaviour (a claim which in the hands of the lawyer becomes the artificial postulate that legal systems are gapless); (ii) they therefore claim to be the supreme authority for their respective community, and to regulate the conditions under which the members of that community can participate in any other normative system or association; (iii) they characteristically purport to 'adopt' rules and normative arrangements (e.g. contracts) from other associations within and without the complete community, thereby 'giving them legal force' for that community; they thus maintain the notion of completeness and supremacy without pretending to be either the only association to which their members may reasonably belong or the only complete community with whom their members may have dealings, and without striving to foresee and provide substantively for every activity and arrangement in which their members may wish to engage.

All these defining features, devices, and postulates of law have their foundation, from the viewpoint of practical reasonableness, in the requirement that the activities of individuals, families, and specialized associations be co-ordinated. This requirement itself derives partly from the requirements of impartiality as between persons, and of impartiality as between the basic values and openness to all of them, given certain facts about the ensemble of empirical conditions under which basic goods such as health, education, science, and art can be realized, and realized in the lives of each person according to the measure of his or her own inclinations and capacities. I shall have more to say of this when I explicitly turn to study justice: see VII.1, VII.3.

Suffice it for the moment to say that, like other forms of community, political community exists partially (and sometimes primarily) as a kind of business arrangement between self-interested associates (the kind of mutual insurance association or 'social contract' derided by Aristotle and all the classics for its meagreness as a form [or account] of community); partially (and sometimes primarily) as a form of play, in which the participants enjoy the give-and-take, the dissension, bargaining, and compromise, for its own sake as a vastly complex and absorbing performance; partially (and sometimes primarily) as an expression of disinterested benevolence, reinforced by grateful recognition of what one owes to the community in which one has been brought up and in which one finds and founds one's family and one's life-plan, and further reinforced by a determination not to be a 'free rider' who arbitrarily seeks to retain the benefits without accepting the burdens of communal interdependence; and characteristically by some admixture of all these rationales.

But we must not take the pretensions of the modern state at face value. Its legal claims are founded, as I remarked, on its self-interpretation as a complete and self-sufficient community. But there are relationships between persons which transcend the boundaries of all *poleis*, realms, or states. These relationships exist willy-nilly, in manifold and multiplying ways, in three of the four orders: for there is physical, biological, ecological interdependence, there is a vast common stock of knowledge (including knowledge of each other's existence, concerns, and conditions), and there is a vast common stock of technology, systems of intercommunication, ideological symbolisms, universal religions... Thus, there is no reason to deny the good of international community in the fourth order, the order of reciprocal interactions, mutual commitments, collaboration, friendship, competition, rivalry... If it now appears that the good of individuals can only be fully secured and realized in the context of international community, we must conclude that the claim of the national state to be a complete community is unwarranted and the postulate of the national legal order, that it is supreme and comprehensive and an exclusive source of legal obligation, is increasingly what lawyers would call a 'legal fiction'.

VI.7   THE EXISTENCE OF A COMMUNITY

Thus far I have been speaking about the rationale(s) of community or association, as forms of relationship. It is now time to explain what is meant by saying that *a* community, or *an* association, exists, or acts, or has members or rules that belong to it. It will be convenient to frame this explanation in terms of 'a group', since that word lacks the ambiguity of 'community' and 'association' to which I have referred. In common usage, however, 'group' has some distracting connotations. So what I now have to say about groups applies as well to two-member teams, couples, or pairs (which are not usually called groups), but is not intended to apply to any group in the sense of a mere aggregation, i.e. a class whose members have something important in common, but which is not spoken of as acting, and in and for which there is no authority (e.g. the group comprised of all English-speakers, or all aunts; or perhaps such groups as a rush-hour crowd).

   In solving the obvious mystery about what it means to say that a group exists, many modern thinkers hoped to be able to do without reference to the practical reasoning ('internal attitudes') of its members. Thus, for A, B, and C to constitute a group, it was said to be sufficient that, over a given period of time, A interacts with B and C *more often* than with P, Q, and R (who are outsiders or members of other groups), while B similarly interacts more often with A and C than with outsiders, and so on.[2] But this analysis will not do. Suppose that (i) in the library A has more interactions with B than with any other reader while B has more interactions with A than with any other reader, and (ii) in the tavern A sees more of C than of anyone else, while C sees more of A there than of anyone else, and (iii) at the sports ground B plays more often with C, and C more often with B, than either of them plays with anyone else. Yet C never goes to the library, B never goes to the tavern, and A has no interest in sport. A, B, and C then may interact more often with one another than with anyone else. But why should they be called a group?

When the inadequacy of simply counting interactions became apparent, an attempt was made to rescue the behaviouristic analytical strategy by stipulating that, to constitute a group, the persons in question must interact with one another more than they interact with anyone else, *in a given context*.[3] But what constitutes a different context? Obviously, it cannot be merely geographical location. Members of a family, or of a secret police service, may be scattered all over the world; or the circus may be simply on the move. Consider the employee, E, who opens and shuts a factory gate for incoming and outgoing lorries of independent contractors who bring supplies for the factory through that gate. E may interact with lorry drivers, or even with particular lorry drivers, more frequently than with other employees or with the management; indeed, E may interact almost exclusively with the lorry drivers at the gate. Yet E is a member of the factory business, and conversely there is no point in talking of a group comprising E and those outside lorry drivers. What makes E a member of the factory business? It is that E's *purpose* in being there, opening and shutting the gate, is to work for the business (to increase its profits, or to earn a wage, or both); E is therefore prepared to adjust his or her conduct to the needs of the factory, as E perceives

---

[2] See G. C. Homans, *The Human Group* (London: 1951), 84; he adds: 'It is possible just by counting interactions to map out a group quantitatively distinct from others'.

[3] See, e.g., W. J. H. Sprott, *Human Groups* (Harmondsworth: 1958), 9.

them (e.g. if E sees it catch fire) or as the factory management directs. Though E's purposes or aims and those of the lorry drivers are (normally) co-ordinated, they are not shared; they are tangential or coincidental aims. Conversely, E and the lorry drivers become a group as soon as they begin to share an aim; if E conspires with them, even by a nod and a wink, to open the gates to let them burgle the factory and make a get-away, then E has teamed up with them, even if only temporarily, and is acting as an associate of their gang...

In short, sharing of aim rather than multiplicity of interaction is constitutive of human groups, communities, societies.[4] (This is fortunate for our understanding of human groups; for if we take no account of the practical reasonings of the actors, which allow us to individuate *actions*, there is in fact no way of individuating *interactions* other than by *ad hoc* stipulation. How many interactions are there between lecturer and audience in an hour?) Outside the 'given context' of a sharing (i.e. in the active sense, community) of purpose, interactions have no significance as constitutive of a group. This remains the case even when the purpose in view is materially identical with the interaction or shared activity, as is the case with games and all forms of play (the shared objective being a good play of the game). Interactions between persons may be unilateral (as where A's act is intended to and does prompt B's) or reciprocal (as where A's act prompts B's and B's prompts A's). No doubt reciprocal interactions are apt to constitute a sustained group existence. But far more important than the form of inter-action is the shared purpose of A and B that their activities be co-ordinated, either for the sake of the co-ordinated interaction itself (as in a game) or for the sake of some further shared objective. (To see the importance of this shared intention to co-ordinate or co-operate, in the constituting of a group, consider the reciprocal interactions of the submarine commander and the destroyer cap-tain who is hunting the submarine down, or of the evasive witness and cross-examining counsel.)

Notice that in this section we have been considering what would be said by people of common sense—historians, sociologists, and the like; we are not considering the quite different problem

---

[4] Despite his initial definition, Sprott concedes that a group, in his sense, only exists when it has a 'purpose collectively pursued': *ibid.*, 11.

of analysing and accounting for settled rules or propositions of law which ascribe existence, rights, liabilities, etc., to corporations, funds, idols, or other 'legal persons' or legal institutions. On the other hand, my analysis of the existence of a group can be relevant when the question is not how such rules are to be analysed, but is whether such rules *should* be extended to such-and-such an alleged group, or conversely whether the protection of such rules *should* be removed by 'lifting the veil' of legal personality to disclose the 'real' group or individuals who *ought* to be held responsible for certain actions or states of affairs.

To summarize: a group, in the relevant sense, whether team, club, society, enterprise, corporation, or community, is to be said to exist wherever there is, over an appreciable span of time, a co-ordination of activity by a number of persons, in the form of interactions, and with a view to a shared objective.

If we ask why common sense tends to require co-ordination over some space of time before being willing to speak of a group existing, the answer is not far to seek. The more the co-ordination of the relevant persons is pursuant to some value or open-ended commitment, or, if directed to some definite and fully realizable project, is nevertheless controlled by concern for some value(s) that require(s) adaptation of the co-ordination in response to contingencies, the more likely we are to be willing to think of the participants as constituting a group; and, as we shall see, the more likely it is that the participants themselves will think of themselves as a group, and look about for practices, usages, conventions, or 'norms' for solving their co-ordination problems, and/or for someone with authority to select among available solutions. Such norms will then be thought of as norms *of* and *for* the group, and the leader(s) will be thought of as having authority *in* and *over* the group. The 'existence' of the group, the 'existence' of social rules, and the 'existence' of authority tend to go together. And what makes sense of these ascriptions of existence is in each case the presence of some more or less shared objective or, more precisely, some shared conception of the point of continuing co-operation. This point we may call the common good.

VI.8   THE COMMON GOOD

Confronted by the term 'the common good', one is first inclined to think of the utilitarian 'greatest good of the greatest number'. When one is persuaded that, outside limited technical contexts, that notion is not merely practically unworkable but intrinsically incoherent and senseless (see V.6), one is inclined to think that reference to the common good must inevitably be empty. But if readers look back at the uses of the term in earlier sections of this chapter, they will see that it need not be vacuous. In the case of the pair of students (VI.3), their common good (some conception of which could guide their co-ordination of actions) was the ensemble of conditions which would enable each to pursue his or her own objective. In the case of a game (VI.3), the common good for the participants was that there should be a good play of the game, which requires not only a substratum of material conditions but also a certain quality (rule-conformity, sportsman-ship, etc.) in the co-ordination itself. In the case of friendship (VI.4), the common good was identified as the self-fulfilment of each of the friends through the sharing of life and affection and activity and material goods (which of course also requires the maintenance of a certain ensemble of material conditions, for intercommunication, etc.). Finally, in the case of political commu-nity (VI.6), the point or common good of such an all-round association was said to be the securing of a whole ensemble of material and other conditions that tend to favour the realization, by each individual in the community, of his or her personal development. In each case, therefore, 'the common good' referred to the factor or set of factors (whether a value, a concrete operational objective, or the conditions for realizing a value or attaining an objective) which, as considerations in someone's practical reasoning, would make sense of or give reason for that individual's collaboration with others and would likewise, from their point of view, give reason for their collaboration with each other and with that individual.

The classical analogy of the 'ship of state', i.e. between governing a political community and navigating a ship, though it is by no means as unwarranted as many have claimed, is indeed misleading in one important respect. Since passengers normally board ships because they wish to get to an advertised destination (or to some set of ports of call), the analogy suggests that the political community, too, has some definite and completely attainable objective. But here, as so often, we must recall the distinction between, on the one hand, values in which we participate but which we do not exhaust and, on the other hand, the particular projects we undertake and objectives we pursue (normally, if we are reasonable, as ways of participating in values) and which can at a given point of time be said to have been fully attained, or not, as the case may be: see III.2–3. There is no reason to suppose that political community has any aim or destination of the latter sort. Equally there is no reason to suppose that the members of a political community each have, or ought to have, any one such aim or determinable set of aims which political community does or should seek to support. Committing oneself to a life-plan is not at all like setting oneself to bake a cake. Nor is there only one reasonable life-plan or determinable set of reasonable life-plans, which the state should seek to get its citizens to commit themselves to. Yet there is a common good of the political community, and it is definite enough to exclude a considerable number of types of political arrangement, laws, etc.

For there is a 'common good' for human beings, inasmuch as life, knowledge, play, aesthetic experience, friendship, religion, and freedom in practical reasonableness are good for any and every person. And each of these human values is itself a 'common good' inasmuch as it can be participated in by an inexhaustible number of persons in an inexhaustible variety of ways or on an inexhaustible variety of occasions. These two senses of 'common good' are to be distinguished from a third, from which, however, they are not radically separate. This third sense of 'common good' is the one commonly intended throughout this book, and it is: a set of conditions which enables the members of a community to attain for themselves reasonable objectives, or to realize reasonably for themselves the value(s), for the sake of which they have reason to collaborate with each other (positively and/or negatively) in a community. The community referred to in this definition may be specialized, partial, or complete; when I speak simply of 'the common good' hereafter, I normally mean the all-round or complete community, the political community subject to my caveat about the incompleteness of the nation state in the modern world: see VI.5. The common good in this sense is a frequent or at least a justified meaning of the phrases 'the general welfare' or 'the public interest'.

Notice that this definition neither asserts nor entails that the members of a community must all have the same values or objectives (or set of values or objectives); it implies only that there be some set (or set of sets) of conditions which needs to obtain if each of the members is to attain his or her own objectives. And that there is, in human communities, some such set (or set of sets) of conditions is no doubt made possible by the fact that human beings have a 'common good' in the first sense mentioned in the last paragraph. The common good in the first sense thus explains the availability and relevance of a common good in the third sense. In this respect we can speak of the common good on different explanatory levels.

What, then, is the content of the common good of the political community, or of the international community that ought to (but in practice cannot yet) assume some though not all of the present justified functions and aspects of the political communities we call states? That is the subject-matter of the following chapters on justice, authority, and law.

NOTES

VI.1

In acting for any common good, one is rejecting the claims of 'self-interest' but is not ignoring one's own interests... For useful preliminary clarifications see B. J. Diggs, 'The Common Good as Reason for Political Action' (1973) 83 *Ethics* 283–93.

VI.2

'Community' and 'society'... Much that Aristotle said or might have said in terms of *koinōnia* is said by Augustine in relation to *societas* and *vita socialis*: see, e.g., *De Civitate Dei*, XIX, 5–9. Ferdinand Tönnies, *Gemeinschaft und Gesellschaft* (1887; trans. C. P. Loomis, *Community and Association*, London: 1957), proposed a broad distinction, rather similar to that made earlier by Maine (in terms of 'status' and 'contract') and later by Durkheim (in terms of 'mechanical solidarity' and 'organic solidarity'), between *community*, in which instinct and tradition are the basis of social union, and *society*, in which rational self-interest prevails. On the other hand, Thomas Gilby, *Between Community and Society: A Philosophy and Theology of the State* (London: 1953), contrasts community (rooted in instinct, natural affections, mass-pressures, etc.), not with the 'rational' order of contractual and similar relations, but with the *communicatio amicorum*,

i.e. friendship in the full sense. (*Communicatio* is the Latin for *koinōnia*.) The fact is that the two words have no settled resonance or connotation, and thus can either be put to stipulative use to make a contrast, or else (as here) be left undifferentiated in the analysis.

Unifying relationships...In Aristotle, *taxis* (see, e.g., *in Pol.* III.4: 1278b9; III.1: 1274b9; VII.4: 1326a30); in Augustine, *ordo* (see, e.g., *De Civitate Dei* XIX, 1; *De Libero Arbitrio* I, 6, 15); in much modern writing, 'system'—as in the common usage of 'the social system', 'the legal system'...

The four orders... See Aquinas, *in Eth.* I, 1 (introduction): 'Order stands to reason in four ways...'. The reintroduction of Aquinas's taxonomy into the modern debate is the work of Germain Grisez, *Beyond the New Theism: A Philosophy of Religion* (Notre Dame and London: 1975), 230–40, 353–6, who adjusts Aquinas's account by recognizing that language is an artefact. The account in the text, above, follows Grisez closely.

Family relationships...The reference, throughout the analysis, is primarily but not exclusively to the 'nuclear family', the procreative community of two parents living in the same household and co-operating in the care of their own children. References in this chapter and elsewhere are not intended to express any judgment on proposed alternatives to the rearing of children in families (e.g. communes, kibbutzim, etc.). The point here is to discuss 'community' in relation to a context very familiar to most readers of this book.

VI.3

Aristotle on three types of 'friendship'...Aristotle's distinction between friendships of utility, friendships of pleasure, and the 'perfect friendship' of those who love each other for their own sake is expressly based on the already traditional threefold distinction between types of good or objective (see notes to III.2): *Nic. Eth.* VIII.2: 1155b17–20; VIII.3–4: 1156a6–1157b6; and it is carefully linked to the classic threefold distinction between types of political constitution: *Nic. Eth.* VIII.9–11: 1159b25–1161b11. In using an analogous threefold distinction between types of co-ordination and community, I do not intend to import all the results of Aristotle's analysis, e.g. that 'friendships of utility seem to occur most frequently amongst the old' (VIII.3: 1156a25), etc., etc. For Aristotle's analysis itself, see John M. Cooper, 'Aristotle on the Forms of Friendship' (1977) 30 *Rev. Metaphysics* 619.

'A good play of the game'... See Rawls, *Theory of Justice*, 525–6. I agree with Rawls that the shared end of a social union (such as a family or a state) is 'clearly not merely a common desire for the same particular thing' (*ibid.*, 526), but I do not agree with him that the 'shared final end of all the members of [a well-ordered society]' is 'the successful carrying out of just institutions' (*ibid.*, 527). The latter view assimilates communities such as the family and the state too closely to games in which 'a good play of the game' *is* the shared final end. In a really well-ordered society the shared final end of each is the well-being of all, to which end the 'carrying-out of just institutions' (an odd phrase, which I interpret very broadly, for the sake of the argument) is the proximate means.

VI.4

Friendship as the central case of community...The classic analysis is by Aristotle, who opens his *Politics* with the statement that the *polis* is a *koinōnia* (*Pol.* I.1: 1252a1; see also the little treatise on politics in *Nic. Eth.* VIII.9–11: 1160a8–1161b11) and who then makes *koinōnia* (which ranges in meaning from any degree of common interest, e.g. between businessmen, to the deepest intimacy and communion of minds in real friendship) the pivot in his analysis of *philia* (roughly, friendship in its various forms): see *Nic. Eth.* VIII.9: 1159b32; IX.12: 1171b33. On *koinōnia*, see W. L. Newman, *The Politics of Aristotle, vol.* I (Oxford: 1887), 41–2; *Gauthier-Jolif* II/2, 696–7, 768.

Friendship in the full sense . . . Although 'friendship' has lost some of its resonance and become rather cool and narrow in modern English, it lends itself better to analysis for present purposes than 'love', which is too charged with special Christian (agapeistic) or, more usually, erotic or merely sentimental overtones. Thomas Aquinas did well to begin his treatise on love *(caritas*, in Greek *agapē)* by showing that *caritas* is a friendship (*amicitia*): *S.T.* II–II q. 23 a. 1. Much of what is said by Aristotle in relation to *philia* and by Aquinas in relation to *amicitia* or *amor amicitiae* is said by Augustine in relation to *amor* and *concordia*. With the intention of superseding this entire range of classical philosophical and theological meanings, Auguste Comte invented the term 'altruism' (in French, *altruisme*): Comte, *Système de politique positive, vol.* I (1851), Introduction, and ch. III (see *System of Positive Polity* (trans. J. H. Bridges, London: 1875), vol. I, 502, 558, 564–70; cf. 10–18). This word has made its way in the world; it has a peculiar thinness, however, related to the important fact that it means 'willingness to live [act, etc.] for the sake of another [person]' (*'vivre pour autrui'*), and lacks the mutuality, and hence the special 'third viewpoint' and sense of *common* good, that are intrinsic to friendship, as the text of this section shows. For a modern discussion close to mine, as far as it goes, see Rawls on 'the idea of social union' and 'the good of community', *Theory of Justice*, 520–9.

Friendship as the central case (focal meaning) of 'philia' . . . Aristotle says: 'But since people do apply the term "friends" [*philoi*] to persons whose regard for each other is based on utility, just as states can be "friends" (since expediency is generally recognized as the motive of international alliances), or on pleasure, as children make friends, perhaps we too must call such relationships friendships; but then we must say that there are several sorts of friendship, that between good men, as good, being friendship [*philia*] in the primary and proper [*protos . . . kai kyrios*: in Latin, *primo et principaliter*] meaning of the term, while the other kinds are friendships in an analogical sense [or: by way of resemblance to true friendship: *kath homoiotetа*: in Latin, *secundum similitudinem*]': *Nic. Eth.* VIII.4: 1157a26–33, trans. Rackham (Loeb). Hence the intimacy (*suzen*) of true friends is the central case *of koinōnia*: cf. *Nic. Eth.* IX.12: 117lb32–33 with *Gauthier-Jolif*, II/2, 768–9.

The dialectic of self-love and love of the friend . . . See Aristotle, *Nic. Eth.* VIII.2: 1156al-5; IX.4: 1166a2–33; IX.8: 1168bl5–1169b2; IX.9: 1170b5–19; IX.12: 1171b33–1172al; *Rhet.* II.4: 1380b36; also Cicero, *De Legibus*, I, xii, 34; xviii, 49; Aquinas, *S.T.* II–II q. 25 a. 4; q. 26 aa. 4, 5.

VI.5

Plato's communism of women, children, and property . . . See *Rep.* V: 457c–465a, where the communizing (*koinōneō*) seems to be restricted to the class of guardians of the *polis*; *Laws* V: 739b–d, where the proposal extends to the whole *polis*. As to the motivations of the proposal, see Eric Voegelin, *Order and History*, vol. 3, *Plato and Aristotle* (Baton Rouge: 1957), 47, 49, 118–19.

Aristotle's critique of Plato's communism . . . See *Pol.* II.1–2: 1260b37–1264b3; for outline and summary, see Newman, *The Politics of Aristotle*, vol. I, 160–8; for the interpretation followed here, see Voegelin, *Order and History*, 319–22.

Aristotle on the family, domestic management, and the economy of the 'polis'... See *Pol.* I.3–4: 1256a1–1259a38. There are many deficiencies in his analysis. The neighbourhood association, having been introduced as the intermediate association between family and *polis*, immediately drops out of view altogether.

'Subsidiarity'...This principle is one important development of the Aristotelian political science, drawing on but going well beyond Aristotle's critique of Plato's communism. It has been popularized by recent Popes under the name of 'subsidiary function' or 'subsidiarity'. Pius XI first referred to it as such in his encyclical letter *Quadragesimo Anno* (1931), para. 79: '...just as it is wrong to withdraw from the individual and commit to a group what private initiative and effort can accomplish, so too it is a wrong...for a larger and higher association to arrogate to itself functions which can be performed efficiently by smaller and lower associations. This is a fixed, unchanged and most weighty principle of moral philosophy...Of its very nature the true aim of all social activity should be to help [*subsidium afferre*] members of a social body, and never to destroy or absorb them...'. Later pronouncements of the Roman Catholic authorities have applied the principle to relationships of production in the economy (1961, 1967), to world political order (1963) and world economic order (1965), to the relationships between families, schools, and the state (1965), to the ecclesiastical community (1969), and to politics at all levels (1971). Being a matter of right (justice), not merely efficiency, it is obviously closely related to what many people refer to as the right to *liberty*.

VI.6

Aristotle and the 'natural' progression from family through neighbourhood association to political community... See *Pol.* I.2: 1252a15–1253a29; Ernest Barker, The Politics of Aristotle (Oxford: 1946), 7; for penetrating analysis and critique, see Voegelin, *Order and History*, 315–17, concluding that 'the polis is a premature generalization from insufficient materials' (317; see also 310–14). My discussion goes beyond Aristotle in a number of respects, and rejects both his fundamental assumption (*Pol.* I.1: 1252b13–30) that the family is merely an association for the sake of life (survival and reproduction) (while the polis is an association for the sake of the good life) and the conclusions which he draws from that assumption, notably that education is exclusively the function of the *polis* and not primarily or at all the responsibility of parents (see *Pol.* VIII.1: 1337a23–32). Nor does my analysis make any claims about the historical priority of one form of association over others.

Comprehensiveness, purported supremacy, and absorptive capacity ('openness') of legal systems... For these characteristics of the central cases of legal systems, see Raz, *Practical Reason*, 150–4.

The state as merely a mutual insurance society: the classical critique...See Aristotle, *Pol.* III.5: 1280a31–1281a5: '...the *polis* was formed not for the sake of life only but rather for the good life...and...its purpose is not [merely] military alliance for defence...and it does not exist [merely] for the sake of trade and of business relations...any *polis* which is truly so called, and is not one merely in name, must devote itself to the aim of encouraging excellence [*aretē*]. Otherwise a *polis* sinks into a mere alliance, which only differs in space from other forms of alliance where the members live at a distance from each other. Otherwise, too, the law becomes a mere covenant—or (in the phrase of the sophist Lycophron) "a guarantor of justice as between one man and another"—instead of being, as it should be, such as will make the members of the *polis* good and just...The *polis* is not merely the sharing of a common locality for the purpose of preventing mutual injury and exchanging goods. These are necessary pre-conditions of the existence of a *polis*...but a *polis* is a *koinōnia* of families and clans [and neighbourhoods] in living well, with the object of a full and self-sufficient life [and for the sake of truly good (*kalōn*) actions, not merely of living together] ...'. In short, analysis of political community should not be based on a view of what would be reasonable in Hobbes's 'state of nature' or in the game-theorist's 'prisoners' dilemma' (cf. E. Ullmann-Margalit, *The Emergence of Norms* (Oxford: 1977), ch. II). On the political theory of the sophists, see Voegelin, *Order and History*, vol. 2, *The World of the Polis* (Baton Rouge: 1957), 305–31.

Aristotle on the complete sufficiency of the 'polis' ... For Aristotle the *polis* is a complete and self-sufficient community because it provides context and resources completely adequate for the full and complete development of a man. On this *autarkeia*, see *Nic. Eth.* I.6–7: 1097b7–17; *Pol.* I.1: 1252b29; III.5: 1281a1. See Voegelin's critique, cited above, of this 'premature generalization'. Aristotle envisages neither the spiritual community of a universal Church nor the international community of all mankind.

VI.7

The existence of a group and the number of interactions between its members ... I follow the lucid critique of this theory by A. M. Honoré, 'What is a Group?' (1975) 61 *Arch.R.S.P.* 161 at 167–76.

Sharing of aim as constitutive of human groups ... See Honoré, 'What is a Group?', at 168–70; Rawls, *Theory of Justice*, 525; Aristotle, *Pol.* I.1: 1252a1–4: 'Observation shows us, first, that every *polis* is a species of association [*koinōnia*], and, secondly, that all associations are instituted with a view to some good—for all men do all their acts with a view to something which is, in their view, good'.

Analysis of the existence, as a matter of law, of corporations and other legal institutions ... See H. L. A. Hart, 'Definition and Theory in Jurisprudence' (1954) 70 *L.Q.R.* 37 at 49–59; D. N. MacCormick, 'Law as Institutional Fact' (1974) 90 *L.Q.R.* 102 at 106–10.

VI.8

Community to be analysed in terms of common good ... Cf. Aristotle, *Pol.* I.1: 1252a2: 'every *koinōnia* is formed with a view to some good (since all the actions of all men are done with a view to what they think to be good)'. This good Aristotle usually calls 'common interest' (*koinon sympheron*) but sometimes calls 'common good' (*koinon agathon*): e.g. *Pol.* III.8: 1284b6.

The common good of the political community ... The definition here given is similar to that worked out by French commentators on Aquinas: see J. T. Delos in *Saint Thomas d'Aquin, Somme théologique: La Justice*, vol. I [II–II qq. 63–6] (1932), 209, 242.

VII

JUSTICE

VII.1 ELEMENTS OF JUSTICE

THE preceding chapter's examination of community enables me to turn to the requirement of practical reasonableness held over from Chapter V (V.8), the requirement of justice—an ensemble of requirements of practical reasonableness that hold because one must seek to realize and respect human goods not merely in oneself and for one's own sake but also in common, in community. (Something of the sense of this 'must', this rational necessity, was indicated in VI.4.) This being my purpose, I use the concept of justice with all the breadth that that concept has had in academic discussion since Aristotle first treated it as an academic topic. That is to say, I set aside all the special and limiting shades of meaning that the word 'justice' may have acquired in common parlance, as in the expression 'courts of justice', or in the contrast that might be drawn by saying that a perfectly *fair* lottery does not necessarily produce a *just* result.

In its full generality, the complex concept of justice embraces three elements, and is applicable to all situations where these elements are found together. The first element might be called *other-directedness*: justice has to do with one's relations and dealings with other persons; it is 'inter-subjective' or interpersonal. There is a question of justice and injustice only where there is a plurality of individuals and some practical question concerning their situation and/or interactions *vis-à-vis* each other. Of course, by a kind of metaphorical extension, we can speak of 'doing oneself justice' (e.g. by performing well in a game or examination, not necessarily competitive): here we preserve the element of other-directedness by implicitly relating subjects and their actual performances to subjects and their performances as they should be. Plato capitalized on another quasi-metaphorical extension by treating justice as concerned essentially with the relation between three aspects of the soul (reasonableness, desire, and the spiritedness which normally allies itself to reason to master desire):[1] justice as order in the soul then becomes the model for and cause of justice as right order in society.[2] I shall not follow Plato in this extension. Suffice it to note, first, that he preserves the element of other-directedness by treating the aspects of the soul as if they were (or could be compared to) distinct individuals; and, secondly, that modern European languages are still more liberal than Plato in their word-play. They embody an immensely complex and extensive web of overlapping notions which shift and play in and between the field of human society (our present concern) and quite other fields: consider the sequence, *'le mot juste'* 'just so', 'correct', 'rectify', *'Recht'*, 'right', *'dirritto'*, *'droit'*, 'direct', 'regular', 'regulate', 'rule'... So we must let our discussion be ruled by the substantive questions we have in mind (about what is reasonable and unreasonable in human conduct), not by the conventions and associations of our language (which provide, nevertheless, a useful assemblage of reminders).

The second element in the relevant concept of justice is that of *duty*, of what is owed (*debitum*) or due to another, and correspondingly of what that other person has a right to (viz. roughly, to what is his or her 'own' or at least 'due', by right). To the complexities of this element I devote the next chapter, and to the roots of all obligation or duty I devote Chapter XI. For the present, suffice it to say that justice concerns not every reasonable relationship or dealing between one person and another, but only those relations and dealings which are necessary or appropriate for the avoiding of a wrong. (There may, of course, be more than one way of avoiding the relevant sort of wrong; but in calling something 'just' we are not asserting that it is the *only* way of avoiding a wrong, and are not assessing it by comparison with other possible ways, but are asserting that it is a way of avoiding something that in reason *must* not be or be done in the relevant, i.e. inter-subjective, field.)

The third element in the relevant concept of justice can be called *equality*. But, even more than in the case of the other two elements, this must be taken in an analogical sense: that

---

[1] *Rep.* IV: 439c–441b.
[2] *Rep.* IV: 441c–444a; and *passim*.

is to say, it can be present in quite various ways. There is, for example, the 'arithmetical' equality of $2 = 2$, and there is also the 'geometrical' equality of $1 : 1 = 2 : 2$, or of $3 : 2 = 6 : 4$; to feed a large adult the same rations as a small child both is and is not to treat the two 'equally'. To avoid misunderstandings and oversimplifications, therefore, it may be better to think of *proportionality*,[3] or even of *equilibrium* or balance. Even so, there remains the question of the terms of the comparison in any assessment of proportions; we may be interested in comparing adults' rations with small children's rations as shares of some available supply, or we may be interested in comparing adults' rations with what they need or with what it is *fitting* for them to have if they are to remain alive and well, regardless of questions of supply and shares. Given the analogical nature of the concept of justice and of each of its three main conceptual components, either sort of comparison suffices to supply the equality/inequality or proportion/disproportion that must enter, at least implicitly, into any assessment in terms of justice/injustice.

By treating these three elements, thus understood, as necessary and sufficient for an assessment to be an assessment of justice, I am seeking to give the concept of justice sufficient precision to be useful in an analysis of practical reasonableness, and sufficient breadth for it to be worthy of its classical and popular prominence in that analysis. My theory of justice, then, is not restricted (like Rawls's) to the 'basic institutions of society'.[4] Nor is it restricted (as Aristotle was tempted to restrict his[5]) to relations between mature and free equals in political community. In my theory parents can treat their child with straightforward injustice. Nor are the requirements of justice in my account restricted (like Hart's) to what can be drawn from the principle 'Treat like cases alike and different cases differently'.[6] My theory includes principles for assessing how one person ought to treat another (or how one person has a right to be treated), regardless of whether or not others are

---

[3] 'Proportion being equality of ratios': Aristotle, *Nic. Eth.* V.3: 1131a31.
[4] See *Theory of Justice*, 4, 7, 84; see also the diagram, *ibid.*, 109: justice as treated in the present chapter would appear not only where Rawls places it in that diagram but also at the foot of arms III, II(b), and both limbs of II(a).
[5] See *Nic. Eth.* V.6: 1134a25–b17.
[6] See *Concept of Law*, 155–6 [159–60]. On the principle, see VII.4.

being so treated; in my usage, a principle forbidding torture in *all* cases is a principle of justice. Finally, it goes without saying that my theory is not restricted (like Rawls's) to the ideal conditions of a society in which everyone complies fully with the principles and institutions of justice.[7] So my theory incorporates theses about war, about punishment, about civil obligation in face of unjust legislation, and about other situations of social breakdown and individual recalcitrance. Many parts of the theory are only mentioned (if that) in this chapter; some others are treated in the chapters on rights (VIII), authority (IX), law (X), and obligation (XI).

VII.2   GENERAL JUSTICE

The requirements of justice, then, are the concrete implications of the basic requirement of practical reasonableness that one is to favour and foster the common good of one's communities. That principle is closely related both to the basic value of friendship and to the principle of practical reasonableness which excludes arbitrary self-preference in the pursuit of good; but it may not be reducible to either or both without remainder, so I referred to it at V.8 as a distinct eighth principle of practical reasonableness. The principle contains, in other terminology, all three elements discussed in the preceding section: other-directedness, in the reference to the community or communities of which one is a member, and whose other members (as well as oneself) one assists in serving the common good; duty, by virtue of the fact that this is a *requirement* of practical reasonableness; and equality or proportionality, since (a) the principle looks to the *common* good of the relevant community, not to the good of any individual or group in disregard of the well-being of the others, and (b) the principle looks to the common *good*, which entails a reference to standards of fittingness or appropriateness relative to the basic aspects of human flourishing, which are pertinent whether or not an interpersonal comparison is being made.

To live up to this principle fully would obviously require that one lived up fully to all the other principles of practical reasonableness; for though one's personal failings do not all on

---

[7] See *Theory of Justice*, 4–5, 8, 454.

every occasion implicate one in injustice, still, any form of per-sonal failing is liable to implicate one in a failure of justice, by act or omission. That is why Aristotle, partly under the influence of Plato's ambitious extension of the analogy of justice, began his treatise on justice by identifying a general sense of 'justice' in which the word signifies *comprehensive* virtue (in my terminology, full practical reasonableness) as displayed in relation to other persons.[8] Since Aristotle wanted to introduce into academic dis-course a technical distinction between two connotations of *dikaion*, the Greek word for that which is just—namely, just *qua* lawful (conforming to standard) and just *qua* equal (taking no more than one's share)—the Aristotelian name for justice in this general sense is 'legal justice'.[9] Since we, on the other hand, are equipped with two technical notions which, as technical notions, Aristotle lacked—namely, the common good and the distinct and enumerable requirements of practical reasonableness—we can discard the confusing term 'legal justice' while retaining the fundamental notion (which I formulated as a principle at the beginning of this section) as an orientation in the subsequent discussion. Justice, as a quality of character, is in its general sense always a practical willingness to favour and foster the common good of one's communities, and the theory of justice is, in all its parts, the theory of what in outline is required for that common good.

VII.3   DISTRIBUTIVE JUSTICE

The requirement of practical reasonableness is not satisfied by a general disposition, in one or all, to favour the well-being of other members of the community or communities in question. Few will flourish, and no one will flourish securely, unless there is an effective collaboration of persons, and co-ordination of resources and of enterprises (including always, in the notion of collaboration and co-ordination, patterns of mutual restraint and non-interference). Such an ensemble of conditions of collaboration which enhance the well-being (or at least the opportunity of flourishing) of all members of a community is, indeed, often called the common good (see VI.8). And when we

---

[8] *Nic. Eth.* V.1: 1129b26–1130a13.
[9] *Ibid.*, 1130b10, 21–5.

wish to consider the concrete requirements of justice ('particular' as distinct from the 'general' justice discussed in the preceding section), we need to consider the term 'common good', used in formulating the general principle of justice, as taking on now this more concrete meaning.

A full analysis of what is for the common good is, of course, far beyond the scope of this chapter or indeed this book. But we can at least orient ourselves in a bafflingly complex field, by observing that the problems of realizing the common good through a co-ordinated ensemble of conditions for individual well-being in community can be divided into two very broad classes. *First*, there are problems of *distributing* resources, oppor-tunities, profits and advantages, roles and offices, responsibilities, taxes and burdens—in general, the *common stock* and the *incidents of communal enterprise*, which do not serve the common good unless and until they are appropriated to particular individuals. The theory of distributive justice outlines the range of reasonable responses to these problems. *Secondly*, there are all the other problems, concerning what is required for individual well-being in community, which arise in relations and dealings between indi-viduals and/or groups, where the common stock and what is required for communal enterprise are not directly in question. The range of reasonable responses to these problems is outlined in what I shall call (for reasons that will appear) the theory of *commutative* justice.

The intentions of this classification should not be misunder-stood. On the one hand, the classification is intended as exhaustive, in the sense that all problems of justice, and all the specific require-ments generated by the requirement of 'general justice', are in-tended to find a place in one or other or (under different aspects) both of these two classes of 'particular justice'. On the other hand, it is not denied that other classifications, and certainly sub-classifications, could be found. But, as will be seen in VII.4 below, the classification here adopted, though academic in inspiration and philosophical in origin, can help towards understanding certain perennial tensions in sophisticated legal systems.

A disposition is *distributively just*, then, if it is a reasonable resolution of a problem of allocating some subject-matter that is essentially common but that needs (for the sake of the common good) to be appropriated to individuals. Now subject-matters may be common in a variety of ways.

(A) A subject-matter is common, in the sense relevant to distributive justice, if it is part of no individual person and has not been created by anybody, but is apt for use for the benefit of anyone or everyone: for example, solar energy and light, the sea, its bed and its contents, land and its contents, rivers, air and airspace, the moon...

(B) Another sort of common subject-matter arises out of the willingness of individuals to collaborate to improve their position. For example, a set of individuals may come under attack by others or by the sea or pestilence or famine. None of them can keep safe by solo, unco-ordinated efforts, but all may be saved by collaboration. Such collaboration involves (B1): the task of deciding what is to be done and how; the task of participating in particular aspects of determinate projects; the responsibility of contributing necessary resources or funds, etc. Such collaboration also yields (B2): a city wall and stock of weapons; a sea wall or dyke; a drainage system and hospitals; a harvest in communal granaries, etc. Both the roles, responsibilities, offices, and burdens mentioned in (B1) and the products in (B2) are intrinsically common. In the general characterization of problems of distributive justice, earlier in this section, I compendiously called the natural resources in (A) and the products in (B2) *common stock*, while the subject-matters in (B1) I called *incidents of communal enterprise*. All these subject-matters are essentially common, and none of them fulfils its beneficial potentialities for anyone or everyone without some appropriation, conditionally or unconditionally, to particular persons (in the limiting case, to everyone in the community, including passing strangers). The problem of distributive justice is: to whom and on what conditions to make this necessary appropriation.

Some of the problems of distributing the responsibilities mentioned in (Bl) above are to be treated later, in our discussion of authority: see IX.4. But here we may notice that, as human experience shows, very many common enterprises are best conducted by charging particular individuals with the responsibility of settling co-ordination problems which *must* be settled if the enterprise is to go forward and which could otherwise be settled only by a unanimity which is in practice impossible to attain or to attain in time. Few are the armies, few indeed the victorious armies, without any officers.

Some who hold office in common ('public') enterprises, civil or military, have responsibilities clearly definable and regulated by rules which require little more than application or administration. Other responsibilities cannot be discharged adequately unless the officers who bear them are permitted to exercise a wide and even unreviewable discretion. Such discretionary authority remains, however, public; it is the good of the common enterprise that the officers are conscientiously to pursue, not their own ('private') advantage. A government that appoints unworthy party hacks to public office violates distributive justice, as does a biased licensing magistrate.

At this point we must recall that the common good is fundamentally the good of individuals (an aspect of whose good is friendship in community). The common good, which is the object of all justice and which all reasonable life in community must respect and favour, is not to be confused with the common stock, or the common enterprises, that are among the means of realizing the common good. Common enterprises and the exploitation and creation of a common stock of assets are alike for the common good because they are for the benefit of the individual members of the community: talk about benefiting 'the community' is no more than a shorthand (not without dangers) for benefiting the members of that community. And here we must further recall that the fundamental task of practical reasonableness is self-constitution or self-possession; inner integrity of character and outer authenticity of action are aspects of the basic good of practical reasonableness, as are freedom from the automatism of habit and from subjection to unintegrated impulses and compulsions; even friendship, in its ordinary sense, and the intense community of family require and entail a certain specialization and limitation of one's attentions; in short, no common enterprise can itself bring about the all-round flourishing of any individual. An attempt, for the sake of the common good, to absorb the individual altogether into common enterprises would thus be disastrous for the common good, however much the common enterprises might prosper (see also VI.5).

It is therefore a fundamental aspect of general justice that common enterprises should be regarded, and practically conducted, not as ends in themselves but as means of assistance, as ways of helping individuals to 'help themselves' or, more precisely, to constitute themselves. And in all those fields of activity, including economic activity, where individuals, or families, or other relatively small groups, can help themselves by their own private efforts and initiatives without thereby injuring (either by act or omission) the common good, they are entitled in justice to be allowed to do so, and it is unjust to require them to sacrifice their private initiative by demanding that they participate instead in a public enterprise; it remains unjust even if the material dividend they receive from the public enterprise is as great as or even somewhat greater than the material product of their own private efforts would have been. The principle of subsidiarity (see VI.5) is a principle of justice.

All this has implications in many fields of activity, not least in that field of work and enterprise which we call economic activity. The implications concern, for example, the proper conditions of employment for wage or salary, i.e. of service which is a *proprium*—something of his or her own—of the person who renders it, but is not within the focal meaning of 'property'. But to illustrate the interrelation of 'private' and 'common' in the notion of justice, I will say something about private ownership.

The good of personal autonomy in community, as we have just traced it in outline, suggests that the opportunity of exercising some form of private ownership, including of means of production, is in most times and places a requirement of justice.[10] It is a requirement that strongly conditions, but also is conditioned by, the concrete application of the general principles and criteria of distributive justice. Clearly, the term 'private property' calls for some explanation. But that explanation

---

[10] All requirements of general justice are specifically requirements either of distributive justice or of commutative justice or of both. The present requirement (i) is a requirement of distributive justice in so far as it is unfair if the opportunity to control the use of natural resources, or of products of, claims to or means of claiming such resources, is not distributed to some but is to others, for inadequate reason, and (ii) is a requirement of commutative justice in so far as, if everyone in a community is deprived of the opportunity of private ownership, for inadequate reasons, then *each* is being treated unfairly, regardless of the like treatment of the others. See the end of VII.6 below.

will be easier if we look first at a second (alternative) basis in
justice for establishing a regime of private property. (As always,
the explanation of social institutions, and of the terms appropriate for talking about them, is primarily a matter of grasping
their rationale.) This second basis rests on a 'rule' of human
experience: natural resources, and the capital resources and
consumer durables derivable therefrom, are more productively
exploited and more carefully maintained by private enterprise,
management, husbandry, and housekeeping than by the 'officials'
(including all employees) of public enterprises. At least for the
times and places and the classes of resources for which this rule
of experience holds true, a regime of private ownership will be a
requirement of justice, provided that the increased stock of
goods yielded by such a regime is not hoarded by a class of
successful private owners but is made available by appropriate
mechanisms (e.g. profit-sharing, trade under competitive market
conditions, redistributive taxation, full employment through productive investment, etc.) to all members of the community, in
due measure. Of course, *if the* active members of the community
were more detached from considerations of private advantage,
from love of 'their own', etc., then common ownership and
enterprise *would* be more productive of benefits for all. But a
theory of justice is to establish what is due to individuals in the
circumstances in which they are, not in the circumstances of
some other, 'ideal' world. And those many members of the
community who reasonably[11] depend for their livelihood upon
the productive efforts and good husbandry of other members can
rightly complain of injustice[12] if a regime of property (exploitation, production, and management of resources) is adopted, on
the basis that it *would* enhance their well-being if the non-
dependent members of the community had characters different
from those that in fact they have, but which *actually* yields the
dependent members (and everyone else) a lower standard

---

[11] In testing the justice of a social arrangement by considering it from the viewpoint of the
'worst-off' member of the community (which is certainly a relevant viewpoint), we ought ordinarily
to exclude from the class of 'worst-off' those who unreasonably *refuse* to contribute by work or
otherwise to the common good. In the pithy phrase of St. Paul (2 Thess. 3:10), quoted (without
acknowledgement) in Art. 10 of the Constitution of the Chinese People's Republic (1978): 'He who
will not work, let him not eat'; likewise Art. 13 of the Constitution of Albania (1946).

[12] Certainly commutative and usually also distributive; cf. p. 169, n. 10.

of living than they would enjoy under a different regime of property operated by the non-dependent members as they *actually* are.

Having mentioned two independent reasons why a system of private ownership (which may co-exist in the same community with more or less extensive public ownership, i.e. management of resources by officials) is typically required for the common good and thus by justice, it remains to clarify what is meant by 'private ownership'. What I mean is summed up in the apparent paradox which Aristotle uses to sum up his rather similar discussion: 'property ought to be common in a sense, but private speaking generally... possessions should be privately owned, but common in use; and to train the citizens to this is the special task of the legislator'.[13] I cite Aristotle partly in order to emphasize that the analyses put forward in this section, even where they are applicable to issues of current political debate in the reader's community, are not to be taken as if they were intended as a contribution to any particular such debate.

For regimes of property are very various and, usually, complex; and not unreasonably so, since what combinations of private and public ownership reasonably answer to the requirements of general justice vary with time, place, and many different circumstances: indeed, the very distinction between 'public' and 'private' may reasonably be treated in some systems as not exhaustive. (See also X.7.) Hence, there is no question here of setting out some model or 'pure case' of private ownership as the relevant demand of justice in all or even in most political communities. Suffice it to say that the two arguments put forward above suggest that individuals, singly or in combination, should have access either directly or (as, for example, in the case of a shareholder in a joint-stock company) indirectly to natural resources, capital goods, and/or consumer durables, such access being more or less exclusive (in that he or they are entitled to exclude other

---

[13] *Pol.* II.2: 1263a26, 38–9; see likewise Aquinas, *S.T.* II–II q. 66 a. 2c; q. 32 a. 5 ad 2. Cf. Basic Law of the Federal Republic of Germany (1949), Art. 14: '(1) Property and the right of inheritance are guaranteed. Their content and limits shall be determined by law. (2) Property imposes duties. Its use should also serve the common weal'. Likewise, Art. 24 of the Constitution of the German Democratic Republic (1949).

individuals from access), more or less immune from divestment by or at the instance of other individuals, and more or less transmissible by him at his choice. The purpose of these rights of exclusion and transmission and immunity from divestment is to give private owners freedom to expend their own creativity, inventiveness, and undeflected care and attention upon the thing(s) in question, to give them security in enjoying the thing(s) or investing or developing them, and to afford the owners the opportunity of exchanging their thing(s) for some alternative item(s) of property seeming to them more suitable to their life-plans. These are the principal features required to meet the demands of the common good referred to in the two arguments put forward above for the justice of private ownership.

Those arguments in no way suggest that private ownership, thus understood, is unconditionally just. On the contrary, by starting from the general notion of the common good, and by emphasizing that natural resources are essentially common stock (though apt for distribution, including distribution as private property), the arguments themselves suggest the conditions which private owners must conform to if their ownership is to be distributively just.

As private owner of a natural resource or capital good, one has a duty in justice to put it to productive use or, if one lacks the further resources required to do so, to dispose of it to someone willing and able to do so. The undeveloped *latifundia* of the rich (as in the Roman Empire and in various regions today) are a sign of injustice, whether or not they are tolerated by law. Similarly, speculative acquisition and disposition of property, for the purposes of merely financial gain uncorrelated with any economically productive development or use, is contrary to distributive justice. So, typically, is the hoarding of gold and in general the withholding of liquid assets from capital markets in which they might be mobilized for productive use. So too are dilapidations and failures of reasonable conservation of consumer durables, such as houses. So is the development of monopolistic and oligopolistic positions or arrangements which, for the profit and power of a restricted class of individuals, restrict the availability of property to other individuals, and prevent the working of a competitive market system which would encourage the unwasteful production and distribution of goods, more widely, in larger quantities and less expensively than is otherwise possible. So, likewise, are various (not all!) privately devised restrictions on alienation and/or on the future use of property.

The point, in justice, of private property is to give owners first use and enjoyment of their thing and its fruits (including rents and profits), for it is this availability that enhances their reasonable autonomy and stimulates their productivity and care. But beyond a reasonable measure and degree of such use for them and their dependants' or co-owners' needs, they each hold the remainder of their property and its fruits as part (in justice if not in law) of the common stock. In other words, beyond a certain point, what was commonly available but was justly made private, for the common good, becomes again, in justice, part of the common stock; though appropriated to management and control by an owner or owners, items of private property ('things') are now not for the owners' private benefit but are held by them immediately for common benefit (as Aristotle, we saw, more tersely said). From this point, owners have, in justice, duties not altogether unlike those of a trustee in English law. They may fulfil them in various ways—by investing their surpluses in production of more goods for later distribution and consumption; by providing gainful employment to people looking for work; by grants or loans for hospitals, schools, cultural centres, orphanages, etc., or directly for the relief of the poor. Where owners will not perform these duties, or cannot effectively co-ordinate their respective efforts to perform them, then public authority may rightly help them to perform their duties by devising and implementing schemes of distribution, e.g. by 'redistributive' taxation for purposes of 'social welfare', or by a measure of expropriation.

VII.4   CRITERIA OF DISTRIBUTIVE JUSTICE

Equality is a fundamental element in the notion of justice and thus of distributive justice. In particular, *all* members of a community *equally* have the right to respectful consideration when the problem of distribution arises: see further VIII.6. This is the moral relevance of the so-called 'formal' principle of justice: 'Treat like cases alike'. But, for resolving problems of distributive justice, equality is a residual principle, outweighed by other criteria and applicable only when those other criteria are inapplicable or fail to yield any conclusion. For the objective of justice is not equality but the common good, the flourishing of all members of the community, and there is no reason to suppose that this flourishing of all is enhanced by treating everyone identically when distributing roles, opportunities, and resources. Thus, to revert to the question of private ownership: what is unjust about large disparities of wealth in a community is not the inequality as such but the fact that (as the inequality suggests) the rich have failed to redistribute that portion of their wealth which could be better used by others for the realization of basic values in their own lives. If redistribution means no more than that more beer is going to be consumed morosely before television sets by the relatively many, and less fine wine consumed by the relatively few at salon concerts by select musicians, then it can scarcely be said to be a demand of justice. But if redistribution means that, at the expense of the wine, etc., more people can be preserved from (non-self-inflicted) illness, educated to the point where genuine self-direction becomes possible for them, defended against the enemies of justice, etc., then such redistribution is a requirement of justice.

There are, of course, no very precise yardsticks for assessing these questions. The all-round flourishing of human beings in community is indefinitely many-sided. There is no one criterion universally applicable for resolving questions of distribution. In respect of the realization of basic human goods, up to a certain threshold level in each member of the community, the primary criterion is *need*. For here we are dealing with the fundamental component of the common good. Even this is, however, subject to considerable discounting in the case of those whose indigence either results from their own unreasonable unwillingness to exert themselves for their own good, or is imposed upon them as lawful punishment for their culpable self-preference and harmful indifference to the good of others (see X.1). And, apart from that, the priority of need as a criterion for distribution is not a straightforwardly 'lexicographical' priority; in situations of emergency, which are not too uncommon, a few or even many may rightly be deprived of much in order that those who can defend the whole community against its dangers may be enabled and encouraged to do so.

A second criterion of just distribution is *function*, that is to say, need relative not directly to basic human good but to roles and responsibilities in the community. And since this book is not a treatise on justice, I may be summary in mentioning the other reasonable criteria. Thirdly, then, there is *capacity*, relative not only to roles in communal enterprises but also to opportunities for individual advancement. 'Flutes to flute-players': if higher education is to be made available (whether by private or by public initiative) it should go only to those capable of benefiting from it. Fourthly, *deserts and contributions*, whether deriving from self-sacrifice or from meritorious use of effort and ability, are a proper criterion of distribution; for the friendliness that is expressed by manifested gratitude is a great human good, for both giver and receiver. Fifthly, in the distribution of the costs and losses of communal enterprise fairness will often turn on whether some parties have *created* or at least *foreseen and accepted avoidable risks* while others have neither created them nor had opportunity of foreseeing or of avoiding or insuring against them: this is a problem familiar to lawyers but rather overlooked by philosophers and (so?) lacks a convenient short label.

Finally, in considering and employing criteria of distributive justice we must not lose sight of the fact that in speaking of justice we are not trying to assess states of affairs and their consequences. Rather, we are trying to assess what practical reasonableness *requires* of particular people (in their dealings with other people). And what is thus required of particular persons depends essentially on what responsibilities they respectively have, whether by virtue of voluntary commitments (e.g. assumption of rulership) or by virtue of past or present receipt of benefits from another (e.g. as children, in relation to their respective parents), or by virtue of the dependence of others upon them (e.g. as parents, in relation to their own children), or by virtue of a network of relationships of actual and potential interdependencies (such as exist strongly, for one set of reasons, amongst members of a family living unit, and strongly, for another set of reasons, amongst members of a sound political community, and to a lesser but increasing extent between the communities that together make up the whole community of mankind).

Here Aristotle's famous and often overworked *dictum* about not demanding too much precision in ascertaining the demands of practical reasonableness[14] has an important application. The claim of Weber, Sartre, and many others, that objective or rational judgements are impossible in the field of values (ethics and politics), has been based partly upon the difficulty ('impossibility') of resolving certain problems of conflicting claims of responsibility. Sartre, for example, proposes the case of a young man trying to decide whether he ought to stay at home to care for his aged and dependent mother or leave home to fight against Nazi occupation of France.[15] But such arguments lack the force ascribed to them by Sartre and Weber. Neither of the courses of action contemplated by the young man need be regarded as incompatible with justice. His dilemma cannot be solved by declaring one of his two prima facie responsibilities to be the exclusive requirement of practical reasonableness. But practical reasonableness certainly convicts of irrational irresponsibility someone who in such a situation decides to do whatever the first person he meets suggests, whether it be to shoot his mother, join the occupying forces, drink himself to stupefaction, commit suicide, or whatever—all of these being possibilities that Sartre simply overlooks.

But the inappropriate demand for precise and unqualified directives of reason in assessing responsibilities also seems to lie behind a quite different development in contemporary thought. For it is becoming common, at least in academic discussion, to propose, in effect, that 'everyone of us is responsible for everyone else in every way'.[16] Here the feeling that it is difficult or impossible to find norms for definitively apportioning one's effort in differing degrees amongst different potential beneficiaries seems to link up with the assumption that justice is primarily a property of states of affairs and only derivatively a property of particular decisions of ascertained persons; and this combination of unformulated assumptions yields the

---

[14] *Nic. Eth.* I.3: 1094b12–14.

[15] J.-P. Sartre, *L'Existentialisme est un humanisme* (Paris: 1946), 40–1.

[16] Cf. Father Zossima's brother, in Dostoyevsky's *The Brothers Karamazov*, quoted by Jonathan Glover, *Causing Death and Saving Lives* (Harmondsworth: 1977), 104, as bearing 'an obvious resemblance to what has been argued' by Glover himself. Perhaps the resemblance is only apparent; cf. Herbert Morris, *On Guilt and Innocence* (Berkeley and London: 1976), ch. 4.

peculiarly utilitarian concept of justice. Here the principle 'Treat like cases alike' becomes, specifically, 'each person counts for one and only one': indeed, the new view is simply drawing out the conclusions of the logic of classic utilitarianism.[17] And a principal conclusion is: one (each of us) is morally bound to devote one's wealth and energy (which one might otherwise have devoted to the interests of oneself, one's 'dependants', one's own local and political communities, etc.) to the interests of the most disadvantaged persons whom one can find anywhere in the world, up to the point where one's (marginal) sacrifice of wealth and energy would render one, and one's 'dependants', worse off than those most disadvantaged persons.[18] Any other use of one's wealth and energy is, on this view, simply unjust.

In so far as this view is a version of utilitarianism, it is subject to the general critique which shows that its substratum of principle is incoherent (see V.6). But, in thinking about justice, we should go further and reject the principle, so plausible prima facie, that 'each person counts for one and only one'; for this principle is not reasonable as a principle for the practical deliberations of anyone. Of each and all of us it is true that, because of one's promises, and/or one's parenthood, and/or one's debts of gratitude, and/or one's relations of interdependence with or assumption of authority in relation to ascertained persons or communities, one cannot reasonably give equal 'weight', or equal concern, to the interests of every person anywhere whose interests one could ascertain and affect.

To say this is not to deny that the problem of assessing the extent of one's responsibilities in reason for the welfare of persons in other political communities (the problem of 'international justice') is one of the most difficult of all practical problems; and its resolution, by each of us (for our situations and thus our responsibilities differ), is constantly threatened by the pull of unreasonable self-preference, group bias, and lukewarmness about human good.

VII.5   COMMUTATIVE JUSTICE

There is a vast range of relationships and dealings between persons (including dealings between officials and individuals)

---

[17] Cf. J. S. Mill, *Utilitarianism* (1863), ch. 5 (ad fin.).
[18] See Glover, *Causing Death and Saving Lives*, 109–10.

in which neither the requirements or incidents of communal
enterprise nor the distribution (whether by public or private
owners) of a common stock are directly at stake, but in which
there can be question of what is fitting, fair, or just as between the
parties to the relationship. A theory of justice must respond to this
range of questions, and as I have used the name 'distributive' for
the justice whereby one gives and puts into practice reasonable
solutions to the problems discussed in the preceding section, so it
will be convenient to have a single name for the justice that
responds to the present range of problems. For want of a satisfactory term from common English, I adopt a traditional academic
term, 'commutative justice'.

This term has a definite origin. Aristotle, too, wished to divide
the whole field of problems of justice into two broad classes. The
first class he named problems of *distributive* justice (*dianemetikon
dikaion*),[19] and he characterized these problems much as I have:
they deal with whatever pertains to the community as common but
divisible by allotment amongst its members. The second class of
problems he named problems of *corrective* justice (*diorthotikon
dikaion*),[20] the justice that rectifies or remedies inequalities which
arise in dealings (*synallagmata*) between individuals. These 'dealings' may be either voluntary, as in sale, hire, and other business
transactions, or involuntary, as where one man 'deals with' another
by stealing from him, murdering him, or defaming him.[21] *Synallagmata* in Aristotle's account must therefore be understood very
broadly, and not restricted (as in modern Roman law systems) to
reciprocal 'exchanges'; the terms 'dealings' and 'deals with' have
several irrelevantly narrow connotations, but I intend their most
general meaning. The real problem with Aristotle's account is its
emphasis on correction, on the *remedying* of the inequality that
arises when one person injures or takes from another, or when
one party fulfils his side of a bargain while the other does not. This
is certainly one field of problems of justice, but even when added to
the field of distributive justice it leaves untouched a wide range of
problems. 'Correction' and 'restitution' are notions parasitic on
some prior determination of what is to count as a crime, a tort, a
binding agreement, etc.

---

[19] *Nic. Eth.* V.3: 1131b28; 1132b24, 1131b32.
[20] *Nic. Eth.* V.2: 1131a1; V.3: 1131b25; V.4: 1132b25.
[21] *Nic. Eth.* V.2: 1131a1–9.

So it was that Thomas Aquinas, purporting to interpret Aristotle faithfully, silently shifted the meaning of Aristotle's second class of particular justice, and invented a new term for it: 'commutative justice'. Many followers of Aquinas have understood *commutativa* as 'pertaining to exchanges'. But the advantage of Aquinas's new term is precisely that, in his usage, it is limited neither to correction nor to voluntary or business transactions, but is almost as extensive as the term *commutatio* in classical Latin (= 'change'), limited only by its contextual restriction here to the field of human interaction. With this term, then, we can cover the whole field in which, problems of allocation of common stock and the like apart, the problem is to determine what dealings are proper between persons (including groups).

The distinction between distributive and commutative justice is no more than an analytical convenience, an aid to orderly consideration of problems. Many actions are both distributively and commutatively just (or unjust). Consider the act of the judge in giving judgment. The subject-matter of the judgment may be a matter of distributive justice (whether that justice has been assessed by the legislator, as with rules of succession on intestacy, or is left to be assessed by the judge, as in apportionment of damages where there is contributory negligence or of the costs of litigation), or again the subject-matter for adjudication may be a matter of commutative justice (as in an action for the price of goods sold and delivered, or for damages for trespass to goods). But, whether the subject-matter of this act of adjudication be a problem of distributive or of commutative justice, the act of adjudication itself is always matter for distributive justice. For the submission of an issue to the judge itself creates a kind of *common* subject-matter, the *lis inter partes*, which must be allocated between parties, the gain of one party being the loss of the other. The biased or careless judge violates distributive justice by using an irrelevant criterion (or by inappropriately using a relevant criterion) in apportioning the merits and awarding judgment and/or costs. But, finally, we can also consider the judge's duty simply in so far as it is a duty to apply the relevant legal rules; in this respect the duty is one of commutative justice: faithful application of the law is simply what is fitting and required of judges in their official dealings with others.

Moreover, to revert to the question of the subject-matter of litigation, mentioned in the preceding paragraph, there may be fields of law of which it is difficult to say (or at least a matter of controversial interpretation) whether the rules are intended to secure distributive or, rather, commutative justice. The modern law of liability in tort for non-intentionally inflicted personal injuries is such a field, and so, perhaps, is the modern law of frustration of contracts.

Consider the common law of torts. In its 'classical' period (say, between 1850 and 1950) this set of rules and principles was regarded as an instrument of commutative justice, indeed of corrective justice in Aristotle's sense. One party, D, was bound to make payment or restitution to another, P, if and (with 'marginal' exceptions) only if D had behaved wrongfully in relation to P (e.g. by carelessly running P down on the road). But in recent times, in some places more than in others, this view of the function of the law has been challenged by another view which implicitly represents the proper function of the law about compensation for personal injuries as an essentially distributive one. In this view, the question is not 'What are the standards of conduct which individuals must live up to in relation to their "neighbours"?', or 'What should be the extent of liability of one who fails to live up to those standards of conduct?', or even 'How should those injured by the wrongs of others be restored to their former condition?'. Those are questions central to the theory of commutative justice. But in the newer view, the question is held to be 'How should the risks of *common life* be apportioned, especially the risks of such essentially *collaborative* enterprises as travel and traffic by road?'. Injury to one of the participants is then treated as an incidental loss to be set against the gains which accrue to all who participate in this sphere of common life. The costs of this loss should then, as a matter of distributive justice, be shared amongst those who gain most from their part in the whole 'enterprise' and/or who are able to pay with least injury to their own interests or position in it; or should even be shared amongst *all* the participants. The question whether the injury was caused by any fault becomes substantially irrelevant.

Mutual participation, bringing common gains, thus calls for mutual insurance. By the same token, the claims of the injured party for compensation, being now treated as incidents in a kind of common enterprise, are treated as claims upon the common resources; and all such claims must therefore be measured by reference not to the fault and ability to pay of any individual wrongdoer, but to all the other claims, of every sort, on public funds or (if the scheme of compensation is funded wholly by the participants in that particular sphere of life) by reference to all the other claims, public and private, on the funds of the participants.

Such a legal scheme for securing distributive justice seeks, then, to compensate *all* who suffer injury in the relevant course of common life, whereas the scheme for securing commutative justice seeks to compensate *only* those who were injured by the act(s) of any who failed to live up to their duties (in commutative justice) of care and respect for the well-being of others, and who are therefore required to make reparation. On the other hand, the distributive scheme will typically be limited by the resources of the common funds, so that *none* of those compensated will receive as much as *some* of them might have received under the commutative scheme. The duties of wrongdoers in commutative justice no doubt remain, discounted to allow for the compensation received by the injured party from the distributive scheme; but these duties are no longer enforced by law. Hence, if a pure distributive scheme is adopted in a context in which it is inappropriate, some injured parties can rightly say that the law fails to secure them justice.

A similar tension between the perspectives of distributive and commutative justice has long been developing within the common law of contract. In one perspective, which informs much of that law, the parties to a contract are treated as individuals dealing with one another at arm's length, each pursuing interests which remain entirely individual and are merely juxtaposed, so to speak, to the other party's interests by and to the extent defined by the contract. Thus, if I fail to perform as I promised, I ought (subject to any contrary provisions of the contract itself) to restore the other party (so far as money can) to a position *equivalent* to that which that other party, the promisee, would have enjoyed but for my (the promisor's) non-performance; in short, a promise is a guarantee of performance or its equivalent in damages. Such is a perspective characteristic of the theory of commutative justice. But as early as *Hadley v Baxendale* (1854),[22] which settled the English law on quantum of damages for breach of contract, we can discern an alternative perspective which sees non-performance as one of the risks that *both* parties accept when they enter upon their mutual agreement, and that therefore can reasonably be *shared* between them, so that neither bears the risk of having to compensate for *all* the losses that the other may suffer through non-performance. As this perspective has won acceptance, so the rules of frustration of contract have been developed to relieve contracting parties of their obligations of performance or compensation in circumstances where the contractual arrangement, viewed (usually implicitly) by reference to its 'point', *rather as if it were a kind of partnership or common enterprise*, has been frustrated by unforeseen external contingencies. Contemporary English law provides that on frustration of a contract a party who has paid money may recover it, and a party who owed money due under the contract before frustration is relieved from payment, while a party who has incurred expenses may, 'as the court considers just', be allowed to recover them, and a party who has received benefits under the contract before frustration may, 'as the court considers just', be required to share their monetary value with, or hand it over to, the other party.[23] The distributive perspective is carried yet further by recent proposals under which every party to a frustrated contract would be entitled to restitution for any performance of any part of his contractual obligations, while losses would be apportioned equally between the parties making and receiving restitution.

There is no need here to take sides for or against any of these changes in perspective. Often enough, legislative debate concerning them turns on matters only mediately related to the criteria of justice, for example on the efficiency with which alternative schemes or perspectives can be implemented and their expense. But the fundamental issue is really: How reasonable is it to regard the persons whose activities are in question

---

[22] 9 Ex. 341.
[23] Law Reform (Frustrated Contracts) Act 1943 (Eng.), s. 1.

as engaged in a common enterprise? The modern developments in relation to compensation for personal injuries spring from schemes for compensating industrial accidents, where the employees who are injured and the employers who are bound to contribute to the scheme are manifestly engaged in a kind of common enterprise (notwithstanding that the form of their relationship is not that of a legal partnership but envisages only the limited participation that pertains to wage-labour). Can this conception of participation in a common enterprise, in which risk of loss should be shared amongst all participants, reasonably be extended to encompass the whole of the national community? It seems not, at least in respect of certain causes and certain forms of loss.

Having stressed at some length the complex relations that hold between the theory of distributive and the theory of commutative justice, it remains to indicate some of the matters securely located within the province of the latter theory. There are, of course, innumerable aspects of commutative justice: so the following examples are intended only to illustrate some outlines.

First, then, commutative justice may concern relations between ascertained individuals. A's failure, without good reason, to perform on a contract with B is commutatively unjust; and in English (unlike French) law A is required in commutative justice to pay damages to B even when the failure was not culpable (subject to the limitations on liability introduced by the doctrines of remoteness and frustration, already mentioned). If A defames B, being careless of the true facts, or communicating the defamation to persons who have no purposeful and good reason to hear ill of B, A wrongs B in commutative justice, even if a particular legal system (as in the United States) in certain contexts denies B a remedy lest political debate be chilled. (Observe, from the two preceding observations about particular laws, that the relation between law and justice is not symmetrical; the existence of a certain legal regime, say of contract, may create legal duties which are also 'moral' duties in justice because of the other party's reliance upon performance according to *that* legal regime, but which would not be duties in justice under another reasonable legal regime; yet it does not follow that, where the law reasonably abstains from enforcing a duty in justice, that duty is cancelled in justice.)

Again, if A commits perjury in litigation against B, A wrongs B in commutative justice; so, too, do those who appeal against judgment, not in the belief that they have a good case in law or justice, but to delay satisfaction of the judgment debt. The reader will think of very many other instances. Having done so, it will be useful to reflect that adherence to these duties of commutative justice between one *individual* and another is an integral and indispensable aspect of respect and favour for the *common* good. How can a society be said to be well-off in which individuals do not respect each other's rights?

Secondly, an individual may have a duty in commutative justice to many more or less ascertained individuals. One's duty of care in the modern law of tort embodies such a duty.

Thirdly, an individual may have duties in commutative justice to many more or less unascertained individuals. If one abuses, exploits, or 'free-rides' on some system which is advantageous to oneself and to others, knowing that one's abuse may bring about the limitation or abandonment of the scheme (*après moi le déluge*), one is commutatively unjust to all those who might in future have enjoyed the benefits of the original scheme.

Fourthly, one (any individual) has duties in commutative justice to the governing authorities of one's community. (The 'duties to the State' which are violated, say, by treason are a complex amalgam of duties of the second, third, and fourth kind here listed.) So perjury and contempt of court offend against commutative justice in this respect as well as others. The general duty of both officials and private citizens to conform to just (and even, sometimes, to unjust) laws is a duty of commutative justice. (I shall return to this topic at length at XI.7 and XII.1–3.)

Finally, persons holding public authority (in the lax terminology of recent centuries, 'the State') owe duties of commutative justice to those subject to their authority. A scheme of taxation and social welfare may be distributively just; its lawful and regular administration is a matter of commutative justice owed to all those who have ascertainable rights, powers, immunities, or duties under it.

VII.6 JUSTICE AND THE STATE

The foregoing enumeration, like much else in the preceding sections, was tacitly directed against an analysis of justice which became so widespread after the sixteenth century that many people consider it the 'classical' analysis. Much discussion, even outside the confines of this 'traditional' analysis, is significantly moulded by assumptions drawn from it.

The origins of the analysis in question can be traced to Cardinal Cajetan's famous commentary on Aquinas's *Summa Theologiae*. Aquinas had devoted an article to the question whether it is proper to divide justice into two species, distributive and commutative, and had argued that it is.[24] In his commentary on this article, Cajetan introduced a novel interpretation of the whole Aristotelian-Thomist schema, which had classified justice into 'general' (or 'legal') and 'particular' and had subdivided particular justice between distributive and commutative. The charm of Cajetan's new analysis of justice was that it used all the language of the old, and indeed appeared at first glance to be based on some reasoning of Aquinas's—but above all, its abiding attraction was its appearance of symmetry:

There are three species of justice, as there are three types of relationships in any 'whole': the relations of the parts amongst themselves, the relations of the whole to the parts, and the relations of the parts to the whole. And likewise there are three justices: legal, distributive and commutative. For legal justice orients the parts to the whole, distributive the whole to the parts, while commutative orients the parts one to another.[25]

In a very short time, certainly by the time of Dominic Soto's treatise *De Justitia et Jure* (1556), the inner logic of Cajetan's synthesis was being worked out. A modern representative of the post-Cajetan tradition puts it thus:

Three kinds of order are required [by justice]: order of parts to whole, order of whole to parts, and order of one part to another. Legal justice pertains to the first sort, since it governs the relationship of subjects to the State. Distributive justice pertains to the second sort, since it governs the relationship of the State to its subjects. Commutative justice pertains to the third, governing the relationship of one private person or entity to another.[26]

---

[24] *S.T.* II–II q. 61 a. 1.

[25] Cajetan (Thomas de Vio), *Commentaria in Secundam Secundae Divi Thomae de Aquino* (1518), *in* II–II, q. 61, a. 1.

[26] 'Triplex exigitur ordo: ordo partium ad totum, ordo totius ad partes, ordo partis ad partem. Primum respicit justitia legalis quae ordinat subditos ad rempublicam; secundum, justitia distributiva, quae ordinat rempublicam ad subditos; tertium, justitia commutativa quae ordinat privatum ad privatum': B.-H. Merkelbach, Summa theologiae moralis (Paris: 1938), vol. II, nos 252, 253.

On Aquinas's view, anyone in charge of an item of 'common stock' will have duties of distributive justice; hence any property-holder can have such duties, since the goods of this earth are to be exploited and used for the good of all. In the newer view (now thought of as traditional), the duties of distributive justice belong only to the State or the personified 'whole' (community). On Aquinas's view, the State and its officials have duties in commutative justice to the subjects of the State; punishment, for instance, is fundamentally though not exclusively a matter of commutative justice,[27] and the framing of an innocent person is a denial of commutative justice.[28] In the newer view, commutative justice concerns only private transactions. On Aquinas's view (though he is not explicit enough about it), 'legal justice' is the fundamental form of *all* justice, the basis of all obligations, distributive or commutative; for it is the underlying duty to respect and advance the common good. In the newer view, legal justice is little more than the citizen's duty of allegiance to the State and its laws.

The historical success of the new, symmetrically triadic schema is of more than merely historical significance. Particularly influential has been, and is, the notion that it is the State or 'the community as a whole' that is responsible for distributive justice. This drastic limitation of perspective helps along the argument (to take only one contemporary instance) which Robert Nozick directs against redistributive taxation. A primary concern of Nozick's *Anarchy, State and Utopia* is to argue that once anyone has justly acquired capacities, endowments, or holdings (property, etc.), it is unjust for anyone, including the State, to deprive him of any of those holdings, or to conscript any of his capacities, for the purpose of aiding other persons. Systems of taxation for purposes of redistribution and social welfare are therefore unjust; they amount to the imposition of forced labour, and an unwarrantable infringement of a man's rights over his own body, effort, and property, and his rights not to be forced to do certain things.[29]

---

[27] *S.T.* II–II q. 62 a. 3c; q. 80 a. un. ad 1; q. 108 a. 2 ad 1.

[28] *S.T.* II–II q. 64, introduction; q. 68 a. 3.

[29] See *Anarchy, State and Utopia* (Oxford: 1974), ix, 167–74 (in the chapter entitled 'Distributive Justice').

Nozick is far indeed from the tradition of the scholastic textbooks, pre- or post-Cajetan. But the plausibility of his argument comes entirely from its focus on the coercive nature of the State's intervention as the agent of (re)distributive justice. Suppose we abandon this perspective. That is to say: leave the State out of consideration for a moment, and ask instead whether a private property-holder has duties of (re)distributive justice. (The question is strictly inconceivable in the post-Cajetan tradition.) Then we will find that Nozick has little indeed to say in favour of his assumption that what one has justly acquired one can justly hold without regard for the needs, deserts, or other claims of others (except such claims as one has actually created, e.g. by contract, and which one has a duty to satisfy in what I, not Nozick, would call commutative justice). If we see no reason to adopt his assumption that the goods of the earth can reasonably be appropriated by a few to the substantial exclusion of all others, and if we prefer instead the principle[30] that they are to be treated by all as for the benefit of all according to the criteria of distributive justice though partly through the mediation of private holdings, then the question of State coercion, which dominated Nozick's argument, becomes in principle of very secondary importance. For in establishing a scheme of redistributive taxation, etc., the State need be doing no more than crystallize and enforce duties that the property-holder *already* had. Coercion, then, comes into play only in the event of recalcitrance that is wrongful not only in law but also in justice. Distributive justice is here, as in most contexts, a relation between citizens, or groups and associations

---

[30] On what is this principle based? Well, in a nicely ironical passage on p. 160 of *Anarchy, State and Utopia*, Nozick remarks: 'Things come into the world already attached to people having entitlements over them. From the point of view of the historical entitlement conception of justice in holdings [which Nozick favours], those who start afresh to complete "to each according to his—" treat objects as if they appeared from nowhere, out of nothing. A complete theory of justice might cover this limit case [which, in the attached end-note, he says is not 'our own' case]; perhaps here is a use for the usual conceptions of distributive justice'. But, whether or not my theory of distributive justice is one of the 'usual conceptions' that Nozick had in mind, it is clear that his irony is misdirected. The decisive fact is that in 'our own' world the natural resources from which all 'things' or 'objects' are made *did* appear 'from nowhere, out of nothing' and did *not* 'come into the world already attached to people having entitlements over them'. This basic fact conditions all the entitlements subsequently derived from labour, contribution, purchase, or other just sources of private title. See also pp. 170–3 above.

within the community, and is the responsibility of those citizens and groups. The role of the governing authorities and the law in determining, for particular political communities, the particular requirements of distributive justice is a decisive but subsidiary (see VI.5) role.

VII.7   AN EXAMPLE OF JUSTICE: BANKRUPTCY

In this final section I try to consolidate, illustrate, and extend the foregoing analysis by reference to some elements of the English law of bankruptcy—a characteristic modern legal regulation of insolvency.

Bankruptcy is a legal process whereby someone who is insolvent (i.e. cannot discharge his or her financial liabilities) is judicially declared bankrupt, whereupon the bankrupt's property vests in a trustee who holds it solely for the purpose of division amongst the bankrupt's creditors. During bankruptcy the opportunities and rights of the bankrupt to engage in business are severely limited. Upon satisfactory division of the property, the bankrupt may be judicially discharged from bankruptcy, and is thereupon relieved from all further liability in respect of his or her former debts.

The first thing to observe about the legal provisions thus roughly described is that they replace provisions under which an unsatisfied creditor could have a debtor imprisoned. The old provisions were unsatisfactory. For they imposed a condition of servitude upon one who might be innocent of any contempt of law or justice. And, by allowing debtors to be removed, by one of their creditors, into prison where (unlike free persons, or even slaves) they could do nothing to improve their financial position or work off their debts, the old provisions tended to frustrate the commutatively just claims of their other creditors.

Next, observe that the bankruptcy law both gives effect to the commutatively just claims of the insolvent's creditors and at the same time subjects all those claims to a principle of distributive justice. Without a law of bankruptcy, and indeed before the provisions of such law are applied to particular debtors, each of their creditors is entitled to satisfy the whole of his or her claim from the whole of the debtor's property, regardless of the claims of any other creditor. Bankruptcy law pools all the claims, and treats the debtor's property as if it were now the common property of the creditors (put technically, the legal ownership vests in the trustee in bankruptcy but the beneficial interest vests in the creditors in common, subject to a division according to law by the trustee). Bankruptcy law thus departs radically from the fundamental principle of Nozick's 'historical entitlement theory' of justice: 'Whatever arises from a just situation by just steps is itself just'.[31] For if a creditor enforces a commutatively just claim, by the normal processes of law (which are themselves quite just), and thereby swallows up the wherewithal for satisfying any of the equally just claims of other creditors, the situation that has thus 'arisen' cannot (so the law of bankruptcy assumes, quite reasonably) be properly regarded as 'itself just'.[32]

Thirdly, in dividing the debtor's property amongst the creditors, the bankruptcy law uses more than one criterion of distributive justice: (i) It recognizes above all the bankrupt's *need* to be preserved from outlawry, slavery,[33] or helpless indigence; excluded, therefore, from the common pool of assets for division among creditors are the bankrupt's tools of trade, the 'necessary wearing apparel and bedding of himself, his wife and his children', and such earnings of his (after adjudication as a bankrupt and before discharge) as are necessary for maintenance of that family. (ii) The law recognizes the similar *need* of those who were presumably wholly dependent on the debtor for their livelihood; high in the list of preferential claims, which must be satisfied in full before further division of the pooled assets, are the wages or salaries of the debtor's 'clerks or servants, labourers or workmen', earned during the four months before bankruptcy.[34] (iii) The law gives preference, over all other claims upon the pooled assets, to those whose claims are *not* based on their having entered into a business arrangement with the debtor: (a) the expenses and remuneration of those who have

---

[31] Nozick, *Anarchy, State and Utopia*, 151.

[32] Indeed, any attempt by an actually insolvent person (even before legally bankrupted) to give one creditor preference over the others is treated by English law as a 'fraudulent preference' (notwithstanding that the debtor could truthfully say 'I am simply paying off one of my just debts'); see Bankruptcy Act 1914, s 44(1).

[33] See *Re Wilson Ex parte Vine* (1878) 8 Ch D 364 at 366 (CA).

[34] Even higher, rightly or wrongly, is ranked the claim of an apprentice or articled clerk to be released from his obligations to the bankrupt master or principal, and to be repaid a proper proportion of his fee for apprenticeship or articles.

to administer the law of bankruptcy and apply it to the debtor's affairs; (b) claims to money or property belonging to a Friendly Society or Trustee Savings Bank where the bankrupt was an officer of the Society or Bank and had these assets in his or her possession (for these are essentially the funds of persons who dealt with the Society or Bank, not with the bankrupt); (c) the claims of central and local governments to one year's unpaid taxes or rates. (iv) Conversely, where someone has entered into an arrangement with the debtor that partakes of the nature of partnership as such, that person's claims under that arrangement are deferred or postponed to the claims of all the ordinary business creditors: such arrangements include loans between spouses, and loans on the basis that the lender will share in profits. (v) Finally, as between all the ordinary creditors, who are neither preferred nor deferred under the law and who have no realizable security (mortgage, charge, or lien over the debtor's property), 'equality is equity'. The debts they prove are paid to them *pari passu*. That is to say, each receives, from the pool remaining after payment of preferred creditors, the same percentage of the debt owed *to him or her* (not the same percentage of that pool); if the pool is insufficient, the claim of each abates proportionately. This is, then, another instance of the 'geometrical' equality which, as opposed to 'arithmetical' equality, is (as Aristotle said) characteristic of distributive justice. In other words, within this class of creditors, the criterion of distributive justice is: 'to each according to his or her (legally recognized) claim upon the debtor in commutative justice'.

Fourthly, as even the foregoing incomplete list of principles for treating the property in the possession of the debtor may have suggested to the reader, the English law of bankruptcy applies principles of justice in ways which are reasonable but not necessarily or always the only reasonable, or even most reasonable, amongst possible ways. Doubts have reasonably, if not compellingly, been raised about, for example, the priority accorded to claims to unpaid taxes, and about the doctrine (expanded by the courts in both England and the United States) that 'traceable' property held by the insolvent on an actual or even a constructive trust can be claimed directly by the 'beneficiary' and is exempted from the common pool.

Fifthly, many features of the law of bankruptcy are devices to deter and/or to circumvent the effects of fraud, i.e. of attempts by debtors to evade their debts or the process of bankruptcy, or to live beyond their means at the expense of their creditors, or to enter into new debts with unsuspecting persons, or to prefer one of their creditors to others without lawful reason. The law has to determine the requirements of justice in a society where persons are only partially compliant and imperfectly just.

Sixthly, the law of bankruptcy itself can be made the instrument of injustice, above all by bankrupts themselves. For it is certainly possible, and in some places not uncommon, that persons who could pay their just debts if they were so minded may choose instead to have those debts cancelled by bankruptcy, submitting themselves to temporary inconvenience for the sake of a future freedom from financial difficulty, a freedom which their own action may deny to their defeated creditors (say, small shopkeepers) or to others (say, fellow students to whom valuable sources of credit may now be closed). No system of law can secure justice if its subjects, let alone its officials, are themselves careless of justice.

Seventh, any law about insolvency must effect an adjustment between aspects of justice which, in particular circumstances, compete. The whole idea of bankruptcy is to make such an adjustment between commutative and distributive justice in the peculiar circumstances of insolvency. But in detail, too, there are numerous compromises between, for example, speed (for it is an aspect of justice that just debts be paid at the time promised and that distribution to the needy be made at the time of their need) and certainty (for it is an aspect of justice that persons who have just claims should not lose them through momentary oversight or temporary absence, and that persons who have no just claim should not be paid on some inadequately tested story). *General* and clear rules about procedure, proof, notification, time, appeals, etc., must be adopted, notwithstanding that their very generality and clarity—the source of their value in the effort to do justice—will sometimes occasion the failure of particular parties to secure the satisfaction of their just claims. It is not that such contingencies were unforeseen, but that to provide exhaustively against them would for practical purposes defeat the just claims of many more.

Finally, the law of bankruptcy is worth attending to, as one of the relatively few instances in which a formal distribution of a common stock or pool is carried out. More commonly, in societies which for the all-round well-being of their members have grown complex and which recognize the value of individual autonomy both as an aspect of human flourishing and as a cause of economic advancement, the claims of distributive justice are met by establishing schemes of property-holding, inheritance, contract, taxation, etc., which *tend* to check the growth of *de facto* inequalities (whether arising from catastrophic loss or from unlimited accumulation) within a framework which, since it looks formally to a *process* of piecemeal satisfaction of particular claims of commutative justice, would otherwise permit unlimited inequalities. This is reasonable, both (a) because the reasonable criteria for assessing distributive justice do not yield any one pattern of distribution (or even any determinable set of patterns) on which all reasonable people would be bound to agree, and more fundamentally (b) because to secure and maintain a pattern of distribution without reference to any of the commutatively just claims, gifts, and liabilities which individuals, families, or other groups create for themselves would be possible only if every individual initiative were stifled *and* every individual's acts of injustice overlooked. No mutually exclusive distinction between 'end-states' which can be assessed as distributively just and 'processes' which create and satisfy claims and liabilities in commutative justice can reasonably be maintained except in relation to very limited projects. On the scale of the full community which seeks the common good of the all-round flourishing of all its members the distinction fails (i) because the flourishing of persons has among its intrinsic aspects (as distinct from mere extrinsic means) the opportunity of engaging in certain processes (such as giving and being given, choosing one's own commitments and investments of skill or effort, etc.), and (ii) because the existence of such a community is radically open-ended, members continually being born into it, departing and dying, so that no one slice of time (by reference to which a pattern could be assessed as just, purely distributively) has the privileged status of an 'end-state'.

Recalling an earlier discussion (see V.6), we can now add: the dream of a purely distributive justice shares with utilitarian consequentialism the illusion that human good is adequately quantifiable, the illusion that pursuit of the common good is pursuit of a once-for-all attainable objective, like *making an omelette*, and the illusion that it is reasonable to postulate a privileged point or slice of time by reference to which the consequences of actions could notionally be summed and evaluated, apportioned, and distributed.

NOTES

VII.1

'Justice to oneself' and 'justice in the soul'...I follow Aristotle in discounting these metaphorical extensions and in focusing on relations between distinct persons: see *Nic. Eth.* V.11: 1138a4–b13.

Word-play about right, rights, etc....This is not restricted to modern European languages. See the analysis of the Barotse word *tukelo* and its cognates, meaning 'right', 'a right', 'straight', 'upright (just)', 'duty', and 'justice': Max Gluckman, *The Judicial Process among the Barotse* (Manchester: 1955), 66.

Other-directedness, duty, and equality...The excavation of these elements from the quarry of Aristotle's treatise on justice (which was itself an excavation from Plato and from common language) is the work of Aquinas: on other-directedness, see *S.T.* II–II q. 57 a. 1c; q. 58 aa. 1c, 2; q. 80 a. un. c; on equality, see I–II q. 114 a. 1c; II–II q. 57 a. 1 ad 3, a. 2c; q. 61 a. 2 ad 2; q. 157 a. 3c; on the *debitum*, which Aquinas owes to both the Latin language and the Roman law, see I q. 21 a. 1 ad 3; I–II q. 60 a. 3c; II–II q. 58 aa. 10c, 11c; also q. 58 a. 1 ad 6, a. 3 ad 2; q. 122 a. 1c. At the head of his analysis of justice, Aquinas places the Roman jurists' tag *'justitia est constans et perpetua voluntas jus suum [uni]cuique tribue[ndi]': Digest* I, 1 (*de Justitia et Jure*), 10; also *Institutes* I, 1, 1. Close to Aquinas's analysis is Cicero's eclectic synthesis, *De Finibus*, V, xxiii, 65–7.

'Arithmetical' and 'geometrical' equality...This is the *differentia* which Aristotle most emphasizes in distinguishing distributive from corrective justice: *Nic. Eth.* V.3–4: 1131a10–1132b20, esp. 1131b12, 1132a2.

VII.2

From 'legal' to 'general' justice...On the importance of Aristotle's effort to clarify the connotations of *dikaion*, see *Gauthier-Jolif*, II/1, 335–6. Aristotle comes close to calling his 'legal justice' also 'general justice': *Nic. Eth.* V.1: 1130b15–16. The terminological emphasis is somewhat shifted by Aquinas from 'legal' towards 'general justice', but 'legal justice' is retained: *S.T.* II–II q. 58 aa. 5c, 6c, a. 7, tit. and obj. 3; I–II q. 60 a. 3 ad 2. On the unfortunate later consequences of Aquinas's retention of the term 'legal justice' see VII.6. Beyond matters of terminology, however, it is important to recognize that Aristotle uses the term 'legal justice' (*dikaion...nomimon*) above all because his whole analysis is focused on the *polis*, in which the whole of human life is regulated by posited law: see *Pol.* I.1: 1253a38–40; *Nic. Eth.* V.1: 1129b12, 18–19; V.6: 1134a30–36, 1134b13–15; this leads to the notorious unclarity of his discussion of natural as distinct from conventional (*nomikon*) justice: V.7: 1134b18–1135a6; for all this, see Eric Voegelin, '*Das Rechte von Natur*' in his *Anamnesis* (Munich: 1966), 116 ff. In Aquinas's account of legal or general justice the restriction to the political community and posited law is clearly transcended: the 'law' that is the *ratio* of the *jus* which is the object of justice is primarily the *lex naturalis* and only secondarily the *lex positiva* which is 'derived' from *lex naturalis*: see, e.g., *S.T.* II–II q. 57, a. 1 ad 2; I–II q. 95 a. 2; see also X.7 below. Notice, finally, the link between Aquinas's adoption of the Aristotelian term 'legal justice' and his own fundamental definition of law as 'an ordinance of reason *for the common good*…': I–II q. 90 aa. 1c, 2c, 4c, explicitly recalled in II–II q. 58 a. 5; also I–II q. 100 a. 8c. On 'general justice' between Plato and the seventeenth century, see G. Del Vecchio, *Justice* (ed. A. H. Campbell, Edinburgh: 1952), ch. II, esp. the notes.

VII.3

Distributive justice, concerns the appropriation to individuals of what is 'common'…See *Nic. Eth.* V.2: 1130b31–33; V.4: 1131b27–32; *S.T.* II–II q. 61, a. 1c ad 5. On the importance of not confusing this divisible '*id quod est commune*' (common stock, incidents of common enterprise, etc.) with 'the common good', see P.-D. Dognin, '*La notion thomiste de justice face aux exigences modernes*' (1961) 45 *Revue des Sciences Philosoph. et Théol.* 601, 615, 620, 627; '*La justice particulière comporte-t-elle deux espèces?*' (1965) 65 *Revue Thomiste* 398, 403, 408. The common good which is the object(ive) of all justice logically cannot be distributed.

The common good requires that individuality not be absorbed in common enterprises…This is no more paradoxical than the related principles that privacy is a good which the organs of the community should defend, or that there is a public interest in maintaining the confidentiality of certain sorts of personal communication.

Common enterprises should be to help individuals to help themselves…On this principle of *justice*, see the note on 'subsidiarity', appended to VI.5. For its application to the question of property, in the 'natural law' teaching of the Catholic Church, see, e.g., Second Vatican Council, *Gaudium et Spes: Pastoral Constitution on the Church in the Modern World* (1965), paras 65, 69, and citations.

Private property…For an analysis of the elements of the focal meaning of 'private property', see A. M. Honoré, 'Ownership', in A. G. Guest (ed.), *Oxford Essays in Jurisprudence* (Oxford: 1961), 107–47. For an ample treatment of the place of private property and enterprise in a just social economy, see J. Messner, *Social Ethics: Natural Law in the Modern World* (St. Louis: 1949), 697–947, esp. 785–800.

VII.4

Equal right of all to respectful consideration in distribution…See R. M. Dworkin, *Taking Rights Seriously* (London: 1977), 180, 227, and (with some ambiguous gloss, and questionable conclusions from a 'thin theory' of human good) 273. Note, moreover, that if it is to be treated as 'the formal principle *of justice*', the injunction 'Treat like cases alike' must be taken in a more than merely formal sense; it must, for example, implicitly treat all human beings as alike in their humanity and in their basic entitlement to be treated differently from animals and to be treated by the agent, to whom the injunction is addressed, as 'like' him in their fundamental capacity to be subjects of human flourishing: see, with reservations, Del Vecchio, *Justice*, ch. 8; see also J. Finnis, 'The Value of the Human Person' (1972) 27 *Twentieth Century* (Australia), 126–37. Those who propose that animals have rights have a deficient appreciation of the basic forms of human good. At the root of their contention is the conception that good consists essentially in sentience (cf. IV.5); for it is only sentience that is common to human beings and the animals which are said to have rights. (For they do not have regard to life as such, or even to animal life as such: they do not propose to stop the phagocytes in their blood from destroying alien life.) Even if we consider the bodily human goods, and those simply as experienced, we see that the quality of this experience is very different from a merely animal consciousness, since it is experienced as expressive of decision, choice, reflectiveness, commitment, as fruition of purpose, or of self-discipline or self-abandonment, and as the action of a responsible personality. The basic human goods are not abstract forms, such as 'life' or 'conscious life': they are good as aspects of the flourishing of a person. And if the proponents of animal rights point to very young babies, or very old and decayed or mentally defective persons (or to someone asleep?), and ask how their state differs empirically from that of a flourishing, friendly, and clever dog, and demand to know why the former are accorded the respect due to right-holders while the latter is not, we must reply that respect for human good reasonably extends as far as human beings, and is not to be extinguished by the circumstance that the incidents or 'accidents' of affairs have deprived a particular human being of the opportunity of a full flourishing.

Does justice demand that we give up virtually everything to feed the starving anywhere in the world?... For the suggestion that it does ('perhaps to the point of marginal utility'), see P. Singer, 'Famine, Affluence and Morality' (1972) 1 *Phil. Pub. Aff.* 229 at 234. Many strands of ethical methodology and of *Weltanschauung* are involved in any discussion of this question. So far as the suggestion rests on a denial of the moral relevance of the distinction between actions and omissions, note that the implications of the denial do not all have the 'edifying' quality of the suggestion itself. Thus Glover, *Causing Death and Saving Lives* (Harmondsworth, 1977), 104–6, qualifies Father Zossima's claim that 'everyone of us is responsible in every way' (see VII.4, fn. 16), by observing that our time is limited, so that selection of priorities is inevitable. From here he argues that his denial of the action-omission distinction 'does not *entail* the view that... parents playing with their children ought to be trying to raise money for Oxfam instead. (But it does make us ask the disturbing question: would we kill people if it were necessary for our pursuit of [such] activities?... (There is always the disturbing question, for those of us who reject the acts and omissions doctrine, of the extent to which we would think it legitimate to kill people, in order to bring about things that make life interesting for the rest of us... This Dostoyevskian question, when taken seriously, is likely to force us to reconsider *both* how justifiable it is for us to spend time playing with our children rather than helping fight starvation *and* the matter of whether positive acts of killing are quite as hard to justify as we usually suppose...)'. Leaving to one side Glover's odd procedure of framing questions for practical reasonableness in terms of what 'we *would* do or think, and what we are 'likely' to do or think, it cannot be said that his very frank book even sketches an answer to *these* questions. This is not to say that the distinction between action and omission is *always* morally decisive or important; nor is it to say that the following maxim, adopted by the Vatican Council II, *Gaudium et Spes* (1965), para. 69, from Gratian's *Decretum* (c. 1140), c. 21, dist. 86, has no application: 'Feed the man dying of hunger, because if you do not feed him you are killing him'.

Classic and latter-day utilitarianism... In assessing the new utilitarian conception of justice developed in Glover's book, and in other recent writings, bear in mind G. E. M. Anscombe's comment on an earlier phase in the development of utilitarianism: 'we may state the thesis thus: it does not make any difference to a man's responsibility for an effect of his action which he can foresee, that he does not intend it. Now this sounds rather edifying; it is I think quite characteristic of very bad degenerations of thought on such questions that they sound edifying' ('Modern Moral Philosophy' (1958)

33 *Philosophy* 1 at 11). The difference between the thesis there mentioned and the new thesis is simply that the new utilitarians condemn as morally irrelevant the distinction between actions and omissions, which the older utilitarians retained from the non-utilitarian moral culture of their upbringing. See Glover, *Causing Death and Saving Lives*, 94.

VII.5

'Synallagmata' *not limited to exchanges*...See *Gauthier-Jolif*, II/1, 350.

'*Corrective justice*'...For the translation of *diorthōtikon*, and for critique of Aristotle's restriction of this second category of particular justice, see *Gauthier-Jolif*, II/1, 358–9; also 369–72; cf. Del Vecchio, *Justice*, 61. The fascination of Aristotle's restriction can be seen in Hart, *Concept of Law*, 154–5 [159], where the 'primary application of justice' is said to be 'to matters of distribution and compensation'. For Hart's ingenious relating of 'redress' to his 'general principle...of justice' ('Treat like cases alike and treat different cases differently'), see *Concept of Law*, 160–1 [164–5].

Aquinas and 'commutative justice'...*Gauthier-Jolif*, 370, argue that the introduction of this term rests on a misunderstanding occasioned by the ambiguous Latin translation of Aristotle that Aquinas used. This seems unlikely, in view of the extremely elaborate treatment of commutative justice that Aquinas undertook in *S.T.* II–II qq. 64–78, and in view of the conceptual gaps left by Aristotle's emphasis on correction. For an example of Aquinas's wide use of '*commutatio*', see, e.g., II–II q. 80 a. un. ad 4; but the real proof is the range of topics he treats under the heading of commutative justice, outlined in II–II q. 61 a. 3c.

Distributive justice, commutative justice, and the act of judicial judgment...See Aquinas, *S.T.* II–II q. 63 a. 4 ad 1.

Compensation for personal injuries...See P. S. Atiyah, *Accidents, Compensation and the Law* (London: 1970). For the conceptual shift of the modern law of torts towards an attempt to 'distribute risks and losses', see, e.g., J. G. Fleming, *Law of Torts* (Sydney: 5th edn, 1977), 9–10.

Limitation of liability in law of contract...For suggestive analysis along the lines adopted here, see F. H. Lawson, *Remedies of English Law* (Harmondsworth: 1972), 336–8, 104–9, 177–9. For a criticism of recent developments, from the perspective of commutative justice, and linking the developments to a 'risk' theory of contractual obligation (itself linked to Holmes's analysis of contractual obligation, criticized at XI.5), see Roscoe Pound, *An Introduction to the Philosophy of Law* (rev. edn 1954), 164–8.

VII.6

The triadic schema: distributive-commutative-legal...For one of the countless expositions adopting this schema, see H. Rommen, *The Natural Law* (St. Louis and London: 1947), 67. For references to some sources, and a recognition that the schema falsifies both Aristotle and Aquinas, see Del Vecchio, *Justice*, 35–6; also 37–9, suggesting rightly that the term 'social justice' used in recent Catholic social teaching is equivalent to Aquinas's 'legal justice', and is used to fill the gap left by the mislocation of legal justice by the triadic schema. To like effect, and more fundamentally, see P.-D. Dognin, 'La notion thomiste de justice face aux exigences modernes' (1961) 45 *Rev. des Sc. Phil. et Théol.* 601–40; 'La justice particulière comporte-t-elle deux espèces?' (1965) *Rev. Thom.* 398–425. For the priority of Cajetan, see *ibid.* (1965) 415–16; (1961) 624–38. For attempts to interpret Aristotle 'triadically' for the purpose (not shared by Cajetan) of assimilating him to the threefold principle of justice proposed by

Digest I, 1, 10 (Ulpian) ('*honeste vivere, neminem laedere, suum cuique tribuere*'), see citations in Del Vecchio, *Justice*, 25–6, 63–4; and G. Grua, *La justice humaine selon Leibniz* (Paris: 1956), 80–3.

Nozick on redistribution of property . . . For criticism of Nozick's position on other grounds, compatible with those advanced here (though too doubtful of the justice of private property), see A. M. Honoré, 'Property, Title and Redistribution' (1977) 10 *Arch.R.S.P.* 107–15.

VII.7

Doubts about the order of priority in distribution in bankruptcy . . . See, e.g., Lawson, *Remedies of English Law*, 181–94, 338–41.

'*End-states' and 'processes'* . . . Nozick's discussion in *Anarchy, State and Utopia*, 153–64, is valuable, but fails to reach the fundamental point made here in the text. This fundamental point is expressed by Aristotle in his important distinction between practical reasonableness (*phronēsis*) and technical ability (*technē*) (in other words, between 'doing something' and 'making something'): 'making aims at an end distinct from the end of making, whereas in doing the end cannot be other than the act itself: doing well [*eupraxia*] is in itself the end [*telos*]': *Nic. Eth.* VI.4: 1140b3–6; see also II.4: 1105a32; and John M. Cooper, *Reason and Human Good in Aristotle* (Cambridge, Mass.: 1975), 2, 78, 111. More vivid, perhaps, is Cicero, *De Finibus* III, vii, 24: 'Wisdom is not like seamanship or medicine, but like the arts of acting and of dancing—for its end, being the actual exercise of the art, is contained within the art, and is not something extraneous to it'. This is the root of the principle of the *subsidiary* function of communal enterprise (a principle of justice: see VII.3 above).

VIII

RIGHTS

VIII.1 'NATURAL', 'HUMAN', OR 'MORAL' RIGHTS

ALMOST everything in this book is about human rights ('human rights' being a contemporary idiom for 'natural rights': I use the terms synonymously). For, as we shall see, the modern grammar of rights provides a way of expressing virtually all the requirements of practical reasonableness. Indeed, this grammar of rights is so extensive and supple in its reach that its structure is generally poorly understood; misunderstandings in discussions about rights, and about particular (alleged) rights and their extent, are consequently rather frequent. For this reason, and also because both the explanatory *justification* of claims of right and the resolution of many conflicting claims of right require us to identify values and principles which need not be expressed in terms of rights, the explicit discussion of rights occupies only this one chapter. But the reader who follows the argument of this chapter will readily be able to translate most of the previous discussions of community and justice, and the subsequent discussions of authority, law, and obligation, into the vocabulary and grammar of rights (whether 'natural' or 'legal').

This vocabulary and grammar of rights is derived from the language of lawyers and jurists, and is strongly influenced by its origins. So, although our own concern is primarily with the human or natural rights that may be appealed to whether or not embodied in the law of any community, it will be useful to devote the next section to a resumé of the results of contemporary juristic analysis of rights-talk. For the logic that we can uncover in legal uses of the term 'a right' and its cognates will be found largely applicable for an understanding of 'moral' rights-talk. (Human or natural rights are the fundamental and general moral rights; particular or concrete moral rights—for example, James's right not to have his private correspondence

read by John during his absence from the office today—can be
spoken of as 'human' or 'natural', but it is more usual to speak of
them as 'moral' rights, derived, of course, from the general forms of
moral, i.e. human rights: the distinction thus drawn by usage is not,
however, very firm or clear.)

VIII.2   AN ANALYSIS OF RIGHTS-TALK

The American jurist Hohfeld, building on earlier juristic work,
published an analysis of rights which, though poorly understood
by many of its exponents, satisfactorily accommodates a wide
range of lawyers' uses of the term 'a right' and its cognates—
though not, as we shall see, all such uses. Departing from Hohfeld's own style of exposition, we may say that the fundamental
postulates of his system are: (i) that all assertions or ascriptions of
rights can be reduced without remainder to ascriptions of one or
some combination of the following four 'Hohfeldian rights': (a)
'claim-right' (called by Hohfeld 'right *stricto sensu*'), (b) 'liberty'
(called by Hohfeld 'privilege'), (c) 'power', and (d) 'immunity'; and
(ii) that to assert a Hohfeldian right is to assert a three-term
relation between one person, one act-description, and one other
person. These two postulates, supplemented by a vocabulary
partly in current use and partly devised *ad hoc*, generate the
following logical relations (where A and B signify persons,
natural or legal, and ϕ stands for an act-description signifying
some act):

(1) A has a *claim-right* that B should ϕ, if and only if B has a *duty* to
A to ϕ.

(2) B has a *liberty* (relative to A) to ϕ, if and only if A has *no-claim-
right* ('a no-right') that B should not ϕ.

(2') B has a *liberty* (relative to A) not to ϕ, if and only if A has *no-
claim-right* ('a no-right') that B should ϕ.

(3) A has a *power* (relative to B) to ϕ, if and only if B has a *liability*
to have his or her legal position changed by A's ϕ-ing.

(4) B has an *immunity* (relative to A's ϕ-ing), if and only if A
has no power (i.e. a *disability*) to change B's legal position by
ϕ-ing.

It will be observed that the reference of 'ϕ' in (3) and (4) is to some act (a 'juridical act')[1] which is defined at least partly by reference to its effect upon juridical relationships, whereas, in (1), (2), and (2'), 'ϕ' may denote either juridical acts or, more commonly, acts ('natural acts')[2] fully definable without reference to their effect upon juridical relationships (even though the act may entail such an effect under a given legal regime and may accordingly be the subject of legal definition in that regime). It may be thought that in discussion of human rights, outside the context of particular legal regimes, relations on the model of (3) and (4) will play little or no part. But, although powers and immunities from the exercise of powers do indeed play a less prominent role in such discussions than claim-rights and liberties, it would be a mistake to overlook them. For wherever A can grant B permission to do something that otherwise B would have the (moral) duty not to do, A can be said to have a right of much the same character as a Hohfeldian legal power; and wherever A's moral claim-rights, liberties, and powers cannot be affected merely by B's purported grants of permission to C, A's rights can be said to involve or be buttressed by a right of the same character as a Hohfeldian immunity.

Still, the most important of the aids to clear thinking provided by Hohfeld's schema is the distinction between A's *claim-right* (which has as its correlative B's duty) and A's *liberty* (which is A's freedom from duty and thus has as its correlative the absence or negation of the claim-right that B would otherwise have). A claim-right is always either, positively, a right to be given something (or assisted in a certain way) by someone else, or, negatively, a right *not* to be interfered with or dealt with or treated in a certain way, by someone else. When the subject-matter of one's claim of right is one's own act(s), forbearance(s), or omission(s), that claim cannot be to a claim-right, but can only be to a liberty (or, in the case of juridical acts, to a power). Of course, one's liberty to act in the specified way may be enhanced and protected by a *further* right or set of rights, viz. the claim-right(s) not to be interfered with by B, C, D...in exercising one's liberty. But a liberty thus protected by a claim-

---

[1] For example, buying, selling, leasing, granting, marrying, paying, adjudicating, enacting...
[2] For example, walking, hitting, travelling by aeroplane, defaming...

right is not a distinct type of Hohfeldian right; it is a conjunction, never logically necessary but always beneficial to the liberty-holder, of two distinct Hohfeldian relationships (each of which, of course, may be and normally is 'multital', i.e. obtains in identical form not only between A and B but also between A and C, A and D, A and . . .). In the law, such conjunctions of a liberty with a claim-right are often supplemented by further conjoined rights; for example, by the claim-right to compensation in the event of wrongful (i.e. duty-breaking) interference with the liberty, and/or by the ancillary liberty to resort to self-help or to approach the courts in defence of one's substantive liberty, and/or by the power to institute legal proceedings or to waive compliance with the duty, etc. Most 'legal rights', even when not multital, are in fact combinations, often very complex, of Hohfeldian rights; Hohfeld's ambition was to enable any legal right, such as the undifferentiated legal 'right of A to £10 under this contract', to be resolved or translated without remainder into its component Hohfeldian rights.

It has, recently, however, been demonstrated that such a translation, while it may always be possible (at least in principle), may none the less fail to provide a full elucidation of lawyers' ascriptions of rights. Lawyers frequently talk about rights, not as three-term relations between two persons and an act of a certain type, but as two-term relations between persons and one subject-matter or (in a broad sense) *thing*: for example, someone's right to £10 under a contract, or to (a share in) a specified estate, or to the performing rights of an opera. The reason why such a two-term ascription of rights is preferred by lawyers, in many contexts, is this: it gives an intelligible unity to a temporal series of the many and varying *sets of* Hohfeldian rights which at different times one and the same set of rules provides in order to secure and give substance to one *subsisting* objective. To take the simplest example: A, who has the right to £10 under a contract, may at one time have a Hohfeldian claim-right to be paid £10 by B, and at a later time (B's debt having been assumed by C) another Hohfeldian claim-right, to be paid £10 by C; and the procedural rights (Hohfeldian claim-rights, powers, etc.) that A enjoys to enforce this right to £10 may be shifting, either in step or out of step with the shift between the earlier claim-right to be paid £10 and the later. Yet this series of differing sets of Hohfeldian rights is intelligibly unified; for the shifting applications of the various relevant legal rules all relate to one topic, the 'right to £10 under that contract', a non-Hohfeldian right of which the benefit, the burden, and the procedural props and incidents can all be shifted more or less independently of each other without affecting the 'right itself' which is the constant focus of the law's concern.

This explanation of the persistence of 'two-term' 'thing-oriented' rights-talk, amongst lawyers familiar with Hohfeld's 'three-term' 'act-oriented' schema of rights, will be worth bearing in mind when we turn to consider natural rights such as 'the right to life' (see VIII.5). At the moment, however, it will be useful to conclude this short account of the logic of contemporary legal rights-talk by referring briefly to the jurisprudential debate about the proper *explanation* of rights and of the logic of rights-talk. This debate is provoked by two different problems, but the principal opposing answers to each of these problems overlap (as if there were only one problem evoking the opposing theses).

The first problem is technical. Before the Hohfeldian schema can be applied to any rule or to the translation of any non-Hohfeldian rights-talk, it is necessary to stipulate at least one further definitional postulate which Hohfeld omitted (at least, expressly) to supply. For, granted that B has a *duty* when, in virtue of a certain rule, B is required to act in a certain way, when shall we say that there is, correlative with this duty, a claim-right? And in whom does the claim-right vest? To these questions there are two opposing answers. The first answer is that there is a claim-right correlative to B's duty if and only if there is some ascertainable person A for whose benefit the duty has been imposed, in the sense that A is to be the recipient of the (presumable) advantage of B's performance of or compliance with the duty; and that that person A has the claim-right correlative to B's duty. The alternative answer is that there is some person A with a claim-right correlative to B's duty, if and only if there is some person A who has the power to take appropriate remedial action at law in the event of B's failure to comply with that duty. It seems that Hohfeld himself would have favoured the latter answer had he squarely faced the question. But neither answer is consistently reflected in legal discourse. Consider, for example, a body of law which (like English law) provides that, where B and C enter into a contract that C shall pay a sum to A, A has no power to enforce C's duty or to take any remedial action at law in the event of C's non-performance. On the first approach, we could express the purport of this law by saying that, under such a contract, A has a claim-right correlative to C's duty but cannot enforce or uphold that claim-right at law.[3] On the second approach, we would be bound to say that, in this state of the law, A simply has no rights under the contract, even though it was made for A's benefit. English lawyers, while agreed about the content of the relevant rules, in fact waver between these two approaches. Most state brusquely that in English law a third party (A) has no rights under a contract. Others, of high authority, say that such a third party does indeed have rights (meaning legal rights) despite being personally unable to enforce them at law.[4]

If one wishes to apply the Hohfeldian analysis, therefore, one must first *stipulate* which of these two meanings of 'claim-right' one is going to adopt, and must bear in mind that, whichever meaning one adopts, one's subsequent ascriptions of claim-rights will not always correspond with legal usage. But beyond this first, technical problem, which is thus to be solved by simply stipulating how one will use the term 'claim-right', there is a philosophical problem not to be solved by stipulation. This is the question: What, if any, is the underlying principle, unifying the various types of relationships that are reasonably said to concern 'rights'? Or, more crudely: Is there some general explanation of what it is to have a right?

The principal competing answers to this broad question parallel and overlap with the above two proposals for providing a specific meaning for 'claim-right'. On the one hand, rights of all forms are said to be *benefits* secured for persons by rules regulating the relationships between those persons and other

---

[3] We could add, on this approach, that: (i) B, too, has a claim-right correlative to C's duty (so that, formally, C has a legal duty comprising two Hohfeldian duties of identical form), since it is always (presumably) for the benefit of a promisee that the promisor should honour the promise (even when the material benefits of the promise go to someone other than the promisee); and (ii) B, unlike A, can enforce this claim-right.

[4] See *Beswick v Beswick* [1968] AC 58 at 71 (Lord Reid), 89 (Lord Pearce).

persons subject to those rules. These benefits are various: there is the advantage of being the recipient of other persons' acts of service or forbearances; the advantage of being legally or morally free to act; the advantage of being able to change one's own or others' legal position, and of being immune from such change (when of a form characteristically disadvantageous to anyone subject to the change) at the hands of others; the advantage of being able to secure any or all of the foregoing advantages by action at law, or at least compensation for wrongful denial of any of them; and finally, if we shift to the two-term thing-focused rights of lawyers' talk, there are the various advantages constituted by the things or states of affairs which are the subject-matter of such rights.

On the other hand, it has been argued by some that the foregoing 'benefit' or 'interest' theory of rights treats rights too undiscriminatingly, as if they were no more than the 'reflex' of rules which impose duties, or relieve from duties, or enable duties to be created, shifted, or annulled. This, it is said, is to miss the point of rights. For, it is said, the point and unifying characteristic of rules which entail or create rights is that such rules specifically recognize and respect a person's *choice*, either negatively by not impeding or obstructing it (liberty and immunity) or affirmatively by giving legal or moral effect to it (claim-right and power). Indeed, in this view, moral rights are said to belong to a 'branch of morality which is specifically concerned to determine when one person's freedom may be limited *by another's* [freedom]'. Just as the 'benefit' theory gives reason for adopting the first approach to fixing the meaning of Hohfeld's claim-right, so the 'choice' theory gives reason for adopting the second approach. As Hart put it: 'The case of a right correlative to obligation then emerges as only a special case of legal power in which the right-holder is at liberty to waive or extinguish or to enforce or leave unenforced another's obligation'.[5]

---

[5] H. L. A. Hart, 'Bentham on Legal Rights', in *Oxford Essays II*, 171 at 196–7; also 192: 'The idea is that of one individual being given by the law exclusive control, more or less extensive, over another person's duty so that in the area of conduct covered by that duty the individual who has the right is a small-scale sovereign to whom the duty is owed'. This image of 'temporary authority or sovereignty' is already present in Hart, 'Are there any Natural Rights?' (1955) 64 *Philosophical Rev.* 175–91 at 184, reprinted in A. M. Quinton, *Political Philosophy* (Oxford: 1967), 70.

But Hart, the principal contemporary exponent of the 'choice' or 'will' theory of rights, has recently conceded (in the course of a firm defence of it as an explanation of lawyers' talk about 'ordinary' law) that that theory is inadequate to explain how the language of rights is deployed by those who, in assessing the justice or constitution-ality of laws, treat 'certain freedoms and benefits... as essential for the maintenance of the life, the security, the development, and the dignity of the individual' and thus speak of these freedoms and benefits as rights. In such discourse, 'the core of the notion of rights is neither individual choice nor individual benefit but basic or fundamental individual needs':[6] in my terminology, basic aspects of human flourishing. In the light of this concession, it is not necessary here to settle the dispute between the 'benefit' and the 'choice' theories, as regards strictly legal rights. It suffices that, for the less restricted purposes of this chapter, we may safely speak of rights wherever a basic principle or requirement of practical rea-sonableness, or a rule derived therefrom, gives to A, and to each and every other member of a class to which A belongs, the benefit of (i) a positive or negative requirement (obligation) imposed upon B (including, *inter alia*, any requirement not to interfere with A's activity or with A's enjoyment of some other form of good), or (ii) the ability to bring it about that B is subject to such a requirement, or (iii) the immunity from being subjected by B to any such requirement.

VIII.3   ARE DUTIES 'PRIOR TO' RIGHTS?

In short, the modern vocabulary and grammar of rights is a many-faceted instrument for reporting and asserting the requirements or other implications of a relationship of justice *from the point of view of the person(s) who benefit(s) from* that relationship. It provides a way of talking about 'what is just' from a special angle: the viewpoint of the 'other(s)' to whom something (including, *inter alia*, freedom of choice) is owed or due, and who would be wronged if denied that something. And the contemporary debate shows that there is a strong though not irresistible tendency to specialize that viewpoint still further, so that the peculiar advantage implied (on any view) by any

---

[6] Hart, in *Oxford Essays II*, 200–1.

ascription of rights is taken to be the advantage of *freedom* of action, and/or *power* to affect the freedom of action of others.

All this can be better understood if we review the history of the word 'right(s)' and its antecedent in the classical language of European culture, viz. '*jus*'. For this history has a watershed, and it is essentially the same watershed as we saw in the classification of types of justice (VII.6) and as we shall see again in the explanation of authority (IX.4) and of the source or justification of obligation (XI.6, XI.8).

The word '*jus*' ('*ius*') begins its academic career in the Roman law. But its meaning in the Roman texts has become an object of controversy, particularly since scholars became aware of the watershed. (The Roman lawyers did not attempt a linguistic analysis of their framework juristic concepts.) So it is more convenient to begin this historical sketch by asking what '*jus*' was taken to mean by Thomas Aquinas, a philosophical theologian but fairly well-acquainted with the Roman law systems of his day (especially the canon law of his Church). Here there is little ambiguity. Aquinas prefaces his elaborate study of justice with an analysis of *jus*, at the forefront of which he gives a list of meanings of '*jus*'. The primary meaning, he says, is 'the just thing itself' (and by 'thing', as the context makes clear, he means acts, objects, and states of affairs, considered as subject-matters of relationships of justice). One could say that for Aquinas '*jus*' primarily means 'the fair' or 'the what's fair'; indeed, if one could use the adverb 'aright' as a noun, one could say that his primary account is of 'arights' (rather than of rights). He then goes on to list secondary and derivative meanings of '*jus*' (relationships of justice): 'the art by which one knows or determines what is just' (and the principles and rules of this art, he adds, are the law), 'the place in which what is just is awarded' (i.e. in modern legal systems, the court), and finally 'the award (even if unjust) of the judge, whose role it is to do justice'.[7]

If we now jump forward about 340 years to the treatise on law by the Spanish Jesuit Francisco Suarez, written c.1610, we find another analysis of the meanings of '*jus*'. Here the 'true, strict and proper meaning' of '*jus*' is said to be: 'a kind of moral power [*facultas*] which every man has, either over his own property

---

[7] *S.T.* II–II q. 57 a. 1c ad 1, ad 2.

or with respect to that which is due to him'.[8] The meaning which
for Aquinas was primary is rather vaguely mentioned by Suarez
and then drops out of sight; conversely, the meaning which for
Suarez is primary does not appear in Aquinas's discussion at all.
Somewhere between the two men we have crossed the watershed.

A few years after Suarez (and not altogether independently of
him), Hugo Grotius begins his *De Jure Belli ac Pacis* (1625) by
explaining that the meaning of the term *jus (jure)* in his title is 'that
which is just';[9] but he then offers an elaborate exposition of 'another meaning of *jus*... which has reference to the person; this
meaning of *jus* is: a moral quality of the person enabling [*competens*]
him to have or to do something justly'. This, he says, is the
meaning that hereafter he is going to treat as the word's 'proper
or strict' meaning. Then he clarifies the reference of the phrase
'moral quality'. Such a quality can be 'perfect', in which case we call
it a *facultas*, or 'imperfect', in which case we call it an *aptitudo*.[10]
When Roman lawyers refer to one's *suum* (as in their defining
principle of justice, *suum cuique tribuere*, which is synonymous
with *jus suum cuique tribu*[*endi*]) they are referring, says Grotius,
to this *facultas*. And '*facultas*' in turn has three principal meanings:
(i) power (*potestas*), which may be power over oneself (called liberty:
libertas) or power over others (e.g. *patria potestas*, the power of a
father over his family); (ii) ownership (*dominium*)...; and (iii)
credit, to which corresponds debt (*debitum*).[11] The last-mentioned
meaning of *facultas* rather complicates the picture; the Roman law
tradition had more of a hold on Grotius than on Suarez. But
Grotius is still on the same side of the watershed as Suarez: *jus* is
essentially something someone *has*, and above all (or at least
paradigmatically) a *power* or *liberty*. If you like, it is Aquinas's
primary meaning of '*jus*' but transformed by *relating it exclusively
to the beneficiary* of the just relationship, above all to that beneficiary's doings and havings.

This shift of perspective could be so drastic as to carry
right-holders, and their rights, altogether outside the juridical
relationship which is fixed by law (moral or posited) and which

---

[8] *De Legibus*, I, ii, 5.
[9] Grotius, *De Jure Belli ac Pacis*, I, I, iii.
[10] *Ibid.*, iv.
[11] *Ibid.*, v.

establishes *jus* in Aquinas's sense: 'that which is just'. For within a few years Hobbes is writing:

> ... *jus,* and *lex, right* and *law*... ought to be distinguished; because RIGHT, consisteth in liberty to do, or to forbear; whereas LAW, determineth and bindeth to one of them: so that law, and right, differ as much, as obligation, and liberty; which in one and the same matter are inconsistent.[12]

Pushed as far as Hobbes's purposes, this contrast between law and rights deprives the notion of rights of virtually all its normative significance. Hobbes wishes to say that one has most rights when one is in the 'state of nature', i.e. a vacuum of law and obligation, since 'in such a condition, every man has a right to everything; even to one another's body'.[13] But we could just as well say that in such a condition of things, where no persons have any duty not to take anything they want, *no one has any rights*. The fact that we could well say this shows that the ordinary modern idiom of 'rights' does not follow Hobbes all the way to his contrast between law and rights. Nor did Locke or Pufendorf; yet they did adopt his stipulation that 'a right' (*jus*) is paradigmatically a liberty.[14] Their successors are those who today defend the 'choice' theory of rights, which as we saw in the preceding section is one eligible way of accounting for most, but not all, of the modern grammar of rights. And even those who defend the 'benefit' theory of rights are far from using the idiom of Aquinas, since (in common with ordinary language-speakers and lawyers in all modern languages) they think of 'a right' as something beneficial which a person *has* (a 'moral [including legal] quality' in Grotius's terminology), rather than 'that which is just in a given situation', the ensemble of juridical relationships established, by rules, between two or more persons in relation to some subject-matter (act, thing, or state of affairs).

---

[12] *Leviathan* (1651), ch. xiv; in Raphael (ed.), *British Moralists,* vol. I, para. 56. Thus, for Hobbes as for Hohfeld, liberty is simply the negation of duty; and this 'liberty-right' is the only right Hobbes has in mind.

[13] *Leviathan* (1651), ch. xiv; Raphael, *British Moralists,* para. 57.

[14] Locke, *Essays on the Law of Nature* (1663; ed. W. von Leyden, Oxford: 1954), 10 (f. 11): '*jus enim in eo positum est quod alicujus rei liberum habemus usum*' (right is predicated on this, that we have the free use of a thing). Pufendorf, *Elementa Jurisprudentiae Universalis* (1660), I, def. xiii, para. 3; cf. def. viii, para. 1; and *De Jure Naturae et Gentium Libri Octo* (1672), I, c. 1, paras 19–20.

There should be no question of wanting to put the clock back. The modern idiom of rights is more supple and, by being more specific in its standpoint or perspective, is *capable* of being used with more differentiation and precision than the pre-modern use of 'the right' (*jus*). But it is salutary to bear in mind that the modern emphasis on the powers of the right-holder, and the consequent systematic bifurcation between 'right' (including 'liberty') and 'duty', is something that sophisticated lawyers were able to do without for the whole life of classical Roman law. This is not the place to argue the translation of the Roman law texts. To establish how differently the term '*jus*' sounded in the ears of a Roman lawyer from the modern term 'a right', suffice it to cite one short passage from a students' manual of the second century AD, the *Institutes* of Gaius:

The jura of urban estates are such as the *jus* of raising a building higher and of obstructing the light of a neighbour's building, or of not raising [a building], lest the neighbour's light be obstructed.[15]

Obviously, we cannot replace the word '*jus*' in this passage with the word 'right' (meaning *a* right), since it is nonsense (or, if a special meaning can be found, it is far from the meaning of this passage) to speak of a 'right *not* to raise one's building, lest the neighbour's light be obstructed'. In Roman legal thought, '*jus*' frequently signifies the assignment, made as between parties, of and by justice according to law; and one party's 'part' in such an assignment might be a burden, not a benefit—let alone a power or liberty of choice.

And in this, the vocabulary of Roman law resembles more than one pre-modern legal vocabulary. Anthropologists study-ing certain African tribal regimes of law have found that in the indigenous language the English terms 'a right' and 'duty' are usually covered by a single word, derived from the verbal form normally translated as 'ought'. This single word (e.g. *swanelo* in Barotse, *tshwanelo* in Tswana) is thus found to be best translated as 'due'; for 'due' looks both ways along a juridical relationship, both to what one is due to do, and to what is due to one. This is linked, in turn, with a 'nuance in tribal societies,

---

[15] *Inst.* II, 14 (as conventionally reconstructed; but the same use of '*jus*' to cover both '*altius tollendi*' and '*non altius tollendi*' is found in the *Digest*, viii, 2, 2, along with similar uses, e.g. '*stillicidium avertendi . . . aut non avertendi*').

in that they stress duty and obligation, rather than the nuance of modern Western society, with a stress on right[s]'.[16]

Let me conclude this review of the shift of meaning in the term 'right' and its linguistic predecessors by repeating that there is no cause to take sides as between the older and the newer usages, as ways of expressing the implications of justice in a given context. Still less is it appropriate to argue that 'as a matter of juristic logic' duty is logically prior to right (or vice versa). But when we come to explain the requirements of justice, which we do by referring to the needs of the common good at its various levels, then we find that there is reason for treating the concept of duty, obligation, or requirement as having a more strategic explanatory role than the concept of rights. The concept of rights is not on that account of less importance or dignity: for the common good is precisely the good of the individuals whose *benefit*, from fulfilment of duty by others, is their *right* because *required in justice* of those others.

VIII.4   RIGHTS AND THE COMMON GOOD

The modern language of rights provides, as I said, a supple and potentially precise instrument for sorting out and expressing the demands of justice. It is often, however, though not inevitably or irremediably, a hindrance to clear thought when the question is: What *are* the demands of justice? The aspects of human well-being are many. The commitments, projects, and actions that are apt for realizing that well-being are innumerable even when, as an individual, one contemplates just one's own life-plan. When we contemplate the complexities of collaboration, co-ordination, and mutual restraint involved in pursuit of the common good, we are faced with inescapable choices between rationally eligible but competing possible institutions, policies, programmes, laws, and decisions. The strength of rights-talk is that, carefully employed, it can express precisely the various aspects of a decision involving more than one person, indicating just what is and is not required of each person

[16] Max Gluckman, *The Ideas in Barotse Jurisprudence* (Manchester: 2nd edn, 1972), xxv; see also xlv, n. 18, and 21; I. Schapera, 'Contract in Tswana Law' in Max Gluckman (ed.), *Ideas and Procedures in African Customary Law* (Oxford: 1969), 319, 326; Max Gluckman, *The Judicial Process among the Barotse* (Manchester 1955), 166.

concerned, and just when and how one of those persons can affect those requirements. But the conclusory force of ascriptions of rights, which is the source of the suitability of rights-talk for expressing conclusions, is also the source of its potential for confusing the rational process of investigating and determining what justice requires in a given context.

The Universal Declaration of Human Rights, proclaimed by the General Assembly of the United Nations in December 1948, has been taken as a model, not only for the United Nations Covenants on Civil and Political Rights and on Economic, Social and Cultural Rights (1966) but also for the European Convention for the Protection of Human Rights and Fundamental Freedoms (1952), itself the model for the very many Bills of Rights entrenched in the Constitutions of countries becoming independent since 1957, especially within the (British) Commonwealth. Such thoroughly pondered documents deserve close attention from anyone wishing to think out problems of human life in community in terms of rights, human, natural, or legal.

Two features of all these documents are immediately noticeable. First: each document employs not one but two principal canonical forms: (A) 'Everyone has the right to...' and (B) 'No one shall be...'.[17] Now it is clear that the formal logic of rights-talk permits, by simple conversion of terms and appropriate negations, a transformation from one form to the other. Hence, a single canonical form would have been possible. The decision to use two different formulae cannot be ascribed to logical ineptitude or mere love of stylistic variation. The rationale of the decision can be detected by attending to the second feature common to all these documents: namely, that the 'exercise of the rights and freedoms' proclaimed is said to be 'subject to limitation'. In some documents (e.g. the European

---

[17] Thus, in the Universal Declaration: Art 3 'Everyone has the right to life, liberty and security of person'; Art 4 'No one shall be held in slavery or servitude...'; Art 5 'No one shall be subjected to torture...'; Art 13(1) 'Everyone has the right to freedom of movement and residence within the borders of each state'; Art 17(1) 'Everyone has the right to own property alone as well as in association with others', (2) 'No one shall be arbitrarily deprived of his property'; etc., etc. Or again, in the European Convention: Art 5(1) 'Everyone has the right to liberty and security of person. No one shall be deprived of his liberty save in the following cases...'.

Convention) these limitations are specified article by article, in conjunction with the specification of the respective rights. In others the limitation is pronounced only once, in generic terms. Thus, Article 29 of the Universal Declaration reads:

(1) Everyone has duties to the community in which alone the free and full development of his personality is possible.
(2) In the exercise of his rights and freedoms, everyone shall be subject only to such limitations as are determined by law solely for the purpose of securing due recognition and respect for the rights and freedoms of others and of meeting the just requirements of morality, public order and the general welfare in a democratic society.
(3) These rights and freedoms may in no case be exercised contrary to the purposes and principles of the United Nations.

The grounds of limitation specified in Article 29(2) are referred to again and again in the particular limiting clauses in the European Convention and other documents. The point to notice is that the limitations in Article 29(2) are said to be on the exercise of the 'rights and freedoms' specified in the document. This suggests that the limitations might *not* be applicable to those articles which do not purport to define a right but instead impose a negative requirement (which *could*, as we have observed, have been expressed as a right, but was not). This in turn suggests a differentiation in the guiding force of the various articles, as criteria for just laws and decisions. The articles expressed in form (B)—'No one shall be subjected to ...'—are intended to be of conclusory force. But the articles in form (A) have guiding force only as items in a process of rational decision-making which cannot reasonably be concluded simply by appealing to any one of these rights (notwithstanding that all are 'fundamental' and 'inalienable' and part of 'everyone's' *entitlement*[18]).

Some of the articles cast in the peremptory (B) form do themselves contain internal qualifications: for example, Article 9 'No one shall be subjected to *arbitrary* arrest...'. But some are quite unqualified: for example, Article 3 'No one shall be subjected to torture...'. And none are subject (if this interpretation of the draftsmanship is correct) to the limitation on exercise of rights, stipulated in Article 29. One's right not to be tortured (as we can

---

[18] See Universal Declaration, preamble and Art 2.

indeed express it) is not a 'right' that one 'exercises' in the sense of Article 29; acts of torture cannot therefore be justified by appeal to 'just requirements of public order'. The right not to be tortured, then, could be called an absolute right, to distinguish it from the rights that are 'inalienable' but subject 'in their exercise' to various limitations. Later in this chapter I consider whether it is reasonable to assert that some rights are absolute, i.e. whether this feature of the Universal Declaration can be justified (see VIII.7).

For the moment, let us examine the specified grounds of limitation more closely. They are fourfold: (i) to secure due recognition for the rights and freedoms of others; (ii) to meet the just requirements of morality in a democratic society; (iii) to meet the just requirements of public order in a democratic society; (iv) to meet the just requirements of the general welfare in a democratic society.

The last-mentioned ground of limitation, (iv), attracts attention, not merely for its breadth and vagueness. Some theorists have treated rights as 'individuated political aims' which are not subordinate to conceptions of 'aggregate collective good'[19] or the 'general interest'[20] or 'general utility'.[21] Such an account of rights would give reason for concluding that the reference to 'general welfare' in Article 29 of the Universal Declaration is inept. That conclusion is indeed correct, but not for the reason just suggested. In defining or explaining rights we must not make reference to concepts which are incoherent or senseless; and, as I explained in V.6, conceptions of 'aggregate collective good' are incoherent, save in limited technical contexts. The ongoing life of a human community is not a limited technical context, and the common good of such a community cannot be measured as an aggregate, as utilitarians suppose.

---

[19] R. M. Dworkin, *Taking Rights Seriously* (London: 1977), 91.

[20] *Ibid.*, 269.

[21] *Ibid.*, 191. But Dworkin continues: 'I must not overstate the point. Someone who claims that citizens have a right against the Government need not go so far as to say that the State is *never* justified in overriding that right. He might say, for example, that although citizens have a right to free speech, the Government may override that right when necessary to protect the rights of others, or to prevent catastrophe, or even to obtain a clear and major public benefit (though if he acknowledged this last as a possible justification he would be treating the right in question as not among the most important or fundamental)'.

The ineptitude of Article 29's reference to 'the general welfare', as a distinct and separate ground for limiting rights, can
be shown if we reflect on the first of the grounds proposed in
that article: to secure 'due recognition and respect for the rights
and freedoms of others'. For amongst the rights proclaimed in
the Universal Declaration are life, liberty, security of person
(Article 3), equality before the law (Article 7), privacy (Article
12), marriage and protection of family life (Article 16), property
(Article 17), social security and the 'realization, through national
effort and international co-operation ... of the economic, social
and cultural rights indispensable for [everyone's] dignity and the
free development of his personality' (Article 22), participation in
government (Article 21), work, protection against unemploy-
ment, favourable remuneration of work (Article 23), rest and
leisure (Article 24), 'a standard of living adequate for ... health
and well-being ...' (Article 25), education (Article 26), enjoyment of the arts and a share in the benefits of scientific advancement (Article 27), and 'a social and international order in
which the rights and freedoms set forth in this Declaration can
be fully realised' (Article 28). When we survey this list we
realize what the modern 'manifesto'[22] conception of human
rights amounts to. It is simply a way of sketching the *outlines
of the common good*, the various aspects of individual well-being
in community. What the reference to rights contributes in this
sketch is simply a pointed expression of what is implicit in the
term '*common* good', namely that *each* and everyone's well-being,
in each of its basic aspects, must be considered and favoured at
all times by those responsible for co-ordinating the common life.
Thus, when the human rights proclaimed in the Universal
Declaration are spelt out, and amplified as in the subsequent
UN Covenants,[23] there is no room left for an appeal, *against* the
'exercise' of these rights, to 'general welfare'. Either 'general
welfare' is a reference to a utilitarian aggregation, in which
case it is merely illusory, or else it is a dangling and confused

---

[22] See Joel Feinberg, *Social Philosophy* (New Jersey: 1973), 67.
[23] For example, the Covenant of Economic Social and Cultural Rights (1966): Art 11 'the right of
everyone to an adequate standard of living ... and to the continuous improvement of living conditions'; Art 12 ' ... the right of everyone to the enjoyment of the highest attainable standard of physical
and mental health ...', etc. etc.

reference to a general concept at the end of a list of (most of)[24] the particular components of that very concept.

What, then, are we to say about the other listed grounds of limitation: (ii) just requirements of morality in a democratic society and (iii) just requirements of public order in a democratic society? The argument of the preceding paragraph suggests that, given the breadth of the rights contemplated by the rest of the Universal Declaration, most of what these limitations import is already implicit in ground (i) in the list of grounds of limitation: viz. (i) due respect for the rights and freedoms of others. It must also be noted that neither 'morality' nor 'public order' is a term clear in its meaning (quite apart from any substantive controversies about the requirements of morality or public order). For in much modern usage, including legal usage, 'morality' signifies almost exclusively sexual morality and the requirements of decency, whereas, in philosophical usage, sexual morality (including decency) is merely one small portion of the requirements of practical reasonableness. This ambiguity affects the use of the term 'morality' even when it is conjoined with 'public' as in the frequent references of the European Convention and the later UN Conventions (1966) to 'public order or morals'. And as for 'public order', this phrase as used in the international documents suffers from the irremediable ambiguity that in common law systems it signifies absence of disorder (i.e. public peace, tranquility, and safety), whereas the expressions *ordre public* and *orden público* used in the French and Spanish versions of those documents signify a civil law concept almost as wide as the concept of public policy in common law. For example, by using a version of the civil law concept of public order, the Second Vatican Council, in proclaiming the right to freedom of religious belief, profession, and practice, found that all the necessary limitations on this right could be expressed in terms of public order:

the protection of civil society, by civil authority, against abuses of this right must not be accomplished arbitrarily or with inequitable favour to any person or group, but must be according to juridical

---

[24] Perhaps the list needs to be eked out, at least in respect of some of the rights which it is to limit, by reference to 'public health' and 'national security', which are among the grounds of limitation specified in the later documents.

norms which are consistent with the objective moral order and which are required for [i] the effective protection of the rights of all citizens and of their peaceful coexistence, and [ii] a sufficient care for the authentic public peace of an ordered common life in true justice, and [iii] a proper upholding of public morality. All these factors constitute the fundamental part of the common good, and come under the notion of *public order*.[25]

In the face of these terminological problems, why not say that the exercise of rights is to be limited only by respect for the rights of others? The answer must be that although it would be possible, given the logical reach of rights-talk, to express *any* desired restriction on rights in terms of other rights, the references to morality, public morality, public health, public order, etc., in all the contemporary declarations of rights, are neither conceptually redundant nor substantively unreasonable.

For, as we have seen, modern rights-talk is constructed primarily on the implicit model of a relationship between two individuals. So, in its primary signification (as distinct from its inherent logical reach), modern rights-talk most fittingly concerns benefits or advantages to individuals (in the limiting cases, to *all* individuals), 'not simply as members of a collectivity enjoying a diffuse common benefit in which all participate in indistinguishable and unassignable shares'.[26] But public morality and public order (even in the restricted, common law sense) are both diffuse common benefits in which all participate in indistinguishable and unassignable shares. Hence, there is reason for referring to them specifically.

The fact is that human rights can only be securely enjoyed in certain sorts of milieu—a context or framework of mutual respect and trust and common understanding, an environment which is physically healthy and in which the weak can go about without fear of the whims of the strong. Consider, now, the concept of public morality, in its oddly restricted, sexual sense. Apart from such special arrangements as marriage, no one's human rights include a right that other men or women should not conduct themselves sexually in certain ways. But the great majority of any community that is reproducing itself will spend

---

[25] Declaration *Dignitatis Humanae*, 7 Dececember 1965, sec. 7.
[26] Cf. D. N. MacCormick, 'Rights in Legislation', in *Essays*, 205.

more than a quarter of their lives as children and then more than another quarter as parents bringing up children—in all, more than half their lifetimes. If it is the case that sexuality is a powerful force which only with some difficulty, and always precariously, can be integrated with other aspects of human personality and well-being—so that it enhances rather than destroys friendship and the care of children, for example; and if it is further the case that human sexual psychology has a bias towards regarding other persons as bodily objects of desire and potential sexual release and gratification, and as mere items in an erotically flavoured classification (e.g. 'women'), rather than as full persons with personal and individual sensitivities, restraints, and lifeplans, then there is reason for fostering a milieu in which children can be brought up (and parents assisted rather than hindered in bringing them up) so that they are relatively free from inward subjection to an egoistic, impulsive, or depersonalized sexuality. Just what such a milieu concretely amounts to and requires for its maintenance is something that is matter for discussion and decision, elsewhere. But that this is an aspect of the common good, and fit matter for laws which limit the boundless exercise of certain rights, can hardly be doubted by anyone who attends to the facts of human psychology as they bear on the realization of basic human goods. And while all this could be, and sometimes has been, expressed in terms of human rights, there is no need to consider inept, still less redundant, the reference to public morality, preferred by contemporary legislators with impressive unanimity.

Similarly, public order, in its restricted, common law sense, concerns the maintenance, not so much of the psychological substratum for mutual respect, but of the physical environment and structure of expectations and reliances essential to the well-being of all members of a community, especially the weak. Inciting hatred amongst sections of the community is not merely an injury to the rights of those hated; it threatens everyone in the community with a future of violence and of other violations of right, and this threat is itself an injury to the common good and is reasonably referred to as a violation of public order. Rioting and bombing, and threats thereof, are not merely prejudicial to the rights of those killed or injured, but to everyone who has now to live in a community where such things happen.

The operation of a grossly noisy aeroplane can be said to violate the rights of those awakened and deafened by it, but the problem is quite reasonably described as one of public order or public nuisance and not pinned down to the rights of those who happen so far to have been affected. The same goes for the notion of public health, a component in the civil law conception of *ordre public*, and a partner of the common law conception of public order.

This long but by no means elaborate discussion can now be summarized. On the one hand, we should not say that human rights, or their exercise, are subject to the common good; for the maintenance of human rights is a fundamental component of the common good. On the other hand, we can appropriately say that most human rights are subject to or limited by each other and by other *aspects* of the common good, aspects which could probably be subsumed under a very broad conception of human rights but which are fittingly indicated (one could hardly say, *described*) by expressions such as 'public morality', 'public health', and 'public order'.

VIII.5   THE SPECIFICATION OF RIGHTS

The foregoing section suggested general reasons for concluding that most assertions of right made in political discourse need to be subjected to a rational process of specification, assessment, and qualification, in a way that rather belies the peremptory or conclusory *sound* of '...have a right to...'. This conclusion can be reinforced by attention to the logical structure of the assertions or claims made or recognized or conceded in Bills of Rights and in political discourse at large. To resume the vocabulary I employed in VIII.2, we can say that these claims assert two-term relations between a (class of) person and a (class of) subject-matter (life, body, free speech, property or ownership of property...). Before such assertions can reasonably be accorded a real conclusory force, they must be translated into specific three-term relations.

This translation involves specification of (a) the identity of the duty-holder(s) who must respect or give effect to A's right; (b) the content of the duty, in terms of specific act-descriptions, including the times and other circumstances and conditions for the applicability of the duty; (c) the identity or class-description of A, the correlative claim-right-holder(s) (in a Hohfeldian sense of 'claim-right'); (d) the conditions under which a claim-right-holder loses the claim-right, including the conditions (if any) under which the holder can waive the relevant duties; (e) the claim-rights, powers, and liberties of the claim-right-holder in the event of non-performance of duty; and, above all, (f) the liberties of the right-holder, including a specification of the limits of those liberties, i.e. a specification of the right-holder's duties, especially of non-interference with the liberties of other holders of that right or of other recognized rights. Since (f) involves specifying the *duties* of right-holder A, it necessarily involves a specification of the claim-rights of B, and this specification in turn requires a complete specification of points (a) to (f) in respect, now, of B; which will require a similar specification in respect of B's duties of non-interference with C...

Employing a useful contemporary jargon, we can say that people (or legal systems) who share substantially the same *concept* (e.g. of the human right to life, or to a fair trial) may none the less have different *conceptions* of that right, in that their specifications under (a) to (f) differ, partly because the circumstances they have in mind differ and partly because specification normally involves choices, by some authoritative process, from among alternatives that are more or less equally reasonable. As I said in relation to the lawyer's preference for two-term rights-talk (VIII.2), shifting and even competing specifications in terms of three-term rights can be intelligibly unified by their shared relationship to one topic, the two-term right (e.g. to life, or to a fair trial).

How is this process of specification and demarcation to be accomplished? How are conflicts of rights to be resolved? That is to say, how much interference with one person's enjoyment of a 'right', by other persons, in the exercise of the same right, and of other rights, is to be permitted? There is, I think, no alternative but to hold in one's mind's eye some pattern, or range of patterns, of human character, conduct, and interaction in community, and then to choose such specification of rights as tends to favour that pattern, or range of patterns. In other words, one needs some conception of human good, of individual flourishing in a form (or range of forms) of communal life that fosters rather than hinders such flourishing. One attends not merely to character types desirable in the abstract or in isolation, but also to the quality of interaction among persons; and one should not seek to realize some patterned 'end-state' imagined in abstraction from the processes of individual initiative and interaction—processes which are integral to human good and which make the future, let alone its evaluation, incalculable (see VII.7).

So one will bear in mind, on the one hand, that art with all its (often competing) forms and canons really is better than trash, that culture really is better than ignorance, that reputation and privacy and property really are aspects of or important means to human well-being, that friendship and respect for human personality really are threatened by hatred, group bias, and anarchic sexuality, that children really do benefit from a formation that defines paths as well as illuminating horizons... and, on the other hand, that servility, infantilism, and hypocrisy really are evils, that integrity and authenticity in self-constitution really are the indispensable centre to human well-being, that where 'paternalism' on the part of the political community is justified it is, like the educative function of parenthood itself, to be no more than a help and support to self-correction and self-direction, and that the resolution of all these problems of human rights is a process in which various reasonable solutions may be proposed and debated and should be settled by some decision-making procedure which is authoritative but which does not pretend to be infallible or to silence further rational discussion or to forbid the reconsideration of the decision. In short, just as the right of free speech certainly requires 'limitation', i.e. specification, in the interests both of free speech itself and of many other human goods, so too the procedure for settling the 'limits' of this and other human rights will certainly be enhanced in reasonableness by a wide freedom of cultural and political debate, in any society in which there is a sufficiently diffused respect for discussion and compromise as ways of being reasonable in community.

Human rights (not to mention the public order and morality which constitute a necessary framework for their enjoyment) can certainly be threatened by uses of rights-talk which, in bad faith or good, prematurely ascribe a conclusory or absolute status to this or that human right (e.g. property, contract, assembly, speech). However, if its logic and its place in practical reasonableness about human flourishing are kept in mind, the modern usage of claims of right as the principal counter in political discourse should be recognized (despite its dubious seventeenth-century origins and its abuse by fanatics, adventurers, and self-interested persons from the eighteenth century until today) as a valuable addition to the received vocabulary of practical reasonableness (i.e. to the tradition of 'natural law doctrine'). For first, the modern usage of rights-talk rightly emphasizes equality, the truth that every human being is a locus of human flourishing which is to be considered with favour in him or her as much as in anybody else. In other words, rights-talk keeps justice in the foreground of our considerations. Secondly, it tends to undercut the attractions of the 'calculations' of consequentialists (though, since many rights are not absolute, the real critique of such calculations must be made more directly: see V.6). Thirdly, since rights must be and are referred to by name, modern rights-talk amplifies the undifferentiated reference to 'the common good' by providing a usefully detailed listing of the various aspects of human flourishing and fundamental components of the way of life in community that tends to favour such flourishing in all.

VIII.6   RIGHTS AND EQUALITY OF CONCERN AND RESPECT

It is sometimes argued that to prefer, and seek to embody in legislation, some conception or range of conceptions of human flourishing is unjust because it is necessarily to treat with unequal concern and respect those members of the community whose conceptions of human good fall outside the preferred range and whose activities are or may therefore be restricted by the legislation. As an argument warranting opposition to such legislation, this argument cannot be justified; it is self-stultifying (cf. III.6). Those who put forward the argument prefer a conception of human good, according to which a person is entitled to equal concern and respect and a community is in bad shape in which that entitlement is denied; moreover, they act on this preference by seeking to repeal the restrictive

legislation which those against whom they are arguing may
have enacted. Do those who so argue and so act thereby necessarily treat with unequal concern and respect those whose preferences and legislation they oppose? If they do, then their own
argument and action is itself equally unjustified, and provides no
basis for political preferences or action. If they do not (and this
must be the better view), then neither do those whom they oppose.
Nor can the argument be rescued by proposing that it escapes self-
stultification by operating at a different 'level of discourse': for
example, by being an argument about entitlements rather than
about good. For there is no difficulty in translating any 'paternalist' political preference into the language of entitlement, by postulating an entitlement of all the members of a community to a
milieu that will support rather than hinder their own pursuit of
good and the well-being of their own particular children, or an
entitlement of each and all to be rescued from their own folly.
Whether or not such entitlements can be made out, they certainly
pertain to the same 'level of discourse'. Nor, finally, can the argument we are considering be saved by a stipulation that arguments
and political programmes motivated, as it is, by concern for 'equal
respect and concern for other people' must be regarded as
showing equal concern and respect for everyone, even those
people whose (paternalist) arguments and legislation they reject
and override. For, on the one hand, such a stipulation is merely an
ad hoc device for escaping self-stultification; if overriding some
persons' political preferences and compelling them to live in a
society whose ways they detest were *ipso facto* to show unequal
concern and respect for those persons in one context, so it would be
in any other. And, on the other hand, there is no difficulty in
supposing that a 'paternalist' political programme may be based
on a conception of what is required for equal concern and respect for
all; for paternalists may well consider that, for example, to leave
people to succumb to drug addiction on the plea that it is 'their
business' is to deny them the active concern one would show for
one's friend in like situation; or that to fail to forbid teachers to form
sexual attachments with their pupils is to deny the children of
negligent or 'wrong-headed' parents the protection that the paternalist legislators would wish for their own children, and is thus
again a failure in 'equal concern and respect'. 'I wish someone had

stopped me from...': if this can rationally be said (as it can), it follows necessarily that even the most extensive and excessive programme of paternalism might be instituted without denial of equal concern and respect to anybody.

The pursuit of any form of human community in which human rights are protected by the imposition of duties will necessarily involve both selection of some and rejection of other conceptions of the common good, and considerable restrictions on the activities of everyone (including the legislators themselves, in their private capacities as persons subject to egoism and indifference to the real well-being of others). Some ways of pursuing the common good through legislation do indeed err by forgetting that personal authenticity, self-direction, and privacy for contemplation or play or friendship are aspects and important adjuncts of human well-being: see VI.5, VII.3. Paternalist programmes guilty of this oversight should be criticized for that—a failure in commutative justice—and not for the quite different vice of discrimination, group bias, denial of equal concern and respect, a kind of refined selfishness, a failure in distributive justice. To judge another person mistaken, and to act on that judgment, is not to be equated, in any field of human discourse and judgment, with despising that person or preferring oneself.

The argument of this section has been dialectical. It has not needed to consider whether the principle 'everyone is entitled to equal concern and respect' is an adequately refined principle of justice. I said earlier (VII.4) that everyone is equally entitled to respectful consideration in the distribution of the common stock and the incidents of common life, including legal protection and roles and burdens. But I also indicated that this does not require 'equality of treatment' (i.e. identical treatment), even in such distributions. And it would certainly be wrong to suggest that any individual is bound or even permitted in justice to show everyone equal *concern*; and the same is true of those in authority in any particular community, with respect to those within and those outside their community: see VII.4, XI.2.

VIII.7 ABSOLUTE HUMAN RIGHTS

Are there then no limits to what may be done in pursuit of protection of human rights or of other aspects of the common good? Are there no fixed points in that pattern of life which one must hold in one's mind's eye in resolving problems of rights? Are there no 'absolute' rights, rights that are not to be limited or overridden for the sake of any conception of the good life in community, not even 'to prevent catastrophe'?[27]

The answer of utilitarians, of course, is clear: there are no absolute human rights, for there are no ways of treating a person of which it can be said, by a consistent utilitarian, 'Whatever the consequences, nobody must ever be treated in this way'. What is more striking, perhaps, is the fact that, whatever may be commonly professed in the modern world, no contemporary government or elite manifests in its practice any belief in absolute human rights. For every government that has the physical capacity to make its threats credible says this to its potential enemies: 'If you attack us and threaten to defeat us, we will kill all the hostages we hold; that is to say, we will incinerate or dismember as many of your old men and women and children, and poison as many of your mothers and their unborn offspring, as it takes to persuade you to desist; we do not regard as decisive the fact that they are themselves no threat to us; nor do we propose to destroy them merely incidentally, as an unsought-after side-effect of efforts to stop your armed forces in their attack on us; no, we will destroy your non-combatants precisely because you value them, and in order to *persuade* you to desist'. Those who say this, and have been preparing elaborately for years to act upon their threat (and most of them acted upon it massively, between 1943 and 1945, to say no more), cannot be said to accept that anyone has, in virtue of his or her humanity, any absolute right. These people subscribe to Bills of Rights which, like the Universal Declaration and its successors, clearly treat the right not to be tortured as (unlike most of the other 'inalienable' rights there proclaimed) subject to no exceptions. But their military policy involves courses of action which in all but name are torture on an unprecedented scale, inflicted for the same motive as old-fashioned torturers seeking to change their victim's mind or the minds of those next in line for the torture. Nor is this just a matter of governments and soldiers; many of these governments are freely elected, and their policy (as distinct from the dangers

---

[27] See Dworkin, quoted above at n. 21.

of pursuing it) arouses scant controversy among their electorates. And who does not notice the accomplished smoothness with which the issue is avoided by many who write about rights?

In its classical representatives the tradition of theorizing about natural law has never maintained that what I have called the requirements of practical reasonableness, as distinct from the basic human values or basic principles of practical reasonableness, are clearly recognized by all or even most people—on the contrary.[28] So we too need not hesitate to say that, notwithstanding the substantial consensus to the contrary, there are absolute human rights. For the seventh of the requirements of practical reasonableness that I identified in V.7 is this: that it is always unreasonable to choose directly against any basic value, whether in oneself or in one's fellow human beings. And the basic values are not mere abstractions; they are aspects of the real well-being of flesh-and-blood individuals. Correlative to the exceptionless duties entailed by this requirement are, therefore, exceptionless or absolute human claim-rights—most obviously, the right not to have one's life taken directly as a means to any further end; but also the right not to be positively lied to in any situation (e.g. teaching, preaching, research publication, news broadcasting) in which factual communication (as distinct from fiction, jest, or poetry) is reasonably expected; the related right not to be condemned on knowingly false charges; the right not to be deprived, or required to deprive oneself, of one's procreative capacity; and the right to be taken into respectful consideration in any assessment of what the common good requires.

Because these are not two-term rights in need of translation into three-term right-duty relationships, but are claim-rights strictly correlative to duties entailed by the requirements of practical reasonableness, the difficult task of giving precision to the specification of these rights has usually been undertaken in terms of a casuistry of duties. And because an unwavering recognition of the literally immeasurable value of human personality in each of its basic aspects (the solid core of the notion of human dignity) requires us to discount the apparently measurable evil of looming catastrophes which really do

---

[28] See, e.g., Aquinas, *S.T.* I q. 113 a. 1; I–II q. 9 a. 5 ad 3; q. 14 a. 1 ad 3; q. 94 a. 4c; q. 99 a. 2 ad 2. See also V.2 and II.3 above.

threaten the common good and the enjoyment by others of *their* rights, that casuistry is more complex, difficult, and controvertible in its details than can be indicated in the foregoing summary list of absolute rights. That casuistry may be framed in terms of 'direct' choices or intentions, as against 'indirect' effects, and of 'means' as against 'incidents': see V.7. But reasonable judgments in this casuistry are not made by applying a 'logic' of 'directness and indirectness' of 'means and ends' or 'intended and unintended', drawn from the use of those notions in other enquiries or contexts. Rather, such judgments are arrived at by a steady determination to respect human good in one's own existence and the equivalent humanity or human rights of others, when that human good and those human rights fall directly into one's care and disposal—rather than trade off that good and those rights against some vision of future 'net best consequences'—consequences which overall, both logically and practically, one cannot know, cannot control or dispose of, and cannot evaluate.

NOTES

VIII. 2

Hohfeld's analysis of rights... W. N. Hohfeld, *Fundamental Legal Conceptions* (New Haven: 1919). For common misunderstandings, see J. Finnis, 'Some Professorial Fallacies about Rights' (1972) 4 *Adel. L. R.* 377 [*CEJF* IV.18]. For limitations of Hohfeld's analysis, see A. M. Honoré, 'Rights of Exclusion and Immunities against Divesting' (1959–60) 34 *Tulane Law Rev.* 453; Raz, *Legal System*, 179–81. For problems in formalizing the schema, see P. Mullock, 'The Hohfeldian Jural Opposite' (1971) 13 *Ratio* 158.

'Juridical acts' and 'natural acts'... 'Juridical acts' are called by Hart 'acts-in-the-law' (*Concept of Law*, 96 [99]; 'Bentham on Legal Rights', in *Oxford Essays II*, 196), and the distinction is explained by him thus: '... [an] act may be called a natural act in the sense that it is not endowed by the law with a special legal significance or legal effect. On the other hand in the case of rights which are powers, such as the right to alienate property, the act ... is an act-in-the-law, just in the sense that it is specifically recognized by the law as having legal effects in varying the legal position of various parties': *Oxford Essays II*, 196. To prevent all commissions of crimes and torts being characterized as 'juridical acts' (and as exercises of Hohfeldian power!) I prefer the characterization in the text, though it is not perfect and may need to be supplemented or qualified by the notion that a juridical act is an act (usually involving one or more natural acts) which is *typically* done *in order to* affect legal relations, and which is regulated or defined by rules on the basis that it is *desirable* to enable officials or individuals to act effectively with that motivation: see Raz, *Practical Reason*, 102–4; cf. 110. The problem of restricting the notion of power, so that we are not obliged to say that A has a power to make himself an offender by hitting X on the nose, has its parallel in the problem of restricting the notion of immunity lest we find ourselves having to

say that, by refusing to testify in court, A gains an immunity from being granted a reward of £10,000, or an immunity from being exempted from military service. It cannot be said that Hohfeldian analysis has mastered these problems. (It may be remarked, incidentally, that each of these problems of reconciling Hohfeldian definition with ordinary legal usage suggests that ordinary legal usage is rooted in the idea that a right is a *benefit*, not in the idea that it is a legally respected *choice*: see below.)

Is the bare Hohfeldian liberty legally or morally significant? . . . Hart argues, rightly ('Bentham on Legal Rights', in *Oxford Essays II*, 171 at 179–82), that (i) it is analytically important to distinguish liberty (mere absence of duty) from claim-right, and (ii) it is important to see that a liberty unprotected by any claim-rights against interference cannot usefully be dignified with the name of a right. (This again suggests, though not to Hart, that common usage treats rights as distinctively *beneficial*, not merely as legally recognized *choice*.) The second of these two points is aimed at Hobbes's notion of a right, discussed at p. 208 above: to like effect, see G. Marshall, 'Rights, Options and Entitlements', in *Oxford Essays II*, 228 at 231.

Inadequacy of Hohfeldian analysis to account for lawyers' talk of 'two-term' rights . . . See D. N. MacCormick, 'Rights in Legislation', in *Essays*, 188 at 200–2; A. M. Honoré, 'Rights of Exclusion and Immunities against Divesting' (1959–60) 34 *Tulane Law Rev* 453; Raz, *Legal System*, 180; and, less rigorously, L. L. Fuller, *Morality of Law*, 134–7. What I am here calling 'two-term' rights are instances of legal 'institutions'; MacCormick, 'Law as Institutional Fact' (1974) 90 *L.Q.R.* 102 at 106, 110, rightly stresses the importance of *persistence through time* as the basic reason for lawyers' conceptions of 'things' or institutions, which are ways of conceptually ordering and controlling the ascription of Hohfeldian rights. J. L. Mackie pointed out to me the analogy with our common-sense account of the material world: the empirical consequences of a statement about material objects may be identical with those of some set of statements about phenomena, but are not exhaustively analysable into such a set; so too the practical legal consequences of any 'lawyers'-right' may be identical with those of some set of Hohfeldian rights, but are not exhaustively analysable into those.

Is the Hohfeldian claim-right-holder the person with the remedy, or the beneficiary? . . . For the need to stipulate, and some problems about stipulating, that it is the remedy-holder, see J. Finnis, 'Some Professorial Fallacies about Rights' (1972) 4 *Adel. L. R.* 377 at 379–80 [*CEJF* IV.18 at 379]. Hart's confidence, in all his defences of the 'choice' theory of rights (see the following note), that English lawyers would unhesitatingly express the clear rules of English law by saying that 'third parties have no rights under a contract', seems misplaced in view of the *dicta* of Lords Reid and Pearce (made without polemical or theoretical animus) cited in the text.

'Benefit or interest' versus 'choice or will' theories of rights . . . The most illuminating introduction to this very long-standing debate is (though I disagree with his preference for the 'choice' theory) Hart, 'Bentham on Legal Rights', *Oxford Essays II*, 171–201. For criticism of Hart's preference, see Marshall, 'Rights, Options and Entitlements', *Oxford Essays II*, 228–41; MacCormick, 'Children's Rights: a Test-Case for Theories of Rights' (1976) 62 *Arch.R.S.P.* 305–16. Even for the strictly legal context, MacCormick provides good reasons for preferring some version of the 'benefit' explanation of rights: 'Rights in Legislation' in *Essays*, 189–209. In his earliest defence of the 'choice' theory, Hart admitted that 'if there are legal rights which cannot be waived these would need special treatment': 'Definition and Theory in Jurisprudence' (1954) 70 *L.Q.R.* 49, n. 15. That 'special treatment' has not been forthcoming, and the existence of such rights does tell against the 'choice' theory.

VIII.3

The meaning of 'jus' *in Aquinas*... For this extensively debated topic, see P. M. Van Overbeke, 'Droit et Morale: Essai de synthèse thomiste' (1958) 58 *Rev. Thorn.* 285 at 304–11 and works there cited; to which add P.-D. Dognin, 'La justice particulière comporte-t-elle deux espèces?' (1965) 65 *Rev. Thorn.* 399 at 412 n. On Aquinas's acquaintance with Roman legal terminology, see J.-M. Aubert, *Le Droit romain dans l'oeuvre de Saint Thomas* (Paris, 1955), 87–139.

The meaning of 'jus' *in Roman law*... For this difficult matter, see H. Maine, *Early Law and Custom* (1891), 365, 390; W. W. Buckland, *A Text-Book of Roman Law* (Cambridge: 3rd edn, 1966), 58; M. Villey, *Leçons d'histoire de la philosophie du droit* (Paris: 1957), chs XI, XIV; Villey, *Seize essais de philosophie du droit* (Paris: 1969), 149–55. *Ibid.*, 155–69 contains a detailed and valuable account of the debate about the meaning of '*jus*' between Pope John XXII (a canon lawyer and devotee of Aquinas) and William of Ockham, in the years between 1323 and c.1332. The novel definition of '*jus*' developed by Ockham can be seen from his definition of '*jus utendi*' (*ibid.*, 166): 'A *jus utendi* is a lawful power of using an external object; a power which one ought not to be deprived of against one's will except for fault or other reasonable cause; a power such that, if one is deprived of it, one can institute legal proceedings against the person so depriving one' ('*jus utendi est potestas licita, utendi re extrinseca, qua quis sine culpa sua et absque causa rationabili privari non debet invitus, et si privatus fuerit, privantem poterit in judicio convenire*'). This can usefully be compared with modern 'choice' theories of right, and with Hart's notion of a right as a 'small-scale sovereignty'. Unfortunately, Villey's treatment of *jus* is marred by an exaggerated distinction between *jus* and *lex* (which are, of course, distinct notions but closely related), which leads him to misplaced distinctions between law and morality, and between justice and the principles of practical reasonableness: see Villey, 'Si la théorie générale du droit, pour Saint Thomas, est une theorie de la loi' (1972) 17 *Arch.Phil.Dr.* 427–31; for correctives, see *ibid.*, 424–5, and G. Kalinowski, 'Le fondement objectif du Droit d'après la "Somme théologique" de saint Thomas d'Aquin' (1973) 18 *Arch.Phil.Dr.* 59 at 64, 69–72; 'Sur l'emploi métonymique du terme "ius" par Thomas d'Aquin...', *ibid.*, 333–6.

Hobbes on rights... For the criticism advanced in the text, see also Marshall, 'Rights, Options and Entitlements', in *Oxford Essays II*, 228 at 231; Hart, 'Bentham on Legal Rights', in *ibid.* 171 at 179–82. Hobbes's claim that *jus* and *lex* were commonly confused is certainly not groundless, in relation to his contemporaries: see e.g. John Selden, *De Jure Naturali et Gentium juxta Disciplinam Ebraeorum* (1640), in his *Opera Omnia* (ed. D. Wilkins, 1726), vol. I: '*Jus peti nequit, unde auctoritas et imperium perspici nequit*' (Right/law cannot be sought where authority and governance cannot be found) (133), or even more strikingly, '*Nulla obligatio juris inter pares*' (There is no bond of right/legal obligation between equals) (140). This is as far as possible from Aquinas's use of '*jus*', and simply equates *jus* with *lex* (a very voluntaristically conceived *lex*, too).

Locke on rights... In *Two Treatises of Government* (1689), Locke uses the term 'a right' and its cognates in a loose and informal manner, but with an overwhelming predominance of the connotations of 'liberty' and 'power', rather than of 'claim-right' or of '*jus*' in its classical sense: see, e.g., Second Treatise, paras 87, 123, 128–9, 137, 190, 220; cf. paras 7, 190.

VIII.4

Contemporary declarations and Bills of Rights...See, e.g., Ian Brownlie, *Basic Documents on Human Rights* (Oxford: 1971).

'Public order' and l'ordre public'... The marked difference in meaning of these terms was noted by the draftsmen of the Covenants of 1966: see UN General Ass. Records Annexes, Tenth Session (1955), Agenda item 28 (Part II), p. 48, quoted in Maurice Cranston, *What are Human Rights?* (London: 1973), 79. The common law conception is preserved in the interpretation of the Constitution of India, Art 19 (2); see Durga Das Basu, *Constitutional Law of India* (New Delhi: 1977), 45.

'Public morality' and 'morality'... The international texts use both expressions and are sometimes grammatically ambiguous so that 'morality' may or may not be qualified by 'public'. The argument in the text concentrates on 'public morality' but there may be a case for allowing 'morality' as a ground of limitation in some contexts, e.g. in relation to incest and paedophilia generally, sado-masochistic practices, and suicide and complicity in suicide.

The rights of children and parents to a certain sort of milieu... Thus, the Child and Youth Welfare Code (Presidential Decree No. 603 of 1974) (Philippines) provides, *inter alia*: Title I, Art 3. 'All children shall be entitled to the rights herein set forth... (3) Every child has the right to a well-rounded development of his personality... (5) Every child has the right to be brought up in an atmosphere of morality and rectitude for the enrichment and strengthening of his character... (9) Every child has the right to live in a community and a society that can offer him an environment free from pernicious influences and conducive to the promotion of his health and the cultivation of his desirable traits and attributes...' Neither this nor the argument in the text exhausts the reasons for legislation concerned with sexual matters. Public decency is a related but distinguishable matter, concerned with the maintenance of (to be very summary) a certain 'distance' from other people's bodily features and sexuality, a distance that most people find essential to maintaining the integration of their own bodily nature and sexuality with their self-possession, friendship, etc.

VIII.5

Translating 'two-term' claims of human rights into 'three-term' relationships... For the problem in relation to 'the right to life' and 'the right to one's own body', see Judith J. Thomson, 'A Defense of Abortion' (1971) 1 *Phil. Pub. Aff.* 47–66, and J. M. Finnis, 'The Rights and Wrongs of Abortion: a Reply to Judith Thomson' (1973) 2 *Phil. Pub. Aff.* 117–45 [*CEJF* III.18] (both reprinted in, e.g., Dworkin (ed.), *Philosophy of Law* (Oxford: 1977)). For an outline of the complexities in relation to 'freedom of speech', see J. Finnis, 'Some Professorial Fallacies about Rights' (1972) 4 *Adel. L. R.* 376 at 385–6 [*CEJF* IV.18 at 384–6]. When thinking about freedom of speech, it is important to bear in mind the law about patents, copyright, contracts in restraint of trade and protection of trade secrets, and intellectual property; misleading or dangerous advertisements, and consumer protection generally; libel, slander; treason; conspiracy to commit any and every crime; incitement to commit any and every serious crime; official secrets; etc., before thinking of the law about pornography.

'Paternalism'... For the significance of the proportion of every human life spent in childhood, see Francis Schrag, 'The Child in the Moral Order' (1977) 52 *Philosophy* 167–77.

VIII.6

'Paternalism', 'liberalism', and equal respect and concern... For the argument criticized in the text, see Dworkin, *Taking Rights Seriously*, 272–7; I do not mention his distinction between 'external' and 'internal' preferences, since that is directed against utilitarianism, not against my position (which is roughly what he describes as an 'ideal argument of policy': 274). It is important to rebut Dworkin's interpretation of the requirements of equal concern and respect, since, properly understood, those requirements are a fundamental component of distributive justice: see VII.3.

Paternalism and violation of commutative justice... To defend paternalism against the charge that it denies equal concern and respect is not to defend all forms of paternalism. Indeed, certain contemporary forms of paternalism seem particularly indifferent to (commutative) justice: especially (i) the new and radical paternalism that kills handicapped people (in the womb, in old age, or at other times) 'for their own good', 'because their life is, or will be, not worth living'; also, less strikingly, (ii) the paternalism that insists that the poor be given 'welfare benefits' only or mainly in kind, not in cash, treating the autonomy and self-direction of the recipients only as a cause of waste and folly, not as an intrinsic good.

VIII.7

'Absolute' rights... Since 'inalienable' and 'inviolable' have been appropriated by manifesto writers and draftsmen of Bills of Rights for describing rights which are confessedly subject to exception-creating balancing and trade-offs with other rights or exercises of the same right, not to mention public order and morality, etc., it is necessary to use another term: here, 'absolute' or 'categorically exceptionless', after Feinberg, *Social Philosophy* (Englewood Cliffs: 1973), 79, 86–8, 94–7.

The right not to be killed as a means to any end... See G. G. Grisez, 'Toward a Consistent Natural Law Ethics of Killing' (1970) 15 *Am. J. Juris.* 64; G. E. M. Anscombe, 'War and Murder', in W. Stein (ed.), *Nuclear Weapons and Christian Conscience* (London: 1961), 46–51, also in R. Wasserstrom (ed.), *War and Morality* (Belmont, Calif.: 1972); J. Finnis, 'The Rights and Wrongs of Abortion...' (1973) 2 *Phil. Pub. Aff.* 117–45 [*CEJF* III.18] (also in Dworkin (ed.), *Philosophy of Law*). The casuistry developed in relation to this absolute right can be extended, *mutatis mutandis*, to the other rights mentioned in the text.

IX

AUTHORITY

QUESTIONS about the need and justification for authority can arise in different ways. Someone reflecting on the fact of human freedom in moral choosing, or on the basic values of authenticity and freedom in practical reasonableness, may be moved to ask how any human person can have authority to require one to choose what one would not otherwise have chosen. Orders and rules may weigh with me because of accompanying threats, or because of my uncritical conformism or my careerism. But can they have for me the authority of a fully critical conclusion of authentic practical reason? Someone else may raise a question about authority in reflecting more speculatively on human community. Is authority in a group required only because of the stupidity and incompetence of its members, their infirmity of purpose and want of devotion to the group, their selfishness and malice, their readiness to exploit and to 'free ride'? In a community free from these vices, would authority be needed, or justified?

It will be helpful to respond first to this last question. The human weaknesses recited in the question do indeed give good reason for having authority. But, more interestingly, it is also true that the greater the intelligence and skill of a group's members, and the greater their commitment and dedication to common purposes and common good (see VI.8), the *more* authority and regulation may be required, to enable that group to achieve its common purpose, common good.

For, as I hinted in relation to the fifth requirement of practical reasonableness (see V.5), dedicated members of the group will always be looking out for new and better ways of attaining the common good, of co-ordinating the action of members, of playing their own role. And intelligent members will find such new and better ways, and perhaps not just one but many possible and reasonable ways. Intelligence, dedication, skill, and commitment thus multiply the problems of co-ordination, by giving the group more possible orientations, commitments, projects, 'priorities', and procedures to choose from. And until a particular choice is made, nothing will in fact be done. Moreover, in some forms of human community, that something be done is not just a matter of optional advantage, but is a matter of right, a requirement of justice. Somebody (e.g. parents) must decide how children are to be educated; in the political community, there must be decisions about the management and use of natural resources, about the use of force, about permitted forms or content of communication, and about the many other problems of reconciling aspects of justice with each other (see VII.7), and of reconciling human rights with each other and with other 'conflicting' exercises of the same right and with public health, public order, and the like (see VIII.4, 5). In the broad sense of 'co-ordination problem', these are all co-ordination problems which need a solution (see VI.7). And for most though not all of these co-ordination problems there are, in each case, two or more available, reasonable, and appropriate solutions, none of which, however, would amount to a solution unless adopted to the exclusion of the other solutions available, reasonable, and appropriate for that problem.

There are, in the final analysis, only two ways of making a choice between alternative ways of co-ordinating action to the common purpose or common good of any group. There must be either unanimity, or authority. There are no other possibilities.

Exchange of promises (see XI.2) is not a third way; rather, it is a modality of the first way, unanimity. For there is no agreement without just that: some meeting of minds on what is to be done, or at least on what is the specific content of that promise. Even a unilateral promise is not binding unless accepted by the promisee. Moreover, the agreed co-ordination of action will occur only so long as the parties either retain their original unanimity, *or* acknowledge the authority of a rule requiring fulfilment of promises, *or* are held to their agreement by some authoritative person or body.

Now there is no need to labour the point that unanimity about the desirable solution to a specific co-ordination problem cannot in practice be achieved in any community with a complex common good and an intelligent and interested membership. Unanimity is particularly far beyond the bounds of practical possibility in the political community. For here we have the most complex common good, which (subject to the principle of subsidiarity) excludes no aspect of individual well-being and is potentially affected by every aspect of every life-plan (see VI.8). The principle of subsidiarity (see VI.5, VII.3) has wide implications here. Experience suggests that individuals and particular groups (this family, this firm, this university, this government department...) should have a certain autonomy, a certain prior concern and responsibility for their own particular good, their own particular interests or speciality. Yet this concern of particular persons and groups for individual goods, for particular common goods and for particular aspects of the over-all common good, will enhance the over-all common good only if the resulting particular options are subject to some degree of co-ordination. And if the particular individuals and groups have as their *prior* concern (as they should) their respective particular interests, such over-all co-ordination can hardly be achieved save by some person or body of persons whose prior concern and responsibility is to care for the over-all common good. Again, the life of the political community is open-ended; its ends are never fully achieved and few of its co-ordination problems are solved once and for all. Finally, it must not be forgotten that unanimity is not a practical possibility in a community in which intelligence and dedication to the common good are mixed with selfishness and folly.

IX.2 THE MEANINGS OF 'AUTHORITY'

One treats something (e.g. an opinion, a pronouncement, a map, an order, a rule...) as authoritative if and only if one treats it as giving one sufficient reason for believing or acting in accordance with it *notwithstanding* that one cannot oneself otherwise see good reason for so believing or acting, or cannot evaluate the reasons one can see, or sees some countervailing reason(s), or would oneself otherwise (i.e. in the absence of what it is that one is treating as authoritative) have preferred not so to believe or act. In other words, one treats something as authoritative when one treats it as, in Joseph Raz's useful terminology, an exclusionary reason, i.e. a reason for judging or acting in the absence of understood reasons, or for disregarding at least *some* reasons which are understood and relevant and would in the absence of the exclusionary reason have sufficed to justify proceeding in some other way.[1]

This is the focal meaning of authority, whether that authority be speculative (the authority of learning or genius) or practical (the authority of good taste, or practical experience, or office...), and whether the authority be ascribed to a person or persons, or to their characteristics, or to their opinions or pronouncements, or to some opinion or prescription which has authority for reasons other than that its author(s) had authority (e.g., as we shall see, custom or convention). I need say no more here about speculative authority, beyond observing in passing that a person or persons' theoretical knowledge is often a good reason for treating them as having practical authority, but is not a necessary condition for so regarding them.

Before going further, it is as well to face up to some linguistic complications which, when not clearly understood, cause serious confusion between 'positivists' and 'natural law theorists' in jurisprudence. The foregoing two paragraphs have treated as focal or primary the meaning which the proposition 'X has authority' has when that proposition is asserted by speakers of a kind (S_1) who treat X (or X's pronouncements, etc.) as authoritative not merely for others but also *for the speakers themselves* (S_1), i.e. as giving anyone (relevant) including *themselves* (S_1) exclusionary reason for action in accordance with X (or X's pronouncement, etc.). But 'X has authority' may be said, truthfully, by speakers of a kind (S_2) who do *not* regard X as having authority over or in relation to them (S_2); for S_2 speakers, the truth of the proposition is established by showing that some people (S_1) in fact treat X as authoritative. In short, S_2 speakers speak as historians, sociologists, or, in general, observers. (They may, of course, be S_1-speaking as observers.) Finally, 'X has authority' may be asserted by speakers of another kind (S_3), who assert it *neither* in recognition of X's authority or authoritativeness in relation to themselves (S_3),

---

[1] *Practical Reason*, 35–48, 58–73.

nor by way of report about other people's attitudes to X, but rather by way of stating what is the case from the viewpoint of S_1 but without either endorsing or rejecting S_1's view. (S_3 speakers may of course be S_1, speaking from a 'detached' or professional viewpoint.) Statements of this third type are very common in textbooks which explain the rules of a game, or of English, Russian, or Roman law, and in professional opinions, advice, and arguments. In what follows I use the notation S_1, S_2, S_3 to refer to statements of the three types respectively, rather than, as above, to (kinds of) speakers.

The difference between these three senses of 'X has authority' is found across the whole range of normative statements: for example, 'that is a binding promise', 'A has a legal duty to ϕ', and even (and above all) 'there is a rule that C must/may/has power to ϕ'. In all these cases one and the same grammatical form may be used to assert (S_1) what there is good reason to do, or what a sufficient reason is for doing ϕ, *or* it may assert (S_2) that a group considers that there is good reason to ϕ, *or* it may assert (S_3) what there is good reason to do from the viewpoint of a certain group or on the basis of certain rules or *if* certain rules give good reason for so acting (but without affirming or denying that that viewpoint is reasonable or correct or that those rules do provide good reason for acting). One and the same person may, even on one and the same occasion, make statements of all three types, switching viewpoint without warning or grammatical indication. This is quite common in legal advocacy.

Joseph Raz has identified and explained these three types of statement. While stressing the importance of not trying to collapse S_3 into either S_1 or S_2, he clearly recognizes that S_1 and S_2 are 'basic' and 'primary'.[2] S_3, though widespread in discourse, is parasitic. And in discussing a closely related distinction between three 'properties or dimensions of norms' he says that 'beyond doubt the primary one' is the dimension or property of actually being a good reason (as distinct from being believed by some people to be a good reason, or being intended by some people to be taken as a good reason by

---

[2] *Practical Reason*, 172. For his account of the three types see 171–7; see also his 'Promises and Obligations', in *Essays*, 225.

others).[3] But to assert that something is or provides a good reason is to make an S_1 assertion. Thus, even for Raz's purposes, which lie within the 'formal part' of 'the philosophy of practical reason' (i.e. that part which is concerned with 'conceptual analysis', as distinct from the 'substantive or "evaluative" part'),[4] the primary and focal type of statement about authority and norms is the S type. For our purposes in this book (which are sufficiently described by Raz's description of substantive practical philosophy),[5] this primacy of S_x statements is even more evident. That is why the explanation of authority advanced in the first sentence of this section is an explanation of that form of recognition of authority which would be expressed by an S_1 statement.

But what is the importance of these technical distinctions between types of statement, or types of recognition of authority? It is this. As is already obvious from the opening section of this chapter, not to mention earlier chapters, my explanation of the need and justification for authority, and of its limits and its proper modes of operation, is going to be an explanation by reference to the common good (including justice and human rights); see, for example, the account of the authority of custom in the next section. To all such explanations, some 'positivists' in jurisprudence have made the following sort of objection:

You claim to be explaining what it is for an authority, an authoritative custom, or a rule, to exist. But at best you succeed in explaining only what it is to believe that such an authority, custom or rule *ought* to exist. For on your explanation it would be *redundant* to say, e.g. '(P_1) an authoritative custom exists and (P_2) it is for the common good that it should

---

[3] *Practical Reason*, 84. 'Existential statements about norms are used for a variety of purposes, among which three are the most important. In saying that there is a norm one may state either that it is valid (that is, justified), or that it is practised, or that it has been prescribed by a certain person or body. These are the three dimensions of norms...': *ibid.*, 80.

[4] *Ibid.*, 10.

[5] *Ibid.*, 10: 'Substantive practical philosophy includes all the arguments designed to show which values we should pursue, what reasons for action should guide our behaviour, which norms are binding, etc'. See also *ibid.*, 11 on 'the most important branches of practical philosophy'.

exist'. But it is odd and counter-intuitive to claim that P_2 is redundant when conjoined with P_1. Or again, on your explanation it would be *contradictory* to say '(P_1) an authoritative custom exists but (P_2) its existence is not for the common good'. But it is odd and counter-intuitive to claim that P_1 contradicts P_2. We conclude that your method of explaining authority and rules is itself unsatisfactory, since it yields results which are counter-intuitive and inconsistent with ordinary language and common sense.

To this 'positivist' objection the reply is now obvious. My programme of explanation does not commit me to condemning as either redundant or contradictory the conjunction of P_1 with P_2. Such a conjunction *does* entail redundancy or inconsistency if and only if P_1 is understood as an S_1 statement. But the positivist objection simply overlooks the fact that 'existential sentences about norms are used for a variety of purposes...'.[6] The 'existential sentence' P_1 can perfectly well be understood as an S_2 or an S_3 statement, and someone who makes either of the conjunctive statements mentioned in the positivist's objection will of course intend the first half of his statement (i.e. P_1) in an S_2 or S_3 sense and the second half (i.e. P_2) in an S_1 sense. His meaning simply is: 'people treat this custom as justified, and indeed it is [or: is not]'; or perhaps, 'speaking from the lawyer's point of view, this is a legally authoritative custom; and, I may add, in my personal opinion it is [or: is not] for the common good that it be treated as such'; 'this is law; but it is too iniquitous to be applied or obeyed'.[7] The fact that I systematically treat S_1 statements as primary, because the focus of my theoretical interest is in justificatory explanations, in no way requires me to regard any of those statements as objectionable (though the history of contemporary jurisprudence shows that they are open to misunderstanding): see II.2, XII.4. Hence this 'positivist' objection to my programme of explanation need not deflect us.

---

[6] *Ibid.*, 80.
[7] Hart, *Concept of Law*, 203 [208], where the 'positivist' objection here under discussion is deployed in a compact form.

IX.3 FORMATION OF CONVENTIONS
OR CUSTOMARY RULES

In this section I show how an authoritative rule can emerge (i.e. begin to regulate a community) without being made by anyone with authority to make it, and even without the benefit of any authorized way of generating rules. The discussion will enable us to deepen our understanding of the relation between acknowledging the authority of a rule and following the principles of practical reasonableness. It will also enable us to understand more adequately both the distinctions and the connections between unanimity and authority in a community. For in studying the formation of custom we are studying the emergence of a substitute for unanimity under conditions which require a substantial degree of unanimity.

It will be convenient to conduct our discussion of the formation of custom by reference to the international community and the formation of customary rules of international law. This is the context in which the problem of custom arouses most interest today, has been most debated, and found most difficult to explain satisfactorily. In what follows, I use the term 'custom' as shorthand for 'authoritative customary rule', and by 'authoritative' in this context I mean 'legally authoritative'. I use the term 'state' as a short form of reference to any entity acting in the sphere of international law as a subject or potential subject thereof.

There is a vast and confused literature on custom as a source of international law. It is generally agreed that custom involves some concurrence or convergence or regularity of practice amongst states. It is further agreed that such concurrence, convergence, or regularity is not enough to constitute custom. There must be a concurrence of deliberate practice, not induced by force or fraud or mistake. More positively, the practice must be accompanied by a certain attitude, belief, intention, or disposition: in the literature this is called the *opinio juris*. It is this last condition for the formation of custom that causes difficulty. The classical accounts of the required content of the *opinio juris* are openly question-begging or paradoxical (but alternative accounts have not been forthcoming). As Oppenheim's treatise says: 'International jurists speak of a custom when a clear and continuous habit of doing certain actions has grown up under the aegis of the conviction that these actions are, according to international law, obligatory or right'.[8] But this is paradoxical, for it proposes that a customary norm can come into existence (i.e. become authoritative) only by virtue of the necessarily erroneous belief that it is already in existence (i.e. authoritative).

The method of analysis and explanation which I have been developing in this Part of the book (and which is only completed in the final chapters of this Part) enables us to offer an analysis of the formation of custom which makes intelligible something like the classic position of international jurists, a position which they themselves, however, have been unable to free from the paradox just mentioned. Technically speaking, the key to a solution of the problem lies in the distinction (expressed in the preceding section as that between S_1 and S_2 statements) between, on the one hand, practical judgments and, on the other hand, empirical judgments about the existence and extent of practices. As throughout this book, 'practical judgment' here refers to judgments made by any person, whether privately or in some official capacity, which explicitly or implicitly state that some action (including always omissions or forbearances) by some (potential) agent should (not) be done, or could (not) appropriately or justifiably be done (in any of the various senses of 'should', 'appropriately', or 'justifiably'): see I.4 (p. 12).

At the root of the formation of custom, and in particular at the core of that factor in the formation of custom which is usually labelled the *opinio juris*, are two different but related practical judgments:

(a) in this domain of human affairs (e.g. passage of warships through coastal waters), it would be appropriate to have *some* determinate, common, and stable pattern of conduct and, correspondingly, an authoritative rule requiring that pattern of conduct; to have this is more desirable than leaving conduct in this domain to the discretion of individual states;

---

[8] Oppenheim, *International Law*, vol. I (London: 8th edn, 1955), sec. 17; to like effect the International Court of Justice in the *North Sea Continental Shelf Cases, I.C.J. Rep.* 1969, 44.

(b) *this* particular pattern of conduct ϕ (e.g. innocent passage on the surface under flag to be permitted by coastal states)[9] is appropriate, or would be *if* generally adopted and acquiesced in, for adoption as an authoritative common rule of conduct.

These are both practical, not empirical, judgments, and they are not yet legal judgments. When the contents of a multilateral treaty, or the resolutions of an international body representative of states, are spoken of as sources or evidence of custom, what is really (or, at any rate, justifiably) being said is that the treaty or resolutions are evidence not of an opinion about what the law already is, but of *opinio juris* in the limited sense expressed in these two judgments. They are indeed judgments that might be made by anyone thinking about the relevant domain. They affirm that something is desirable (a) in general, (b) in particular. In a well-ordered international community, the frame of reference for assessing desirability would be primarily the common good of the whole community and its members (including considerations of justice and rights), and only secondarily the interests of the person or state making the judgments. Very commonly, of course, this ranking of the frames of reference is in fact reversed. This fact is an obstacle to the formation of custom, but only an obstacle, not insuperable.

The next step in the analysis is to observe that both the foregoing practical judgments are distinct from the empirical judgment that many (or few) states in fact subscribe to them. And this empirical judgment is, in turn, to be distinguished from two further empirical judgments: (i) that the practice of many (or few) states, in the relevant domain, is convergent in pattern and is of the pattern referred to in the second (b) of the aforementioned practical judgments; and (ii) that other states do (or do not) acquiesce in that pattern of conduct.

Empirical judgments of the three sorts just mentioned are prerequisites to the making of a new, practical judgment. This new practical judgment is a further aspect of the undifferentiated '*opinio juris*' of the classic treatises. (Indeed, it is the aspect

---

[9] Note that the relevant pattern of conduct ϕ may be procedural or 'framework' in nature: e.g. *negotiation of agreements,* as the appropriate and required method of settling disputed questions about (substantive) conduct in such-and-such a domain.

which, by its undue or even exclusive emphasis, renders the whole doctrine of those treatises paradoxical.) It affirms that the empirically widespread making of the two practical judgments ((a) and (b)), and the empirical concurrence of practice and generality (not necessarily universality) of acquiescence, together warrant the claim that a custom exists as an authoritative legal norm. Notice that the latter claim is a practical or S_1 statement; like S_2 statements it uses the indicative grammar of 'existence', but unlike S_2 statements it is not empirical. It expresses the view that the norm imposes *justified* requirements on all actors in the relevant domain. Even more obviously practical is the judgment that that claim is warranted in the circumstances. This judgment builds on the three empirical judgments mentioned above, but it relates the relevant empirical facts about state practice and opinion to some principle(s) about what is required for the common good of the international community. The action-guiding and requirement-imposing force of the legal norm which this judgment is affirming to be justified derives from some such meta-legal principle of practical reasonableness about the needs of international community. About this meta-legal principle I shall say more when I have completed and reviewed the analysis in outline.

The practical judgments identified in the preceding paragraph are to be distinguished from the empirical (S_2) judgment (often expressed in the same grammatical forms) that 'there is a legal norm requiring such-and-such', in the sense that states empirically do generally recognize such a norm, i.e. that the norm is more or less 'effective'. Those practical judgments are also to be distinguished, of course, from the S_3 statements which neutral jurists make. Although juristic statements are, quite properly, the ones most frequently on lawyers' lips, I say no more about them here, since they are parasitic upon the attitudes of, and corresponding statements open to, those persons who consider that the relevant body of norms ought to be adhered to in practice, i.e. who actually use those norms to guide their own conduct: see IX.2. Our problem about the formation of custom is to explain how a course of international practice can become a legal rule imposing requirements that *those* persons should and would recognize.

The distinctions made in the preceding four paragraphs can now be summarized. For brevity and clarity we can use an ad hoc and elementary notation, merely as a shorthand: PJ signifies a practical (S_1) judgment, EJ an empirical (S_2) judgment, and JJ a juristic (S_3) judgment in the sense explained above:

PJ_0—(a) it is desirable that in this domain there be some determinate, common, and stable pattern of conduct and corresponding authoritative rule;

(b) this particular pattern of conduct, ϕ, is (or would be if generally adopted and acquiesced in) an appropriate pattern for adoption as an authoritative common rule.

EJ_1—there is widespread concurrence and acquiescence in this pattern of conduct, ϕ, by states.

EJ_2—the *opinio juris* (i.e. PJ_0) is widely subscribed to by states.

PJ_1—the widespread subscription to PJ_0, and the widespread concurrence or acquiescence in the pattern of conduct ϕ, are sufficient to warrant the judgment (PJ_2) that there is now an authoritative customary rule requiring (or permitting) ϕ...

PJ_2—ϕ is required (or permitted), by virtue of an authoritative customary rule of international law.

EJ_3—states generally accept the rule that ϕ is to be done (or may be done)...

JJ_1—according to international law, ϕ is required (or permitted) ...

What are the virtues of this analysis? First, by differentiating between PJ_0 and PJ_1, it enables us to see that there need be no paradox or circularity in the classic notion that, in order to amount to an authoritative custom, a course of practice must be accompanied by a particular sort of attitude or *opinio*. Secondly, by differentiating between PJ_0 and PJ_2, it enables us to see that the legal judgment PJ_2, while in various ways dependent upon prior political or moral judgments PJ_0 (not necessarily made by the person now making the legal judgment), is quite distinct and 'positive' (*de lege lata*, not merely *ferenda*). Thirdly, by separating out EJ_1, EJ_2, and EJ_3 from the other judgments, the relation of authoritative rules to facts is clarified: an authoritative rule can be said to be a fact, but it is more than the fact of concurrent practice, and more even than the fact of concurrence of opinion; and it is a fact only because it is treated as an exclusionary reason for action (i.e. as more than a fact).

Fourthly, the analysis enables us to see clearly the real problems involved in explaining (for practical reasonableness) the formation of custom. The main problem emerges clearly in PJ_1, the immediately proximate preliminary to the judgment that a norm is in force and authoritative. For PJ_1, if it is not to be a mere *non sequitur*, must have a suppressed practical premiss; this premiss, I think, is the meta-legal or framework principle PJ^m:

PJ^m—the emergence and recognition of customary rules (by treating a certain degree of concurrence or acquiescence in a practice and a corresponding *opinio juris* as sufficient to create such a norm and to entitle that norm to recognition even by states not party to the practice or the *opinio juris*) is a desirable or appropriate method of solving interaction or co-ordination problems in the international community.

In turn, the clear identification of the meta-principle PJ^m enables us to see that the formation of custom is possible only because PJ^m enjoys wider favour among states than does the PJ_0 relating to almost any particular problem of conduct. Just as it is easier to get agreement that *some* rule would be desirable ($PJ_0(a)$) than to get agreement that *this* particular rule is desirable ($PJ_0(b)$), so it is easier still to get agreement that the international community needs methods of solving its interaction and co-ordination problems and that custom, *if* there is sufficient acceptance that custom is an appropriate method, is an appropriate method (since it often is the only practicable method). This way of expressing PJ^m shows that the desirability or appropriateness of accepting PJ^m is conditional upon a sufficient number of other states also accepting PJ^m. This is not a paradox or vicious circle!

Thus, although there are direct 'moral' arguments of justice for recognizing customs as authoritative (e.g. arguments against unfairly defeating reasonable expectations or squandering resources and structures erected on the basis of the expectations), the general authoritativeness of custom depends upon the fact that custom-formation has been *adopted* in the international community as an appropriate method of rule-creation. For, given this fact, recognition of the authoritativeness of particular customs affords all states an opportunity of furthering the common good of the international community by solving interaction and co-ordination problems otherwise insoluble. And this opportunity is the root of all legal authority, whether it be the authority of rulers or (as here) of rules.

In short, the 'framework' practice of treating custom-formation as a source of authoritative norms is itself one instance of the pattern-of-conduct 'ϕ' in the analysis. In other words, the requirements, preconditions, and forms of custom-formation are themselves determined, in large part, by custom (i.e. by a framework custom whose source is similar in form to the customs for the formation of which it itself provides the framework). The authoritativeness of this framework custom derives not from some yet further custom, but from the opportunity of advancing the common good, the opportunity which is afforded by widespread (not necessarily universal) recognition of the framework custom, and of the particular substantive customs, as authoritative. But it is also very important to see that the authoritativeness of particular customs should not be explained by saying that their formation was 'authorized' by the framework custom. The framework custom does indeed regulate the making of PJ_1 judgments by states, and thus to some extent controls the emergence of customs, and determines the range of their authoritativeness (e.g. by determining what degree, if any, of prior protest exempts a state from adhering to the emergent custom). But it is artificial and unnecessary to say that the framework custom 'authorizes' states to make customs, or that it is 'the source' of the authority of particular customs. Both the framework custom and the particular customs which become authoritative within its framework derive their authoritativeness directly from the fact that, if treated as authoritative, they enable states to solve their co-ordination problems—a fact that has normative significance because the common good requires that those co-ordination problems be solved.

Finally, the analysis reveals the further problems that must be solved if custom-formation is to work at all well as an instrument of international order and community. If it is to work, there must be a sufficient degree of agreement in answering these questions, amongst others:

(i) What actions of what persons in what contexts count as state practice?
(ii) What degree of practice counts as 'widespread' in a given domain, and for how long?
(iii) What expressions or silences, and whose, count as subscribing to the *opinio juris* (PJ_0(a) and (b))?
(iv) To what extent can custom be localized geographically, granted that the interaction and co-ordination problems of the international community, in a given domain, are perhaps not peculiar to a particular geographical area (but perhaps have local variations)?

Answers to these and similar questions go to make up the content of the framework custom. Although they will reflect assessments of what is for the common good of the international community, they are none the less answers that have to be *adopted* by most members of the community if they are to *count as* answers. They therefore can change, i.e. be changed—not necessarily by the exercise of authority (custom is authoritative but not the result of anyone's exercise of international authority) but, authoritatively, by change in practice and opinion.

IX.4 THE AUTHORITY OF RULERS

The clumsiness of custom-formation as a method of generating authoritative solutions to co-ordination problems is obvious enough. Although the process does not require unanimity, it does require a substantial convergence of practices and of opinions, not merely on the desirability of *some* solution but on the desirability of a particular solution. And, as my analysis showed, there are numerous potential causes for doubt about whether an authoritative custom has emerged, whom it binds, and so on. The need for somebody, or some body, to settle co-ordination problems with greater speed and certainty is apparent in any community where people are energetic and inventive in pursuit of their own or of common goods, not to mention any community threatened with military, economic, or ecological disaster.

Authority (and thus the *responsibility* of governing) in a community is to be exercised by those who can in fact effectively settle co-ordination problems for that community. This principle is not the last word on the requirements of practical reasonableness in locating authority; but it is the first and most fundamental.

The *fact* that the say-so of a particular person or body or configuration of persons will in fact be, by and large, complied with and acted upon, has normative consequences for practical reasonableness; it affects the responsibilities of both ruler and ruled, by creating certain exclusionary reasons for action. These normative consequences derive from a normative principle—that authority is a good (because required for the realization of the common good)—when that principle is taken in conjunction with the fact that a particular person, body, or configuration of persons can, for a given community at a given time, do what authority is to do (i.e. secure and advance the common good).

Of course, this derivation of the relevant normative consequences is not indefeasible. That is to say, the conjunction of the principle with the opportunity is only presumptively sufficient to justify the claim to and recognition of authority. Those who use their empirical opportunity, or even their legally recognized authority, to promote schemes thoroughly opposed to practical reasonableness cannot then reasonably claim to have discharged their own responsibilities in reason, and may be unable to justify their claim to have created a good and sufficient exclusionary reason affecting the responsibilities of those whose compliance they are seeking or demanding. I take up the problem of unjust exercise of authority more fully in Chapter XII.

It is for political science to examine the empirical conditions under which particular persons, bodies, or configurations of persons can make stipulations for action, with empirical effectiveness. It will, for example, be pointed out immediately that the state of affairs I am calling simply 'acquiescence', 'compliance', and 'effectiveness' is in reality more complex: while the mass of a population may passively obey, each 'for his own part only' and out of fear of sanctions, there must also be a class of more active, willing, 'consenting' supporters including many if not most officials. But for present purposes it is quite sufficient to say, in simple terms, that the motives or reasons which people have for complying with and acting upon stipulations presented to them as authoritative (and for being willing to do so should occasion arise) vary widely—fear of force, hope for (perhaps fraudulently suggested) profit, respect for age or for wisdom or for numbers or for the fall of the lot, belief in divine designation (charisma) or world-historic mission, adherence to convention or custom (which in turn may designate blood-lineage, or lot, or age, or . . .) . . . Some of these motives are more reasonable than others, either absolutely or at least in given situations. Political science can say important things about this relative reasonableness, and thus about the legitimacy, for reasonable people, of various forms of constitution. But, for an understanding of the authoritativeness of rulers, as a concern of practical reasonableness, it is the sheer fact of effectiveness that is presumptively (not indefeasibly) decisive.

In fact, political theorists pondering the location of authority have frequently erred by carrying certain legal modes of thought beyond the origins of law. Lawyers (reasonably, as we shall see: X.3), when confronted by a claim to a certain status, title, power, or right, inquire after the root of the alleged title; they ask to be shown the conveyance or enactment or other transaction which gave rise to the title, and in turn they will want to be satisfied that those who made that conveyance or enactment had been given authority to do so by some further enactment or transaction which in turn . . . From this train of thought arise the theories of governmental legitimacy and political obligation which tacitly assume that the present authority of particular rulers must rest on some prior authority (of custom; or of the community over itself, granted away to the ruler by transmission or alienation; or of individuals over themselves, granted away by promise or implied contract or 'consent').

The legalistic theories which seek to justify the authority of rulers by reference to the prior authority of some presumably self-authorizing transaction such as a 'contract of subjection' or an act of 'consent', have often been reinforced by a train of reasoning which employs the quite correct premise that *all* the members of a community are entitled in justice to a certain concern and respect. An argument along these lines became popular amongst scholastic writers in the sixteenth century. At the beginning of the seventeenth century, Cardinal Bellarmine formulated this argument with precision: Natural reasonableness requires that there be governmental authority; but natural reasonableness does not identify any particular human person or class as the bearer of governmental authority; therefore natural reasonableness requires that the bearer of governmental authority be the multitude, the whole community itself. (And the multitude, or community, then *transmits* its authority to representatives, be they kings, councils, or assemblies.) Bellarmine's 'syllogism' is helpfully clear; it reveals the fallacy in his theory, and in all such 'transmission' theories (which secular writers later developed, of course, into theories that governmental authority rests for its legitimacy on 'the consent of the governed'[10]). The argument's two premisses are certainly correct; but the conclusion obviously does not follow from them.

Indeed, the conclusion is intrinsically implausible. For the need for authority is, precisely, to substitute for unanimity in determining the solution of practical co-ordination problems which involve or concern everyone in the community. To say 'the community has authority over itself' *either* amounts to saying that there is no authority in this community (so that co-ordination problems are solved by unanimity, or are dissolved by sheer force), *or* it amounts to saying something else, by way of a confusing legal fiction or ideological manner of speaking, about the location of authority in *some* communities; for example, that each member of such and such a community has an opportunity to participate in determining that location (though such acts of participation, while not devoid of significance, do not themselves amount to an exercise of authority, as every outvoted voter in a parliamentary election is well aware).

Consent, transmission, contract, custom—none of these is needed to constitute the state of affairs which (presumptively) justifies someone in claiming and others in acknowledging his authority to settle co-ordination problems for a whole community by creating authoritative rules or issuing authoritative

---

[10] American Declaration of Independence, 1776.

orders and determinations. Rather, the required state of facts is this: that in the circumstances the say-so of this person or body or configuration of persons probably will be, by and large, complied with and acted upon, to the exclusion of any rival say-so and notwithstanding any differing preferences of individuals about what should be stipulated and done in the relevant fields of co-ordination problems.

This emergence of authority without benefit of prior authorization requires, of course, the definite solution of a vast preliminary or framework co-ordination problem: *Whose* say-so, if anyone's, are we all to act upon in solving our co-ordination problems? Necessarily the solution will require virtual unanimity; *here* there will be no solution unless the preferences of the individual members of the community are brought into line. Such unanimity of practical judgment is, obviously, not easy to come by. Individual motivations for concurring in the relevant judgment will vary, and very commonly those who aspire to benefit from the judgment (i.e. who aspire to authority) will be busy ensuring that anyone who is failing to appreciate their claims to intrinsic fitness to rule will be supplied with some extrinsic motive to concur—fear or favour. The effort to bring everyone to at least an acquiescence in this judgment is usually very taxing and exhausting for all concerned, and makes clear to all what is indeed the case: that those general needs of the common good which justify authority, certainly also justify and urgently demand that questions about the location of authority be answered, wherever possible, by authority. I have been stressing that there are situations where this is not practically possible, and that the emergence of particular bearers of authority in such situations is, nevertheless, neither impossible nor unduly mysterious. Now it is time to recall that, very commonly, the first authoritative act of unauthorized bearers of authority is to lay down directions for ensuring that in future the location of authority (whether in themselves or in their successors) shall be determined, not by the hazards of those processes of arriving at unanimity from which they have just emerged as the beneficiaries,[11] but by authoritative rules.

---

[11] 'Beneficiaries': the *hereditas* can, however, be *damnosa*; in any event, authority is (in reason, as in modern British constitutional draftsmanship) responsibility.

Of course, some rulers are content to rule charismatically, and to leave their succession to the movements of a spirit which blows where it listeth (not perhaps without some huffing and puffing by those who would like it to breathe on them). But Weber was well justified in his tendency (contrary, perhaps, to some of his own methodological notions) to speak of the 'legal' type-form of ruler-ship as the 'rational' type-form.[12] Once the problems of social order, and of authority as a rational response to such problems, have become the object of practically reasonable reflection in a community, 'constitutional' provision for the location of authority becomes a first priority. If the ruler does not make it his business to determine the location of authority for later times (not to mention for lower levels), thoughtful members of such societies will commonly make it their business to try, as best they can, to reach some understandings about it. The tendency of political thinkers to utter legalistic fictions about the original location of authority has its excuse, and perhaps its occasion (but not a justification), in the urgent need to legalize the devolution of undevolved authority.

It remains true that the sheer fact that virtually everyone *will* acquiesce in somebody's say-so is the presumptively necessary and defeasibly sufficient condition for the normative judgment that that person has (i.e. is justified in exercising) authority in that community. But to this perhaps scandalously stark principle there are two significant riders. First: practical reasonableness requires (because of the self-same desirability of authority for the common good) that, faced with a purported ruler's say-so, the members of the community normally should acquiesce *or withhold* their acquiescence, comply or *withhold* their compliance, precisely as the purported ruler is, or is not, designated as the lawful bearer of authority by the constitutional rules authoritative for that time, place, field, and function—*if*, by virtue of custom or authoritative stipulation, *there are such rules*. The second rider

---

[12] *On Law*, 336, xxxi: 'Indeed, the continued exercise of every domination (in our technical sense of the word) always has the strongest need of self-justification through appealing to the principles of its legitimation. Of such ultimate principles, there are only three...(a) A domination can be legitimately valid because of its rational character: such *legal domination* rests upon the belief in the legality of a consciously created order and of the right to give commands vested in the person or persons designated by that order...'

is this: while 'consent' as distinct from acquiescence is not needed to justify or legitimate the authority of rulers, the notion of consent may suggest a sound rule of thumb for deciding when someone should be obeyed even though general acquiescence is not likely, and for deciding when someone whose stipulation will be generally acquiesced in should nevertheless be treated as having no authority in practical reason. This rule of thumb is: someone's stipulation has authority when practically reasonable subjects, with the common good in view, would think they *ought* to consent to it.

The standing temptation of lawyers, and of political philosophers in a culture saturated with legal ideals and legalistic assumptions, is to treat these riders not as riders but as the fundamental principle—shutting their eyes to the fact which the lawyer and political philosopher, Sir John Fortescue, squarely faced during the turbulent emergence of nation-states in Europe: 'amongst *nearly all* peoples, realms have come into being by usurpation, just as the Romans usurped the government of the whole world'.[13] The fact that bad people happen to originate a government does not (Fortescue explained) affect the truth that governing power has its beginnings under, and by virtue of, the 'law of nature', and at all times was and remains regulated by that natural law. (Where Fortescue speaks of the law of nature, I have preferred to speak of the principles of practical reasonableness that call for co-operative life in the wide 'political' community, and for the authority that alone makes that life practicable.) In the very frequent case where bad people establish their rulership over a realm, there as elsewhere the law of nature itself (said Fortescue) operates to initiate the rulership, for the sake of human well-being: 'in one and the same act both the force of justice and the malice of wrongfulness effect the operation of the law of nature'—one can say that these persons establish governing power through the law of nature, but in the last analysis it is better to say (he concluded forcefully) that it is the law of nature that establishes that power through such persons, be they good or bad.[14] In these formulations,

---

[13] *De Laudibus Legum Angliae* (c. 1470), c. 12: '*Sic et Romani orbis imperium usurparunt qualiter fere in omnibus gentibus regna inchoata sunt*'.

[14] Fortescue, *De Natura Legis Naturae* (c.1463) I, c. 18 (entitled '*Lex naturae statum regium in eius initio operata est, licet iniqui eundem statum primordiarunt*').

his lawyers' jargon about powers being created by operation of (natural) law does not obscure this English judge's moral realism which refuses to trace the ultimate origin of authority to any fiction of transmission, contract, or actual consent, or to anything other than the principles of practical reasonableness and the basic values of the common good, generating practical conclusions ('I have the responsibility of ruling'; 'They have authority...') from the sheer fact of ability to co-ordinate action for the common good.[15]

IX.5 'BOUND BY THEIR OWN RULES'?

The foregoing section was not a defence of the rule of the few over the many. For convenience, I referred often to 'the ruler'. But nothing turned on the number of persons entitled, in a given community, to participate in rulership. As the classics said, the ruler may be one, or few, or many ('the multitude', 'the masses'). There are social circumstances where the rule of one will be best, and other circumstances where the rule of a very narrow, or a very wide, class will be best. (The classical 'preference' for the rule of one—'mon-archy'—was not a preference for life tenure of office, hereditary titles, or the paraphernalia of royal courts, but expressed a concern for effectiveness of co-ordination, for unity and consequently effectiveness in the pursuit of common good; and the preference was carefully qualified by the proviso that the conditions must be right—for where the conditions are wrong, the rule of one is the absolutely worst form of rule: tyranny.) The discussion of the best forms of rule under given conditions is for political science. My concern is with the distinction, which all social thought easily employs and recognizes and which legal thought formalizes with convenient fictions, between acting in the capacity of ruler and acting in the capacity of subject.

Nothing in the notion of authority which I have been expounding requires that authority rest in some permanently or even quasi-permanently distinct governing personnel. The

---

[15] Thus, there was sound philosophy behind the formula employed to claim jurisdiction for the Crown in British 'protectorates': 'Whereas by treaty, grant, usage, *sufferance* and other lawful means, Her Majesty has power [sc. authority] and jurisdiction in the said territories...' (emphasis added).

axiom that authority is required as a substitute for unanimity in no way entails that authority cannot vest in an assembly of all the sane adults of a community, or even in such an assembly determining issues only by unanimous vote. Provided that the determinations of such an assembly are treated by the members as authoritative after the determination, and after its members have returned to their own private affairs, we have co-ordination of action in the community by authority rather than by unanimity of judgment (for minds can change; assemblymen can come to regret their vote, and yet comply, and be bound to comply, with the determination). Of course, any requirement of unanimity amongst those who exercise authority tends to render authority inefficient as a substitute for unanimity amongst the members of the community: hence, some form of majority rule will ordinarily meet with general acquiescence, at least 'in principle', i.e. as a method of generating authoritative determinations. But the axiomatic distinction remains conceptually clear: as Yves Simon said, imagining a small farming community practising direct, non-representative government by participatory democracy: 'Between [a] few hundred farmers scattered in their fields, busy with their own private affairs, and the same farmers gathered in an assembly in charge of the community's affairs, the qualitative difference is just as great as between the President of the United States and any of us United States citizens'.[16]

There is nothing mysterious about this distinction between the assemblymen in their 'collegiate capacity' (as John Austin aptly put it)[17] and each assemblyman in his individual capacity as subject to 'the assembly's' stipulations (i.e. the stipulations which have met the approval of that number of assemblymen—and according to that manner and form of expressing such approval—which wins general acquiescence, either merely *de facto* or, more usually, because of rules so providing). The distinction simply corresponds to two distinct though related human excellences which Aristotle summed up when he said that a citizen, in the focal sense of that word, is one who shares in rulership (whether in the deliberative assemblies or in the courts of law), and added that 'the good citizen must possess

---

[16] Yves Simon, *Philosophy of Democratic Government* (Chicago: 1951), 151.
[17] Austin, *Province*, 254, 259, 279, etc.

the knowledge and capacity requisite both for ruling and for being ruled, and the excellence of a citizen may be defined as consisting in a practical knowledge of the governance of free men from *both* points of view'.[18]

Just as it is obvious that each and every member of a governing assembly is bound by its authoritative stipulations, in so far as these stipulate what the member is (not) to do, so it is obvious that a ruler who rules alone may stipulate what he or she is (not) to do, and is then bound by this stipulation. If we are to call these stipulations 'laws', and their obligation 'legal', so far as they touch and bind any mere subject, why should we not call them laws and their obligation legal so far as they touch a person who also rules? It will not do to object that monarchs (sole rulers) may have the authority to relieve themselves of their obligations by amendment or dispensation—for the question relates to their position, in reason's contemplation of law, *while* the law which embraces them is not thus amended or dispensed from. Nor is it helpful to declare that such a monarch's obligations must be merely 'political' or 'moral', not legal—for commonly they are obligations deriving not from this or that political 'factor', nor (directly) from any general moral rule, but directly and precisely from that very manner and form of acting which, in that society at that time, counts as authoritative laying-down-of-law.

The elementary distinction needed for present purposes—made clearly in medieval terminology and only gradually slipping out of English legal language during the two centuries dividing St. German, through Hale, from Blackstone—is that between the 'directive' and the 'coercive' force of authority. But when we speak of the coercive force of rules, we are beginning to speak of law (which, as we shall see, is not the same as saying that one cannot conceive of law without coercion).

NOTES

IX.1

It works to the common good that particular goods be properly defended by particular persons... For insistence on this, and a vivid illustration, see Aquinas, *S.T.* I–II q. 19 a. 10c; also Yves Simon, *The Philosophy of Democratic Government* (Chicago: 1951), 41, 55–8, 71. The first chapter of Simon's book

[18] *Pol.* III.2: 1277b14–16; also III.7: 1284a1–3.

also provides an excellent analysis of the reasons why, and differing ways in which, authority is natural to human beings, i.e. is required for their good but not (only) because of the deficiencies of individuals. Discount, however, his theory (taken from Maritain) of 'affective knowledge'.

Co-ordination problems... The concept of co-ordination problem recently developed for analysis of games, strategies, and conventions is summarized by Edna Ullmann-Margalit, *The Emergence of Norms* (Oxford: 1977), 78: 'Co-ordination problems are interaction situations distinguished by their being situations of interdependent decision. That is, they are situations involving two or more persons, in which each has to choose one from among several alternative actions, and in which the outcome of any person's action depends upon the action chosen by each of the others... The specific difference of co-ordination problems within this class is that in them the interests of the parties coincide'. Ullmann-Margalit rightly employs central case/focal meaning analysis here: 'When the coincidence of interests is perfect we speak of a *pure* co-ordination problem. In the non-pure co-ordination problems the convergence of the parties' interests is less than perfect, but still outweighs any possible clash of interests'. In my discussion, 'co-ordination problem' ranges from the pure to the very non-pure instances, approaching asymptotically the 'pure conflict case' where 'the parties' interests diverge completely and one person's gain is the other's loss'. For a legislator or judge, considering the problems of social order generically, the pure conflict situation cannot be conceded to exist as between the members of a community: A and B may be in a pure conflict situation here and now; but A might have been in B's position, and vice versa; so, in advance or generically (i.e. for the purpose of selecting rules and conventions), people of A's and B's sorts have a convergent interest in containing, modulating, and conditioning the possible loss (and gain).

IX.2

'Exclusionary' and 'protected' reasons... Joseph Raz has developed the concept in his *Practical Reason and Norms*. An exclusionary reason is a reason to exclude, or refrain from acting upon, a relevant reason for acting: see *ibid.*, 39, 42, 62; sometimes, as where someone is under orders, it is a reason for not acting on 'the merits of the case' at all—the order operates as a reason for not acting on an assessment of the pros and cons of the action ordered and alternative courses of action: see 42. As Raz rightly observes at 64: 'if authority is to be justified by the requirements of co-ordination [as he thinks it is: *ibid.*] we must regard authoritative utterances as exclusionary reasons. The proof is contained in the classical analysis of authority. Authority can secure co-ordination only if the individuals concerned defer to its judgment and do not act on the balance of reasons, but on the authority's instructions...'. Raz, 'On Legitimate Authority', in R. Bronaugh (ed.), *Philosophical Law* (Westport: 1978), 6–31, is a useful analysis of authority in terms of 'protected reasons', a protected reason being one that is both a reason to ϕ and an exclusionary reason for disregarding reasons against doing ϕ.

Distinction between S_1 and S_3 statements... See also Raz, 'Kelsen's Theory of the Basic Norm' (1974) 19 *Am. J. Juris.* 94 at 107–9. A similar point is made by, e.g., Winston Nesbitt, 'Categorical Imperatives' (1977) 86 *Phil. Rev.* 217 at 221: 'The judgment that from the point of view of etiquette one should do a certain thing is not "a 'should' statement based on rules of etiquette"...; it is not a "should"-judgment at all, but a theoretical judgment about what etiquette requires, and is quite consistent with "But of course, it's nonsense that you should do any such thing". A "should" statement based on the rules of etiquette is not a judgment to the effect that one should from the point of view of etiquette do *A*, because the rules of etiquette require it...' See also Neil MacCormick, *Legal Reasoning and Legal Theory* (Oxford: 1978), 62.

IX.3

'*Opinio juris*' *as belief in obligatory character of the practice*...Besides Oppenheim, see (amongst countless other sources) Judge Manley Hudson's Working Paper (dated 3 March 1950) on Art 24 of the Statute of the International Law Commission: 'The emergence of a principle or rule of customary international law would seem to require presence of the following elements: (a) concord-ant practice by a number of States with reference to a type of situation falling within the domain of international relations; (b) continuation or repetition of the practice over a considerable period of time; (c) conception that the practice is required by, [surely too strong a requirement for the *opinio juris*] or consistent with [surely too weak a requirement] prevailing international law; and (d) general acquiescence in the practice by other States': *International Law Commission Yearbook 1950*, II, 26. Hudson's element (b) is rejected (so far as concerns the modern world) by Tanaka J. (dissenting) in *Ethiopia v South Africa*, *I. C. J. Rep.* 1966, at 291; already Suarez and the earlier jurists whom Suarez cites were clear that custom can be established in a short period provided that knowledge of the custom is quickly spread to all concerned (which is Tanaka J.'s point): *De Legibus*, VIII, xv, 8–9, reading '*princeps*' in the light of xiii, 1. Critical questions could also be raised about the sense in which Hudson intended his element (d). The International Court of Justice employed the classic doctrine *of opinio juris*, almost in Oppenheim's words, in the *North Sea Continental Shelf Cases*, *I. C. J. Rep.* 1969, at 44. But in the *North Sea Fisheries Case (Great Britain v Iceland)*, *I. C. J. Rep.* 1974, at 23, 26, can be seen an understanding of custom-formation rather closer to that set out in our analysis.

'*Appropriateness*' *of a practice as a solution to a co-ordination problem*...The text simplifies matters here. A rational judgment of appropriateness, which is made both as a component of the PJ$_0$ judgments and again (but now taking more facts into account) as a component of PJ$_1$ judgments, will consider not only the intrinsic features (so to speak) of the relevant co-ordination problem, but also the extent to which concurrent practice in the relevant sphere has created structures (whether physical, economic/ financial, or of habit, 'goodwill', etc.) the dismantling of which would involve sheer loss to many (for what gain? and to whom?). It will also consider whether (as is likely) many have benefited from the regularity and concurrence of practice and the consequent relative stability of expectations and predictions; and will ask whether it would be reasonable for those who have so benefited (or who had the free opportunity of so benefiting) to depart from the practice whenever they consider it burdensome to them. These considerations tend in practice to reduce somewhat the difficulty occasioned by the fact that, as D. K. Lewis stresses in his book *Convention: A Philosophical Study* (Ithaca: 1969), 24, 'co-ordination problems' are typically 'situations of interdependent decision...in which there are two or more proper co-ordination equilibria'; for his account of the relation between practice, opinion (expectations and preferences), and convention, see *ibid.*, 42. See also the analysis of 'conformative behaviour' in David Shwayder, *The Stratification of Behaviour* (London: 1965), 233–43, 247–80.

'*Appropriateness*' *of custom as a method of settling both substantive and framework questions*... This appropriateness does not derive from any abstract principle that what has always been done ought to continue to be done; or from any principle that what a majority of individuals or states want to be done (or to be authoritative) intrinsically ought to be done (or to be regarded as authoritative). (Majority rule is often a highly convenient, and therefore reasonable, principle of authority for a community to adopt—but it is not, *pace* Locke, a 'natural law' principle; it must be *adopted*, by unanimity or by authoritative, e.g. customary, rule: see Burke, *Appeal from the New to the Old Whigs*

(1791) in *Works* (1826), vol. VI, 212–16, summarized in J. W. Gough, *The Social Contract* (Oxford: 2nd edn, 1957), 194–5; contrast Locke, *Second Treatise of Government* (1689), para. 96, and see the tangle of opinions recorded by Otto Gierke, *Natural Law and the Theory of Society, 1500–1800* (trans. E. Barker [1934], Cambridge: 1950), 110, 120, 127, 247, 315, 321, 372, 387.) This judgment of appropriateness rests not only on the considerations mentioned in the text and the preceding note on appropriateness (which apply not in all but in many particular cases), but also on the consideration (parasitic, but reinforcing) that where this method of creating authoritative rules is accepted, those who take the benefits of the resulting system of practice, restraints, etc., will normally be acting unreasonably (partially or unfairly) if in particular cases they claim to be free from the products of the method.

Failure to disentangle PJ_0 from PJ_2 judgments... Hart's notion of the 'internal viewpoint' and the 'internal aspect of rules' has a close relationship to the notion of *opinio juris*; certain problems in understanding and applying Hart's notion arise from his conflation of elements which I have here tried to disentangle. See *Concept of Law*, 86–8 [88–91], 54–7 [56–8], 99–100 [102–3].

IX.4

Defeasibility, or only presumptive sufficiency, of effectiveness as the basis of authority... For this use of 'defeasible' and, especially, 'presumptive', see MacCormick, 'Law as Institutional Fact' (1974) 90 *L.Q.R.* 102 at 123–7.

Empirical conditions for effective rulership... An early study is Aristotle, *Pol.* V: 1301a–1316b27. Hart, *Concept of Law*, 111–14 [114–7], 59–60 [60–1], 197–8 [201–3], 226 [232], 86–8 [89–91], 242 [289], 247 [295], regularly and sharply distinguishes between 'the ordinary citizen's obedience' and 'acceptance on the part of officials of constitutional rules' (though he fails to reserve the word 'acceptance' exclusively for the latter attitude of voluntary, critical acceptance of the rules as common public standards of conduct); likewise Raz, *Practical Reason*, 124–6. Classical political science also regularly distinguished between the two classes of persons likely to be found in any society: those who need to be compelled to keep the peace, and those who freely make the law their own—as Aquinas says, *S.T.* I–II q. 96 a. 5c, these are the two principal ways of being 'subject to law' (or 'subject to authority'). On the empirical concerns of political science as conceived by Aristotle, see Eric Voegelin, *Plato and Aristotle* (Baton Rouge: 1957), ch. 9, esp. 357.

Differing motives for compliance... See Hart, *Concept of Law*, 198 [203], 226 [232]; Weber, *On Law*, 328.

Bellarmine's transmission theory... His syllogism (in fact, of course, an enthymeme) actually runs: '[Political] power is of divine right; But divine right did not give it to any particular person; Therefore it gave it to the multitude'; or again: 'apart from positive law, there is no greater reason why, out of many equals, one rather than another should dominate; therefore power belongs to the whole multitude': *Controversiarum de membris ecclesiae* (1588), III, c. 6, trans. Simon, *Philosophy of Democratic Government*, 166. For an earlier formulation, see Francisco de Vitoria, *De Potestate Civili* (1528), c. 7: 'Nam cum de iure naturali et divino sit aliqua potestas gubernandi rempublicam, et sublato communi iure positivo et humano, non sit maior ratio ut potestas illa sit in uno quam in altero, necesse est ut ipsa communitas sit sibi sufficiens et habeat potestatem gubernandi se'. For Cajetan's looser formulation in 1512, see Simon, *Philosophy of Democratic Government*, 160–5. All these theorists took encouragement from some ambiguous and unsatisfactory remarks of Aquinas, especially *S.T.* I–II q. 90 a. 3c; q. 97

a. 3 ad 3. For an elaborate discussion, which evasively recognizes that in the not infrequent case of a conquered people mere acquiescence suffices for 'transmission' of authority from the people to the new rulers, see Suarez, *De Legibus*, III, c. iv, para. 2; also paras 3–5, 8; also c. ii, paras 3, 4; c. iii, para. 6.

From transmission (or translation) theories to social contract theories... See Otto Gierke, *Political Theories of the Middle Age* (trans. F. W. Maitland, Cambridge: 1900), notes 138–65, 305–8; for the distinction between the supposed contract of social union and the supposed contract of subjection to a ruler, see Gierke, *Natural Law and the Theory of Society, 1500–1800*, 107–11 (sec. 16, para. iv). Generally, see Gough, *The Social Contract*, esp. ch. VI.

Usurpation and conquest as modes of acquiring authority ... The frequency with which authority (i.e., as always throughout this discussion, authority which ought to be respected by a reasonable citizen) is acquired by these methods is rightly stressed by David Hume, 'Of the Original Contract' [1748] (*Social Contract*, ed. E. Barker, Oxford: 1947, 230–5). The US Dept. of the Army, *The Law of Land Warfare* (1956), para. 358, sums up the principle on which the International Regulations respecting the Laws and Customs of War on Land, annexed to The Hague Convention IV (1907), implicitly proceed: '... military occupation ... does not transfer the sovereignty to the occupant, but simply the authority or power to exercise some of the *rights of sovereignty*. The exercise of these *rights results from the established power of the occupant and from the necessity of maintaining law and order, indispensable* both to the inhabitants and to the occupying force' (emphasis added). See also A. D. McNair, 'Municipal Effects of Belligerent Occupation' (1941) 57 *L.Q.R.* 33, stressing that 'the morality or immorality of the occupation is irrelevant' (36); and that the occupying ruler acquires 'a right against inhabitants who remain that they should obey his lawful regulations for the administration of the territory' (35). On the authority of usurpers, according to English law, see Honoré, 'Allegiance and the Usurper' [1967] *Camb. L. J.* 214; J. Finnis, 'Revolutions and Continuity of Law' in *Oxford Essays II*, 44 at 46–7 [*CEJF* IV.21 at 409–10].

Fortescue on the origins of authority ... See also *De Laudibus Legum Anglie* (ed. S. B. Chrimes, Cambridge: 1942), cc. 12, 13, (and the analysis of c. 13 in Voegelin, *The New Science of Politics* (Chicago: 1952), 41–5). The full title of Fortescue's treatise on natural law is significant: *De Natura Legis Naturae et de ejus Censura in Successione Regnorum Suprema* ('On the nature of the law of nature, and on its judgment on the succession to supreme office in kingdoms'). Despite the value of its teaching (aimed against a teaching of Cicero (*De Re Publica*, I, 25, 39) and Augustine (*De Civitate Dei*, XIX, 24) lying at the root of later social contract doctrine) that a people without authoritative rulership cannot be called a body, c. 13 of Fortescue's *De Laudibus* is not as wholly free from assumptions about transmission of authority as a reading of Voegelin's valuable analysis might suggest. By 1670, a similarly philosophically inclined judge, Sir Matthew Hale CJ, is denying the frequency of conquest as an origin of authority and is looking assiduously for a 'consent of the governors and the governed': see his 'Reflections on Hobbes's Dialogue of the Common Law', in Holdsworth, *A History of English Law*, vol. V (London: 2nd edn, 1937), 507.

IX.5

The ruler may be one, few or many (even 'all')... Plato, *Statesman*, 291d–303d; Aristotle, *Pol.* III.5: 1279a28; IV.11: 1298a7–9; *Nic. Eth.* VIII.10: 1160a32–35; V.III.11: 1161a30; Aquinas, *De Regimine Principum*, c. 1, para. 11; Blackstone, I *Comm.*, 49.

Classical preference for monarchy ... The argument is simply from the need for efficiency (*not* to be contrasted here with justice) in co-ordination: Aquinas, *De Regimine Principum*, c. 2; and the rule of one *bad* (self-interested) person ('tyrant') is the worst form of government, *ibid.*, c. 3 (also Plato, *Statesman*, 302c–303b; Aristotle, *Nic. Eth.* VIII.11: 1161a31–33). Plato particularly stresses that these questions about the form and number of the ruling authority are of little moment compared with questions of substance about what this authority *does*: loc. cit., and Voegelin, *Plato and Aristotle*, 158–61.

Aristotle on citizenship as participation in government ... *Pol.* III.1: 1275a22–24, a33, b17–22. (These pages of the *Politics* are the *locus classicus* on definition of terms in social science; and see I.3 above and XII.4 below.)

Single rulers may be bound by their own stipulations, just as members of governing assemblies are ... The argument in the text is that used by Vitoria, *De Potestate Civili*, 21.

Can laws made by a sovereign be binding upon him? ... This question is not of great practical moment in polities where governing powers are distributed amongst various persons and bodies, and the distribution is judicially supervised. Indeed, it has never been of great practical moment for lawyers, since sovereign monarchs of the sort supposed in the discussion will not lack powers of self-dispensation. But the question remains significant for uncovering basic assumptions and confusions about law and legal obligation—just as a critique of Austin's conception of law can most profitably begin by assessing the adequacy of his reason for asserting that a sovereign is legally illimitable; see *Province*, 253–4. For the late scholastic ('voluntarist') view of obligation as a force whereby a *superior* by an act of will moves an *inferior* to the performance of a particular act, see Suarez, *De Legibus*, I, c. v, 24; c. iv, 7 (and see XI.8 below, and II.6 above). For the English legal doctrine that 'the King can do no wrong', see Blackstone, I *Comm.*, 235–40, 243–4; esp. 237: the King himself can do no wrong; since it would be a great weakness and absurdity in any system of positive law, to define any possible wrong, without any possible redress': III *Comm.*, 254–5; IV *Comm.*, 32.

The single ruler is under the 'directive' though not the 'coercive' obligation of the law ... The fundamental discussion is Aquinas, *S.T.* I–II q. 96 a. 5 ('Is everybody subject to the law? Yes'), ad 3: 'A [supreme, single] ruler [*princeps*] is said to be "exempt from the law" in relation to the coercive power of law, for one does not compel oneself, in the strict sense of the word (and the law only has its coercive force from the power of the ruler) ... But in relation to the directive authority of the law, such rulers are subject to the law made by their own will ... Before God's judgment, such rulers are not "exempt from law" in relation to its directive authority, and ought to fulfil the law freely, not under coercion (though they are each above the law, in so far as each of them can change it if expedient, and grant dispensations from it adapted to place and season)'. The distinction is found in Bracton, *De Legibus Angliae* [c. 1250] I, 38 (and see Maitland, *The Constitutional History of England* [1888] (Cambridge: 1919), 100–1), in Matthew Hale, *Pleas of the Crown* [c.1670] (1st edn, 1736) I, 44; Hale, 'Reflections on Hobbes's Dialogue of the Common Law' [c.1670], in Holdsworth, *A History of English Law*, vol. V, at 507–8; and as a vestigial relic, in a discussion of 'the King can do no wrong', muddied with fiction and shifting rhetoric, in Blackstone, I *Comm.*, 235, 237; and esp. IV *Comm.*, 33. For the undifferentiated proposition that the ruler should (save in extraordinary circumstances) be subject to the law, see Plato, *Seventh Letter*, 337a, d; *Laws*, IV: 715b–d, 875d.

For an account of the *vis directiva*, the 'directive' force of law, see XI.4.

X

LAW

THE central case of law and legal system is the law and legal system of a complete community, purporting to have authority to provide comprehensive and supreme direction for human behaviour in that community, and to grant legal validity to all other normative arrangements affecting the members of that community (see VI.6). Such large claims, advanced by or on behalf of mere human beings, would have no plausibility unless those said to be subject to legal authority had reason to think that compliance with the law and with the directions of its officers would not leave them subject to the assaults and depredations of their enemies, inside or outside the community. The authority of the law depends, as we shall see at length, on its justice or at least its ability to secure justice. And in this world, as it is, justice may need to be secured by force; failure to attempt to resist by force the depredations of invaders, pirates, and recalcitrants will normally be a failure in justice. If 'effectiveness' is to be contrasted (as it need not be) with 'justice', the coercive force of law is not merely a matter of effectiveness.

Aristotle gave currency to a regrettable oversimplification of the relationship between law and coercion. He was aware that law typically has two modes of operation—directive and coercive. But he suggested that the need for coercion arises from the recalcitrance of the selfish, the brutish many whose unprincipled egocentricity can be moderated only by a direct threat to their self-interest. But the fact is that recalcitrance—refusal or failure to comply with authoritative stipulations for co-ordination of action for common good—can be rooted not only in obstinate self-centredness, or in careless indifference to common goods and to stipulations made for their sake, but also in high-minded, conscientious opposition to the demands of this or that (or perhaps each and every) stipulation. Practical reasonableness—

from the genuine authority of which conscience, in the modern sense of that term, gets the prestige it deserves (see V.9)—demands that conscientious terrorism, for example, be suppressed with as much conscientious vigour as other forms of criminality.

Not all lawful coercion is by way of sanction or punishment. Even the most developed legal systems rightly allow a use of force not only in resistance to forcible assaults but also for expelling certain sorts of intruders. All allow the arrest of certain suspected offenders or potential offenders, and of persons and things (e.g. ships) likely otherwise to escape due processes of adjudication. Judgments may be executed, and some other classes of debts satisfied, by seizure, distraint, and forced sale. But the context of restrictions with which these measures of coercion are surrounded in a mature legal system is best understood by looking more closely at a threat and use of force employed for a quite distinct purpose: punitive sanctions ('punishment').

The prohibitions of the criminal law have a simple justifying objective: that certain forms of conduct including certain omissions shall occur less frequently than they otherwise would. But the 'system' of criminal law is more than that set of prohibitions. The 'goal' of the familiar modern systems of criminal law can only be described as a certain form or quality of communal life, in which the demands of the common good indeed are unambiguously and insistently preferred to selfish indifference or individualistic demands for licence but also are recognized as including the good of individual autonomy, so that in this mode of association no one is made to live his life for the benefit or convenience of others, and each is enabled to conduct his own life (to constitute himself over his span of time) with a clear knowledge and foreknowledge of the appropriate common way and of the cost of deviation from it. Thus, the administration, or working-out, of the criminal law's prohibitions is permeated by rules and principles of procedural fairness ('due process of law') and substantive fairness (desert, proportionality), which very substantially modify the pursuit of the goal of eliminating or diminishing the undesired forms of conduct—such principles as *nulla poena sine lege* (and rather precise *leges*, at that), and the principles which outlaw retroactive proscription of conduct (at the known cost of letting some dubious characters slip through the net) and restrain the process of investigation, interrogation, and trial (even at the expense of that *terror* which a Lenin knows is necessary for attaining definite social goals).

One can rightly debate the details of these criminal law systems, and adjust them to changing circumstances. But, in their main features and intent, they are justified because the common good of the community is the good of all its members; it is an open-ended good, a participation in all the basic values, and its maintenance is not a simple objective like that of keeping a path free from weeds.

The legal sanction, then, is to be a human response to human needs, not modelled on a campaign of 'social defence' against a plague of locusts or sparrows. There is the need of almost every member of society to be taught what the requirements of the law— the common path for pursuing the common good—actually are; and taught not by sermons, or pages of fine print, but by the public and (relatively!) vivid drama of the apprehension, trial, and punishment of those who depart from that stipulated common way. There is the need of the actually or potentially recalcitrant (which includes most members of society, in relation to at least some activity or other) to be given palpable incentive to abide by the law when appeals to the reasonableness of sustaining the common good fail to move. And there is the need to give the law-abiding the encouragement of knowing that they are not being abandoned to the mercies of criminals, that the lawless are not being left to the peaceful enjoyment of ill-gotten gains, and that to comply with the law is not to be a mere sucker: for without this support and assurance the indispensable co-operation of the law-abiding is not likely to be continued.

Quite distinct from the foregoing set of defining purposes or requirements, which derive from the 'psychology' of citizens, there is a further defining purpose or requirement, by reason of which legal sanctions constitute *punishment*, rather than merely the 'social hygiene' of quarantine stations, asylums for the insane, and preventive detention. Sanctions are punishment because they are required in reason to avoid injustice, to maintain a rational order of proportionate equality, or fairness, as between all members of the society. When someone, who really could have chosen otherwise, manifests in action a preference (whether by intention, recklessness, or negligence) for his own interests, his own freedom of choice and action, as against the common interests and the legally defined common way-of-action, then in and by that very action he gains a certain sort of advantage over those who have restrained themselves, restricted their pursuit of their own interests, in order to abide by the law. For is not the exercise of freedom of choice in itself a great human good? If free-willing criminals were to retain this advantage, the situation would be as unequal and unfair as it would be for them to retain the tangible profits of their crimes (the loot, the misappropriated funds, the office of profit...). If those in authority allowed the retention of unfairly gained advantages they would not only lose the allegiance of the disadvantaged law-abiding but indeed forfeit their title, in reason, to that allegiance. The authority of rulers derives from their opportunity to foster the common good, and a fair balance of benefits and burdens within a community is an important aspect of that common good.

Punishment, then, characteristically seeks to restore the distributively just balance of advantages between the criminal and the law-abiding, so that, over the span of time which extends from before the crime until after the punishment, no one should actually have been disadvantaged—in respect of *this* special but very real sort of advantage—by choosing to remain within the confines of the law. This restoration of the order of fairness is accomplished by depriving criminals[1] of what they gained in their criminal acts (in the presently relevant sense of 'gain'): viz. the exercise of self-will or free choice.

What is done cannot be undone. But punishment rectifies the disturbed pattern[2] of distribution of advantages and disadvantages throughout a community by depriving convicted criminals of their freedom of choice, proportionately to the degree to which they had exercised their freedom, their personality, in the unlawful act. Such deprivation is very commonly by fine;

---

[1] Remember: not all who are defined as offenders by this or that legal system will actually be 'criminals' in the sense here relevant, that is people who (a) really exercised their freedom in their unlawful act and (b) were not prior to that time themselves disadvantaged by a social order substantially unfair in some *relevant* respect.

[2] 'Pattern' here must be understood, not as a 'current time-slice' pattern (for that could never be 'rectified'), but as the diachronic pattern whose justice is assessable only by examining how advantages and disadvantages are gained, incurred, and shifted over a stretch of time.

the removal of pecuniary means removes opportunities of choice. But deprivation of freedom may also be accomplished by actual imprisonment, or by the removal of civil liberties. There is no absolute 'natural' measure of due punishment: the 'law of talion' (life for life, eye for eye, etc.) misses the point, for it concentrates on the material content or consequences of criminal acts rather than on their formal wrongfulness (unfairness) which consists in a will to prefer unrestrained self-interest to common good, or at least in an unwillingness to make the effort to remain within the common way. But some unlawful acts are premeditated, some impulsive, some involve trivia while others are big choices, for high stakes, really pitting the self-will of individual offenders against their fellows; accordingly, there emerges a rough-and-ready 'function' or, more crudely, 'scale' of *relatively* appropriate punitive responses.

Finally, sanctions are part of the enterprise of legally ordering society, an enterprise rationally required only by that complex good of individuals which we name the common good. The criminal is an individual whose good is as good as anyone's, notwithstanding that the criminal ought in fairness to be deprived of some opportunities of realizing that good. On the supposition (which I have been making, for simplicity, throughout this section) that the legal system and social order in question are substantially just, we are bound by our whole analysis of human good to say that those who defy or contemn the law harm not only others but also themselves. They seized the advantage of self-preference, and perhaps of psychological satisfactions and/or of loot, but all at the price of diminishing their personality, their participation in human good; for such participation is only through the *reasonable* pursuit, realization, and enjoyment of basic goods. The punitive sanction ought therefore to be adapted so that, within the framework of its two sets of defining purposes already indicated, it may work to restore reasonable personality in offenders, reforming them for the sake not only of others but of themselves: 'to lead a *good* and useful life'.[3]

---

[3] Prison Rules (England and Wales) 1964, SI 1964/388, r 1.

X.2 UNJUST PUNISHMENT

The foregoing discussion of the role of coercion in the legal ordering of community is a fragmentary illustration of method in jurisprudence. The method is not squeamish about human evil. It is not restricted to the problems of an imaginary 'well-ordered' society. Nor does it suppose for a moment that those in authority are exempt from criminality and injustice. But someone pursuing this method will not participate in debates about whether 'we would call it punishment' if a judge knowingly sentenced an innocent person, using that person as a scapegoat to avert civil commotion. The problem in jurisprudence is not to find or devise definitions which will extend to *all* circumstances in which, regardless of particular points of view, the word being defined could 'correctly' be employed. There is place in jurisprudence, of course, for stipulative definitions of words, in order to avert misunderstandings of discourse; and for lexical explorations, in order to assemble reminders of the complexity of human affairs, concerns, and reasonings. But the point of a jurisprudence such as is exemplified in this chapter is to explain certain human institutions by showing how they are responses to the requirements of practical reasonableness.

Authoritative institutions justified by the requirements of practical reasonableness may be, and quite commonly are, deflected to meet the requirements of individual or group bias. In other circumstances (e.g. the international community) these malign influences, or other practical obstacles, work to prevent the full development of such institutions. A sound jurisprudential method will recognize this, but will not water down its explanations of the links between human institutions and the values and requirements of practical reasonableness. So the explanation of punishment will refer to features which are absent from the punishment of scapegoats. This absence does not require us to amend the explanatory definition of punishment. Nor does that definition require us to forbid the use of the term 'punishment' in the scapegoat case. Still less does it require us to banish the study of abuse of authority to some other discipline. It simply requires us to recognize the unjust punishment of scapegoats for what it is: an abusive, corrupt use of a justified human institution or procedure, an abuse aptly referred to by a secondary or non-focal use of the term 'punishment', a term which in its focal use has a proper role in any satisfactory account of what is required for human well-being. The reasons for this role, and the corresponding features of the central case of the institution and the focal use of the term, have been set out in my account.

X.3 THE MAIN FEATURES OF LEGAL ORDER

Law needs to be coercive (primarily by way of punitive sanctions, secondarily by way of preventive interventions and restraints). But other main features of legal order will come into view if we pursue the question: Would there be need for legal authority and regulation in a world in which there was no recalcitrance and hence no need for sanctions?

Max Weber decided to define 'law' by reference to the problem of recalcitrance and the availability of authorized sanctions.[4] This was explicitly offered as a stipulative definition, and as such is unobjectionable. But it is significant that the complexity and richness of Weber's data, and of the Western language in which he had to discuss those data, overcame his definitional decision. For he felt obliged to distinguish, from among three 'pure types' of authoritative co-ordination (*Herrschaft*), one type that could best be described as *legal*. The characteristics of this type, as Weber himself described them, had nothing in particular to do with coercion or with a staff of persons authorized to impose sanctions. Indeed, he considered legal order to be most purely exemplified in the internal order of a modern bureaucracy, in whose workings coercion, even 'psychic' coercion, is characteristically replaced, in large measure, by a sense of duty motivated by a sense of the worth 'for its own sake' of compliance with the organization's internal rules. This departure from his own stipulated definition of law is evidence of Weber's sensitivity to data and language—for the many senses or facets of the term 'law' (and its equivalents

---

[4] 'An order will be called *law* if it is externally guaranteed by the probability that coercion (physical or psychological), to bring about conformity or avenge violation, will be applied by a *staff* of people holding themselves specially ready for that purpose': *On Law*, 5.

in German, etc.) simply reflect the many concerns, aspirations, and motivations of the societies which use that term for the purposes, and in the course, of the communal life and practices that in turn constitute Weber's sociological data (see I.1).

For Weber, then, authoritative co-ordination is legal in character when it operates by way not of an attitude of obedience to persons but of a disposition to comply with 'the law', a legally established order of consistent, abstract rules (normally established intentionally) and principles to be applied to and followed in particular cases—so that those in authority are regarded as 'officials' whose office or authority is defined by these rules, and who are to be obeyed only while they act within their legal powers. Here we can leave Weber, observing that the features of law which he thus found, intelligibly clustered in a historically significant constant in many (not all!) phases of human social order, are features enabling us to distinguish law from politics, conventions, manners, etiquette, mores, games, and indeed from every other form or matrix of communal interaction—and to distinguish it with complete adequacy *even in the absence of any problem of recalcitrance* and hence of any need for coercion or sanctions.

The preceding paragraph's description of what is distinctive of legal authority and order does not in fact carry us much further than Aristotle's suggestive but teasing notion of 'the rule of law and not of men'.[5] Taking for granted the already-mentioned (see VI.6) features of comprehensiveness, purported supremacy, and absorptive or ratificatory capacity (features which do not by themselves distinguish legal order from the charismatic personal governance of a sovereign administering 'palm-tree justice' by ad hoc decrees), we may now briefly list the main features which as a set (characteristically but not invariably found together) are distinctive of legal order. It will be evident from the list that the ways in which law shapes, supports, and furthers patterns of co-ordination would be desirable even in a society free from recalcitrance. Just as authority is not required exclusively by human malice or folly, so these features of legal order, though adaptable to handling problems of recalcitrance or negligence, are not neces-

---

[5] Cf. *Pol.* III.10: 1286a9; *Nic. Eth.* V.6: 1134a35–b1.

sitated exclusively, either individually or as a cluster, by the need to meet or remedy those human deficiencies.

First, then, law brings definition, specificity, clarity, and thus predictability into human interactions, by way of a system of rules and institutions so interrelated that rules define, constitute, and regulate the institutions, while institutions create and administer the rules, and settle questions about their existence, scope, applicability, and operation. There is thus a characteristically legal 'circle', a sense in which the system (as the interrelated rules and institutions are significantly but loosely called) 'lifts itself by its own bootstraps'—a sense captured by the more scientific but still literally paradoxical axiom that 'the law regulates its own creation'. My analysis of custom-formation (see IX.3) showed, of course, that the circle can be broken and the paradox avoided; but legal thought systematically avoids answering the question which I there answered: how an authoritative rule can be generated without prior authorization.

The primary legal method of showing that a rule is valid is to show (i) that there was at some past time, t_1, an act (of a legislator, court, or other appropriate institution) which according to the rules in force at t_1 amounted to a valid and therefore operative act of rule-creation, and (ii) that since t the rule thus created has not determined (ceased to be in force) by virtue either of its own terms or of any act of repeal valid according to the rules of repeal in force at times t_2, t_3 ... It is a working postulate of legal thought (so fundamental that it is scarcely ever identified and discussed) that whatever legal rule or institution (e.g. contract, settlement, corporation) has been once validly created remains valid, in force or in existence, in contemplation of law, until it determines according to its own terms or to some valid act or rule of repeal.

Thirdly, then, rules of law regulate not only the creation, administration, and adjudication of such rules, and the constitution, character, and termination of institutions, but also the conditions under which a private individual can modify the incidence or application of the rules (whether in relation to himself or to other individuals). That is to say, individuals may perform juridical acts which, if performed in accordance with rules in force at the time of the performance, count as making a contract or sale or purchase or conveyance or bequest, contracting a marriage, constituting a trust, incorporating a company, issuing a summons, entering judgment... All the legal entities thus created have the quality of persistence through time.

Fourthly, we can say that legal thinking (i.e. the law) brings what precision and predictability it can into the order of human interactions by a special technique: the treating of (usually datable) past acts (whether of enactment, adjudication, or any of the multitude of exercises of public and private 'powers') as giving, *now*, sufficient and exclusionary reason for acting in a way *then* 'provided for'. In an important sense the 'existence' or 'validity' of a legal rule can be explained by saying that it simply is this relationship, this continuing relevance of the 'content' of that past juridical act as providing reason to decide and act in the present in the way then specified or provided for. The convenience of this attribution of authoritativeness to past acts is twofold. The past is beyond the reach of persons in the present; it thus provides (subject only to problems of evidence and interpretation) a stable point of reference unaffected by present and shifting interests and disputes. Again, the present will soon be the past; so the technique gives people a way of now determining the framework of their future.

Fifthly, this technique is reinforced by the working postulate ('no gaps') that every present practical question or co-ordination problem has, in every respect, been so 'provided for' by some such past juridical act or acts (if only, in some cases, by provisions stipulating precisely which person or institution is now to exercise a discretion to settle the question, or defining what precise procedure is now to be followed in tackling the question). There is no need to labour the point that this postulate is fictitious and, if taken literally, is descriptively misleading and would restrict unnecessarily the development of the law by non-legislative means. The postulate is significant simply as a reinforcement of the other four characteristics of law and legal thought already mentioned.

All this, then, stands as a sufficiently distinctive, self-contained, intelligible, and practically significant social arrangement which would have a completely adequate rationale in a world of saints. In the world as it is, these five con-

stellated formal features of legal order are amplified and elaborated in order to meet the problems of fraud and abuse of power,
and are supplemented by the law of wrongs and of offences,
criminal procedure, and punishment (see X.1). So it is that legal
order has two broad characteristics, two characteristic modes of
operation, two poles about which jurisprudence and 'definitions of
law' tend to cluster. They are exemplified by the contrast
between Weber's formal definition of law and his extensive employment of the term 'legal'; and they can be summed up in the
two slogans: 'law is a coercive order' and 'the law regulates its
own creation'.

X.4 THE RULE OF LAW

The account just given of five formal features of law's regulation of
its own creation and operation was more incomplete than the very
brief account of punitive sanctions in X.1 above. For it lacked any
systematic account of the relation between these formal features
and the requirements of justice and the common good. Such an
account may best be developed through some consideration of the
conditions under which we can reasonably say that the 'legal
system' is working well.

The name commonly given to the state of affairs in which a
legal system is legally in good shape is 'the Rule of Law' (capitalized simply to avoid confusion with a particular norm within a
legal system). The Rule of Law, the specific virtue of legal systems,
has been well analysed by recent writers; so my discussion can be
brief. A legal system exemplifies the Rule of Law to the extent (it
is a matter of degree in respect of each item of the list) that (i) its
rules are prospective, not retroactive, and (ii) are not in any other
way impossible to comply with; that (iii) its rules are promulgated,
(iv) clear, and (v) coherent one with another; that (vi) its rules are
sufficiently stable to allow people to be guided by their knowledge
of the content of the rules; that (vii) the making of decrees and
orders applicable to relatively limited situations is guided by
rules that are promulgated, clear, stable, and relatively general;
and that (viii) those people who have authority to make, administer, and apply the rules in an official capacity (a) are accountable
for their compliance with rules applicable to their performance

and (b) do actually administer the law consistently and in accordance with its tenor.

The eighth desideratum should remind us that what is loosely called 'the legal system' subsists in time, ordering the affairs of subsisting persons; it therefore cannot be understood as merely a set of 'rules' as meaning-contents. None of the eight desiderata is merely a characteristic of a meaning-content, or even of the verbal expression of a meaning-content; all involve qualities of institutions and processes. *Promulgation*, for example, is not fully achieved by printing numerous legible official copies of enactments, decisions, forms, and precedents; it requires also the existence of a professional class of lawyers whose business it is to know their way around the books, and who are available without undue difficulty and expense to advise all who want to know where they stand. Or again, *coherence* requires not merely an alert logic in statutory drafting, but also a judiciary authorized and willing to go beyond the formulae of intersecting or conflicting rules, to establish particular and if need be novel reconciliations, and to abide by those reconciliations when relevantly similar cases arise at different times before different tribunals. Or again, the *prospectivity* of the law can be secured only by a certain restraint in the judicial adoption of new interpretations of the law. At each point we see that the Rule of Law involves certain qualities of process which can be systematically secured only by the institution of judicial authority and its exercise by persons professionally equipped and motivated to act according to law. Obviously, much more could be said about this institutional aspect of the Rule of Law—of what historical experience has shown to be further desiderata, such as the independence of the judiciary, the openness of court proceedings, the power of the courts to review the proceedings and actions not only of other courts but of most other classes of official, and the accessibility of the courts to all, including the poor.

To complete this review of the content of the Rule of Law, before proceeding to inquire into its point, we need only observe that concern for the Rule of Law does not merely shape or modulate projects which a ruler already has in mind. It also works to suggest new subject-matters for authoritative regulation. Consider, for example, the extension of law into a field such as consumer-supplier relations. Just as a rule authorizing a tyrant to do what he wills *is* 'a rule of law' (in a thin, rather uninteresting sense) but departs from the Rule of Law, and *is* 'a constitution' (in a thin, uninteresting sense) but fails to establish constitutional government, so likewise a rule such as *caveat emptor* is 'a rule of law in respect of consumer-supplier relations' but fails to extend legal order into that field. The decision to extend legal order into the field, by way of criminal law, contract and tort law, new institutions for inspection, complaint-investigation, arbitration, etc., is justified not only by the desirability of minimizing tangible forms of harm and economic loss but also by the value of securing, for its own sake, a quality of clarity, certainty, predictability, trustworthiness, in the human interactions of buying and selling, etc.

And here we touch, at last, the reason why the Rule of Law is a virtue of human interaction and community. It is the reason that I touched upon in discussing the law of criminal procedure. Individuals can only be *selves*—i.e. have the 'dignity' of being 'responsible agents'—if they are not made to live their lives for the convenience of others but are allowed and assisted to create a subsisting identity across a 'lifetime'. This is the primary value of the predictability which the law seeks to establish through the five formal features discussed above (see X.3). But it is also the primary value of that notion of *constitutional* government (*Rechtsstaat*) which, often at the expense of some certainty about the precise location of authority, seeks to guarantee that rulers will not direct the exercise of their authority towards private or partisan objectives. The motive of constitutional devices such as the so-called 'separation of powers' is characteristically expressed not merely by reference to the unjust schemes of arbitrary, partisan, or despotic rulers but also by appeal to the positive good of a certain quality of association and interaction between ruler and ruled: 'to the end it may be a government of laws and not of men'.[6] Implicitly, a principal component of the idea of constitutional government (which itself is one aspect of the idea of the Rule of Law) is the holding of the rulers to their side of a relationship of reciprocity, in which the claims of authority

---

[6] Massachusetts Declaration of Rights [1779], Art 30 (providing for the strict separation of legislative, executive, and judicial powers).

are respected on condition that authority respects the claims of the common good (of which a fundamental component is respect for the equal right of all to respectful consideration: see VII.4)

In short, the five formal features of law (see X.3) are the more instantiated the more the eight desiderata listed above are fulfilled. The fundamental point of the desiderata is to secure to the subjects of authority the dignity of self-direction and freedom from certain forms of manipulation. The Rule of Law is thus among the requirements of justice or fairness.

X.5 LIMITS OF THE RULE OF LAW

Just as I followed my discussion of punishment (X.1) with a discussion of unjust punishment (X.2), so we should now briefly consider the abuse of the Rule of Law. Lon Fuller and his critics raised the question whether a tyranny devoted to pernicious objectives can pursue those ends through a fully lawful Rule of Law. The debate failed to clarify the relevant sense of 'can'. It is clear enough that 'logical' or 'conceptual' possibility is not, and should not be, the focus of discussion here. As we have to stress again and again in an age of conceptual dogmatism, concepts of law and society are legitimately many, and their employment is subordinated to matters of principle rooted in the basic principles and requirements of practical reasonableness (which themselves generate many concepts and can be expressed in many reasonable forms). Fuller himself seemed to rest with a very different but equally unsatisfying claim that as a matter of historical fact you will not find a tyranny that operated consistently through law. But Fuller's discussion had more underlying sense than his critics were willing to allow, who could see in it no more than either a 'logical' or a 'historical' claim.

The truly relevant claim, emerging in muted form in Fuller's references to 'reciprocity', is this. A tyranny devoted to pernicious ends has no self-sufficient *reason* to submit itself to the discipline of operating consistently through the demanding processes of law, granted that the rational point of such self-discipline is the very value of reciprocity, fairness, and respect for persons which the tyrant, *ex hypothesi*, holds in contempt.

The sort of regime we are considering tends to be (i) exploitative, in that the rulers are out simply for their own interests regardless of the interests of the rest of the community; or (ii) ideological, in that the rulers are pursuing a goal they consider good for their community, but pursuing it fanatically (cf. V.6, VII.7), overlooking other basic aspects of human good in community; or (iii) some admixture of exploitative and ideological, such as the Nazi regime. None of these types of tyranny can find in its objectives any rationale for adherence (other than tactical and superficial) to the disciplines of legality. For such regimes are in business for determinate results, not to help persons constitute *themselves* in community (cf. VI.5, VI.8, VII.3, VIII.5–6).

So it is a mistake to say, as some of Fuller's critics have said, that the Rule of Law (his set of eight desiderata) is simply an efficient instrument which, like a sharp knife, may be good and necessary for morally good purposes but is equally serviceable for evil. Adherence to the Rule of Law (especially the eighth requirement, of conformity by officials to pre-announced and stable general rules) is always liable to reduce the efficiency for evil of an evil government, since it systematically restricts the government's freedom of manoeuvre. The idea of the Rule of Law is based on the notion that a certain quality of interaction between ruler and ruled, involving reciprocity and procedural fairness, is very valuable for its own sake; it is not merely a means to other social ends, and may not lightly be sacrificed for such other ends. It is not just a 'management technique' in a programme of 'social control' or 'social engineering'.

To this, however, we must add something not sufficiently emphasized in Fuller's account of the virtue of the Rule of Law, but not overlooked in Plato's. In any age in which the ideal of law, legality, and the Rule of Law enjoys an ideological popularity (i.e. a favour not rooted in a steadily reasonable grasp of practical principles), conspirators against the common good will regularly seek to gain and hold power through an adherence to constitutional and legal forms which is not the less 'scrupulous' for being tactically motivated, insincere, and temporary. Thus, the Rule of Law does not guarantee every aspect of the common good, and sometimes it does not secure even the substance of the common good.

Sometimes, moreover, the values to be secured by the genuine Rule of Law and authentic constitutional government are best served by departing, temporarily but perhaps drastically, from the law and the constitution. Since such occasions call for that awesome responsibility and most measured practical reasonableness which we call statesmanship, one should say nothing that might appear to be a 'key' to identifying the occasion or a 'guide' to acting in it. Suffice it to make two observations—one practical, the other reflective. The practical corollary is the judicially recognized principle that a written constitution is not a suicide pact, and that its terms must be both restrained and amplified by the 'implicit' prohibitions and authorizations necessary to prevent its exploitation by those devoted to its overthrow. (I return to the question of 'implied' principles, their source, and their place in legal thought in XI.3 and XII.3.) The reflective observation one may add here is that at this point in our analysis we have visibly returned to the basic principle with which we began (IX.4): authority, of which legal rulership is one species, is the responsibility that accrues, as Fortescue said, 'by operation of the law of nature'—i.e. for the sake of the standing needs of the good of persons in community—from the sheer fact of power, of opportunity to affect, for good, the common life.

An exploration of the limits of the Rule of Law is an exploration not only of the judicial methodology developed to embody and buttress the Rule of Law, but also of the 'general theory of law' which, even when eschewing all concern with 'ideologies' and values, faithfully mirrors that methodology and thus, willy-nilly, the concern for values that informs the methodology. Judges unconscious of the limits of a methodology which suffices for normal times will respond inadequately to abnormal problems. In face of a revolution they will say, for example: 'A court which derives its existence and jurisdiction from a written constitution cannot give effect to anything which is not law when judged by that constitution'.[7] This proposition, like any unqualified statement of constitutionalism (whether

---

[7] *Madzimbamuto v Lardner-Burke, N.O.* 1968 (2) SA 284 at 432, per Fieldsend A. J. A. (High Court of Rhodesia, Appellate Division). See my fuller discussion in [1968] *Annual Survey of Commonwealth Law* 108–12; and in 'Revolutions and Continuity of Law', in *Oxford Essays II*, 44 at 54, 70 [*CEJF* IV.21 at 415, 429].

judicial or jurisprudential), is self-defeating. For the proposition itself cannot be derived from, and applied in any particular instance simply by reference to, the constitution alone. Usually a constitution will be quite silent on this sort of question. (And why should the matter be affected fundamentally by the written or unwritten character of the constitution?) But even if a written constitution did contain a rule embodying the proposition, there would remain the question whether any given court derives its existence, jurisdiction, or authority from the written constitution alone, whatever that document may assert. Test the matter further. Suppose a constitution specifically provided that no rule or person should have any authority save by virtue of the constitution. There would still remain the question whether acceptance of one part of, or acceptance of authority under, a constitution requires one to accept the whole constitution, including the part which demands that the whole be accepted as exclusive. A constitution may stipulate, so to speak, 'All from me or nothing from me'. But it cannot thereby prevent anyone from raising the question whether he need accept *that* norm or stipulation. The very raising of the question shows that the answer cannot be determined by any positive rule (written or unwritten) of the 'system'—not even a rule stipulating that the question is illegitimate.

X.6 A DEFINITION OF LAW

Throughout this chapter, the term 'law' has been used with a focal meaning so as to refer primarily to rules made, in accordance with regulative legal rules, by a determinate and effective authority (itself identified and, standardly, constituted as an institution by legal rules) for a 'complete' community, and buttressed by sanctions in accordance with the rule-guided stipulations of adjudicative institutions, this ensemble of rules and institutions being directed to reasonably resolving any of the community's co-ordination problems (and to ratifying, tolerating, regulating, or overriding co-ordination solutions from any other institutions or sources of norms) for the common good of that community, according to a manner and form itself adapted to that common good by features of specificity, minimization of arbitrariness, and maintenance of a quality of reciprocity between the subjects of the law both amongst themselves and in their relations with the lawful authorities.

This multi-faceted conception of law has been reflectively constructed by tracing the implications of certain requirements of practical reason, given certain basic values and certain empirical features of persons and their communities. The intention has not been lexicographical; but the construction lies well within the boundaries of common use of 'law' and its equivalents in other languages. The intention has not been to describe existing social orders; but the construction corresponds closely to many existing social phenomena that typically are regarded as central cases of law, legal system, Rule of Law, etc. Above all, the meaning has been constructed as a *focal* meaning, not as an appropriation of the term 'law' in a univocal sense that would exclude from the reference of the term anything that failed to have all the characteristics (and to their full extent) of the central case. And, equally important, it has been fully recognized that each of the terms used to express the elements in the conception (e.g. 'making', 'determinate', 'effective', 'a community', 'sanctioned', 'rule-guided', 'reasonable', 'non-discriminatory', 'reciprocal', etc.) has itself a focal meaning and a primary reference, and therefore extends to analogous and secondary instances which lack something of the central instance. For example, custom is not *made* in the full sense of 'made'—for making is something that someone can set himself to do, but no one sets himself (themselves) to make a custom. Yet customs are 'made', in a sense that requirements of practical reason are not made but discovered. The way in which each of the other crucial terms is *more or less* instantiated is quite obvious. (If the term 'reasonable' arouses misgivings, see VI.1.) Law, in the focal sense of the term, is *fully* instantiated only when each of these component terms is fully instantiated.

If one wishes to stress the empirical/historical importance,[8] or the practical/rational desirability, of sanctions, one may say, dramatically, that an unsanctioned set of laws is 'not really law'. If one wishes to stress the empirical/historical importance, or the practical/rational desirability of determinate legislative

---

[8] Remember, incidentally, that empirical or historical *importance* can, in the last analysis, only be measured by reference to the values or principles of practical reason: see I.1, I.4.

and/or adjudicative institutions, one may say, dramatically, that a community without such institutions 'lacks a real legal system' or 'cannot really be said to have "a legal system"'. If one wishes to stress the empirical/historical importance, or the practical/rational desirability, of rules authorizing or regulating private or public change in the rules or their incidence, one may say, dramatically, that a set of rules which includes no such rules 'is not a legal system'. All these things have often been said, and can reasonably be said provided that one is seeking to draw attention to a feature of the central case of law and not to banish the other non-central cases to some other discipline.

I have by now sufficiently stressed that one would be simply misunderstanding my conception of the nature and purpose of explanatory definitions of theoretical concepts if one supposed that my definition 'ruled out as non-laws'[9] laws which failed to meet, or meet fully, one or other of the elements of the definition. But I should add that it would also be a misunderstanding to condemn the definition because 'it fails to explain correctly our ordinary concept of law which does allow for the possibility of laws of [an] objectionable kind'.[10] For not only does my definition 'allow for the possibility'; it also is not advanced with the intention of 'explaining correctly our [sc. the ordinary person's] ordinary concept of law'. The truth is that the 'ordinary concept of law' (granting, but not admitting, that there is *one* such concept) is quite unfocused. It is a concept which allows 'us' to understand lawyers when they talk about sophisticated legal systems, and anthropologists when they talk about elementary legal systems, and tyrants and bandits when they talk about the orders and the customs of their syndicate, and theologians and moralists...There is no point in trying to explain a common-sense concept which takes its meanings from its very varied contexts and is well-understood by everyone in those contexts. My purpose has not been to explain an unfocused 'ordinary concept' but to develop a concept for use in a theoretical explanation of a set of human actions, dispositions, interrelationships, and conceptions which (i) hang together as a set by virtue of their adaptation to a

---

[9] See Raz, *Practical Reason*, 164.
[10] *Ibid.*

specifiable set of human needs considered in the light of empirical features of the human condition, and (ii) are accordingly found in very varying forms and with varying degrees of suitability for, and deliberate or unconscious divergence from, those needs as the fully reasonable person would assess them. To repeat: the intention has been not to explain a concept, but to develop a concept which would explain the various phenomena referred to (in an unfocused way) by 'ordinary' talk about law—and explain them by showing how they answer (fully or partially) to the standing requirements of practical reasonableness relevant to this broad area of human concern and interaction.

Lawyers are likely to become impatient when they hear that social arrangements can be *more or less* legal, that legal systems and the rule of law exist as a matter of degree... and so on. Lawyers systematically strive to use language in such a way that from its use they can read off a definite solution to definite problems—in the final analysis, judgment for one party rather than the other in a litigable dispute. If cars are to be taxed at such and such a rate, one must be able, as a lawyer, to say (i.e. to rule) of every object that it simply is or is not a car: qualifications, 'in this respect... but in that respect', *secundum quids*, and the like are permissible in argument (and a good lawyer is well-aware how open-textured and analogous in structure most terms and concepts are); but just as they do not appear in statutory formulae, so they cannot appear in the final pronouncement of law. And lawyers, for the same good practical reasons, intrinsic to the enterprise of legal order as I have described it in this chapter, extend their technical use of language to the terms 'law', 'rule', 'legal', 'legal system' themselves. To make their point propositionally they will say that a purported law or rule is either valid or invalid. There are no intermediate categories (though there are intermediate states of affairs, e.g. voidable laws, which now are valid, or are treated as valid, or are deemed to be valid, but are liable to be rendered or treated as or deemed invalid). Equipped with this concept of validity, the lawyer aspires to be able to say of every rule that, being valid, it is a legal rule, or, being invalid, is not. The validity of a rule is identified with membership of the legal system (conceived as a set of valid rules), which thus can be considered legally as the set of all valid rules, including those rules which authorized the valid rule-originating acts of enactment and/or adjudication which are (in this conception) the necessary and sufficient conditions for the validity of the valid rules.

There is no need to question here the sufficiency of this set of concepts and postulates for the practical purposes of the lawyer—though questions could certainly be raised about the role of principles (which have no determinate origin and cannot without awkwardness be called valid) in legal argumentation. Rather it must be stressed that the set is a technical device for use within the framework of legal process, and in legal thought directed to arriving at solutions within that process. The device cannot be assumed to be applicable to the quite different problems of describing and explaining the role of legal process within the ordering of human life in society, and the place of legal thought in practical reason's effort to understand and effect real human good. It is a philosophical mistake to declare, in discourse of the latter kinds, that a social order or set of concepts must either be law or not be law, be legal or not legal.

For our purposes, physical, chemical, biological, and psychological laws are only metaphorically laws. To say this is not to question the legitimacy of the discourse of natural scientists, for whose purposes, conversely, what we call 'law strictly speaking' is only metaphorically a set of laws. The similarity between our central case and the laws of arts and crafts and applied sciences is greater; in each case we are considering the regulation of performances by self-regulating performers whose own notions of what they are up to affects the course of their performance. But the differences are still systematic and significant; as I said before (see VII.7, X.1), ordering a society for the greater participation of its members in human values is not very like following a recipe for producing a definite product or a route to a definite goal. 'Natural law'—the set of principles of practical reasonableness in ordering human life and human community—is only analogically law, in relation to my present focal use of the term: that is why the term has been avoided in this chapter on law, save in relation to past thinkers who used the term. These past thinkers, however, could, without loss of meaning, have spoken instead of 'natural right', 'intrinsic morality', 'natural reason, or right reason, in action', etc. But no synonyms are available for 'law' in our focal sense.

X.7 DERIVATION OF 'POSITIVE' FROM 'NATURAL' LAW

'In every law positive well made is somewhat of the law of reason ...; and to discern ... the law of reason from the law positive is very hard. And though it be hard, yet it is much necessary in every moral doctrine, and in all laws made for the commonwealth'.[11] These words of the sixteenth-century English lawyer Christopher St. German express the fundamental concern of any sound 'natural law theory' of law: to understand the relationship(s) between the particular laws of particular societies and the permanently relevant principles of practical reasonableness.

Consider the law of murder. From the lay person's point of view this can be regarded as a directive not to intentionally kill (or attempt to kill) any human being, unless in self-defence ... The legal rule, conceived from this viewpoint, corresponds rather closely to the requirement of practical reason, which would be such a requirement whether or not repeated or supported by the law of the land: that one is not to deliberately kill the innocent (in the relevant sense of 'innocent'). Now this requirement is derived from the basic principle that human life is a good, in combination with the seventh of the nine basic requirements of practical reason (see V.7). Hence, Aquinas says that this sort of law is derived from natural law by a process analogous to deduction of demonstrative conclusions from general principles; and that such laws are not positive law only, but also have part of their 'force' from the natural law (i.e. from the basic principles of practical reasonableness).[12] Hooker calls such laws 'mixedly human', arguing that their matter or normative content is the same as reason necessarily requires, and that they simply ratify the law of reason, adding to it only the additional constraining or binding force of the threat of

---

[11] *Doctor and Student*, I, c. 4. As St. German remarks, *ibid.*, 1, c. 5, English lawyers are not used to reasoning in terms of what is and is not a matter of 'the law of nature'; instead they frame their reasoning 'in that behalf' in terms of what is and is not 'against reason' (i.e. unreasonable).

[12] *S.T.* I–II q. 95 a. 2c.

punishment.[13] Aquinas's general idea here is fundamentally correct, but vaguely stated and seriously underdeveloped; and Hooker's clarifications and developments are not in the most interesting direction.

True, some parts of a legal system commonly do, and certainly should, consist of rules and principles closely corresponding to requirements of practical reason which themselves are conclusions directly from the combination of a particular basic value (e.g. life) with one or more of those nine basic 'methodological' requirements of practical reasonableness. Discussion in courts and amongst lawyers and legislators will commonly, and reasonably, follow much the same course as a straightforward moral debate such as philosophers or theologians, knowing nothing of that time and place, might carry on. Moreover, the threat of sanctions is indeed, as Hooker remarks,[14] an 'expedient' supplementation for the legislator to annex to the moral rule, with an eye to the recalcitrant and wayward in his own society.

But the process of receiving even such straightforward moral precepts into the legal system deserves closer attention. Notice, for example, that legislative draftsmen do *not* ordinarily draft laws in the form imagined by Aquinas: 'There is not to be killing'[15]—nor even 'Do not kill', or 'Killing is forbidden', or 'A person shall not [may not] kill'. Rather they will say 'It shall be [or: is] an offence to...' or 'Any person who kills... shall be guilty of an offence'. Indeed, it is quite possible to draft an entire legal system without using normative vocabulary at all. Why do professional draftsmen prefer this indicative propositional form? At the deepest level it is because they have in their mind's eye the pattern of a future social order, or of some aspect of such an order, and are attempting to reproduce that order (on the assumption, which need not be stated or indicated grammatically because it is contextually self-evident, that the participants are to, shall, must, may, etc., act conformably to the pattern). More particularly, a lawyer sees the

---

[13]   Richard Hooker, *Of the Laws of Ecclesiastical Polity* (1594), Book I, c. 10, sec. 10.

[14]   *Ibid.*

[15]   *S.T.* I–II q. 95 a. 2c: 'Derivantur ergo quaedam [leges] a principiis communibus legis naturae per modum conclusionum: sicut hoc quod est "non esse occidendum", ut conclusio quaedam derivari potest ab eo quod est "nulli esse faciendum malum" ...'

desired future social order from a professionally structured view-point, as a stylized and manageable drama. In this drama, many characters, situations, and actions known to common sense, sociology, and ethics are missing, while many other characters, relationships, and transactions known only or originally only to the lawyer are introduced. In the legally constructed version of social order there are not merely the 'reasonable' and 'unreasonable' acts which dominate the stage in an individual's practical reasoning; rather, an unreasonable act, for example of killing, may be a crime (and one of several procedurally significant classes of offence), and/or a tort, and/or an act which effects automatic vacation or suspension of office or forfeiture of property, and/or an act which insurers and/or public officials may properly take into account in avoiding a contract or suspending a licence...etc. So it is the business of the draftsman to specify, precisely, into which of these costumes and relationships an act of killing-under-such-and-such-circumstances fits. That is why '*No one may* kill...' is legally so defective a formulation.

Nor is all this of relevance only to professional lawyers. The existence of the legal rendering of social order makes a new train of practical reasoning possible, and necessary, for the law-abiding private citizen (see also XI.4). For example, the professionally drafted legislative provision, 'It is an offence to kill', contextually implies a normative direction to citizens. For there is a legal norm, so intrinsic to any legal ordering of community that it need never be enacted: criminal offences are not to be committed. Behind this norm the citizen need not go. Knowing the law of murder (at least in outline), he need not consider the value of life or the requirement of practical reason that basic values be respected in every action. So Hooker is mistaken in suggesting that what the positive law on murder adds to the permanent rule of reason is merely the punitive sanction. As part of the law of the land concerning offences, it adds also, and more interestingly, (i) a precise elaboration of many other legal (and therefore social) consequences of the act and (ii) a distinct new motive for the law-abiding citizen, who acts on the principle of avoiding legal offences as such, to abstain from the stipulated class of action.

Thus, in a well-developed legal system, the integration of even an uncontroversial requirement of practical reasonableness into the law will not be a simple matter. The terms of the requirement *qua* requirement (e.g., in the case we were considering, the term 'intentionally') will have to be specified in language coherent with the language of other parts of the law. And then the part which the relevant acts are to play in the legal drama will have to be scripted—their role as, or in relation to, torts, contracts, testamentary dispositions, inheritances, tenures, benefits, matrimonial offences, proofs, immunities, licences, entitlements and forfeitures, offices and disqualifications, etc., etc.

Very many of these legal implications and definitions will carry legislators or judges beyond the point where they could regard themselves as simply *applying* the intrinsic rule of reason, or even as deducing conclusions from it. Hence the legal project of *applying* a permanent requirement of practical reason will itself carry the legislator into the second of the two categories of human or positive law discerned by Aquinas and Hooker.

For, in Aquinas's view, the law consists in part of rules which are 'derived from natural law like conclusions deduced from general principles', and for the rest of rules which are 'derived from natural law like implementations [*determinationes*] of general directives'.[16] This notion of *determinatio* he explains on the analogy of architecture (or any other practical art), in which a general idea or 'form' (say, 'house', 'door', 'door-knob') has to be made determinate as this particular house, door, doorknob, with specifications which are certainly derived from and shaped by the general idea but which could have been more or less different in many (even in every!) particular dimension and aspect, and which therefore require of the artificer a multitude of choices. The (making of the) artefact is controlled but not fully determined by the basic idea (say, the client's order), and until it is fully determinate the artefact is non-existent or incomplete. To count as a door in a human habitation, an object must be more than half a metre high and need not be more than 2.5 metres, but no doors will be built at all

---

[16] *S.T.* I–II q. 95 a. 2c. There seems to be no happy English equivalent of '*determinatio*': perhaps Kelsen's 'concretization' would do; 'implementation' is more elegant.

if artificers cannot *make up their minds* on a particular height (whether or not it is the same, or different, for each door). Stressing, as it were, each artificer's virtually complete freedom in reason to choose, say, 2.2 rather than 2.1 or 2.3 metres, Aquinas says that laws of this second sort have their force '*wholly* from human law', and Hooker names his second category '*merely* human laws'.[17]

These last formulae, so strongly emphasizing the legislator's rational freedom of choice in such cases, can be misleading unless one bears in mind that they enunciate only a subordinate theorem within a general theory. The general theory is that, in Aquinas's words, '*every* law laid down by men has the character of law just in so far as it is derived from the natural law',[18] or in St. German's words, already quoted, 'in *every* law positive well made is somewhat of the law of reason'. The compatibility between this theory and the subordinate theorem can be best understood by reference to one or two concrete examples.

A first example is hackneyed, but simple and clear. Consider the rule of the road. There is a sense in which (as the subordinate theorem implies) the rule of the road gets 'all its force' from the authoritative custom, enactment, or other determination which laid it down. Until the stipulation 'drive on the left, and at less than 70 miles per hour' was posited by one of these means, there was no legal rule of the road; moreover, there was no need for the legislator to have a reason for choosing 'left' rather than 'right' or '70' rather than '65'. But there is also a sense in which (as the general theory claims) the rule of the road gets 'all its normative force' ultimately from the permanent principles of practical reason (which require us to respect our own and others' physical safety) in combination with non-posited facts such as that traffic is dangerous and can be made safer by orderly traffic flows and limitation of speed, that braking distances and human reaction times are such-and-such, etc.

A second example is richer. If material goods are to be used efficiently for human well-being (cf. V.6), there must normally be a regime of private property: see VII.3. This regime will be

---

[17] *Ibid.*: 'ea quae sunt secundi modi, ex sola lege humana vigorem habent'; Hooker, loc. cit.

[18] *S.T.* I–II q. 95 a. 2c: 'omnis lex humanitus posita intantum habet de ratione legis inquantum a lege naturae derivatur'.

constituted by rules assigning property rights in such goods, or many of them, to individuals or small groups. But precisely what rules should be laid down in order to constitute such a regime is not settled ('determined') by this general requirement of justice. Reasonable choice of such rules is to some extent guided by the circumstances of a particular society, and to some extent 'arbitrary'. The rules adopted will thus for the most part be *determinationes* of the general requirement—derived from it but not entailed by it even in conjunction with a description of those particular circumstances: see VII.4, 5, 7.

Moreover, in the vast area where the legislators are constructing *determinationes* rather than applying or ratifying determinate principles or rules of reason, there are relatively few points at which their choice can reasonably be regarded as 'unfettered' or 'arbitrary' (in the sense that it reasonably can be when one confronts two or more feasible alternatives which are in *all* respects equally satisfactory, or equally unsatisfactory, or incommensurably satisfactory/unsatisfactory). The basic legal norms of a law-abiding citizen are 'Do not commit offences', 'Abstain from torts', 'Perform contracts', 'Pay debts', 'Discharge liabilities', 'Fulfil obligations', etc.; and, taking these norms for granted without stating them, the lawmaker defines offences (from murder to road-traffic offences), torts, the formation, incidents, and discharge of contracts, etc., etc. But this task of definition (and redefinition in the changing conditions of society) has its own principles, which are not the citizen's. The reasonable legislator's principles include the desiderata of the Rule of Law (see X.4). But they also include a multitude of other substantive principles related, some very closely, others more remotely, some invariably and others contingently, to the basic principles and methodological requirements of practical reason.

What are these basic norms for the legislator? Normally they are not the subject of direct and systematic enquiry by lawyers. But it should be recalled that 'legislator' here, for convenience (and at the expense of some significant differentiations), includes any judiciary that, like the judge at common law, enjoys a creative role. The principles that should guide judges in their interpretation and application of both statutory and common or customary law to particular issues are the subject of scientific discussion by lawyers. *These* principles are almost all 'second-order', in that they concern the interpretation and application of other rules or principles whose existence they presuppose. They therefore are not directly the concern of legislators who have authority not merely to interpret and supplement but also to change and abolish existing rules and to introduce novel rules. Nevertheless, the second-order principles are themselves mostly crystallizations or versions (adapted to their second-order role) of 'first-order' principles which ought to guide even a 'sovereign legislature' in its acts of enactment. Moreover, legislators who ignore a relevant first-order principle in their legislation are likely to find that their enactments are controlled, in their application by citizens, courts, and officials, by that principle in its second-order form, so that in the upshot the law on the particular subject will tend to turn out to be a *determinatio* of that principle (amongst others).

Many of the second-order principles or maxims employed by lawyers express the desirability of stability and predictability in the relations between one person and another, and between persons and things. Such maxims[19] are obviously connected very closely not only with the formal features of law (see X.3) and the desiderata of the Rule of Law (see X.4), but also with the willingness of lawyers and indeed of people in society in every age to attribute authoritative force to usage, practice, custom (see IX.3). And there is a corresponding first-order principle or set of principles to which any legislator ought to give considerable weight—that those human goods which are the fragile and cumulative achievements of past effort, investment, discipline, etc., are not to be treated lightly in the pursuit of future goods. More prosaically, the tangible expenses and waste of dislocative change are to be taken fully into account—the legislative choice between 'drive on the left' and 'drive on the right' is a matter of indifference in the abstract, but not in a society where by informal convention people already tend to drive on the left, and have adjusted their habits, their vehicle construction, road design, and street furniture accordingly.

[19] For example: '*qui prior est in tempore, potior est in jure, in aequali jure*'; '*ex diuturnitate temporis omnia praesumuntur solenniter esse acta*'; '*communis error facit jus*' ('*multitudo errantium tollit peccatum*'; '*consensus tollit errores*'); '*interest reipublicae res judicatas non rescindi*'; '*ut res magis valeat quam pereat*' ...

Starting with these second-order maxims favouring continuity in human affairs—i.e. favouring the good of diachronic order, as distinct from the good of a future end-state—we can trace a series of related second-order principles which include the principle of stability but more and more go beyond it to incorporate new principles or values. In each case these are available in first-order form to guide a legislator. Prose-form requires a linear exposition here which oversimplifies and disguises their interrelations: (i) compulsory acquisition of property rights to be compensated, in respect of *damnum emergens* (actual losses) if not of *lucrum cessans* (loss of expected profits); (ii) no liability for unintentional injury, without fault; (iii) no criminal liability without *mens rea*; (iv) estoppel (*nemo contra factum proprium venire potest*); (v) no judicial aid to those who plead their own wrong (those who seek equity must do equity); (vi) no aid to abuse of rights; (vii) fraud unravels everything; (viii) profits received without justification and at the expense of another must be restored; (ix) *pacta sunt servanda* (contracts are to be performed); (x) relative freedom to change existing patterns of legal relationships by agreement; (xi) in assessments of the legal effects of purported acts-in-the-law, the weak to be protected against their weaknesses; (xii) disputes not to be resolved without giving both sides an opportunity to be heard; (xiii) no one to be allowed to judge his or her own cause.

These 'general principles of law' are indeed principles. That is to say, they justify, rather than require, particular rules and determinations, and are qualified in their application to particular circumstances by other like principles. Moreover, any of them may on occasion be outweighed and overridden (which is not the same as violated, amended, or repealed) by other important components of the common good, other principles of justice. Nor is it to be forgotten that there are norms of justice that may never be overridden or outweighed, corresponding to the absolute human rights (see VIII.7). Still, the general principles of law which have been recited here do operate, over vast ranges of legislative *determinationes*, to modify the pursuit of particular social goods. And this modification need not be simply a matter of abstaining from certain courses of conduct: the principles which require compensation, or ascertainment of *mens rea*, or 'natural justice'... can be adequately met only by the positive creation of complex administrative and judicial structures.

In sum: the derivation of law from the basic principles of practical reasoning has indeed the two principal modes identified and named by Aquinas; but these are not two streams flowing in separate channels. The central principle of the law of murder, of theft, of marriage, of contract... may be a straightforward application of universally valid requirements of reasonableness, but the effort to integrate these subject-matters into the Rule of Law will require of judge and legislator countless elaborations which in most instances partake of the second mode of derivation. This second mode, the sheer *determinatio* by more or less free authoritative choice, is itself not only linked with the basic principles by intelligible relationship to goals (such as traffic safety...) which are directly related to basic human goods, but is also controlled by wide-ranging formal and other structuring principles (in both first- and second-order form) which themselves are derived from the basic principles by the first mode of derivation.[20]

In the preceding chapter (see IX.1) I said that a principal source of the need for authority is the luxuriant variety of appropriate but competing choices of 'means' to 'end'. Now we can see how this range of choices is both increased *and* controlled by the complex of interacting 'principles of law'. True, the reasoning of those in authority frequently ends without identifying any uniquely reasonable decision; so the rulers must choose, and their choice (*determinatio*) determines what thereafter is uniquely just for those subject to their authority. But, having stressed that it is thus authority, not simply reasoning, that settles most practical questions in the life of a community, I now must stress the necessary rider. To be, itself, authoritative in the eyes of a reasonable person, a *determinatio* must be consistent with the basic requirements of practical reasonableness, though it need not necessarily or even usually be the *determinatio* one would oneself have made had one had the opportunity; it need

---

[20] Hence the standing possibility of a jurisprudence which would disclose the 'jural postulates' of a particular legal system and trace their diverse relationships with universal rational requirements—the kind of jurisprudence adumbrated and practised by Sir William Jones, the first great English comparative lawyer, but eclipsed by the Benthamite misunderstanding of practical reason. See, e.g., Jones's *Essay on the Law of Bailments* (1781).

not even be a rule or decision one would regard as 'sensible'. Our jurisprudence therefore needs to be completed by a closer analysis of this authoritativeness or 'binding force' of positive law (see Chapter XI), and by some consideration of the significance of wrongful exercises of authority (see Chapter XII).

It may, however, be helpful to conclude the present discussion by reverting to the textbook categories, '[positive] law', 'sources of law', 'morality'. The tradition of 'natural law' theorizing is not characterized by any particular answer to the questions: 'Is every "settled" legal rule and legal solution settled by appeal exclusively to "positive" sources such as statute, precedent, and custom? Or is the "correctness" of some judicial decisions determinable only by appeal to some "moral" ("extralegal") norm? And are the boundaries between the settled and the unsettled law, or between the correct, the eligible, and the incorrect judicial decision determinable by reference only to positive sources or legal rules?' The tradition of natural law theorizing is not concerned to minimize the range and determinacy of positive law or the general sufficiency of positive sources as solvents of legal problems.

Rather, the concern of the tradition, as of this chapter, has been to show that the act of 'positing' law (whether judicially or legislatively or otherwise) is an act which can and should be guided by 'moral' principles and rules; that those moral norms are a matter of objective reasonableness, not of whim, convention, or mere 'decision'; and that those same moral norms justify (a) the very institution of positive law, (b) the main institutions, techniques, and modalities within that institution (e.g. separation of powers), and (c) the main institutions regulated and sustained by law (e.g. government, contract, property, marriage, and criminal liability). What truly characterizes the tradition is that it is not content merely to observe the historical or sociological fact that 'morality' thus affects 'law', but instead seeks to determine what the requirements of practical reasonableness really are, so as to afford a rational basis for the activities of legislators, judges, and citizens.

NOTES

X.1

Aristotle on the dual operation of law and the need for coercion... 'law [*nomos*] is a rule [*logos*], emanating from a certain practical reasonableness [*phronēsis*] and intelligence [*nous*] and having compulsory force [*anagkastikē dynamis*]': *Nic. Eth.* X.9: 1180a21–22; for the whole discussion of the dual operation of law (i.e. in relation to the reasonable citizen and to the unreasonable), see 1179b30–1180b28. The medievals translated *anagkastikē* in 1180a22 as *coactiva* (coercive) (cf. IX.5 above and note).

'Conscientious objection' not a 'principle', or generally valid ground for exemption from law ... See note to V.9. A pungent brief discussion is Eric Voegelin, 'The Oxford Political Philosophers' (1953) 3 *Philosophical Q.* 97 at 102–7. But when conscientious objection witnesses to basic values such as life or religion and is not radically incompatible with the genuine common good it may be tolerated notwithstanding the conscientious judgment of the rulers that the law objected to is really necessary. See, e.g., Vatican Council II, *Gaudium et Spes* (1965), 79; *Dignitatis Humanae* (1965) 3, 7.

Punishment as the restoration of fairness...See J. Finnis, 'The Restoration of Retribution' (1972) 32 *Analysis* 132 [*CEJF* III.11]. Paul C. Weiler, 'The Reform of Punishment', in Law Reform Commission of Canada, *Studies on Sentencing* (Ottawa: 1974); Herbert Morris, *On Guilt and Innocence* (Berkeley: 1976), 32–6.

There is no 'natural' measure of due punishment...This proposition is for Aquinas the classic illustration of his wider thesis that much just law is *not a conclusion* from principles of reason (natural law): see *S.T.* I–II q. 95 a. 2c, following the hint given by Aristotle, *Nic. Eth.* V.7: 1134b22–23 (quoted in note to X.7 below).

Compulsory measures of 'reformative treatment' ... Note that what is said in the text about reform applies to the 'free-willing' criminals who are the subject of the whole discussion of punishment in X.1. Many discussions, and measures, of reform are directed, in fact, towards offenders considered (sometimes *a priori*, sometimes not) to be immature, mentally ill, etc.—i.e. considered not to be 'criminals' in the sense I intend.

X.3

Weber on the 'legal' type of Herrschaft...See *On Law*, 8–9, 336, xxxi–xxxii. On bureaucracy, the legal character of its internal order, and the bureaucrat's sense of duty, see *ibid.*, 1, 3; Weber, *The Theory of Social and Economic Organization* (ed. T. Parsons) (New York: 1947), 328–36. For an excellent instance of Weber's working use of 'legal', 'rational', and 'bureaucratic', see *From Max Weber: Essays in Sociology* (eds H. H. Gerth and C. W. Mills, London: 1948), 298–9.

'Law regulates its own creation'...For this most concentrated formulation of his jurisprudence, see Kelsen, *General Theory*, 126, 132, 198, 354, 124.

What has been validly enacted (or transacted) remains valid until...For the significance and source of this fundamental legal postulate, see J. Finnis, 'Revolutions and Continuity of Law', in *Oxford Essays II*, 44 at 63–5, 76 [*CEJF* IV.21 at 423–5, 434].

Law regulates the conditions under which individuals can modify the incidence or application of rules...Here we touch on an interesting difference between contemporary analytical jurisprudence and its classical/medieval forerunners. In modern jurisprudence, e.g. Hart, *Concept of Law* [ch. III.1 and *passim*], the law 'confers powers' upon citizens, e.g. to contract, to lease, to marry, etc., etc., and this is one of the fundamental 'functions' of the law. This manner of speaking, which is appropriate in a rigorously intra-systemic context, is quite novel. In Suarez (e.g. *De Legibus*, I, c. 17; III, c. 33, para. 1; V, cc. 19–34) or Hale (e.g. *On Hobbes' Dialogue of the Common Law* [c.1670], in Holdsworth, *History of English Law*, vol. V, 507–8) there is certainly a recognition that the law 'does' more than merely command, forbid, permit, and punish (as the Roman lawyers (see *Digest* I, 3, 7 (Papinian)) and Aquinas (*S.T.* I–II q. 92 a. 2) supposed); but the further 'effect' or 'force' of law is not 'power conferring' but rather 'laying down a definite form for contracts and similar acts-in-the-law, so that an act performed in other form may be treated as not valid' (*De Legibus*, III, 33, 1). In this perspective, one can marry, buy, sell, promise, lend, etc., etc., without having any power to do so conferred on one by law, but the law may, for good reasons, *nullify* one's acts (*lex irritans*). This perspective (in which the law has a moulding, *subsidiary* function) seems more appropriate to an analysis of the role of law within the wider context of human life and practical reason in society; it is revived in, e.g., Jonathan Cohen, 'Critical Notice of Hart's *The Concept of Law*' (1962) 71 *Mind* 395, and J. R. Lucas, 'The Phenomenon of Law', in *Essays*, 85 at 91; see also A. M. Honoré, 'Real Laws', in *Essays*, 99 at 106–7.

The postulate of gaplessness of legal systems... This is of course a lawyer's desideratum rather than a plain fact; as a description of the range and coverage of settled rules it is a fiction, but as a postulate of method it is central to legal thought. Formally it is secured by 'closing rules' such as 'whatever is not prohibited is permitted'; in legal process it is secured by the principle concerning *non liquet*, i.e. by the rule that a court cannot decline jurisdiction to settle a controversy on the ground that there is no law covering the matter in dispute. See generally J. Stone, *Legal System and Lawyers' Reasonings* (London: 1964), 188–92.

X.4

The Rule of Law ... See Raz, 'The Rule of Law and its Virtue' (1977) 93 *L.Q.R.* 195; Fuller, *Morality of Law*, chs II and V; J. R. Lucas, *The Principles of Politics* (Oxford: 1966), 24–31; Rawls, *Theory of Justice*, 235–43; Alexander Solzhenitsyn, *The Gulag Archipelago*, Part VII (1976), ch. 3 ('The Law Today').

Desirability of reciprocity between ruler and ruled... This principle is exploited but misconstrued by social contract theories. See, e.g., Cicero, *De Legibus*, II, v, 11, reporting an argumentation, standard in his time, that the first lawgivers convinced their people that it was their intention to enact such rules as would make possible an honourable and happy life for them; so that 'those who formulated wicked and unjust commands, *thereby breaking their promises* [*polliciti*] *and agreements* [*professi*], put into effect anything but "laws"'. Locke's use of the notion is very well-known: *Second Treatise of Government*, e.g. sec. 134; see also Blackstone, I *Comm.*, 47–8. Less well-known is Aquinas's cautious reference to the *lex statuta* as amounting to 'something like a kind of pact between king and people: *quasi quoddam pactum inter regem et populum*': see his *Commentary on the Epistle to the Romans*, 13, lect. 1 (para. 1041). See also the remarks of the sociologist Georg Simmel cited by Fuller, *Morality of Law*, 217, 39.

X.5

Fuller and his critics on law and tyrannical wickedness... See Fuller, *Morality of Law*, 154, appearing to assert that 'history does [not] in fact afford significant examples of regimes that have combined a faithful adherence to the internal morality of law [sc. the eight desiderata] with a brutal indifference to justice and human welfare'. Hart, in his review of Fuller's book, (1965) 78 *Harv. L. Rev.* 1281 at 1287–8, identifies and (rightly) attacks a special argument that the desideratum of clarity is incompatible with evil aims, but sees no further issue than 'the varying popularity and strength of governments'.

Rule of Law not a neutral tool of managerial direction... See Fuller's useful clarifications in his 'A reply to critics', ch. V of the revised edition of *Morality of Law*, esp. 210, 214, and 216 n. The comparison of the Rule of Law with a sharp knife is to be found in Joseph Raz, 'The Rule of Law and its Virtue' (1977) 93 *L.Q.R.* 195 at 208; in other respects the article is a valuable study of the content and point of the Rule of Law.

'Social engineering' and 'social control'... These misleading notions of the nature of law have been popularized by Roscoe Pound, e.g. *Social Control through Law* (New Haven: 1942). They are directly linked with that form of utilitarianism (associated with William James and Bertrand Russell: see note to V.7) which (in the spirit of John Rawls's 'thin theory of the good') maintains that every desire of every person is in itself equally worthy of being satisfied, so that, in Pound's words, *Social Control through Law*, 64–5, 'there is, as one might say, a great task of social engineering... of making the goods of existence, the means of satisfying the demands and desires of men being together in a politically organised society, if they cannot satisfy all the claims that men make upon them, at least go round as far as possible'. Or again, '... we come to an idea of a maximum satisfaction of human wants or expectations. What we have to do in social control, and so in law, is to reconcile and adjust these desires or wants or expectations, so far as we can, so as to secure as much of the totality of them as we can': Pound, *Justice According to Law* (New Haven and London: 1951), 31; see also Pound, *Jurisprudence* (St. Paul, Minn.: 1959), vol. III, 334; and see J. Stone, *Human Law and Human Justice* (London: 1965), ch. 9. For a critique of this pure utilitarianism, see V.7.

Plato on abuse of legality... See *Statesman*, 291a–303d; for accurate interpretation see Eric Voegelin, *Plato and Aristotle* (Baton Rouge: 1957), 158–66.

Illegal acts for the sake of the values of legality... For a partial formulation of this principle in the language of one polity, see A. V. Dicey, *Introduction to the Study of the Law of the Constitution* (1908; London: 10th edn, 1959), 412: 'There are times of tumult or invasion when for the sake of legality itself the rules of law must be broken. The course which the government must then take is clear. The Ministry must break the law and trust for protection to an Act of Indemnity'. See also Blackstone's reference, I *Comm.* 250–1, to 'those *extraordinary* recourses to first principles, which are necessary when the contracts of society are in danger of dissolution, and the law proves too weak a defence against the violence of fraud and oppression... [It is] impossible, in any practical system of laws, to point out beforehand those eccentrical remedies, which the sudden emergence of national distress may dictate, and which that alone can justify'. See also David and Brierley, *Major Legal Systems in the World Today* (London: 1968), 117: 'According to the court of Constitutional Justice of the German Federal Republic, one can imagine extreme circumstances in which the *idea* of law itself should prevail over positive constitutional law; the... Court... might then be led to appraise such "unconstitutionality"'. See also Eric Voegelin, *Plato and Aristotle* (Baton Rouge: 1957), 161; *The New Science of Politics* (Chicago: 1952), 144.

'A constitution is not a suicide pact'... 'No one could conceive that it is not within the

power of Congress to prohibit acts intended to overthrow the Government by force and violence': *Dennis v United States* (1951) 341 US 494 at 501 (and certainly neither the dissentient justices nor later decisions suggest such a conception). In reaching, in the same year, a very different decision about the constitutionality of proscribing a revolutionary party, the High Court of Australia nevertheless affirmed the existence of an inherent self-protecting legislative power, arising 'on an essential and inescapable implication which must be involved in the legal constitution of any polity': *Australian Communist Party v Commonwealth* (1951) 83 CLR 1 at 260, also 187–8, 193.

X.6

The focal meaning of 'law'... With the focal meaning of 'law' gradually constructed, and employed and identified, in this chapter, compare the 'definition of law' (*definitio legis*) offered by Aquinas, *S.T.* I-II q. 90 a. 4c: '*quaedam ordinatio rationis ad bonum commune, ab eo qui curam communitatis habet, promulgata*': 'a certain ordinance of reason, directed to the common good, promulgated by the person or body that has responsibility for the community'.

Law that is defective in rationality is law only in a watered-down sense... This proposition is not offered as immediately applicable in a court of law (or other intra-systemic context); nor does it entail that a court or a citizen ought not to comply with such a law: see XII.3, and Aquinas, *S.T.* I-II q. 96 a. 4c. The proposition is, however, offered as philosophically inevitable in any reflection upon law which seeks to answer questions about the place of law and legal system in human efforts to extend intelligence into action.

Lawyers tend to regard legality in 'either-or', 'black-and-white' terms... Fuller notices this, *Morality of Law*, 199, but fails to connect it with the very features of the legal enterprise which he himself underlines.

Laws of nature, studied by natural sciences, are for us only metaphorically laws... See Suarez, *De Legibus*, I, c. i., para. 2: '*non proprie sed per metaphoram*'. Rules of art, he continues, are laws only *secundum quid* (para. 5). Finally, 'although iniquitous precepts or rules customarily go by the name of law... none the less, speaking strictly and without qualification [*proprie et simpliciter loquendo*], only a rule which is a criterion of moral rectitude (in other words, a morally right and proper rule) can be called law... For an unjust law is not a criterion of the rectitude of human conduct... Therefore, it is not law, but partakes of the name of law by a kind of analogy [*per quandam analogiam*] in so far as it does prescribe a certain mode of action in relation to a given end' (para. 6). See XII.4 below.

Natural law is only analogically law, for our purposes... For a stimulating argument (not in every respect beyond cavil) that in the Thomist analysis of law, natural law is law only by analogy of attribution (that is, by a loose form of analogy, not the strict analogy of proportionality) to the primary analogate which is human positive law, see Mortimer J. Adler, 'A Question about Law', in R. E. Brennan (ed.), *Essays in Thomism* (New York: 1942), 207–36.

X.7

Positive law is derived from natural law in two ways... Aquinas discovers this analysis in Aristotle, *Nic. Eth.* V.7: 1134b18–24, Aristotle's principal discussion of *physikon dikaion* (natural right): see *in Eth.* V, lect. 12 (nn. 1016–23). In both Aristotle (above) and 'Cicero' (*Rhetoric*, II, 14; 16; 19) Aquinas finds the important notion that (human, positive) law *includes* natural law (as well as many elements that are not of natural law, but are consistent with it and intelligibly, but *not* deductively, derived from it). Aristotle's distinction, in *Rhetoric*, I.13: 1373b3–8, between particular law (written or unwritten) and universal natural law, is much less subtle and serviceable.

Legal systems can be promulgated without normative vocabulary ... For reflections on this, see A. M. Honoré, 'Real Laws', in *Essays*, 99 at 117–18. Because the citizen/subject, the legislator, and the judge, all have different practical perspectives, there is no reason to take sides, or to adjudicate, in the debate about whether or not there is a canonical form of legal rule, or a single method of individuating the units of meaning of which any 'legal system' is composed.

The legal drama ... For use of this figure, see Honoré, 'Real Laws', 112; cf. Honoré, *Tribonian* (London: 1978), 36 ('the esoteric legal universe, neither natural nor supernatural'); also M. Villey, 'Le droit subjectif et les systèmes juridiques romains' [1946] *Rev. Historique de Droit* 201, 207, explaining the Roman lawyers' categorization of the objects of legal science as *personae*, *res*, and *actiones*.

'First-order' and 'second-order' principles ... For a lucid discussion of legal principles, employing this distinction, see Genaro R. Carrió, *Legal Principles and Legal Positivism* (Buenos Aires: 1971). Speaking historically, or sociologically, the principles discussed in the text exist mainly in the form of judicial customs; but very many of them are of such intrinsic or inevitable appropriateness for human life in society that judges do not need to demonstrate the existence of such a custom and can appeal, fully reasonably, to that appropriateness as the sufficient basis of their applicability in judicial reasoning.

The relation of determinationes to natural law ... See *S.T.* I–II q. 95 a. 2c; q. 99 a. 3 ad 2; q. 100 a. 3 ad 2.

Do many laws relate to matters 'indifferent in themselves'? ... Aristotle launched the notion that *determinationes* relate to matters indifferent in themselves, in his set piece on natural right: *Nic. Eth.* V.7: 1134b18–24: 'Political right is of two kinds, one natural, the other conventional [*nomikon*]. Natural right has the same validity everywhere, and does not depend on our accepting it or not. Conventional right is *that which in principle may be settled in one way or the other indifferently* [*outhen diapherei*], though once settled it is not indifferent: e.g. that the ransom of a prisoner shall be a mina, that a sacrifice shall consist of a goat and not of two sheep ... [1135a1] Right based on convention and expediency is like standard measures—measures for corn and wine are not the same everywhere, but are larger in wholesale and smaller in retail markets ...' The notion of *adiaphora*, 'things naturally indifferent', became, via the Stoics, a scholastic commonplace; it was extensively used by Blackstone (see also Locke, *Two Tracts on Government* (c. 1660/1; ed. P. Abrams, Cambridge: 1967). It is important to notice that the problem is much more complex than the simple Aristotelian and scholastic terminology suggests. For example, in Blackstone's *Commentaries* the category of 'things indifferent in themselves' shifts its meaning uneasily between (i) matters so 'indifferent' that legislation on them is unjustified (e.g. *Comm.* I, 126); (ii) matters so 'indifferent' that a legislator should be content with either performance or payment of penalty (e.g. I, 58) (for this 'purely penal law' theory, see XI.6 below); (iii) matters 'indifferent' in that, though of considerable moment in a given society, they are not of moment in all conceivable societies (e.g. I, 299); and (iv) matters 'indifferent' only in the sense that, though of great moment to social living, they would not be of great moment in the 'state of nature' which Blackstone (departing altogether, with Locke, from the Aristotelian and high scholastic tradition) postulates (e.g. I, 55). Moreover, Blackstone makes it clear that the matters in categories (iii) and (iv) include matters the regulation of which is of great moment, but which could be regulated in a variety of alternative but more or less equally reasonable ways (e.g. property to descend on intestacy to the eldest rather than the youngest son). (See further J. Finnis, 'Blackstone's Theoretical Intentions' (1967) 12 *Nat. L. F.* 163 at 172–4, 181 [*CEJF* IV.8 at 198–200, 209].) Parallel distinctions can be found in Stoic writings: see Diogenes Laertius, *Lives of Eminent Philosophers* [c.225?], VII, 104–6 (Zeno).

'*Basic norms for the law-abiding citizen*'... See A. M. Honoré, 'Real Laws', 118.

Creative role of judges... To refer to this is not to dispute A. W. B. Simpson's pertinent observations, in 'The Common Law and Legal Theory', *Oxford Essays II*, 85, 86, that 'the production of [judicial] authority that this or that is the law is not the same as the identification of acts of legislation... [Judges'] actions create precedents, but creating a precedent is not the same thing as laying down the law... [T]o express an authoritative opinion is not the same thing as to legislate'.

'*General Principles of Law*'... The 13 principles listed in the text are evidenced in recent research: see the sources cited in R. P. Dhokalia, *The Codification of Public International Law* (Manchester: 1970), 344–50. They are not themselves first principles of practical reason, and some of them contain elements contingent upon the existence of certain social institutions (e.g. courts). But they are so closely related to the first principles in combination with the basic methodological requirements of practical reasoning that they should be regarded as derivable *by reasoning* from natural law and thus, in a sense, a part of the natural law. At the same time, they are essentially principles for systems of positive law, and are in fact to be found in virtually all such systems. Hence, they are the (or part of the) *jus gentium* in the sense explained (not without obscurity) by Aquinas, *S.T.* I–II q. 95 a. 4c ad 1; II–II q. 57 a. 3; *in Eth.* V, lect. 12, no. 1019. The essence of Aquinas's concept of *jus gentium* is that the principles of *jus gentium* are part of the natural law by their mode of derivation (by deduction, not *determinatio*), and at the same time part of positive human law by their mode of promulgation. Aquinas's own examples of *deduced* principles of natural law (i.e. of *jus gentium*) may be found in *S.T.* I–II q. 100 a. 1; a. 7 ad 1.

Analytical jurisprudence in Jones and Bentham... Sir William Jones, *Essay on the Law of Bailments* (1781) has three parts, styled 'analytical', 'historical', and 'synthetical'. For Jones, to treat a set of rules *analytically* is to trace 'every part of it up to the first principles of natural reason' (4); to treat it historically is to show the extent to which various legal systems conform to these first principles; and to treat it synthetically is to restate the law by way of (a) definitions, (b) rules, (c) propositions derived from the combination of (b) with (a), and (d) exceptions to the propositions (127). The definitions are to derive principally from the experience and complexity of English law (i.e. of the legal system under particular study), while the rules 'may be considered as axioms flowing from natural reason, good morals and sound policy' (119) as verified against the vast comparative learning of the 'historical' survey (11–116). With all this compare the programme announced five years earlier by Bentham in his *Fragment on Government* (1776), more or less closely followed thereafter by analytical jurisprudence: 'To the province of the *Expositor* it belongs to explain to us what, as he supposes, the Law *is*: to that of the *Censor*, to observe to us what he thinks it *ought to be*. The former, therefore, is principally occupied in stating, or in enquiring after *facts*: the latter, in discussing *reasons*. The *Expositor*, keeping within his sphere, has no concern with any other faculties of the mind than the *apprehension*, the *memory*, and the *judgment*: the latter, in virtue of those sentiments of pleasure or displeasure which he finds occasion to annex to the objects under his review, holds some intercourse with the affections' (Montague ed., Oxford: 1891), 98–9; Bentham's italics). (Somewhat inconsistently, Bentham introduced, at 117–22, the notion that an expositor could not properly, i.e. 'naturally', carry out this work of arrangement without first establishing a complete 'synopsis' or 'map' of the legal system, indeed for all legal systems, in terms of the tendency of actions to produce pain or pleasure. But this suggestion, not surprisingly, was not followed up extensively by Bentham—though cf. his *An Introduction to the Principles of Morals and Legislation* (1789; ed. J. Burns and H. L. A. Hart, London: 1970), 5, 270–4)—and died with him.)

XI

OBLIGATION

XI.1 'OBLIGATION', 'OUGHT', AND RATIONAL NECESSITY

DISCUSSION of obligation is burdened by the cultural particularity of the word 'obligation'. Philosophers and moralists find the grammatical substantive form 'obligation' convenient for signifying a wide range of notions: that there are things, within our power either to do or not to do, which (whatever we desire) we *have* to do (but not because we are forced to), or *must* do, which it is our *duty to* do, which it is *wrong not to* do, or *shameful not to,* which one *morally* (or *legally*) *ought to* do, which (in Latin) *oportet facere* or (in French) *il faut faire,* one's *devoir* in French, *to deon* in the Greek of Aristotle and Euripides, *swanelo* among the Barotse of southern Africa (see VIII.3). And the philosopher's decision to comprehend all these expressions or notions under 'obligation' does not seem unjustified: they all seem to relate to what can be experienced as a demand of conscience, a claim upon one's commitment, decision, action. Or again (since those experiences are characteristically related to the process of responsible rational assessment and practical judgment), all those expressions and notions may be related to some form or forms of rational necessity. The purpose of this chapter is to explore some of these forms of rational necessity, these (derivative) *requirements* of practical reasonableness.

On the other hand, the word 'obligation' etymologically relates particularly to the 'binding force' (*ligare,* to bind) of promissory or quasi-promissory commitments. In several modern languages, as in English, obligations to other persons, deriving from particular roles, arrangements, or relationships, remain the central cases signified by the word. It thus becomes possible to say that there are things one ought to do which one has no obligation to do (since no one has a right to demand their performance). This serves as a warning that within the class of *rational necessity* we should expect to find significant subclasses connected with a particular range of problems, those of justice and rights (other-directedness, owing, equality...: see VII.1). At the same time, we need not reserve the word 'obligation' exclusively to that particular range of problems. For the basic principles and requirements of practical reasonableness which, as we have seen, underlie our response to those problems, are certainly wide enough to make good sense of the moralist's question: If one is irretrievably marooned alone on an island, has one an obligation not to drink (etc.) oneself to death?

For the purposes of this book we need not tackle that particular moral question. Nor, incidentally, need we be concerned with the important moral distinctions between the obligatory and the meritorious or supererogatory, or between the excusable and the forbidden. At the same time we must set aside as spurious the categorizations of a textbook tradition which divides all moral thought between 'deontological ethics of obligation' and 'teleological ethics of happiness or value'. Finally, observe that I will not here deal with logical and grammatical refinements such as whether 'obligation' refers primarily to the act required or primarily to the relationship between the person-subject and the act required of him or her.

This said, it will be convenient to start the analysis by discussing that form of obligation with which the word has a particular affinity, and with which theorists of political (and therefore legal) obligation have often been peculiarly concerned: promissory obligation. To what extent, and why, do promises bind?

XI.2 PROMISSORY OBLIGATION

First, what is a promise or undertaking? Being a human practice, engaged in and maintained for diverse practical purposes, promising has its central cases (its focal meaning) and its secondary or borderline cases. Centrally, then, a promise is constituted if and only if (i) A communicates to B his intention to undertake, by that very act of communication (in conjunction with B's acceptance of it), an obligation to perform a certain action (or to see to it that certain actions are performed), and (ii) B accepts this undertaking in the interests of himself, or of A or of some third party, C. In other words, the giving of a promise is the making of a sign,[1] a sign which signifies the creation of an obligation, and which is knowingly made with the intention of being taken as creative of such obligation. It is this that makes the giving of a promise distinct from the expression of an intention to perform an action—which is not to deny that there are circumstances in which the expression of an intention to perform an action, particularly when one is aware that one's addressee may rely on one, will create an obligation to perform it: only, *this* form of obligation is not strictly promissory (but rather, perhaps, an extended form of estoppel).

This definition of promising takes a stand on some issues controverted amongst philosophers (e.g. whether promises are complete and binding without acceptance, but can always be released from by their addressee). But it leaves aside many other controverted questions (e.g. as to the circumstances under which what would otherwise amount to a binding promise either fails to constitute a promise—say, because of fraud, mistake, or duress—or fails to bind—say, because it is to do an intrinsically wrongful deed). Moreover, it leaves aside borderline cases, upon which a mature law of contract must take a stand. Indeed, my definition is both wider and narrower than typically modern notions of legally binding contracts. For example, it includes no requirement of consideration, or of communication of acceptance by B to A. On the other hand, a promise as defined above will not be constituted in circumstances where a legal contract is—for by getting on to a bus one concludes, whether or not one knows or intends it, a legally binding contract of carriage for reward and incurs in law the contractual obligation to pay; but one does not *promise* or *undertake* to pay. The informal human practice or institution of promising, not the law of contract, is my present concern.

The striking thing about promises is that their obligation is taken to be created by, or at any rate to arise upon, an intentional reference (express or implied) to that obligation. An expression signifying the undertaking of an obligation brings about (or at any rate tends to bring about) that obligation. But there

---

[1] In special circumstances, remaining silent can be significant and amount to a sign.

is no obligation-creating *magic* in uttering a sign signifying the
creation of obligation. How, then, do promises bind?

A first level of explanation penetrates below the linguistic phenomena of signs and expressions of obligation, and points to the
complex practice in which promissory undertakings are rooted. In
this practice, expressions of obligation are not merely offered or
given, they are accepted as such by other persons; subsequently and
consequently, demands for corresponding performance are made,
with express or tacit reference back to the prior giving of the
promissory signs; criticism and reproach for non-performance,
and threats and pressures, all likewise refer back to the undertaking
given, as do self-criticism, apologies, demands for and offers of
amends, compensation, restitution, or recovery of losses and/or
anticipated profits, etc. To give those linguistic signs that do
amount to a promise (signs which may of course be very various
in form and implicit in expression) is precisely to communicate a
willingness to enter into and go along with that whole practice, i.e.
by performing one's undertakings or at least by acknowledging the
propriety of demands for performance, compensation, etc. It need
not, incidentally, be assumed that there is only one 'promising'
practice in any given community; there can indeed be many, containing the same basic elements in varying forms, some wider,
some narrower, some more relaxed, others more stringent. Moreover, such practices can have a datable beginning. But it remains
true, I think, that if someone utters a sign signifying the undertaking of an obligation, in a context in which no one is inclined to
criticize him, etc., for non-performance, it seems odd to say that he
has an obligation.[2]

Because it thus explains how some expressions purporting to
signify the undertaking of an obligation do not bring into being
any such obligation, while other, perhaps quite similar, expressions do (by virtue of their place in an interpersonal practice
that involves more than merely linguistic signs), this first-level
explanation has some explanatory power. An analysis which
yields the conclusion that one is under a promissory obligation
if and only if there is a social practice according to which one's
expression of an undertaking is taken as justifying demands and

---

[2] Unilateral vows and oaths require a special analysis, not undertaken here.

pressure for performance, criticisms of non-performance, etc., is not a negligible analysis. But it fails to capture the significance or 'meaning' of promissory obligation, for it fails to give an account of the role of the notion of obligation in the practical reasonings both of the person under that obligation and of those other persons who take his being under an obligation as giving good (justifying) reason for their demands, pressure, criticisms, etc. This failure is readily brought to light by asking, for example: Granted that there is this social practice in which the linguistic or quasi-linguistic act of promising gives rise to such-and-such practical expectations, reactions, etc., why should I go along with the practice? Why not, at any stage along the way, *break the spell*?

In response to such questions, there emerges a second level of explanations, independent of but quite consistent with the first, and typically capable of giving reason for the attitudes, dispositions, reactions, etc., referred to in the first-level explanation. For example, Hume explains that 'the [promising-] conventions of men...create a new motive...After these signs are instituted, whoever uses them is immediately bound by his interest to execute his engagements, and must never expect to be trusted any more, if he refuse to perform what he promised'; in short, someone who uses the conventional form of words 'subjects himself to the penalty of never being trusted again in case of failure'.[3] Hume is here explaining the obligation of promises—in effect, the rational 'necessity' they create—and is doing so by implicit reference to the following sort of schema of practical reasoning: 'I have made what is conventionally regarded by my fellows as a promise. Given the expectations and attitudes that are part of that convention, I will never again be trusted by my fellows if I fail to perform as I promised and they expect. But it is in my own interests to be trusted (i.e. I want/need to be trusted). Therefore it is necessary for me to perform'. In short, continued trust in me being *impossible* without performance, performance is *necessary* if I am to get what I want (continued trust in me). And so, as Hume says,

---

[3] David Hume, *A Treatise of Human Nature* (1739), Book III, Part II, sec. V, 'Of the Obligation of Promises' (e.g. *British Moralists*, II, para. 541). I here ignore some peculiarities of Hume's treatment of obligation and motive: see II.5, pp. 41–2, 53–4 above.

'interest is the *first* obligation to the performance of promises'.[+]

Just as, when we come to consider the obligation of laws, we will encounter again the first-level type of explanation, so we will then encounter again this second-level type of explanation. It is not a negligible explanation. The schema of practical reasoning to which it appeals is quite genuine, applicable, and forceful. And who is there who does not reason thus, quite frequently? Still, as an explanation of obligation it leaves much to be desired. Someone sensitive to language will say that it is really an explanation, not of obligation, but of the 'prudential' *ought* (as in 'You ought to change your wet clothes'). Moreover, there are many circumstances in which failure to perform a promise, which everyone involved in the social prac-tice would agree was a binding one, will in fact expose one to no more than a risk of 'never being trusted again'. That risk may be quite remote, even negligible. Indeed, there are cases where (for lack of observers, or by skill in cover-up...) there is no danger that the violation of obligation will even be known, let alone taken as an indication of general untrustworthiness. Yet, even in such cases, no one involved in the practice may doubt that there *is* an obligation; and there is no reason for the reflective analyst to adopt an explan-ation of obligation which would oblige him to say that when self-interested motives for performance are lacking, obligation, as a factor relevant to its subject's practical reasoning, is absent. The same goes for all explanations of obligation in terms purely of self-interest, for example the argument (insinuated by Hume in tandem with that already discussed) that if I do not perform my obligations to others, others will not perform their obligations to me. For in all such cases it remains that my violation of obligation may go undiscovered or be disregarded, without thereby ceasing to be a violation of a subsisting obligation.

Still, the strategy of locating obligation as the conclusion of a train of practical reasoning, about what is *necessary* if one is to get what one wants, needs, or values, is a strategy that can

---

[+] Hume, *A Treatise of Human Nature* (Raphael, para. 542). By 'interest' Hume means 'self-interest': see *ibid.*, sec. II ('Of the Origin of Justice and Property') ad fin. (Raphael, para. 534). Hume goes on to refer sketchily to a 'new obligation' which arises 'afterwards', as an 'effect' of, *inter alia*, 'public interest': Raphael, para. 543; see also Hume, *A Treatise of Human Nature*, Book III, Part III, sec. IX (ninth paragraph).

yield ampler and more powerful explanations. Though these better explanations could be called 'second-level', it will be convenient to call them 'third-level', in recognition of the extra explanatory dimension introduced by any reference to the common good. For these explanations will take for granted what we have previously laboured to explain: that one (everyone) has reason to value the common good—the well-being alike of oneself and of one's associates and potential associates in community, and the ensemble of conditions and ways of effecting that well-being—whether out of friendship as such, or out of an impartial recognition that human goods are as much realized by the participation in them of other persons as by one's own (see VI.4, VI.6, VII.2).

It is not difficult to establish that the practice or institution of promising-and-therefore-performing-or-accepting-the-justice-of-reproaches-etc. is greatly to the common good. The 'purchase' it gives one individual on another's action is a uniquely appropriate means of attaining both the (private) purposes of individuals and purposes conceived and executed as common enterprises for the advantage of the 'community' or the 'public' rather than of ascertained persons. It provides an effective means of maintaining co-operation, once initiated, over the span of time necessary for the fulfilment of any human project (whether a straightforwardly attainable goal, such as building a bridge, or an essentially open-ended commitment, such as undertaking to raise and educate a family and give mutual support in old age...). Like the law, it enables past, present, and predictable future to be related in a stable though developing order; it enables this order to be effected in complex interpersonal patterns; and it brings all this within reach of individual initiative and arrangement, thus enhancing individual autonomy in the very process of increasing individuals' obligations. ('From status to contract...' is a movement of, on the whole, increasing 'individual liberty'.) So if one is to be a person who favours and contributes to the common good, one *must* go along with the practice of promising. Similarly, and secondarily, if one is not to be a 'free-rider' who unfairly takes the benefits of beneficial social institutions but repudiates the burdens, then one *must* go along with the practice when one has promised, as much as when one has been promised. And these necessities, unlike the necessity adverted to in the second-level explanation (in terms of the promisor's own reputation), are not affected by the fact that breach of the promise will go undetected either by the promisee or by others. The practice of promising gains much of its value, as a contribution to the common good, precisely from the fact that the obligations it involves hold good even when breach seems likely to be undetectable. Those who renege on their promise(s) simply because they judge that the non-performance will go undetected are therefore doing what they can to defeat the common good in this particular aspect.

To these necessities, derived from the needs of the common good at large, we must add a further necessity derived from the requirement of practical reasonableness (see V.4) that one do as one would be done by (impartiality). One has no general responsibility to give the well-being of other people as much care and concern as one gives one's own; the good of others is as really good as one's own good, but is not one's primary responsibility, and to give one's own good priority is not, as such, to violate the requirement of impartiality. But one can incur responsibilities which give certain other people's claims upon one's care and concern a due measure of priority. Promising is one way of incurring such responsibilities. The making of the promise creates a new criterion of impartiality, relative to the persons concerned and the subject-matter of the promise. The promise constitutes a special frame of reference, or vantage point, in relation to which the conduct of the parties can be assessed for its impartiality. That is to say: given the institution or practice of promising and its appropriateness for the common good as an instrument of co-operation, an impartial observer, with the common good and the interests of all concerned with the promise at heart, would use the promise as such a frame of reference. A promise thus gives each party (and normally, I think, a beneficiary who is not actually party in a strict sense: cf. VIII.2) a special *locus standi*, a right to claim performance. Performance is not merely an obligation in the general (philosophers' and moralists') sense (see XI.1); it is also *owed* to the other party. Given the 'general justice' of the institution of promising, breach of promise is (presumptively) a commutative injustice (see VII.5). All this is homogeneous with the third-level explanation in terms of the common good 'at large'. Indeed, it is a development of that explanation. The good of an individual party to (or beneficiary of) the promise—the good which, by virtue of the promise, gains some priority of claim upon the care and concern of the promisor—is not something distinct from the common good. It is part of the common good. That the good of ascertained individuals should be respected in the way required by these considerations is itself a further component of the common good—it is one of the conditions for the well-being of each and all in community.

Indeed, it is a truth of wide application that one acts most appropriately for the common good, not by trying to estimate the needs of the common good 'at large', but by performing one's contractual undertakings, and fulfilling one's other responsibilities, to ascertained individuals, i.e. to those who have particular rights correlative to one's duties. Fulfilling one's particular obligations in justice, even within the restricted sphere of private contracts, family responsibilities, etc., is necessary if one is to respect and favour the common good, *not* because 'otherwise everyone suffers', or because non-fulfilment would diminish 'overall net good' in some impossible utilitarian computation, or even because it would 'set a bad example' and thus weaken a useful practice, but simply because the common good *is* the good of individuals, living together and depending upon one another in ways that favour the well-being of each.

All these *necessities*, derived from basic requirements of practical reasonableness, have a feedback into the obligation which is expressed, undertaken, argued about, etc., *within* the practice of promising. That is to say, the meaning of 'obligation' at the level of practice (i.e. in the uttering of promises, etc.) becomes charged with its meaning in the first, second, and third levels of explanation, whenever the people engaged in the practice are at all reflective. Then the expressions of and references to obligation which are integral to the practice will not have merely the force of moves in a game (though in Wittgenstein's sense of 'language-game' they *are* that) but will be regularly intended and taken as involving (and/or expressing the involvement of) the participants and their community, and relative to practical reasonableness itself.

Without presupposing that this third level of explanation of obligation is the deepest (cf. XIII.5), let me dwell for a moment on its strategy. It is an explanation parallel in form to the explanation offered (see IX.3) for the authoritativeness of custom. Custom was explained as a complex practice involving: (i) concurrent patterns of conduct; (ii) claims and opinions ('judgments') about (a) the appropriateness of uniformity of conduct in this particular field of action and (b) the appropriateness of *this* pattern of conduct; and (iii) acceptance of the conjunction of the concurrence of conduct with the concurrence of claims and opinions as constituting an authoritative custom warranting compliance, claims, demands for compliance, reproaches for non-compliance, amends, etc. In this account, the authoritativeness of custom was explained (in third-level fashion, the first-level form of explanation being taken for granted) as deriving from (A) the need (for the common good) for some authoritative solution to co-ordination problems, taken with (B) a certain set of facts (about conduct, opinions, degrees of acceptance, etc.) which pragmatically afford an answer to that need (or afford an opportunity of answering to it).

So with promises. A certain set of facts affords an opportunity of answering to a standing need of the common good, the need for individuals to be able to make reliable arrangements with each other for the determinate and lasting but flexible solution of co-ordination problems and, more generally, for the realizing of the goods of individual self-constitution and of community. (Mutual trustworthiness is not merely a means to further distinct ends; it is in itself a valuable component of any common life.) The set of facts that affords this opportunity comprises: (a) the framework fact that a practice (involving more than one party and extending over a span of time and applicable to many and various promises) exists or can readily be initiated (given the underlying facts about human foresight, memory, desire for security, ability to understand, co-operate, rely, etc.), whereby the intentional giving of certain signs will be linked by the participants with expectations of future performance, demands for that performance, etc., etc.; (b) the particular fact that one has entered into the practice by voluntarily and intentionally giving the relevant signs; (c) the fact that if one, like others, goes along with the practice by trying to perform as one promised to perform, even when performance is at the expense of some inconvenience, foreseen or even unforeseen, to oneself, one will thereby not only contribute to the well-being of the person for whose benefit one's promise was accepted (a contribution which might in the particular case be outweighed by the loss to one's own well-being) but will also be playing one's part in a pattern of life without which many of the benefits of community could not in fact be realized.

Given these empirical facts and the aforementioned standing need of the common good, that common good (including the good of the promisee or other ascertained beneficiary) can be realized with reasonable impartiality *only* if one performs on one's promise; and this necessity *is* the obligation of one's promise (both the general, moralists' obligation, and the obligation owed to the promisee or beneficiary). 'I *cannot* be one who acts for the common good *unless* I go along with the practice by performing on this promise'. Secondarily, 'I *cannot* be one who is rationally impartial *unless* I take the burdens of the practice as well as the benefits, and perform on this promise...'. The conclusion, in each case, is: '*Therefore*, I *must* perform...'. Both the authorities responsible for the common good at large, and the promisee or other ascertained beneficiary, have the right to demand that the promise be performed. Hence, it is appropriate that there be a judicially enforceable law of contract (and judicial doctrines of good faith, equity, etc.) and a right of parties (and sometimes beneficiaries) to sue on the promises covered by that law.

The reason for repeating and emphasizing this analysis of obligation in terms of the necessity, given certain facts, of determinate actions as means to valuable ends, is the prevalence, for many centuries, of an analysis of obligation, not least of the obligation of promises, in terms of 'bonds' created by 'acts of will': see XI.7. Suffice it to observe here that although promissory obligations do not come into being without some voluntary and intentional act such as might be said to manifest an 'act of will' on the part of the promisor, the occurrence of that act is only one of the several facts relevant to the emergence of the necessity which we call obligation, and has no special role in explaining the *obligation* of the performance promised.

The reason why *this* source of obligation, unlike some others, requires, *inter alia*, a voluntary act, and indeed a voluntary act intended to express willingness to create an obligation, is that the point of this institution, unlike others, is particularly to enable individuals to exercise a control over their own relationships in community. A practice or practical doctrine according to which obligation came into being whenever one made certain signs (whether or not voluntarily, and whether or not intending them to be signs with *that* significance), or whenever one expressed one's intentions of acting in the future, or whenever one expressed such intentions knowing that others might rely on one, would in each case be a practice or practical doctrine too restrictive of individual autonomy and self-direction, too cramping of human expressiveness and communication. So one's willingness, as promisor, to be bound (or to be taken as willing to be bound) is one of the necessary conditions of one's being bound; but this fact itself has no peculiar explanatory power in an account of obligation.

XI.3 VARIABLE AND INVARIANT
OBLIGATORY FORCE

Though recent philosophers have often overlooked or minimized the fact, the obligation of promises is very variable, and is often quite weak. This is a fact about the practice as commonly understood and carried on. Without any expressed 'doctrine of frustration' or *clausula rebus sic stantibus*, people who make and receive promises commonly understand that a change in the circumstances of the parties, affecting the interests of one or both of them (especially but not necessarily if unforeseen at the time of the promise), may exempt from the obligation of performance and, quite often though not always, from the obligation of amends (and even of apology) for non-performance. (If the promisee has been inconvenienced by this justified non-performance it will still be in order to express regret, as distinct from contrition.) A promise properly made is always an exclusionary reason, that is, always gives a reason for disregarding *some* reasons, which are genuine and relevant and which in the absence of the promise to do ϕ would have sufficed to justify not doing ϕ (see IX.2). But a promise is usually an exclusionary reason that can be defeated by some countervailing reasons, often by a wide range of readily available reasons (though never by *any and all* of the reasons that would, in the absence of the promise, have warranted not doing the thing promised). When it is intended by the parties that the promise shall afford a virtually indefeasible exclusionary reason, the promise will have to be expressed with solemnity and precision as being one that binds them 'for better for worse, for richer for poorer, in sickness and in health... till death...'[5] (and even such a form of words may be given a reduced obligation-creating significance by the practice in which it is rooted).

Of course, all this renders the practice of promising subject not only to obvious abuses and exploitation, but also to frequent bona fide differences of opinion about the strength of particular promissory obligations and even of promissory obligation in general. The practice is permeable by virtually all evaluative considerations, not only by those which in the third level of explanation give promises their obligatory force, but also by all other comparable considerations (whether or not incommensurable). That is to say, the feedback of considerations about individual and communal good is not only of considerations tending to show why it is necessary to perform promises in general and therefore this promise in particular, but is also of considerations tending to show that in this or that particular set of circumstances the general rule of obligatoriness can reasonably be considered inapplicable or supplanted. This feedback of various forms and requirements of practical reasonableness lends the extra-legal practice a flexibility without which it doubtless could not survive, but also an elusive variability or unreliability, of a sort that legal thought strives to exclude from legally regulated transactions.

This, then, is the first thing to observe about legal obligation. Whereas, at the level of language, common attitudes, and practice, the obligation of promises is understood by parties to promises as varying from one promise to another, the obligation of all laws and hence of all legally regulated transactions is understood by lawyers as being of the same legal force in every case. There are, legally speaking, no degrees of legal obligation, just as there are (see X.6) no degrees of legal validity.

---

[5] *Book of Common Prayer* (1662), Form of Solemnization of Matrimony.

The fact that, legally, all legal obligations are of the same strength can be obscured from casual view by the fact that many legal obligations are of variable content and incidence. The duty of drivers or manufacturers to take reasonable care, or of employers to fence machines adequately, is in each type of instance likely to involve conduct different at one time from another, at one place from another. But this sort of variability should be understood with precision. Consider, as a representative instance, the following provisions of the (English) Sale of Goods Act 1893, as amended by the Supply of Goods (Implied Terms) Act 1973:

Section 14(2). Where the seller sells goods in the course of a business, there is an implied condition that the goods supplied under the contract are of merchantable quality, except that there is no such condition—
(a) as regards defects specifically drawn to the buyer's attention before the contract is made; or
(b) if the buyer examines the goods before the contract is made, as regards defects which that examination ought to reveal.

Section 62(1A). Goods of any kind are of merchantable quality within the meaning of this Act if they are as fit for the purpose or purposes for which goods of that kind are commonly bought as it is reasonable to expect having regard to any description applied to them, the price (if relevant) and all the other relevant circumstances.

The seller's duty, then, is to supply goods 'as fit [for the usual purposes of purchasers of such goods] as it is reasonable to expect having regard to all relevant circumstances'. Such a duty is obviously variable in content, in two different ways: it will vary as the goods vary, and as other circumstances of the sale vary; and it will vary as the opinions of lawyers and judges vary concerning the relevance of particular types of 'circumstance'. But all these potential variations should not be allowed to obscure from our view the invariant elements which the law stipulates: if sellers are selling in the course of a business they have a duty to supply goods of a certain type of quality except as regards two defined types of defect; but if they are not selling in the course of a business then they simply do not have *any* duty of this type, though they have others; and if they do have this duty, the consequences of failure to conform to it, though not always the same, are well-defined and, legally, inevitable.

There is simply no room for them to plead that, although they fall within the terms of section 14(2) and their goods fail to meet the specifications of the provision, nevertheless their prima facie duty was *outweighed* and *diminished* or *deferred* or in some other way *modified* by other considerations, however 'reasonable'. Of course, the law makes provision for exceptional circumstances in which the whole contract of sale is frustrated and the parties are relieved of their obligations (see VII.5); but even here the legal method of analysing the situation produces the conclusion that what would otherwise have been the sellers' duty is *not* their duty and has been *replaced* either by some *other* duty or by a legal liberty (*absence* of duty).

This invariability in the formal force of every legal obligation has as its methodological counterpart the legal postulate (shared by 'legalistic' moral thought) that there are no overlapping and conflicting legal duties; for any such overlap would oblige the lawyer to weigh one obligation against the other and to declare the weightier obligation to be the more binding. A lawyer will always seek to define (in terms of subject, subject-matter, act-description, time, and circumstance), the limits of each potentially applicable obligation so that the unique legal obligation in the situation under consideration can be identified, and all competing claims of obligation simply dismissed (for that situation). Hence the casuistical refinement of legal rules, their lists of conditions and exceptions, the unwearying legal effort for exhaustiveness and coherence of stipulation. The famous 'inflexibility' of the law goes far deeper than one would suppose if one merely called to mind, for example, well-known instances of criminal prohibitions so bluntly, naively, or widely drafted as to catch what all would agree is praiseworthy or at least acceptable conduct. Rather, the law's inflexibility is rooted in the invariance (in contemplation of law) of the action-guiding force of each and every obligation-imposing legal provision; and in mature legal systems this inflexibility should have as one principal consequence an exquisite refinement and narrowness of draftsmanship.

But my mention of the doctrine of 'frustration of contracts in exceptional circumstances' should remind us (if we had not already been reminded by the reference to 'reasonableness' at the heart of that refined commercial code, the amended Sale of Goods Act) that legal thought is not unaware of policies and principles which cannot be, or have not been, reduced to definite legal rules. That is to say, mature legal thought does not banish altogether those considerations, touching the common good, which in general are scarcely more closely definable than the basic values and principles discussed in earlier chapters of this book, but which in particular circumstances can lead reasonable people to agree on a course of action *not* provided for by the existing legal rules or the network of contractual or other obligatory arrangements subsisting under those rules. Nevertheless, unlike the informal social practice of promising, the legal system does not allow an unrestricted feedback of such 'value' or 'policy' considerations from the justificatory level of straightforward practical reasonableness back into the level of practice. Instead, the legal system systematically restricts such feedback by establishing institutions, such as courts, arbitrators, and legislatures, and then requiring that any shifting of the obligations imposed by existing rules and subsisting arrangements shall be authorized only by those institutions. Moreover, the institutions are themselves placed under legal rules (differing according to the nature and functions of the institutions) which make it obligatory that only in certain circumstances, and according to defined procedures and within certain limits, may they admit, accept, or act upon the 'extra-legal' policies, or upon the legally indeterminate (or not fully determinate, e.g. justificatory rather than strictly obligatory) principles. Thus, the legal system buttresses and gives practical effect to a framework principle of legal thought, that legal obligation is of legally invariant force.

The black-and-white quality of legal obligation (like the all-or-nothing quality of legal validity)[6] is part of the data, which an explanation of law must take into account and explain (and not explain away). It is a feature of legal thought which obviously renders incomplete and unsatisfying any form of first-level explanation which is restricted to asserting that 'rules are conceived and spoken of as imposing obligations when the

---

[6] See X.6; see also, e.g., Dworkin, *Taking Rights Seriously* (London: 1977), 79: 'The rule that unreasonable restraints of trade are invalid remains a rule if every restraint that is unreasonable is invalid, even if other reasons for enforcing it, not mitigating its unreasonableness, might be found'.

general demand for conformity is insistent and the social pressure brought to bear upon those who deviate or threaten to deviate is great'.[7] As I observed in relation to the analogous first-level explanation of statements of promissory obligation, such location of the 'logic of obligation' in a context of regularities of practice is not devoid of explanatory power. But over and above the general deficiency of first-level explanations—that they fail to uncover or explain the practical reasoning which by motivating and justifying the practice in the eyes of its participants gives the practice its specific unity and significance—there is a special deficiency in any explanation of a black-and-white, invariant obligation in terms only of 'social pressures' which must inevitably be very variable in their pressure and insistence.

The formal invariance of legal obligation equally renders inadequate all those forms of second-level explanation which account for the force and role of obligations and obligatory rules in practical reasoning by pointing to *human reactions to non-performance of the obligatory behaviour* (reaction of a kind which is standardly undesired by persons subject to the obligation, and which therefore gives them a reason to perform-in-order-to-avoid-it). The most well-known forms of such explanation are, of course, the theories of legal obligation in terms exclusively of exposure to (the threat of, or liability to) sanctions. I stressed the importance of sanctions in any general account of law (see X.1). But my remarks on Hume's theory of promissory obligation (see XI.2) should make clear why the threat of, or liability to, sanctions does not account for the nature and role of obligation in practical reasoning. This has, indeed, been elaborately shown by H. L. A. Hart;[8] his distinction between being obliged (under threat of unpleasant consequences) and being under an obligation in virtue of a mandatory rule was put forward not so much as an independent argument (which could be accused of verbalism) but rather as a summary reminder of features of the logic of obligation which give it a distinct place in the map of rational motivations of, or justificatory reasons for, action. But his own account of obligation (given in the last paragraph), when transposed from the first on to the second level of explana-

---

[7] Hart, *Concept of Law*, 84 [86]; also 214 [220].
[8] *Concept of Law*, 80–3 [82–4].

tions (i.e. in his terminology, into an explanation from the 'internal point of view'), suffers from analogous defects. The threat of adverse critical reactions to one's breaches of the law is variable in intensity and immediacy (as is one's own distaste for those reactions in differing contexts and circumstances).

In short, the 'directive' force of law is not to be reduced to, or explained by reference only to, the 'coercive' force of law (see IX.5). In the next section I advance an explanation of that *vis directiva*.

XI.4 'LEGALLY OBLIGATORY': THE LEGAL SENSE AND THE MORAL SENSE

Obligation-imposing legal rules, as we saw earlier (see X.7), are rarely drafted imperatively or even in terms of 'ought' or 'obligation'. Nevertheless, for analytical purposes they can be cast into the schematic form 'If p, q, r, then XOϕ'—where 'p, q, r' signify the circumstances under which the legal obligation arises, 'ϕ' [*phi*] stands for an act-description signifying the obligatory act (being or to-be) done by X, the relevant person-subject of the norm in those circumstances, and 'O' is a deontic modal operator signifying that ϕ is in those circumstances obligatory for X (rather than merely permitted or discretionary; and also rather than being actually the case or not the case or possible or necessary, as might be signified by some non-deontic operator).

Using this analysis, we can say that the problem discussed in the preceding section is the problem of explaining (i) how an obligation-imposing law provides a reason for action which would not exist independently of that law and is indeed provided by 'the law' or legal system itself, and (ii) why the obligation of such a law has, for legal thought, the black-and-white quality characteristic of legal obligations, i.e. how the modal operator 'O' has an all-or-nothing deontic force even when 'ϕ' stands for some vague or variably instantiated act-description such as 'supplying goods of reasonable quality'.[9]

---

[9] Notice that this section does not deal with those 'legal principles' which some writers (e.g. Dworkin, *Taking Rights Seriously*, ch. 2) consider to be legally binding although not legal *rules*. Such principles, while 'part of the law', do not legally require particular actions or decisions, although they (a) may *justify* particular decisions that particular actions are required, and (b) may be the subject of obligation-imposing rules *requiring* a judge to take them into account.

The answer to the problem consists in the correct identification of the law-abiding subject's practical reasoning—reasoning to which such a norm is directed and which such a norm is intended to direct in a distinctively 'obligatory' way.

The answer to the problem, then, consists in a third-level explanation similar in strategy to the explanations I offered in respect of custom (see IX.3) and promissory obligation (see XI.2). The relevant schema of practical reasoning runs something as follows (formulations could vary widely in detail):

Step *A.* For *all* co-ordination problems legally specified as appropriate for legal solution [including the problem of which such problems to specify and solve, and in what manner and form to specify and solve them] I must act in the legally specified way if I am to respect the common good.

Step *B.* Where a pattern-of-action has been legally specified as obligatory [i.e. where it has been legally stipulated that 'if p, q, r, then $XO\phi$'] the *only* way of satisfying the need postulated in step *A* is to act according to the pattern so specified [i.e. is to ϕ].

Step *C.* So, in the cases mentioned in step *B*, I must [ought to] act in the way specified as obligatory [i.e. where 'if p, q, r, then $XO\phi$' is a legal norm, and p, q, r, and I am X, then $XO\phi$].

At first glance, this schema may appear empty and/or viciously circular. Step *A* will sound gratuitous or question-begging unless it is treated as a summary formulation of my earlier, rather elaborate contentions about the need for authority in community and for that authority to be treated as authoritative in practice, and about law as one form of authoritative solution to co-ordination problems (see IX.1, X.1, X.3). But the appearance of vicious circularity in the schema derives particularly, perhaps, from the peculiar feature (mirrored in steps *B* and *C*) which legal obligation shares with promissory obligation, namely, that the obligation is standardly created by a sign which expressly or impliedly *signifies* that obligation. In steps *B* and *C* of the schema, the legal sign signifying a specific legal obligation is indicated by the formula ' "if p, q, r, then $XO\phi$" '. (Recall that this is a schematic formula rarely adopted by draftsmen, but well-understood by lawyers as contextually signified by a variety of legislative expressions and/or as derivable from judicial precedent or practice, with or without the interpretative assistance of accepted legal principles: see X.7.) When the formula 'if p, q, r, $XO\phi$' appears in step C without enclosing quotation marks, it refers not to the legal sign, the legal stipulation of obligation, but to the rational necessity, given steps A and B, of acting in the way characterized as ϕ.

The schema is not redundant. For if it were not possible to find any means-end schema of practical reasoning generating a conclusion such as C, then the legal signification or stipulation '$XO\phi$' referred to in step B would be empty words (save as a threat of sanctions). But since the schema is indeed available, the notion of obligation which it generates is available for use in the law-maker's act of 'obligation'-stipulation, an act which has its peculiar action-guiding relevance and force precisely because it can play its role in a train of practical reasoning whose conclusion it expressly anticipates. (Here again we are observing the 'feedback' which we noticed in analysing the practice of promising, and which is made possible by human reflectiveness: see XI.2.)

What, then, is the rational source and force of steps A and B? Perhaps these steps can be more readily understood if I translate the whole schema into the following simplified form:

A. We need, for the sake of the common good, to be law-abiding.
B. But where ϕ is stipulated by law as obligatory, the *only* way to be law-abiding is to do ϕ.
C. Therefore, we need [it is obligatory for us] to do ϕ where ϕ has been legally stipulated to be obligatory.

It will be objected that the force of step A varies according to circumstances; sometimes the common good may best be preserved or realized by deviation from the law. That is true; step A can take its place in the unrestricted flow of practical reasoning and, since it is not itself one of the *basic* principles or requirements of practical reasoning, will then vary in force and applicability. Whence, then, the legally invariant force of legal obligation? The answer is: from step B, taken together with an interpretation of step A as an undiscussed postulate, isolated by legal thought from the general flow of practical reasoning.

Step *B* proposes that if you are to have and retain the quality 'law-abiding citizen' you *must* perform each action which the law has stipulated to be 'obligatory', whenever and in all the respects in which such stipulations are applicable. This fundamental principle implicit in legal thought is not empty. It embodies the postulates that each obligation-stipulating law is a member of a system of laws which cannot be weighed or played off one against the other but which constitute a set coherently applicable to all situations, and exclude all unregulated or private picking and choosing amongst the members of the set. When you are confronted by an obligation-stipulating legal rule applicable to your circumstances there is no legally recognized rule or principle to which you can appeal to relieve you of your obligation. In this sense, at least, your allegiance to the whole system ('the law') is put on the line: either you obey the *particular* law, or you reveal yourself (to yourself, if not to others) as lacking or defective in allegiance to the *whole*, as well as to the particular.

In short, the law forbids any feedback (save through institutionalized channels and procedures) into step *B* from those general values and principles which can give step *A* a varying force; they can be systematically ignored by treating step *A* as a framework principle or postulate. Thus, the law, as a system of practical reasoning offered to the person who wants (and sees the need) to be law-abiding, seeks to give an invariant force to the rational necessity expressed in step *C*, the law-abiding person's conclusion. That is why I have stressed that it is only 'in contemplation of law' that legal obligation is invariant in force. In fact, in strictly legal thought the basis and force of step *A* never becomes a topic of consideration (except perhaps in 'public emergencies' of the sort mentioned in X.5). That right or justice is to be done *according to law* is the judge's oath of office; it is a formulation of step *A* for intra-systemic legal purposes (rather than for private moral reasoning about the law) and so is not a subject-matter for judicial reasoning or pronouncement. But the formulae expressive of legal obligation have their specific intelligibility from the fact that they are self-consciously designed not only to fit into the recalcitrant citizen's sanction-dominated practical reasonings, but also and most characteristically to fit into and to give a special conclusory force to the practical reasonings of those who see and are generally willing to act upon the need (for the common good) for authority.

The law thus anticipates and seeks to capitalize upon, indeed to absorb and take over, the 'good citizen's' schema of practical reasoning, and to give it an unquestioned or dogmatic status. It tries to isolate what I have been calling 'legal thought' or 'purely legal thought' from the rest of practical reasoning. But the good citizen can always recover step *A* from its status, in legal thought, of undiscussed postulate or framework principle. By relocating step *A* in the whole flow of practical reasoning, one gives it as a premiss a moral force. Thus, we can and should distinguish, *on the one hand*, both (i)(a) the moral principle, embodied in this interpretation of step *A*, that laws provide directly applicable and authoritative guidance for reasonable people and eliminate the need for them to weigh up (as the legislature had to weigh up) the pros and cons of many possible courses of actions, and (i)(b) the moral theorem, embodied in step *C*, that one of the forms of moral obligation is legal obligation, from, *on the other hand* (ii) the legal principle (or theorem of strictly legal science) that legal obligation is invariant. The *equal* obligation in *law* of each obligation-imposing law is to be clearly distinguished from the moral obligation to obey *each* law.

Like the obligation of promises, the moral obligation to obey *each* law is variable in force. It will vary according to the subject-matter of the law and the circumstances of a possible violation; for some subject-matters are in greater need of legal regulation than others, and some violations of law make a greater rent in the fabric of the law than others. On the one hand, the moral obligation to obey the law as such is usually, but in differing measures, reinforced by moral obligations that would exist in the same form (e.g. not to murder) or at least inchoately (e.g. to contribute towards the expenses of good government) even if the law did not re-enact them (as in murder) or concretize them (as in the law imposing income tax, estate tax, etc.): see X.7. On the other hand, the moral principles and theorems with which we have been dealing in this section (e.g. those in step *A* and step *C*) are all to be understood as giving *presumptive* and *defeasible* (see IX.4) exclusionary reason for action. For simplicity I have omitted this qualification from the schema of practical reasoning, and from my elaboration of it. (The nature and effect of the defeating conditions will be examined in XII.2–3.)

Still, the reasons that justify the vast legal effort to render the law, unlike the informal social institution of promising, relatively impervious to discretionary assessments of competing values and conveniences are reasons that also justify us in asserting that the moral obligation to conform to legal obligations is relatively weighty. These reasons relate particularly to the extent, complexity, and depth of the social interdependences which the law, unlike promises between individuals, attempts to regulate. Such an ambitious attempt as the law's can only succeed in creating and maintaining order, and a fair order, in as much as individuals drastically restrict the occasions on which they trade off their legal obligations against their individual convenience or conceptions of social good. Moreover, just as promising creates a special frame of reference in which to assess impartiality, giving to the promisee (and to any ascertained beneficiary) a basis for claiming performance as a matter of right, so too the law creates a similar frame of reference and gives, at least to those directly responsible for superintending the common good, a right to demand compliance, not merely as something morally obligatory in the broad, moralists' sense, but as something morally owed 'to the community'. The law provides the citizen, like the judge, with strongly exclusionary moral reasons for acting or abstaining from actions.

Once it is understood that the schema of practical reasoning discussed in this section can be read both in the restricted, legal sense (in which its first premiss is a postulate detached from extra-legal practical reasoning) and in the unrestricted, moral sense, it should be clear that the schema satisfies the demands both of third-level strategies of explanation (which must display the location and role of the *explicandum* in unrestricted practical reasoning) and of specifically legal science, which reasonably insists both that legal obligation be understood as invariant and that legal obligation (whether or not it is *also* a form of moral obligation) be sharply distinguished from all those moral (or other) obligations which would subsist apart from or in the absence of the law.

This last-mentioned demand or insistence of legal thought is not of interest only to 'positivists'. A 'natural law' jurist can also make the demand, and can observe that it is satisfied by step B in the schema. This step expresses the fact that, wherever it reasonably can, legal thought looks to distinct sources for legal rules and obligations, viz. to the acts which lawyers treat as authoritative, i.e. as giving *now* (in the ambulatory present) good and conclusive (or at least determinate exclusionary) reason for acting *now* in the way *then* stipulated. This derivation of present sufficient reasons for action from past acts or facts, themselves identified by reference to other past acts or facts, ... etc., is thoroughly characteristic of legal thought: see X.3. Those past acts or facts include the acts of deliberate or at least datable creation or amendment to which legal rules, *qua* legal, are always subject, in contrast to moral rules, which *qua* moral rules morally considered have no datable origins and cannot be amended. The dual role of the schema that I have been discussing goes to explain why legal rules, like promises, can generate moral obligations which (in a sense to be elaborated: see XI.8) *are* subject to deliberate creation and amendment. It also, incidentally, helps to explain why it is often so difficult to tell whether a legal, especially an advocate's, utterance is intended to express the demands of unrestricted practical reasonableness in the situation, or is intended only from a professionally structured and systematically restricted 'purely legal' viewpoint—see the distinction between S_1 and S_3 statements, drawn in IX.2.

XI.5 CONTRACTUAL OBLIGATION IN LAW:
PERFORMANCE OR COMPENSATION?

The foregoing section offered a schema of practical reasoning. When artificially isolated from the unrestricted flow of practical reason, the schema explains the specific action-guiding force of an obligation-imposing legal rule in contemplation of law; when integrated into the unrestricted flow of practical reasoning, it explains the specific moral force of such a rule. The remainder of this chapter seeks to consolidate the analysis of both these senses of 'legal obligation', i.e. the purely legal sense, and the moral sense. I do so, first, by considering two long-standing controversies in which lawyers have disputed with lawyers, and moralists with moralists, about these respective senses; and, secondly, by using that discussion to clarify the precise role of the legislator's or, *mutatis mutandis,* promisor's 'will' in the creation and explanation of obligation.

The two controversies which we are to consider have very different origins and concerns, but raise overlapping and parallel questions. There is the controversy amongst lawyers about the legal obligation created by a contract: Is it to perform what was undertaken, or is it no more than an obligation to pay compensatory damages to the other party in the event of one's non-performance? And there is the controversy amongst moralists about the moral obligation to obey a legal-obligation-creating rule of law: Is it to do what that rule of law implicitly or explicitly directs the subject to do, or is it no more than an obligation to submit to the 'penalty' provided for by the law on certain conditions which concern the actions or omissions of the subject?

At the root of the lawyers' controversy is, it seems, the fact which we observed in the preceding section when discussing the appearance of circularity in the schema of practical reasoning which concludes: '*C*. Hence one must [is under an obligation to] ϕ when ϕ is stipulated by an obligation-imposing legal rule'. The schema requires one to identify those legal rules to which one *must* conform if one is to be a law-abiding citizen. Where there is a legislative text which employs distinctive terms, such as 'X shall ϕ, if p, q, r', the task of identifying the rules is relatively easy. But even in such cases, there will be problems about the range of circumstances in which the rule imposes the legal requirement to ϕ. Typically, it will be for courts to interpret the rule and pronounce upon its scope. But the courts do not generally make such pronouncements for the purpose of enlightening the curious or conscientious; rather, they act only on the motion of a party who is seeking from the court some *remedy*, whether punitive or compensatory (e.g. damages) or compulsory (e.g. an order for specific performance). And they tend to use the availability of a remedy as an indication that a rule is of the obligation-imposing type. Thus, it is easy to leap to the supposition that the boundaries of legal obligation are coter-minous with the availability of remedies.

This supposition is even easier to arrive at in those areas of law in which the very content of the law is discoverable not from any legislative text using a clear terminology of obligation-stipulation but only (or primarily) from the pronouncements of judges in the act of granting or refusing enforceable remedies; here the availability of a remedy is often the principal, sometimes the only, sign of the existence and extent of an obligation-imposing legal rule. The supposition, finally, is reinforced by a practical lawyer's professional involvement with the concerns of those citizens who are only interested in the law to the extent that it may affect them adversely, and who care nothing for any train of practical reasoning which proceeds from concern for the common good or for the value of legal order as such.

From such roots emerges the view of an Oliver Wendell Holmes. Aspiring to 'wash with cynical acid' all idealistic fancies about the law, he argues that 'the test of legal principles' is 'the bad man's point of view'. 'What does the notion of legal duty mean to a bad man?' 'Mainly, and in the first place, a prophecy that if he does certain things he will be subjected to disagreeable consequences by way of imprisonment or compulsory payment of money'. So much for 'the widest concept which the law contains—the notion of legal duty'.[10] But, more specifically, 'the duty to keep a contract at common law means a prediction that you must pay damages if you do not keep it,—and nothing else'.[11] More precisely: 'the only universal consequence of a legally binding promise is, that the law makes the promisor pay damages if the promised event does not come to pass. In every case it leaves him free from interference until the time for fulfilment has gone by, and therefore free to break his contract if he chooses'.[12]

Discussions of this analysis of contractual obligation often focus on Holmes's references to prediction, and critiques of his

---

[10] Holmes, 'The Path of the Law' (1897) 10 *Harv. L. Rev.* 457 at 461; also in Holmes, *Collected Legal Papers* (New York: 1920), 167.

[11] Holmes, 'The Path of the Law', at 462.

[12] Holmes, *The Common Law* (1881; ed. M. deW. Howe, Cambridge, Mass.: 1963), 236. For the link between the general strategy of analysing law from the 'bad man's' point of view and this analysis of contract, see *ibid.*, 317.

argument often get little further than showing that it fails to reproduce or account for the 'internal point of view' of judges, who are interested not in predicting what they are about to do, but in reasons they have for doing it. But, as the last passages quoted from Holmes make clear, his argument can readily be stated without any reference to prediction; for X to be under a contractual duty to ϕ means that X must *either ϕ or* pay damages—and this 'must' can (though it need not) be regarded as the conclusion of a genuine 'internal' schema of practical reasoning.

Reflection on Holmes's contention should begin with the recognition that a legal system certainly *could* interpret all its obligation-imposing rules in this disjunctive sense: *either ϕ or* undergo the stipulated 'penalties' (whichever you please). Or, more narrowly, it could construe all contracts in that sense. Still, the fact is that legal systems do not (though many do, of course, permit people to make such a disjunctive contract if they choose to). It is a maxim of civil law systems that contracts are made to be performed, and common law systems have worked on the same principle. Executors or personal administrators, for example, have been held bound to carry out the contracts entered into by the deceased person whose estate they are administering, even when it would be more advantageous to the estate and its beneficiaries for them to refuse performance and pay damages for the breach. The reason judicially advanced for this rule is significant: 'the breaking of an enforceable contract is an unlawful act'.[13] And again: 'The administrator has...a clear duty to perform. The moral duty is distinct. It is to perform the contract entered into by his intestate. The legal duty, in this instance, as...it is in all cases where it is fully understood and examined, is identical with the moral duty'.[14] Similar reasons are advanced for other rules exemplifying the same general principle, for example the rule that it is a civil wrong for C to incite me to break my contract with B, even when C is *not* inciting me to avoid paying damages for the suggested breach: in the view of the judges there is a

---

[13] *Ahmed Angullia v Estate and Trust Agencies (1927) Ltd* [1938] AC 628 at 635 (Privy Council).
[14] *Cooper v Jarman* (1866) LR 3 Eq 98 at 102, quoted and approved in *Ahmed Angullia* (above) at 634 as 'both good law and good sense'.

'chasm' between cases where the act incited or induced was a breach of contract and cases where the act was the not entering into a contract, and there is this chasm precisely because the breach of contract is unlawful.[15] In short, allegiance to the legal system as a whole requires, according to the self-interpretation of these legal systems, that one perform what one undertook; offering or being willing to pay damages, or paying damages when assessed, does not suffice.

This virtually universal legal interpretation of contracts and contractual obligation has its significance, for us, as an indication that contracts are upheld by the law for the sake of the common good, which is positively enhanced (i) by the co-ordination of action, and solution of co-ordination problems, made possible by performance of contracts (in the ordinary, not the Holmesian, sense of 'performance'), and (ii) by the continued existence of a social practice which actively encourages such fully co-ordinated performance and discourages non-performance. If all contracts were interpreted and upheld in the Holmesian disjunctive sense, the common good of co-ordination might still, of course, be served to some extent. But it is served to a much greater extent if the law, as it does, (a) allows parties to enter into disjunctive contracts if they choose to, but (b) refuses to interpret other contracts disjunctively, and thus (c) allows the parties to a contract to know with precision what *unique* course of action is required of the other party by law, in all those cases (the great majority) in which it is to the advantage of each party *not* to give the other party a free option between more than one course of action (as Holmes's contract *does* give).

The ineptness of the Holmesian contract as an instrument for advancing the common good by collaborative works will be even more apparent when one observes that the duty to pay damages arises only, on his view, when a court has settled and ordered them, i.e. after the expense of social resources in litigation. And even then, what is this 'duty to pay'? Is it only a duty *either* to pay *or* to submit to the sheriff or bailiff when he comes to enforce payment by seizing one's goods? And is the 'duty to submit' only the duty to *either* submit *or* accept liability for assault and/or contempt of court? Without collaps-

---

[15] *Rookes v Barnard* [1964] AC 1129 at 1168, 1201.

ing the clear distinction between law and morals, it is possible to see and say that the law's ambitions are higher than this, and its distinctive schemata of thought quite different.

An important theoretical motivation for Holmes's construction, as appears from the immediate context of his formulation of it in *The Common Law*, was his desire (like Hume) to avoid and discredit any attempt to explain contractual obligation as the 'product' of an act (or acts or conjunction of acts) of will which could subsequently somehow 'bind' or 'subject' the (wills of the) parties. This motivation was entirely reasonable. But Holmes failed to see that contractual obligation, like legal obligation in general, can be explained as the necessity of a type of means uniquely appropriate for attaining a form of good (e.g. the standing availability of co-ordination of constructive action) otherwise attainable only imperfectly if at all. He failed to see, or at any rate to make sufficient allowance for the fact, that the social importance of law (as of the practice of promising) derives not only from its ability to mould the 'bad man's' practical reasoning, but also from its capacity to give all those citizens who are willing to advance the common good precise directions about what they *must* do if they are to follow the way authoritatively chosen as the common way to that good (it being taken for granted that having a defined and commonly adhered-to 'common way' is, presumptively, a peculiarly good way of advancing the common good).

XI.6 LEGAL OBLIGATION IN THE MORAL SENSE: PERFORMANCE OR SUBMISSION TO PENALTY?

It is now time to turn to the far more wide-ranging and long-standing controversy amongst moralists about the obligatory force of various common forms of legal stipulation. The controversy about 'purely penal' laws, which anticipates several of the debates of our contemporary analytical jurists, emerges in the later fifteenth century, and finds a classic expression in the work of Suarez at the beginning of the seventeenth century.

The term 'purely penal law' comes from an elementary analysis of the form of legal stipulations. Such stipulations may be in (or be analytically reduced to) one or other of three forms: (i) 'If p, q, r, then $XO\phi$'; this form was often, confusingly, labelled a *lex moralis*; (ii) 'If *p*, *q*, *r*, then XOφ: the penalty for non-compliance is P'; this two-clause form was labelled *lex poenalis mixta*, since it combined a stipulation of action (or, of course, omission) with a stipulation of penalty; (iii) 'If *p*, *q*, *r*, and X does (not) do φ, a penalty P is to be imposed on him'; this conditional directive to officials was labelled a *lex pure* (or *mere*) *poenalis*, since its formulation dealt only (*pure*, or *mere*) with the sanction.[16]

So elementary a piece of analysis could not be dignified with the name of 'theory'. The 'purely penal law theory' is the theory that asserts that some laws which might otherwise be interpreted as imposing a legal (and therefore, by the presumptive entailment we have been exploring, a moral) obligation on subjects to φ should rather be interpreted as imposing on them no more than the obligation to undergo the penalty P—or, in some versions of the theory, as imposing on them only the disjunctive obligation to *either* φ *or* undergo the penalty P. A law which should be so interpreted was a 'purely penal law'.

The reason for this description is as follows. The first systematic treatise devoted to the theory was Alphonsus de Castro's *De Potestate Legis Poenalis* (1550). In his version of the theory the decisive ground for interpreting a law as imposing only the obligation to undergo the penalty was simply the *form* of the law. If the legislative formulation was a conditional directive to impose a penalty (i.e. the *pure poenalis* form), then the law must[17] be interpreted as imposing on the subject no obligatory directive to do the act, φ, whose non-performance was the condition of the penalty. If, on the other hand, the legislator used the *poenalis mixta* form, incorporating an express direction to the subject to φ, then the law *must* be interpreted as imposing on the subject an obligation to φ. In short, for Castro the only class of enforceable laws that failed to impose on the citizen a straightforward obligation to φ was the class of laws

---

[16] The labels can be traced to Castro, *De Potestate Legis Poenalis* (1550); the distinctions are recognized by earlier authors: see Suarez, *De Legibus*, Book V, c. 4, para. 2.

[17] '...unless one can consult the lawgiver personally, and he tells you orally what he really meant': Castro, *De Potestate Legis Poenalis*, Book I, c. 5.

pure poenalis in form.[18] (The modern reader will have observed that in Kelsen's 'pure theory of law' all laws are to be analytically rendered into the *pure poenalis* form, but are then to be interpreted as imposing on the citizen an obligation (purely legal, of course) to do the act whose non-performance is the condition for the application of the penalty.[19] The reader should reflect, not that Kelsen is wrong and Castro right, or vice versa, but that both the analytical reduction and the inter-pretative construction of a 'secondary norm' involve Kelsen in many more assumptions about the practical point and value of law than he is wont to admit.)

Castro's motive in linking obligation with verbal forms was to *limit* the effects of a notion of legal/moral obligation which, he said, he found widespread amongst laymen and ill-educated preachers and confessors—the notion that wherever a penalty is stipulated by the lawgiver there is no obligation on the subject to do (or refrain from) the act (or omission) to which the penalty is attached, and indeed no obligation to do any-thing other than to submit to the penalty if and when it is enforced. Castro's strategy was to restrict this wide exemption from positive obligation to the relatively narrow class of cases in which the lawgiver's formulae contained no directive to the subject at all.

This formalistic strategy is, of course, exposed to many objections. Above all, does not the lawgivers' use of the term 'penalty' (and/or of the machinery of criminal law enforcement) indicate an implicit directive to the subject to abstain from the penalized act or omission? Unless we admit the presence of this implicit directive, do we not extinguish the basic distinc-tion between a *tax* (on conduct which the lawgivers regard as compatible with the common good) and a *penalty* (for conduct which they regard as inimical to the common good)?[20] In short,

---

[18] Such laws, according to Castro, impose only (a) an obligation on the judge to impose the penalty P, and/or (b) an obligation on the citizen to undergo P: *ibid.*, c. 9. John Driedo, who anticipated Castro in his *De Libertate Christiana* (published posthumously in 1546), makes it clear that the latter obligation arises only 'when one has been caught': Book 2, c. 1.

[19] See Kelsen, *General Theory*, 58–62.

[20] The point is made by two opponents of all 'purely penal law theories': Dominic de Soto, *De Iustitia et Iure* (1556), Book 1, q. 6, a. 5, and Louis Molina, *De Iustitia et Iure*, vol. III (1600), tr. 2, disp. 674. Cf. Hart's criticism of Kelsen and Holmes on similar lines: *Concept of Law*, 38–41 [38–42].

is it not 'verbal and childish'[21] to attend exclusively to the lawgivers' formulae in gauging their intention?

In reaction to Castro, there very soon emerged in a number of writers[22] a new version of 'purely penal law theory'. In this second version, the verbal form of a law was of little or no consequence; all laws imposing or concerning penalties were in substance directive or preceptive, incorporating a directive to citizens as well as to sanction-imposing officials, just as if they had been expressed in the *lex poenalis mixta* form. But 'directive' or 'preceptive' were given a special interpretation by these writers. Lawgivers, in their view, had two methods available to give action-guiding force to their directive: they could *either* attach to it the threat of a sanction P, to be imposed by officials in the event of non-compliance with the directive, *or* attach to it a moral obligation (with the result that the non-complying subject would in the next life undergo the penalties imposed by God for sin). So if lawgivers chose to stipulate a penalty P, they should be *presumed* to be withholding all moral obligation from their directive (express or implied) to ϕ. This presumption was founded on the lawyers' tag *'expressio unius est exclusio alterius'*: 'And so the legislator who has power to oblige to both eternal [divine] and temporal [human] punishment, by invoking the latter seems to exclude the former'.[23] In a new sense, therefore, a law stipulating a penalty could be presumed to be 'purely penal', i.e. to impose no moral obligation on the subject.

It is hard to imagine a theory which detaches obligation more radically from all questions of the rational necessity of means uniquely appropriate to a common good. On this new version of the purely penal law theory, legal obligation (in both its

---

[21] Sylvester Prierias, *Summa Summarum de Casibus Conscientiae* (1515), s.v. 'inobedientia', para. 3, criticizing Castro's principal predecessors, Henry of Ghent (c. 1280) and the *Summa Angelica* (1486).

[22] Notably Martin de Azpilcueta, commonly called Navarrus (1557), and Gregory de Valencia (1592); but their views differ in various respects, and the synthesis in the text above is not to be attributed precisely to either.

[23] Navarrus, *Enchiridion sive Manuale Confessariorum* (1557), c. 23, n. 55. The presumption is not conclusive; contrary evidence as to the lawgiver's real intention is relevant if available.

purely legal sense and its moral sense)[24] amounts to nothing
more than liability to sanctions human or divine; for this reason, if no other, it is (in both its senses) wholly at the disposition of lawgivers to impose or withhold, in any degree, as they
please.

Suarez, in his *De Legibus* (1612), objected to this second
version of the theory on two closely related grounds: (a) because
it eliminated from most enforceable laws all traces of a positive
direction to the law-abiding citizen, and (b) because it assumed a
reductionist account of obligation as equivalent to liability to
penalty. But, while rejecting this radical elimination of differences commonly accepted and plainly relevant to practical reasonableness, Suarez (and his many followers) shared not only
the new theorists' desire[25] that the consciences of citizens should
not be burdened by too many and too onerous obligations, but
also their belief that the intention of the lawgiver is decisive in
determining the incidence of obligation. Thus, there emerges in
Suarez a third version of the purely penal law theory, skillfully
combining elements of both the earlier versions, and foresha-
dowing Holmes in its principal analytical device.

In Suarez's account, a 'purely penal law' is one that, whatever its form, is to be interpreted as imposing on the subject
(citizen) a disjunctive obligation: to *either* ϕ *or* submit to a
'penalty' P.[26] (It now seems desirable to enclose the word
'penalty' in inverted commas in stating the theory, since the
theory's most obvious, though not most basic, difficulty is in
explaining how P is a penalty at all; for the theory's essential
contention is precisely that, in the case of a purely penal law, a
citizen who fails to ϕ *has not violated the law at all* and *has not
failed to comply with any directive* whether express or implied,
obligatory or non-obligatory.) Suarez rejects the appeal to
the tag *expressio unius est exclusio alterius*; not every law which
stipulates or concerns a penalty is to be interpreted as 'purely

---

[24] This distinction between the senses of legal obligation is mine (see XI.4), and is not explicit in
the debates we are here analysing. I do not think the course of these debates would have been
substantially affected if the participants had made the distinction.

[25] Expressed, e.g., by Blackstone in his discussion of 'purely penal law': I *Comm.* 58.

[26] *De Legibus*, Book I, c. 14, para. 7; Book III, c. 27, para. 3. Sometimes Suarez calls it a
'hypothetical precept', i.e. to submit to penalty if ϕ is not done: e.g. Book V, c. 4, para. 8. Not
surprisingly, Suarez also recognizes 'purely penal' contracts, promises, or vows: Book III, c. 22,
para. 6; Book V, c. 4, para. 8.

penal' in his view. Rather, the intention of the lawgiver to impose only the disjunctive obligation is to be declared explicitly, or else conveyed 'through tradition, custom or unwritten law'.[27] In the absence of any such customary principle of interpretation in a given community, Suarez suggests that Castro's criterion be used (i.e. that laws *pure poenalis* in *form* impose on the citizen no obligation to do or abstain from the acts referred to in the conditional clause). But Suarez avoids pure formalism by adding a proviso: the severity of the penalty or the intrinsic importance of the law's subject-matter[28] may indicate that the lawgiver (notwithstanding his form of stipulation) must have intended to impose a straightforward (not a merely disjunctive) obligation on the citizen.

What is the importance for us of these old theories? It is twofold. First, they force us to refine our conception of the role of legislative will (lawgivers' acts of choice or decision) in the imposition of legal and moral obligation. This point is developed in the following section. Secondly, they suggest a closer attention to the problems of conscience created by burdensome and insensitive laws, which are to be found today in legal systems that on the whole are just, as often as they were found by moral theologians in the legal systems of sixteenth- and seventeenth-century Europe. This point is developed in the next chapter.

XI.7 OBLIGATION AND LEGISLATIVE WILL

All versions of the purely penal law theory share the assumption that obligation is an effect of lawmakers' will, is to be explained by reference to the moving force of this will, and can be imposed or withheld by lawmakers at their choice when they are indicating a rule or common pattern of action which they consider desirable for the common good. Some versions of the theory (e.g. Vazquez's[29]) propose that lawgivers can withhold all obligation from the pattern of action which they expressly or

---

[27] *Ibid.*, Book V, c. 4, para. 8.

[28] i.e. the matters referred to in the conditional clause of the law: in my notation, ϕ. See *ibid.*, Book V, c. 4, paras 10, 12.

[29] *In Primam Secundae*, disp. 159, cc. 2, 3. Vazquez's theory is a less formalistic version of Castro's, emphasizing legislative intention rather than legislative formulae.

impliedly are stipulating to the citizen. Others propose that lawgivers can regulate the degree of obligation. Others (e.g. Suarez's[30]) propose that, while obligation is essential if a stipulation is to count as a legal rule at all, this obligation may be directed by lawgivers either (i) to the action, ϕ, which they desire or (ii) disjunctively to that action *or* the penalty (which amounts to saying that, on a certain condition, they can withhold all obligation from the stipulated pattern of action, ϕ).

A first difficulty, then, with all the purely penal law theories is that they almost inevitably trade in fictions. The fact is that very few lawmakers have any wish to distinguish between making conduct legally obligatory and subjecting it to a penalty, and even fewer have any will or intention about the moral implications of their enactments. Rarely do they go beyond the straightforward train of reasoning that common adherence to some single pattern of action ϕ is desirable for the common good, that ϕ should therefore be a legal requirement, and that a sanction P should be laid down (a) to indicate that it is henceforth a legal requirement, (b) to dissuade the recalcitrant from recalcitrance, and (c) with an eye to the range of pedagogical, retributive, and reformative considerations sketched in X.1. To look for a legislative intention to impose or withhold legal obligation in the moral sense, whether by looking to the drafting forms employed, or by searching behind them, is to look for something that typically is not there to be found. The upshot is a comedy of fictions: confronted by the stipulation of a 'disproportionately' severe penalty, some purely penal law theorists[31] presume that the severity indicates a legislative intention to impose a strict obligation to ϕ, while others[32] presume that it indicates the intention to impose no obligation to ϕ at all. Both presumptions are quite arbitrary, the latter (more popular) perhaps more so than the former.

A second difficulty goes a little deeper. All versions of the theory (and not just Castro's) muddy the distinction between

---

[30] *De Legibus*, Book I, c. 14, para. 4; Book III, c. 20, para. 4.

[31] See, e.g., Castro, *De Potestate Legis Poenalis*, Book I, c. 11; Suarez, *De Legibus*, Book V, c. 4, para. 10.

[32] For example A. Lehmkuhl, *Theologia Moralis* (Freiburg: 12th edn, 1914), vol. I, para. 312; J. Messner, *Social Ethics: Natural Law in the Modern World* (St. Louis: 1949), 211; for an early version of this line of thought, Alphonsus de Liguori, *Theologia Moralis* (1755), Book III, n. 616.

tax and penalty. In various situations this distinction inevitably is hard to draw in practice: legislators imposing taxes can be uncertain whether they wish to discourage a certain form of conduct (e.g. smoking) or to raise revenue from it, or both. But it remains importantly desirable that law-abiding citizens should know where they stand in relation to any form of conduct they are considering: Is this (i) a form of conduct authoritatively declared to be incompatible with the authoritatively chosen common way (and *therefore* subjected to penalty) or is it (ii) a form of conduct which the legislator perhaps (a) approves but finds convenient as an occasion for raising revenue, or perhaps (b) disapproves of but is willing to concede to citizens (including the law-abiding) but only at a discouraging price? The distinction between (i) and (ii) is much more significant for the enterprise of ordering a community fairly through law than the distinction between (ii)(a) and (ii)(b). But 'purely penal law' theorists argue that the device of declaring an 'offence' and/or stipulating a 'penalty' is systematically ambivalent as between form (i) and form (ii)(b). In truth it is perhaps the legislator's most distinctive device for indicating form (i). Thus, the 'purely penal law' theorists make legal regulation less finely tunable and so less apt as a way to the common good.

But the really basic difficulty lies in the very notion which gives the theory its perennial plausibility and popularity. Obligation, it is argued, results from the lawmakers' decision to create an obligation-imposing rule. Can they not therefore decide to create a non-obligation-imposing rule, or a lesser-obligation-imposing rule, or a disjunctive-obligation-imposing ('either ϕ or P') rule? Does not power to do the greater include power to do the lesser? Only a rigorous analysis of the role of legislative will or decision in creating legal or legal/moral obligation will allow us to resist these rhetorical questions, as we should.

The necessary distinctions, though basic, are fine, as the failure of so many to see them shows. They can be made clear by reference to a legal analogy. (This analogy is intended to capture a single distinction, to rebut a single supposed entailment, not to be on all fours with law in general as it appears in the problematic of this section.) Consider a federal state,[33] in which the constitution requires lawyers to distinguish between 'federal' duties and 'provincial' duties, for example because 'federal' (i.e. central, as opposed to 'provincial') courts have exclusive jurisdiction in cases involving 'federal' rights and duties or obligations. A federal duty is one imposed by, under, or by virtue of federal law. Now suppose that a federal law stipulates that all persons who are certified to belong to class C shall have the duty to ϕ; and suppose further that under the constitution no provincial legislature could impose such a duty. This duty is imposed by federal law (and thus enforceable in federal courts). It remains a federal duty or obligation whether or not only federal officials have the power to certify that given persons belong to class C. Suppose that provincial officials are empowered by federal or provincial law to issue the relevant certificates: the duty of the certified persons to ϕ remains a federal duty. It will remain an exclusively federal duty even if the provincial officials are empowered to issue the certificates on criteria specified by provincial law, or by some foreign law, or in their own discretion. It will remain an exclusively federal duty whether the form of the provincially issued certificate is 'X is hereby certified to belong to class C', or 'X, being hereby certified to be a member of class C, shall ϕ', or 'X is hereby certified to be under an obligation to ϕ', or 'X is hereby required to ϕ'. None of these variations in verbal forms, or in width of delegation to non-federal officials, affects the *source* of the obligation, which is exclusively federal. The decisions of the non-federal officials to issue certificates are simply facts the occurrence of which attracts the federal obligation to a particular person—just as reaching the age of 18 is a fact which attracts federal obligations under federal laws relating to adults.

In short, although it is true that the decision (act of will) of a provincial official to bring it about that X is under an obligation to ϕ has the result that X is under that obligation, it is not true that therefore 'the source' of X's obligation is that

---

[33] The analogy could also be developed for a unitary state, in terms of a Minister, or local authority, or other functionary, empowered to classify persons for the purposes of an existing parliamentary enactment which imposes various obligations on various classes of persons.

official's act of will. Some official's act of will is indeed a necessary condition for X to incur this particular obligation; but that act of will has no more intrinsic importance (or explanatory significance in an explanation of X's obligation) than any other fact (e.g. turning 18) which is a necessary condition for X to incur that (or some other) obligation. And note that an official cannot decide to issue a certificate but to withhold the obligation that flows from that issue.

The foregoing analysis is not affected if we widen the range of choices open to the non-federal officials, e.g. to certify X as a member of class C, or class C_1, or class C_2, or class C_n, with the result that X would have the duty to ϕ,... or ϕ_n, respectively. The only consequence of thus widening the range of options is that the officials' decisions can affect people in more various ways and are perhaps more difficult to make, and in these senses more 'weighty'; the decisions are still not 'the essential source' of the various obligations, any more than X's own decision would be 'the source' of X's obligations under a federal law which imposed obligations on specified classes of persons but authorized and required people to *choose their own class* (whether periodically, or once and for all).

By their decision to stipulate that ϕ is legally obligatory for X, persons with authority to make laws bring it about that (i) ϕ is legally obligatory and thus (presumptively) that (ii) ϕ is morally obligatory. But, as the foregoing analysis of the imagined federal legal situation should have helped to make clear, these consequences flow not from any 'force' of the law-givers' 'superior will', but from the interrelationship between (a) the fact that they have thus decided and (b) a 'higher' (or 'deeper') principle that makes that fact legally and/or morally significant.[34] In a strictly legal analysis, that further principle will consist in some law which imputes legal effect to specified types of legislative act (but which equally, though less commonly in the modern world, might impute normative effect to

---

[34] This explains how one should understand the *quia* ('because') in Aquinas's famous remark, still alive in English juristic parlance, that 'there are some things commanded because good, or prohibited because bad, but other things good because commanded, or bad because prohibited [*mala quia prohibita*]': *S.T.* II–II q. 57 a. 2 ad 3; cf. I–II q. 71 a. 6 ad 4.

events or facts which involve nobody's act of will or decision to impose such-and-such an obligation: see IX.3). In the wider perspective of practical reasoning which includes but goes beyond the confines of legal reasoning, the relevant further principles will be the principles that the common good is to be advanced, that authoritative determination of co-ordination problems is for the common good, and that legal regulation is (presumptively) a good method of authoritative determination.

Hence, the question whether lawgivers can withhold moral obligation from their stipulations, or modify the extent or degree of the obligations' moral force, is not to be settled by asking what moral obligations they can or do intend or 'will' to impose. Rather, that question is to be settled by asking what, in view of the common good, is the significance, for practical reasonableness, of certain facts—in this case, the fact that an authoritative lawgiver has decided and stipulated that ϕ is 'legally obligatory'. The correct answer to that question is the one given in the preceding sections of this chapter, viz. that because of (a) the importance of law as a specific way of realizing a fundamental element of the common good, i.e. a fair, predictable, positively collaborative, and flexibly stable order of human interrelationships, and (b) the fact that the law will not be effective for that purpose unless its subjects are generally willing to accept and act upon its stipulations (even when they would rather they had been otherwise), it follows (c) that where the authorized lawgiver stipulates that ϕ is obligatory, the effect, for the lawyer, is that ϕ is obligatory (there being no grades or degrees of legal obligation), and the effect for conscientious citizens as such (whether or not they are also lawyers) is that ϕ is (presumptively) morally obligatory. Thus, the lawgiver's acts of will have their significance for the practical reason of other people only because they can take their place in a normative framework *which is not of the lawgiver's making*. That framework has no place for legislative 'intentions' (or 'acts of will') to withhold or modify moral obligations; for such intentions, if they had their intended effect, would seriously weaken the clarity, certainty and uniformity of application which are the very bases of law's utility as a specific way of realizing the common good. Therefore, *these* intentions or acts of will are of no effect, i.e. are irrelevant to moral reasoning about one's obligations as a citizen.

To say this is not, of course, to deny that a legislator can expressly (or by a genuine implication) make a stipulation of which the correct legal analysis is that it is of the disjunctive sort identified by Suarez. But such legislative acts should be regarded by lawyers and citizens alike as muddled and abusive attempts to impose a tax on the doing of ϕ. They impose *no* form of obligation not to do ϕ. So far as concerns the doing of ϕ they are to be treated rather like a legislator's exhortations not to do ϕ. Though such exhortations have some relevance to the citizen's own assessment of the requirements of the common good, they have *no* legal effect and hence do not create *any* degree of legal obligation in either the legal or the moral sense.

Nor, finally, does my basic argument against the 'purely penal law' theories in any way diminish the breadth and freedom of the legislator's authority to choose the obligatory pattern of action from amongst all the possible alternative patterns that might reasonably be made obligatory for the common good. Nor does it entail or suggest that the legislator is confined to crystallizing obligations that were somehow already 'there' (by virtue of 'natural law'): see X.7. If the analogy I developed with a certain federal legal situation seems to suggest such consequences, consider a further partial analogy. It sometimes happens that a central legislature, which has *exclusive* legislative jurisdiction over, say, the federal capital city, will provide for the criminal law for that city by simply enacting that the criminal law there shall be the criminal law of the surrounding province, whatever that law may be from time to time. In such a situation all the acts of choice about the *content* of the criminal law to be in force in the city are made by the provincial (i.e. non-federal) legislature—yet it remains true that that provincial legislature has *no* authority over the capital city, and no power to withhold, prevent, or modify the applicability of its laws to that city. The validity and obligatory force of the province's laws in that city are to be explained by reference essentially to the overriding federal law. So, too, in the analysis of law in general. The wide discretion of lawmakers to choose and mould the content of their subjects' obligations is not incompatible with the principles we have insisted upon, that the obligatory force of their acts of legislative choice is not essentially[35] explicable by reference to those acts of choice as such, and is not theirs to impose, withhold, modify, or otherwise dispose of.

XI.8 'REASON' AND 'WILL' IN DECISION, LEGISLATION, AND COMPLIANCE WITH LAW

There the matter could be left. But a deeper understanding of the centuries-long debates among the moralists is available. *Why* did the purely penal law theorists (and indeed many others) attribute to acts of will a significance in the explanation of law that they do not truly have, and that seriously obscures the positively[36] explanatory role of the various relevant aspects of and appropriate means to the common good? In answering this it will be helpful to follow up the assumption or principle, shared by all parties to the debate, that the interplay of reasonableness and sheer decision in the politico-legal arena is illuminated by developing an analogy with an individual's own decision-making and action. We immediately notice that the most influential purely penal law theorist, Suarez, has developed an analysis of individual action (which he shares with Vazquez, another purely penal law theorist) in explicit opposition to the analysis offered by Aquinas, whose followers became the principal opponents of the purely penal law theory.

Like Aquinas, Suarez understands any free and deliberate human action in terms of a series (not necessarily chronologically extended) of interacting components. There is the intelligent grasp of an end, value, or objective: let this be attributed to one's 'reason', one's capacity to 'see the point' or understand the good of that end. But this will not result in action unless one is actively interested in, i.e. desirous of, that end, for oneself:

---

[35] But for the ambiguity of 'formal' in modern speech, it would be preferable to say 'formally': in short, our argument is aimed against the view, expressed by Locke in his sixth *Essay on the Law of Nature*, that 'the formal cause of obligation [is] the will of a superior' (von Leyden ed., Oxford: 1954, 185). Retaining the Aristotelian terminology used by Locke, our argument is that the will of a superior is one amongst several possible 'efficient', *not* formal, causes of obligation.

[36] Suarez of course allows the common good and justice a negative or limiting role in his account of law: a lawgiver's will does not have its moral effect if it is *unjust*: *De Legibus*, Book I, c. 9.

let this desire of the end be attributed to one's 'will', one's capacity to pursue objectives which one understands, or considers, to be valuable. Then there is the intelligent consideration of ways of achieving that end, and assessment of their respective efficacy, availability, advantages, and disadvantages: let this be attributed to one's 'reason'. But this consideration and assessment will not result in action unless one is not only attracted by the various respective advantages but is also willing to bring the potentially interminable process of comparing possibilities, advantages, and disadvantages to a close by choosing a specific means and *deciding* so to act: let this be attributed to one's 'will'. So far Aquinas and Suarez agree.[37]

But at this point in the analysis Suarez (like Vazquez) says: one's *decision* moves one to bestir oneself and carry out one's action. Decision being attributed by him, as by Aquinas, to 'will', we arrive at the same axiom as dominates Suarez's political and legal philosophy: it is will that moves human beings to action— in the political arena, the will of the superior; in the quasi-political arena of one's control over one's own faculties and limbs, one's own will. Aquinas, on the other hand, draws a distinction at this point. Between the decision, by which one settles, for oneself, what one is to do, and the physical or psychosomatic activity by which one actually executes one's own decision, Aquinas discerns by analysis a last component; he calls it *imperium* ('command', imperative). He attributes it to one's 'reason', and claims that what moves one to act is not, very strictly speaking, one's decision but this *imperium*, this 'direction to oneself'.[38] Suarez protests: Aquinas's *imperium* is,

---

[37] Suarez would not dissent from Aquinas's view that 'reason' and 'will' are not to be personified or reified; it is only the person that acts; and, moreover, the alternating activations of the two capacities in question are psychologically entirely interdependent and only analytically distinguishable. *'Voluntas est in ratione'* and *'est appetitus rationalis'* [will is *in* one's reason and is a *rational* appetite/inclination]: *S.T.* I q. 87 a. 4; I–II q. 6 prol.; q. 8 a. 1; II–II q. 58 a. 4c and ad 1.

[38] *S.T.* I–II q. 17 a. 1: 'Hence, in conclusion, to order [or ordain: *imperare*] is an act of one's reason, presupposing an act of will in virtue of which one's reason moves [one], by way of the *imperium*, to the execution of the act'. Speaking more broadly, in the prologue to the same *Quaestio* 17, Aquinas refers to phases of action which are 'commanded by *the will*' (*imperatis a voluntate*). See also q. 90 a. 1 sed contra, and ad 3.

he says, unnecessary and indeed impossible, 'certainly a fiction'.[39]

What, then, is the *imperium*, in Aquinas's analysis? It is an 'act of intelligence' by which one, so to speak, sets one's decided-upon course of action before oneself. Such an act of mind is necessary in order to guide, shape, direct the physical or psychosomatic activity which will carry one's intention into effect. So far, so good. But how can we say that this holding of the plan in one's mind's eye, however necessary it may be to the shaping of movement into 'an action', is what *moves* one to act? Certainly if, like Suarez both here and in the political context, we regard movement as the effect of a driving or pushing force,[40] we will be unable to accept Aquinas's claim about *imperium*. But Aquinas regards human movement not as the effect of a push (whether from within or from an external agent, for example a superior), but rather as a person's response to the attraction of (something considered to be) good. So for Aquinas, the final component in any deliberate action, viz. the actual bodily or other exertions, is an active response to (a) the good of the end and (b) the appropriateness of the means, both (a) and (b) being summarily held before one's attention by a representation (which could be expressed in propositions about what is-to-be or must-be done) of the pattern of action which one has settled upon. This representation, the *imperium*, is to be attributed to one's reason rather than one's will, because it is representational (of a series of relationships between particular ends and particular means) and because it in turn enables intelligible (because intelligent) order to be brought into physical or psychosomatic exertions.

The *imperium* certainly presupposes 'exercises of will', i.e. the desire of this particular end, the preference for these means, the sheer decision to bring deliberation to an end in choice.

---

[39] Suarez, *De Legibus* (1612), Book I, c. 5, para. 6; c. 4, para. 4. It is often overlooked that, in this, Suarez was preceded by the 'rationalist', Gabriel Vazquez, who argued elaborately that Aquinas's postulation of an *imperium* between one's decision and one's performance was 'unnecessary', 'inept', and 'futile': *in Primam Secundae*, disp. 49, c. 4 (on *S.T.* I–II q. 17 a. 1). Indeed people were protesting along these lines within a few years of Aquinas's death.

[40] See, e.g., *De Legibus*, Book I, c. 5, para. 15: 'The first [of the characteristics of law that are to be found in the will not the reason] is that the law moves and applies [one] to action ...'; c. 4, para. 7: 'law does not merely enlighten, but also provides motive force and impels; and, in intelligent processes, the primary faculty for moving to action is the will'.

For without these exercises of will there would as yet be no plan of action and thus no fully determinate basis for exerting oneself in this way rather than that. But, granted those indispensable 'acts' of will (whose efficacy continues right through one's deliberation and one's action to its completion), it is the *imperium*, the fully determinate formulation to oneself of one's intention, that most directly moves one to act. For, being a representational 'act' of intelligence, there can (so to speak) shine through the *imperium* the attractiveness of the end or values at stake, and the adjudged appropriateness of the means selected; and it is *these* that account for one's carrying out this total action. Persons are moved by their perceptions and assessments of good, of value, of advantage; one's decisions mature into corresponding consummated actions not so much because, having being made, they somehow push one along 'of their own force', but rather because one can continue to express one's decision to oneself in a form that allows an understood relationship, between an end perceived as valuable and a means perceived as appropriate, to remain 'visible' to one, 'making sense' of one's exertions throughout their course.

There would be no point in taking sides in this debate about the 'faculties', were it not the case that Aquinas's analytical 'psychology' of the deliberate human act is simply one expression of his understanding of all such action by reference to the values which persons can seek and are seeking through action. At a decisive point in his explanation of obligation (itself the decisive aspect of law, for Suarez), Suarez allows the end and the means assessed as appropriate to it to drop out of view behind the sheer fact of decision.[41] To repeat: Aquinas regards the decision as a wholly necessary condition for any full human action; but he considers that the most precise reason for (and cause of) one's now acting is not that one has at some time (however proximate) decided so to act, but that one now sees the point of acting on one's decision: and this 'seeing the point' is accomplished by a rational representation-to-oneself-of-the-

---

[41] For example, *De Legibus*, Book I, c. 5, para. 21: 'if one has in mind the moving force in law, so that law is said to be the power in the ruler which moves and makes action obligatory, then in that sense, it is an act of will. If, on the other hand, we are referring to and considering that force in law which directs us towards what is good and necessary, then law pertains to the intellect'. Note the disjunction between the 'obligatory' and the 'good and necessary'.

selected-course-of-action, in a form homogeneous with and transparent for the intelligent grasp-of-value-and-assessment-of-means that has made one's decision a 'rational decision' rather than an 'impulse'. And as a Suarez denies this in his analytical psychology of individual action, so he correspondingly sees no need to explain obligation by setting in a framework of ends and means the ruler's decision that his subjects shall ϕ and shall be under an obligation to ϕ.[42]

In their politico-legal analysis, Suarez and Vazquez of course use a concept of *imperium*, command.[43] But there it is conceived by them primarily as an expression of the lawgiver's decision (to impose an obligation); the important thing for them is the act of will (decision) thus expressed and addressed to subjects. Again and again, Suarez makes the point that unless the lawgiver decides to make obligatory the pattern of action which he prefers, it will not be obligatory.[44] This proposition need not be denied. Suarez's mistake is to infer from it that what makes the conduct *actually* obligatory is, precisely and simply, the lawgiver's decision that it should be. The federal analogy should have put us on our guard against this inference. For Aquinas, on the other hand, the important thing about the lawgiver's *imperium* is not that it represents an act of decision, and indeed of decision to 'impose an obligation'; that fact is taken for granted. The important thing is that the expressed *imperium*, the promulgated 'intention of the legislator', represents to the subject an intelligible determinate pattern of action, which, having been chosen by the lawgiver to be obligatory, can actually *be* obligatory in the eyes of a reasonable subject because the ruler's *imperium* can (for the sake of the common good) be reasonably treated by the subject as if it were his own *imperium*.[45]

---

[42] By contrast, for Aquinas, obligation is simply a rational necessity of certain sorts of means to certain sorts of ends: *S.T.* I–II q. 99 a. 1c; II–II q. 58 a. 3 ad 2.

[43] See, e.g., *De Legibus*, Book I, c. 5, para. 13; Book II, c. 2, paras 9, 14; c. 4, para. 1; c. 5, para. 13; c. 6, para. 6; etc.; *in Primam Secundae*, disp. 150, c. 3, no. 19; disp. 49, c. 2, no. 6. See notes to II.6.

[44] *De Legibus*, Book I, c. 4, paras 7, 8; c. 5, paras 16, 19.

[45] See Aquinas, *S.T.* II–II q. 50 a. 2c and ad 3; q. 47 a. 12c. Cf. Weber, *On Law*, 328: 'In our terminology domination shall be identical with authoritarian power of command. To be more specific, domination will mean the situation in which: The manifested will (command) of the ruler or rulers is meant to influence the conduct of one or more others (the ruled) and actually does influence it *in such a way that their conduct to a socially relevant degree occurs as if the ruled had made the content of the command the maxim of their conduct for its very own sake*' (emphasis added).

For, just as an individual's *imperium*, his formulated resolve to act, motivates his exertions by being transparent for the value of his objectives and the appropriateness of the chosen means to them, so in the eyes of the subject the ruler's *imperium* is compelling precisely by being transparent for the common good, to the needs of which the ruler's stipulation is treated by the subject (who recognizes the need for authoritative resolutions of social problems) as a relevant response.[46]

In short, in examining the purely penal law theories, with their attribution of all moving and obligatory force to the lawgiver's will, we are examining one limited aspect or offshoot of that vast movement of thought which has sought, with overwhelming historical success, to expel from the analysis of individual and political action all systematic attention to the intelligibility of the goods which are realizable in action.

XI.9 MORAL OBLIGATION AND GOD'S WILL

Those who founded legal obligation on the will of the ruler tried to be consistent in their understanding of obligation. They explained the obligation to act reasonably (i.e. morally) by appealing to a special exercise of the divine will, whereby God commands that good (the reasonable) be done and evil (the unreasonable) be avoided: see II.8. For what could moral obligation consist in, if not in the movement of an inferior's will by a superior's?

Such an approach to the explanation of obligation is conceptually misdirected, because based on a reduction of the logic of practical reason to a kind of mechanics, in which one force moves or overrides another. Moreover, it invites the questions: Why should I obey God's will? How can obligation arise from what seems, after all, to be just one more *fact*? In the Suarezian tradition (which had antecedents, of course, and has followers to this day) such questions cannot be coherently answered. In

---

[46] This is why, at the very beginning of his treatise on law, Aquinas argues that 'law pertains to reason. For law is a rule and measure of action...and the rule and measure of human acts is the reason, which is the basis [*principium*] of such acts. For ordering things to an end is the function of reason—and the end is the first *principium* of actions': *S.T.* I–II q. 90 a. 1c. And, of course, the end or objective figures in one's practical reason(ing) under the description of 'good', 'valuable', etc.: q. 94 a. 2c; see III.2 above.

II.5–6 above I briefly traced the aftermath of the Suarezian impasse, down to its spectacular dénouement in Hume's dismantling of the moral philosophy of several centuries. The grounding of ethical obligation in God's will becomes a prize specimen amongst conceptual fallacies collected for exhibition in elementary philosophy books.

Things are not, however, so simple: an unravelling of conflated issues is called for. Moreover, the topic should serve as a reminder that my explanation of obligation is as yet incomplete. Certainly it is possible to ask why the needs of the common good (taken as ultimate in this chapter) impose an obligation on you or me. It is possible to inquire, too, concerning the basic requirements of practical reasonableness which we discussed in Chapter V. Just what is meant by 'requirement'? And such questions are not merely conceptual or speculative. They arise, sometimes quite urgently, as part of or extensions to the effort to make practical sense of one's action and of one's life as a whole. There is room, therefore, for a deeper explanation, which I try to provide in Chapter XIII.

NOTES

XI.1

Obligation in Aristotle... It is sometimes suggested that Aristotle has no concept of (what we would call moral) obligation at all. But for much evidence to the contrary, see *Gauthier-Jolif*, II/2, 568–75.

Obligation, 'ought', and supererogation... See, e.g., Joel Feinberg, 'Supererogation and Rules' (1961) 71 *International J. Ethics* 276–88; Roderick M. Chisholm, 'Supererogation and Offence' (1963) 5 *Ratio* 1–14 (both in J. Thomson and G. Dworkin (eds), *Ethics* (New York: 1968)).

Division of ethics into 'deontological' and 'teleological'... Aristotle's certainly escapes this categorization: see J. M. Cooper, *Reason and Human Good in Aristotle* (Cambridge, Mass.: 1975), 87–8. So does Aquinas's, and so does the ethics in this book.

XI.2

Promising and contract... On the relationship between promises and the modern Anglo-American law of contracts (and its antecedents), see E. Allan Farnsworth, 'The Past of Promise: an Historical Introduction to Contract' (1969) 69 *Columbia L. Rev* 576–607.

The focal meaning of 'promising'... For much of the following analysis of promissory obligation, see G. E. M. Anscombe, 'On Promising and Its Justice, and Whether It Needs be Respected *in foro interno*' (1969) 3 *Crítica* 61–78. For a similar account, differing in details, see J. Raz, 'Promises and Obligations' in Hacker and Raz, *Essays*, 210–27; in the same tradition, Grotius, *De Jure Belli ac Pacis* (1625), Book II, c. xi, paras ii–iv.

Obligation based, via 'estoppel', on relied-upon expressions of intention to act... See Neil MacCormick, 'Voluntary Obligation and Normative Powers' (1972) *Proc. Aris. Soc.*, Supp. vol. 46, 59–78; *Australia v France, I. C. J. Rep.* 1975, 253 at 267–8, and the comment by Thomas M. Franck (1975) 69 *Am. J. Int. L.* 612–20. Reliance rather than promise is increasingly the basis of American contract law, but this develops in tandem with a 'risk' theory of liability which bypasses, or at least radically reinterprets, the 'obligation' of contracts: see Roscoe Pound, *Introduction to the Philosophy of Law* (rev. ed., New Haven: 1954), 159–68; for the origins of the risk theory, see Oliver Wendell Holmes, *The Common Law* (1881; ed. Mark deWolfe Howe, Cambridge, Mass.: 1963), 235; for criticism of Holmes's corresponding theory of obligation, see XI.5.

'First-level explanations' of promissory obligation... See Raz, *Practical Reason*, 52–3, 56–8, for exposition and criticism of the analogous 'practice theory of norms'.

'From status to contract'... See Henry Sumner Maine, *Ancient Law* (10th edn, 1884; ed. F. Pollock [1906], Boston: 1963), 165; on 'The Early History of Contract', see *ibid.*, ch. ix; for the wider relevance of the main lines of Maine's analysis of contract, see Max Gluckman, *The Ideas in Barotse Jurisprudence* (Manchester: 2nd edn, 1972), ch. 6 and xvi, xxiv. Both Maine and Gluckman show how the emergence of the modern concept of promissory contract is, in widely differing legal systems, (i) the struggle to detach the focal notion of an expressed and accepted intention to undertake an obligation from the notion that no obligation can arise without some transfer, or partial execution, or at least some formalities; and (ii) the struggle to admit that the obligations created by contract need not conform to any pre-existing type of proprietary or status obligation. It matters little whether or not this line of development is, as a linear progression, universal: Leopold Pospisil, *Anthropology of Law* (New York: 1971), 150, gives some reason for thinking that it is not.

XI.3

Legal obligation is of invariant force... Dworkin, *Taking Rights Seriously* (London: 1977), chs 2 and 3, stresses that the obligation derived from legal *rules* is not a matter of weight. Although he also argues that there are legal *principles* which do create legal obligations of varying weight, he is primarily concerned to argue that such principles have legal weight precisely by virtue of their moral weight, and that 'legal theory' is a branch of moral or political theory or ideology. In this way, he minimizes the extent to which legal thought can and does insulate itself from the general flow of practical reasoning. The present chapter is not concerned to assert or deny that in 'sociological fact' all legal obligations are (treated as) of the same weight, or that in a moralist's 'theory of law' all legal obligations are of the same weight; its concern is to explain the practical reasons for a working postulate of legal thought, and the consequences of the postulate in legal reasoning.

No conflicts between duty-imposing rules... Dworkin's view that 'such conflicts would be occasions of emergency, occasions requiring a decision that would alter the set of standards in some dramatic way', and his supporting reasons (*Taking Rights Seriously*, 74–7), are to be preferred to Raz's view that 'conflicts' are commonplace ('Legal Principles and the Limits of Law' (1972) 81 *Yale L. J.* 823).

Explanation of obligation by reference to human reactions to non-performance... The best attempt, supplementing Kelsen's with Hart's ideas, is Raz, *Legal System*, 147–59. Other well-known sources are Hobbes, *De Cive* [1651], ch. XIV, paras 1, 2; Austin, *Province*, 14–15.

XI.4

Schematic representation of obligation-imposing rules...For a fuller version on similar lines, see G. H. von Wright, *Norm and Action* (London: 1963), ch. V. In my notation ϕ corresponds to what is called 'a pattern of conduct' by Hart, 'a norm act' by Raz, 'an action-idea' by Alf Ross, 'a phrastic' by R. M. Hare, 'norm-contents' or more precisely 'generic acts' by von Wright...

Moral obligation to obey the law...M. B. E. Smith, 'Is There a Prima Facie Obligation to Obey the Law?' (1973) 82 *Yale L. J.* 950–76, argues that there is no obligation, even prima facie, to obey the law as such ('generically'); when confronted with a legal demand (e.g. to stop at a traffic light) one is morally entitled to start with a clean slate, i.e. to assess what is morally required in the situation apart from the fact that there is a rule of law demanding certain conduct in that situation. But in evaluating the fate of a society whose members showed this approach, i.e. who held that there was no prima-facie obligation to obey the law, Smith says (969) 'we must assume that the members of that society accept other moral rules (e.g. "Do not harm others", "Keep promises", "Tell the truth") which will give them a moral incentive to obey the law in most circumstances'. He fails to see that all the arguments he brings against the generic obligation to obey the law could equally be brought against those other moral principles or norms—the general strategy of his argument being to postulate circumstances in which, if one started with a clean slate, one would conclude that there was no sufficient reason to do what a law stipulates, or, alternatively, that there was sufficient reason to do it even in the absence of that law. That general strategy would easily dispose of the obligations to keep promises, tell no lies, etc. Even on its own quasi-utilitarian terms, the strategy is unsound because it overlooks the drastic 'second-order' effects of many people holding themselves ready to start with a clean slate in each situation, i.e. ready to pick and choose amongst the options while prescinding from 'framework' considerations derived from past agreements and undertakings, general adherence to basic values, or authoritative stipulations in community. Some of these effects are well explored in D. H. Hodgson, *Consequences of Utilitarianism* (Oxford: 1967).

Exclusionary force of legal rules...For very strong illustrations, consider two of Aquinas's teachings: (i) that public officials do not do wrong by carrying out a judicial sentence which they know to be mistaken (not because the law applied was unjust, but because the defendant was innocent), since 'it is not for them to discuss the sentence of their lawful superior': *S.T.* II–II q. 64 a. 6 ad 3; (ii) similarly, judges must not defy the laws about evidence, proof, verdicts, etc., in order to bring about the acquittal of someone they *know* (from legally inadmissible evidence) to be innocent. The most they can do is to subject any legally found 'fact' to stringent tests in an effort to find some error in the process of its determination: *S.T.* II–II q. 64 a. 6 ad 3; q. 67 a. 2c. Note that Aquinas's older contemporary, Saint Bonaventure, disagreed with the rigorism of the second teaching.

XI.5

Obligation and penalty in contract...Since the mid-seventeenth century, English law has treated 'penalties' (as distinct from genuine covenanted pre-estimates of damages) as irrecoverable: see A. W. B. Simpson, *A History of the Common Law of Contract* (Oxford: 1975), 118–25. But the standard-form written contract of medieval Europe, the conditioned bond on which in English law the action of debt would lie, might be regarded as a disjunctive contract, as Simpson seems to regard it: *ibid.*, 6. 'Performance of what may be called the underlying agreement is not imposed as a duty; instead performance is only relevant as providing a defence to an action of debt for the penalty': 112. But he also cites much evidence that the courts and jurists never lost sight of the underlying substantial agreement 'to which the obligee is primarily bound' (per Stanton J, in the Eyre of Kent, 1313–14, quoted in Simpson, *A History of the Common Law of Contract*, 115). Indeed, rather inconsistently with his earlier remarks, Simpson concludes (123) that 'the institution of the penal bond and the practice of the courts in upholding such bonds exemplified' 'the idea that the real function of contractual institutions is to make sure, as far as possible, that agreements are performed'—and here 'agreements' must refer to the 'underlying, substantial agreement' concealed 'beneath the legal form' (112). So there is nothing Holmesian about the medieval technique, adapted to a time 'where men cannot trust each other, and the machinery of the law is weak' (124).

Influence of the Summa Angelica *and other* Summae Confessariorum *on English Law*... See Simpson, *A History of the Common Law of Contract*, 337–405.

Holmes on contract... See Mark deWolfe Howe, *Justice Oliver Wendell Holmes: The Proving Years 1870–1882* (Cambridge, Mass.: 1963), 224, 233–40. Note the evidence (*ibid.*, 234 n. 25) that Holmes did not himself accept that his analysis amounts to saying that the promisor undertakes a disjunctive obligation (to either perform or be liable in damages). The fact is that Holmes really wished to get rid of the concept of obligation ('duty') in this context: see *ibid.*, 236, 76–9.

XI.6

History of the 'purely penal law' theories... A 'purely penal law theory' is first clearly formulated in Angelo de Clavasio's *Summa Angelica de Casibus Conscientialibus* (1486; at least 30 editions by 1520), a manual for confessors which influenced the development of English law (e.g. of contract) through the English law student's first and most long-lasting textbook, St. German's *Doctor and Student*. The theory was still producing confused textual echoes in the seventh and later editions of Blackstone's *Commentaries*. See I *Comm.* (7th edn, 1775), 58n, claiming misleadingly to follow Robert Sanderson's *De Obligatione Conscientiae* (1660). The best accessible discussion is William Daniel, *The Purely Penal Law Theory in the Spanish Theologians from Vitoria to Suarez* (Rome: 1968), which gives references and quotations from all the writers here cited. He effectively criticizes (112) D. G. Bayne, *Conscience, Obligation and the Law* (Chicago: 1966), which is, however, of value. The history of the theory is, of course, considerably more complex than our brief account can suggest.

'Obligation' in the purely penal law theories... Throughout the moralists' controversy about 'purely penal laws', 'obligation' signifies, primarily (since the disputants were moralists) the moral obligation to ϕ that presumptively is entailed by any legal obligation to ϕ, and secondarily the legal obligation itself as it might be recognized in a judge's reasoning or conclusions (to be sharply distinguished, of course, from 'legal obligation' in the restricted [Holmesian] sense of mere liability to penalty P in the event of failure to ϕ). Note, however, that even a moralist strongly opposed to the 'purely penal law' theories might surrender to the misleading simplification according to which one has a 'legal obligation' if and only if one is liable to P on failure to ϕ: see Dominic Soto, *De Justitia et Jure* (1556), Book X, q. 5, a. 7.

Motives of Castro's formalist strategy ... See Daniel, *The Purely Penal Law Theory in the Spanish Theologians from Vitoria to Suarez*, 46, 77–83, 164–70. Castro's principal follower in this respect was Gabriel Vazquez, *in Primam Secundae*, disp. 159, c. 2. To the objection that 'purely penal' stipulations do not deserve the name of law, Vazquez is inclined to reply that he agrees, or that they can be called laws because they impose an obligation on the judge to inflict a penalty: *ibid.*, c. 3.

Navarrus, Gregory de Valencia, and the 'second purely penal law theory'...See Daniel, *The Purely Penal Law Theory in the Spanish Theologians from Vitoria to Suarez*, 64–70, 82–8, 175–200, labelling the theory one of 'benign supposition' (sc. as to the legislator's intention (not) to bind). Suarez's objections to this version of the theory are discussed: *ibid.*, 188, 205: see Suarez, *De Legibus*, Book III, c. 22, para. 10; Book V, c. 3, paras 11–12. Daniel, *The Purely Penal Law Theory in the Spanish Theologians from Vitoria to Suarez*, 86–7, 91, rightly stresses the importance of the assumption of Navarrus and many others (encouraged by the unfortunate medieval legal, canonical, and theological idiom which distinguished between *obligatio ad culpam* and *obligatio ad poenam*) that (moral) *guilt*, like a human penalty, was a kind of sanction, which the legislator could either impose or withhold.

'Purely penal law theory' as a relief from burdensome laws...See especially Daniel, *The Purely Penal Law Theory in the Spanish Theologians from Vitoria to Suarez*, ch. 4, on the theological discussion of (i) the harsh Spanish laws, of the sixteenth century, forbidding the gathering of wood and (ii) sales tax (the *alcavala*, first imposed in Spain in 1341, and rising to 10 per cent or more in the sixteenth century).

Suarez and the 'third purely penal law theory'...See Daniel, *The Purely Penal Law Theory in the Spanish Theologians from Vitoria to Suarez*, 88–92, 94–113, 158–62, 200–6. Suarez's theory has remained influential to the present day.

XI.7

Distinction between tax and penalty...As Soto, Bartholomew Medina (1577), and others (see Daniel, *The Purely Penal Law Theory in the Spanish Theologians from Vitoria to Suarez*, 41–4) have been aware, the distinction, used also by the US Supreme Court (see, e.g., *United States v La Franca* (1930) 282 US 568 at 572), representing a tax as a compulsory contribution to the expenses of maintaining the common good, is too simple. There is a third category, of laws imposing a levy on conduct (e.g. the export of grain, the smoking of cigarettes) in order to discourage it (or to allow it at a price: *lex concessoria*). Holmes boldly used the existence of borderline tax/penalty cases to buttress his denial of the distinction altogether (from the 'strictly legal' point of view, i.e. the 'bad man's' point of view, of course): 'The Path of the Law' (1897) 10 *Harv. L. Rev.* 457 at 461.

XI.8

Aquinas and Suarez on 'reason' and 'will'...For Aquinas, see *S. T.* I–II qq. 10–17. Useful syntheses are provided by S. Pinckaers in the Editions du Cerf edition of the *Somme Théologique*, 1a–2ae, qq. 6–17 (Paris: 2nd edn, 1962), 408–49, and more briefly by Thomas Gilby in vol. 17 of the Blackfriars translation (1966), appendix I. Behind Aquinas in these matters lies Aristotle, *Nic. Eth.* esp. VI.2: 1139a17–b6 (notwithstanding Aquinas's misunderstandings of Aristotle on various points of detail: see *Gauthier-Jolif* on 1139b4–5 and III.5: 1113a6–7). For Suarez, see *De Legibus*, Book I, cc. 5 and 6; Book II, c. 3, paras 4–9, and the texts cited in T. E. Davitt, *The Nature of Law* (St. Louis: 1951), ch. VI; D. P. O'Connell, 'Rationalism and Voluntarism in the Fathers of International Law' (1964) 13 *Indian Yearbook Int. Aff.*, Part II, 3–32. The real differences between Aquinas and Suarez, stressed in the text, should not be taken to entail that Suarez was a pure voluntarist; rather, he inclines to the view (*De Legibus*, Book I, c. 5, paras 20–2) that for law there are two requisites: impulse and direction, or (so to speak) goodness and truth, i.e. right judgment concerning the things to be done and an efficacious will impelling to the performance of those things; and so law may consist of both an act of the will and an act of the reason. A good summary of similarities and differences is Walter Farrell, *The Natural Moral Law according to St. Thomas and Suarez* (Ditchling: 1930).

Excursus on 'Will' Theories of Obligation

Many accounts of obligation, both promissory and legal, have employed, more or less obscurely, the notion that it is created by the will—of the promisor, or of a superior whose will 'moves' the inferior's. Often this goes along with the notion that the subject's will is moved by the threat of sanction (or, sometimes, by prospect of reward): Bentham's *Of Laws in General* is a good example, and can be interpreted as both asserting and denying that sanction (or reward) is strictly essential to legal obligation in its formal essence (as distinct from its efficacy). (For similar ambiguity, or ambivalence, see Pufendorf, *De Jure Naturae et Gentium* (1672) I, c. vi, para. 9.) In *A Fragment of Government* (1776), ch. V, paras vi, vii, Bentham had defined duty in terms of sanction: 'That is my *duty* to do, which I am liable to be punished, according to law, if I do not ... One may conceive three sorts of duties; *political, moral,* and *religious*; correspondent to the three sorts of *sanctions* by which they are enforced ... Political duty is created by punishment: or at least by the will of persons who have punishment in their hands ...'. See also *ibid.*, ch. I, para. xii, note, where duty is defined simply in terms of expressions of the will of a superior; likewise *Of Laws*, 93, 294. See *Of Laws*, 54, 134, 136n, 248, 298, for passages emphasizing the importance of sanctions, in the absence of which 'obligation would be a cobweb' (136n) [but would not be inconceivable?] and the law 'could not have any of the effect of what is really a law' (248). On p. 298 Bentham wrestles directly with the question and concludes: 'an expression of will, and the expression of the motive relied on for the accomplishment of that will, may actually exist the one without the other ...' This is reflected in his formal definition of 'a law' in the opening sentence of his work (p. 1). In all, the evidence for a change of view after the *Fragment* is insubstantial, but the ambiguities are significant evidence of the strength of the will-theory of obligation.

At any rate, it is clear that in the vast jurisprudence of Francisco Suarez, for example, obligation as the motive force of superior will moving inferior will (and see II.6) is clearly and fairly firmly distinguished from liability to penalty or sanction (as one would expect of a theorist who still subscribes to the medieval distinction between the 'directive force' of law, and its 'coercive force'). On obligation as the motive force of superior will, see, e.g., *De Legibus* (1612), Book II, c. vi, paras 7, 10, 22 (where no reference to sanction is ever made). For the distinction between 'directive' and 'coercive' 'power' or 'binding force' of laws, see e.g., Book III, c. xxxii, paras 5, 6 (which, however, confuses imposing an obligation with successfully inducing or 'obliging'), c. xxxiii, paras 1, 8, 9; Book VII, c. xix, para. 3. Suarez's central proof of his version of the 'purely penal law theory' (see XI.6 above) is as follows: 'the lawmaker can make a law obliging in conscience and at the same time imposing a penalty on law-breakers, and he can also make a law obliging in conscience without attaching any penalty to violation; therefore he can also make a law which obliges only to [undergo] the due penalty ...': Book V, c. iv, para. 3. In short, the fact that one is liable to legally stipulated penalty in the event of failing to ϕ simply does not entail, in Suarez's view, that ϕ-ing is obligatory (whether legally or morally).

A special, but not historically insignificant variant of the will theory of promissory obligation was suggested by Hobbes in his *De Corpore Politico* (1650), Part I, c. 3 (Raphael, *British Moralists*, para. 102): 'There is a great similitude between what we call *injury* or *injustice* in the actions and conversations of men in the world, and that which is called absurd in the arguments and disputations of the Schools. For as he which is driven to contradict an assertion by him before maintained, is said to be reduced to an absurdity ... there is in every breach of covenant a contradiction properly so called. For he that covenanteth, willeth to do, or omit, in the time to come. And he that doth any action, willeth it in that present, which is part of the future time contained in the covenant. And therefore he that violateth a covenant, willeth the doing and the not doing of the same thing, which is a plain contradiction. And so injury is an absurdity of conversation [sc. actions and transactions], as absurdity is a kind of injustice in disputation'. The argument reappears in slightly different form at a critical juncture of the *Leviathan* (1651), c. 14 (*British Moralists*, paras 59, 61), with particular reference to the duty, or state of being 'obliged', created by 'contracts' ('covenant' here being given a special meaning, more restricted than in the *De Corpore Politico*). In the *Leviathan* the argument from self-contradiction is simply juxtaposed with Hobbes's better-known view that 'the bonds, by which men are...obliged...have their strength, not from their nature, (for nothing is more easily broken than a man's word,) but from fear of some evil consequence upon the rupture'. The argument from self-contradiction has two obvious weaknesses. The first is its equivocation between willing to ϕ at a certain time and willing at a certain time to ϕ. The second is that where two propositions contradict each other, *either* may be false, and there is no *a priori* reason to prefer one to the other; but a promissory act of will must *a priori* be preferred to the violative act of will if the former is to be counted as obligation-imposing.

When Kant took up the argument from self-contradiction, he seems to have identified the first weakness (of equivocation) but not the second: see Kant, *The Science of Right* (trans. Hastie) (Edinburgh: 1887), First Part, sec. 7: 'This right [to what has been promised] is not to be annulled by the fact that the promiser having said at one time, "This thing shall be yours", again at a subsequent time says, "My will now is that the thing shall not be yours." In such relations of rational right, the conditions hold just the same as if the promiser had without interval of time between them, made the two declarations of his will, "This shall be yours", and also "This shall not be yours"; which manifestly contradicts itself'. With this read secs 10, 17, and 19 and Second Part, secs 45, 46, and 47.

The whole strategy of explaining obligation in terms of acts of will inducing, blocking, or overriding each other fails because it has turned aside from the genuine 'logic of the will', which is the logic of practical reasoning, that is, of values and their realization, of the requirements of basic principles which *must* be satisfied if human goods (including the good of reasonableness) are to be as fully participated in as they can be. The rational necessity which we call obligation (in any of its forms) can be accounted for only by attending (as one in practice attends when 'willing' anything) to the goods at stake in compliance or non-compliance with a proposed or stipulated course of action.

In modern jurisprudence, the theory that attributes significance to 'acts of will' and their 'contents' is not advanced directly for the purpose of explaining obligation, but to explain the 'nature' or 'ontological status' of norms. See G. H. von Wright, *Norm and Action* (London: 1963) 120–1, where von Wright announces his adherence to 'the *will-theory* of norms'. He asks (148): 'Can commands or norms in general, ever contradict one another? I wish I could make my readers see the serious nature of this problem...It is serious because, if no two norms can logically contradict one another, then there can be no logic of norms either...So therefore, if norms are to have a logic, we must be able to point to something which is impossible in the realm of norms...' After further discussion he concludes (151): 'The only possibility which I can see of showing that norms which are prescriptions can contradict one another [sc. so that their co-existence in a corpus of norms is logically impossible] is to relate the notion of a prescription to some idea about the unity and coherence of a will...a *rational* or *coherent* or *consistent* will'. His 'will-theory' prevents him, however, explaining why inconsistency *is* irrational. Well known are Kelsen's struggles with the problem, which start and (after many attempts) end with the admission that in a pure will-theory of norms contradictory norms *can* co-exist within the same system: see Kelsen, *General Theory*, 401–6, 437; for the intermediate efforts, see *The Pure*

Theory of Law (Berkeley: 1967), 72, 74, 205–8; for the final admission, see (1963) XIII *Österreichische Zeitschrift für öffentliches Recht* 2, quoted in translation in Alf Ross, *Directives and Norms* (London: 1968), 157–8.

XI.9

Moral obligation 'explained' by reference to God's will... For example, see Suarez, *De Legibus* (1612), Book II, c. 6, paras 5–24: e.g. 'the law of nature, as it is true divine law, may also superimpose its own moral obligation, derived from a precept, over and above what may be called the natural evil or virtue inherent in the subject-matter in regard to which such a precept is imposed' (para. 12); '...in view of the fact that no real [*propria*] prohibition or preceptive obligation is created solely by a judgment [i.e. as to the evil of a particular action], since such an effect cannot be conceived of apart from volition, it is consequently evident that there exists, in addition, the [divine] will to prohibit the act in question, for the reason that it is evil' (para. 13): '...and if no such prohibition existed, that action would not possess the consummate and perfect character (so to speak) of guilt...' (para. 19); '...the mere dictate of intelligence apart from will...cannot impose upon another being a particular obligation. For obligation is a certain moral impulse [*motio*] to action; and to impel [*movere*] another to act is a work of will' (para. 22). Since Suarez is under pressure from theological tradition to admit that an action can be identified as contrary to one's obligation, and that the doing of it can be described as guilty, *without reference to God's will*, his effort to be consistent with his own concept of obligation is only verbally successful; again and again in these paragraphs he is brought to the brink of saying that even without reference to any divine precept, acts (or their avoidance) can be obligatory (or guilty/sinful); this is betrayed in his repeated statement that the obligation imposed by the divine will underpinning natural law is 'some sort of *additional* obligation' (paras 12, 13,) a 'special obligation' (paras 11, 17, 22).

Antecedents of Suarez on the obligation-imposing force of God's will... See Suarez, *De Legibus*, Book II, c. 6, para. 4, citing a number of fourteenth-century writers, most relevantly Ockham, *Super quatuor libros Sententiarum* (c. 1318), Book II, q. 19, ad 3 and 4, and Peter d'Ailly, *Quaestiones...super libros Sententiarum* (1375), Book I, q. 14, a. 3. Between these and Aquinas, Suarez tries to hold a 'via media' (para. 5). Especially forthright for the view that obligation can derive only from the will of a superior is Suarez's great predecessor in the Spanish revival of scholasticism, Vitoria: see his *De eo ad quod tenetur homo cum primum venit ad usum rationis* (1535), Part II, para. 9, cited by Suarez, *De Legibus*, Book II, c. 6, para. 5; quoted in II.6 above (p. 45, n. 61).

XII

UNJUST LAWS

XII.1 A SUBORDINATE CONCERN OF
NATURAL LAW THEORY

THE long haul through the preceding chapters will perhaps have convinced the reader that a theory of natural law need not have as its principal concern, either theoretical or pedagogical, the affirmation that 'unjust laws are not law'. Indeed, I know of no theory of natural law in which that affirmation, or anything like it, is more than a subordinate theorem. The principal concern of a theory of natural law is to explore the requirements of practical reasonableness in relation to the good of human beings who, because they live in community with one another, are confronted with problems of justice and rights, of authority, law, and obligation. And the principal jurisprudential concern of a theory of natural law is thus to identify the principles and limits of the Rule of Law (see X.4), and to trace the ways in which sound laws, in all their positivity and mutability, are to be derived (not, usually, deduced: see X.7) from unchanging principles—principles that have their force from their reasonableness, not from any originating acts or circumstances. Still, even the reader who has not been brought up to believe that 'natural law' can be summed up in the slogan *'lex injusta non est lex'* will wish a little more to be said about that slogan and about the effect of unjust exercises of authority upon our responsibilities as reasonable persons.

The ultimate basis of rulers' authority is the fact that they have the opportunity, and thus the responsibility, of furthering the common good by stipulating solutions to a community's co-ordination problems: see IX.4. Normally, though not necessarily, the immediate source of this opportunity and responsibility is the fact that they are designated by or under some authoritative rule as bearers of authority in respect of certain aspects of those problems: see IX.4, X.3. In any event, authority is useless for the common good unless the stipulations of those in authority (or which emerge through the formation of authoritative customary rules) are treated as exclusionary reasons, i.e. as sufficient reason for acting notwithstanding that subjects would not themselves have made the same stipulation and indeed considers the actual stipulation to be in some respect(s) unreasonable, not fully appropriate for the common good...: see IX.1, IX.2. The principles set out in the preceding three sentences control our understanding both of the types of injustice in the making and administration of law, and of the consequences of such injustice.

XII.2   TYPES OF INJUSTICE IN LAW

First, since authority is derived solely from the needs of the common good, the use of authority by rulers is radically defective if they exploit their opportunities by making stipulations intended by them not for the common good but for their own or their friends' or party's or faction's advantage, or out of malice against some person or group. In making this judgment, we should not be deflected by the fact that most legal systems do not permit the exercise of 'constitutional' powers to be challenged on the ground that that exercise was improperly motivated. These restrictions on judicial review are justified, if at all, either by pragmatic considerations or by a principle of separation of powers. In either case, they have no application to reasonable people assessing the claims of authority upon them. On the other hand, it is quite possible that an improperly motivated law may happen to be in its contents compatible with justice and even promote the common good.

Secondly, since the location of authority is normally determined by authoritative rules dividing up authority and jurisdiction amongst separate office-holders, office-holders may wittingly or unwittingly exploit their opportunity to affect people's conduct, by making stipulations which stray beyond their authority. Except in 'emergency' situations (see X.5) in which the law (even the constitution) should be bypassed and in which the source of authority reverts to its ultimate basis (see IX.4), an *ultra vires* act is an abuse of power and an injustice to those treated as subject to it. (The injustice is 'distributive' inasmuch as these officials improperly assume to themselves an excess of authority, and 'commutative' inasmuch as they improperly seek to subject others to their own 'official' decisions.) Lawyers sometimes are surprised to hear the *ultra vires* actions of an official categorized as abuse of power, since they are accustomed to thinking of such actions as 'void and of no effect' in law. But such surprise is misplaced; legal rules about void and voidable acts are 'deeming' rules, directing judges to treat actions, which are empirically more or less effective, *as if* they had not occurred (at least, as juridical acts), or *as if* from a certain date they had been overridden by an *intra vires* act of repeal or annulment. Quite reasonably, purported juridical acts of officials are commonly presumed to be lawful, and are treated as such by both fellow officials and laymen, unless and until judicially held otherwise. Hence, *ultra vires* official acts, even those which are not immune-for-procedural-or-pragmatic-reasons from successful challenge, will usually subject persons to effects which cannot afterwards be undone; and the bringing about of (the likelihood of) such effects is an abuse of power and an unjust imposition.

Thirdly, the exercise of authority in conformity with the Rule of Law normally is greatly to the common good (even when it restricts the efficient pursuit of other objectives); it is an important aspect of the commutative justice of treating people as entitled to the dignity of self-direction (see X.4), and of the distributive justice of affording all an equal opportunity of understanding and complying with the law. Thus, the exercise of legal authority otherwise than in accordance with due requirements of manner and form is an abuse and an injustice, unless those involved consent, or ought to consent, to an accelerated procedure in order to cut out 'red tape' which in the circumstances would prejudice substantial justice (cf. VII.7).

Fourthly, what is stipulated may suffer from none of these defects of intention, author, and form, and yet be substantively unjust. It may be distributively unjust, by appropriating some aspect of the common stock, or some benefit of common life or enterprise, to a class not reasonably entitled to it on any of the criteria of distributive justice, while denying it to other persons; or by imposing on some a burden from which others

are, on no just criterion, exempt. It may be commutatively
unjust, by denying to one, some, or everyone an absolute
human right, or a human right the exercise of which is in the
circumstances possible, consistent with the reasonable requirements of public order, public health, etc., and compatible with
the due exercise both of other human rights and of the same
human rights by other persons (see VII.4–5, VIII.7).

XII.3 EFFECTS OF INJUSTICE ON OBLIGATION

How does injustice, of any of the foregoing sorts, affect the obligation to obey the law?

It is essential to specify the exact sense of this question. Any
sound jurisprudence will recognize that someone uttering the
question might conceivably mean by 'obligation to obey the law'
either: (i) empirical liability to be subjected to sanction in event
of non-compliance; or (ii) legal obligation in the intra-systemic
sense ('legal obligation in the legal sense') in which the practical
premiss that conformity to law is socially necessary is a framework principle insulated from the rest of practical reasoning; or
(iii) legal obligation in the moral sense (i.e. the moral obligation
that presumptively is entailed by legal obligation in the intra-
systemic or legal sense); or (iv) moral obligation deriving not
from the legality of the stipulation-of-obligation but from some
'collateral' source (to be explained shortly). None of these interpretations is absurd, and a sound jurisprudence will show to
what extent the answers to each will differ and to what extent
they are interrelated.

An unsound jurisprudential method will seek to banish the
question, in some of its senses, to 'another discipline',[1] or even
declare those senses to be nonsense. Thus, John Austin:

Now, to say that human laws which conflict with the divine law are
not binding, that is to say, are not laws, *is to talk stark nonsense.*
The most pernicious laws, and therefore those which are most opposed
to the will of God, have been and are continually enforced as laws by
judicial tribunals. Suppose an act innocuous, or positively beneficial,
be prohibited by the sovereign under the penalty of death; if
I commit this act, I shall be tried and condemned, and if I object

---

[1] Cf. Hart, *Concept of Law*, 205 [209].

to the sentence, that it is contrary to the law of God, who has commanded that human lawgivers shall not prohibit acts which have no evil consequences, the Court of Justice will demonstrate the inconclusiveness of my reasoning by hanging me up, in pursuance of the law of which I have impugned the validity.[2]

I need not comment on the tone of this treatment of unjust law and conscientious objection. What concerns us is the methodological obtuseness of the words here italicized, the failure to allow that one and the same verbal formulation may bear differing though not necessarily unrelated meanings, and express questions whose interrelations and differences can fruitfully be explored.

The first of the four conceivable senses of the question listed above is the least likely, in practice, to be intended by anyone raising the question. (Nevertheless, it is the only sense which Austin explicitly recognizes.) If one asks how injustice affects one's obligation to conform to law, one is not likely to be asking for information on the practically important but theoretically banal point of fact, 'Am I or am I not likely to be hanged for non-compliance with this law?'

The second of the four listed senses of the question of obligation might seem, at first glance, to be empty. For what is the point of asking whether there is a legal obligation in the legal sense to conform to a stipulation which is in the legal sense obligatory? This objection is, however, too hasty. In my discussion of the formal features of legal order (X.3), of the Rule of Law (X.4), and of legal obligation (XI.4), I emphasized the way in which the enterprise of exercising authority through law proceeds by positing a system of rules which derive their authority not from the intrinsic appropriateness of their content but from the fact of stipulation in accordance with rules of stipulation. I emphasized the degree to which the resulting system is conceived of, in legal thought, as internally complete ('gapless') and coherent, and thus as sealed off (so to speak) from the unrestricted flow of practical reasoning about what is just and for the common good. I treated these 'model' features of legal system and legal thought not as mere items in some 'legal logic' (which as a matter of logic could certainly differ widely from that model!), but as practically reasonable

---

[2] *Province*, 185 (emphasis added).

responses to the need for security and predictability, a need which is indeed a matter of justice and human right. But all this should not disguise the extent to which legal thought in fact (and reasonably) does allow the system of rules to be permeated by principles of practical reasonableness which derive their authority from their appropriateness (in justice and for the common good) and not, or not merely, from their origin in some past act of stipulation or some settled usage. The legal system, even when conceived strictly as a set of normative meaning-contents (in abstraction from institutions, processes, personnel, and attitudes), is more open than the model suggests—open, that is to say, to the unrestricted flow of practical reasoning, in which a stipulation, valid according to the system's formal criteria of validity ('rules of recognition'), may be judged to be, or to have become, unjust and, therefore, after all, wholly or partially inapplicable.

In some legal systems this openness to unvarnished claims about the injustice of an existing or purported law is particularly evident, as in the United States. In others, as in English law, it is less obvious but is still familiar to lawyers, for example from the 'golden rule' that statutes are to be interpreted so as to avoid 'absurdity' or injustice, and from the debates, quite frequent in the highest courts, about the propriety of amending or abandoning even well-established rules or 'doctrines' of common law. Those who doubt or minimize the presence of open-ended principles of justice in professional legal thought will usually be found, on close examination, to be making a constitutional claim, viz. that the judiciary ought to leave change and development of law to the legislature. Conversely, those who stress the pervasiveness of such principles and minimize the coverage of practical problems by black-and-white rules will usually be found to be advancing the contradictory constitutional claim. In other words, what is presented[3] as a dispute about the 'legal system' *qua* set of normative meaning-contents is in substance, typically, a dispute about the 'legal system' *qua* constitutional order of institutions.

In short, even in well-developed legal orders served by a professional caste of lawyers, there are (and reasonably) quite a few opportunities of raising 'intra-systemically', for example

---

[3] As in Dworkin, *Taking Rights Seriously* (London: 1977), chs 2–4.

before a court of law, the question whether what would otherwise be an indubitable legal obligation is in truth not (*legally*)
obligatory because it is unjust. On the other hand, since there is
little point in meditating about the legal-obligation-imposing
force of normative meaning-contents which are not treated as
having legal effect in the principal legal institutions of a community (viz. the courts), it is idle to go on asking the question
in this sense (the second of the four listed) after the highest
court has ruled that in its judgment the disputed law is not
unjust or, if unjust, is none the less law, legally obligatory, and
judicially enforceable. It is not conducive to clear thought, or to
any good practical purpose, to smudge the positivity of law by
denying the legal obligatoriness *in the legal or intra-systemic sense*
of a rule recently affirmed as legally valid and obligatory by the
highest institution of the 'legal system'. (Austin's concern to
make this point, in the 'hanging me up' passage, was quite reasonable.
What was unreasonable was his failure to acknowledge (a) the
limited relevance of the point, and (b) the existence of questions
which may be expressed in the same language but which are not
determinately answerable intra-systemically.)

The question in its *third* sense therefore arises in clear-cut
form when one is confident that the legal institutions of one's
community will not accept that the law in question is affected by
the injustice one discerns in it. The question can be stated thus:
Given that legal obligation presumptively entails a moral obligation, and that the legal system is by and large just, does a
particular unjust law impose upon me any moral obligation to
conform to it?

Notoriously, many people (let us call them 'positivists') propose that this question should not be tackled in 'jurisprudence'
but should be left to 'another discipline', no doubt 'political
philosophy' or 'ethics'. Now it is not a purpose of this book to
conduct a polemic against anybody's conception of the limits of
jurisprudence. Suffice it to mention some disadvantages of
this proposal. First, the proposed division is artificial to the
extent that the arguments and counter-arguments which it is
proposed to expel from jurisprudence are in fact (as we observed
in the preceding paragraphs) to be found on the lips of
lawyers in court and of judges giving judgment. Of course,

the arguments about justice and obligation that find favour in the courts of a given community at a given time may be arguments that would be rejected by a sound and critical ethics or political philosophy. But they are part of the same realm of discourse. One will not understand either the 'logic' or the 'sociology' of one's own or anyone else's legal system unless one is aware (not merely in the abstract but in detail) how both the arguments in the courts, and the formulation of norms by 'theoretical' jurists, are affected, indeed permeated, by the vocabulary, the syntax, and the principles of the 'ethics' and 'political philosophy' of that community, or of its elite or professional caste. In turn, one will not well understand the ethics or political philosophy of that community or caste unless one has reflected on the intrinsic problems of 'ethics' and 'political philosophy', i.e. on the basic aspects of human well-being and the methodological requirements of practical reasonableness. Finally, one will not well understand these *intrinsic* problems and principles unless one is aware of the extent to which the language in which one formulates them for oneself, and the concepts which one 'makes one's own', are themselves the symbols and concepts of a particular human civilization, a civilization which has worked itself out, as much as anywhere, in its law courts and law schools. This set of considerations affords the first reason why I would not myself accept the proposal to banish to some 'other discipline' the question of the moral obligation of an unjust law.

The second reason, not unconnected with the first, is to be found in the argument, developed in my first chapter and not to be repeated here, that a jurisprudence which aspires to be more than the lexicography of a particular culture cannot solve its theoretical problems of definition or concept-formation unless it draws upon at least some of the considerations of values and principles of practical reasonableness which are the subject-matter of 'ethics' (or 'political philosophy'). Since there can be no sharp distinction between the 'two disciplines' at that basic level, it is not clear why the distinction, if such there be, should be thought so very important at other levels.

The third reason is that (not surprisingly, in view of what I have just said) the programme of separating off from jurisprudence all questions or assumptions about the moral significance of law is not consistently carried through by those who propose it. Their works are replete with more or less undiscussed assumptions such as that the formal features of legal order contribute to the practical reasonableness of making, maintaining, and obeying law; that these formal features have some connection with the concept of justice and that, conversely, lawyers are justified in thinking of certain principles of justice as principles of *legality*;[4] and that the fact that a stipulation is *legally* valid gives some reason, albeit not conclusive, for treating it as *morally* obligatory or *morally* permissible to act in accordance with it.[5] But none of these assumptions can be shown to be warranted, or could even be discussed, without transgressing the proposed boundary between jurisprudence and moral or political philosophy—in the way that I have systematically 'transgressed' it in the preceding five chapters. Thus, the state of the scholarly literature testifies, so to speak, to what a sound philosophy of practical reason establishes abstractly: the principles of practical reasonableness and their requirements form one unit of inquiry which can be subdivided into 'moral', 'political', and 'jurisprudential' only for a pedagogical or expository convenience which risks falsifying the understanding of all three.

What, then, are we to say in reply to the question whether an unjust law creates a moral obligation *in the way* that just law *of itself does?* The right response begins by recalling that the stipulations of those in authority have presumptive obligatory force (in the eyes of the reasonable person thinking unrestrictedly about what to do) only because of what is needed if the common good is to be secured and realized.

All my analyses of authority and obligation can be summed up in the following theorem: rulers have, very strictly speaking, no right to be obeyed (see XI.7); but they have the authority to give directions and make laws that are morally obligatory and that they have the responsibility of enforcing. They have this authority for the sake of the common good (the needs of which can also, however, make authoritative the opinions—as in custom—or stipulations of people who have no authority). Therefore, if they use their authority to make stipulations against the common

---

[4] See Hart, *Concept of Law*, 156–7 [160–1], 202 [206].
[5] See *ibid.*, 206–7 [211].

good, or against any of the basic principles of practical reasonableness, any such stipulation altogether lacks the authority it would otherwise have *by virtue of being theirs*. More precisely, stipulations made for partisan advantage, or (without emergency justification) in excess of legally defined authority, or imposing inequitable burdens on their subjects, or directing the doing of things that should never be done, simply fail, of themselves, to create any moral obligation whatever.

This conclusion should be read with precision. First, it should not be concluded that an enactment which itself is for the common good and compatible with justice is deprived of its moral authority by the fact that the act of enacting it was rendered unjust by the partisan motives of its author. Just as we should not be deflected from adjudging the act of enactment unjust by the fact that improper motivation is not, in a given system, ground for judicial review, so we should not use the availability of judicial review for that ground, in certain other systems of law, as a sufficient basis for concluding that private citizens (to whom is not entrusted the duty of disciplining wayward officials or institutions) are entitled to treat the improper motives of the author of a just law as exempting them from their moral duty of compliance. Secondly, it should not be concluded that the distributive injustice of a law exempts from its moral obligation those who are *not* unjustly burdened by it.

Understood with those precisions, my response to the question in its third sense corresponds to the classical position: viz. that for the purpose of assessing one's legal obligations in the moral sense, one is entitled to discount laws that are 'unjust' in any of the ways mentioned. Such laws lack the moral authority that in other cases comes simply from their origin, 'pedigree', or formal source. In this way, then, *lex injusta non est lex* and *virtutem obligandi non habet* [does not have authority to bind],[6] whether or not it is 'legally valid' and 'legally obligatory' in the restricted sense that it (i) emanates from a legally authorized source, (ii) will in fact

---

[6] Aquinas, *S.T.* I–II q. 96 a. 6c; he is referring back to the discussion in a. 4, which (having quoted Augustine's remark (see XII.4 below) about unjust laws not seeming to be law) concludes: 'So such [unjust] laws do not oblige in the forum of conscience (except no doubt where the giving of a corrupting example [*scandalum*] or the occasioning of civil disorder [*turbationem*] are to be avoided—for to avoid these, one ought to yield one's right)'. He adds that the last-mentioned

be enforced by courts and/or other officials, and/or (iii) is commonly spoken of as a law like other laws.

But at the same time I must add that the last-mentioned facts, on which the lawyer *qua* lawyer (normally but, as I have noted, not exclusively) may reasonably concentrate, are not irrelevant to the moralist—to reasonable persons with their unrestricted perspective.

At this point there emerges our question in the *fourth* of the senses I listed at the beginning of this section. It may be the case, for example, that if I am *seen* by fellow citizens to be disobeying or disregarding this 'law', the effectiveness of other laws, and/or the general respect of citizens for the authority of a generally desirable ruler or constitution, will probably be weakened, with probable bad consequences for the common good. Does not this collateral fact create a moral obligation? The obligation is to comply with the law, but it should not be treated as an instance of what I have called 'legal obligation in the moral sense'. For it is not based on the good of *being* law-abiding, but only on the desirability of not rendering ineffective the just parts of the legal system. Hence, it will not require compliance with unjust laws according to their tenor or 'legislative intent', but only such degree of compliance as is necessary to avoid bringing 'the law' (as a whole) 'into contempt'. This degree of compliance will vary according to time, place, and circumstance; in some limiting cases (e.g. of judges or other officials administering the law) the morally required degree of compliance may amount to full or virtually full compliance, just *as if* the law in question had been a just enactment.

So, if an unjust stipulation is, in fact, homogeneous with other laws in its formal source, in its reception by courts and officials, and in its common acceptance, the good citizen may (not always) be morally required to conform to that stipulation to the extent necessary to avoid weakening 'the law', the legal

'exceptional' source or form of obligation to obey the law does not obtain where the injustice of the law is that it promotes something which ought never to be done (forbidden by divine law). Later he speaks similarly of unjust judgments of courts (for 'the sentence of the judge is like a particular law for a particular case': II–II q. 67 a. 1c): e.g. II–II q. 69 a. 4c, mentioning again *scandalum* and *turbatio*. See also II–II q. 70 a. 1 ad 2 (the obligation *de jure naturali* to keep a secret may prevail over human law compelling testimony).

system (of rules, institutions, and dispositions) as a whole. The rulers still have the responsibility of repealing rather than enforcing their unjust law, and in this sense have no right that it should be conformed to. But the citizen, or official, may meanwhile have the diminished, collateral, and in an important sense extra-legal obligation to obey it.

The foregoing paragraphs oversimplify the problems created for the conscience of reasonable citizens by unreasonableness in lawmaking. They pass over the problems of identifying inequity in distribution of burdens, or excessive or wrongly motivated exercise of authority. They pass over the dilemmas faced by conscientious officials charged with the administration of unjust laws. They pass over all questions about the point at which it may be for the common good to replace a persistently unjust lawmaker, by means that are prohibited by laws of a type normally justified both in their enactment and in their application. They pass over the question whether, notwithstanding the normal impropriety of bringing just laws into contempt, there may be circumstances in which it is justified to use one's public disobedience, whether to an unjust law itself or to a law itself quite just, as an instrument for effecting reform of unjust laws. And they pass over the question whether, in the aftermath of an unjust regime, the responsibility for declaring its unjust laws unjust and for annulling and undoing their legal and other effects should be undertaken by *courts* (on the basis that a court of justice-according-to-law ought not to be required to attribute legal effect to radically unjust laws), or by retrospective *legislation* (on the basis that the change from one legal regime to the other ought to be explicit).

Much can be said on such questions, but little that is not highly contingent upon social, political, and cultural variables. It is universally true that one has an absolute (liberty-)right not to perform acts which anyone has an absolute (claim-)right that one should not perform (see VIII.7). But beyond this, one should not expect generally usable but precise guides for action in circumstances where the normally authoritative sources of precise guidance have partially broken down.

XII.4 'LEX INJUSTA NON EST LEX'

St. Augustine in his early dialogue on Free Will makes one of his characters say, rather breezily, 'a law that was unjust wouldn't seem to be law'.[7] Plato and Cicero had made the same point in less contorted a fashion,[8] and Aristotle often made similar remarks;[9] but the Augustinian formulation for long enjoyed more prominence. Aquinas quoted it, but at that point and elsewhere offered his own more measured renderings: unjust laws (by which he meant, as he carefully explained, laws defective in any of the ways mentioned in XII.2 above) are 'more outrages than laws',[10] 'not law but a corruption of law'.[11] More precisely, he says that such a law is 'not a law *simpliciter* [i.e. straightforwardly, or in the focal sense], but rather a sort of perversion of law'; but, as he immediately adds, it does have the character of law in one important respect: it is the command of a superior to subordinates (and in this respect is calculated to render the members of the community 'good', through their compliance with it—not (of course) good *sim-*

---

[7] *De libero arbitrio*, I, v, 11: '*nam mihi lex esse non videtur quae justa non fuerit*'.

[8] Plato, *Laws*, IV: 715b: 'Societies [in which the winners of the competition for office reserve the conduct of public affairs wholly to themselves] are no constitutional states [*out einai politeias*], just as enactments, so far as they are not for the common interest of the whole community, are no true laws [*out orthous nomous*]; men who are for a party, we say, are factionaries, not citizens, and their so-called rights are empty words' (trans. A. E. Taylor); cf. also IV: 712e–713a; *Statesman*, 293d–e; *Rep.* IV: 422e; Cicero, *De Legibus*, II, v, 11 (quoted at p. 292 above); *De Re Publica*, III, xxxi, 43.

[9] E.g. *Pol.* III.4: 1279a17–22; III.5: 1280b7–9; IV.4: 1292a31–34 ('... it would seem to be a reasonable criticism to say that such a rule-of-the-many is not a constitution at all; for where the laws do not govern there is no constitution... an organization of this kind, in which all things are administered by [*ad hoc*] resolutions of the assembly is not even a democracy in the proper sense...' (trans. Barker).

[10] '*magis sunt violentiae quam leges*': *S.T.* I–II q. 96 a. 4c. Cf. q. 90 a. 1 ad 3: '*magis iniquitas quam lex*'.

[11] '*non lex sed legis corruptio*': *S.T.* I–II q. 95 a. 2c. This is the phrase adopted by St. German, *Doctor and Student*, First Dialogue (Latin) (1523, 1528), c. 2 ('*non sunt statuta sive consuetudines sed corruptele*', rendered in the English version [1531] as 'no prescriptions statutes nor customs but things void and against justice'; the English of the Second Dialogue [1530], c. 15, is elliptical but happier: 'where the law of man is in itself directly against the law of reason or else the law of God and then properly it cannot be called a law but a corruption'.

pliciter, but good relative to that (tyrannical, unreasonable) regime).[12]

Thus, Aquinas carefully avoids saying flatly that 'an unjust law is not a law: *lex injusta non est lex*'. But in the end it would have mattered little had he said just that.[13] For the statement either is pure nonsense, flatly self-contradictory, or else is a dramatization of the point more literally made by Aquinas when he says that an unjust law is not law in the focal sense of the term 'law' (i.e. *simpliciter*) notwithstanding that it is law in a secondary sense of that term (i.e. *secundum quid*).

Perhaps we can dwell on this a little. The central tradition of natural law theorizing in which the *'lex injusta ...'* doctrine is embedded has not chosen to use the slogans attributed to it by modern critics, for example that *'what is utterly immoral* cannot be law',[14] or that *'certain rules* cannot be law because of their moral iniquity',[15] or that *'these evil things* are not law',[16] or that *'nothing iniquitous* can *anywhere* have the status of law',[17] or that 'morally iniquitous *demands...*[are] *in no sense* law',[18] or that *'there cannot be* an unjust law'.[19] On the contrary, the tradition, even in its most blunt formulations,[20] has affirmed that unjust LAWS are not law. Does not this formula itself

---

[12] 'lex tyrannica, cum non sit secundum rationem, non est simpliciter lex, sed magis est quaedam perversitas legis. Et tamen inquantum habet aliquid de ratione legis intendit ad hoc quod cives sint boni; non enim habet de ratione legis nisi secundum hoc quod est dictamen alicujus praesidentis in subditis: et ad hoc tendit ut subditi legis sint bene obedientes; quod est eos esse bonos, non simpliciter sed in ordine ad tale regimen': *S.T.* I–II q. 92 a. 1 ad 4; see also the notes to this section, below.

[13] He does say that an unjust judgment of a court is not a judgment (*injustum judicium judicium non est*): *S.T.* II–II q. 70 a. 4 ad 2. But recall (p. 206) that in listing the meanings of *jus*, Aquinas had noted that even an unjust judgment can be called a *jus* (because it is the judge's *duty* to do justice): *S.T.* II–II q. 57 a. 1 ad 1. What we see here (as so often in classical social philosophy) is not self-contradiction but a supple subordination of words to a shifting focus of interest.

[14] Hart, 'Positivism and the Separation of Law and Morals' (1958) 71 *Harv. L. Rev.* 593, reprinted in Dworkin (ed.), *The Philosophy of Law* (Oxford: 1977), 17 at 33 (emphasis added).

[15] *Ibid.* (emphasis added).

[16] *Ibid.,* 34 (emphasis added).

[17] Hart, *Concept of Law,* 206 [210] (emphasis added).

[18] *Ibid.,* 205 [210] (emphasis added).

[19] Arthur C. Danto, 'Human Nature and Natural Law', in S. Hook (ed.), *Law and Philosophy* (New York: 1964), 187 (emphasis added), ascribing this *'dictum'* to 'the Thomistic defenders of natural law'.

[20] E.g. Blackstone, I *Comm.* 41 (quoted in notes to II.2).

make clear, beyond reasonable question, that the tradition is not indulging in 'a refusal, made *once and for all*, to recognize evil laws as valid *for any purpose*'?[21] Far from 'den[ying] legal validity to iniquitous rules',[22] the tradition explicitly (by speaking of 'unjust *laws*')[23] accords to iniquitous rules legal validity, whether on the ground and in the sense that these rules are accepted in the courts as guides to judicial decision, or on the ground and in the sense that, in the judgment of the speaker, they satisfy the criteria of validity laid down by constitutional or other legal rules, or on both these grounds and in both these senses. The tradition goes so far as to say that there may be an obligation to conform to some such unjust laws in order to uphold respect for the legal system as a whole (what I called a 'collateral obligation': see XII.3).[24]

There is no need to repeat here the analysis of normative statements offered in IX.2. It will be recalled that such statements may, in one and the same grammatical form, intend to assert (S_1) what is justified or required by practical reasonableness *simpliciter*, or (S_2) what is treated as justified or required in the belief or practice of some group, or (S_3) what is justified or required if certain principles or rules are justified (but without taking any position on the question whether those principles or rules *are* so justified). And it will be recalled how natural and frequent it is to shift from the expository (S_3) or sociological/historical (S_2) viewpoint to the fully critical (S_1) viewpoint within the space of a single sentence. *Lex injusta non est lex* is such a sentence: it implies (i) that some normative meaning-content has for some community the status (S_2/S_3) of law, (ii) that that law is unjust (a critical judgment of practical reasonableness, whether correct or incorrect), and (iii) that compliance with that law is (S_1) *not* justified or required by the derivative and defeasible principle of practical reasonableness that laws impose moral obligations.

Plato, Aristotle, Augustine, and Aquinas did not draw attention to the distinction between the intra-systemic expository

---

[21] Hart, *Concept of Law*, 206–7 [211] (emphasis added); and see 152 [156], ascribing that view to 'the Thomist tradition'.

[22] *Ibid.*, 207 [211].

[23] And such references are not merely in the context of '*non est lex*' formulations: see e.g. *S.T.* I–II q. 94 a. 6 ad 3.

[24] *S.T.* I–II q. 96 a. 4c and ad 3.

viewpoint, the historical/sociological viewpoint, and the viewpoint of unrestricted practical reasonableness. They took it for
granted, and shifted easily from one to another while treating
the last-mentioned viewpoint as their primary concern: 'we hold
that, in all such matters [pertaining to human passions and
actions], whatever appears to the mature person of practical
wisdom [the *spoudaios*] to be the case really is the case'.[25]
They did employ a technical device to signal their consciousness
of differing viewpoints, and of the consequently different intentions of identical sentences. It was the device of distinguishing
between focal meaning ('X *simpliciter*', '*vere* X', 'X *proprie*', etc.)
and secondary meanings ('X *secundum quid* [in some respect]', 'X
secundum aliquem modum [in a certain way]', 'X *secundum similitudinem*', 'X *cum aliqua adjectione* [with some modification]', etc.)
within one and the same discourse or theoretical discipline.[26]

This technical device is justified and indeed indispensable in
any philosophy of human affairs, given the variety of human
concerns and projects, reasonable and unreasonable (see I.3). But
while it enables us to register the degrees to which the elements
of some complex concept are instantiated by various particular
states of affairs, all assessed from one viewpoint, the device does
not register, with all the explicitness that could be desired, the
difference between the meanings of statements which results
from differences in *viewpoint* or theoretical or practical *purposes*.
The device does allow a use of terms which is the primary or
exclusive use from one viewpoint to be admitted as a secondary
use in discourse which is controlled by some other viewpoint.
But it fails (i) to make explicit what the difference of viewpoints
is, and (ii) to clarify the relationship of interdependence or one-
way dependence or, as the case may be, independence between
the different viewpoints and their respective usages. Hence, the
need to supplement the traditional formulations (see also X.2) in
the way I have attempted in IX.2 and in the present section.

---

[25] Aristotle, *Nic. Eth.* X.5: 1176a16–17; the first set of bracketed words is inserted by Aquinas
in his commentary *ad loc*, *in Eth.* X, lect. 8, para. 2062. See also *Nic. Eth.* I.8: 1099a11–15; III.4:
1113a22–33; X.6: 1176b26; and notes to V.1 above.

[26] The Latin phrases are all to be found in Aquinas's commentary on Aristotle's discussion of
'citizen' and citizenship (*Pol.* III.1: 1274b32–1275b34); Aquinas, *in Pol.* III, i. See I.3–4, esp. pp. 9, 11
and 15 n. 37 above.

NOTES

XII.2

Types of injustice of laws...See Aquinas, *S.T.* I–II q. 96 a. 4c; St. German, *Doctor and Student*, First Dial., c. 4; Suarez, *De Legibus*, Book I, c. 9, paras 12–16.

XII.3

Consequences of injustice of laws...See Suarez, *De Legibus*, Book I, c. 9, paras 11–12, 20.

Unjust legislative motives may be disregarded if the enactment itself is reasonable...See *De Legibus*, Book I, c. 9, paras 11–12, 20; *Doctor and Student*, I, c. 26.

Collateral moral obligation to obey the law ...See *S.T.* I–II q. 96 a. 4. Such an obligation may arise from quite different sorts of reasons; e.g. from one's duty to one's family to avoid the punishment that would come from breaking the law.

Undoing the effects of unjust laws... The celebrated debate between Hart and Fuller on this point comes down to a question of constitutional niceties, of purely symbolic implications, and of convenience in settling details: cf. (1958) 71 *Harv. L. Rev.* 618–20 (Hart) and 655 (Fuller); Fuller, *Morality of Law*, Appendix.

XII.4

'Lex injusta non est lex'...A vigorous modern formulation is P. T. Geach, *The Virtues* (Cambridge: 1977), 128: 'University people argue mightily about whether laws that violate these principles are laws or (as Aquinas called them) mere violence. Of course it doesn't matter whether you *call* them laws or not: the question is what consequences follow. An unjust piece of legislation exists *de facto*, as an institution: but it is no debt of justice to observe it, though it may be imprudent to ignore it. And though a private person should not lightly judge a law to be unjust, its contrariety to the Law of Nature and the peace and justice of society may be so manifest that such a judgment is assured. A sufficient mass of unjust legislation may justify a man in deciding that the civil authority is a mere Syndicate. I think Old John Brown rightly so judged about the slave-owning U.S. commonwealths of his time. Rebellion, however, is another matter, because the evils it may bring about are so great: whether Old John Brown judged rightly about this is a matter we must leave between Old John Brown and his Maker...'. Aquinas himself was something of a 'University person', and his account is (as I have tried to show) a little more nuanced than Geach's. But he would certainly have agreed that (except for some special purpose) 'it doesn't matter whether you *call* them laws or not: the question is what consequences follow'.

Aquinas on tyrannical laws and 'law' and 'good' simpliciter...The passage from *S.T.* I–II q. 92 a. 1 ad 4, translated in the text and reproduced in the footnotes, is Aquinas's reply to someone who objected (against his claim that the point of law is to make people good) that there are tyrannical laws, intended by their makers for their own benefit and not to make people good. Aquinas's reply significantly concedes that there are indeed such laws, and tries to show that, though not in the strictest sense 'laws', they share in the nature of law not only as being the directives of rulers to their subjects *but also* as having (in a misdirected way) the same sort of social function. See also the body of the article which further illustrates Aquinas's resolute use of focal meaning: 'If the law-maker's intention bears on true good, namely the common good measured according to divine justice, the consequence will be for men through law [i.e. by complying with it] to become good *simpliciter*. If, however, the intention is not for good without qualification [*simpliciter*], but for what serves his own profit or pleasure, or against divine justice, then the law will make men good, not *simpliciter* but relatively [*secundum quid*], namely in relation to that regime. This sort of goodness can be found even in things intrinsically bad; as when we speak of a "good thief", meaning that he operates efficiently'. Cf. also *Nic. Eth.* VI.9: 1142b30–31.

Part Three

XIII

NATURE, REASON, GOD

XIII.1 FURTHER QUESTIONS ABOUT THE POINT OF HUMAN EXISTENCE

WHAT further explanations are required? After all, the basic forms of human flourishing are obvious to anyone acquainted, whether through his or her own inclinations or vicariously through the character and works of others, with the range of human opportunities. And the general requirements of reasonableness (itself one of those basic forms of good) are, likewise, as obvious as the norms of rationality, principles of logic, and canons of explanation that are presupposed in *any* explanation, whether in our practical context or in natural science or analytical philosophy. (Which is not to say that the implications of those requirements, for anyone's commitments, projects, or actions, are all obvious!) Certainly, an analytical exploration of possible and actual social structures, practical norms, individual virtues and vices, and the like, is both possible and not easily exhaustible. But would it not be a mistake to expect any deeper level of explanation of the practical reasonableness of community, authority, law, rights, justice, and obligation, once their explanation has been pursued from practice to self-interest, and thence to the common good which both friendship and rational impartiality require us to respect and favour?

The answer must be: No, we cannot reasonably rest here. There are further practical questions; and there are also further relevant theoretical questions about both the whole structure of norms and requirements of good that has been identified, and the whole structure of explanations already advanced.

The range of relevant further practical questions can be indicated as follows. The basic aspects of human well-being are really and unquestionably good; but after all, they are not abstract forms, they are analytically distinguishable aspects of the well-being, actual or possible, of you and me—of flesh-and-

blood individuals. This is equally true of the common good; it
is the well-being of you and me, considered as individuals with
shared opportunities and vulnerabilities, and the concrete
conditions under which that well-being of particular individuals may be favoured, advanced, and preserved. But of each
and every individual person, and therefore of each and every
community of individuals, it is true that his or her participation
in the various forms of good is, even at best, extremely limited.
Our health fails, our stock of knowledge fades from recall, our
making and appreciation of play and art falters and finishes,
our friendships are ended by distance, time, death; and death
appears to end our opportunities for authenticity, integrity,
practical reasonableness, if despair or decay have not already
done so. We notice the succession of human persons (and of
their communities), evidently separated beyond all contact with
one another by time and distance; and the question arises
whether my good (and the well-being of my communities) has
any *further* point, i.e. whether it relates to any more comprehensive human participation in good.

That question is an extension of, or analogous to, some not
yet adequately settled questions about friendship itself. An
aspect of my well-being is the well-being of my friend; if he
or she is ruined or destroyed, I am worse off. What then is
to be said of (and done in) situations in which his or her well-
being can be secured only by my ruin or destruction? 'What
is the good of it?' This question does not question the good
of my friend's good, either as his or hers or as an aspect of
mine; but it asks whether *further* sense can be made of the
whole situation, in which the limitation on one's participation
in human good arises not from time and decay but from a kind of
conflict of opportunities. Similarly, those who clearly see their
responsibilities to their family or their political community, and
who do not doubt that these responsibilities reasonably may require
self-sacrifice, still may reasonably inquire whether there is any
further *point*, to which both their reasonable self-sacrifice and
the resultant well-being of their community (which itself will
sooner or later come to an end) contribute. (By 'contribution'
is not necessarily meant some cause of chronologically distinct
effects; what is looked for might be some wider pattern in which
the particular situation-and-response in question might 'take

its place', corresponding to some less limited perspective in which it could be seen to 'make [more] sense'.)

Or again, each of us is an item not only in the succession of persons (and their communities) but also in a universe, indefinitely extended in space and time, of entities and states of affairs, many of which have intelligible patterns of flourishing and decay. Of each, and of the ensemble, it is possible to ask whether it too has a good, a point, a value—and, in any case, how that entity or state of affairs, or ensemble of entities and of states of affairs, relates to anybody's good, not to mention my good and my community's.

In the absence of any answers to such questions, the basic human values will seem, to any thoughtful person, to be weakened, in their attractiveness to reasonableness, by a certain relativity or subjectivity—not so much the 'subjectivity' of arbitrary opining, but rather the 'subjectivity' of the *merely* relative to us' (where 'us' has an uncertain but restricted reference).

The urgency with which thoughtful persons press these questions is amply evidenced by the course of human specula-tion. In modern times, the questions, as experienced, create a ready market for interpretations of history which allow questioners to believe that they and their community, race, class, or party are contributing to the attainment of some future plateau to which History will, with their assistance, progress. The assumption about the plateaux of progress, from which Humanity will not regress, can be seen in Mill as plainly as in Marx.[1] The assumption that the basic point of good actions, projects, and commitments consists in their realizing some future good condition of the (then-existing) human race, can be observed in many versions of utilitarianism. The defect (questions of fact and probability aside) in all such responses was noted, near the beginning of the period of their popularity, by Kant:

What remains disconcerting about all this is firstly, that the earlier generations seem to perform their laborious tasks only for the sake of the later ones, so as to prepare for them a further stage from which they can raise still higher the structure intended by nature; and

---

[1] J. S. Mill, *On Liberty* (1859), ch. 1.

secondly, that only the later generations will in fact have the good fortune to inhabit the building on which a whole series of their fore-fathers (admittedly, without any conscious intention) had worked without themselves being able to share in the happiness they were preparing.[2]

Still, Kant himself brushes the problem aside; he will not be deflected from his 'assumption' that 'nature does nothing un-necessarily' (not in the individual, who is mortal, but 'in the species, which is immortal'), not indeed 'by instinct or by the guidance of innate knowledge', but by the 'reason' which 'nature gives' man in order 'to reach its ends'.[3]

In these remarkable passages, Kant makes plain the usually half-expressed assumptions of much modern thought about the point of human life and human good. And, above all, he is resuming, but in relation to a supposed course of 'history', the most important themes touched upon 2,000 years earlier in Stoic thought about *natura*. Since the Stoic speculations (and word-play) on *natura* are an immediate source of the rather un-happy term 'natural law', it is important for us to observe how those speculations are motivated by the same practical questions about the objectivity (as opposed to 'subjectivity' in the already indicated sense) of human goods.

If, for example, we attend to the word *natura* in its 52 appearances in paragraphs 16 to 48 of the first book of Cicero's *De Legibus*,[4] we can readily understand the Stoic opinion, reported by him in his *De Finibus*, III, 73: 'he who is to live

---

[2] 'Idea for a Universal History with a Cosmopolitan Purpose' [1784], trans. H. B. Nisbet in Hans Reiss (ed.), *Kant's Political Writings* (Cambridge: 1970), 44.

[3] All the words, phrases, and ideas are to be found in the first four 'Propositions' in Kant's essay. The anxiety underlying the 'assumption' is revealed by the last sentence of the First Proposition: 'For if we abandon this basic principle, we are faced not by a law-governed nature, but with an aimless, random purpose, and the dismal reign of chance replaces the guiding principles of reason'. See also Kant's essay 'On the Common Saying: "This may be true in theory, but it does not apply in practice"', Part III, 'On the relationship of theory to practice in international right considered from a universally philanthropic, i.e. cosmopolitan point of view' [1792], *ibid.*, 87–91.

[4] Here Cicero is reporting Stoic opinions, explicitly bracketing out the Academic-sceptical opinions to which he himself adhered (with waverings towards Stoic ethics): see *De Legibus*, I, 39. The word-count includes *naturalis*, but excludes one use of *natura* to mean, neutrally, 'the concept of (natura iuris*: I, 17).

[as Stoic ethics commends][5] in accordance with nature [*convenienter naturae*] must reason on the basis of the whole world and its government. Nor can anyone judge truly of good and evil, save by knowledge of the whole plan of nature [*omni ratione naturae*] as well as of the life of the gods, and of whether the nature of man is or is not in harmony with universal nature [*utrum conveniat necne natura hominis cum universa*].[6]

Being scholastics, interested in establishing a technical vocabulary, the Stoics were aware that *natura* was a word with a variety of meanings and shifting references. So a characteristic elaboration of a Stoic ethics would refer: (i) to the *prima naturae*,[7] the primary inclinations, needs, or objects of natural impulse, which in human nature are to live (in health of mind and body) and to know;[8] (ii) to the possibility of pursuing the *prima naturae* in a particular and appropriate manner, i.e. reasonably, i.e. by way of a plan harmonious with itself, with human *natura*, and with universal *natura*;[9] (iii) to the aspects of human and universal *natura* which reason (in natural philosophy: i.e. *physica*, the *explicatio naturae*)[10] discovers by investigation and comparison, for example, the fact that familial affection, being conducive to procreation and education, is natural not only as instinctive but also as being consistent with the maintenance of particular human beings in being[11] or that there is a *cosmopolis*, a universal community of gods and men, into which each of us is born, and which it is therefore fitting (*conveniens naturae*) for each of us to prefer, as any whole takes precedence over its parts;[12] (iv) to the fact that virtue, i.e. living-according-to-reason, not only is guided by (a) the

[5] See *De Finibus*, III, 26, 31, 34; *De Republica*, III, 33.

[6] Likewise *De Finibus*, II, 34: for the Stoics the supreme good is harmony with nature (*consentire naturae*), which they interpret as meaning living virtuously, i.e. *honeste*, which they explain as living 'with an understanding of the natural course of events [*cum intelligentia rerum earum quae natura evenirent*], choosing those things that are in accordance with nature [*secundum naturam*] and rejecting contrary things'; similarly IV, 14.

[7] Cicero, *De Finibus*, III, 21. Synonyms are *prima secundum naturam* (V, 18, 19, 45); *prima naturalia* (II, 34); *prima natura data* (II, 34); *initia naturae* (II, 38); *principia naturae* (III, 22, 23); *principia naturalia* (II, 35; III, 17); *res quae primae appetuntur* (III, 17); etc.

[8] *Ibid.*, III, 16–18.

[9] *Ibid.*, III, 23.

[10] *Ibid.*, III, 73; IV, 12.

[11] *Ibid.*, III, 62.

[12] *Ibid.*, III, 64.

principle that choice is to be in accordance with nature [*secundum naturam*][13] and (b) the object of maintaining one's being *in statu naturae*,[14] but also is actually most characteristic of (natural to) men and gods, these being the only beings, in the whole of *natura*, whose proper *natura* it is to be reasonable;[15] and (v) to the final speculative inference that, by virtue of being reasonable, the human virtue of living-according-to-[human]-nature is also in accordance with the universal *ratio* (intelligence/intelligibility) which informs the whole of nature (the universe or cosmos), and which, being a governing or directive *ratio*, should be called the law of nature (*lex naturae*), establishing a universal rightness or justice (*jus naturale*).[16]

In such an elaboration, the phases of the argument are fairly distinct, or at any rate distinguishable; but it is virtually impossible to prevent the meaning or reference of *natura*, as used in one phase, from flooding into its use in the other phases. And it is the meaning of *natura* in phase (v) which is most pervasive, and which by implication and anticipation most helps forward the 'argument'. For the Stoic, human life has its meaning, choice its significance, practical reason its objectivity, just in so far as they fit into the vast divine plan (*logos*) of the cosmos, one aspect of which is the cosmopolis of gods and men in the harmony (*homologia*) of their respective communities.

Phases (i) and (ii) of the foregoing elaboration may have reminded the reader of my distinction between (i) the basic forms of human good, and (ii) the basic requirements of practical reasonableness. Indeed, there are obvious similarities. But the Stoic conception of ethics or natural law (in both its Hellenistic/Roman and its post-Renaissance formulations) differs in a fundamental respect from the conception advanced both in earlier chapters of this book and in the Platonic and Aristotelian teachings which the Stoics were recasting. In my explication of practical reasonableness, the fundamental term is 'good(s)'; in the Stoic explication, 'good' has virtually

---

[13] *Ibid.*, III, 12.
[14] *Ibid.*, III, 20.
[15] Cicero, *De Legibus*, I, 25.
[16] Cicero, *De Re Publica*, III, 18; *De Finibus*, III, 71; *De Legibus*, I, 18, 23; II, 10, 16: etc.

disappeared[17] (along with, correspondingly, the difference between practical reasoning and theoretical or speculative reasoning). Of course, the Stoics are more than willing to join in the great Hellenistic debate about the identity of the highest form of good (the *summum bonum* or *finis bonorum*). But their answer is: there is only one good for human beings, namely, virtue—living-according-to-reason/living-according-to-nature.[18] They will invent a whole series of neologisms to avoid calling the *prima naturae* 'good' or 'goods'. Boldly they will declare that, if you wish to compare one's choice of aim in life with someone aiming a spear at a target, then you must admit that the ultimate good, end, or aim that such a person has in view is *not* the target, *nor* the hitting of it, but the aiming straight![19] The concept of good (*notio boni*) is for the Stoic a concept which one only arrives at by a process of inference (*collatio rationis*) which takes off from a prior recognition of things as being in accordance with nature (*secundum naturam*).[20] Hence, Stoics will not choose to formulate their basic practical questions in the way I formulated them at the beginning of this section.

But their teaching is a response to the same anxiety about the 'subjectivity' of human effort. To that anxiety they respond by pointing to the all-embracing order-of-things, intelligible because intelligently ordered; human intelligence has its objectivity and worth by understanding that order; human activity has its objectivity and worth by conforming to the order thus understood, by corresponding, in intention if not in effect, to the intentions of the superintending universal-intelligence. This imposing vision of order and reasonableness is taken as rendering superfluous all further questions, either about the point or good of the whole in itself, or about the point or good-for-man of conforming to it.

Certainly the Stoic thesis has more to commend it than Kant's. Kant postulates a future order-of-things by sheer extrapolation on the basis of nothing more than a hope (or anxiety) which even as hope is, on his own admission, 'disconcerting'. In the bad sense of the term, his thesis is a 'projection'; the

---

[17] The replacement was deliberate and occurred at the very beginning of the Stoic school: see Cicero, *De Legibus*, I, 55.

[18] Cicero, *De Finibus*, III, 36.

[19] *De Finibus*, III, 22; also V, 20.

[20] *Ibid.*, III, 33.

identification and denunciation of such projections is perhaps the principal *modus operandi* of the post-Kantian sceptic. But the Stoic thesis, too, seems to be essentially an expression of piety directed towards a world-order whose order might well be regarded as not altogether admirable, and whose outcome might equally be regarded as a matter of indifference to us. And without the support of that piety, the Stoic cultivation of virtue would be no more than the 'athleticism', the self-cultivation whose vanity Augustine of Hippo remorselessly exposed. Indeed, the Augustinian critique of the athleticism of virtue remains in many respects the most searching objection to any theory of natural law (or of morality) that is restricted to tracing the requirements of practical reasonableness and refuses or fails to respond to the practical questions raised at the beginning of this section.

XIII.2 ORDERS, DISORDERS, AND THE EXPLANATION OF EXISTENCE

Let me restate those practical questions in terms of that 'reasonableness' which is central both to the Stoic analysis and to my own. To be reasonable (well-informed, intelligent, consistent, free from arbitrariness...) is primarily understood as obviously a good for me and for any person, a good as self-evidently and underivatively good as life itself, as play, art, friendship... But is the point of being reasonable simply to be better-off, myself—to be flourishing in one more aspect (even if that aspect be rather strategic or architectonic)?

The proper way to begin an answer to such searchingly reflexive practical questions is to tackle the strictly theoretical (non-practical) questions mentioned but not identified at the beginning of the preceding section. The exploration of these theoretical questions will occupy the next three sections; in XIII.5 the results of that exploration will be brought to bear on the practical questions about the point of reasonableness, the reasonableness of self-sacrifice, the relevance of history and the universe, and the most basic explanation of obligation.

Because the practical questions were, or could well be, framed in terms of 'reasonableness', the theoretical questions start with 'reason'. Reason, intelligence, the mind and its powers, are to be understood not by trying to peer within oneself but by reflecting upon the forms and cumulation of explanations in any of the many fields in which it is possible to advance from ignorance and confusion to some degree of knowledge and clarity. It matters little which field is selected for this reflection.

Consider, therefore, by way of example, the explanations advanced in Chapter XI. In that chapter I was trying to explain (i) certain judgments which (it was assumed) the reader, like the writer, sometimes makes and (ii) secondarily, certain terms and patterns of word-usage that actually obtain in a number of cultures, including our own. The explanations, first of promises and then of obligation(s) in general, themselves fell into a recognizable and intelligible pattern: analysis in terms of the practical context of word-usage could be supplemented by analysis of rational necessities relative first to self-interest and then to the common good. That is to say, phenomena of existent practices, and the instruments and products of collaboration and interaction, could all be related intelligibly to the principles which guide and shape reasonable individual actions, projects, commitments, habits, and attitudes. The pragmatic state of affairs in human conduct and culture and the order of practical reasonableness, while thus related, remained nevertheless distinct; the pragmatic state of affairs, as it actually exists, can be understood only if the effects not only of human unreasonableness, inertia, ignorance, and malice, but also of chance or coincidence are recognized (cf. I.4).

Moreover, the explanatory reference to the common good was itself a summary reference to an elaborate order of explanations in earlier chapters. There, too, I was concerned to explain, first, the practical judgments which we find ourselves making and, secondly, the cultural phenomena of language-usage, customs, institutions, etc., concerning actual and possible human activities. My explanations distinguished inclinations from judgments of value; and distinguished good, considered as a definite objective capable of complete attainment by definite means, from value, considered as a form of good to which one can be committed but which one can realize or attain only by way of a participation which is never completed. Basic values (treated in practical thinking as principles) were identified, and found to be, in their content, parallel with basic inclinations, drives, or urges. A multi-faceted notion of human flourishing was thus developed, such flourishing being understood as capable of realization in a multitude of particular ways, as well as in varying degrees of fullness. Friendship was identified as one aspect of this flourishing, and community as a 'means' indispensable to the realizing of most aspects of human well-being. Parallel with the urge to question, and to reject the unintelligible, were found to be the value of knowledge and understanding (including the understanding being accumulated in this series of explanations itself) and the value of establishing (partly by discovery and partly by commitment and *determinatio*) an intelligible order in one's own actions and one's own interaction with other intelligent beings.

The fact that human beings have a certain range of urges, drives, or inclinations; the fact that these have a certain correspondence, parallelism, or 'fit' with the states of affairs that anyone intelligent would consider constitute human flourishing; the fact that without reasonable direction the inclinations will bring about individual and communal ruin ('natural sanctions'); and the fact that certain psychological, biological, climatic, physical, mechanical, and other like principles, laws, states of affairs, or conditions affect the realization of human well-being in discoverable ways—all these are facts in an order, external to our own understanding, which our understanding can only discover. This order is often called the order of nature. But alongside this are (i) the order of human artefacts (including language, technologies, the formulations of laws, and the design and manifestations of institutions employed to exploit nature for real or supposed human good); (ii) the order of attitudes, habits ('second nature'), commitments, and principles of action, by which individuals shape their lives and interactions more or less intelligently; and (iii) the order of the operations of thought as such, the order of logic, of investigations, critiques, analyses, and explanations (including the reflexive explanation of this order itself, as well as of the others): see VI.2.

The remarkable fact that there is an order of nature which, like the orders of human artefacts, actions, and thoughts, is amenable to human understanding calls for some explanation. Often it has been explained by attributing the order(s) to an ordering intelligence and will, creating or in some other way causing the whole world-order. Kant, for example, considered that, to have an orientation in the scientific investigation of nature, one must postulate 'that a supreme intelligence has ordered all things in accordance with the wisest ends'. 'Moreover', he adds, 'the outcome of my attempts [in explanation of nature] so frequently confirms the usefulness of this postulate, while nothing decisive can be cited against it, that I am saying much too little if I proceed to declare that I hold it merely as an opinion'.[21] Hume, too, in his *Dialogues concerning Natural Religion* [1779], not merely concedes but forcefully stresses and strikingly illustrates the orderliness of the world, and seems to ascribe it to an 'internal, inherent principle of order'[22] which 'first arranged, and still maintains, order in this universe' and 'bears...some remote inconceivable analogy to the other operations of Nature and among the rest to the economy of human mind and thought'.[23]

But, as there is order, so there is lack of order in the world, in terms of all four orders: waste in physical nature, error in reasonings, breakdown in culture, unreasonableness in human attitudes and actions...'The utmost...that the argument [from order] can prove', says Kant, 'is an *architect* of the world who is always very much hampered by the adaptability of the material in which he works, not *creator* of the world to whose idea everything is subject'.[24] 'Look round this universe', says Hume's protagonist: 'the whole presents nothing but the idea of a blind Nature, impregnated by a great vivifying principle, and pouring forth from her lap, without discernment or parental care, her maimed and abortive children!'[25] At any rate, he remarks in more measured terms, the proposition that the cause or causes of order in the universe probably bear some remote analogy to human intelligence, while

---

[21] Immanuel Kant, *Critique of Pure Reason* [1781, 1787], B854; see also B651. On the postulate as a 'regulative ideal' of reason, see B728.

[22] David Hume, *Dialogues concerning Natural Religion* (ed. Kemp Smith, London: 2nd edn, 1947), Part VI, 174.

[23] *Ibid.*, Part XII, 218.

[24] Kant, *Critique of Pure Reason*, B655.

[25] Hume, *Dialogues concerning Natural Religion*, Part XI, 211.

acceptable, is 'ambiguous, at least undefined' and 'not capable
of extension, variation, or more particular explication' and
'affords no inference that affects human life, or [that] can be
the source of any action or forbearance'.[26]

In short, *direct* speculative questions about the significance,
implications, or source of the orderliness of things yield, *by
themselves*, no clear or certain answers. But this is not the end of
the matter. As well as the orderliness of the order(s) of things,
there is their sheer existence—the fact that propositions
picking out states of affairs are sometimes true.[27] Philosophical analysis has gradually refined our undifferentiated
wonder (Why?) about the origin of things, by differentiating
the fact that entities and states of affairs are *what* they are
from the fact *that* they are. There thus remains an alternative
route for investigation, starting with the sort of fact with
which we start in the investigations by which we gain our
knowledge of order, viz. the fact that this or that particular
state of affairs exists (or existed, or will exist). If we are
to understand a number of issues of importance in answering
the practical questions raised at the beginning of this chapter,
and in the history of theories of natural law, we must try to
see what this alternative investigation yields (and has often
been taken to yield).

Consider, for example, this state of affairs: Someone reading
a sentence in this book tomorrow (the day after you, the
present reader, read a sentence in it). Such a state of affairs
may or may not exist. If it does, its existence will be the factor,
distinct from *what* the state of affairs is, that makes true a
proposition picking out that state of affairs. (The proposition
which may thus be made true can be variously stated,
depending on the time of the statement: viz., as stated today,

---

[26] *Ibid.*, Part XII, 227. See also Hume, *An Enquiry concerning Human Understanding* (1748),
sec. XI.

[27] For a much ampler and more rigorous version of the argument in the rest of this section, see
Germain Grisez, *Beyond the New Theism: A Philosophy of Religion* (Notre Dame and London: 1975), chs
4 and 5. In order to avoid the ambiguities of the verb 'to be' and the noun 'existence', and the
consequent well-known philosophical complications, Grisez uses the verb 'to obtain' to refer to the
factor, distinct from *what* a state of affairs is, that makes true a proposition picking out that state of
affairs. Since I am here only sketching the argument, I retain the less artificial word 'exists' (and its
cognates), but giving it the sense just defined in the text (so that it corresponds to Grisez's use of
'obtains').

'Tomorrow someone will read a sentence in *Natural Law and Natural Rights*'; as stated at the time of that reading, 'Someone is reading a sentence in ...'; and as stated the day after tomorrow, 'Yesterday someone read a sentence in ...'.) Since the state of affairs which we are considering may or may not exist (or, retrospectively, might or might not have existed), it is reasonable to ask why it will exist if it exists (... is existing if it is existing; ... existed if it was an existing state of affairs). History, biography, sociology, natural sciences ... all proceed by raising such questions. What conditions or prerequisites will have (had) to be fulfilled for that state of affairs to exist?

Some of the prerequisites for this state of affairs are included in the state of affairs itself: for example, for one to read the sentence, one has to be able to see the words on the page. But there are many other conditions, prerequisite to the existing of this state of affairs, which are not included in the state of affairs itself. There must be enough light to read by (but it might be sunlight or candlelight or electric light); there must be someone alive and conscious and able to understand English. There will be no one alive and conscious unless a very great many physical, physiological, and psychological processes are then going on (including many processes which one need not, however, understand or even be aware of in order to know that the state of affairs exists). There would be no one able to understand English if there were not a whole English-speaking culture. If we elaborate the state of affairs to include the fact that the sentence being read is being read with understanding, it is easy to see that in this instance the conditions that must be satisfied (i.e. the states of affairs that must exist) for the relevant state of affairs to exist include states of affairs in all four orders—the physical order, the cultural order, the order of meaning and thought, and the order of human choices, attitudes, and actions.

All these prerequisite states of affairs may or may not exist (might or might not have existed). And they in their turn exist only if further prerequisites not included in themselves are satisfied. That *all* these prerequisites and their own prerequisites are so disposed (whether simultaneously or in temporal succession or both) as to provide what is required for the first-mentioned state of affairs to exist, is itself a state of affairs. This whole prerequisite state of affairs (which might or might not extend to include the whole universe)[28] can be said to cause the first-mentioned state of affairs.[29] But, just as we began by asking why the first-mentioned state of affairs will exist if it exists (is existing...; did exist...), so we can now ask why the whole causing state of affairs itself exists (or will exist...; or did exist...).

Must there be an answer to this question? The rationalists of the late seventeenth and the eighteenth centuries, against whom Kant and Hume were arguing on many fronts (and whose doctrines of natural law I have not reproduced or defended), considered that indeed there must. For is there not a 'principle of sufficient reason'? Leibniz had identified such a principle, and formulated it thus: 'No fact can be real or existent, no statement true, unless there be a sufficient reason why it is so and not otherwise, although these reasons usually cannot be known to us'.[30] But, in fact, this principle should not be conceded. No *reason* can be given or need be sought to explain why two identical individuals (e.g. two pins or two atoms) are distinct and different. No reason can or need be given for a choice that was really freely made as between eligible alternatives. And no reason can or need be given why it is *this* world-order *rather than some other* possible world-order that exists. (Leibniz held that *this* world-order exists because God chose it, but his principle of sufficient reason compelled Leibniz to offer a reason for *this* choice. The reason offered had to be that *this* is the best of all possible worlds.[31] But we must reject the very notion of a best possible world as 'merely incoherent, like the idea of a biggest natural number'.[32] For goodness, as I argued in V.7, has irreducibly distinct and

---

[28] For the sake of the argument, we should grant that this whole prerequisite state of affairs comprises an *infinite* number of states of affairs, notwithstanding that contemporary scientific cosmology tends to favour Einstein's view that the universe is not infinite. If an infinite series of states of affairs happens to exist, it is still reasonable to ask why.

[29] In saying this one stipulates a sense of 'cause', such that where state of affairs A includes conditions which are not included in state of affairs B, but which must be satisfied for B to exist, one calls A a cause of B. See Grisez, *Beyond the New Theism: A Philosophy of Religion*, 54, 128; Richard Taylor, 'Causation', in *Encyclopedia of Philosophy* (ed. Paul Edwards, London and New York: 1967), vol. 2, 63.

[30] Leibniz, *Monadology* [1714], sec. 32.

[31] *Ibid.*, secs 53–5.

[32] P. T. Geach, *The Virtues* (Cambridge: 1977), 98.

incommensurable aspects.) So, in the absence of any universal, necessary principle such as that of 'sufficient reason', our question remains: Must we answer the question why the whole state of affairs causing the first-mentioned state of affairs to exist itself exists?

In III.4, I referred to some norms or principles of theoretical rationality, with which I compared the basic principles and requirements or norms of practical reasonableness discussed in Chapters III, IV, and V. These norms or principles of theoretical rationality underpin all our thinking, even in logic and mathematics: for although the basic forms of deductive inference, such as *modus ponens*,[33] cannot be theoretically 'justified', it would be quite unjustified, i.e. irrational, to refuse on that score to accept and use them—it is, in short, a principle of theoretical rationality that one ought to accept deductive arguments that seem valid, even though no justification of the inference is possible. As I said in III.4, there are many norms of theoretical rationality. Among them are certainly such norms or principles as: If a question of a certain form has been asked and answered, one can expect another question of the same general form to be answerable; and: If a theoretical question can be partially answered by positing a theoretical entity, and to do so allows the raising of further questions which, if answered, might well provide a more satisfying answer to the initial question, then one ought to posit such a theoretical entity—unless there are good reasons for not doing so.

Well, the substantive question on hand is of the same general form as questions that can be answered fairly satisfactorily: for it is simply the question 'Why does X exist?' (the question underlying much of the sciences), applied to the case where X is the whole set of states of affairs which initially explain why the particular state of affairs first under consideration itself exists. And it is possible (as we shall shortly see) to answer this further question about the whole causing state of affairs, by positing one or more states of affairs, of which we may have no experience, but the positing of which is fruitful of further questions, the answers to which can more adequately answer the substantive question on hand. This being so, it is rationally (not logically)

---

[33] If *p* then *q*; but *p*; therefore *q*.

necessary to entertain this answer, and to accept it unless there are reasons not to.

The explaining of the whole causing state of affairs is not the empty project of 'explaining a group' after all the group's members have been fully explained—of absurdly demanding to know, for example, why there is a set of five Eskimos standing at the street corner, *after* the presence of *each* of the five has been explained. Rather, it is a matter of explaining more fully the existing of one particular state of affairs. The existing of that (first-mentioned) state of affairs is partially explained by the already postulated causing state of affairs, but only on the assumption that that whole causing state of affairs exists; so the relation between 'member', 'group', and 'explanation' is quite different, here, from in the case of the Eskimos. The only available explanation of the whole causing state of affairs is this: that there is some state of affairs causing that whole causing set of prerequisites or conditions of the first-mentioned state of affairs, but which is not itself included in that causing set of conditions precisely because, unlike all the members of that set, its existing does not require some prerequisite condition (not included in itself) to be satisfied. This newly postulated state of affairs can (and should, given the sense we are giving to 'cause') be called an uncaused causing.

In so far as it is causing, this uncaused causing might or might not be an existing state of affairs: otherwise it would not be the case, as it is, that the first-mentioned state of affairs (somebody reading a sentence in this book) might or might not be an existing state of affairs. In this respect—contingency—the uncaused causing state of affairs does not differ either from the first-mentioned state of affairs or from the whole causing state of affairs which can partially explain the existing of the first-mentioned state of affairs. Where the un-caused causing must differ, if it is to explain what needs to be explained, is in this: that to exist, it requires nothing not included in itself. (That is the fact about it that we signify by 'uncaused'.)

Since the uncaused causing might or might not be an existing state of affairs, its existing needs explanation. (In saying this, one appeals to the same principle of theoretical rationality as underpins scientific inquiry, and the whole of our present inquiry thus far.) The explanation of its existing can only be this: that the uncaused causing state of affairs includes, as a prerequisite to its existing, a state of affairs that exists because of *what* it is, i.e. because it is what it is. It will be convenient to label this last-mentioned state of affairs D. In the case of all states of affairs except D, we can describe the state of affairs, say *what* it is, without knowing *that* it is (i.e. without knowing whether it is an existing state of affairs). But, of D the argument requires us to say that *what* it is is all that it requires to exist. So, although the argument provides us with no further description of this state of affairs, of what it is, than that, still the argument does require us to say that we know *that* D exists. For what the whole argument shows, with rational (not logical) necessity, is that if *any* state of affairs, that might not exist, exists, then D *must* exist; without it, no state of affairs that might not exist could exist. But some state of affairs, that might not exist, does happen to exist (e.g. the reader reading this sentence). So D must (this is *not* logical necessity) exist.

To this line of argument, many objections have been raised. Since this is not a book on natural theology or the philosophy of God, I may be excused for doing no more than referring the reader to at least one place where the objections I am aware of are fairly and sufficiently dealt with.[34] The purpose of this section has been twofold. The first purpose has been to show how concern for the basic value of truth is essential if reasoning is to lead from questions about states of affairs which we experience to knowledge of the existing of a state of affairs which we do not as such experience. For principles of theoretical rationality, although they do not describe anything (as Leibniz's mistakenly unqualified principle of sufficient reason purported to), are objective, not conventional or relative to individual purposes or commitments. But one can choose to ignore or flout them; the cost is not self-contradiction but simply loss of knowledge of what one might come to know if one cared enough for the value of truth to adhere to principles which, as experience confirms, guide our reasoning towards knowledge and away from ignorance.

---

[34] Grisez, *Beyond the New Theism*, chs 4–13. Chapters 6–13 alternately state and criticize empiricist, Kantian, Hegelian, and some contemporary relativist arguments and alternatives.

The second purpose of the section has been to show that a truth-seeking reasoning can provide an explanation of the existing of things (including the orders of things, and the goods which we can make exist by our choices, actions, projects, and commitments, and the acts of understanding whereby we understand these orders and these goods), an explanation more securely based than the earlier-mentioned purported inference directly from order and good to transcendent intelligence and wisdom. The explanation that we have found warranted is, of course, incomplete. It affirms nothing about the explanatory state of affairs, D, other than that it has what it takes to make all other states of affairs exist. What more can be said about it?

XIII.3 DIVINE NATURE AND 'ETERNAL LAW': SPECULATION AND REVELATION

Before answering the question what can be said about D, it may be as well to indicate why that question is worth tackling in this book, here. The reason is that arguments (which are rather common) about whether or not God is, or could be, the 'basis' or explanation of moral obligation, or of principles of practical reason, are quite futile in the absence of a clear grasp of (i) what reasons, if any, there are for speaking of anything that might be termed 'God' at all (I offered some reasons in the preceding section); (ii) what can be predicated of the entity termed 'God', in what sense any terms can be so predicated, and what reasons there are for so predicating them; and (iii) the precise questions in answer to which God or some aspect of God's causality is advanced by way of explanatory answer. Very commonly, none of these three sorts of clarification is made before argument is joined about whether, for example, God's 'will' is the basis of obligation, or could not possibly be such a basis ('For why *ought* we to obey God's will?'); or about whether God's 'goodness' is that basis, or could not possibly be ('How could one respect the author of the evils of this world?').

'God' is a term burdened with very varying associations. So the argument set out in the preceding section terminates in the affirmation of the existing, not of God (since I do not know what the reader understands by 'God'), but of D, of which all that has been affirmed is that it is a state of affairs which exists simply by being what it is, and which is required for the existing of any other state of affairs (including the state of affairs: D's causing all caused states of affairs).

And beyond this the argument will not, I think, take us. Still, it is philosophically possible to speculate that D's causing of all caused states of affairs, being an uncaused causing which determines between contingent possibilities, is in some respects analogous to the free choices of human persons. Of course, human choosing, unlike D's causing, requires many prerequisites; so the analogy must be imperfect. But the analogy may be justified in as much as human persons, by free acts of thinking, choosing, and using or making, bring into being entities (e.g. arguments, friendships, poems, and constitutions) that simply would not exist but for these not-wholly-determined human acts.

If there is any such analogy, then, D's uncaused causality can be described as an *act*, and can be thought of as presupposing something like our *knowledge* of the alternative possibilities available to be brought to realization by choice and creation. We only act freely when we know what the possibilities were, and when we know what we are doing. This knowledge is propositional: we can say what we are up to in doing what we are doing. The Augustinian and Thomistic speculation on Eternal Law is a development of the analogy in this respect: what we do is guided, shaped, directed by the formally (and often chronologically) prior plan we have in mind; if we are trying to get the members of a community themselves to act in the way we have it in mind for them to act, our plan of action can be presented as a law of their actions. So too the ensemble of caused states of affairs can be thought of as a quasi-community of entities or states of affairs which exist in intelligible orders in accordance with physical and other laws of nature (both 'classical' and statistical), with principles of logic and theoretical rationality, with requirements of practical reasonableness for human flourishing, and with the flexible norms of arts and technologies. Thus, the theory of Eternal Law proposes that the laws, principles, requirements, and norms of the four orders be regarded as holding for their respective orders precisely because they express aspects, intelligible to us, of the creative intention which guides D's causing of the categorially variegated 'community' of all entities and all states of affairs in all orders.

The purport of the theory of Eternal Law can easily be misunderstood. *First*, it must not be treated as a theory which could guide investigation and verification of suggested norms in any of the four orders; rather, it is a speculation about why those norms whose holding has been appropriately verified or established do hold. *Secondly*, the creative 'plan' of D which the theory hypothesizes (by a speculative inference not altogether unlike 'reading off' artists' or architects' intention from their work) must not be imagined on some single model of 'law' or 'norm' drawn from any one of the four orders; rather, it must comprise elements as categorially diverse as the four orders which we directly understand. As it is a mistake to confuse the laws in human legal systems with laws of nature such as the classical and statistical laws of physics, so it is a mistake to suppose that the Eternal Law could be described on the model of any of the norms of any of the four orders. *Thirdly*, the sense of 'eternal' must not be misunderstood. To exist, D requires nothing other than to be what it is; thus, D cannot be incomplete, cannot be changing in any sense of 'change' that we could apply to contingent entities or states of affairs in any of the four orders. But, for just the same reason, D cannot be 'static' or 'unchanging' in any sense applicable to such contingent entities or states of affairs. To say that D is eternal, and to call the act(s) and intention(s) of D eternal, is simply a way of indicating that D (and anything that can be predicated of D) neither develops nor declines, that D is outside the range of application of the concepts of change and changelessness, and hence of time. *Fourthly*, the speculation that the norms intelligible to us in any of the four orders are expressions or indications of D's creative plan in no way warrants the further speculation that D's creative plan is understood by us. All that we *know* about D is that D has what it takes to bring it about that every state of affairs which exists exists. But what states of affairs do in fact exist is not at all fully explained by the laws and norms of natural sciences, or of reasoning, or human arts, or of practical reasonableness and human flourishing. Much is coincidental, 'fortuitous'. Yet every state of affairs,

however 'fortuitous', requires D's creative causality if it is to
exist. So the speculation on the 'plan' of that causality, i.e.
on Eternal Law, suggests that much of that Law is quite unknown
to us.[35]

The *fifth* and final point to be mentioned here is related to
the fourth. It concerns the relation between the supposed
creative plan or intention of D and the evils and disorders
that, as I have already stressed, are to be found in all four created
orders. A careful analysis of evils and disorders shows that
evil, strictly speaking, is a defect, a lack, the non-existing of
what ought (in terms of the norms of the relevant order) to have
existed but in fact does not exist. Evil is real, indeed, but is
not something that itself exists. Therefore it is not caused by D.
But D does cause all the states of affairs that involve evil; in
this sense D is responsible for evil. Does this entail that D's
creative causality is somehow defective? It does not; for we
could only judge D's causality to be evil or imperfect or
defective if we knew what the norms applicable to creative
causality are. But the creative causality of D is not a state of affairs
within any of the four orders whose norms we more or less know.
While we can speculate that the norms known to us do reflect the
plan 'underlying' creative causality, such an assumption does not
warrant an inference that that plan is 'captured' by the norms
which we know (or could come to know by any means imaginable
to us). The norms in terms of which we judge states of affairs to be
evil, in any of the four orders, are not applicable to D as creator.
Thus, we have no ground to judge that D's creative causality is
defective. In short, if there is an Eternal Law, we do not know
enough of it to be able to judge D's creative performance defective
in terms of it.

---

[35] Thus Aquinas, *S.T.* I–II q. 19 a. 10c; q. 91 a. 3 ad 1; q. 93 a. 2. The text, above, oversimplifies.
Aquinas sometimes distinguishes between Eternal Law and Providence: *ibid.* I q. 22 a. 1; I–II q. 93
a. 4, obj. 3; see also *Summa contra Gentiles* III, cc. 97, 98, 113, 114: the distinction seems similar to that
between the principles of an art like seamanship and the incommunicable skill of the seaman in
applying them and adapting their application to unforeseen circumstances. The Eternal Law (on
Aquinas's conception of it) would be known by us imperfectly, not only because its over-all point is
unknown to us, but also because the boundaries between Eternal Law ('general') and Providence
('particular') are opaque to us (and, indeed, Aquinas sometimes speaks of the Eternal Law as
extending to all particular contingencies: *S.T.* I–II q. 91 a. 3 ad 1; q. 93 a. 5 ad 3).

The foregoing discussion of the theological topic of Eternal Law has been in hypothetical form, since the speculation on creative causality, as analogous to an act of choice made in pursuance of a logically prior intention, is a speculation which (unlike the conclusion that D obtains and is an uncaused cause) cannot, I think, be rigorously established by philosophical argumentation. Verification of the speculation, and clarification of the meaning of the concepts employed in it, will depend upon some other mode of access to D. Inasmuch as the speculation suggests that D *acts* and *knows*, it suggests that D's existing is conceivable on the model of *personal life*. It therefore suggests that some sort of communication from or self-disclosure of D might occur. Whether this does occur is a question of fact, of experience and history.

It must never be overlooked that, for nearly two millennia, the theories of natural law have been expounded by theorists who, with few exceptions, believed that the uncaused cause has in fact revealed itself to be all that the foregoing analogue model of creative causality hypothesized, to be indeed supremely personal, and to be a lawgiver whose law for human persons should be obeyed out of gratitude, hope, fear, and/or love.[36] The supposed revelation of God has been conceived of as more or less public and empirically accessible, i.e. as something more than an event in the intellectual or spiritual life of a meditating individual. But it also must not be overlooked that the originators of natural law theorizing, who did not suppose that God has revealed himself by any such act of informative communication, believed none the less that through philosophical meditation one can gain access to the transcendent source of being, goodness, and knowledge. Nor is this belief of Plato and Aristotle irrelevant to their development of a teaching about practical reasonableness, ethics, or natural right, in opposition to the sceptics, relativists, and positivists of their day. For at the foundation of such teachings is their faith in the power and objectivity of reason, intelligence, *nous*. And there is

---

[36] So the Ten Commandments of Israel are introduced by the words 'I am the Lord your God, who brought you out of the land of Egypt, out of the house of bondage ...': Exodus 20:2. And the second promulgation of the Commandments is ratified by the self-identification of 'The Lord, the Lord, a God merciful and gracious, slow to anger, and abounding in steadfast love and faithfulness...': Exodus 34:5; cf. also Deuteronomy 5:29; 5:33–6:6.

much reason to believe that their confidence in human *nous* is itself founded upon their belief that the activity of human understanding, at its most intense, is a kind of sharing in the activity of the divine *nous*.[37]

Neither Plato's nor Aristotle's conception of the divine nature and causality is the same as the notion of D and D's causing expounded in this chapter (or as the Jewish and Christian notion of God and God's creation). But their conceptions certainly have a similarity to the speculative analogue model discussed in this section, and to the confirmation of that speculation by the public divine revelation(s) believed in by Jews and Christians; so much similarity, indeed, that Augustine of Hippo felt obliged to raise the hypothesis that Plato had had some access to the divinely inspired prophets of Israel.[38] In the end, Augustine rather preferred the vague suggestion that Plato's knowledge of the divine nature and causality had been revealed to Plato by God 'through His created works'.[39]

Neither of Augustine's hypotheses is too satisfactory. But the issue is not unimportant. For there has been pressure in some theological traditions to distinguish sharply between revelation and reason (or 'natural reason'), and to appropriate the term 'revelation' rather exclusively to the Judaeo-Christian orbit. Plato and Aristotle, on the other hand, do not trade on any such distinction. Certainly they think they have reasons, arguments, for judging that the ordered goods of this world (among them our own *nous*, power of understanding) are caused by something beyond this world.[40] These arguments are perhaps unsatisfactory to the extent that they proceed by too straight and narrow a path from the order of the world to an ordering intelligence.[41] But this need not concern us here, since they can in any case be treated as arguments towards the development of an analogue model for speculatively interpreting the possible or likely nature of the uncaused causing

---

[37] See Plato, *Rep.* VI: 508a–509b; VII: 514a–518e; Aristotle, *Meta.* XII.7: 1072b13–25; *Nic. Eth.* X.7: 1177b26–1178a1.

[38] *De Civitate Dei*, VIII, c. 11. The suggestion had been mooted by earlier Christian writers.

[39] *Ibid.*, c. 12 (cf. c. 10), quoting Romans 1: 19–20.

[40] See Plato, *Rep.* VI: 509b.

[41] See, e.g., Plato, *Laws*, X: 888d–889d; Aristotle, *Meta.* I.3: 984b7–24; and cf. XIII.2 above. Notice that they are well aware of evils and disorders; Plato indeed considers them more extensive than good and order: *Rep.* II: 379c.

which can be affirmed on the basis of a sound argument which these philosophers were moving towards but had not yet differentiated from the arguments in question. What does concern us here is that, besides their arguments, both Plato and Aristotle seem to claim a certain experiential access to the divine. In particular they both affirm, usually meditatively rather than argumentatively, that man can participate in the divine through the activity of his intelligence, first, inasmuch as one's wondering desire to know is the result of a divine attraction stirring one from one's incuriosity to a curiosity that can be satisfied by, and only by, a knowledge of the divine origin of things; and, secondly, in as much as the act of understanding is itself a kind of sharing in the divine intelligence which by its practical exercise has made an intelligible world.

It is necessary to mention these matters because the distinctions later drawn by Christian theologians between natural law and divine law, and between natural reason and revelation, have given some encouragement to the supposition that 'natural law' or 'natural reason(ableness)' signify properties of a purely immanent world ('nature') or an intelligence which has no knowledge of, or concern for, the existence of any transcendent ('supernatural') uncaused cause. But this supposition is mere muddle and is not, and was not intended to be, entailed by the aforementioned distinctions. When, for example, Aristotle speaks of the 'right (or just) by nature' (*physei dikaion*),[42] or of what every person desires 'by nature' (*physei*), he is in no way contrasting 'by nature' with 'by divine appointment'. Indeed, he insists that when Anaxagoras first said 'that there is mind [*nous*] in nature [*physei*], as in animals, and that this is the cause of *all* order and arrangement, he seemed like a sane man in contrast with the haphazard statements of his predecessors'.[43] More pointedly, Aristotle opens his fundamental philosophical work with the affirmation that 'by nature [*physei*] all men desire to know'.[44] From there he proceeds not only to the affirmation (i) that the most desirable object of knowledge is 'the highest good in the whole of nature [*physei*]',[45] a good which he identifies

[42] *Nic. Eth.* V.7: 1134b18–1135a5; cf. I.3: 1094b11–16.
[43] *Meta.* I.3: 984b15–17. And 'the first principle upon which depend the sensible universe and nature [*physis*]' is God (*ho theos*): XII.7: 1072b14.
[44] *Meta.* I.1: 980a22.
[45] *Ibid.* I.2: 982b7–8.

as God,[46] but to the further affirmations (ii) that understanding (or thought) 'in the highest sense' is concerned with God;[47] (iii) that the supreme object of understanding or thought is God and that 'intelligence [or thought] [*nous*] understands [or thinks] itself through participation [*metalēpsis*] in the object of under-standing [or thought]; for it becomes an object of understanding by being touched and understood, so that intelligence [*nous*] and the object of understanding are the same';[48] and (iv) that the best and most pleasant state, which is enjoyed only intermittently by us but always by God, is the contemplation (*theoria*) of that actuality which understanding has, as a divine (*theion*) possession, when it thus participates in its supreme object.[49] In these intense passages the subject of Aristotle's attention, *nous*, is intended by him to be taken as something in a sense shared between God and man, in that human understanding participates in the divine *nous* which is its source, its attracting mover, and its object, while the divine *nous* participates in the human *nous* which it moves, illuminates, and satisfies. And all this is Aristotle's unfolding of what, he says, everybody desires *by nature*.

   Plato and Aristotle do not use the existence of God or the gods as an argument to justify their claim that there are objective norms of human flourishing and principles of human reasonableness. But their arguments in justifying that claim, and their reflection upon the nature, point, and source of those (and all such) arguments, lead them to affirm that there is a transcendent source of being (i.e. of entities and states of affairs, and of their existing) and in particular of our capacity and desire to understand being (or nature) and its many forms of good. Thus, in realizing one's nature, in flourishing (*eudaimonia*), and (what is the same thing from another aspect) in recognizing the authoritativeness of practical reasonableness, its principles, and its requirements, one is responding to the

---

[46] *Ibid.* I.2: 982b4–11, 983a6–10; XII.7: 1072a26–b31.
[47] *Ibid.* XII.7: 1072b19–20.
[48] *Ibid.* XII.7: 1072b20–23.
[49] *Ibid.* XII.7: 1072b23–27.

divine pull[50] and recognizing the mastery of God.[51] So when Plato speaks of God's law, his meaning is rather close to what a Christian theologian, such as Aquinas, means in speaking of natural law as the Eternal Law in so far as it is addressed to human practical reasonableness. Thus, Plato:

> God, as the old saying says, holds in his hand the beginning, end and middle of all that is, and straight he travels to the accomplishment of his purpose, as is (his) nature [*kata physin*]; and always by his side is Right [*dikē*: justice] ready to punish those who disobey the divine law [*theiou nomou*]. Anyone who wants to flourish [*eudaimonēsein*] follows closely in the train of Right, with humility... What line of conduct, then, is dear [*philē*] to God and a following of him?... Well, it is God who is for us the measure [*metron*] of all things; much more truly so than, as they [sophists, notably Protagoras] say, man. So to be loved by such a being, a man must strive as far as he can to become like that being; and, following out this principle, the person who is temperate-and-ordered is dear to God, being like him.[52]

Plato has no conception corresponding to Aquinas's differentiated[53] concept of divine law, i.e. the law which supplements the natural law and is promulgated by God for the regulation of the community or communities (Israel and then the universal Church) constituted through God's public self-revelation and offer of friendship. For Plato, while he would affirm that God can be apprehended by us in the act and experience of human understanding, has no conception of a revelation accessible to men without the effort of rational dialectic and contemplation—of the sort of empirical revelation, for instance, that would be 'folly to the Greeks' (but would be offered to them none the less).[54]

---

[50] Plato, *Laws* I: 644d–645b; V: 803, 804b. See also *Rep.* VII: 515c, e, on the dragging of the prisoner from the cave, the pulling of him into the light of the sun. For Aristotle, see *Eud. Eth.* VII.14: 1248a16–28.

[51] *Laws* IV: 713a, 716c; VII: 803c; VI: 762e; Aristotle, *Eud. Eth.* VIII.3: 1249b6–21.

[52] *Laws* IV: 715e–716d. See also *Rep.* VI: 500c.

[53] In the *Summa contra Gentiles* III, cc. 114–18, Aquinas also uses an undifferentiated concept of *lex divina*, embracing what in the *Summa Theologiae* (*S.T.* I–II q. 91 aa. 1–5) he distinguishes as *lex aeterna*, *lex naturalis*, and *lex divina* (Old and New).

[54] As by Paul: 1 Corinthians 1: 22–4. Of course, on Aquinas's view, this revelation does not oppose reason; in going beyond what is accessible either to argument or to meditative rational experience, the revealed truths, he thinks, incorporate truths accessible to reason and answer questions raised, pressed, but found insoluble by reason. Correspondingly, the divine (i.e. revealed) law, for Aquinas, incorporates and repromulgates many elements of natural law: *S.T.* I–II q. 100 aa. 1, 3; q. 99 a. 2.

In short, Plato and Aristotle consider that what I have called a speculative analogue model of D's nature and causality is in some measure verified in the experience of the true philosopher.[55] By this belief they are encouraged to treat reason as more than a skill, knack, or characteristic that men, unlike animals, happen to have; and to treat the nature or reality that both includes and is illuminated by our understanding as more than a fortuitous agglomeration of entities and states of affairs devoid of any significance that could attract human admiration and allegiance. Practical reasonableness gains for them the significance of a partial imitation of God;[56] the basic values grasped by practical reason gain an objectivity;[57] and practical reason's methodological requirements of constancy and impartiality are reinforced by the worth of adopting the viewpoint of the God who 'contemplates all time and all existence'.[58]

Still, there is deep uncertainty in their knowledge of God's nature and relation to this world and its goods. This uncertainty could be illustrated in many ways. Suffice it here to take a representative instance. Aristotle quite often speaks of the friendship (*philia*) of God or the gods for men and of men for God or the gods;[59] but in his fundamental analysis of friendship he expresses his considered opinion: God is so remote from man that there can be no friendship between God and man.[60] Both the vacillation and the fundamental conclusion on this point entail a deep uncertainty about the content of human flourishing and the significance of human life. Very well-known is Aristotle's uncertainty about the relation between contemplation of divine things and a practical life of all-round flourishing in the context of the *polis*. Not quite so well-known is Aristotle's attempt to explain the reasonableness of self-

---

[55] Plato adds that *every* human being possesses the capacity of learning this truth: *Rep.* VII: 518; cf. VI: 505.

[56] See *Rep.* II: 383c; VI: 500; VII: 540a.

[57] See *Rep.* VI: 504b, 508b–e.

[58] *Rep.* VI: 486a.

[59] See *Nic. Eth.* X.9: 1179a23–32; VII.12: 1162a5; IX.1: 1164b5; *Eud. Eth.* VII.3: 1238b18; VII.10: 1242a32.

[60] *Nic. Eth.* VIII.7: 1158b35, 1159a4.

sacrifice for one's friend;[61] the attempt seems laudable, inevitable, right; but the explanation offered is curiously inadequate. Every reader of Aristotle's *Ethics* becomes aware of such uncertainties, though not all trace them to their roots.

This uncertainty of Plato and Aristotle corresponds to D's objective inaccessibility to the argumentations and inferences of rational inquiry. Without some revelation more revealing than any that Plato or Aristotle may have experienced, it is impossible to have sufficient assurance that the uncaused cause of all the good things of this world (including our ability to understand them) is itself a good that one could love, personal in a way that one might imitate, a guide that one should follow, or a guarantor of anyone's practical reasonableness.

XIII.4 NATURAL LAW AS 'PARTICIPATION OF ETERNAL LAW'

Most people who study jurisprudence or political philosophy are invited at some stage to read Thomas Aquinas's 'treatise on law' (Questions 90–7 of the First Part of the Second Part of his *Summa Theologiae*). Here they read his definition of natural law as *participatio legis aeternae in rationali creatura*:[62] the participation of the Eternal Law in rational creatures. In fact the treatment of natural law in that 'treatise on law' is barely intelligible to one who has not read Aquinas's account of the moral measure and significance of reasonableness;[63] or his account of *prudentia*, practical reasonableness;[64] or any of his discussions of particular moral questions, not to mention his treatment of *beatitudo*, the happiness of human flourishing;[65] and of *caritas*, friendship with God.[66] Still, what has been said about the first two of these topics, in Chapters III–V of this book, has sufficient similarities (as well as additions) to Aquinas's line of thought to afford the present reader some indispensable orientation and complementary material for

---

[61] *Ibid.* IX.8: 1169a18–26.
[62] *S.T.* I–II q. 91 a. 2c.
[63] *Ibid.* I–II qq. 18–21.
[64] *Ibid.* I–II q. 57 aa. 4–6; q. 65 a. 1; II–II q. 47.
[65] *Ibid.* I–II qq. 1–5.
[66] *Ibid.* I–II qq. 62, 65; II–II qq. 23–7.

understanding Aquinas's formal discussion of natural law. The present section, then, seeks to provide a summary elucidation of that famous phrase: *participatio legis aeternae in rationali creatura*.

The term *participatio* translates into Latin a number of Greek terms (especially *methexis*) which Plato used in a semi-technical manner, as well as the term *metalēpsis* which, in the previous section, we observed Aristotle using, non-technically, to express the significance of the supreme activation of human intelligence as a kind of sharing in God's self-understanding. Aquinas is inclined to dissociate himself from Plato's semi-technical meanings as he understands them,[67] and is not here concerned with Aristotle's contemplative experience. Nor does he mean what I mean by 'participation' in a value, in earlier parts of this book (see III.3). For Aquinas, the word *participatio* focally signifies two conjoined concepts, causality and similarity (or imitation). A quality that an entity or state of affairs has or includes is participated, in Aquinas's sense, if that quality is *caused by* a *similar* quality which some other entity or state of affairs has or includes in a more intrinsic or less dependent way.

Aquinas's notion of natural law as a participation of the Eternal Law is no more than a straightforward application of his general theory of the cause and operation of human understanding in any field of inquiry. His bases for inference are the power of human insight and the imperfection of human intelligence. The power of human understanding far exceeds (or rather is incommensurable with) what we would expect to be the intrinsic capacity of the brain-material, however complex, that is its substratum; under-standing an equation, a series or an inference, or somebody else's intention and meaning, or that a proposition indeed answers a question, or that a certain event really occurred, or that a certain scientific law really holds, or that a pointer-reading verifies a scientific hypothesis about the universe—all this amounts to a unique capacity-in-action quite irreducible to any material con-ditions. On the other hand, it is not difficult to postulate an intelligence that would far exceed human intelligence; for our pursuit of understanding is laborious, developmental, and never nearly completed; we need images, figures, symbols, to help us

---

[67] See, e.g., *ibid.* I q. 6 a. 4c.

understand even the most abstract terms and relations; and our learning and discovery are always harassed by oversight, muddle, and lapse of memory. Thus, Aquinas follows Plato and Aristotle in postulating a 'separate intellect' which has the power of understanding without imperfection, and which causes in us our own power of insight, the activation of our own individual intelligences—somewhat as a source of light activates in us our power of sight.[68] He then relies explicitly on revelation ('the *documenta* of our faith')[69] to identify the supposed 'separate intellect' as God. In short (he concludes): 'it is from God that the human mind shares in [*participat*] intellectual light: as Psalm 4 verse 7 puts it "The light of thy countenance, O Lord, is signed upon us."'[70] The same scriptural quotation caps his account of natural law as a *participatio* of Eternal Law.[71]

So, for Aquinas, there is nothing extraordinary about our grasp of the natural law; it is simply one application of our ordinary human power of understanding. None the less his account of this practical *participatio* of the Eternal Law draws attention to some related points worth recapitulating here.

Aquinas begins by drawing a sharp distinction (which runs through all his work)[72] between the intelligent nature of human beings, and the intelligible but not intelligent nature of animals, vegetables, and the rest of 'nature'. The latter participate in the Eternal Law 'somehow',[73] since that is the ultimate source of all their tendencies (*inclinationes*) (which have and follow intelligible patterns). Human beings, on the other hand, provide for themselves (and for others); so we can say that

---

[68] On this analogy, admitted by Aquinas to be inadequate, see his *Summa contra Gentiles* III, c. 53.

[69] *S.T.* I q. 79 a. 4c.

[70] *Ibid.* He is quoting the Vulgate version of the Psalm, and considers the verse peculiarly relevant in relation to practical reasoning because it is preceded by the verse 'Many say: "Who showeth us good things?"': see *De Veritate*, q. 16 a. 3c.

[71] *S.T.* I–II q. 91 a. 2c. In q. 93 a. 3 he remarks that *all* knowledge of truth is a kind of *irradiatio* and *participatio* of the Eternal Law. The quotation from Psalm 4: 6 recurs e.g. in q. 19 a. 4c, where Aquinas is arguing that reasonableness is the standard of moral judgment because our practical reason participates in the Eternal Law, the primary standard.

[72] See, e.g., *S.T.* I–II q. 1 a. 2c; q. 6 a. 1c; *De Potentia*, q. 1 a. 5c; *in Meta.* V, lect. 16, nn. 999–1000.

[73] 'Aliqualiter': *S.T.* I–II q. 91 a. 2c; in ad 3 he remarks that their participation can be called (a following of) law only metaphorically (*per similitudinem*).

each of us is not only subject to God's providence, but is actually a participant (*particeps*) in it.[74] In brief, animals (and the rest of 'lower creation') are *not* subject to natural law. And their nature is not a basis for inference about the principles of human reasonableness.

Next, Aquinas specifies the basic manner in which the eternal reason is participated in us: through our 'natural inclination to the due [*debitum*] act and the due end'. This terse formulation needs expansion. It is elaborated a few pages later, when he explains that amongst our natural inclinations is the inclination to act *secundum rationem*, i.e. reasonably.[75] But the formula also looks right back to the beginning of Aquinas's discussion of human self-direction.[76] There his first exploration is of our inclination towards our last (or all-embracing)[77] end (*ultimus finis*), a completeness of flourishing (*beatitudo*) which will be found when our natural desire for understanding (i.e. for the satisfaction of our reason) is satisfied by that undying contemplation of God which, he says, can be anticipated only on the basis of revelation and can be attained only by a divine gift.[78] Finally, the formula in the discussion of natural law looks forward to his resumption of the Aristotelian meditation on the divine causality that underpins all our inclinations and capacities, including our desire to know and to be intelligent, reasonable, responsible, and our capacity to choose freely and responsibly.[79] All these themes Aquinas draws together in explaining this aspect of the participation of Eternal Law in us as natural law: 'every activity of reason and of will derives, in us, from that which is according to nature... For all reasoning derives from principles [or sources: *principiis*] naturally[80] known; and all desire for things which are for an end derives from natural desire for an end beyond which

[74] See also *S.T.* I–II q. 93 a. 5c; a. 6c.

[75] *S.T.* I–II q. 94 a. 3c.

[76] See *S.T.* I–II, Prologue, and qq. 1–5.

[77] For the meaning of *ultimus* here as 'completely adequate, fully actuating, perfecting', see, e.g., *S.T.* I–II q. 3 a. 2; and p. 46 at n. 62 above.

[78] *Summa contra Gentiles,* III, cc. 52–4; *S.T.* I–II q. 5.

[79] *S.T.* I–II q. 109 a. 2 ad 1; similarly I q. 82 a. 4 ad 3; Aristotle, *Eud. Eth.* VII.14: 1248a16–28.

[80] But not without experience; for the intelligence of each of us starts as a *tabula rasa: S.T.* I q. 79 a. 2c. Like Aristotle (*Post. Anal.* B, c. 19: 99b14–100b17), Aquinas has no truck with 'innate ideas'.

is no further end [*ultimus finis*]; and so it must be that the first directing of our acts towards an end [or: the end] is through natural law'.[81]

Having thus stressed the inclinations which, prior to any rational control of ours, underlie all our effort, including our effort to make our efforts intelligent and reasonable, Aquinas turns to that aspect of our participation of God's practical reason which I mentioned earlier: our power of understanding. For, by this power, we grasp the basic forms of good (and thus the basic principles of natural law);[82] the data for this act of understanding include the desires and inclinations which we experience, but like all understanding, this act of understanding goes beyond the data as experienced, to concepts accessible or available not to experience but only to understanding. I have already indicated (briefly!) Aquinas's general account of the source of our power of illuminating the data of imagination and experience by the insights of common sense, natural science, philosophy, and practical reasonableness. So now he cites again the words of Psalm 4:7, and adds that 'the light of natural reason, whereby we discern what is good and what is bad (which is what natural law concerns), is simply the impress in us of the divine light'.[83]

This metaphorical language is not to be understood in a mystical way. There is a touch of mysticism (i.e. a suggestion of direct experience of God) in Aristotle's account of the participation of divine and human *nous* in contemplation. (To say this is not to comment on the validity of that account.) But Aquinas's account, though sometimes metaphorically expressed, works with no more than the ideas of causality and similarity. There is no suggestion that the mode of divine causality can be further explained, or that the causing or its source are experienced as such. The Thomist theory of participation is not a report of experience, but a theorem in the general explanation of all states of affairs by reference, ultimately, to creative uncaused causality. And so far as it concerns similarity, and also in its metaphorical colouring, the

---

[81] *S.T.* I–II q. 91 a. 2 ad 2.
[82] I–II q. 94 a. 2c; q. 10 a. 1c.
[83] *S.T.* I–II q. 91 a. 2c. Some people are more receptive of this light than others, though every (sane and conscious) person grasps the general principles of practical reasonableness: I–II q. 93 a. 2.

theorem is derived simply by taking the analogue model of divine intelligence, intentionality, life, personality, etc.; treating the model as verified; and then applying it in reverse to the explanation of the human inclinations, intelligence, deliberations and decisions, etc., on which the analogy was founded.

The account of the *source* of natural law thus focuses first on the experienced dynamisms of our nature, and then on the intelligible principles which outline the aspects of human flourishing, the basic values grasped by human understanding.[84] A few pages later Aquinas formulates one of the fundamental theoretical principles of his account of the *content* of natural law: 'all those things to which the human being has a natural inclination, one's reason naturally understands as good (and thus as "to be pursued") and their contraries as bad (and as "to be avoided")'.[85] It is certainly possible to raise the question: Whence this parallelism, this fit, this *convenientia*, of felt inclinations with valuable aspects of human well-being?[86] And it is easy to see what Aquinas's answer to this question would have been, had he bothered to raise it.

XIII.5 CONCLUDING REFLECTIONS ON THE POINT AND FORCE OF PRACTICAL REASONABLENESS

I have not presented natural law or the principles of practical reasonableness as expressions of God's will. And I have positively declined to explain obligation in terms of conformity to superior will. But what I have said in this chapter should show why appeals to God's will, and explanation of obligation by reference to it, cannot be refuted (as it often is supposed they can) by the apparently available question: 'But why should we obey God?' (cf. XI.9). For that question implicitly treats 'God' as referring simply to one more superior in an ascending series of superiors, of each of whom the question can reasonably

---

[84] In *S.T.* I–II q. 93 a. 6c, at the end of his discussion of Eternal Law and immediately before his main discussion of natural law, Aquinas focuses on the two themes explicitly and together.

[85] *S.T.* I–II q. 94 a. 2c.

[86] On the *convenientia* of *appetitus naturalis* with the nature of the being that has these 'appetites' or inclinations or tendencies (for this is, for Aquinas, a quite general metaphysical principle), see *S.T.* I q. 78 a. 1 ad 3; q. 80 a. 1c and ad 2; I–II q. 26 a. 1c. This *convenientia* is not, for Aquinas, the decisive principle of ethical reasoning: see II.6 above.

be asked (so that it would seem arbitrary to treat the last member of the series as immune from the questioning). But the perspective of those who assert that God wills such-and-such, and that that will should be obeyed, is (or certainly can be) quite different.

To the extent that they follow something like the train of argument leading to the affirmation that D exists (see XIII.2), those who speak of God intend to refer to an entity and state of affairs that by its existing explains the existing of all entities and states of affairs in all four orders of contingent being. Consequently, by 'D' or 'God' is meant (i) that which explains the very possibility of explanation, of there being answers to questions about any order of being, and in particular explains (a) the existing of any and every entity or state of affairs to be explained, (b) the existing of all our powers of understanding and explaining, and (c) the order of entities or states of affairs (and the corresponding order of concepts) that afford or figure in the partial explanations available to us in every discipline or field of inquiry. By 'D' or 'God' is further meant: (ii) that which explains the existence of the questioning subject; (iii) that which explains the existing of good states of affairs, and the opportunity of making them exist; (iv) that which explains our ability to recognize goods, to grasp values and their equivalent practical principles; and (v) that which explains our ability to respond to the attractiveness of those goods, to the rational appeal of the principles. How D (or God) thus is the explanation of all this is not known; what is considered to be known is simply that D (or God) is whatever is required to explain them. Already, therefore, it should be clear that to ask for an explanation of D (or God) is to miss the sense and reference of claims made about D (or God).

But those who claim to know what God wills in some human context, and that that will should be obeyed, are (as I have said) going beyond what can be affirmed about D on the basis of philosophical argumentation.[87] They are claiming (like Plato,

---

[87] Aquinas, who will not be suspected of minimizing the range of philosophical reasoning, says: 'the will of God cannot be investigated by reasoning, except for those items that it is absolutely necessary for God to will. Now, as we have said before [q. 19 a. 3c], such items do not include what God wills in regard to creatures': *S.T.* I q. 46 a. 2c.

but relying unlike him upon some definite revelation) that God positively favours both the basic goods and human adherence to the principles and requirements of practical reasonableness in the pursuit of those goods; that the evils and disorders of this world are not favoured so, but are merely tolerated by God for the sake of some positive good (what, and how attained, we do not know); and that friendship with God, some sharing in God's life and knowledge and love-of-goods, is available to those who positively favour what God positively favours. In the context of such beliefs—and it is only in such a context that claims about the authoritativeness of God's will for man are plausibly made—the question 'Why should God's will be obeyed?' has no bite.

After these preliminary remarks about a problem that is not mine (since I have asserted nothing about God's will), I can at last return to the practical problems raised at the beginning of this chapter: the possibility of a deeper explanation of obligation; the reasonableness of self-sacrifice in human friendship; the relevance of our limited place in human history and the universe; the point of living according to the principles and requirements of practical reasonableness. In view of all that has been said in this and earlier chapters, I can perhaps afford to be summary.

In the first place, what can be established, by argumentation from the existence and general features of this world, concerning the uncaused cause of the world, does not directly assist us in answering those practical questions.

In the second place, this limitation of 'natural reasoning' leaves somehow 'subjective' and 'questionable' the whole structure of basic principles and requirements of practical reasonableness and human flourishing discussed in Chapters III to XII. On the other hand, it does not unravel that structure or affect its internal order or weaken its claim to be more reasonable than any logically possible alternative structures.

In the third place, 'natural reasoning' can speculatively postulate that the uncaused cause exists in something like the mode of personal life, and that its causality has some analogy to the intelligent self-direction and intentionality of human creative decision. Such a model for thinking about the uncaused cause allows the further speculation that the uncaused cause might somehow disclose itself to human understanding, by an act of intelligible communication. This further specula- tion in turn permits the speculating thinker to hope that the uncaused cause might reveal itself to be lovable, and that the 'ideal observer' which practical reasonableness postulates as a test of arbitrariness might prove to have a real and substantial counterpart (cf. V.4).

In the fourth place, if these speculations and hopes were confirmed, a more basic account of obligation would become possible. For if the uncaused cause were revealed to favour the well-being of everyman, for no other reason than its (D's, God's) own goodness (in a sense of goodness going, now, beyond the perfection of being all that is required to make all states of affairs exist), the common good could be pursued by us for a new reason, viz. out of love or friendship for the personal being ('God') who not only makes possible whatever well-being of persons there can be and actually is, but also positively favours (though in ways often unintelligible to us) that common good. This would not entail that we no longer favoured the common good for its own sake, nor that we no longer loved our friends for their own sakes. Rather, it would mean that 'for their own sakes' would gain a further (and explanatory) dimension of meaning. For then other persons (and ourselves!) could be regarded not simply as persons whose good we happen to favour, rather inexplicably (in view of their inevitable imperfections), but as persons whose good is favoured also by one whose own goodness is unrestricted and whose love is in no way blind but rather is given knowing fully the true worth and all-explaining point of every- thing, of the existence of every person, and of the history of every community. And this would not only explain, in principle, how self-sacrifice in friendship can make sense; it would also account for our obligation to favour the common good.

Our earlier accounts of obligation terminated at the common good: those actions, projects, and commitments are obligatory which are necessary if the common good of persons in our communities is to be realized. This left an unanswered question: In what sense are we to take it to be *necessary* to favour that common good, which after all will end, sooner or later, in the death of all persons and the dissolution of all communities? That question could now be answered. In friendships (see VI.4) one values what one's friends value (save where the friends are mistaken in their valuation), for no other reason than that they value it. (No other reason is called for.) So if God could be recognized to be our friend (in, of course, an unusual sense of 'friend'), and to be one who favours the common good of human persons, we would have a new and pertinent reason for loving that common good, pertinent even though we could not see how that love would work out in the perspective of all times and all places. And, if we wanted to use the rather vague terms of contemporary philosophy textbooks, we could say that the considerations advanced in this paragraph show how 'God is the basis of obligation'.

In the fifth place, the foregoing speculations or anticipations, if verified, would enable a deeper understanding of the basic values with which our exploration of natural law began in Chapter IV. Here I propose to reconsider only three: practical reasonableness, religion, and play: cf. IV.2.

Plato has carried out such a reconsideration of those three basic human values, through the central philosophical myth in his last work, the *Laws* (*Nomoi*). The symbol in the myth is introduced in Book I [644c–5b] immediately after a first theoretical account of a central meaning of *nomos*, law. Plato, through the Athenian stranger, has begun the parable by remarking that one (each human being) is indeed one person, but has within oneself unwise and conflicting sources of direction, namely pain and pleasure, and their concomitants, aversion and audacity. But also there is *logismos*, reflective insight and reasonable judgment concerning the better and the worse among these basic movements in the psyche. And when this *logismos* is embodied in a public decree (*dogma*) of the *polis*, it is called *nomos*. To explain this, the Athenian stranger invites us to suppose that each of us is a puppet of the gods, created perhaps as a plaything (*paignion*), perhaps for some serious purpose—we do not know. What is certain is that all those basic movements within us are, so to say, the cords by which we puppets are worked, with opposite tensions pulling us in opposite directions; herein lies the division between virtue and vice. The myth is not to be understood mechanistically or as treating us as each an automaton, for the account goes on to say that there is one

cord which works only with our support, and that each of
us ought to follow the pull of this cord against the pull of all
the others. For this is the golden and sacred cord of practical
reasonableness (*logismos*) or, 'to give it another name', the
common law (*koinos nomos*) of the *polis*. The pull of this cord is
soft and gentle. But the other cords are of iron and various
other materials. Against their hardness one ought always to
co-operate with the pull of the *nomos*, lest the other pulls
prevail over one. If one understands all this, one understands
self-mastery and self-defeat; one has true understanding (*logos
alēthēs*) of the tensions in the soul; and one understands that the
individual ought to live according to the golden cord of reason,
and that the *polis* ought to embody it in a law regulating both
the internal and the foreign relations of the *polis*.

Up to this point, Plato's discussion amounts to a compressed
anticipation, in deliberately undifferentiated language (playing
upon the various meanings and references of *nomos* and *logos*),
of the themes we have discussed in terms of natural law,
positive law, inclinations, practical reasonableness, and participation in the Eternal Law. This is one of the foundation texts
in the tradition of theorizing about natural law. But in Book VII
of *Laws*, at the middle point of the whole work, Plato's Athenian
returns to the symbol of the plaything (*paignion*) of God:

We should keep our seriousness for serious things [*spoudaion*], not
waste it on non-serious things. While God is by nature [*physei*] the
goal of all beneficent serious endeavours, human beings (as we have
said before) have been made as God's playthings, and this is, indeed, the
finest thing about us. All of us, men and women, ought to fall in with this
role, and spend our lives in playing this noblest of plays.

The usual view is that our serious work must be attended to for
the sake of our play. Thus people think that war is serious work which
ought to be well discharged in order to secure peace. In truth, however, in war we do not find, and we never will find, either real
play [*paidia*] or real formation [education: *paideia*]—which are the
things I count most serious for us human creatures. So it is in
peace that each of us should spend most of his life and spend it
best. This, then, is the right course: That we should pass our lives
in playing the games [or play] of sacrifice, song and dance, so that
we may gain the grace of the gods and be able to repel and defeat
our enemies when we have to fight...[We are to bring up those
in our care so that they] will live out their lives as what they are by

nature [*physeōs*], puppets for the most part, though having a little bit of reality, too.

Megillus: You give us a very poor opinion of the human race, Stranger.

Athenian: Do not be surprised, Megillus. Bear with me. The one who just spoke was looking and feeling towards God, when he was speaking.[88]

Perhaps the mood of Plato's symbolism is what the Christians would call pagan; man the plaything is not, perhaps, man the fellow player in the divine drama of history and eternity, who might be redeemed for friendship with God by God become man. But Christianity has not offered, nor has philosophy provided, any reason to doubt Plato's more fundamental point, that obligation, while real enough (and referred to again and again in the passages just cited), is not the framework or finally authoritative category of 'moral' thought. The requirements of practical reasonableness (which generate our obligations) have a 'point' beyond themselves. That point is the *game* of co-operating with God. Being *play*, this co-operation has no point beyond itself, unless we wish to say that God is such a further 'point'. By analogy with human friendship, we may be able to say that, but only in a special, restricted sense. For if we simply said that we act for the sake of God, we would suggest that God somehow needs us, needs creation, the success of creation, the achieving of the creative purpose. But D needs and lacks nothing. And has God been revealed as needing or lacking anything? So if we ask why God creates, no answer is available other than the one implicitly given by Plato: play—a free but patterned expression of life and activity, meaningful but with no further point.[89] Hence, even one who goes beyond Plato to accept that man is called to a friendship of devotion to God will grant that such friendship takes the form of sharing, in a limited way, in the divine play.

Practical reasonableness, therefore, need not be regarded as ultimately a form of self-perfection. That is not its final significance. Nor, on the other hand, are its requirements sheer

---

[88] *Laws*, VII: 803b–c. In A. E. Taylor's translation the last words are finely rendered: 'Bear with me. I had God before my mind's eye, and felt myself to be what I have just said'.

[89] Cf. Proverbs 8: 30–1.

categorical imperatives; they gain practical force from the most basic explanation that can be provided for them—that they are what is needed to participate in the game of God.

Play, too, can now be more adequately understood. It is to be contrasted with business, with responsibilities, with the serious things of life. But, in the last analysis, there is a play that is the *only* really serious matter. In such a 'final analysis', in which we seek an understanding going beyond our feelings, the 'serious things of life', even atrocious miseries, are really serious only to the extent that they contribute to or are caught up into a good play of the game of the God who creates and favours human good.

Finally, the assumptions about God necessary to justify the two preceding paragraphs would, if verified, entitle us to remove the question mark with which I originally introduced the basic human value of religion: see IV.2. In doing so, I spoke hesitantly, constrained by the anthropological and psychological evidence to postulate an inclination and a corresponding basic value which, however, I could describe only vaguely. The present chapter has illustrated some of the questions and concerns which exemplify, or provide the basis for, 'religious concern'; and my discussion suggests the conditions on which an adequate object of that wondering concern could be found. It only remains to avert a possible misunderstanding. The assumptions I am making or postulating in this section would entitle us to say that God is an unrestricted, 'absolute' value and that harmony with God ('religion') is a basic human value. They would not entitle us to say that religion is a more basic value than any of the other basic human values, so that 'for the sake of religion' one might rightly choose directly against any of those other values or ignore any of the other requirements of practical reasonableness: see IV.4, V.5–6. There is nothing to justify treating God as an objective to be attained by the skilful disposition of concrete means. (The fanatic acts as if God were such an objective.) Due allowance made for the direct expression of religious concern (say, as Plato says, by 'sacrifice, song, and dance'), the human person's way of realizing the proposed friendship with God builds on all the requirements of practical reasonableness in the pursuit of, and respect for, all the basic forms of human good.

NOTES

XIII.1

Stoic ethics based moral principles on theoretical knowledge of the universe...Besides the cited texts from Cicero, see, e.g., Diogenes Laertius, *Lives of Eminent Philosophers* [c.225?], VII, 87–9: 'Zeno [of Cyprus] in his work *On the Nature of Man* [early third century BC] was the first [?Stoic] to declare that "life lived according to nature" [*homologoumenos te physei zen*] is the ultimate moral end...Again, living virtuously is equivalent to living in accordance with experience of the actual course of nature, as Chrysippus states in the first book of his *Concerning Ends* [late third century BC], because our individual natures are parts of the nature of the whole universe. And this is why the [human] end may be defined as life in accordance with nature, i.e. in accordance with our human nature as well as with that of the universe—a life in which we refrain from every action forbidden by the law common to all things. But this law is nothing other than right reason, which pervades all things and is identical with God...And this very thing constitutes the virtue of the truly happy man...when all his actions promote the harmony of the spirit dwelling within individual man with the will of Him who orders the universe...By the nature with which our life ought to be in accordance, Chrysippus understands both universal nature and more particularly the nature of man. Cleanthes, on the other hand, accepts the nature of the universe alone as the standard of all actions without referring to the nature of individual man'. The account I am giving of Stoicism is synthetic, ignoring important differences and developments within a school of thought that flourished for many hundreds of years and was strongly eclectic.

Hope and projection in Kant...On the question 'What may we hope?', see Kant, *Critique of Pure Reason*, B833 ff. On the 'fictitious' character (from the viewpoint of pure reason) of the immortality we may hope for, see *ibid.*, A780/B808. For the origins of the idea that immortality, God, etc., are merely *projections* of human longings, relationships, etc., see L. Feuerbach, *The Essence of Christianity* (1841; trans. Marian Evans, 1854), *passim*; e.g. 226: 'The personality of God is nothing else than the projected personality of man'. On the idea of immortality, see, e.g., 181: 'As God is nothing other than the nature of man purified from that which to the human individual appears...a limitation...so the future life is nothing else than the present life freed from that which appears a limitation or an evil'. For the exploitation of these ideas by Marx, see his 'Towards a Critique of Hegel's Philosophy of Right: Introduction' [1843/4].

Augustine's critique of the athleticism of virtue...See Augustine, *De Civitate Dei*, Book XIX, cc. 5, 10, 25.

XIII.2

'Natural sanction'...On the *poena naturae* ('self-avenging laws of conduct'), see Arnold Brecht, *Political Theory* (Princeton: 1959), 431–3; cf. Plato, *Rep.* IX: 571a, 577c; Xenophon, *Memorabilia*, IV, 4, 21–4.

The distinction between 'what' and 'that'...The distinction is fairly clearly drawn by Aquinas in his early treatise *De Ente et Essentia* (c.1255) and is exploited in cc. 4 and 5 of that work, in an argument somewhat similar to Grisez's (which, however, works with 'obtaining' rather than 'existence'), to conclude to the existence of God.

'Sufficient reason' and 'the best of all possible worlds' ... Leibniz's 'great principle of sufficient reason' has three principal senses or applications: nothing happens without a cause; God cannot act without a motive; God must always act for the best (since there could be no reason to prefer the less good to the best). Four points may be noted here. (i) The Leibnizian argument for the existence of God starts with the principle in its first form, which Leibniz considers 'entitles' one to raise the question 'Why does something exist rather than nothing?': *Principles of Nature and of Grace* [1714], secs 7–8. This is not the question with which my argument begins. (ii) One consequence of the principle for Leibniz is the 'identity of indiscernibles', the view that there are never two beings which are perfectly alike (i.e. lacking in any intrinsic difference): *Monadology*, sec. 9. (iii) In Leibniz's work the principle of sufficient reason is sometimes rendered as 'the principle of fitness [*convenance*]'. On the significance of fitness or *convenientia* in the natural law theorizing of the period, see II.6. (iv) Leibniz's successors, notably Christian Wolff, author of influential 'rationalist' treatises on natural law, debased the Leibnizian principle of sufficient reason and the Leibnizian theorem that this is the best of all possible worlds by taking 'best' to mean 'best for mankind': so the stars are to give us light. Leibniz's principle is unacceptable but Wolff's teleology is ridiculous, which helps to explain the thorough discredit into which theories of natural law soon fell.

Explaining states of affairs ... It is often supposed that an uncaused cause need not be postulated, because any causing state of affairs can be adequately explained by further causing states of affairs in a series which is either infinite or circular. But neither an infinite series of causes nor a circle of causes is capable of adequately explaining any state of affairs. See Grisez, *Beyond the New Theism*, 59–67; Barry Miller, 'The Contingency Argument' (1970) 54 *The Monist* 368–71. Grisez suggests that the appeals to infinite or circular series, so obviously unsatisfactory as explanations, are usually merely the outposts of ('a symbolic way of suggesting') the central fortress of the sceptic, which is the claim (attended to in my text) that no explanation is required beyond the conditional explanations of science. The ways in which these scientific explanations demand to be completed by 'metaphysical' explanations, such as the one indicated in this section, are abundantly illustrated in Stanley L. Jaki, *The Road of Science and the Ways to God* (Chicago and Edinburgh: 1978).

Explaining the 'five Eskimos' ... The image is taken from a well-known objection by Paul Edwards, 'The Cosmological Argument' in Donald R. Burrill (ed.), *The Cosmological Arguments: A Spectrum of Opinion* (New York: 1967), 114–22.

'D exists' ... Here the meta-predicable 'exists' is used in an unusual sense (as are all terms applied to D), unusual because in the case of D, *what* it is is all that it requires to exist, so that D's existing is only 'logically' distinct from what D is.

XIII.3

Eternal Law ... See Cicero, *De Legibus*, II, 9; Augustine, *Contra Faustum*, XXII, 27; *De Libero Arbitrio*, I, 6; Aquinas, *S.T.* I–II q. 19 a. 4; q. 91 a. 1; q. 93 aa. 1–6; St. German, *Doctor and Student*, First Dial., c. 1; Richard Hooker, *Of the Laws of Ecclesiastical Polity* (1593), I, secs ii–v.

Evil and creation ... For a careful and realistic treatment of obvious objections (e.g. 'pain is an evil and is not a mere lack'), see Grisez, *Beyond the New Theism*, ch. 19. As to pain, I may very briefly note that, while it is *felt* by us as an evil, it is *understood*, by anyone who reflects, as having a number of important functions, in particular as good for warning us of threats to our bodily constitution.

Our understanding of it as, at least sometimes, a good does not diminish our horror of it; but, conversely, our dislike of it is not to be taken as a rational judgment on its character. This does not, of course, settle all objections based on pain; but it allows them to be tackled.

Aquinas on providence... For a sophisticated explanatory account, see Bernard Lonergan, *Grace and Freedom: Operative Grace in the Thought of St. Thomas Aquinas* (New York: 1970), ch. 4.

Access to the God in contemplation: Plato and Aristotle... For the view adopted in the text, and particularly for the analysis of *Metaphysics*, XII.7, see *Gauthier-Jolif*, II/2, 848–60, esp. 857–60; Eric Voegelin, *Order and History*. vol. 4, *The Ecumenic Age* (Baton Rouge: 1974), 189–90, 228–38. On *Eud. Eth.* VIII.3, see A. Kenny, *The Aristotelian Ethics* (Oxford: 1978), 173–80.

XIII.4

Aquinas on 'participation'... See *S.T.* I q. 3 a. 8c; q. 8 a. 1c; q. 44 a. 1c and ad 1; q. 61 a. 1c; q. 75 a. 5 ad 1 and ad 4; q. 79 a. 4; q. 96 a. 1c.

Aristotle and Aquinas on God's moving the will... For a discussion of this, and of the obvious problems concerning human freedom, see Lonergan, *Grace and Freedom*, ch. 5; Grisez, *Beyond the New Theism*, ch. 18. See also notes to V.2, on contingency, providence, and freedom.

XIII.5

Plato and the origins of theorizing about natural law ... See J. P. Maguire, 'Plato's Theory of Natural Law' (1947) 10 *Yale Classical Studies* 151–78.

God, man, and play ... For the history of the exegesis of *Laws*, VII, 803b–c and Proverbs 8: 30–1, see Hugo Rahner, *Man at Play* (London: 1964), esp. 19–25.

POSTSCRIPT

1.

The book was commissioned by the editor of the Clarendon Law Series, H.L.A. Hart, soon after I became a colleague of his as a Fellow of University College Oxford, in the autumn of 1966. He asked me to write a book for his series, a book called *Natural Law and Natural Rights*; he repeated this title, to make clear what he wanted. I was very pleased to be asked, and said I would try to have it done by Christmas 1970. He said 'Don't hurry'.

It took me until 1972 or 1973 to begin any real writing of the book. From 1967 I gave at least one lecture course in the Law Faculty every year on General Theory of Law. In these, and in the six-month course in Jurisprudence I gave in Adelaide University's Faculty of Law in 1971, I developed most of the ideas in the book concerning law, its complex point and structure, its relation to the underlying society, and much else. Like my college tutorials in Jurisprudence (which I gave along with a number of other subjects including Criminal Law, Constitutional Law, Administrative Law, Public International Law, and Penology, and later Roman Law instead of the others), these lectures extensively and intensively treated Kelsen, as well as Austin and Hart. At the same time, I read a good deal on the methodological issues which both Strauss and Voegelin had explored in the opening chapter of *Natural Right and History* and *The New Science of Politics* respectively. And from 1968 I was commenting extensively on developments in constitutional law over wide geographical areas for the *Annual Survey of Commonwealth Law*, with an immediate theoretical by-product, the theory of revolutions and *coups d'état*. Like my work on some foundational issues in value theory, action theory, or act-analysis, and normative ethics, this theory can be tracked in the Bibliography appended to each volume of the *Collected Essays* [*CEJF*], or in the select Bibliography following this Postscript, especially items

1967b (now essay IV.8), 1970a (I.6), 1970b, 1970c, 1971a (IV.21), 1972a (III.11), 1972b (IV.18), 1972d, 1973a (III.3), 1973b (III.18), 1976b, 1977a (I.3), and 1977b.

I have always supposed that Hart included 'Natural Rights' in the title because of his interest both in Hohfeld's analysis of rights (on which he lectured for a number of years: I heard the series in October–November 1963) and in Michel Villey's vigorously elaborated writings contending that both Roman Law and mediaeval philosophy and theology before Ockham were innocent of the modern idea of a right and therefore of natural or human rights. Hart had met Villey in Paris, had been given Villey's then main book, *Leçons d'histoire de la philosophie du droit* (1957), and had read it before he lent it to me (along, I think, with Chaim Perelman's *La théorie de l'argumentation* (1963)). So far as I know, Hart never took a position on this thesis, whether in the form put forward by Villey, or in other forms such as Strauss's. But it certainly interested him, and he thought it should get a discussion within the context of a legal philosophy centred on the range of issues and authors discussed in his *The Concept of Law*. As the sole supervisor of my doctoral thesis (1962–5), he knew of my interest in foundational questions about practical reason, as well as in conceptual analysis, Bentham, Kelsen, Fuller, and Aristotle, and juridical framework-concepts. But beyond this specification that the book deal with rights as well as natural law, he never gave the least indication of what he hoped the book would or would not say. He read it as it developed between 1974 and 1977, made the argument which appears as a '"positivist" objection' at pp. 236–7, discussed the placing of Chapter XIII, and beyond that left the book to its author.

2.

Reading my way into the natural law tradition, as a final-year law student and then during my doctoral studies, I was disconcerted by the inability or unwillingness of the modern writers in that tradition to meet modern secular students as and where they are— equipped by schoolteachers and journalists with views derivative from Hume and Russell or other varieties of modern scepticism about good and bad, right and wrong in human action, and with scientistic determinism, materialism, and conceptions (e.g. Logical Positivistic) of the limitations of reason. So I ought not to have been surprised, yet I was, at the inability or unwillingness of reviewers and other readers from the more or less Thomistic tradition to take into account the book's genre, and its primary intended audience as a part of the Clarendon Law Series. Of course, that audience was envisaged as including philosophers, both inside and far outside that tradition, and a book should speak accurately whatever its audience. Still, these reviewers and readers, seeing things done quite out of traditional orders of treatment, and reading occasional programmatic declarations more or less in isolation from contexts, endnotes, and later argumentation, all too quickly wrote the book down or off as a sell-out. It was, they thought, a capitulation to Hume on 'Is and Ought'. There was never, I think, real evidence that they had read the root-and-branch critique of what Hume does, says, and does not say, about *Is* and *Ought*, in secs II.5–6; nor that they faced up to my claim on p. 47 that Aristotle and Aquinas would have agreed that *ought* cannot be deduced from *is* (without some *ought* premise).

Still, it was a serious weakness of the book that it did not deploy or indeed envisage the proper response to these would-be Aristotelian-Thomistic critics, the response that points to their own inattention to a cardinal principle of Aristotle's and Aquinas's methodology and working methods. That is the principle, pervasive in their work but conspicuously lost to view in the work of their modern would-be representatives, that we do not know natures of things without knowing those things' capacities, which in turn we cannot know without knowing their actualization in activity, which in turn we cannot understand with any adequacy except by knowing the activities' objects. That is the prime epistemological axiom for Aristotle and Aquinas, and its application to human action and practical reason is clear. *Adequate knowledge of human nature is not the source of our coming to understand human ends, goods, or flourishing.* Rather it is a resultant of our understanding of the intelligible objects of human willing and action, objects which are the intelligible goods (called 'values' in this book).

Of course, ontologically the order of dependence is precisely the reverse: objects of will are attainable only by actions made possible only by capacities which we have only by virtue of having the human (not ape, mouse, or asteroid) nature we have. But the doubts pressed about the book's coherence with the *natural*-law tradition are epistemological, and the doubters should have been challenged in advance, and sooner, on their own territory. The book's nearest approach to the epistemological axiom is in the first endnote to sec. III.5, on p. 78, which is enhanced by the immediately following endnote, on pp. 78–9. But these seemed to gain no detectable attention from those whom it most concerned (e.g. Ralph McInerny and Henry Veatch, and later Alasdair MacIntyre). It was not until *Fundamentals of Ethics* in 1983 that I deployed the axiom, while also challenging writers such as Mortimer Adler and Veatch on the home ground of their claims to be able to derive practical from theoretical principles.

There I also showed, I think, the groundlessness of the claim that the book is Kantian in inspiration. Kant does not have a patent on the term 'practical reason', a term central to Aquinas and important to Aristotle; and Kant knows only one underived practical principle, an empty and formal one at that. His not infrequent appeals to nature are innocent of the axiom that might have given them sense (at the expense of what is distinctively Kantian). His work is not a sound guide to practical reasoning.

3.

Among critics unencumbered by those 'tradition'-based concerns, the two most common misapprehensions have been, first, an assumption that Chapter I's discussion of method in descriptive-explanatory social science and jurisprudence is a necessary preliminary to the account of practical reason and of moral, social-political, and legal theory in Chapters II–XII; and secondly, an assumption that the first principles identified in Chapters III and IV provide a sufficient basis for understanding the social-political and legal theory in Chapters VI–XII—so that Chapter V can be skipped over.

But, as the title of Chapter I suggests and the title of its first section makes clear, *descriptive social science* is the subject-matter of this chapter. Accordingly, the chapter's last paragraph sets the scene for the rest of the book:

A theory of natural law need not be undertaken primarily for the purpose of … providing a justified conceptual framework for descriptive social science. It may be undertaken, *as this book is*, primarily to assist the practical reflections of those concerned to act … (p. 23)

And the first page of Chapter II, introducing the book's subject-matter and theses about principles of natural law, says that those

principles *justify* authority and *require* that it be exercised with
respect for human rights and common good, and generally in
accordance with the Rule of Law. In other words, the book's
concern after Chapter I is normative, practical, moral. Description
is henceforth subordinate, and relevant only insofar as (i) all practical reasoning to a conclusion about what ought to be done has
amongst its premises at least one descriptive (including predictive)
premise about circumstances and causalities; (ii) 'a knowledge of
the whole range of human possibilities and opportunities, inclinations and capacities, a knowledge that requires the assistance of
descriptive and analytical social science' is needed for normative
theory to be done 'securely' (pp. 18–19); and (iii) attention to the
facts about our language provides (as Hart says) 'reminders' about
human possibilities and opportunities, etc. The book's programme
and explanations are justificatory (p. 237), to 'explore the requirements of practical reasonableness', and 'trace the ways in which
sound laws, in all their positivity and mutability, *are to be derived...*
from unchanging principles... that have their force from their reasonableness' (p. 351).

To say this is not to retreat in the least from the argument of
Chapter I, that descriptive social theory is a legitimate project but
dependent, for the critical formation of its own concepts, on fully
normative considerations such as those introduced in Chapter II
and proposed, defended, and elaborated through the ten chapters of
Part Two. That argument has its own intrinsic interest and importance, and provides a free-standing ground and motive for
investigating the question whether practical reason is truly reason,
capable of reaching and vindicating true judgments and thus sur-
mounting relativism and 'demonic' (Weber) 'selection of values' by
the social theorist. Still, that ground and motive is secondary to
practical reason's significance for deliberation and choice across
the whole field of individual and group life. And putting the
secondary first, in the book's order of treatment, had the bad side
effect of encouraging the myth (or *déformation professionelle* of believing) that the default position in jurisprudence or legal philosophy is legal positivism, and that anyone who upholds law's
appropriate positivity is 'conceding' or 'admitting' something
rightly affirmed by positivists—as if the loose cluster of positions
labelled by textbooks 'positivism' were not (as it is) a latecomer to
the philosophy of law, with not too many important discoveries to

its name and a vast capacity and willingness to misread the philosophical tradition from which it emerged.

As to the second misapprehension, about the main principles of
practical reason, suffice it to say that although the articulation and
defence of first principles in Chapters III and IV deserve to be
considered the book's primary confrontation with ethical and political scepticism, the unfolding of those principles' moral/ethical
content and force, in Chapter V, is critically important for the
grounding of the book's political and legal theory. Indeed, any
defensible normative political or legal theory will need some such
account, distinguishing the principles which give action intelligible
point from those that guide morally sound choices and moral
judgments about possible or actual choices.

4.

That makes all the more significant the failure of Chapter V to
identify the unifying source of the nine 'methodological principles'
or 'requirements' of practical reasonableness that it articulates. The
short bridging paragraph in the middle of p. 102 finds for them
only the extrinsic unity of historical fact: that each has been
identified, at some time or other, by 'some philosopher', as (or as
if it were) *the* 'controlling and shaping' requirement of practical
reasonableness.

That fact is indeed significant. But these principles and requirements do have an intrinsic, normative source of unity and intelligibility, a source which therefore counts as morality's master principle.
Each first principle of practical reason picks out and directs us
towards an intrinsic intelligible good, a basic aspect of human
fulfilment, and so we can understand the possibility of an integral,
that is overall, directiveness of the whole set of first practical principles, a directiveness not deflected or reduced by sub-rational
motivations. Since each of the basic goods is as good in the lives of
others as in the life of the person deliberating, the content of this
integral directiveness will be *integral* human fulfilment, that is, the
flourishing of *all* human persons and groups, considered not as an end
which might be attained by skilful and/or fortunate disposition of
means but rather as a kind of ideal of reason against which plans of
action can be measured. Thus the requirements of practical reason,
which are the most general *moral* principles, are to be understood

as specifications of the most general (and thus 'master') moral principle: all one's choices and other kinds of willing should be *open to* integral human fulfilment. The Golden Rule (sec. V.4), for example, picks out a way of not being open, in one's choosing or other forms of willing, to integral human fulfilment. That is to say: to violate the Golden Rule is to allow emotional motivations for self-interested preference—independent of rational grounds for prioritizing among persons—to override the rational rule of fair impartiality. (Which is not to overlook the fact that emotional motivations enter legitimately into that part of the Golden Rule's content that refers to 'as *you yourself would* (i.e. would be willing to) be done by…'.) And the same goes for the other requirements discussed in Chapter V.[1] Contrary to p. 102 (last paragraph), failure to live up to these requirements is not so much irrational as *unreasonable*, and wrong.

5.

It may be helpful to make a synoptic comment on the book's other main omissions or *corrigenda*, leaving detailed treatment of them to later points in this Postscript.

Free choice and intention

The fact that we can make free choices, for which we are responsible, and which have self-determining (self-constituting) significance, is clearly affirmed, and if one reads all the pages indicated in the index under 'Freedom' and 'Self-constitution', and the note on p. 127, one will have a fair idea of the fact's significance. But no clear definition is articulated, though the needed definition is presupposed on, and indeed inferable from, p. 384. It was given in *Fundamentals of Ethics* VI.1: 'a choice is free if and only if it is between open practical alternatives (i.e. to do this, or to do that…) such that there is no factor but the choosing itself which settles which alternative is chosen'.[2] The radical character of such freedom was already emphasized in the argument on p. 384 above, that free choice is

---

[1] Openness to integral fulfilment is identified as the master principle of morality in *FoE*, at 70–4, 120–4, 151–2; in *CEJF* I.10 at 159, 167 (1984a); in Grisez, Boyle, and Finnis, 'Practical Principles, Moral Truth, and Ultimate Ends', AJJ 32: 99 (1987f) at 126–9; in *NDMR* at 283–4; and then in *CEJF* I.14 at 215 (1992a) and various later works.

[2] *FoE* 137; this is substantially the definition proposed and defended by Grisez, Boyle, and Tollefsen in the work cited above on p. 127. *FoE* 137 proceeds to set out a summary version of the Grisez-Boyle-Tollefsen argument that it is self-refuting to argue (or critically hold) that there are no free choices. *Ibid.*, 139–42, 152–3, spell out the significance of free choice for self-constitution, as an intransitive consequence

incompatible with Leibniz's asserted 'principle of sufficient reason'; and its incompatibility with contemporary 'soft determinism', in any form, is brought out in *Nuclear Deterrence, Morality and Realism* IX.6. The definition's references to 'open practical alternatives' can be clarified and tightened by referring instead to *proposals* shaped in deliberation precisely as options, each proposal/option describing a set of ends and means in some respect(s) incompatible with alternative proposal(s), and choice being then understood as the adoption of one such proposal/option in preference to the other(s). The concepts employed in the preceding sentence are discussed in *CEJF* II, Introduction at pp. 2–4 and 11; *ibid.*, pp. 4–10 elaborate on the remarkable, 'strange' character of ordinary human freedom, and point to the relevant links with meaning, intention, and person-hood—realities absolutely central to an adequate idea of law and its rationale and importance; *ibid.*, pp. 13–14 focus on intention. The highly significant inter-definability of *proposal* and *intention* is expounded in detail—and in a legal context—in essay II.10 (1991b). The link enables, for the first time, a clarified and stable theoretical concept of intention. This theoretical concept is no more and no less than a distillation and purification of the commonsense understanding of intention—an understanding displayed not only in 'intention' and 'intend' but also in 'purpose', 'aim', 'in order to', 'with a view to', 'to...', 'trying to', etc.[3] This common sense is also the core of the legal concept of intention when the latter is freed from such fictions as the doctrine that whatever is foreseen by A as a certain or even very probable effect of A's conduct is intended by A.

Virtues and principles

The book says little about virtue(s). That was deliberate, but it would have been appropriate to explain both the decision and the intrinsic relationship between virtues and principles, the priority of the latter, and the bearing of free choices' intransitive aspects (their lasting in the dispositions of the chooser) on the formation of virtues and vices. *Aquinas*, 124, explains why principles, propos-

---

or effect of choice, an effect ineluctable and permanent unless cancelled by a contrary, repudiatory choice (repentance). These pages, drawing on Grisez and Wojtyla and contradicting Hume, enhance and clarify what is said in *NLNR* about self-constitution and self-determination. See also, especially, essay I.15, p. 239 (1997b).

[3] For other equivalent words and phrases, see e.g. essay II.14 (2010a). For a full-dress treatment, see essay II.13 (2001a), co-authored with German Grisez and Joseph Boyle, architects of this clarification as of the substance of my works' other main clarifications in ethics and action theory.

itional practical truths, are more fundamental than virtues, even
than the master virtue of practical reasonableness (*prudentia*): 'for
virtues are the various aspects of a stable and ready willingness to
make good choices, and like everything in the will, are a response
to reasons, and reasons are propositional'.[4] And the relevant propositions are the first principles of practical reason(ing) (Chapters
III and IV above) and the requirements of practical reasonableness
(Chapter V), together with the more specific moral norms which
result from bringing these two levels of principle to bear on one
another. Some of this is hinted at in the paragraph on p. 102 above
concerning Aristotle's idea of the 'mean' (virtue's mean between
the vices of 'too much' and 'too little'—where reasons are the
measure of the excessive and the fitting). But spelling out the
inherent connection between principles and virtue(s), the logical
and rational primacy of the former (a primacy acknowledged by
Aquinas[5]), and the grounds on which, nonetheless, Aquinas could
judge it reasonable to arrange his largest discussion of morality
under the various cardinal virtues, would have helped avoid the
suspicion that 'virtue ethics' was or is an unexamined alternative to
the kind of moral theory deployed in this book. It is not.

Incommensurability

The discussion on pp. 112–23 points to a number of reasons why it
is not rationally possible to measure and compare the goods and
bads in alternative options in such a way as to identify (as utilitarians propose) the option that is morally required because promising most overall net good. With one exception, the points made
seem to me sound, though they might profitably be rearranged.
The exception is the sentence on p. 115: 'But the different forms
of goods, like the different kinds of quantities, are objectively
incommensurable'. Though true, this suggests (though it does
not assert)[6] that different instantiations of a single 'form of good',
i.e. a single basic human good (e.g. life), *can* be commensurated
objectively as is demanded and presupposed by utilitarianism. But
incommensurabilities between morally significant options defeat
utilitarian-style methods even when only one basic human good is
at stake. This is pointed out already in *Fundamentals of Ethics* at

---

[4] *Aquinas* 124; see also ibid. 187–8.

[5] *Id.*, nn. 103, 104.

[6] The assertion is made, concessively, in essay I.8 at 141 (an unpublished paper of 1975).

p. 89, by reference to the fact that 'the basic human goods are not abstract entities but aspects of the *being* of persons each of whom is distinct from and no mere means to the well-being of any other person'. But the matter is tackled much more explicitly and clearly in essay IV.17 at 357 (1990d): inter-categorial incommensurability is an important source of the incommensurability in issue, but is by no means necessary for such incommensurability, or its only source.

There is incommensurability also between choosable instantiations of one and the same basic good. For instance, what makes vacationing at the beach appealing and what makes vacationing in the mountains appealing—such alternatives are incommensurable in the sense that each possibility has some intelligible appeal not found in what makes the other appealing.

Essay I.15 at 241–2 (1997b) considerably deepens and extends the explanation, in the graver context of choices such as Socrates': to suffer the loss of two lives (including his own) rather than kill one innocent. The points it makes overlap with some of the points in *NLNR*'s discussion of incommensurability, but enhance that earlier discussion with explicit attention to (a) choice's capacity to create a new world, (b) the lack of an objective theory of probabilities and of the weight of probabilities against values and disvalues, and (c) the self-constitutive intransitive effects of choice on the chooser and on any who approve the chooser's choice.

Justice, ius, *and rights*

Chapter VII's discussions of justice would have done well to pay more attention to its definition in Justinian's *Digest*, adopted nearly seven hundred and fifty years later by Aquinas: the steady and lasting willingness to give to each what is his or hers or, synonymously, his or her right(s) (*jus*). The definition is given on p. 207, but its significance is not sufficiently grasped. To say that *jus* is something people, one by one, *have* is to say that it is 'subjective' in the sense that it belongs to subjects (persons). And this *having* (to which others have the duty actively to respond) is by no means exhausted, or even most centrally exemplified, as Grotius thought, by the possessor's power or liberty of acting, but rather extends also, and centrally too, to being the proper beneficiary of the duties (negative and positive) of another or others. This in turn entails that the 'watershed' in the history of *jus* and right(s), asserted on p. 206 and explored in the remainder of sec. VIII.3, must be judged much less substantial and significant than even the limited significance accorded to it in that section. (This implication is drawn and explained in *Aquinas* V.1–2 and in 2002c ('Aquinas on *jus* and Hart on Rights').)

The nature of God

As essay V.13 says at 193:

NLNR takes a very austere, minimalist view of what can be affirmed on the basis of reason alone about the nature of God. The argument that we are, not logically, but rationally required to affirm the existence of a transcendent explanation/cause 'which exists simply by being what it is, and which is required for the existing of any other state of affairs' is said on p. 389 to be unable, 'I think', to take us further. That God's nature is personal, that 'the uncaused cause of all the good things of this world (including our ability to understand them) is itself a good that one could love, personal in a way that one might imitate, a guide that one might follow, or a guarantor of anyone's practical reasonableness' is said on p. 398 to be a set of propositions of which 'it is impossible to have sufficient assurance ... without some revelation more revealing than any that Plato or Aristotle may have experienced'. Hence the negative conclusion stated bluntly on p. 405: '... what can be established, by argumentation from the existence and general features of the world, concerning the uncaused cause of the world, does not directly assist us in answering' the practical questions set up in the chapter's first pages—about the possibility of a deeper explanation of obligation, the reasonableness of self-sacrifice in human friendship, 'the point of living according to the requirements of practical reasonableness',[7] that is, 'whether any *further* sense can be made of the whole situation ...'.[8] This limitation of 'natural reasoning', I added, though it 'leaves somehow "subjective" and "questionable" the whole structure of basic principles and requirements of practical reasonableness and human flourishing ... does not unravel that structure or affect its internal order or weaken its claim to be more reasonable than any logically possible alternative structures'.[9]

Later, working further on Aquinas's arguments, I came to think that rational reflection and argumentation on what p. 406 calls 'the perfection of being all that is required to make all states of affairs exist' can establish significantly more, even without the benefit of

---

[7] *NLNR* 405.　　[8] *Ibid.*, 372.　　[9] *Ibid.*, 405.

any divine communication, than Chapter XIII allows. The arguments summarized in *Aquinas* X.1–4 enable us to say enough about the divine nature, and about the divine causing, shaping, and sustaining of the universe, to establish a good deal about the *point* of the existence and flourishing of created realities and about the special point of human persons as each ends in themselves.[10]

6.

So the book has significant weaknesses. But its main purposes and main positions remain intact. Primary among its purposes, as p. 46 says, is to resume those lines of thought about human choices, action, institutions, and well-being that were carried forward from Plato by Aristotle and Aquinas. Aquinas's contribution to that great conversation was powerfully but incompletely clarifying, and in some key respects was misunderstood by his successors and would-be followers—misunderstandings which rendered the tradition needlessly vulnerable, and enfeebled in its response, to the crude attacks of Hobbes, Locke, and Hume, attacks to which Kant responded quite inadequately and Bentham by compounding their errors. At the root of scholastic misunderstandings of Aquinas was the resort to *will* as purported source of normativity, a resort which Grotius's (Suarezian) appeal to 'rational nature' avoids only by leaving the source simply obscure. *NLNR* is resolutely 'intellectualist', as opposed to 'voluntarist' in its strategies for explaining and justifying moral—and then legal—predicates, not least 'is obligatory' or 'must be done' but more broadly all the normative predicates and concepts such as responsibility and virtue/vice. But the understanding connoted by 'intellectualist' is the understanding not, in the first instance, of nature, rational or otherwise, but of human *good* and of the means necessary or appropriate to pursuing and actualizing it integrally. The book's articulation of many good-identifying principles, and more than one level of principles, is the price of avoiding, so far as possible, the appeal to ungrounded and unintegrated 'moral intuitions' which pervades the post-Kantian and post-utilitarian ethics and political philosophy of our time.

---

[10] See especially *Aquinas* 312–14, or the discussion of and quotations from those pages in essay V.13 at 196–8. On the importance for law of a secure grasp of the priority of persons, each one, over the subpersonal, see essay II.1 (2000a).

CHAPTER I: EVALUATION AND THE
DESCRIPTION OF LAW

I.1 The Formation of Concepts for Descriptive Social Science

The title of this section points to the theme of the whole chapter, whose subsequent sections are steps along the way in an *argument*. That argument's conclusion is stated in the last two sentences of the first paragraph of I.5. The decisive steps in the argument are taken in I.4, on pp. 14 and 15; the paragraph that begins on p. 16 gives a first statement of the conclusion. The most well-known published challenges to the chapter's conclusion ignore or, at best, unwarrantably truncate, its argument.

Of decisive importance for the argument are the words 'science' and 'theory', which are used synonymously with 'general theory'. For the argument takes for granted, and indeed implies, that there can be non-evaluative, neutral, value-free descriptions of evaluations, i.e. of the value judgments that particular people or peoples make (and give effect to in normative institutions of many kinds). The decisively important contrast, between *particulars* such as these and *general* features of the human condition and situation is made in the italicized sentence high on p. 4. It is the only whole sentence italicized in the book—yet, despite the precaution, is often ignored as a statement of the question being tackled in the chapter. Social theory or science deals with the general (while using the device of central cases and focal meanings to avoid overlooking or neglecting the particulars).

So the chapter's main theme is its argument that (1) theory descriptive in purpose must be evaluative in method if it concerns human actions (as societies or social relations do). But it is worth noting two less visible themes: (2) jurisprudence is not a matter of 'conceptual analysis'; its subject-matter is the reality of human persons as subjects and objects of the intelligent purposes of securing peace, justice, and prosperity. Conceptual analysis, simply as such, could yield only local history, lexicography, ethnography. (This theme is revisited, precisely in the context of 'the concept of law', on pp. 278–9.) And (3) social theory (in its centrally important and appropriate forms) is not modelled on natural science and the proper replacement for conceptual analysis is not 'naturalism'. All these themes are pursued, and the proper reading of this chapter is explored, in essay IV.1 (2003b); the essay supplements considerably what is said in this Postscript, and should itself be read along with the Introduction to *CEJF* IV at 1–9.

The section needs no change. But it (like the first endnote to it, on p. 19) could usefully have said explicitly, on its first page, that biography and history describe individual and social actions, arrangements, and institutions by reference to their point (purpose, rationale) *as conceived by the acting persons* under study. R.G. Collingwood's thesis that history is the rethinking of the thoughts of past persons brings out this truth with only a touch of exaggeration. His own successful practice as an archaeologist in his spare time exemplified this truth about historical method, notably by his success in inferring where Roman generals would have sited forts on the coasts south of Hadrian's Wall in the early second century AD. The same truth is exemplified by the fictional detective practices of Sherlock Holmes, and the actual practices of real detectives and cryptographers, of some chess-players and of most successful generals—all those who anticipate their foe's manoeuvres on the basis of his or his associates' past performance, understanding the opponent's or other subjects' evaluations without sharing them. I had this all in mind in writing the chapter, and might fittingly have referred to it.

Ronald Dworkin's subsequent claim to have expounded a theory of interpretation, and of law as subject-matter of interpretation, makes it necessary to add that what I have just said about understanding the intentions and meaning of particular persons or groups approximates to what Dworkin calls 'ordinary conversational interpretation, in which the interpreter aims to discover the intentions or meanings of another person' (*Law's Empire*, 54). But there seems no case for drawing the sharp distinction that Dworkin draws between understanding one's interlocutors in conversation and understanding the meaning and intentions embodied or put into effect in a social practice. There seems no ground for assuming in advance, about every social practice, that 'it is essential to the structure of such a practice that interpreting the practice be treated as different from understanding what other participants mean by the statements they make in its operation' (*ibid.*, 55)—by which Dworkin means, *so different* that interpreting a practice (unlike a conversation) can *only* be done by participants (*id.*), must try to put the practice 'in its best light' (*ibid.*, 54), involves 'imposing purpose' (purposes of the interpreter!) on the practice 'in order to make of it the best possible example of the form or genre to which it is taken to belong' (*ibid.*, 52), and so forth. For reasons suggested in essay IV.12 (1987e), sec. I, the 'constructive' or 'creative' interpretation which Dworkin thus (implausibly) claims is the only form of interpretation available for understanding social practices such as law would be much better spoken of, not as interpretation, but as a process of practical reasoning about the requirements of justice and common good, reasoning that appropriately takes different, more constrained and stylized forms in adjudication than in legislative deliberation: see essay IV.20 at 399–402 (1999c). For present purposes, however, suffice it to say that Chapter I proceeds on the assumption that there can be description of social practices (including essentially linguistic practices such as law) which is value-free and imposes no evaluations or purposes of the person observing and describing.

I.2 Attention to Practical Point

At this stage of the argument, what is primary is still the ideas about (= conceptions of) practical point that particular persons, private or public, in particular societies, actually have or have had in mind in doing what they or we count as law-making, law-applying, etc. (Even when descriptive social theory starts to generalize, its first regard must be to the ideas, not of the theorist, but of the people whose activities and dispositions provide social theory with its subject-matter: see, for example, the last part of the final sentence in the full paragraph on p. 12.) But in the strategic passages from Hart recalled in the first paragraph (pp. 6–7), the ideas are assumed by Hart to be ones that his readers will concur in thinking appropriate for the governance of a society. As the account from Raz summarized in the second paragraph (pp. 7–8) makes clear, the kind of society in question is one that in the tradition running from Plato or Aristotle through Aquinas is called a *perfecta communitas*, that is, a 'complete community', also called political or (synonymously, and thus not in Hegel's more specialized sense) civil.

For the purposes of the chapter's primary argument, about concept-formation in descriptive *social* theory, the key paragraph is the middle one on p. 8: one has to *justify* using a concept like law or legal system or Rule of Law in a truly general descriptive/explanatory theory of human affairs; the chapter's argument is exploring the grounds for and logic of such justification. The paragraph following that (pp. 8–9) loses momentum. Still, what it says is I think correct, and the link it makes between the concept of law and the concept of the Rule of Law is important in its own right.

The section's final paragraph, taken in isolation from the points made on pp. 12–16 (when the argument proper resumes), is open to the misunderstanding that importance and significance, for the purposes of descriptive social theory/science, are matters of typicality or of 'consilience'[11] with natural phenomena and natural-science accounts of them. But they are not (see p. 10 after cue 23). Rather, they are a matter of instantiation of, or serviceability for, human flourishing, or, in non-central cases, of opposition or disservice to that well-being.

I.3 Selection of Central Case and Focal Meaning

'Selection' is an unhappy term to the extent that it suggests that this is matter for an option between equals or incommensurables, rather than (as I intended) a matter of sound theoretical judgment about importance and significance in the sense just mentioned. (As the argument will show, sound theoretical judgment, in relation to the theory of these human affairs, even descriptive or descriptive/explanatory theory, will be dependent upon sound practical judgment.)

The philosophical discussion of 'focal meaning' in the decades since 1978 can be studied in Ward, *Aristotle on Homonymy: Dialectic and Science* (CUP: 2008), or Shields, *Order in Multiplicity: Homonymy in the Philosophy of Aristotle* (OUP: 1999); an introductory summary is Ward, 'Aristotelian Homonymy', Philosophy Compass 4 (2009) 575–85. These authors tend to speak of 'core' rather than 'central' cases, and of 'dependent' rather than 'secondary' or 'marginal' or 'watered-down' or 'deviant' cases; but their discussion broadly confirms the approach to analogy taken throughout *NLNR*.

Essay 2008d ('Grounds of Law & Legal Theory'), sec. I, reaffirms that what is central in a range of types or instances, or focal in a range of meanings, is relative to viewpoint and purposes, including

---

[11] William Whewell, in *The Philosophy of the Inductive Sciences* (1840), introduced this term: 'The Consilience of Inductions takes place when an Induction, obtained from one class of facts, coincides with an Induction obtained from another different class. Thus Consilience is a test of the truth of the Theory in which it occurs'. Corroboration by concurrence of phenomena or coincidence or convergence of hypotheses, in other words.

theoretical purposes. The central case of law, e.g. as identified by Hart in *The Concept of Law* or as identified (differently) in *NLNR*, is of course not the central case of law, or focal meaning of 'law', for the purposes of a historian (or philosopher or practitioner) of natural science(s). As sec. 5 of this chapter says, natural law theory undertakes a critique of viewpoints, and as the rest of the book shows, carries forward this critique on the basis of a robust account of principles of practical reason picking out and directing us to basic human goods and, by implication, to judgments of right and wrong as the practically reasonable or unreasonable in choices and actions. What then is to be said of widespread and well-rooted practices which oppose important human goods? Are there central cases of prostitution? Slavery? Concentration camps? Extermination camps? Tyrannies? Burglaries? From the viewpoint of those who choose such acts or ways of life or institutions or ideologies, *efficacy and sustainability* in service of their individual purposes, whatever the cost to the victims, is doubtless a primary criterion of centrality. From the viewpoint of practical reasonableness, such acts and practices earn a place in social *theory* only by their opposition (harm, threat) to and/or parasitism on those goods and requirements of practical reasonableness that they harm and flout, or imitate with unreasonable deviations and restrictions. Slavery is parasitical on wage labour and on property in things. Concentration camps are deviant forms of reasonable prisons, detention centres, holding centres, and quarantine arrangements. Prostitution imitates miniature love affairs which in confused ways imitate marital relations, arrangements for which are a major part of social theory. And so forth.

More generally:

The idea of central cases and focal meanings is itself an analogical idea. That is, we should expect the application and even the meaning of 'central case' and 'focal meaning' to shift as we move from (1) natural orders (physical and other natural sciences, metaphysics and so forth) to (2) logical orders (of thought bringing order into its own operations), to (3) the order of morally significant deliberation and action, and on fourthly (4) to the arts and techniques that bring order into matter beneath our control. We should expect the centrality of central cases in the natural and/or metaphysical sciences to be grounded in kinds of reasons (among them doubtless statistical frequency) notably different from the kinds of reasons that ground the centrality of central cases in the domain of self-shaping and community-shaping morally significant action.

But since human action, like human persons themselves, can often be worth studying not as the carrying out of self-shaping deliberation, free choice and execution of that choice but rather as an event in the natural world, or as an example or outcome of valid or invalid reasoning, or as a technological feat or fumble, we need to be alert to the theoretical purposes of the person carrying out the study.[12]

I.4 *Selection of Viewpoint*

The section deploys two arguments for its conclusion that it is the practical (moral and political) judgments of the practically reasonable person that are the correct criterion for settling whether law earns a place in the general descriptive theory of human affairs, and what is the understanding, conception, or idea of law that is fit to be deployed as the focal meaning of 'law', picking out the central type-case of law, in that theory. One is the dialectical argument in the text, opening in the last paragraph on p. 12, running through to the conclusion on pp. 12–13, and itself prepared for by the scrutiny of method in descriptive legal theories beginning in the last paragraph on p. 4 and running through to the end of sec. I.2 on p. 9. The other is the distinct, short, and powerful Platonic-Aristotelian argument set out in the footnote on p. 15—the chapter's only discursive footnote.

These arguments could usefully be supplemented by the one deployed in conjunction with an analysis of Max Weber's method in concept-formation (in relation to his concept of *Herrschaft*, authority, or domination), in essay IV.9 (1985c), sec. II, esp. 215–17. Legal-rational authority is treated by Weber as having explanatory priority over charismatic and traditional authority, not only for the reasons he tersely offers ('most rational and most familiar'), but also because it is defined by a richer, fuller cluster of features or elements, from which the other two kinds differ mainly by subtraction from that cluster. The same theory-formation phenomena are found in Hart's *The Concept of Law*; primitive law and international law differ from the central type-case of law largely by subtraction from its defining or characterizing features (union of primary with secondary rules of recognition, change, and adjudication). This all

---

[12] 2008d at 315–16. On the four enumerated kinds of order see pp. 135–9 above (where the third and fourth are reversed in numbering).

goes to confirm Aristotle's methodological thesis that the non-central differ from the central cases (of friendship, citizenship, constitution, or whatever) by *watering down* (as wine can be diluted by water).

The 'Thus' with which the main dialectical argument opens on p. 12 looks back, not to the preceding sentence but to the *first sentence* of the preceding paragraph. (The intervening discussion of the word 'practical' is distracting, not least because the ideas of 'critical' reflection and requirements of practical reasonableness are neither needed nor properly available at this stage of the argument—but only from p. 15 on.) The core of the argument is going to be that there is no good reason for denying that the 'internal' or 'legal' point of view itself has a central case, and that the viewpoints of (in turn) an anarchist judge, or of traditionalist, careerist, or conformist judges, officials, or citizens, cannot be the central case: for the reasoning see the top paragraph on p. 14.[13] Rather, that central case internal or legal viewpoint must have the character-istics set out in the long last sentence on p. 14 and the first full sentence on p. 15. That yields the interim conclusion articulated in the sentence ending the top paragraph on p. 15. That interim conclusion is then refined and sharpened in the succeeding para-graph in the centre of p. 15, whose own argument is supplemented by the above-mentioned Platonic-Aristotelian argument set out in footnote 37.

The ultimate conclusion of the whole argument opens the first distinct paragraph on 16: 'Thus by a long march...'. The conclu-sion is first stated in terms (Weber's terms) of 'the evaluations of the theorist himself'... But then, crucially, the first-person view-point ('his' or 'theirs') is dissolved: theorists must each 'decide [better: judge] what the requirements of practical reasonableness really are' (*id.*). The concept of transparency, expounded by Roy Edgley in *Reason in Theory and Practice* (1969) [a book cited in

---

[13] Neither these reasons, nor the setting up of the issue on p. 13, nor the conclusions articulated on pp. 14–15, have anything to do with the position attributed to pp. 13–14 (and to the whole chapter) by Dickson, *Evaluation and Legal Theory* (2001), 44, a position which is essentially Joseph Raz's (law invariably and by its nature claims to be morally obligatory, and the belief that the law's rules are morally obligatory is what needs to be explained) and not mine (since many rules of law, being unjust, are not morally obligatory), and it is possible that some legal systems abstain from claiming to be morally obligatory. My argument, in these pages, concerns the viewpoint of those who think it is practically reasonable to try to introduce or reintroduce law where it is not yet developed or where it has been corrupted or overthrown.

another connection on p. 77] and in *FoE* I.1 and III.5, would have been helpful. Edgley says (as quoted at *FoE* 23):

'my own present thinking, in contrast to the thinking of others, is transparent in the sense that I cannot distinguish the question "Do I think that p?" from a question in which there is no essential reference to myself or my belief, namely "Is it the case that p?" ' (*Reason in Theory and Practice*, 97 [and later, at *ibid.* 127: "thinking that the thing to do is x is one form of thinking that p"])

But the top paragraph on p. 17, though trying to do too much all at once, makes the key point that in critical reflection, one's own judgments are open to correction, not only on factual grounds (the focus of the paragraph) but also by the implicit challenge consti-tuted by other people's views about the good and the reasonable ('what other persons have considered practically important'). In the implicit dialogue here envisaged, the question is not what I think, or others think, but what ought to be thought, *what any of us should think* (e.g. about what to do). Reasons only count for me as reasons if I think of them as accessible to other people, as reasons and thoughts that other people can and (if in like circumstances) should adopt for themselves, and would (in like circumstances) adopt if they could clear their minds of faulty preconceptions, oversights, distracting images and connotation, and other sources of error. To think of something as a reason is to think of it as something about which I can be *mistaken* and some (perhaps many) other people doubtless are mistaken.

Notice that although the term 'moral' was introduced in the course of the dialectical argument with Hart, who employs it to describe one possible kind of internal viewpoint, the argument concludes not that the central case of the internal viewpoint is the moral viewpoint, but that that central case is the practically reasonable viewpoint about law, and the need for introducing, having, and maintaining law in political societies. Morality can earn its place in the picture only if an investigation of practical reasonableness yields the idea of morality as the definitively critical and appropriately 'all-things-considered' form of practical reason-ableness—a conclusion that is reached only on p. 126. In *Aquinas* II.6 ('Social Theory is General Because Practical'), I (very rapidly) sum up the argument entirely in terms of reason and reasons:

One understands, and can describe, what acting persons are doing when one understands their reasons for behaving as they do. The reasons people have for doing what they do hang together to structure a social science just to the extent that good reasons—reasons good as reasons for action—hang together in a coherent set of principles and conclusions, general or strategic reasons, and particular or tactical applications. The reasons which, as a clear-headed theorist, one counts as good when considering human affairs in reflective social theory—even theory intended primarily as explanatory *description*—are the very reasons one counts as good reasons when considering what to do. (*Aquinas* 42)

I.5 The Theory of Natural Law

The first paragraph introduces the natural law *theory* as a critique of practical viewpoints, and as indispensable (as the argument has shown) to any critically warranted analytical, descriptive jurisprudence or any other social science. The paragraph, taken as a whole, articulates the position reached by way of the argumentation of the preceding sections. That position is rearticulated in the Introduction to *CEJF* IV in terms of social *needs* and the responses appropriate for meeting those needs. ('Social needs' were mentioned, in passing but at a significant juncture in the argument, in the middle of p. 14 above.)

The second paragraph, in its first two sentences (often overlooked), states that the rest of the book is *not*, primarily, about 'analytical', i.e. descriptive,[14] jurisprudence or any other descriptive social science or social theory. The book, instead, is going to be directed to assisting the practical reflections and deliberations of those concerned to *act* (as judges, political leaders, or citizens) in response to such needs. It will be about the justification not (as in this chapter) of theoretical concept-selection but of choices and actions, individual and social. Even the theoretical reflections in the final chapter on the world's transcendent cause are directed towards a practical (evaluative) judgment about the point and worth of human existence and action. But in turning away to this normative, point-seeking, justificatory concern, the book does not, of

---

[14] Since conceptual analysis is either local history (ethnography and lexicography) or else a misleading name for the *development* of theoretically adequate concepts for describing and explaining a range of human affairs manifested more or less universally, the term 'analytical jurisprudence' in the last sentence of the first paragraph of sec. I.3 (cf. also 'descriptive and analytical jurisprudence' in second endnote on p. 21) should have been clarified more explicitly than the rest of the sentence accomplishes. On 'conceptual analysis' see also the long paragraph beginning on p. 278; and essays IV.5 at 106–7 (2002a); IV.11 at 259–65 (2009b).

course, abandon its contention that even a theory that aspires to do no more than describe human society (and law's place in it) will need to include, and be guided by, a sound understanding of the worth, the complex point and value of, and justification for, political society, government, and law. That being so, it seems right to push on beyond this chapter's position to the position developed in essay IV.1 (2003b), suggesting that there is no *need* for a social theory purely descriptive in aim (though of course there will always be need for purely descriptive accounts of particular cultures, institutions, practices, and group or individual actions).

On p. 19, as on p. 17, there is a cross-reference to sec. II.4. The earlier passage said that 'there is no question of deriving one's basic judgments about human values and the requirements of practical reasonableness by some inference from the facts of the human situation'; the later says that 'evaluations [of human options with a view, at least remotely, to acting reasonably and well] are in no way deduced from the descriptions [of human affairs by way of descriptive theory/social science]'. Thus the question arises whether the book intends to distinguish between 'inference' and 'deduction'. The issue recurs in much starker form in sec. II.4, which has occasioned endless trouble, and suggestions that the book betrays natural law theory, Aristotle, Aquinas, and the whole tradition, and is Kantian. It is certainly not Kantian, still less neo-Kantian.[15] But how it relates to the tradition could have been made much clearer, as is noted below in considering sec. II.4.

Since Weber had an important role in the dialectic of the earlier sections about concept-formation, it is worth noting that essay IV.9, in secs III and IV (1985b), surveys the misunderstandings that blocked Weber's perception of the implications of his identification of legal-rational authority as the central type-case of authority, in particular the implication that there is need and place for a rational critique of viewpoints on authority (and on other concepts and features in social life). The historic and not outdated locus, form, and name for such a critique is natural law theory, as Weber, in a sense, acknowledges.

[15] See the critique of Kant in *FoE* 73–4, 122–4, 134; essays I.1 at 26 (2005a); I.15 at 236–7 (1997b); IV.5 at 97–8, 111 (2002a).

*Page 21 endnote: Descriptive social theory is not about
what ought to be done*

The account of Dworkin's theory can be updated by essay IV.12 (1987c). It may be worth adding, in relation to Hart's theory, that in the decisive parts of this chapter's argument, law is envisaged as a 'significantly differentiated type of social order' (see pp. 14 end of top paragraph and after cue 36, and 15 top). That is how Hart presents his theory in his Postscript (CL^2 239–40). But there Hart also conceded, or perhaps just granted, that it may be one of the tasks of the general descriptive theorist to state conclusions about 'the meaning of propositions of law in many different legal systems' (*ibid.*, 244). Now there is an important sense in which law is most really, empirically real (fact) precisely *as* a proposition of law in the minds of judges deciding to follow the law rather than their own preferences, and in the minds of those lawyers and law students and professors envisaging that moment of decision. Understanding law in that essential respect, even descriptively, involves more than just reporting that Judge A thinks this, Judge B that, Professor C another thing. It can hardly be other than thinking out what is reasonable *given* this society's and system's 'sources' and 'principles' 'of law'. (The sort of thing that last-period Kelsen anathematized.) That is essentially what Dworkinian jurisprudence undertakes, insofar as it understands itself as 'the general part of adjudication, silent prologue to any decision at law' (*LE* 90) and admits[16] that it is not universal in its theoretical intentions (as Weber is in his sociology, and natural law theory is in its normative, justificatory account of morality, political community, and law). Of course, there are aspects of Dworkin's work that locate his culturally relative jurisprudence in wider horizons of truly general theory, e.g. of authority, but these remain fragmentary and undeveloped. And as for Hart's tentative concession that 'the general descriptive theorist' might articulate 'general descriptive conclusions as to the meaning of . . . propositions of law' in 'all the legal systems' taken into account by the theorist,[17] the project he thus had in mind remains deeply obscure, poised at it is ambiguously (rather like the Roman jurists' *jus gentium*) between the culture-relative and the universal.

---

[16] Thus *LE* 216: 'I am defending an interpretation of our own political culture, not an abstract and timeless political morality'.

[17] CL^2 244.

CHAPTER II: IMAGES AND OBJECTIONS

II.1 Natural Law and Theories of Natural Law

The chapter concerns images of, and objections to, both natural law (moral norms and principles) and natural law theory.

The first two paragraphs summarize the whole of the rest of the book.

The remainder of the section is about the distinction between natural law and natural law theory or theories. One does not have to have any theory of natural law to understand basic principles of practical reasoning and basic requirements of practical reasonableness. A sound theory of natural law is one that accurately identifies true principles of practical reason and practical reasonableness, and vindicates their truth and their interrelationship with each other and with the rest of human knowledge and the realities made known to us in the body of human knowledge. The book is written in the knowledge that 'natural law theory' is a doubly inconvenient label: (1) it is a theory of, amongst other things, *positive* law; and the supposition of self-styled 'positivists' that 'positivism' has a superior and perhaps even historically primary understanding of law's positivity simply overlooks both the history of the explicit idea of positive law (see essay IV.7 (1996c)) and the solidity if not superiority of the accounts of law's positivity that non-'positivist' theories can and do propose; and (2) natural law theory, as a theory of ethics (or morality) and of political communities and institutions, understands itself to be not an ideology or historically conditioned theory in need of a name, but to be, simply, ethics and political philosophy adequately done.

II.2 Legal Validity and Morality

The section's title might better have been *Positive Law, Legal Validity, and Morality.* The section, like the book as a whole, has de facto failed to dispel the radical misunderstandings or misrepresentations of natural law theory. Thus, to the quotations from Raz on p. 26, one can add what his latest work says on its first page:

Theories of law tend to divide into those which think that, by its very nature, the law successfully reconciles the duality of morality and power, and those which think that its success in doing so is contingent, depending on the political realities of the societies whose law is in question.[18]

---

[18] Raz, *Between Authority and Interpretation: On the Theory of Law and Practical Reason* (OUP: 2009), 1.

The suspicion that the primary instances of the first of these 'kinds of theory of law' are, in Raz's view, theories of the 'natural law' kind is confirmed by his later reference to 'Thomist natural law views which regard the law as good in its very nature', a remark the appended footnote to which points to *NLNR* 'esp. chs 1 and 10' as 'a modern version'.[19] So it is necessary to say once again, what p. 26 above already insists upon: that distinction between kinds of theory is a phantasy; there are no representatives of the first kind; and 'Thomist natural law views', and *NLNR*, hold just as firmly as Raz that law's success in reconciling the duality of power and morality is contingent and depends upon the political realities of the societies whose law is in question. The misunderstanding is inexplicable save as yet another—frustrating—instance of what p. 26 calls

the failure of the modern critics to interpret the texts of natural law theorists in accordance with the principles of definition which those theorists have . . . used, . . . principles [sketched in sec. I.3] under the rubric 'central cases and focal meanings'.

It is as if these commentators read in a logic book the statement 'An invalid argument is no argument' and then declared that this school of logicians believes that by their very nature arguments successfully and validly unite known premises with a new proposition (conclusion)—ignoring the fact that much in the logic book is devoted to identifying invalid *arguments* in which the combination of premises yields no support for the 'conclusion'. In the statement thus misunderstood, the first use of the word 'argument' refers to non-central-case (deviant) arguments and the second to central-case arguments.

The focal sense of 'legally valid' is said on p. 27 to be (in Aquinas's theory) the moral sense, and that is true of unrestrained practical reasonableness (which is Aquinas's concern). But the law seeks to insulate itself, to a significant extent, from the general flow of practical reasoning, as is explored in secs XI.3 (esp. p. 312) and XI.4 (esp. pp. 317–18). And a term's focal sense is relative to the concerns, including theoretical concerns, of a speaker (see this Postscript at sec. I.3 above). So what is said here on p. 27 should not be taken as holding universally.

---

[19] *Ibid.*, 167.

II.3 The Variety of Human Opinions and Practices

Leaving behind the two paragraphs discussing the strange statement by Hart with which it begins, the section starts off the book's
extended response to that stock objection which rejects the idea of
natural law and/or of moral truth by pointing to a fact external to
the idea and to arguments for it, the fact that opinions differ, from
which it is inferred that, at least in this domain, one opinion is as
good as another. The book's response is concluded on p. 127 in the
last paragraph of Chapter V.

The section's last paragraph begins the discussion of *self-evidence*
that is continued in sec. III.4.

II.4 The Illicit Inference from Facts to Norms

The section ought to have included, early on, a clarification of the
terms 'inference' and 'derived'. Only in the light of such a clarification might it have been safe to say (p. 34 top) that first principles
of natural law 'are not inferred or derived from anything'. Here
'anything' meant 'any prior, more knowable proposition' and 'inferred' meant 'deduced' as when one proposition is deduced from
another proposition or propositions. In sec. III.4 ('*The self-evidence
of the good of knowledge*'), on p. 66 (discussing the self-evidence of
the first principles of practical reason), what is being denied in
saying 'are not deduced, inferred or derived' is clarified with many
examples of kinds of argument purportedly '[concluding] to' value
which are not being employed in affirming such first principles.
And the second endnote to sec. III.4, on p. 77, reports at some
length Aristotle's and Aquinas's account of the 'induction' of indemonstrable first principles, including practical principles, 'by
insight working on observation, memory, and experience...'. It
would have been helpful to work through an example of the way in
which non-practical knowledge and experience constitutes the
matrix in which our insights into the first principles of practical
understanding occur. The first section of the Introduction to *CEJF*
I works through an example—insight into the good and pursuit-
worthiness of knowledge, on the basis of experience of asking
questions and having them answered, and the non-practical insight
that *knowledge is possible*.

The further essential clarification was only made later, in *FoE*
21–2, distinguishing between the ontological (or metaphysical)

order of reality and the epistemological order of discovery and vindication. This introduces the vital and greatly neglected epistemological and methodological principle that natures are known from capacities, capacities from their actuations, and acts and actuations from their objects—which in the case of human acts are the intelligible goods (basic values) our knowledge of which is what the first principles of practical reason articulate. See also sec. 2 of the Overview to this Postscript, and *Aquinas* II.3.

The quotation from Aquinas on pp. 35–6 above makes the further essential point that nothing can soundly and critically be said to be contrary to human nature (in a morally relevant sense) unless it is first shown to be unreasonable. What is unreasonable is shown by reference not (save implicitly, by a kind of entailment) to human nature but to human good and goods, the intelligible goods picked out in the first principles of practical reason. The metaphysics of human nature comes later in the order of human knowing (though of course earlier in the order of nature—the first of the four kinds of order: the order of things that are what they are independently of our thinking about them).

The statement on p. 34, that 'Aquinas considers that practical reasoning begins . . . by experiencing one's nature, so to speak from the inside, in the form of one's inclinations' is inaccurate as an account of Aquinas and misleading in its implications. Aquinas's account of the relation between natural inclinations and the understanding of first practical principles (propositions) is ambiguous and has been very variously interpreted. There are ways in which pre- or sub-rational inclinations can provide a kind of data for one's originating insights into intelligible goods and the principles which pick them out and direct us towards them; and there are the inclinations of the will that respond to those insights precisely because will, strictly speaking, is responsiveness to practical understanding of goods. It is far from clear that the data on the basis of which the originating practical insights occur must include pre-rational inclinations, let alone that such inclinations are the only relevant data: as Stephen Brock asks, in n. 25 of the article discussed below, under sec. IV.3 at n. 24 (p. 449),

Even as regards goods to which sense-appetite also extends, is it true in every case that we experience sense-desires for them before we understand their goodness? For instance, can a child not understand the good of *coniunctio maris et feminae* [the union of man and woman in marriage] before he feels any urge toward it himself?

II.5 Hume and Clarke on 'Is' and 'Ought'

The important proposition is the statement near the end of p. 37, that the logical principle that no set of non-moral or non-evaluative premises can entail a moral or evaluative conclusion is a principle both significant and true. Those who dissent from the proposition argue in vain unless they identify at least one set of premises none of which is moral or evaluative while the conclusion validly drawn from them is moral or evaluative. No such set of premises is going to be identified. See 1982a, 1981e, and *FoE* 14–17 (pages which conclude with a showing that Henry Veatch—one of those who claim that conclusions about human good can be deduced from facts ('physics') about human function—justifies his judgments about human good by appealing not to such facts but to his readers' understanding of what is—or is not—desirable and valuable).

Footnote 43, running over to p. 38, points to Hume's own defiance of the logical law which, though usually attributed to him, is one that he not only never clearly articulates but frequently violates—p. 41 gives an example and p. 42 a generalization about Hume. (The footnote concludes by referring to the fact that, in different ways, it is violated also by many modern authors who proclaim their adherence to it.) The first part of p. 47's second paragraph will point out that Aristotle and Aquinas would readily grant the soundness of the logical law.

II.6 Clarke's Antecedents

The pages (pp. 38–42) on Samuel Clarke seem to be generally neglected. So, more regrettably, is the discussion on pp. 43–6 of Vazquez, Suarez, and Grotius,[20] and how they differ from Aquinas in ways the importance of which is brought out much later, in sec. XI.8, in which the explication of *imperium* on pp. 338–40 is of great importance to understanding *NLNR* as a whole.

The book's ambition is stated on p. 46: to put together the materials for a satisfactory development of the sort of position espoused by Aquinas but abandoned by his would-be successors.

---

[20] In the first quotation from Grotius on p. 43, 'grant [*etiamsi daremus*]' replaces 'concede [*etiamsi daremus*]'. The sentence shows that Grotius loosely confounded 'grant' and 'concede', using *dare* for both; so the translation now makes him more precise than he was.

Why so? Because this is a position 'untouched by the objections which Hume and after him the whole Enlightenment and post-Enlightenment current of ethics was able to raise against the tradition of rationalism eked out by voluntarism' (p. 47), that is, the tradition or traditions of post-Thomist—and not authentically Thomist—scholastic Aristotelianism. The paragraph with which sec. II.6 ends is a series of challenges to critics, challenges which have not been squarely taken up or met.

II.7 The 'Perverted Faculty' Argument

The argument employed by Aquinas against lying is given fairly close study in *Aquinas* 154–63, pages which show that Aquinas was in all probability indeed not advancing a perverted-faculty argument; *ibid.*, 143–54 show that his sex ethics, too, is not structured on any such argument, and is much more significant and illuminating than is commonly supposed.[21]

II.8 Natural Law and the Existence and Will of God

The important proposition here is articulated in the long second sentence of the paragraph beginning on p. 49; the issues here are taken up again on pp. 371ff. A commentary on this p. 49 sentence is essay V.13 at 194 (from 2008d sec. V).

CHAPTER III: A BASIC FORM OF GOOD: KNOWLEDGE

III.1 An Example

The example is the *basic value*—or, better, the basic intelligible good—of knowledge, and the corresponding *basic principle* of practical reason(ing). The basic practical principles pick out the basic values as *goods and to be pursued* (pursuit-worthy)—that is, they are normative principles which, in informing us, *direct* us. As the first sentence says, they are not moral principles—affirming them just as such is not a matter of making moral judgments. But the next sentence(s), in saying that they are the 'evaluative substratum of all moral judgments', might helpfully have added that, though as such 'pre-moral', they are not outside the realm of moral judgments when moral judgments come into play. Though they only have a moral force or moral normativity once they are modulated and

---

[21] For a summary account, in my own words, see essay IV.5 at 135–8 (2002a, sec. 19).

regulated by practical reasonableness, they do have that force when so regulated and so are not merely pre-moral but also—so to speak, eventually (and always incipiently or *virtualiter*)—moral.

Moreover, this section, though its second paragraph links the basic values to 'good reasons for action', could already have indicated more plainly that the basic values *are* the basic *reasons for action*. To refer to 'reasons' is well short of giving a reason. What 'gives a reason' is the good (value) that is referred to in spelling out the reason—the good picked out by the principle thus articulated. These reasons are the reasons for our basic interests and, if we are functioning at all intelligently, our basic purposes.

III.2 *From Inclination to Grasp of Value*

The word 'value' is used throughout *NLNR* for the reason which is stated in the second complete paragraph on p. 61 and explained further by e.g. the last sentence on p. 62. But I soon regretted it and in *FoE* more or less completely abandoned it for 'understood good' or more commonly 'intelligible good' (for short: 'human good'), the terms used in all my later writings.

The second and third sentences of the first complete paragraph on p. 61 give a not very perspicuous account of the key, non-inferential insight by which one moves from having the urge/inclination of curiosity, via non-practical insight into the possibility of knowledge (getting the concept of knowledge), to practical understanding of knowledge's worth as an intrinsic intelligible good, for me or anyone like me. This shift is described in theoretical terms, and a bit more adequately, in the first complete paragraph on p. 66. For a better, more detailed account, see *CEJF* I, Introduction sec. I, esp. at 2–4. See also p. 449 below, last sentence.

III.3 *Practical Principle and Participation in Value*

This section makes the link between *good* and *principle*, and reaches the Aristotelian point that there is a kind of choice and action—and of what the section finishes by calling 'commitment'—which does not fundamentally seek (like technologies) an end simply outside the means and the actions devoted to it, but rather participates in the good and enables one as an acting person to integrate the good into one's character and identity. The sense and significance of this participation and integration is clearer when one takes into account, as *NLNR* does inadequately, that choices—which are of objectives considered to be beneficial as ends or means or both—last in one's character until reversed by some kind of repentance or other contrary choice: see *CEJF* II, Introduction at 10, essay II.2 at 37–8 (2005c), and essay II.8 at 135–7 (1987b).

III.4 *The Self-evidence of the Good of Knowledge*

Some readers, of course, grumble about appeals to self-evidence. But self-evident propositions, though they cannot and need not be proved, can be defended sufficiently against objections. The section's discussion of self-evidence is sound; the reference forward to rationality norms, on pp. 68–9, is to p. 385; see now also *CEJF* V.9 at 150–4.

The section, on p. 66, somewhat incidentally and belatedly gives the above-mentioned theoretical sketch of the non-inferential 'induction' of the basic good of knowledge and the practical principle picking out and directing us to that good.

III.5 *'Object of Desire' and Objectivity*

About desire, it is advisable not to overlook the endnote on p. 78 about the rather unhelpful saying, 'the good is what all things desire'; and especially the second endnote to the section (pp. 78–9) about the desirable—a word which is really a significant 'equivalent' (not synonym) for 'good' and 'to be pursued' (*prosequendum*) and 'makes better-off'. The later endnote begins to make explicit the connection between human good and human nature, the connection which many have thought is underplayed, and some have imagined is denied, by sec. II.4. To understand some prospective state of affairs attainable by one's own or others' action as desirable, good, a contribution to the flourishing of oneself and others, is to have begun to understand it as good for beings of a certain nature, and thus to have begun to understand that nature more adequately than one did before that practical insight.

About objectivity, see the very next endnote on p. 79, about John Mackie's arguments from 'queerness' and his claim that value-judgments are 'projections' of desire. The Mackiean objectification argument is stated in the last paragraph beginning on p. 70, and is parried through the rest of the section. The queerness argument is stated in the top paragraph on p. 72. The explicit answer to it is

given in Chapter III of *FoE* ('Objectivity, Truth and Moral Principles'), sec. III.2 ('The argument from queerness'), which shows
the objection's roots in Hume and then, *ibid.*, 58–60, directly rebuts
the supposed queerness by pointing to the 'queerness', relative to
perceiving physical objects, of understanding sounds and marks as
meaningful and as propositions; and of understanding arguments
as valid, and conclusions as not merely valid but true. These objects
and relationships are all utterly queer, compared to the bowl of
milk in front of the cat. (This dialectic resembles, but greatly
extends, Dworkin's remarks[22] about the dubious move of sceptics
who seek to advance their doubt or denial by attributing to their
opponents the belief that values or moral principles are 'part of the
fabric of the universe' (a phrase the tacitly sceptical Hart uses in
CL^2 at 168; on his scepticism see e.g. essay IV.10 (2007b) sec. V).)

III.6 *Scepticism about this Basic Value is Indefensible*

The first sentence is important—the argument is not available for
the other basic goods. But of course its availability for this one robs
scepticism of its force as a universal dismissal.

The argument is extensively revisited, in response to Matthew
Kramer's objections, in essay I.4 (2005b). On the basic character of
arguments from self-refutation, that essay says, near the beginning,
at 82:

On this account [the one used in *NLNR*: see p. 74, last paragraph], the
work to be done by an argument from self-referential inconsistency
consists in bringing to light performative inconsistency by drawing out
the 'implicit commitments' of the interlocutor. [That is the argumentative
strategy used in this connection by Mackie.] Or one can skip the machinery of implicit commitments, and the quest for *logical* incoherence or
self-contradiction, and say instead that the work to be done consists in
bringing to light the propositions entailed by 'someone is asserting
that . . .', *i.e.* the facts given in and by the interlocutor's statement. For
even when it is cast into logical form, an argument from self-referential
inconsistency achieves its effect by appealing to facts, which have to be
recognized by the interlocutor(s) not by some purely logical operation
but in the ordinary 'empirical' ways. For p does not entail 'someone
asserts that p'. So the peculiar force of arguments from self-referential

---

[22] *A Matter of Principle* (Harvard U.P.: 1985), 168, 172–3. Note, however, that Dworkin, *ibid.*,
171–2, seems to deny that it is a mark of objective, true propositions that under ideal epistemic
conditions everyone would agree to them. His position is unclear, however, since he uses only the
phrase 'under favorable conditions for reflection'.

inconsistency comes from the unavoidable *proximity* of the relevant facts. Self-refuting interlocutors overlook these facts, but are themselves creating or instantiating them in and by their acts of asserting (disputing).

Arguments from self-refutation broaden out into fruitful arguments from the presuppositions of discourse: see essay I.2 (1999a).

CHAPTER IV: THE OTHER BASIC VALUES

IV.1 Theoretical Studies of 'Universal' Values

This is an important section, because both those engaged in careful practical deliberation, and anyone engaged in theoretical-practical (ethical or political-philosophical) reflection on practical reason, not to mention anyone engaged in the descriptive social theory discussed in Chapter I, will wish to be aware of the manifested range of human interests and evaluations and of their clustering around the basic goods picked out by first practical principles.

IV.2 The Basic Forms of Human Good: A Practical Reflection

The first paragraph might helpfully have recalled that in each case, grasp (understanding) of the practical principle is grasp that a possibility—a goal achievable, in favourable or not too unfavourable circumstances, by action(s)—is an opportunity, for an advantage, a benefit, an aspect of flourishing, a *perfectio*. As the matter is put in *Aquinas* at 94:

One cannot understand that a possibility (e.g. of acquiring knowledge or becoming a friend) is an opportunity, a good, to-be-pursued, unless one first knows, to some extent, that it is a possibility (e.g. that questions sometimes have answers, or that one can communicate and interact with another person). Still, since the goods of human existence are each open-ended, the practical knowledge of basic human goods will outrun, by anticipation, the theoretical knowledge it presupposed. (By reflection, the theoretical can appreciate what was known practically.)

A. *Life*. In face of theories and attitudes that treat the life of the very young or the very decayed or the unconscious as not the life of a human person and no instance of the basic good, the meaning of 'life' in 'human life is an intrinsic good...' needs more explication than it here gets. So it is carefully discussed in *NDMR* (1987) XI.4, 304–9, and essay III.14 (1995b), sec. IV; see also essay II.19 (1993c).

The discussion on pp. 86–7 of procreation as transmission of life contemplates an 'analytical' separating out of sexuality, mating, and family life despite the 'anthropological [ethnographic] convention' that treats these as a single category or unit for investigation. What this discussion misses is the basic good which had long ago been identified not only by the social anthropologists but also by Aquinas, correctly edited and translated (*Aquinas*, 83)—marriage, the committed union of man and woman with a commitment to expressing the good of marriage itself as both friendship and pro-creative. In essay III.20 at 319 (2008c) the rationale is put like this:

Marriage is a distinct fundamental human good because it enables the parties to it, the wife and husband, to flourish as individuals and as a couple, both by the most far-reaching form of togetherness possible for human beings and by the most radical and creative enabling of another person to flourish, namely, the bringing of that person *into existence* as conceptus, embryo, child and eventually adult fully able to participate in human flourishing on his or her own responsibility.

But that way of putting it underplays, perhaps, the aspect that Shakespeare has the god of marriage point to when he stages that god, Hymen, presiding over the simultaneous weddings of four couples with the 'wedlock hymn'—

> O blessed bond of board and bed!
>
> 'Tis *Hymen peoples every town*;
>
> High wedlock then be honoured.
>
> Honour, high honour, and renown,
>
> To Hymen, god of every town!

As You Like It 5.4 (emphasis added)

The good in question, thus, is indeed, in one of its two fundamental elements or aspects, the transmission of the life not just of the mother or just of the father but of this couple and their family and their people (the 'town' that if not thus peopled will fail or, as likely as not, be peopled by quite another people, more willing to sustain itself).

That marriage is a basic human good is a thesis that meets with resistance and doubts; the Introduction to *CEJF* I, at 9, responds to such doubts, and to the objections of an otherwise sympathetic critic.

C. *Play.* The brief treatment (p. 87) fails to articulate what is implied in it, and in the second endnote on play on p. 98, where the reference to playful statutory drafting suggests what (I now think) would be the more adequate and accurate characterization of the good in question: excellence-in-performance, for its own sake, whether in 'work' or 'play'.

The list as a whole was revisited in later essays, such as essay I.14 sec. I,[23] but best, I think, in essay I.15, at 244 n. 25, where at last marriage gets its due:

A list: (1) *knowledge* (including aesthetic appreciation) of reality; (2) *skilful performance*, in work and play, for its own sake; (3) *bodily life* and the components of its fullness, viz. health, vigour, and safety; (4) *friendship* or harmony and association between persons in its various forms and strengths; (5) the sexual association of a man and a woman which, though it essentially involves both friendship between the partners and the procreation and education of children by them, seems to have a point and shared benefit that is not reducible either to friendship or to life-in-its-transmission and therefore (as comparative anthropology confirms and Aristotle came particularly close to articulating [e.g. *Nic. Eth.* VIII.12: 1162a15–29] not to mention the 'third founder' of Stoicism, Musonius Rufus) should be acknowledged to be a distinct basic human good, call it *marriage*; (6) the good of harmony between one's feelings and one's judgments (inner integrity), and between one's judgments and one's behaviour (authenticity), which we can call *practical reasonableness*; (7) *harmony with* the widest reaches and most *ultimate source* of all reality, including meaning and value.

This treatment further improved on *NLNR* by understanding aesthetic appreciation as a kind of knowledge, and recognizing that artistic creation belongs with work and play as mastery of materials for its own sake.

The Introduction to *CEJF* I, at 10–12, briefly reviews others' recent efforts of two kinds: to come up with alternative lists of basic 'capacities/capabilities' or 'freedoms' or 'functionings'; and to test the *NLNR* list against the experience and self-understanding of persons in elemental circumstances, a test which yielded a list essentially the same as *NLNR*'s as modified in essay I.14, sec. I.

[23] This list still omitted marriage, which is *sui generis*, not merely transmission of life nor merely harmony (friendship) between friends, but (as Grisez puts it in *LCL* (1993), ch. 9 Q. A. 2.f): 'marital communion is unlike friendship in that it fulfills a man and a woman precisely insofar as they can be together the principle of new persons, [though] it also is like friendship by being fulfilling for them in itself, apart from the fruitfulness of their cooperation', and (I add) since the parenthood of both the spouses will, if it ensues, require them both and each to shape the whole of their lives with a view to the demands of being not only a good mother or good father but also a good partner for the whole of life—for richer for poorer, in sickness and in health—with a kind of commitment to exclusiveness and permanence which is not required for friendship as such.

IV.3 An Exhaustive List?

Before taking up the question whether the list is complete (see pp. 447–8), this section, in the second of the paragraphs beginning on p. 91, adverts to the relation between inclinations and basic human goods, a relation already implicitly under consideration in sec. III.2, as its title indicates. The point made in the first sentence of this p. 91 paragraph is discussed much more fully in *Aquinas* at 92–3 in the long paragraph straddling those pages. The sentence in Aquinas's discussion of first practical principles, *ST* I–II q.94 a.2c, where he says that the goods to which the first principles of practical reason and natural law direct us are the objects of natural inclinations, has generated a considerable literature in much of which the inclinations are treated as the basis for our coming to understand the principles of natural law and practical thought and reasonableness. So to treat them is, at best, a confusion of the metaphysical with the epistemological, of the order of ontological dependence with the order of coming to know. As to the latter, the coming to know: the fact that I find in my make-up a regular and strong inclination to (Aristotle's four stock examples) eat coal or other people or copulate with beasts or people of the same sex as myself, does not provide a reasonable or even an intelligent basis for thinking that the satisfying of those inclinations is a good either as end or means. The same is true of more common inclinations, too, such as (to use Aquinas's examples) desperation, or fear that disarms resistance, or (to use the examples at p. 91 above) the inclination to take more than one's share, or the urge to gratuitous cruelty, or to selfishness. These are inclinations whose objects—however appealing to emotional motivations as source of some emotional satisfaction—lack the character of being intelligibly good, beneficial prospective states of affairs, making me and anyone like me really better-off. The best interpretation of Aquinas's sentence is to take it as referring not to sub- or pre-rational inclinations of desire or aversion or inertia, but to the inclinations of the will (i.e. of intelligent appetite) which *follow* our understanding of such prospective states of affairs as intelligibly good, desirable.[24]

---

[24] This interpretation is set out carefully in Stephen L. Brock, 'Natural Inclination and the Intelligibility of the Good in Thomistic Natural Law', *Vera Lex* 6 (2005): 57–78, though his accounts at nn. 5 and 62 of the theory in *NLNR* are defective. See also p. 440 above.

IV.4 All Equally Fundamental?

'[T]here is no objective hierarchy amongst them' (p. 92). This proposition in the first paragraph of the section would better have been: there is 'no single, objective hierarchy'[25] of value amongst them. There are various hierarchies. Life is most necessary, as precondition for the others; transmission of life shares in that kind of necessity. As for practical reasonableness, its very intelligibility as a good is as being *in charge of* (and in that sense, above) the pursuit and realization of all the other basic human goods.

IV.5 Is Pleasure the Point of It All?

It could well have been noted that pleasure, though important, delightful, and intrinsic to the full realization of some basic goods (and in certain senses of pleasure, to the full realization of all of them), is not itself an intelligible good; and pain, though important and horrible, is not an intelligible evil. To be born without a susceptibility to pain is to be doomed to an early death; so pain is a benefit, at least as a means of preservation of life and thus of other basic goods. Pain tends, however, to be a vehement proximate cause of the intelligible evil of inner disharmony and loss of integrated psychological functioning and 'personality', the intrinsic harm/evil at stake in the intrinsic wrongfulness of torture.

For a fuller account of the experience machine thought-experiment, and of its implications, see *FoE* 37–42.

CHAPTER V: THE BASIC REQUIREMENTS OF PRACTICAL REASONABLENESS

V.1 The Good of Practical Reasonableness Structures our Pursuit of Goods

The first five paragraphs bring the discussion to the point where it would have been well completed by the line of thought indicated in sec. 4 of the Overview, above. (The succeeding five parts of sec. 5 go on to consider other, less central aspects of practical reason's predicament and means of response.) The point made in sec. 4 was that this chapter does not identify the unity and intelligible explanation of the various principles of practical reasonableness that it correctly identifies. That identification relies on a dialectical

---

[25] Thus *FoE* 51.

method (see p. 126, first paragraph of sec. V.10): attending to what serious philosophers have counted as the master moral principle. What is missing is the real master moral principle, of which all the requirements are specifications. Essay I.14 at 215 (1992a) works up to that principle:

Moral thought is simply rational thought at full stretch, integrating emotions and feelings but *undeflected* by them. Practical rationality's fundamental principle is: take as a premise at least one of the basic reasons for action, and follow through to the point at which you somehow bring about the instantiation of that good in action. Do not act point-lessly. The fundamental principle of moral thought is simply the demand to be fully rational: in so far as it is in your power, allow nothing but the basic reasons for action to shape your practical thinking as you find, develop, and use your opportunities to pursue human flourishing through your chosen actions. Be entirely reasonable.[26] Aristotle's phrase *orthos logos*, and his later followers' *recta ratio*, right reason, should simply be understood as 'unfettered reason', reason undeflected by emotions and feelings. And so undeflected reason, and the morally good will, are guided by the first moral principle: that one ought to choose (and otherwise will) those and only those possibilities whose willing is compatible with a will towards the fulfilment of all human persons in all the basic goods, towards the ideal of integral human fulfilment.

Even this passage fails to state a key premise: each of the first practical principles picks out and directs us to a good which it identifies, in its initial, not fully reflective formulation, as a good 'for me and anyone like me'. Reflection eventually comes to under-stand the true extent and rationale of the 'anyone like me': any human person. Fulfilment (flourishing) is *as good* in and for any human person as it is in and for me; and the same is true of each of fulfilment's basic aspects (basic human goods). So reason un-deflected by sub-rational motivations directs us to the fulfilment of all human persons in all societies.

That fulfilment is not a goal, but an ideal of reason. The more specific general requirements of practical reasonableness, listed and discussed in the chapter, specify ways of *not* being open to integral human fulfilment. These requirements by no means ex-clude prioritization of oneself and one's dependants, familial, con-tractual, political, and so forth. They require rather that the

---

[26] See *NDMR* 119–25.

prioritization proceeds on the basis of reasons, not emotional preferences as such. What is wrapped up in those words 'as such' is articulated in the set of basic requirements of practical reasonableness. For a restatement of the main elements in this whole chapter, in terms of specifications of the master moral principle, a restatement carried forward into a consideration also of legal reasoning, see essay I.15 sec. IV at 243–53 (1997b).

A further, more abstract reflection on the above-mentioned 'key premise' is offered in the opening paragraphs of *Aquinas* IV.3 at 111:

> Many today[27] think that the fundamental problem of ethical and political theory is to escape egoism—to show how and in what sense one can be required, in reason, to give weight to others' interests against one's own, and to recognise at least some moral duties to other people. Theories are constructed to expound the rationality and/or natural primacy of egoistic 'prudence', and to explore the question how we may 'bridge the gap' between such prudence (on the near bank) and morality (on the farther shore). In Aquinas's view, such thoughts and theories are radically misconceived.
>
> For: the only *reasons* we have for choice and action are the basic reasons, the goods and ends to which the first practical principles direct us. Those goods are *human* goods; the principles contain no proper names, no restrictions such as '... for *me*'. [Footnote omitted] So it is not merely a fact about the human animal, but also and more importantly a testimony to people's practical understanding, that they can be interested in the well-being of a stranger, whom they will never meet again but now see taking the wrong turning and heading over a cliff [see Cicero, *De Officiis* 3.5]; for it is the same good(s) that the stranger can share in or lose and that I can: specifically human good(s). [Footnote omitted].

Elsewhere in *Aquinas* it is repeatedly indicated and explained that, and how, emotions not only can deflect reason, but also are a constant accompaniment to and, in a well-ordered psyche, *support* for intelligent and reasonable motivations.

V.2 A Coherent Plan of Life

It is worth repeating what is already said in the endnote on p. 129: 'plan of life' is hazardously metaphorical—hazardously because the primary meaning and connotations of 'plan' come from the technical rather than the moral order. Morality is a matter of practical

---

[27] Henry Sidgwick, *Outlines of the History of Ethics for English Readers* ([1886] 1902) (London: Macmillan), 198: 'in the modern ethical view, when it has worked itself clear [of Greek moral philosophy], there are found to be two [regulative and governing faculties recognized under the name of Reason],—Universal Reason and Egoistic Reason, or Conscience and Self-Love'.

reasonableness in choosing in the *open horizon* of what Aquinas calls, with deliberate ambiguity, 'human life as a whole': one's individual lifetime, whose late/last circumstances one cannot foresee, and the whole human community's living extension into its unknown future. What is said in the section is not unconscious of this predicament, and does not depend for its meaning on the title label 'plan of life'.

V.4 No Arbitrary Preferences Amongst Persons

Here 'arbitrary' points to the deflection of reason by sub-rational preferences or aversions. Reflection on the Golden Rule is a ready way to understanding the sense and force of the master principle of morality as an ideal of reason (rather than a goal).

Still, in such a reflection one must bear in mind the complexity introduced by the fact that while the Golden Rule is a requirement of reason and reasonableness, its application in concrete cases depends on what 'you (I) would be willing for others to do to you (me)', and such a willingness normally includes a rationally under-determined component. This is explained at some length in essay I.14 sec. VII at 227–8 (1992a) and again in essay I.15 sec. IV at 247–8 (1997b).

The critique of Rawls's version of social contractarianism and liberal state-neutrality theory on pp. 108–9, in the section's last two paragraphs, goes to the very heart of *A Theory of Justice*. But it needs to be supplemented now, as it can be, by carrying the critique forward to his *Political Liberalism*, and to the fallacies involved in thinking that reciprocity (that kind of respect for persons) inherently demands that people not be treated in ways that they could not agree to *without rethinking the matter and changing their minds* about important practical truths—about which they may well be mistaken (a simple and undeniable truth that Rawls never faces up to) with effects on themselves and others, often including bad effects which even state authorities whose jurisdiction is limited (as it should be) to *public* good can reasonably be concerned to prevent or reduce.

V.6 The (Limited) Relevance of Consequences: Efficiency, Within Reason

The second paragraph lists an important and neglected set of ways in which rational commensuration of choices' consequences is feasible. *NDMR* IX.7 ('*Why common speech sounds consequentialist*'), at 261–3 lists a further set of ways in which it is reasonable to speak of 'greater good' and 'lesser evil': some of these are non-moral, though often of some relevance to morality; the others are moral, in that they presuppose that the morally good or better (or morally bad or more immoral) choice or type of choice has already been identified. Consequentialist ethics, of course, attempts to work with a sense or senses of 'greater good' and 'lesser evil' which do *not* presuppose some prior moral judgment but instead direct moral judgment by identifying the option promising greater good or lesser evil. The whole matter is further reviewed, systematically, in essay I.15 (1997b): 'Commensuration and Public Reason'. But this section of *NLNR* can stand.

V.7 Respect for Every Basic Value in Every Act

This section, on the other hand, needs supplementation and substantial correction by clearer understanding of intention, as the adoption of a proposal for action, by choice, such that what is included in one's intention—and defines one's action—is (just) the whole set of ends and means which make the proposal attractive to one as an immediate option, under the description of ends and means which makes them seem as a set choiceworthy and to be chosen by me here and now. With that in place one can state the requirement as: not choosing (acting, or planning to act, with intent(ion)) to destroy, damage, or impede any basic good in anyone's existence, whether out of malice/hatred or as a means to a supposedly greater good. (Here there comes to bear the critique of consequentialism given in the previous section, pp. 114–18.) On this clarified account of intention, see all the essays in Part Three of *CEJF* II (*Intention and Identity*).[28] Essay II.11 at 196 (1995a) states the matter in summary form:

Intention is a tough, sophisticated, and serviceable concept, well worthy of its central role in moral and legal assessment, because it picks out the central realities of deliberation and choice: the linking of means and ends in a plan or proposal for action *adopted* by *choice* in preference to alternative proposals (including to do nothing). What one intends is what one chooses, whether as end or as means. Included in one's intention is everything which is part of one's plan (proposal), whether as purpose or as way of effecting one's purpose(s)—everything which is part of one's

---

[28] See especially II.13 (2001a), in which, at 257, Grisez and I reject an element ('indivisibility in performance') in the 1970 article prominent in the endnote on intention on p. 132 above and influential in the conceptual structure of sec. V.7 as a whole.

reason for behaving as one does. In reading the words 'plan', 'proposal', 'deliberation', and 'choice', one should ignore all connotations of formality and 'deliberateness'; in the relevant sense there is a plan or proposal wherever there is *trying*, or doing (or refraining from doing) something *in order to* bring about something *or as a way of* accomplishing something. And there is deliberation and what I am calling adoption of a proposal by choice wherever one course of conduct is preferred to an alternative which had attraction. On all these matters there is a substantial and well-grounded measure of agreement among philosophers. [Footnote omitted]

Accordingly, common speech has many ways of referring to intentions and the intentional. It deploys not only the cognates of 'intend', but also such phrases as 'trying to', 'with the objective of', 'in order to', 'with a view to', 'so as to', and, often enough, plain 'to', and many other terms.

With this clarified idea of intention in place, the bearing of *NLNR*'s secs IV.6 and IV.7 combined is stated in essay I.15 at 245–6 (1997b):

Another specification of the master principle is the principle which every form of consequentialist, proportionalist, or other purportedly aggregative moral theory is tailor-made to reject: do not do evil—choose to destroy, damage, or impede some instance of a basic good—that good may come. The previous principle excludes making harm to another one's end; the present principle excludes making it precisely one's means (as distinct from causing it as a side effect of what one intends and does). In such a case, one unreasonably treats a good end as justifying the bad means. For: the instantiation of good which one treats as end (call it E), and for the sake of which one acts *against* the reason constituted by that instantiation of a basic good which one is choosing to harm (call this reason M), could not constitute a *reason* thus to act against M unless E could be weighed and balanced against, commensurated with, M and—prior to moral judgment—*rationally* judged to be greater, more weighty, the greater good (or, where both reasons concern avoiding evil, the lesser evil). But by virtue of, inter alia, the considerations set out in sec. II, *that* sort of rationally commensurating *judgment* is not possible. So one's preference for E over M is motivated not by reason but by differential *feelings* as between E and M, and choosing to act on it violates the master principle of morality. The feelings which thus motivate the judgment that E is the greater good or lesser evil may well, of course, be veiled (more or less in good faith) by rationalizations or by conventional 'wisdom', which prescribes or licenses some narrowing of horizons or ranking of persons or other way of making the incommensurable seem rationally commensurable.

The principle that evil may not be done for the sake of good, interpreted in this way, is the foundation of truly inviolable (absolute) human rights and is the backbone of decent legal systems. For a decent legal system excludes unconditionally the killing or harming of innocent persons [see *NDMR* 309–19] as a means to any end, whether public or private. On the basis of other specifications of morality's master principle, it also excludes the use of perjured testimony, the choice to render false judgment, judicial or other official support of fraud, resort to sexual seduction as an instrument of public policy, and chattel slavery. These unconditional norms, and the associated absolute or truly inviolable human rights not to be mistreated by the violation of any of those norms, give the legal system its shape, its boundaries, the indispensable humanistic basis (at least some necessary conditions) for its strong claim on our allegiance. Without these norms, and respect for the underlying principle, the legal system becomes an organization of powerful people willing to treat others as mere means.[29]

This principle excluding all *intentional* harm to persons (in any basic aspect of their well-being) also rules out the economistic ambition to explain and justify the main institutions of our law as devices for maximizing economically assessable (commensurable) value. For central to Economic Analysis of Law is the assumption, or thesis, that (though there might be a difference in the purchase price) there is no difference of principle between buying the right to inflict intentional personal injury even on non-consenting persons and buying the right not to take precautions which would (supposedly) eliminate an equivalent number of injuries caused accidentally.[30] But in every decent legal system, the former right is not available, whether by purchase or otherwise. For a decent legal system is in the service of human persons, and its first and most fundamental service is in protecting and vindicating their right not to be made the object (end or means) of someone's will to harm them.

For a response to various objections and pertinent counter-examples raised by David Luban, see essay IV.17, sec. IV at 356–69 (1990d).

V.8 *The Requirements of the Common Good*

Once the master principle of morality is articulated, it seems clear that this eighth requirement is no more than an application of that principle to one's conduct in the communities that exist or should exist in the pursuit of the basic goods, not only of sociability and

---

[29] Kant's second/third formulation of his categorical imperative ('treat humanity in oneself and others always as an end and never as a means only'; *Grundlegung*, 429) is another formulation of this specification of morality's master principle. Kant's own interpretation of it is unsatisfactory because his conception of 'humanity' is too thin, and this because he fails to acknowledge the basic human goods and reasons for action. See *FoE* 120–4.

[30] See e.g. Calabresi and Melamed, 'Property Rules, Liability Rules, and Inalienability' at 1126 n. 71; and *CEJF* IV.16 (1990b), secs V–VI.

marriage but also of every other basic good insofar as its actualization depends upon cooperation.

V.9 Following One's Conscience

This requirement seems to be no more than a re-articulation of the content of sec. V.1, the requirement of practical reasonableness itself (which, when unfolded, is the master principle of morality).

CHAPTER VI: COMMUNITY, COMMUNITIES, AND COMMON GOOD

VI.1 Reasonableness and Self-interest

See the quotation from *Aquinas* at the end of the Postscript to sec. V.1, p. 452 above. See also the discussion of the ambiguity of the term 'rational choice', in essay IV.17 at 358–9 (1990d).

VI.2 Types of Unifying Relationship

The book, beginning here, lists and discusses the four kinds of unifying relationship in an order unfortunately different from Aquinas and Grisez and my other writings, where the moral order is listed third and the technical fourth.

Moreover, since the treatment of the four kinds of order is here tucked into the discussion of community, the relevance of the irreducible differences between them—relevance to social theory and understanding of human nature—is never adequately brought out (even though it is fairly extensively revisited in sec. XIII.2 on order and disorder). A number of my later writings strive to bring out that relevance, most fully in *Aquinas*, 21–2, and essay II.2 secs I and IX (2005c); but also in the discussion of law and legal reasoning as both technical and moral, in essay I.14 secs III and IV at 216–20 (1992a).

VI.4 Friendship

This discussion of the most intense form, the central case, of friendship, important though it is for the overall thesis and architecture of the book, should not be allowed to obscure the significance of a non-central case which is neither of Aristotle's two non-central cases (business and play friendship) but is nonetheless important (as Cicero and the ancients stressed): fellow-feeling among human persons such that it makes sense to warn the stranger from the precipice. (See at the end of Postscript to sec. V.1, p. 452 above.)

In relation to altruism, discussed in the first full endnote on p. 158, see also Anselm Müller, 'Radical Subjectivity', Ratio 19 (1977): 115 at 128.

VI.5 'Communism' and 'Subsidiarity'

In the endnote on subsidiarity on p. 159, the translation of the definition of subsidiarity proposed in the encyclical *Quadragesimo Anno* has been made more exact.

VI.6 Complete Community

The last paragraph needs some revision. There is certainly a common good of humankind, and central to that common good is the equal dignity of all human persons and, consequently, natural human rights prior to all convention, agreement, or other positive sources of obligation; and these natural rights include the right to a share in the resources of the earth (and of any other places that come under human occupation). But it was a mistake to call 'ideological symbolisms [and] universal religions' a common stock of humankind in the same breath as technology and systems of intercommunication. For some or all ideologies, insofar as they misstate the truths about human good and the conditions for its realization, tend to disrupt the universal common good; and false universal religions certainly do so (all the more so as their mischaracterization of the transcendent requires that they be rejected). The injustices which international law has shown itself capable of perpetrating or embodying are, of course, no greater than those perpetrated by or in many states. But it would be premature to think that either international law's *jus cogens* rules or international organs of governance with compulsory powers should be presumed to have morally rightful authority over and against the law or organs of states whose governance is broadly just. The foundations of the proposition articulated in the preceding sentence are proposed and defended in essays II.7 (2008a secs IV and V) and II.6 (2008b); see also essays III.7 (1992b), III.8 (2003a), and III.9 (2007a). The last paragraph of VI.8 needs similar modification.

VI.7 The Existence of a Community

This section's discussion of groups fails to say clearly that group *action* is possible and indeed common and normal. When members of a group coordinate their activity not merely with a common objective but according to a shared plan of action, their individual acts pursuant to the plan are elements in the group's carrying out of the plan by its own action(s). See essays II.4 (which includes some discussion of 'corporate personality') and II.5 (1989a); and *NDMR* 113–24, 128–31.

VI.8 The Common Good

The discussion of the common good is too resolute in giving primacy to the 'third sense' mentioned in the second paragraph on p. 155. This conception—in terms of a set of conditions for the attainment of individual or common objectives—makes the common good (at least seem) *instrumental*. It omits the intrinsic desirability of a communal flourishing which consists not merely in the individual flourishing of each member of the community (family, club, association, team, state...), but also in the reality that this flourishing was and is assisted by, and in good measure consists in, mutual assistance through all the forms of friendship (though not all the instances of friendship between each person and each other person). There is, in short, the common good that consists in the all-inclusive and intrinsically desirable flourishing of that community (and those communities) as such. This is brought out in *Aquinas* at p. 235, together with this rider: it does not follow, and Aquinas himself does not think it follows, that there is or should be someone—even government and law as a whole—responsible for coercively bringing this about, or that the coercive jurisdiction of the state's government and law is defined by this all-inclusive common good. Indeed, that jurisdiction is to be defined rather by the *public good* which, as Aquinas says, is limited to interpersonal relations and external acts which impact directly or indirectly on others.

CHAPTER VII: JUSTICE

VII.1 Elements of Justice

Here and throughout the chapter, the discussion of justice focuses on its relevance to practical reasoning and deliberation as a *norm of action*, a principle (basis) for discriminating (judging) between proposals (options) shaped up for choice. That is, it treats justice as justice is treated in Justinian's *Digest* in the famous triad of *imperative-principles* (which Kant took very seriously), 'honeste vivere, neminem laedere, suum cuique tribuere' (quoted in the endnote to sec. VII.6 at the top of p. 197)—'live rightly, harm nobody, render to each what belongs to each'. The equivalent of the last limb, the definition of justice that opens both the *Digest* and the *Institutes*, is quoted in the third endnote to sec. VII.1 on p. 193, but as one in a heap of references. (It appears again in the middle of p. 207, in sec. VIII.3, as part of the discussion of Grotius.) Although 'justice as a quality of character' is the subject of the sentence that wraps up sec. VII.2, the opportunity is missed to reflect a little, somewhere in the chapter, on the fact that the classic definition picks out a *virtue*—'*constans et perpetua voluntas* jus suum cuique tribuere'—a steady and lasting willingness to give to each the right(s) that belong(s) to each ['his or her right']. As noted above, the book could with advantage have given more attention to virtue as stability of disposition, shaped up by choices as lasting, i.e. as an immanent, intransitive effect of choosing, the virtuous and virtue-making choices being those guided accurately by practical reasonableness.

Neither this chapter nor Chapter VIII on rights reports that Aquinas adopts that same definition as his own definition of justice, at the outset of an account of justice that extends over hundreds of pages and hundreds of substantive issues. Since his definition is preceded by a careful argument that the object (defining goal or point) of justice is right(s) (*jus*), due attention to this transforms sec. VIII.3's discussion of the question whether he had the modern conception of rights as *belonging* to persons ('subjects' of justice)—belonging ('mine', 'theirs', etc.) to them as the advantageous end of relationships. It shows, in short, that Aquinas did have such a conception. So, although the treatment of justice in Chapter VII is essentially Thomist (and opposes most of the neo-scholastic interpretations of justice since Suarez and Grotius), it is not Thomist enough.

On the other hand, it is perhaps, in another respect, too Aristotelian and Thomist. For it continues to distinguish, prominently and structurally, between distributive and commutative justice. Eventually, in sec. VII.5 on p. 179, it is pointed out that the distinction is 'no more than analytical convenience'. (Already in sec. VII.3 the second full paragraph on p. 166 indicates the distinction's relativity.) *Aquinas* VI.1 argues that it is more convenient to get rid of this convenience, which yields 'no really clear and stable analytical pattern' (188), and to focus on more specific ranges of issues of justice. Doing so leaves intact the discussion in *NLNR* VII.1 of the three elements of justice, though it would perhaps be better to say about the third element—equality—that beyond the basic equality in dignity and thus in entitlement to be counted a subject of justice, equality is of less significance than its prominence in Aristotle's discussion in *Nic. Eth.* V (and thus in this section) suggests. 'Treat like cases alike *and different cases differently*', the principle taken by Hart to be definitive of justice, is perhaps more illuminating as a pointer to the relevant third element besides other-directedness and duty; and, for that matter, the Hartian formulation too is firmly grounded in Aristotle's other major discussion of justice (neglected in the endnotes to *NLNR* VII), namely *Politics* III.12–13: 1282b14–1284a3, esp. 1282b21 and 1283a26–31. (Here Aristotle suggests, inter alia, that it is a characteristic perversion of democracy to hold that because all persons are equals in some respects, all persons should be considered equal in all respects.)

VII.2 General Justice

This section is not substantially affected by the recognition (see Postscript to sec. V.8 above) that there is no need to treat advancing/protecting the common good as a distinct requirement of practical reasonableness. Indeed, the first sentence of the last paragraph on p. 164 is approaching a realization that justice is a direct implication of the master principle of morality.

But the discussion of general justice here should have been linked with the discussion in sec. VII.6 of the historic blunder made by Cajetan, transforming Aquinas's theory that distributive and commutative justice are *the two* species of general justice into a new theory, subsequently widely adopted, that there are three species of justice: distributive justice of the state (whole) in relation to its citizens (parts); commutative justice between citizens (between parts); and legal justice of loyal citizens (parts) performing their duties to the state (whole). For that Cajetanic and post-Cajetanic schema (still to be found in a corner—sec. 2411—of the *Catechism of the Catholic Church* (1993)) leaves empty the place occupied by general/legal justice in the modified Aristotelian analysis of justice employed by Aquinas. That place is precisely the place occupied by *social justice* in the encyclical, *Quadragesimo Anno* (1931), which introduces that term (increasingly found in political and political-theoretical discourse after the 1830s and fairly widespread from the 1880s) into a modern quasi-Aristotelian discourse. For there (see secs 57–8,

110, etc.) social justice is defined in terms of the needs of the common good, understood as the good, in due measure, of each and every one of the members of a community (centrally, a political community) whose institutions and forms of life satisfy the preconditions for long-term sustainable flourishing. Social justice, occupying the place of Aristotle's and Aquinas's general/legal justice, clearly has the character attributed to the latter by Aquinas (in stark contrast to the pseudo-interpretation of Cajetan), namely, that social/general/legal justice is centrally a virtue of the ruler(s): *ST* II–II q.58 a.6c. It is a concern of the citizen only insofar as citizens have the character ascribed to them (in the central case of citizenship) by Aristotle: participants in governance, i.e. in ruling.

This understanding of social/general justice is of substantive importance. It confronts an understanding which, looking only to equality, may overlook inequalities (diversities) that bear sooner or later on the common good. *Quadragesimo Anno*'s main concern was that the justice of maintaining a system of property rights (including rights to rents) should be maintained along with rights to wages sufficient to sustain a family but consistent with maintenance of high levels of employment. Other kinds of example can be given. In present and foreseeable conditions of diversity, it would be unjust to very many potential victims to make qualification as an airline pilot or neuro-surgeon the subject of ethnic quotas or other arrangements designed to secure equal representation of every ethnicity among pilots and neuro-surgeons. And it will equally be a matter of social justice, properly understood, that admission to a political community should *not* proceed on a 'social justice/equality' basis—whether of non-discrimination among applicants, or of pro rata shares for every foreign ethnicity—*if* doing so would render the community governable, if at all, only at the cost of gravely impaired freedom of speech and debate; corrupt and racialized and/or sectarian politics, adjudication, and governance; civil disorder and widespread destruction of life and goods; and loss of long-term sustainability of the political community's Rule of Law, economy, territorial integrity, and self-governance. One of the conditions of the political maintenance of social justice is that there be substantial unity, not diversity, in the conceptions held by the law's subjects (the state's citizens) about the 'preliminary' or framework issue: to *which* community do I really belong in any contest of allegiances? (See also essays II.6 (2008b) and II.7 (from 2008a).)

VII.3 Distributive Justice

The discussion of appropriation, begun in this section, runs through the chapter, for example in sec. VII.6's discussion of the duties of distributive justice which individuals and private enterprises owe to others, such that in establishing a scheme of redistributive taxation the state government and law need be doing no more (*pace* Nozick) than crystallize and enforce duties that property-holders already had (p. 187, last full text sentence), or make reasonable *determinationes* of such duties. But some of the discussion of the justice of appropriation probably belongs in an enhanced treatment of general justice. For the decision *what* wholes or common stock are up for distribution depends, explicitly or tacitly, on a judgment (and if need be a decision) about what forms of coexistence, cooperation, and community will tend in the long-run to serve most adequately the sustainable common good of *everybody*. The same kind of '"rule" of human experience' (p. 170 top) as underpins the Aristotelian arguments for having a regime of private property within each political community also grounds the thesis that general justice supports the division of humankind into distinct political communities with distinct territories and populations. Already p. 169 says, at the top, that the other line of argument (from subsidiarity) for property rights and responsibilities is an argument of general justice, and it should doubtless be acknowledged that the same is true of the basic Aristotelian productivity rationale. Both in their application to appropriation of resources within a political community and their application to the more fundamental appropriation of territory by political communities, these are considerations of social justice. In both contexts, superficial and short-sighted claims to equality of treatment ('communism') are negated in favour of arrangements which will tend to serve better the wider, deeper, and more long-term interests of everyone. (See similarly the last paragraph on p. 219, on the specification of rights; and again essays III.7 (1992b) and III.8 (2003a), sec. VII of essay III.9 (2007a), essay II.7 (from 2008a), and secs III and IV of essay II.6 (2008b).)

VII.4 Criteria of Distributive Justice

The fundamental question of human equality in dignity and basic rights over against the diverse interests of other kinds of animal, the question discussed briefly in the first endnote to the section, on pp. 194–5, is discussed in the Introduction to *CEJF* III, at 4–9. The discussion of the question of responsibility raised in the succeeding endnote, on p. 195, should have drawn upon considerations about the conditions for creating and sustaining the level of civilization and measure of prosperity that tend to be advantageous (compared with alternatives such as anarchic resort to *res nullius*) even— indeed, especially—for the worst-off classes of persons.

VII.5 Commutative Justice

It was not correct to say, on pp. 179 and 196 of the first edition, that Aquinas invented the term 'commutative justice', but it seems clear that he brought it into general use and gave it the scope it has in his work and the subsequent tradition, such that 'commutative' extends far beyond its original connotations of exchange.

Oddly, in the years since the first edition, Aristotle's discussion of corrective justice has received wide attention and a surprising measure of acceptance from philosophers of law and of common law—surprising because this is a rather weak part of his *Ethics*, since it quite fails to discuss the *duties* of justice which, if violated, give rise to claims of corrective justice.

VII.7 An Example of Justice: Bankruptcy

The relevance of this was underlined when the countries of Eastern Europe emerged from the legal/political darkness of communism and began inspecting and establishing the institutions needed for a political economy and corresponding law justly founded on the *public* interest in there being *private* property including equitable interests, and choses in action such as contractual undertakings, loans, and debts.

CHAPTER VIII: RIGHTS

VIII.1 'Natural', 'Human', or 'Moral' Rights

For a discussion of the positive-law character of human rights in contemporary national and international law, see the Introduction to *CEJF* III at 2–4. The present section speaks of human rights as natural and moral rights, such as provide—or are available to provide—foundations for positing human rights provisions constitutionally or by treaty or other forms of law-making.

VIII.2   An Analysis of Rights-talk

This section does not seem to need amendment in the light of more recent work[31] on the matters it traverses.[32] The conclusions of the section are stated in the first paragraph of sec. VIII.3.

The serviceability of Hohfeldian analysis for even moral rights is suggested by its deployment in essay III.18 (1973b), and its applicability to the sophisticated and precise logical framework of the 'right to religious liberty' (as a claim-right not to be coerced in religious matters) expounded in Vatican II's declaration on that matter, *Dignitatis Humanae*, discussed in essay V.4 (2006a); the fact that the draftsmen described this right in non-Hohfeldian terminology as an immunity does not affect the logic of their position.

VIII.3   Are Duties 'Prior to' Rights?

The Postscript to sec. VII.2 has already mentioned that the discussion of the history of the word '*jus*' in the present section fails to notice how Aquinas's definition of justice, and his prior identification of *jus* as the very object (proximate goal and rationale) of justice, entail that—though it does not clearly appear from his formal account of the senses of '*jus*'—in his view, *jus* (a right) is something that belongs to the subjects of law or moral relationships, and therefore has the essential characteristic of a subjective right. This being so, the 'watershed' spoken of in the first full paragraph on p. 206 must be regarded as much more a matter of appearance and idiom than of conceptual, let alone political or philosophical, substance. Evidence for this conclusion is in *Aquinas* 133–8; and 2002c (to which Tierney's reply, in the same issue of the Review of Politics, seems ineffective, because he misunderstands the *modern* concept of rights). As to the meaning of '*jus*' in Roman and mediaeval canon law (see the second endnote on p. 228), Tierney's rapprochement with Villey in 2002 is the more surprising in light of his refutation of Villey, in Tierney, 'Villey, Ockham and the Origin of Individual Rights', J. Witte and F. Alexander (eds), *The Weightier Matters of*

---

[31]   e.g., Matthew Kramer and Nigel Simmonds (eds), *A Debate over Rights* (OUP: 2000) or Pavlos Eleftheriadis, *Legal Rights* (OUP: 2008).

[32]   The suggestion on p. 202 about Hohfeld's views is not (*pace* Kramer, *A Debate about Rights* at 61 n. 23) that he might have favoured the will theory, but that in response to the strictly technical problem of identifying the legal claim-right holder, he might well have favoured the view (which is not a theory) that the proper candidate is the person with the remedy against the duty bearer.

the Law (Atlanta, Scholars Press: 1988), 1–31. The willingness of a scholar as historically informed and linguistically sensitive as Honoré to attribute thoughts about human rights to classical Roman jurists such as Ulpian is important evidence against the strong watershed theory.

VIII.4 *Rights and the Common Good*
VIII.5 *The Specification of Rights*

The need to read these two important sections together is suggested by the use to which some main aspects of them are put in Grégoire Webber, *The Negotiable Constitution: On the Limitation of Rights* (OUP: 2010); see *CEJF* III.1 at 45 (1985a); also Bradley W. Miller, 'Justification and Rights Limitation', in Huscroft (ed.), *Expounding the Constitution* (CUP: 2008), 93–116. And on both the relation of human rights to the common good, and their specification, see essay III.1 (1985a) as a whole; this chapter does not deal explicitly with the issues discussed in that Maccabaean lecture, whose predictions about the misdirection of judicial power and legal learning in the service of the administration of mis-specified and/or ungrounded and illusory 'human rights' are being fulfilled in a good many judgments of the European Court of Human Rights and the English courts, not least the House of Lords and now the Supreme Court: see the first, second, and fourth endnotes to essay III.1 at 44–5; essay III.9 (and 2007a at 423–42); and essay II.14 (2010a).

VIII.6 *Rights and Equality of Concern and Respect*

This critique of Dworkin (which could with advantage have noted that it parallels part of the 1973 response to Dworkin by Hart, *Essays in Jurisprudence and Philosophy* (OUP: 1983) at 218–19) was followed by adjustments of Dworkin's position. The sequence of these adjustments is traced, and the adjusted arguments are responded to, in essays III.2 at 51–3 (1987c) and II.6 at 108–12. The critique's discussion (not affirmation) of (what amounts to) paternalism, and the prefatory discussion of public morality on p. 217, would be improved by introducing the thesis clarified for me during the writing of *Aquinas* c.VII: that there are strong arguments of political theory for regarding the coercive jurisdiction of state government and law as limited to the domain of *public good*—defined by Aquinas as the domain of external acts that impact on others directly or indirectly. True, government and law need a clear and true conception of virtue, in order to be able to regulate, for example, spending and education reasonably, as well as to determine appropriately which aspects of the public conduct of private persons to prohibit. But that does not authorize the Platonic-Aristotelian concept of coercive paternalism extended from the regulation of children through their whole life-times as free adults.

VIII.7 Absolute Human Rights

The discussion of nuclear deterrence on p. 224 is greatly amplified in *NDMR*, in which Chapter IX on the futility of consequentialist arguments is particularly germane. See also essay V.20 (1988b).

Meanwhile the European Court of Human Rights has confirmed the interpretative suggestion made in sec. VIII.4 at p. 213, that the right not to be tortured in Article 3 is indeed *absolute* (the term used by the Court). Essay III.1 describes the presence of absolute rights in the European Convention on Human Rights as a cardinal virtue of the Convention. But the Court has given them an unreasonable interpretation (a) in extending the absoluteness to the prohibition of activities in no way involving or intended to result in torture, and (b) in extending it to an extravagant conception of the 'inhuman or degrading'. See the second endnote to essay III.1, and n. 58 in essay III.9 at 145 (2007a).

The brief discussion of incommensurability, at the foot of p. 225, like the treatment in pp. 114–17, fails to make clear that the incommensurability is not merely between one basic good and another, but also between instantiations of one basic good, and between persons: see the discussion of incommensurability on pp. 422–3 in the Overview above.

CHAPTER IX: AUTHORITY

IX.1 The Need for Authority

This section sets the problem of practical, governmental authority in the framework of coordination. It refers to a number of earlier passages in the book,[33] but fails to note the passage most important

---

[33] Thus in sec. VI.7, p. 153, coordination is spoken of as what makes a number of people a group or community (that *acts* socially); the idea is of a shared objective to which coordination is a means, and how to achieve that coordination is the problem. In discussing distributive justice on p. 167, coordination reappears as collaboration, in the context of kinds of *incidents of communal enterprise* up for distribution.

at this juncture in the argument: the introduction of the idea of coordination in the last paragraph of sec. VI.2, on pp. 138–9. There it was pointed out, inter alia, that coordination includes 'negative coordination', the effort to avoid collisions. When p. 232 speaks, in the top paragraph, of the need for e.g. parents to decide, and so forth, it would have been helpful to recall negative coordination. It would also have been helpful to give, at the same time, a clear statement that coordination is an idea that extends to such more or less passive, 'cerebral' states of affairs as: everyone in the law school regarding the law library as the responsibility of the Law Librarian, not of the Governor of the National Bank; or everyone accepting (when the question arises) that this house is yours and that house is mine and not yours, and so forth. Such coordination of thoughts, attitudes, dispositions, and rules of thought and action needs to extend to essentially all the matters with which the law deals, and all the instruments employed by the law for dealing with them.

Neglect of the second endnote to the section, on p. 255, has shipwrecked some critiques of the book's account of authority, critiques foundering on the assumption that the references to 'coordination problems' are to the very narrow game-theoretical concept of coordination problems arising in the dealings of persons who have a complete convergence of interests in the problem and its resolution. (See e.g. essay 2008d sec. IV.) The (real but limited) relevance of game theory, and of other deliberately emaciated conceptions or models of practical reasoning, is explored in two essays concerned to contest Joseph Raz's thesis that law can be authoritative without creating even a prima facie or presumptive obligation to obey: essay IV.2 (1984b) and essay IV.3 (1989b); see also *CEJF* IV, Introduction at 6–7. The hypothesis of authority without coextensive obligation is given a distinct critique in essay IV.4 (1987d), an essay which incidentally clarifies the relation between conceptual analysis (and conceptual possibility) and practical reason.

On p. 232, the last full paragraph says that exchange of promises is a modality of unanimity. But it is really a modality of both unanimity and of authority—as the penultimate line of the paragraph partly acknowledges in speaking of 'the authority of a rule requiring fulfilment of promises' (sc. even when the initial unanimity has been replaced by the desire of one of the parties not to perform in accordance with the promise on its terms).

IX.2 The Meanings of 'Authority'

The discussion of kinds of statement, on pp. 234–7, is a response to objections (both of which appear together as 'the "positivist" objection') raised to the first draft of the chapter by Hart.

IX.5 'Bound By Their Own Rules'?

The parenthesis in the first paragraph (p. 252) seems to imply that tyranny, in the classic conception, is bad *one-man* rule; none of the later references to tyranny removes the impression. But tyranny is any self-interested rule (where self is any number, not concerned with the common good but with their own interests).

CHAPTER X: LAW

X.1 Law and Coercion

Defensive and punitive coercion was taken up at the beginning of this chapter for mainly extrinsic reasons. It seemed important to fend off any suspicion (see p. 29) that the view of law promoted by the tradition being expounded and developed in this book is an 'idealistic' view, unrealistic about the fact that immoral, unjust behaviour is, and is going to be, widespread, persistent, and severely threatening to the common good and every just individual. More-over, the discussion of punishment could compactly display the *variety* of ways in which moral purposes can justify and shape even as raw a genus of actions as coercion.[34] And the discussion of unjust punishment could, again compactly, provide an early occasion for rebutting the absurd but widespread assertion that the tradition shuts its eyes to unjust, wicked instances of official and legal action.

In the result, the chapter fails to expound the link between authority and law as clearly as the matter deserves, both in itself and in the confusing terrain of contemporary jurisprudence. Debate about authority with Raz, around 1984, provided oppor-tunities to rectify the omission. The concluding part of essay IV.3 (my response to his reply to my critique of his 1979 account of law and authority) sums up as follows, indicating the inherent

---

[34] See now essay III.12 (1999b).

connection—indeed inter-definability—between the practically reasonable idea of law and the practically reasonable idea of the Rule of Law as a desirable modality of law and legal order:

The law... makes itself salient in identifying and solving particular coordination problems, not by the merits of its particular solutions, but by having the features which are characteristic of 'the law', notably:

(a) The law presents itself as a seamless web by forbidding its subjects to pick and choose. To say this is not (as Raz thought)[35] to beg the question of law's moral authority; it is merely to point to the fact that, by virtue of this empirical feature of a healthy legal system, all the subjects of the law are, in at least one significant respect, put in like case, and indeed are actually, in many more than one respect, linked to each other by that network of protections and other benefits which the law secures for each by imposing restraints and exactions upon all. Where burdened by a legally enforced coordination scheme he thinks misguided, each can reflect that he has been or at some time will be benefited by the burdens which the law has in other respects (other ways, other contexts) imposed and will impose on others, including those misguided individuals whose exhortations, propaganda, or customs have inspired this new and unmeritorious law.[36]

(b) The 'procedural' features of law give reason for regarding it as authoritative in identifying and solving coordination problems. By comparison with propaganda, exhortation, and custom, the law's legislative capacities hold out the prospect of generating relatively prompt but also relatively clear and subtle solutions to coordination problems as they emerge and change. Its forms and its modes of application and enforcement, too, tend to ensure that its solutions will be relatively discriminating but non-discriminatory, and will be imposed on free-riders and other deviants so that the willing collaborator in the legally required coordination solution can have some assurance that he is not a mere sucker or fall-guy. And the legal process of detecting and penalizing free-riders and deviants is so structured as to minimize the unfairnesses perpetuated by enthusiasts who demand conformity to their exhortations, propaganda, or customs, and would press these demands in ways ill-adapted to finding and acting on the truth.

For these two (related) sorts of reasons,... the existence of the legal order creates a shared interest which gives everyone moral reason to collaborate with the law's coordination solutions, that is, moral reason to regard the law as (morally) authoritative. Most specifically, that shared interest is in the regular, impartial upholding of the law itself. More

---

[35] 'For [Finnis], if this is how the law presents itself, then this is how we ought to take it.... a most vicious circle indeed': Raz, 'The Obligation to Obey: Revision and Tradition', Notre Dame J Law, Ethics & Pub Policy 1 (1984): 139–55 at 150.

[36] 1984b at 120 (essay IV. 2 at 50–1).

generically, the shared interest is in the good of there being and continuing to be (and not merely patchily) a fair method of relating benefits to burdens, and persons to persons, over an immensely wide, complex, and lasting, though shifting, set of persons and transactions—a method which nothing other than law plausibly offers.[37]

The remainder of that summary, considering obligation in more detail, is quoted below in relation to sec. XI.4.

X.2 Unjust Punishment

The last sentence of the first paragraph on p. 265 complements and perhaps supplements the first sentence of Chapter I.

X.3 The Main Features of Legal Order

The discussion of Weber on pp. 266 and 291 misses (perhaps deliberately) the opportunity, not taken up elsewhere, to reflect on why Weber calls *legal* rule/authority *rational* ('legal-rational').[38] This can only be because rules, even when they are *determinationes*, are elements in a rational plan for an end, by means adapted both to that end and to all the other ends that a legal order should be promoting and respecting. Otherwise it would be rule-fetishism, and so no more central as a kind of authority or governance than charismatic or traditional rulership/governance/authority.

Those are the grounds, no doubt, for Weber's own conclusion, alluded to above at p. 431 in discussing him in the second paragraph of the Postscript to sec. I.4 (see also p. 435, the fourth paragraph of the Postscript to sec. I.5): '[Natural law] is *the specific and only consistent type of legitimacy of a legal order* which can remain once religious revelation and the authoritarian sacredness of a tradition and its bearers have lost their force'.[39]

X.5 Limits of the Rule of Law

The argument in the first three paragraphs (pp. 273–4) is put very tersely, but has proven sound in the stress of the extensive debate in which Simmonds defended a similar line of thought against the objections of Kramer.

---

[37] *CEJF* IV.3 at 70–2 (1989b at 136–7). Earlier, essay IV.2 at 50–1, 63–5 (1984b).

[38] See essay IV.9 at 214–17 (1985b).

[39] For citation and commentary see essay IV.9 at 220–2.

X.6 A Definition of Law

'I have by now sufficiently stressed' (p. 278) alludes particularly to what is said about concepts and definition on pp. 265 and 273; those passages, along with pp. 277–80 and 365–6, make clear, I think, an issue that has remained murky in jurisprudential discussion. The points made in the last paragraph on p. 277 can be reinforced by reflection on 'invalid arguments are not arguments': see p. 438, and much more fully: Introduction to *CEJF* IV, at 7, and essay IV.1 at 30 and 35 (2003b).

X.7 Derivation of 'Positive' from 'Natural' Law

The arguments and conclusions of this key section are illustrated and confirmed in dialectic with Economic Analysis of Law, in essay IV.16 (1990b); with Critical Legal Studies, in essay IV.13 (1985c); and with Ronald Dworkin, in essay IV.12 (1987e) and sec. XIV of essay IV.5 (2002a). An overview of legal reasoning can be found in essay I.14 (1992a), earlier in essay IV.17 (1990d).

The remarks about the creative role of judges, in the last paragraph of p. 286 read with the endnote on p. 296, are amplified and nuanced in essay IV.20 (1999c).

The second sentence of the first full paragraph on p. 290 needs qualification if it conveys a stance of complete neutrality about the 'exclusive social-fact sources thesis'. For the idea that 'all law is identified by reference to social facts [of legislation, adjudication, etc.] alone' is unsustainable, for the reasons set out briefly in the Introduction to *CEJF* IV, at 4–5. Juristic thought about sources and validity conditions cannot reasonably proceed (and does not) without reference to a wide range of 'evaluative arguments' such as the desirability of coherence here and now, of stability across time, of fidelity to undertakings, respect for legitimate expectations, avoidance of tyranny, preservation of the community and its capacity for self-governance, protection of the vulnerable, incentives for investment, maintenance of the condition of communal life called the Rule of Law, and many others. Note also 'wherever it reasonably can', at the top of p. 320 above.

CHAPTER XI: OBLIGATION

XI.3 Variable and Invariant Obligatory Force

The statement in the top paragraph on p. 312 that 'the legal system does not allow an unrestricted feedback of such "value" or "policy" considerations from the justificatory level of straightforward practical reasonableness back into the level of [legal] practice' introduces a line of thought developed not only in the rest of that paragraph but also on pp. 316, 317, 318, and 319. It is taken up again in sec. XII.3 near the end of p. 355 and on p. 356, where the phrase 'the unrestricted flow of practical reasoning' might on each occasion have been better put as 'the flow of general ("extra-legal") straightforward practical reasoning'.

XI.4 'Legally Obligatory': The Legal Sense and the Moral Sense

This section perhaps spends too much time showing that the intra-systemic sense (or kind) of 'legal obligation' involves a schema of means-ends practical reasoning. When the moral sense of the term comes into view on pp. 318–19, insufficient mention is made of the consideration which loomed large in the discussion of promissory obligation on p. 307: *fairness* in the sense emphasized by Rawls[40] and Hart[41] in this very context: I cannot be one who is rationally impartial unless I take the burdens of the practice as well as its benefits, and perform on this promise... —that is, unless I take the burdens of upholding the law as well as the benefits that flow to me from others' willingness to uphold, comply with, the law.

Here it is convenient to continue the quotation from essay IV.3 begun in the Postscript to sec. X.1 above:

Raz replies that laws striving to achieve coordination, having to address masses of people and be adapted for judicial and administrative enforcement, will sometimes oversimplify. Those individuals who understand the situation will then, on occasion, have 'no reason' to conform to legal requirements which are simplifications ill-suited, in those circumstances, to the goal of the coordination. And this non-conformity does not threaten the effectiveness of government and the law; for some offences never become known, and many torts and breaches of contract violate the interests of one individual only.[42]

[40] *Theory of Justice*, secs 18 and 52.
[41] *Hart, Essays in Jurisprudence and Philosophy* (OUP: 1983): 119.
[42] Raz, 'The Obligation to Obey: Revision and Tradition', Notre Dame J Law, Ethics and Public Policy 1 (1984): 139–55 at 149.

My rejoinder: 'effectiveness' for what? The point of law is not merely to ensure the survival of government or the future conformity of the potentially recalcitrant. Part of the law's point is to maintain real (not merely apparent) fairness between the members of a community; and this aspect of law's point is unaffected by the detection or covertness of breaches of law. The institution of law gains much of its value, as a contribution to the common good, precisely from the fact that the obligations it imposes hold good even when breach seems likely to be undetectable.[43]

Of course, for Raz undetectability was not a licence for non-conformity but one of the pre-conditions for a justified breach motivated and licensed by the violator's superior understanding of what is needed for the particular goal of a law's coordinative scheme. And it would be foolish to deny that in some circumstances an individual can serve fairness or other aspects of the common good better by breach than by conformity. But Raz's claim that in those situations the law gives 'no reason' for doing what it commands, that is, has *no* moral authority at all, seems extravagant. The thesis which Raz and others deny [footnote omitted] is that law creates a prima facie generic moral obligation and thus has prima facie and generic moral authority. Although on this thesis a prima facie reason and authority of this sort can be *overridden* by countervailing reasons, there is no reason to say that, morally speaking, the law (and its authority) never extended at all to the situations in which it is overridden.

The reason (I suggested) for taking the law seriously to the full extent of its tenor and intended reach—and never regarding it as giving *no* reason for doing what it commands—is a reason connected with that irreducible multiformity of human goods (and that plurality of human persons) which imposes intrinsic limitations on human practical reasoning and makes nonsense (and injustice) of totalitarian projects. Generally speaking, an individual acts most appropriately for the common good not by trying to estimate the needs of the community 'at large' nor by second-guessing the judgments of those who *are* directly responsible for the common good, but by performing his particular undertakings and fulfilling his other responsibilities to the ascertained individuals who have contractual or other rights correlative to his duties. For the common good simply *is* the good of individuals living together and depending upon one another in ways that tend to favour the well-being of each.[44]

---

[43] See pp. 303–5, 319, above.

[44] If one must locate a party to whom the obligation to obey the law is owed, it should be one's fellow-subjects rather than the rulers (legislators, judges, administrators, police, et al.). [See pp. 359–60 above.] Hart saw this. [See his 'Are There Any Natural Rights?', *Phil. Rev.* 64 (1955): 175–91 at 185—quoted in the endnote ('On Law and Obligation') to essay IV.5 at 155–6.] But certain writings denying the generic prima facie obligation to obey the law are shipwrecked by their authors' supposition that such an obligation would have to be (or is commonly supposed to be) *to officials*: see e.g. Postema, 'Coordination and Convention at the Foundations of Law', J Legal Studies 11 (1982): 165–203 at 196.

Correspondingly, those who do have legislative or other constitutional responsibility for the common good as such, do well to regard it as quite other than a goal which could be defined and attained by skilful disposition of efficient means, such as a bridge or an omelette. Attempts to absorb the individual or particular groups into a vast overall coordination 'solution', so as to eliminate all *private* purposes and all enterprises launched for reasons other than the advancement of the public coordinative scheme, confuse the idea of a national common good with the idea of a national common enterprise or scheme of coordination. Such attempts, indeed, thereby do grave damage to the common good. Their injustice *is* a reason for regarding laws made pursuant to them as morally *ultra vires* and devoid of law's generic moral authority—though not of the possible 'collateral' moral significance which both Raz and I admit.[45]

XI.8 'Reason' and 'Will' in Decision, Legislation, and Compliance with Law

The discussion of *imperium* on pp. 338–41 takes up a matter important for understanding ethics and human nature, and the history of ethical, political, and legal theory. It can be clarified further by keeping in mind that will is one's *responsiveness* to reasons for action that one has understood and can shape up, or has shaped up, into proposals for choice and action. On p. 339, near the middle, the contrast with 'push' would be better expressed as: 'one's interest in a reason for action'.

CHAPTER XII: UNJUST LAWS

XII.3 Effects of Injustice on Obligation

On the references on pp. 355–6 to 'unrestricted flow of practical reasoning', see the Postscript to sec. XI.3 above.

To supplement the examples given, in the top paragraph on p. 359—of instances where legal philosophers (notably Hart) dedicated to separating their account of law from moral issues[46] nevertheless include in their accounts of law assumptions or assertions that cannot be defended without venturing into moral or moral/political philosophy—see the second edition of *The Concept of Law* at 275 ('a judge will often have to choose between [different principles], relying, like a conscientious legislator, on his sense of

---

[45] See pp. 361–2 above [and Postscript to sec. XII.3 below]; Raz, 'The Obligation to Obey' at 146–7n.
[46] On Hart, see essays IV.10 (2007b) and IV.11 (2009b).

what is best . . .'); *ibid.*, 270 ('Principles which are morally sound by the standards of what Dworkin has called "background morality" . . . may indeed provide moral limits or constraints upon what can count as law').

The discussion of a 'collateral' obligation to obey the law,[47] in the second full paragraph on p. 361, is rather loosely argued and has been widely misunderstood. There is no reason to suppose that the bad side effects of disobedience or non-compliance will *normally* or *frequently* be so significant that the relevant moral considerations will impose the kind of collateral obligation in question. It is essentially an obligation not to be observed defying the unjust law. And the relevant moral considerations concern fairness (especially to those liable to be harmed by widespread non-compliance) judged in the light of the probabilities that one's non-compliance will be taken as an example, and of other factors relating to one's role in society, etc., against the background of the (variable) factor mentioned in the paragraph (desirability of not rendering ineffective the just parts of the system).

The section—reasonably enough, given the book's purposes—does not consider 'civil disobedience' (mentioned, without the label, on p. 362), a conventionally defined or recognized category of morally motivated disobedience, characteristically to a law not itself unjust, in protest against an unjust law or state policy, the disobedience itself being characterized by openness in violating the law, non-violence even under provocation, and ready submission to legal penalties not disproportionate to the offence. See *NDMR* 352, 354–7; on related issues, essay V.20 at 283–5 (1988b).

XII.4 'Lex Injusta Non Est Lex'

The statement in the first full sentence on p. 365 that the tradition 'accords to iniquitous rules legal validity' is loose. The tradition accepts that iniquitous rules may satisfy the legal system's criteria of legal validity, and where they do, it does not seek to deny that fact unless the system itself provides a juridical basis for treating these otherwise valid rules as legally invalid by reason (directly or indirectly) of their iniquity.

---

[47] In Aquinas's formulation of this, p. 360 n. 6, I have adjusted the translation in line with *Aquinas*, 274 Note D.

CHAPTER XIII: NATURE, REASON, GOD

XIII.1 Further Questions about the Point of Human Existence

The chapter's strategy is discussed at some length in essay V.13 (from 2008a); a passage from this is quoted above in sec. 6 of the Overview to this Postscript. The limitations of this chapter's approach were retained in the briefer discussion in *Fundamentals of Ethics*, 145–7. But the last chapter of *Aquinas* advances well beyond those limitations, adopting the substance of Aquinas's primary arguments for the existence, and about main aspects of the nature, of God. These arguments, especially the first (concluding to God as pure act(uality)) and the fifth (concluding to God as source of the world's intelligible orders), enable much more to be said about the relevance of these facts of divine creation and providence to an understanding of the deepest foundations of, and full rationale for, practical principles and the human fulfilment to which they point and direct us. Chapter X of *Aquinas*, in its first four sections (at 294–319), follows much the same sequence of issues as the present chapter, and those sections should be read as a whole to envisage the revisions that would be appropriate for this chapter. Such revisions would not significantly affect this section of the chapter.

XIII.2 Orders, Disorders, and the Explanation of Existence

The second paragraph on p. 381, in seeming to acquiesce in Kant's and Hume's downplaying of the significance of order and of any inference to divine creation and providential ordering, concedes too much to their objections. Order of any significant kind needs explanation; chance is not that explanation, nor did Darwin think it is (see essay V.1 at 21–5 (2009c)); and the imputations of defect implicit in Kant's word 'hampered' and Hume's words 'without discernment . . . maimed, abortive' are premature and question-begging, in view of the responses to the 'argument from evil' at the end of p. 391 and in the passage from *Aquinas* quoted under sec. XIII.3 below.

The book's argument to creation, from the existence of things each of whose *what it is* does not include *that it is* to the existence of D, whose *what it is* includes *that it is*, is sound but can be supplemented or substituted by the arguments sketched in *Aquinas* X.2 (just as Aquinas substituted the arguments he deploys in *Summa Theologiae* for the argument in his youthful *De Ente et Essentia*).[48]

---

[48] Grisez's book is republished with a new preface and title: *God? Philosophical Preface to Faith* (St Augustine's Press, South Bend: 2004).

XIII.3 Divine Nature and 'Eternal Law': Speculation and Revelation

The first full paragraph on p. 389 and the first paragraph on p. 392 are mistaken in saying that nothing can be established philosophically about God (D) beyond existence and causality; accordingly the intervening paragraphs need not have been put in hypothetical form.

The response to the problem of evil given in the main paragraph on p. 391 can be supplemented by the summary from *Aquinas* 304, of Aquinas's broad response:

> Straining to ascribe everything to chance rather than a creative intelligence, materialists object that in some respects the pattern and evolution of things is wasteful, pointless, badly ordered, *unintelligent*. They do not attend to the fact that much which seems to them pointless or wasteful is still somehow a describable and to that extent stable and intelligible pattern. And in judging it defective or unintelligent because they do not understand its point, they resemble a country bumpkin (*rusticus*; *idiota*; *ignorans*) who, from the true premise that he does not understand what is going on in a busy laboratory or hospital theatre, draws the conclusion that what is going on is random, unintelligible, pointless, or foolish, or perhaps just needlessly complex. [Footnote omitted: given in essay V.1 at 24] The intention of an intelligence capable of projecting and actualising the entire cosmos and all its interlocking orders vast and miniscule (including human minds with all their capacities to understand and reason logically, mathematically, and interpretatively) is not an intention we could ever reasonably hope to understand *fully* by reasoning from those truths about it which, in our fruitful but laborious inferences from experience, we do manage to understand.

XIII.4 Natural Law as 'Participation of Eternal Law'

Perhaps it is needless to remark that the statement at the top of p. 401, that animals etc. are not subject to natural law, refers to natural law in its central sense in which it is addressed by (divine) mind to (human) *mind*. For the purposes of natural sciences, studying orders and systems in the first of the four orders, natural law in that moral sense, central for bringing order into intelligent human choices, is natural law (or a law of nature) only by analogy.

The discussion of the fit between inclinations and first principles of practical reason in the section's last paragraph on p. 403 will be redundant if the sentence quoted there from *ST* I–II q.94 a.2 is understood in the way suggested now in the last paragraph of the Postscript on sec. II.4 above, that is, understood as referring to the inclinations of the will responding to the intelligible goods picked out and directed to by such principles.

XIII.5 Concluding Reflections on the Point and Force of Practical Reasonableness

The hypothetical and/or speculative form of the sequence of observations ('In the first place...' etc.) on pp. 405–7, and the limitations asserted in the first two of those observations (on p. 405), are unnecessarily agnostic, as has been foreshadowed several times already in this Postscript.

The suggestion, at the beginning of the book's final paragraph on p. 410, that the basic human good of religion was introduced in Chapter IV by way of 'postulat[ing] an inclination and a corresponding basic value', and only because 'constrained' by 'anthropological and psychological evidence', needs amendment, in the light both of this Postscript's remarks under secs II.4 and XIII.4 above, and of the sheer intelligibility, and rational urgency, of the questions which press for explanations beyond the reach of natural-scientific method. These questions, and with them an anticipation, at least, of the appropriate answers to them, are truly available to all who approach or attain the age of reason.

BIBLIOGRAPHY OF CITED ESSAYS
OF JOHN FINNIS

1967a   I.17   'Reason and Passion: The Constitutional Dialectic of Free Speech and Obscenity', University of Pennyslvania L Rev 116: 222–43

b   IV.8   'Blackstone's Theoretical Intentions', Natural L Forum 12: 63–83

1970a   I.6   'Reason, Authority and Friendship in Law and Morals', in Khanbai, Katz, and Pineau (eds), *Jowett Papers 1968–1969* (Oxford: Blackwell), 101–24

b   'Natural Law and Unnatural Acts', Heythrop J 11: 365–87

c   i. 'Abortion and Legal Rationality', Adelaide L Rev 3: 431–67
ii. 'Three Schemes of Regulation', in Noonan (ed.), *The Morality of Abortion: Legal and Historical Perspectives* (HUP)

1971a   IV.21   'Revolutions and Continuity of Law', in A.W.B. Simpson (ed.), *Oxford Essays in Jurisprudence: Second Series* (OUP), 44–76

1972a   III.11   'The Restoration of Retribution', Analysis 32: 131–5

b   IV.18   'Some Professorial Fallacies about Rights', Adelaide L Rev 4: 377–88

c   'The Value of the Human Person', Twentieth Century [Australia] 27: 126–37

d   'Bentham et le droit naturel classique', Archives de Philosophie du Droit 17: 423–7

1973a   III.3   Review of John Rawls, *A Theory of Justice* (1972), Oxford Magazine 90 no. 1 (new series) (26 January)

b   III.18   'The Rights and Wrongs of Abortion: A Reply to Judith Jarvis Thomson', Philosophy & Public Affairs 2: 117–45

1976b   Chapters 18–21 (with Germain Grisez), in R. Lawler, D.W. Wuerl, and T.C. Lawler (eds), *The Teaching of Christ* (Huntingdon, IN: OSV), 275–354

1977a   I.3   'Scepticism, Self-refutation and the Good of Truth', in P.M. Hacker and J. Raz (eds), *Law, Morality and Society: Essays in Honour of H.L.A. Hart* (OUP), 247–67

b   'Some Formal Remarks about "Custom"', in International Law Association, Report of the First Meeting [April 1977] on the Theory and Methodology of International Law, 14–21

1978a   'Catholic Social Teaching: Populorum Progressio and After', Church Alert (SODEPAX Newsletter) 19: 2–9; also in James V. Schall (ed.), *Liberation Theology in Latin America* (San Francisco: Ignatius Press, 1982)

b   'Conscience, Infallibility and Contraception', The Month 239:
            410–17

1984b IV.2 'The Authority of Law in the Predicament of Contemporary
             Social Theory', J Law, Ethics & Pub Policy 1: 115–37

1985a III.1 'A Bill of Rights for Britain? The Moral of Contemporary
              Jurisprudence' (Maccabaean Lecture in Jurisprudence), Proc
              Brit Acad 71: 303–31

b   IV.9 'On "Positivism" and "Legal-Rational Authority" ', Oxford J
           Leg St 3: 74–90

c   IV.13 'On "The Critical Legal Studies Movement" ', American J Juris
            30: 21–42; also in J. Bell and J. Eekelaar (eds), *Oxford Essays in
            Jurisprudence: Third Series* (OUP, 1987), 145–65

1987b II.8 'The Act of the Person' *Persona Veritá e Morale*, atti del Con-
             gresso Internazionale di Teologia Morale, Rome 1986 (Rome:
             Città Nuova Editrice), 159–75

c   III.2 'Legal Enforcement of Duties to Oneself: Kant v. Neo-Kantians',
            Columbia L Rev 87: 433–56

d   IV.4 'On Positivism and the Foundations of Legal Authority: Com-
            ment', in Ruth Gavison (ed.), *Issues in Legal Philosophy: the
            Influence of H.L.A. Hart* (OUP), 62–75

e   IV.12 'On Reason and Authority in Law's Empire', Law and Philoso-
            phy 6: 357–80

1988b V.20 'Nuclear Deterrence, Christian Conscience, and the End of Chris-
             tendom', New Oxford Rev [Berkeley, CA] July–August: 6–16

1989a II.5 'Persons and their Associations', Proc Aristotelian Soc, Supp.
             vol. 63, 267–74

b   IV.3 'Law as Coordination', Ratio Juris 2: 97–104

1990b IV.16 'Allocating Risks and Suffering: Some Hidden Traps', Cleveland
              State L Rev 38: 193–207

d   IV.17 'Concluding Reflections', Cleveland State L Rev 38: 231–50

1991a II.9 'Object and Intention in Moral Judgments according to St
             Thomas Aquinas', The Thomist 55: 1–27; rev. version in
             J. Follon and J. McEvoy (eds), *Finalité et Intentionnalité: Doctrine
             Thomiste et Perspectives Modernes*, Bibliothèque Philosophique de
             Louvain No. 35 (Paris: J. Vrin, 1992), 127–48

b   II.10 'Intention and Side-effects', in R.G. Frey and Christopher
            W. Morris (eds), *Liability and Responsibility: Essays in Law and
            Morals* (CUP), 32–64

1992a I.14 'Natural Law and Legal Reasoning', in Robert P. George (ed.),
             Natural Law Theory: Contemporary Essays (OUP), 134–57

b   III.7 'Commentary on Dummett and Weithman', in Brian Barry
            and Robert E. Goodin, *Free Movement: Ethical Issues in the
            Transnational Migration of People and of Money* (University
            Park, Pennsylvania: University of Pennsylvania Press),
            203–10

d V.9 *'Historical Consciousness' and Theological Foundations*, Etienne Gilson Lecture No. 15 (Toronto: Pontifical Institute of Mediaeval Studies) (32 pp)

1993c II.19 '*Bland*: Crossing the Rubicon?', LQR 109: 329–37

1994a II.12 'On Conditional Intentions and Preparatory Intentions', in Luke Gormally (ed.), *Moral Truth and Moral Tradition: Essays in Honour of Peter Geach and Elizabeth Anscombe* (Dublin: Four Courts Press), 163–76

1995a II.11 'Intention in Tort Law', in David Owen (ed.), *Philosophical Foundations of Tort Law* (OUP), 229–48

1996c IV.7 'The Truth in Legal Positivism', in Robert P. George (ed.), *The Autonomy of Law: Essays on Legal Positivism* (OUP), 195–214

1997b I.15 'Commensuration and Public Reason', in Ruth Chang (ed.), *Incommensurability, Comparability and Practical Reasoning* (HUP), 215–33, 285–9

1999a I.2 'Natural Law and the Ethics of Discourse', American J Juris 43: 53–73; also in 'Natural Law and the Ethics of Discourse', Ratio Juris 12: 354–73

b III.12 'Retribution: Punishment's Formative Aim', American J Juris 44: 91–103

c IV.20 'The Fairy Tale's Moral', LQR 115: 170–5

2000a II.1 'The Priority of Persons', in Jeremy Horder (ed.), *Oxford Essays in Jurisprudence, Fourth Series* (OUP), 1–15

2001a II.13 '"Direct" and "Indirect": A Reply to Critics of Our Action Theory' (with Germain Grisez and Joseph Boyle), The Thomist 65: 1–44

2002a IV.5 'Natural Law: The Classical Tradition', in Jules Coleman and Scott Shapiro (eds), *The Oxford Handbook of Jurisprudence and Philosophy of Law* (OUP), 1–60

c 'Aquinas on *jus* and Hart on Rights: A Response', Rev of Politics 64: 407–10

2003a III.8 'Natural Law & the Re-making of Boundaries', in Allen Buchanan and Margaret Moore (eds), *States, Nations, and Boundaries: The Ethics of Making Boundaries* (CUP), 171–8

b IV.1 'Law and What I Truly Should Decide', American J Juris 48: 107–30

2005a I.1 'Foundations of Practical Reason Revisited', American J Juris 50: 109–32

b I.4 'Self-referential (or Performative) Inconsistency: Its Significance for Truth', Proceedings of the Catholic Philosophical Association 78: 13–21

c II.2 '"The Thing I Am": Personal Identity in Aquinas and Shakespeare', Social Philosophy & Policy 22: 250–82; also in Ellen Frankel Paul, Fred. D. Miller, and Jeffrey Paul (eds), *Personal Identity* (CUP), 250–82

2006a   V.4   'Religion and State: Some Main Issues and Sources', American
                  J Juris 51: 107–30

2007 a   III.9   'Nationality, Alienage and Constitutional Principle', LQR 123:
                  417–45

     b   IV.10   'On Hart's Ways: Law as Reason and as Fact', American J Juris
                  52: 25–53; also in Matthew Kramer and Claire Grant (eds), *The
                  Legacy of H.L.A. Hart: Legal, Political & Moral Philosophy* (OUP,
                  2009), 1–27

2008a   I.5/II.7/V.8   'Reason, Revelation, Universality and Particularity in
                  Ethics', American Journal of Jurisprudence 53: 23–48

     b   II.6   'Universality, Personal and Social Identity, and Law', address,
                  Congresso Sul-Americano de Filosofia do Direito, Porto Alegre,
                  Brazil, 4 October 2007; Oxford Legal Studies Research Paper 5;
                  <http://ssrn.com/abstract=1094277>

     c   III.20   'Marriage: A Basic and Exigent Good', The Monist 91: 396–414

     d   [V.13]   'Grounds of Law & Legal Theory: A Response', Legal Theory
                  13: 315–44

2009b   IV.11   'H.L.A. Hart: A Twentieth Century Oxford Political Philoso-
                  pher', American J Juris 54: 161–85

2010a   II.14   'Directly Discriminatory Decisions: A Missed Opportunity',
                  LQR 126: 491–6

INDEX

abortion, 117, 124, 133
Abril, V., 54
Ackrill, J. L., 77
acts, action(s), 60–4, 100, 122–3, 152, 197,
  338–41, 420–1
  and omissions, 195–6
acts-in-the-law, *see* juridical acts
Adler, Mortimer J., 294
aesthetic experience, 87–8, 98, 448
Albania, 170
Almond, G. A., 8
Alphonsus de Liguori, 331
altruism, 116, 158, *see also* love
Ambrose, 76
America(n), 60, 183, 248, 253, 258, 272, 293–4,
  347, 356
Amin, Idi, 11
analogy, 10, 20, 35, 158, 162–3, 279–80, 294,
  389, 392–3, 403, 409, 430, *see also* focal
  meaning
Angelo de Clavasio, 346
animals, 194–5
Anscombe, G. E. M., 76, 132, 195, 230, 343
anthropology, 34, 81–5, 97, 209, 278
Aquinas, Thomas
  on conscience, 125, 133
  on *convenientia*, 45, 55, 403
  on deficiencies in philosophy of, 46–7, 425
  on definition in philosophy of human affairs,
    365–6
  on derivation of positive from natural law,
    27–8, 281–9, 291, 295, 334, 360
  on distinction and relation between 'natural'
    and 'reasonable', 35–6, 440
  on essence and existence, 410–11
  on Eternal Law, 389, 391, 398–403, 412
  on folly and corruption, 30, 128, 225
  on four orders, 157, 457
  on freedom, 127, 130, 401
  on friendship, 158
  on God, 32, 46, 48, 52, 95, 130, 391, 396, 404,
    411–13
  on good, 75–6, 78–9, 367–8
  on human goods and ends, 31, 46, 52, 94–5,
    98, 130, 398, 401–3
  on inclinations, 34, 401–3, 449, 478
  on 'innate ideas', 32, 401
  on intelligence, 399–400
  on 'is' and 'ought', 33, 36, 47, 55, 416
  on *jus gentium*, 296

  on justice, 179, 185, 186, 193–4, 196, 360,
    367, 460, 465
  on law (positive, human), 28, 129, 194, 257,
    259, 292, 294, 342, 360–1, 363–5, 367–8,
    438, 476
  on legal validity, 27–8, 360, 363–5
  on marriage, 447
  on natural law, 29–30, 33–4, 45–8, 51–3,
    76–8, 101, 128, 129, 225, 296, 334, 361,
    396, 398–403
  on obligation, 45–6, 48, 55, 193, 334, 340–1,
    345, 360–1
  on participation, 399–403, 413
  on *perfecta communitas* (complete community,
    political or ecclesial), 428
  on 'practical', 20
  on practical principles and reason(ing), 34,
    36, 45, 52, 53, 77–8, 98, 417, 449
  on primacy of principles over virtue(s), 422
  on property, 171, 186
  on *prudentia*, 51, 52, 102, 128, 398
  on public good, 466–7
  on reason and will, 46, 54–5, 337–42, 347, 413
  on *recta ratio*, 451
  on right (*jus*), 206–8, 228, 360–1, 364, 439
  on rulership, 257–9
  on self-evidence, 32, 51, 67, 78, 101
  on self-love, 131
  on social contract, 257
  other references, vi, 55, 160, 254, 435
Arendt, Hannah, 77
Aristotle (and Aristotelian)
  on cannibalism, 449
  on chance, 130
  on citizenship, 253–4, 259, 366
  on coercion in law, 29, 260, 291
  on community and common good, 145–6,
    148, 156, 157, 160
  on corrective justice, 178, 464
  on democracy, 461
  on doing *v* making, 197, 443, *see also*
    intransitivity
  on ethics, 31, 101–3, 128–9, 176, 343, 365–6,
    392
  on focal meaning and central cases, 9–11, 20,
    129, 253, 363, 365–6, 429, 431–2
  on friendship, 144–5, 157, 158, 397–8, 457
  on God, 392–3, 394–6, 397, 401, 402, 413,
    424
  on indemonstrable principles, 32, 67, 77, 439

Lightning Source UK Ltd.
Milton Keynes UK
UKOW06f1213090615

253158UK00001B/1/P